D0455726

MIND-BODY THERAPY

Ideodynamic Healing in Hypnosis

A NORTON PROFESSIONAL BOOK

MIND-BODY THERAPY

Ideodynamic Healing in Hypnosis

Ernest Lawrence Rossi and David B. Cheek

W. W. Norton & Company • New York • London

Continued on page 500 which constitutes an extension of the copyright page

Published simultaneously in Canada by Penguin Books Canada Ltd., 2801 John Street, Markham, Ontario L3R 1B4

Printed in the United States of America.

Library of Congress Cataloging-in-Publication Data

Rossi, Ernest Lawrence.
   Mind-body therapy: ideodynamic healing in hypnosis / Ernest Lawrence Rossi and David B. Cheek. — 1st ed.
      p.   cm.
   1. Hypnotism — Therapeutic use.   2.   Mind and body.   3.   Medicine, Psychosomatic.   4.   Psychotherapy.   I.   Cheek, David B.   II.   Title.
RC497.R67 1988   616.89′162 — dc19   87-34852

ISBN 0-393-70052-6

W. W. Norton & Company, Inc., 500 Fifth Avenue, New York, NY 10110
W. W. Norton & Company Ltd., 37 Great Russell Street, London WC1B 3NU

5   6   7   8   9   0

Acknowledgments

We wish to express our appreciation to Fred Altman and Sanford I. Cohen of The National Institute of Mental Health for their leadership in assembling the Airlie House I and II Scientific Workshops on the Behavioral and Psychosocial Effects on Physical Health in 1987 and 1988.

The following members of the Airlie Workshops, among others, have contributed inspiration, support, and expertise to our efforts to articulate the leading edge of mind-body research:

Jeanne Achterberg	Steven Locke
Robert Ader	Theodore Melnechuk
Paul Black	Mortimer Mishkin
Susan Blumenthal	Karen Olness
Joan Borysenko	Brendan O'Regan
Thomas J. Carew	Martin Orne
Nicholas Cohen	Candace Pert
Bernard Fox	Michael Ruff
Ronald Glaser	Stephanie Simonton
Elmer E. Green	George Solomon
Nicholas R. S. Hall	Marvin Stein
Janice Kiecolt-Glaser	Jon Kabat-Zinn

Special thanks to Susan Barrows, our editor at Norton, whose continuing enthusiasm, guidance, and creative input have brought yet another volume to fruition; to Aline Lapierre, for her attentive and skillful rendering of the conceptual diagrams; and to Margaret Ryan, whose dedicated editorial and organizational assistance remains an ongoing source of support and actualization.

Contents

SECTION III
State-Dependent Memory, Meaning, and Healing

SECTION IV
The New Psychosomatic Medicine

SECTION V
Psychosomatic Networks: Perception, Pain, and Pleasure

SECTION VI
Women's Consciousness and Psychobiological Clocks

SECTION VII
Sexual Development and Dysfunction

SECTION VIII
Dreams, Illness, and Healing

SECTION IX
Birth Experience and the Construction of Reality

Boxes

Tables

Figures

Introduction

This volume of mind-body therapy methods in hypnosis is being published at an exciting and critical turning point in the history of therapeutic hypnosis. For over 200 years, since the generally recognized beginnings of hypnosis in the work of Anton Mesmer, there has been a continuing controversy about its fundamental nature: Does hypnosis produce real healing at the physiological level within the body, or is its therapeutic effect merely the result of suggestion and imagination in the mind only?

For the most part, the practitioners of therapeutic hypnosis have been "true believers": They have maintained that real biological healing does, indeed, take place. The evidence they have presented usually takes the form of clinical case histories, however, which remain unconvincing for skeptical scientists who require well-documented laboratory experimentation as a criterion of validity. This skeptical point of view maintains that so-called therapeutic hypnosis is actually a form of placebo; it is a nuisance variable, an unreliable phenomenon of spontaneous healing due to as yet unknown factors that beguile the unwary therapist into believing that his "suggestions for healing" have had a real effect.

As is often the case with controversy, no satisfactory solution has been possible because we simply have not known enough to be able to resolve the issue in a manner that is convincing for both sides. Over the past few decades, however, there has been a series of fundamental breakthroughs in the fields of the neurobiology of emotion, memory, and learning; the endocrinology of stress; psychosomatic medicine; and the molecular genetics of "information substances and their receptors." *These breakthroughs are providing a new research database for conceptualizing state-dependent memory, learning, and behavior as one of the major psychobiological foundations of therapeutic hypnosis.* The recent data and theory emerging in these fields may enable the true-believing clinician and the skeptical laboratory researcher to join hands at last in a united effort to create a new science of mind-body healing.

The original clinical work of David Cheek over the past 40 years has evolved a special technique of therapeutic hypnosis that is admirably suited for current investigations of mind-body communication and healing. This is the technique of *ideodynamic or ideomotor* signaling,* the sources of which date back to antiquity. Ideodynamic signaling was rediscovered by Milton H. Erickson in his early investigations of hypnosis in the 1930s, and was taught as a more streamlined approach to therapeutic hypnosis by Leslie LeCron in the 1950s.

David Cheek began his medical career as a specialist in gynecology and obstetrics. When he first learned about ideodynamic signaling in professional hypnosis training seminars taught by Erickson and LeCron, he was very skeptical about the value and validity of such an approach. His earliest papers, in fact, are marked by a cautious attitude of exploration; he was carefully seeking convincing criteria of the validity of ideodynamic signaling.

The first section of this volume traces the evolution of the theory and techniques of ideodynamic signaling for facilitating mind-body communication and healing. Many refinements in the early methods of ideodynamic finger signaling led to approaches that could maximize the validity of therapeutic explorations of the sources of mind-body problems. Cheek's investigations led him to formulate what we may designate here as his "basic clinical hypothesis": There are at least three levels at which mind-body information can be encoded: the *physiological,* the *ideodynamic,* and the *verbal* levels. Most conventional psychotherapy and "conversational hypnosis" deal only with information that is available to normal memory at the verbal level.

Information that is encoded at deeper psychobiological levels by the release of hormones and "messenger molecules" during times of emotional, physical, and surgical stress, however, becomes state-dependent or state-bound to that specific psychophysiological state of stress. When patients later apparently recover from their acute stress and return to their "normal" psychophysiological conditions, the statebound memories frequently are not accessible by the ordinary processes of memory accessed by the verbal level of conversational psychotherapy. The repetitive scanning of the stress-encoded psychobiological sources of memory and problematic behavior by use of ideodynamic signaling during a light state of hypnosis, however, can apparently serve as a mediator or bridge between the physiological and verbal levels. The ideodynamic accessing and reframing of state-dependent memories that encode stress and psychosomatic problems thus become the essence of the mind-body healing methods that are the focus of this volume.

Cheek's basic clinical hypothesis about the way ideodynamic signaling

---

*While Rossi prefers *ideodynamic* and Cheek *ideomotor,* both words refer to the same psychobiological process.

works raises a most provocative and profound question: *Does ideodynamic signaling really reach deeper into our psychobiological matrix to access sources of mind-body healing not usually available to verbally oriented psychotherapy?* The pioneering clinical case studies that comprise the *Practice* portion of each section of this volume suggest an affirmative answer to this question. Because Cheek's therapeutic success is apparently related to the careful series of questions he developed to ideodynamically access and reframe the psychobiological sources of specific problems, they have been outlined and highlighted with boldface print in special instructional boxes throughout this volume. These boxes can serve as a central focus of study for clinicians interested in learning this therapeutic approach; they may also serve as a methodological guide for investigators who may wish to pursue the very necessary research that is now needed to explore the general validity of Cheek's basic hypothesis and its implications for the further study of mind-body communication and healing.

Each section of this volume integrates a new area of *theory, clinical practice*, and *research*. The theoretical introductions were conceptualized and written by Rossi; the middle portions focusing on clinical practice and case histories are usually updated papers originally written by Cheek; the suggestions for further research to integrate theory and practice were conceived and written primarily by Rossi.

The first section begins by tracing the evolution of our current *psychobiological theory* of ideodynamic healing in hypnosis. It then introduces everything the beginning therapist needs to know about learning the *practical methods* of using ideodynamic approaches to psychological and psychosomatic problems. This section ends with suggestions for the types of *research* that are now needed for the further integration of clinical theory and practice.

The second section deals with motivation, stress, and the mind-molecule connection in therapeutic hypnosis. It explores the implications of the psychopharmacological method of "structure-activity analysis" for deepening our understanding of mind-body relationships.

The third section on state-dependent memory, meaning, and healing explores the theory, practice, and research concerned with unconscious perception of meaningful sound during surgical anesthesia. The research section reviews experimental data that support the intriguing notion that classical Pavlovian conditioning is actually a form of state-dependent learning.

The chapters in the fourth and fifth sections deal with new views about the molecular basis of psychosomatic medicine, emotion, and pain. They document the applicability of our ideodynamic approach to a wide range of problems that are not easily resolved by conventional medicine and psychotherapy. These chapters will explore how recent advances in our understanding of neuropeptides and their receptors as a new psychosomatic network may be providing us with the ultimate molecular basis of mind-body healing. We now refer to this new psychosomatic network as the "information substance-receptor communication system" (Is-receptor system). We believe that it may become the ultimate molecular basis for integrating biology and psychology in a common frame of reference.

Since Cheek began his medical career as a specialist in gynecology and obstetrics, one might expect that he would have made some interesting studies on the use of ideodynamic methods in these fields. This, indeed, is the case, and may in part explain why Cheek was in a most fortunate professional position to make such fundamental contributions. We now know, for example, that many of the hormones that are involved in the birth process (such as oxytocin and vasopressin) are also implicated in the state-dependent encoding of memory. Because of this, many women experience varying degrees of amnesia for what happened during the birth of their children, even when they deliver naturally or with the use of local anesthesia. The implications of these and many other hormonally-encoded state-dependent phenomena associated with the birth experience, sexuality, sleep, and dreaming are explored in the next four sections.

This volume ends with reflections on the use of hypnosis as a forensic tool. Forensic hypnosis is a highly controversial area in which the subtle insights of the clinician are often lost in the heat of public debate. The methods and aims of healing often conflict with the adversarial structure of the legal encounter. The issues that are raised in this area are of profound significance because they are at the growing edge of methodology in the legal and court arena, as well as in the continuing evolution of ethical consciousness itself. In this final section, we explore the implications of the special point of view we are presenting throughout this volume: Human memory, learning, and behavior are encoded on many psychobiological levels in sickness and in health, in normal and traumatic circumstances. A comprehensive and responsible understanding of human behavior can only come about by accessing these many levels in a valid and reliable manner for facilitating optimal communication and healing.

—Ernest Lawrence Rossi

SECTION I

The Evolution of Ideodynamic Concepts in Therapeutic Hypnosis

THEORY

Since ancient times, healers have been aware of the effects of words and ideas upon our physical well-being. Ideas can evoke real, dynamic physiological responses; hence the term *ideodynamic* to designate all the relationships between *ideas* and the *dynamic* physiological responses of the body. In the history of hypnosis, four stages have been recognized in the evolution of ideodynamic communication and healing (Erickson & Rossi, 1981):

Stage One: The ancient and medieval periods of prophecy, divination, and magic;
Stage Two: The beginning of hypnosis and the early theories of the Chevreul pendulum and ideomotor movement in the 1800s;
Stage Three: Behaviorism and the clinical rediscovery of ideodynamic movement and signaling in the 1900s;
Stage Four: The psychobiology of ideodynamic healing in hypnosis.

Our earliest records of the first stage of ideodynamic healing in the Western tradition go back to the Papyrus Ebers, which were written around 1,500 B.C. They describe the practice of magical incantation and ritual that evidently evoked healing by facilitating the experience of altered states, belief, and expectancy. Archeological evidence suggests that temples to gods such as Isis Serapis in Egypt and Asclepius and Apollo in Greece were used to facilitate healing around 400 B.C. Such practices were continued almost unchanged up to the Middle Ages, when the "healing touch" was used to evoke ideodynamic processes of cure. The early philosophers-physicians, such as Albert Magnus (1206–1280), Paracelsus (1434–1541), and Robert Fludd (1574–1637), still utilized incantations, faith, and essentially magical or archetypal (Jung, 1959) belief systems to facilitate healing.

The second stage of ideodynamic healing began with the classical period of Mesmerism and early hypnosis in the 1800s. In 1854 a French chemist, Chevreul, published *De la Baquette Divinatorie*, an experimental critique of the ancient beliefs and uses of devices of divination. At that time it was believed that pregnant women could hold a pendulum over their stomachs to determine the sex of their baby. If the pendulum swung in one direction it was a girl; if it swung in the other, it was a boy. Chevreul was able to demonstrate that such movements of the pendulum were actually due to the woman's unconscious knowledge and belief that gave rise to minimal muscular movements that could set the divinationary pendulum in motion.

This discovery was followed up by Bernheim (1886/1957), who recognized that the essential nature of hypnosis could be explained as an ideodynamic process. He formulated this idea in the terminology of his day as follows (Bernheim, 1886/1957, pp. 137–139):

> The mechanism of suggestion in general may then be summed up in the following formula: *increase of the reflex ideo-motor, ideo-sensitive, and ideo-sensorial excitability* . . . is increased in the brain, so that any idea received is immediately transformed into an act, without the controlling portion of the brain, the higher centers, being able to prevent the transformation.

Bernheim's theory is summarized in Box 1.

Such formulations of the essence of hypnotic healing in ideodynamic (primarily ideomotor and ideosensory) responsiveness provided the background for the third stage of experimental and clinical research in hypnosis during the early 1900s by Erickson (1932/1980) and Hull (1933). Weitzenhoffer (1953, p. 259) has summarized the influence of behaviorism on this early work as follows:

> The psychophysiological basis of suggestibility is *ideomotor action,* itself a form of conditioning. . . . The physiological bases of hypersuggestibility are (a) *neuromuscular enhancement* . . . and (b) *abstract conditioning.* . . . The psychophysiological basis of the hypnotic alteration of awareness is a combined selective inhibition and excitation of various cerebral regions leading to a dissociation of awareness from all stimuli except the voice of the hypnotist, unless otherwise specified by suggestions.

It is evident from this quotation that the behavioristic idea of *conditioning* was regarded as the basis of therapeutic suggestion. This was the dominant conception of therapeutic hypnosis when Cheek began his training and clinical work in the 1950s. As we shall see in the chapters of this volume, Cheek used the concept of conditioning; but his focus on the ideomotor approaches gradually led to the idea of *information transduction* from the physiological to the ideomotor to the verbal levels as his *basic clinical*

Hyppolyte Bernheim (1837–1919) was a professor in the Faculty of Medicine at Nancy, France when he described the ideodynamic basis of "suggestive therapeutics" in which ideas are transformed into acts (1886/1957, pp. 137–138):

> The one thing certain is that a *peculiar aptitude for transforming the idea received into an act* exists in hypnotized subjects who are susceptible to suggestion. In the normal condition, every formulated idea is questioned by the mind. . . . In the hypnotized subject, on the contrary, the transformation of thought into action, sensation, movement, or vision is so quickly and so actively accomplished, that the intellectual inhibition has not time to act. When the mind interposes, it is already an accomplished fact, which is often registered with surprise, and which is confirmed by the fact that it proves to be real, and no intervention can hamper it further. If I say to the hypnotized subject, "Your hand remains closed," the brain carries out the idea as soon as it is formulated. A reflex is immediately transmitted from the cortical centre, where this idea induced by the auditory nerve is perceived, to the motor centre, corresponding to the central origin of the nerves subserving flexion of the hand; —contracture occurs in flexion. There is, then, *exaltation of the ideo-motor reflex excitability, which effects the unconscious transformation of the thought into movement, unknown to the will.*
>
> The same thing occurs when I say to the hypnotized subject, "You have a tickling sensation in your nose." The thought induced through hearing is reflected upon the centre of olfactory sensibility, where it awakens the sensitive memory-image of the nasal itching, as former impressions have created it and left it imprinted and latent. This memory sensation thus resuscitated, may be intense enough to cause the reflex act of sneezing. There is also, then, *exaltation of the ideo-sensorial reflex excitability, which effects the unconscious transformation of the thought into sensation, or into a sensory image.* . . .
>
> The mechanism of suggestion in general, may then be summed up in the following formula: *increase of the reflex ideo-motor, ideo-sensitive, and ideo-excitability.*

While Bernheim's words sound a bit antiquated, he well describes information transduction as a basic process of therapeutic hypnosis. All modern approaches to mind-body healing attempt to facilitate this process of converting words, images, sensations, ideas, beliefs, and expectations into the healing, physiological processes in the body. Bernheim's use of the patient's own inner resources (suggestion "awakens the sensitive memory-image") anticipates Erickson's later development of the *naturalistic or utilization approach to therapeutic hypnosis* (Erickson 1958/1980, 1959/1980).

hypothesis about the mechanism by which stress-induced mind-body problems could be accessed and resolved.

Any serious effort to assess empirically the validity of Cheek's basic clinical hypothesis must deal with the question of how the physiological, ideomotor, and verbal levels are to be conceptualized as interacting with each other. What are the psychobiological mechanisms and connecting links between them? Why are these levels separated so that communication does not flow naturally between them? Why do dissociations and amnesias (giving rise to psychosomatic and psychological problems) exist between these levels? Obviously, processes of learning, conditioning, and imprinting are involved, but why should ideodynamic hypnosis be of special value in accessing and reframing these processes?

The well-known stimulus-response psychology of early behaviorism that was based on Pavlov's concept of conditioning was not able to answer these clinical questions in a satisfactory manner. The world view of behaviorism in the 1950s and 1960s seemed to inhibit clinical theory from dealing with such mental issues. Something more was needed to understand the rich complexity of clinical phenomena with human beings. Unknown to most psychotherapists, neuroscientists during this period were accumulating new facts and theories about the molecular biology of neural transmission and modulation that could greatly expand our clinical understanding of mind and behavior. In this and the following sections of the book, we will review some of these new ideas in order to expand our perspective about the psychobiology of ideodynamic healing in hypnosis.

The Psychobiology of Ideodynamic Healing in Hypnosis: A Clinical Introduction

Most of us still have a fairly naive conception of the nervous system as some sort of telephone exchange: a *stimulus* from the outside world evokes a *response* in a sense organ, which in turn transmits impulses along the nerves to our brain like messages along a telephone wire. We know that nerves (neurons) are separated from one another by small gaps called "synapses" and that "neurotransmitters" carry the message across the synapses from one neuron to another. This is called neuro*transmission*. More recent research over the past few decades, however, has gradually determined that there is another broad class of hormonal messenger molecules (also called "information substances") that modulate neurotransmission. These are the neuro*modulators* which stimulate or inhibit neural action, as well as the activity of most other cell, tissue, and organ systems of the body (Bloom, 1986; Iversen, 1986; Schmitt, 1984). The profound implications of the differences between *neurotransmission* and *neuromodulation* for ideodynamic healing in hypnosis will be discussed as a research issue at the end of this section.

One of the most significant developments in psychobiology during the past decade has been the finding that memory, learning, and behavior are influenced by a variety of these neuromodulators (Gold, 1987; Izquierdo & Dias, 1984; McGaugh, 1983; Stewart, 1985; Zornetzer, 1978). It has been found that hormonal information substances released by the stress of any novel life situation can act as neuromodulators. These information substances can modulate the action of neural systems of the brain so as to encode memory and learning in a special manner.

During the shock and stress of an automobile accident, for example, the special complex of information substances that are suddenly released by the limbic-hypothalamic-pituitary-adrenal system encodes all the external and internal sensory (visual, auditory, propioceptive, etc.) impressions of the accident in a special state or condition of consciousness. The accident victim is often recognized as being "dazed" and in an altered state of psychophysiological shock. Hypotherapists describe such shock states as *hypnoidal*: The memories of these traumatic events are said to be *deeply imprinted* as *physiological memory*, *tissue memory*, or *muscle memory*. We propose that all these designations are actually metaphors for the special *state-dependent encoding of memories by the stress released hormonal information substances*.

When accident victims recover from their acute trauma and return to their "normal" psychophysiological states a few hours or days later, they find to their surprise that the details of the accident that were so vivid when it took place are now quite vague and more or less forgotten. This is because the special complex of stress-released information substances that encoded their traumatic memories has changed as their mind-body returned to normal; the memories are thus not available to normal consciousness. We say they are now experiencing a traumatic amnesia. That the traumatic memories are still present and active, however, is evidenced by the fact that they may influence the accident victim's dreams, for example, and/or be expressed as psychosomatic problems. Clinicians typically hypothesize that the memories are *dissociated* from normal consciousness and encoded on "*deeply imprinted physiological levels*" where they form the nuclei of psychosomatic and psychological problems.

Essentially similar psychobiological processes of stress-encoded problems can take place in many other traumatic life situations. These range from what has been called the "birth trauma" to child abuse and molestation, from "shell shock" under battle conditions to the extremes of social and cultural upheaval and deprivation. There can be widely different responses to each of these situations, depending on the age of the person, the degree to which the traumatic situation is acknowledged and reviewed within oneself or with others, and the type of emotional support received. An effective mind-body therapy must take all these factors into account.

How does the hypnotherapist facilitate the resolution of these problems?

Presumably the ideodynamic focusing of attention on the reliving of the sensory details, cues, emotions, and circumstances of these special life events can associatively access the state-dependent encoding of the traumatic memories. Since these state-dependent memories are often encoded on *nonverbal levels* during the shock of these special life experiences, however, they may be more available to ideodynamic (ideosensory and ideomotor) finger signaling that is designed to access *nonverbal processes*.

We hypothesize that the repeated "mini stress" involved in the ideodynamic reviewing of the sensory and emotional circumstances of a traumatic event in hypnosis can partially reactivate the stress-released hormonal information substances that originally encoded that event in a statebound condition. The statebound information is thus brought into contact with the patient's ordinary cognitive and verbal ego processes that are usually still present during light and medium states of hypnosis. This allows the statebound or dissociated memories of the traumatic event to be accessed, discussed, and therapeutically reframed. This conceptualization has become the basis of a new psychobiologically oriented *state-dependent memory, learning, and behavior theory of hypotherapy* (Rossi, 1986c, d, 1987; Rossi & Ryan, 1986). A more extensive presentation of the research basis of this theory is presented in the research portion of this section under the heading: "The Psychobiology of Ideodynamic Healing in Hypnosis: Research Foundations."

The ideodynamic approaches to mind-body healing presented in this volume evolved out of classical hypnotherapeutic methods of the past, but they may find their most useful expression in the future as we develop even more sophisticated research into the psychobiology of state-dependent memory, learning, and behavior. At this point, our ideodynamic approach is still a clinical art based upon a combination of practical therapeutic success and clinical hypotheses about "how it works." The instructional boxes of this first section are centered about the practical details of evoking ideomotor and ideodynamic signaling in therapeutic hypnosis; they outline the major methodological approaches to mind-body communication and healing, as we use it today.

PRACTICE

1

An Introduction to Ideodynamic Methods in Hypnosis

The ideodynamic finger signaling method of mind-body communication and healing in hypnosis has evolved into a safe and flexible general approach to psychotherapy. This method is of value in providing a standardized clinical setting wherein the beginning therapist can learn to recognize the subtle behavioral signs of light, therapeutic hypnosis. It is also an ideal way of introducing patients to a modern, permissive, psychobiologically oriented form of hypnotherapy.

The History of Psychotherapy

AMNESIA AND DISSOCIATION AS THE CRITERIA OF TRANCE AND HYPNOSIS: BRAID, BREUER, FREUD, JUNG, ERICKSON

People often do not recognize the source of their problems. The history of psychotherapy, in fact, could be summarized as an effort to understand the amnesia surrounding the origins of psychological problems. The fascinating story of how such psychological "dissociation" is at the source of the ordinary amnesias of everyday life, as well as the psychopathology of neurosis, can be traced back to ancient times (Ellenberger, 1970). The beginnings of hypnosis over 200 years ago in the ideas of Mesmer, and continuing through the work of the fathers of hypnosis such as Braid (1795–1860) (see Box 2), Esdaile (1808–1859), and Bernheim (1837–1919), contain continual references to amnesia and dissociation as the criteria of trance and hypnosis (Tinterow, 1970).

The origins of psychoanalysis can be found in the detailed case studies of the same basic phenomenon: There is usually an amnesia for the source of psychological problems and neurosis. Psychoanalysis can be said to have begun with the publication of "On the Psychical Mechanisms of Hysterical Phenomena" in 1893 by Breuer and Freud. This paper was used by them again later as the first chapter of their classic *Studies on Hysteria* (1895),

---

BOX 2: JAMES BRAID'S ORIGINAL DEFINITION OF HYPNOSIS

James Braid (1795–1860), a Scottish physician generally regarded as one of the founders of hyponotism, recommended that it be defined as follows:

> Let the term *hypnotism* be restricted to those cases alone in which . . . the subject has no remembrance on awakening of what occurred during his sleep, but of which he shall have the most perfect recollection as passing into a similar stage of hypnotism thereafter. In this mode, *hypnotism* will comprise those cases only in which what has hitherto been called the double-conscious state occurs.
>
> And, finally, as a generic term, comprising the whole of these phenomena which result from the reciprocal actions of mind and matter upon each other, I think no term could be more appropriate than *psychophysiology*. (Tinterow, 1970, pp. 370–372)

In the first part of the quotation, Braid defines hypnotism as a process that modern researchers would term *state-dependent memory and learning*: What is learned and remembered is dependent on one's psychophysiological state at the time of the experience. Memories acquired during the state of hypnosis are forgotten in the awake state but are available once more when hypnosis is reinduced. In actual clinical practice today, patients rarely have a complete amnesia for their experience of therapeutic hypnosis; they tend to have partial amnesias that are associated with their personal complexes.

In the second part of the quotation, Braid's use of the generic term *psychophysiological* to denote all the phenomena of "the reciprocal actions of the mind and matter upon each other" was another prescience of our current psychobiological approach.

---

where it was presented as a "preliminary communication." They wrote (Breuer & Freud, 1895/1955, pp. 11–12):

> We have stated the conditions which, as our experience shows, are responsible for the development of hysterical phenomena from psychical traumas. In so doing, we have already been obliged to speak of abnormal states of consciousness in which these pathogenic ideas arise, and to emphasize the fact that the recollection of the operative psychical trauma is not to be found in the patient's normal memory but in his memory when he is hypnotized. The longer we have been occupied with these phenomena the more we have become convinced that *the splitting of*

consciousness which is so striking in the well-known classical cases under the form of 'double conscience' *is present to a rudimentary degree in every hysteria, and that a tendency to such a dissociation, and with it the emergence of abnormal states of consciousness (which we shall bring together under the term 'hypnoid') is the basic phenomenon of this neurosis.* In these views we concur with Binet and the two Janets, though we have had no experience of the remarkable findings they have made on anaesthetic patients.

We should like to balance the familiar thesis that hypnosis is an artificial hysteria by another—the basis and *sine qua non* of hysteria is the existence of hypnoid states. These hypnoid states share with one another and with hypnosis, however much they may differ in other respects, one common feature: the ideas which emerge in them are very intense but are cut off from associative communication with the rest of the content of consciousness. Associations may take place between these hypnoid states, and their ideational content can in this way reach a more or less high degree of psychical organization. Moreover, the nature of these states and the extent to which they are cut off from the remaining conscious processes must be supposed to vary just as happens in hypnosis, which ranges from a light drowsiness to somnambulism, from complete recollection to total amnesia.

In the final chapter of *Studies on Hysteria*, Freud summarized his early view of psychotherapy as follows (p. 255):

In our 'Preliminary Communication' we reported how, in the course of our investigation into the aetiology of hysterical symptoms, we also came upon a therapeutic method which seemed to us of practical importance. For 'we found, to our great surprise at first, that *each hysterical symptom immediately and permanently disappeared when we had succeeded in bringing clearly to light the memory of the event by which it was provoked and in arousing its accompanying affect, and when the patient had described that event in the greatest possible detail and had put the affect into words*'.

We further endeavoured to explain the way in which our psychotherapeutic method works. '*It brings to an end the operative force of the idea which was not abreacted in the first instance, by allowing its strangulated affect to find a way out through speech; and it subjects it to associative correction by introducing it into normal consciousness (under light hypnosis) or by removing it through the physician's suggestion, as is done in somnambulism accompanied by amnesia.*'

Unfortunately, it was often found that the initial problem started at birth or during the first two years of life. Since conscious memory does not begin until age two or three, it seemed impossible to access such early experience. Breuer initially had some success using hypnosis to access such amnesic experience; however, neither Breuer nor Freud was able to break through the traumatic amnesias and repressions of their hypnotized patients in a reliable manner.

Indeed, they found that their patients sometimes fabricated traumatic memories as the source of their current problems (Ellenberger, 1970).

Jung (1975) also relinquished the trauma concept and the practice of hypnosis. He was a forceful hypnotist who used the traditional, authoritarian approach characteristic of his time. His patients remembered traumatic experiences that probably had some factual basis, but under the stress of the authoritarian approach they were unable to convert these memories into a valid form of verbal communication. It is reasonable to infer that under this pressure, they, too, fabricated experiences. From our modern perspective we can recognize that Jung, like many other psychotherapists, demonstrated only the *unreliability of the authoritarian approach to hypnosis* when he said, "I gave up hypnotic treatment for this very reason, because I did not want to impose my will on others. I wanted the healing process to grow out of the patient's own personality, not from suggestions by me that would have only a passing effect" (Jung, 1964). (For a summary of Jung's views, see Box 3.)

A Revolutionary Shift

THE UTILIZATION APPROACH TO HYPNOSIS AND THERAPEUTIC SUGGESTION:
ERICKSON, FREUD, JUNG, ROGERS

The permissive, exploratory, and ideodynamic approach to therapeutic hypnosis pioneered by Milton Erickson eliminates the types of emotional pressure that encourages patients to fabricate (Erickson, 1980a). Freud, Jung, and most others in the psychoanalytic traditions would probably approve of Erickson's *utilization approach to therapeutic suggestion*, which he outlined as follows (1948/1980, p. 38):

> The next consideration concerns the general role of suggestion in hypnosis. Too often the unwarranted and unsound assumption is made that, since a trance state is induced and maintained by suggestion, and since hypnotic manifestations can be elicited by suggestion, whatever develops from hypnosis must necessarily be completely a result of suggestion and primarily an expression of it.
>
> Contrary to such misconceptions, the hypnotized person remains the same person. His or her behavior is altered by the trance state, but even so, *that altered behavior derives from the life experience of the patient* and not from the therapist. At the most the therapist can influence only

BOX 3: SPONTANEOUS TRANCE IN THE PSYCHOPATHOLOGY OF EVERYDAY LIFE

The experience of "spontaneous trance" or hypnoid states in the normal stream of everyday life was called an *abaissement du niveau mental* (a lowering of mental energy) by Janet (1907), who believed it was the source of mental dissociation and psychopathology. Jung noted that any stimulus or emotion that alters consciousness evokes "a disturbance of attention resembling hypnosis" (1957, pp. 234–235):

> Earlier writers maintain that [excessive *stimulation*] has a deleterious effect on the mental state. Allowing for diagnostic errors, the impairment will probably be confined to a *disturbance of attention resembling hypnosis*; this may offer a plausible explanation of our case. It should not be forgotten, however, that an alteration of this kind never occurs as a result of a mere decision: a certain predisposition is needed (what Forel would call a "dissociation"). And this is where, in my view, the decisive importance of *affects* comes in. As we have already explained at some length, *affects have a dissociating (distracting) effect on consciousness*, probably because they put a one-sided and excessive emphasis on a particular idea, so that too little attention is left over for investment in other conscious psychic activities. In this way all the more mechanical, more automatic processes are liberated and gradually attain to independence at the cost of consciousness. [Italics added]

Jung recognized that if spontaneous hypnosis was associated with the induction of psychological problems, then therapeutic hypnosis could be used to access and resolve these problems (1960a, pp. 234–235):

> If you study the association tests of neurotics, you will find that their normal associations are disturbed by the spontaneous intervention of complex contents typical of an *abaissement*. The dissociation can even go so far as to create one or more secondary personalities, each apparently with a separate consciousness of its own. But the fundamental difference between neurosis and schizophrenia lies in the maintenance of the potential unity of the personality. Despite the fact that consciousness can be split up into several personal consciousnesses, *the unity of all the dissociated fragments is not only visible to the professional eye but can be re-established by means of hypnosis*. [Italics added]

The importance of recognizing the ease with which spontaneous trance can inadvertently lead to the transference or iatrogenic induction of psychological problems has been described by Haberman (1986, 1987).

Erickson and Rossi (1976/1980) have outlined two dozen behavioral signs of spontaneous trance (relaxation, body immobility, eye changes, etc.) that can be utilized in a naturalistic approach to therapeutic hypnosis.

the manner of self-expression. *The induction and maintenance of a trance serve to provide a special psychological state in which patients can reassociate and reorganize their inner psychological complexities and utilize their own capacities in a manner in accord with their own experiential life.* Hypnosis does not change people nor does it alter their past experiential life. It serves to permit them to learn more about themselves and to express themselves more adequately.

Direct suggestion [authoritarian] is based primarily, if unwittingly, upon the assumption that whatever develops in hypnosis derives from the suggestions given. It implies that the therapist has the miraculous power of effecting therapeutic changes in the patient, and disregards the fact that *therapy results from an inner resynthesis of the patient's behavior achieved by the patient himself.* It is true that direct suggestion can effect alteration in the patient's behavior and result in a symptomatic cure, at least temporarily. However, such a "cure" is simply a response to the suggestion and does not entail that reassociation and reorganization of ideas, understandings, and memories so essential for an actual cure. *It is this experience of reassociating and reorganizing his own experiential life that eventuates in a cure,* not the manifestation of responsive behavior which can, at best, satisfy only the observer. [Italics added]

Erickson later noted how his utilization approach to therapeutic suggestion is particularly appropriate in stress situations (1959/1980, pp. 204–205):

These methods are based upon the *utilization of the subject's own attitudes, thinking, feeling, and behavior, and aspects of the reality situation*, variously employed, as the essential components of the trance induction procedure. In this way they differ from the more commonly used techniques which are based upon the suggestion of the subjects of some form of operator-selected responsive behavior. *These special techniques, while readily adaptable to subjects in general, demonstrate particularly the applicability of hypnosis under various conditions of stress* and to subjects seemingly not amenable to its use. They also serve to illustrate in part some of the fundamental psychological principles underlying hypnosis and its induction.

From this perspective we can now understand how Freud's development of "free association" and Jung's "active imagination" are both "utilization approaches" to accessing state-dependent memory and reframing problems. All the utilization approaches to therapy are in striking contrast to those behavior therapies and traditional styles of hypnosis that involve overt or covert conditioning, suggestion, and programming in the conventional sense of attempting to put an idea into the patient's mind. Gunnison (1985) has noted how the utilization approach is the common denominator between the seemingly different approaches of Erickson and Carl Rogers (p. 562):

> Erickson expressed his understanding of the inner world of his patients in a way different from Rogers. It was "through the use of the client's own vocabulary and frames of reference, pacing, and matching, a powerful kind of empathy developed that forms the interpersonal connection." He recognized that this was similar to the approach Rogers took to therapy.

Rogers has recently commented on the fundamental similarities behind the superficial differences between his approach and that of Erickson and Kohut (1978, 1981) in utilizing and reframing a patient's self-understanding (1987, p. 184):

> Erickson used different words, but it is clear that these changes in perception were also important to him. He spoke of the process of therapy as a loosening of the cognitive maps of the patient's experience, "helping them break through the limitations of their conscious attitudes to free their unconscious potential for problem-solving" (Erickson, Rossi, & Rossi, 1976, p. 18). This is very similar to my view that in a sound therapeutic relationship "all the ways in which the self has been experienced can be viewed openly, and organized into a complex unity" (Rogers, 1947, p. 366).
>
> Kohut is in general agreement. The restructuring of the self is central to his whole concept of therapy, and we share many common ideas.

Breaking through the limitations of conscious attitudes to free unconscious potentials for problem-solving often involves accessing state-dependent memories that remain cloaked (dissociated) under a traumatic amnesia. In one particularly dramatic case, for example, Erickson (1937/1980) learned how to break a traumatic amnesia by *the repetitive, recursive, and sequential reviewing of the original experience* during four hours of deep hypnosis. No authoritarian commands were given. Rather, Erickson ideodynamically facilitated the recovery of the traumatic memories by utilizing the patient's own sensory-perceptual processes and natural mental mechanisms. The patient was then able to use the recovered memories to better organize his life.

We believe that it is this simple but revolutionary shift from the early, error-prone authoritarian technique to Erickson's permissive and naturalistic approaches to accessing and creatively utilizing state-dependent memory, learning, and behavior (the essence of the patient's "inner resources") that accounts for the renaissance we are currently witnessing in the professional use of therapeutic hypnosis.

Ideomotor Signaling: A Utilization Approach

DEVELOPMENT OF LECRON AND CHEEK'S METHOD: USE OF THE CHEVREUL
PENDULUM; RESOLUTION OF A GAGGING PROBLEM

LeCron (1954) and Cheek and LeCron (1968) gradually built upon Erickson's work by developing ideodynamic signaling as a utilization approach that was consistently productive, easily taught and learned. Moreover, although this method eventually led to varying depths of hypnosis, it could be initiated and utilized with an apparently unhypnotized person. The therapist introduces the method as follows: **"We can use this little pendulum to find out about things that you cannot consciously remember. Notice that there are four major directions it can take that are easy to recognize and remember. It can circle clockwise or in the opposite direction; it can go transversely, or at right angles in a straight line. Your inner mind can select one of these swings for four different ideas:** *yes, no, I'm not ready to answer consciously yet, I don't know.*"

Either by thinking these words or by asking themselves questions to which the answer was an obvious yes or no, most subjects quickly learned ideodynamic signaling (see Box 4). LeCron then shifted into therapeutic work by asking his subjects to pretend they were observers in responding to questions about their problem. They were to avoid consciously thinking what the answer should be; rather, they could *wonder* what answer the pendulum would be giving. This observer attitude is an indirect approach to facilitating a light state of hypnotic dissociation.

At a hypnosis symposium given in 1956 in San Diego, I (DBC) watched LeCron help one of the participants solve a gagging problem of approximately 45 years' duration. This man would start to vomit whenever he brushed his back molars, and he was unable to tolerate placement of the little x-ray films in the back of his mouth. The total treatment time from introduction to the pendulum until resolution took less than 20 minutes. I have seen this subject many times in subsequent years; the problem recurred briefly in his dentist's office a few weeks later, but since that time he has remained free of his gagging difficulty.

This subject was not in hypnosis at the beginning of his treatment with LeCron, but he slipped into a light state as he saw the pendulum signaling yes to the question:

"Does the inner part of your mind know of some past event that could have caused this gagging problem?"

He then came out of hypnosis and turned toward the panel saying, "I have no idea of any past event like that."

He turned back to watch the pendulum. His facial expression ironed out as he waited for the response to the next question,

---

BOX 4: FACILITATING IDEODYNAMIC SIGNALS
WITH THE CHEVREUL PENDULUM

This approach is useful for introducing patients to hypnosis and ideodynamic signaling, particularly those who fear they cannot use hypnosis satisfactorily.

1. *Introduction to Chevreul Pendulum*
   "The pendulum simply reflects very slight body movement in response to thoughts of *yes*, *no*, and *I'm not ready to know the answer consciously yet*."

2. *Experiencing Ideodynamic Signals*
   "Hold the pendulum and think and feel, *yes-yes-yes*. Watch the pendulum carefully and let's see whether it will follow a repetitive circular or straight swing that will symbolize the *yes* answer." [Pause. If movements are not evident within a minute or so, continue as follows.]
   a. **"At first you may help it with your repeated conscious thought of *yes-yes-yes*! But soon the movement will happen all by itself on an unconscious level."** [Pause until both therapist and patient can identify the *yes* signal.]
   b. **"Now think and feel, *no-no-no*, and let's see which movement it makes."** [Pause until there is agreement about the *no* signal.]
   c. **Now let's see what kind of movement it makes to signal, *I'm not ready to know the answer consciously yet*.** [Pause until this signal is identified.]

3. *Ratification of Ideodynamic Pendulum Signaling*
   a. **"Ask yourself a question with an obvious yes answer. For example, "Is the sun shining?"** [Pause to verify that the pendulum signals with the agreed upon movement for *yes*.]
   b. **"Now ask yourself a question with an obvious no answer."** [Pause to verify that the pendulum signals with the agreed upon movement for *no*.]
   c. **When you are not sure the response is valid ask, "Does your inner mind agree with what you have just told me?"**

"Would that event have taken place before you were 30 years old?"
He was back in hypnosis again by the time he saw the pendulum signaling
yes. The pendulum continued to signal yes when he was asked if the event
took place before he was 20, and then ten years old. The next question was,
"Could it have taken place before you were five years old?"
At this stage the subject came out of hypnosis as the pendulum changed
its swing to indicate no. He put the pendulum down in his lap and launched
into a series of statements connected by several *and*s, until his concluding
shrug and slight movement of his right hand told us that he had finished. In
essence he said:

"Now I remember what it was. When I was a little boy in Chicago they
worried about me, and I was put in an open air school because they thought
I might have tuberculosis, and because I was underweight my mother forced
me to eat eggnog and extra amounts of milk until I felt constantly stuffed,
and then I began having sore throats and they took out my tonsils, and I
remembered that I hemorrhaged after the operation, and the house doctor
put a clamp in my throat and left it there all night."

This type of personal, spontaneous insight that is expressed in one rush
of free association is highly characteristic of the ideodynamic approach.

LeCron now asked his subject to hold the pendulum again and to let his
inner mind answer this question:
**"Now that you have remembered these things, can you be free of your
overactive gag reflex?"**
The pendulum answered yes. LeCron invited a dentist to come up to the
platform and test the subject's tongue and throat. There was no gag response. The subject took the tongue blade from the dentist and wiggled it
around the back of his throat without any discomfort.

The Evolution of Ideomotor Questioning

With further experience, LeCron and I learned that the signal *I don't know*
rarely reflected precisely that, but was rather being used as a polite way of
signaling, *I don't want to answer*. This was equally true of both finger
signals and pendulum responses. It seemed undesirable to let subjects get
away with an *I don't know* when they could be recognizing that something
was too stressful for them to face at the moment. If the question is poorly
constructed or confusing, the subject will look troubled. The question can
then be restated.

With the more recent recognition of the state-dependent encoding of
traumatic memories (Rossi, 1986d; Rossi & Ryan, 1986), we now know that
it may take time and adroit questioning to access the meaningful emotional
and mental sets associated with the amnesic material. Hence it is entirely
appropriate to allow the inner mind the option to signal, *I'm not ready to
know the answer consciously yet.* This is particularly true during the early

stages of questioning, when neither therapist nor patient has any idea about the source and psychodynamics of a problem. The *yet*, of course, frames a powerful implication and expectation that a satisfactory understanding will be forthcoming.

It was observed that signals given partly on the right hand and partly on the left hand frequently were reversed as subjects went deeper into hypnosis. When tested after arousal, a hypnotic anesthesia might be found on the opposite arm. A suggestion that the right arm would eventually lift to indicate a certain achievement might be accepted in a light hypnotic state, but later the left arm lifted instead. Eventually I did a study of the chronological development of handedness (Cheek, 1978), and found that about half of the population begins life with a preference for using the left hand to explore and grasp.

Reversal of finger signals was no longer a problem when we took the suggestion of Doctor Ralph Stolzheise, a psychiatrist from Seattle, to have our subjects keep all the signals on one hand. Then if the subject reversed hand dominance later, it would make no difference because the finger movements would retain their original meanings. (See Box 5 for a summary.)

It was less easy to determine what to do with pendulum swings that began shifting their meaning. We would stop the questioning when this happened and start the selection of responses again. Usually, however, it was easier to simply shift from using the pendulum to finger signals. The changed meaning of pendulum movements usually meant that the subject was in a hypnotic state that was already deep enough to use ideomotor finger signals.

Partial Versus Total Age Regression

In the early symposiums, endless hours were spent demonstrating deep trance phenomena and total age regressions to childhood. The methods often utilized visual imagery to "get on a magic carpet and float back up the river of life . . . further and further, younger and younger . . . and now you are just a little boy." Sometimes it was suggested that subjects look at an imaginary clock that was going backwards, "faster and faster . . . and now it is 1940 . . . getting younger and younger . . . now 1930 . . . " After a few months, however, we realized that much of this procedure was a waste of time; our subjects were usually ahead of us and impatient with our lengthy tactics. By adhering to preconceptions about the need for total age regression, we had mistakenly assumed that our hypnotized subjects needed to be able to talk, see, feel, and behave as if they were really reexperiencing an earlier age level. Such a process of total age regression takes a long time and is not necessary for most therapeutic work.

Indeed, a therapeutically useful *partial age regression* can occur within a moment or two when a very important incident of an individual's emotional

---

BOX 5: FACILITATING IDEODYNAMIC FINGER SIGNALS

Useful for resolving traumatic, emotional, and psychological problems associated with amnesia.

1. *Introduction to finger signaling*
   **"The inner part of your mind often knows what you have forgotten,
   or never even knew consciously. You can let your fingers do the
   talking for you."**

2. *Experiencing finger signals*
   a. **"Think and feel, *yes-yes-yes*, and wonder which finger your inner
   mind will lift to signal *yes*."** [Pause. If a definite movement is not
   evident within a minute, continue with: "Sometimes it feels as if an
   invisible string was pulling it up."]
   b. **"Now think and feel, *no-no-no*, until another finger on the same
   hand lifts to signal *no*."** [Pause. If a definite movement is not evident within a minute, continue with: "Really review deeply inside
   yourself something you definitely know you do not want."]
   c. **"Sometimes the inner mind is just not ready to let your conscious
   mind know something. So let yourself wonder for a moment until
   your inner mind signals, *I'm not ready to know consciously yet*,
   with another finger on the same hand."**

3. *Ratification of ideodynamic finger signals*
   **"Go back now to the beginning of last night's sleep. As you are
   falling asleep, your *yes* finger will lift. Each time you are dreaming,
   your unconscious will let your *no* finger lift. When you awaken,
   your *I'm not ready to know consciously yet* finger will lift."**

---

life is accessed. Behavioral and physiological indicators of partial age regression to a significant life event are sought. The most obvious of these indicators are emotional reactions such as tears, frowning or smiling, facial and
neck color alterations, sweating, sighing, and so forth. The more subtle
behavioral indications that meaningful material is being accessed include
changes in breathing patterns and heart rate, and the appearance of perspiration on the hand used for signaling. In the right light, the accumulation of
perspiration before a finger lifts to signal can be noted. Similarly, muscle
twitches on the back of the hand may be visible before a finger signal
becomes manifest.

Careful observation of many old-fashioned efforts at total age regressions indicated that the significant memories could be accessed rapidly with-

in a moment or two at this initial emotional and physiological level. We speculated that this affective response accessed the limbic-hypothalamic and reticular activating systems. It took longer for such memories to be expressed by action potentials moving skeletal muscles at the ideodynamic finger signaling level. Finally, at the highest integrative, cortical level, the memory could be expressed within cognitive frames of reference as a verbal communication. The time required for each step apparently depended on the degree of stress associated with the memory.

Thus we have developed a series of three observable steps to indicate the successful retrieval of forgotten or repressed experiences. This ideodynamic approach is fail-safe in that it places the responsibility of creative therapeutic work within the patient where it belongs, rather than on the therapist. The therapist is able to focus his or her efforts on helping patients access their own creative inner resources for resolving their problems in their own way. Successful experiences in therapy can then be more easily generalized to other life situations by the patients.

Is Ideomotor Information Valid?

Clinicians can be fooled by using ideodynamic questioning techniques, just as they can be fooled by the hallucinations and fabricated verbal reports of hypnotized subjects. We must always be wary of memories that are verbalized before or at the same time as an ideodynamic signal. We must also be concerned about the validity of reports that follow a single strong movement of a designated finger. These are initiated consciously and are not the best path for the accessing of statebound information that may never have been registered at the conscious level. Rapid verbal responses before an appropriate ideodynamic signal may be fabricated to please the hypnotist.

True unconscious ideodynamic signals are always repetitive and often barely visible. Sometimes we must rely on the slight vibratory movements shown by the tendon leading to a designated finger. With recall of stressful experiences, it is sometimes possible to see an accelerated release of droplets of perspiration around the tip of the finger that eventually will lift. This is a physiological response preceding the skeletal muscle lifting that finger. My basic clinical hypothesis is that there is a definite three-stage sequence involved in the valid recall of meaningful material (see Box 6).

We use the many special approaches outlined in the instructional boxes of this book to access the more stressful statebound memories. The three-stage process of accessing highly meaningful but amnesic memory is a clinical art that requires careful observation and sensitivity to the demand characteristics of the social setting and the transference situation, as well as to the personal, behavioral patterns of the patient. It proceeds best in an open and supportive atmosphere of positive therapeutic expectation that engages a sense of curiosity and wonder in both therapist and patient.

**BOX 6: THREE-STAGE CRITERIA FOR ASSESSING
VALIDITY OF IDEODYNAMIC SIGNALING**

1. *Emotional and physiological memory* can be seen first through changes in respiration, pulse rate, and emotional reactions. These occur very rapidly and must appear *before* a designated finger lifts to show an inner orientation to the time of an important experience.

2. *Ideodynamic signals* indicate the accessing of memory at an unconscious level. They usually occur a few seconds after the appearance of physiological memory. At the moment the finger lifts signaling this second, higher level of memory, the patient still does not have a verbal level of awareness of the experience; there are only feelings of anticipation, vague unrest, or discomfort.

3. *Verbal reporting* of the experience follows these physiological and ideomotor indications of the inner accessing of meaningful material. To reach this conscious horizon of verbal thought, the entire experience may have to be reviewed repeatedly. The patient is told that one finger will lift to signal the beginning of an experience and another finger to signal its ending. The number of required repetitions to elevate the memory from deep unconscious zones of memory storage depends upon the gravity of the experience.

Problems with Ideomotor Questioning Methods

No Signals. Some individuals cannot or will not develop either pendulum swings or definite finger signals. Such behavior is most often seen with patients who have had a series of failures with other modes of treatment at the hands of highly competent physicians. No signals may be an unconscious defense against the possibility of another failure. Obviously, the hypnotherapist needs to access and correct this problem.

A practical psychological approach that I typically use involves a training procedure to heighten a patient's sensitivity to his or her own ideodynamic processes with postural suggestions. A number of authors have described a variety of these procedures as methods of assessing and facilitating suggestibility (Erickson & Rossi, 1981; Weitzenhoffer, 1953, 1957). A flexible routine I call "postural suggestion training" is outlined later in Chapter 14. Its use in a variety of therapeutic situations is illustrated throughout this volume.

Individuals unable to allow ideomotor responses may be the ones most in need of help. If their initial difficulty persists even after the postural suggestion training, we would not persist in the search for causes but rather teach the patient self-hypnosis and do what is possible in the way of symptom alleviation and ego strengthening.

Substitutions of Unimportant Events. This is common in any form of psychotherapy. Individuals in hypnosis are economical in their energy output; they will try to "get away with" the least amount of work. The therapist can be led astray. When ideomotor methods are used and a patient has released what seems important, we ask further:

"Could there have been some earlier experience that set the stage for the one you have just reported?"

We continue to regress in time until the patient is emotionally satisfied and the problem is resolved.

This process has often led to birth as a source of a number of maladjustment problems: feelings of rejection at not hearing a mother's voice; headaches conditioned by pressure on the head during a labor that was painful or frightening for the mother; respiratory difficulties stemming from exhaustion of the baby's resources during a long labor with the mother heavily sedated; gastrointestinal problems with babies that were not nursed by their mothers after a difficult labor. LeCron (1963) wrote about his observations in a cautious paper; we explore these birth trauma issues in Section IX of this volume.

Signals Given but Refusal to Answer Verbally, or Signals that Change or Become Multiple and Unreadable. This gives the therapist immediate knowledge about resistances. Recognition of this fact can save time and cost to the patient and can also stimulate the patient into thinking about the necessity to continue resisting. There may be a resolution of the problem between visits. The reader will find a discussion of these factors in Section II, which deals with motivation and resistance.

Two major classes of typical resistance are:

1. *Intrinsic factors* arising within the patient:
   • "flashback" to a previous unpleasant spontaneous hypnoidal state;
   • previous frightening association (e.g., watching demonstrations);
   • unresolved need for symptom or problem.
2. *Extrinsic factors* arising from the environment:
   • unfavorable reaction to therapist;
   • rebellion against request for therapy by someone else;
   • association with critical or resistant people.

The first of these, the "flashback" to a previous unpleasant spontaneous hypnoidal state, is of special theoretical interest, since it is a clear manifestation of the type of state-dependent memory, learning and behavior that is the basis of many dissociative, hypnotic, and psychosomatic phenomena (Rossi & Ryan, 1986). Ways of dealing with this source of "resistance" are described in Section II of this volume. The other sources of resistance listed above usually can be dealt with by a combination of traditional verbal level therapy and further exploratory efforts using ideodynamic signaling.

Initial Inability to Signal No. Another form of resistance that is usually associated with cultural, religious, or family training in passivity is seen with the patient who is easily able to give a yes signal but initially cannot give a no signal. This is an important psychodiagnostic clue. These people simply don't know how to say no at an inner ideodynamic level. It is likely that many of their life problems stem from this difficulty. Training them to give the no signal then becomes a very effective initial approach to ego strengthening. A variety of ideomotor postural training experiences usually will heighten patients' sensitivity sufficiently for them to learn to make the ideomotor no response. Once it is achieved, ego strengthening can proceed by asking a number of simple and obvious questions that enable patients to rehearse the no response (e.g., "Are you standing up? Is it raining outside?").

Persistent Inability to Signal. A persistent inability to give any apparent ideomotor signal may indicate a difficulty in the transference situation between therapist and patient. The therapist's attitude, approach, or frames of reference may not be appropriate for this particular patient. Therapist and patient may need to take a fresh look at the problem and/or the dynamics of their interaction. Both may need to feel more secure before they can proceed successfully.

Ideosensory Signals. Occasionally, very sensitive subjects will experience such vivid sensory responses (the finger may feel a shock, tingle, or jolt of energy; it may become warm or cool, and so forth) that they may be reluctant to actually move it. Their fingers and/or their entire hand and arm can remain stiff (cataleptic), even while a strong sensory response is experienced. The therapist can utilize these ideo*sensory* responses just as well as the ideo*motor* responses. With the ideosensory responses, however, the patient must verbalize whether a yes or no response is being experienced. Alternatively, the therapist can suggest that the patient's unconscious can translate the ideosensory response into a slow, repetitive head nodding for yes, or a slow head shaking from side to side to signal no.

Summary

The ideodynamic approach to healing in hypnosis has the following characteristics:

1. It is a fail-safe procedure that places the locus of therapy within the patient, where it belongs. The patient is treated as a colleague in the therapeutic process.
2. Pendulum and finger signaling accesses statebound information that

may not be available to the patient's typical conscious verbal levels of functioning.

3. Approaching the significant life experience in a progression of steps often facilitates a rapid desensitization of the original traumatic or stressful experience.

4. The method of ideodynamic questioning is simple and easy to learn. It rapidly facilitates the therapist's sophistication in accessing and therapeutically reframing a wide range of psychological and psychosomatic problems.

5. Resistance to constructive change is immediately evident. An accessing and therapeutic reframing of the sources of such resistance is immediately possible.

6. The unknown psychological needs of the patient are respected at all times. The patient's own unconscious inner repertory of creative resources is continually accessed to facilitate healing.

7. Troublesome abreactions and negative iatrogenic reactions to therapy can be avoided easily.

8. Ideodynamic signaling can be initiated with the patient in an unhypnotized state and therefore is of special value to the beginner in hypnotherapy.

9. The introduction of the Chevreul pendulum and finger signaling sets up an inherently interesting and absorbing clinical situation that focuses the patient's attention and facilitates the experience of mild, carefully controlled therapeutic dissociations.

10. This safe ideodynamic approach provides both therapist and patient with a relaxed setting in which they can learn to observe and use altered states and clinical hypnosis in a therapeutic manner.

2

Two Basic Ideodynamic Approaches to Psychosomatic and Psychological Problems

The usual approach to stressful life events that are responsible for symptomatic and maladaptive behavior is to hypnotize a subject and ask for a verbal report. The desired outcome may not be reached in this way, however; ordinary conversational hypnosis may fall short of its goal. In this chapter, I (DBC) will discuss the reasons for the failures of ordinary conversational methods of hypnoanalysis and the reasons for using ideomotor methods. Then I will present two general approaches to ideomotor signaling that are appropriate for most psychobiological and psychosomatic problems. Each approach has its values and its limitations.

Talking depends on associative pathways within the cortex of the brain. The ability to report verbally on visual, auditory, olfactory, tactual, and positional stimuli depends on the highest levels of cortical activity. Unless the original stressful experience has also reached the highest levels of the central nervous system integration, the therapist may witness a patient's emotional distress and physical discomfort but be unable to help the person talk about the causal experience. Rarely will experiences prior to two years of age be registered at conscious levels of awareness. Rarely will they be reached in a hypnotic state light enough to permit easy, conversational communication. They may be accessed by the subject in very deep hypnosis, but this frequently inhibits the ability to talk. The same observation applies to experiences under general anesthesia, unconsciousness due to trauma, the ideation of deep, natural sleep, and experiences too stressful to be allowed into conscious recognition.

Although the brain stem and limbic-hypothalamic paths of sensory input usually remain functional during these stressful experiences, they may be encoded in a statebound form so that they are not available to consciousness. Retrieval with ordinary conversational hypnotic methods is seldom possible (Cheek, 1959, 1962c,d).

An authoritarian and forceful approach to such experiences with conversational hypnosis may result in defensive action by the subject. There may be initial refusal to confront the event followed by refusal to enter hypnosis again. The pressured subject may substitute an earlier or later unimportant "trauma" in the hope of escaping further discomfort. As a last resort, if pressed too hard, the subject may invent an experience that never happened. As noted earlier, it was this inventiveness of the unconscious mind that led to Jung's abandonment of hypnosis as an untrustworthy tool (1975).

A coercive approach to a traumatic experience may lead to an outpouring of emotional distress. Some authorities believe this to be a requirement for successful therapy. All too often, however, an authoritarian approach may lead to further entrenchment of troubled behavior. Emotional catharsis offers no problem for the experienced hypnotist but it can have a devastating effect on the beginner. Any expression of fear or confusion from the therapist is quickly perceived by the hypnotized subject and can eliminate any benefits that might have come from the revivification of the traumatic event. It may so shake the therapist that he or she abandons hypnosis entirely.

These unsettling problems can be avoided with the ideodynamic approach. Ideodynamic signaling with the Chevreul pendulum or the fingers allows a rapid accessing of the sources of psychosomatic symptoms and psychological problems. The mild, dissociative reaction that usually takes place during ideodynamic signaling permits the patient to be an onlooker or "objective witness" to the process. One patient illustrated this mild, dissociative, and therapeutic reaction by saying, "I'm not to blame. It's my fingers that are talking." Resistance due to guilt, self-punishment, unfavorable identifications, fear of facing unknown threats and unconscious manipulative needs are quickly revealed at the start of therapy and are usually obvious to both patient and therapist. The therapist can then deal with all these therapeutic issues with a systematic "20 questions" method.

The Retrospective Approach: 20 Questions Method

LeCron developed a very useful retrospective approach going from the present moment back to earlier life experiences for exploring the traumatic source of problems; this is particularly valuable for the beginner in the uses of hypnosis. The method sometimes meets with obstruction as the patient gets closer to a very traumatic event, but there are ways of dealing with such a temporary resistance. The retrospective approach has two major virtues. The first is that patients are led to review their primary traumatic events at an unconscious level each time they give an ideodynamic response to questions about the events. In so doing, the impact of the original traumas tends to become desensitized. A second virtue is that this unconscious desensitization process eliminates the risk of patients' suddenly abreacting and disrupting the therapeutic process in a way that the therapist is unable to deal with effectively.

First, the patient is asked if there is some past event responsible for a problem. After getting a yes response, the therapist determines when the event took place, keeping in mind that an unconscious economy of effort may lead a patient toward an event that is relatively unimportant. Discussion of this event may make the therapist believe the solution has been found. It is important to ask,

"Is there some earlier event that might have set the stage for what you have just told me?"

When the goal seems to have been reached the therapist asks,

"Knowing this, does the inner part of your mind feel you can now be well?"

If the answer is affirmative, it is helpful to ask for an orientation into the future when the patient knows he is well and unafraid of the trouble returning. Inability or refusal to access such a time is an indication of previously unrecognized resistance. (See Box 7.)

The "20 questions" technique moves rapidly. It is best to start with a Chevreul pendulum. There is no need to induce hypnosis formally because it will occur spontaneously as the patient becomes interested in the unconscious responses.

AN ILLUSTRATION OF THE RETROSPECTIVE APPROACH: PSEUDOCYESIS WITH
AMENORRHEA OF 18 MONTHS

(Total interview time is 60 minutes.)

An intelligent, healthy woman was referred by the resident in obstetrics because she wanted very much to have children. Her last menstrual period had occurred 18 months earlier. There had been eight negative pregnancy tests contradicting evidence of "milk" in her breasts, nausea, weight gain, and protuberance of her abdomen. Her answers to the following questions were given with the Chevreul pendulum.

Q: Does the inner part of your mind know you can have babies?
A: (No.)*

---

*All nonverbal pendulum-ideomotor answers are indicated by parentheses.

BOX 7: THE RETROSPECTIVE APPROACH TO IDEODYNAMIC SIGNALING

This approach is useful for the beginning therapist as a safe approach to desensitizing traumatic problems.

1. *Accessing a problem*
   a. **"Is there some past event responsible for your trouble?"**
      [If answer is no, ask if there could be a group of events.]
   b. **"Was it before you were 20 years old? Ten years old? Eight years old?" Etc.**
   c. **"Review what is happening at that time. When you know what it is, your yes finger will lift. As it lifts, the memory will come up and you will be able to talk about it."**

2. *Therapeutic reframing*
   a. **"Is it all right to tell me about it?"**
      [Allow the patient to verbalize the memories and facilitate therapeutic reframing as needed.]
   b. **"Is there an earlier experience that might have set the stage, or made you vulnerable to what you have just told me?"**
      [If answer is yes, proceed as in Step 1 above.]

3. *Ratifying therapeutic gains*
   a. **"Now that you know this, can you be well?"**
      [A no response means that further insight and reframing is required, as in Steps 1 and 2 above.]
   b. **"Is there anything else we need to know before you can be free of this problem?"**
      [If it is evident that the patient's symptom, habit, or problematic behavior cannot be resolved completely at that time, find a date for a more complete cure, as follows:]
   c. **"Let your inner mind give a yes signal when it is ready to pop the date of a completely satisfactory resolution of that problem into your conscious mind."**
      [If there is no satisfactory response, more therapeutic work is required, as in Step 2 above.]

Q: Would it be all right for you to know why you feel this way?

A: (No.)

Q: Would it be all right for me to know?

A: (I don't want to answer.)

Q: Would it be all right for your husband to know why you feel you cannot have children?

A: (Yes.)

Q: Is there some past event that has made you feel this way?

A: (Yes.)

Q: Was it before you were 20 years old?

A: (Yes.)

Q: Before you were 10 years old?

A: (Yes.)

Q: Before you were five years old?

A: (Yes.)

Q: Before you were two?

A: (Yes.)

At this point the patient put the pendulum down on her lap and said, "How could I be so stupid?" She then went on to say, "My father died of pneumonia when I was three months old and I guess I have been afraid that if I had a child my husband would die." I asked her to hold the pendulum up again and let it answer this question:

"Is this the whole answer?"

The pendulum said yes. I then asked her to go forward to the time when she could start her next period. She visualized a date on an imaginary black-board about two weeks from the time of my interview. Her breast swelling and secretion stopped in a few days. The nausea disappeared at the end of the interview. She missed the selected day for menstruation by 24 hours and continued then on schedule. At a second interview her fingers indicated that she would be ready to begin a pregnancy without fear in a few months.

The Progressive Chronological Approach
to Traumatic Life Experience

In searching for the traumatic sources of a problem via the retrospective approach, patients often block on unpleasant memories. It seems that later reliving of a troublesome experience at unconscious levels of awareness tends to put up resistances to retrieving the memory at the upper levels of thought associated with speech. Two tactics are useful in dealing with such resistance. One is to ask the patient to go over the experience as it might have been, if all the right things had been said and done to have made it a pleasant memory. The patient then fabricates an idealized experience. For example, a patient might say, "The surgeon is saying that I do not have cancer."

The second approach is to go back to a time *before* the event could possibly have occurred. In the case of an operation, it would be the time of admission to the hospital. By advancing in a progressive, chronological manner, it is easy to have the patient observe what is happening. I have found that it is possible to obtain traumatic information previously inaccessible with the retrospective approach by using this progressive, chronological method (see Box 8).

An Illustration of the Progressive Chronological Approach: Hemorrhaging Two Weeks After Delivery

An obstetrical patient calls on the telephone for an emergency consultation. She is home with her two-week-old baby boy. She had just started nursing him when she began profuse vaginal bleeding. Her voice is tense and fearful as she envisions having to return to the hospital.

Doctor (Dr): There probably is an emotional reason for your bleeding now. You are an excellent hypnotic subject, so let's find out why this happened. Let me see, which is your yes finger? Think *yes*, and tell me which finger goes up.

[The reason for asking this question was to dissociate the patient from the immediate problem of hemorrhage. Later she reported that she had felt the bleeding stop as soon as she shifted her attention to communications that in the past had been associated with comfort in the doctor's office.]

Patient (Pt): My index finger is lifting.

Dr: Now let you inner mind go back to the moment when you were sitting down to nurse your son, just before you began bleeding. When you are there, your yes finger will lift. When it lifts, just say "Now," so I can keep up with you.

Pt: [After about 10 seconds] Now.

Dr: Now come up to the moment when you know you have started bleeding. When you are there, your yes finger will lift again. As it lifts, please tell me what is going on around you in your home that might have something to do with triggering your bleeding.

Pt: It's lifting! Oh, my! My daughter has been with her grandmother for the

BOX 8: THE PROGRESSIVE CHRONOLOGICAL APPROACH
TO IDEODYNAMIC SIGNALING

This approach is useful for the more experienced therapist to access significant but forgotten life events.

1. *Accessing a problem*
   a. **"When you are there at the time before there was any trouble, your yes finger will lift. Let that picture develop and tell me where you are and what is happening."**
   b. **"Now come forward in time to the very first moment you are feeling that something important is happening in relation to this problem. When you are there, your yes finger will lift."**

2. *Therapeutic reframing*
   a. **"As it lifts, please tell me the first thing that comes into your mind. Don't edit it. Just say it, even if it seems ridiculous."**
   [Allow time for emotional catharsis and/or spontaneous insights.]
   b. **"Now come forward in time to the next thing that makes that first experience important in causing the problem you have had."**
   [Allow patients to verbalize spontaneous insights and facilitate therapeutic reframing as needed.]
   c. **"Is there any other experience we should know about?"**

3. *Ratifying therapeutic gains*
   a. **"Please come forward in time to the moment you know you are completely well. When you are there, your yes finger will lift."**
   b. **"Look over to one side and see a blackboard with the date written on it in chalk. When you see that at an unconscious level, your yes finger will lift. As it lifts, tell me the date."**
   [Any difficulty in verbalizing this date of "cure" means that more work is needed in Steps 1 and 2 above.]
   c. **"When your inner mind knows that it can continue with that curative process all by itself—letting your conscious mind have whatever insights it needs to facilitate it—your yes finger will lift again."**

past two weeks. She has just come home. She opened the door as I began nursing. I saw that look in her eyes. It reminded me of my own return home to find my mother nursing my little sister. The thought I had was, *Will I have enough love to give her, too?*

Dr: Let me ask your finger. Now that you have discovered this, can you stop your bleeding?

Pt: My finger signals yes, and I can feel that the bleeding has stopped already.

Dr: You are great! Now finish this nursing, but when you are through, please sit down and explain to your daughter what you have just discovered. She needs to know that she is an important part of the family. Call me back in about half an hour and let me know how you are doing.

Pt: [Thirty minutes later] The bleeding has stopped completely, and I spoke with my daughter. She told me that she felt that her visit with her grandmother was arranged because we wanted to spend all our time with the baby.

The ease and simplicity of using this progressive chronological approach are well illustrated by this emergency case. The healing emotional response and insight the woman experienced came as a spontaneous accompaniment to the ideodynamic signaling process. Overt psychoanalysis or direct suggestion by the therapist was not required. The therapist simply set in motion an ideodynamic search that allowed the patient's own unconscious process to access the traumatic source of her problem. The seemingly spontaneous insight that followed is a natural consequent of the successful accessing of the statebound memory that triggered her bleeding.

Recursion, Healing, and the Creation of Meaning

It may have been noticed that the retrospective (Box 7) and progressive (Box 8) approaches to ideodynamic signaling are repetitive, iterative, and recursive. That is, they are circular processes; if a satisfactory therapeutic gain cannot be ratified by the third step, then we return to step one and repeat the entire process again. Each time we repeat the process anew, however, we begin with whatever therapeutic gain we have already achieved. Each repetition builds on what preceded it. A final satisfactory therapeutic gain often proceeds by this iterative process of successive approximations. Cybernetic theory describes this circular feedback process wherein the output becomes the input as a *recursive function* (Hofstadter, 1979).

Recursive functions are built into our nervous system; it is found, for example, that the output of a nerve cell often feeds back to the same cell to modulate its further activity. This recursive function is found to be a fundamental feature of virtually all of our sensory and motor processes at the cellular and molecular levels (Segal, 1986; von Foerster, 1984). A series of theoretical developments and experimental findings in the cybernetics of living systems, from Schrodinger's 1947 classic *What is Life?* to Maturana's (1970, 1971) "Biology of Cognition," and Hofstadter's *Gödel, Escher, Bach* (1979), implicate the recursive function as the essential operation that allows for the generation of ever new forms of complexity from the molecular, genetic, and cellular levels to that of the whole organism.

More recently, Watzlawick (1984) and the constructivist philosophers have described how the recursive function is the essence of all processes of self-reflexivity, self-awareness, and self-reflection. Ultimately, the recursive function leads to the creation of meaning and identity for society as a whole, as well as for individuals. We will explore the fuller implications of the recursive function for the "invention of reality" (Watzlawick, 1984) in Section IX of this volume. For now, it is enough to recognize that much of the efficacy of the ideodynamic signaling methods we summarize in our boxed outlines probably comes from the utilization of this recursive function to generate new therapeutic frames of reference for facilitating healing.

3

Ideodynamic Head, Hand, and Arm Signaling

In teaching ideodynamic signaling to psychotherapists with many different theoretical backgrounds, the author (Rossi) has discovered its useful generalizability to almost any therapeutic situation. One need not describe ideodynamic signaling as a form of hypnosis because there is no valid empirical method for assessing whether or not an altered state is involved. When used by hypnotherapists, these ideodynamic approaches can facilitate states of dissociation and hypnotic phenomena because the hypnotist knows how to facilitate such experiences. When used by Gestalt, Rogerian, psychoanalytic, behavioral, cognitive, movement practitioners or family therapists, however, these same ideodynamic approaches can be usefully employed within their frameworks without calling it "hypnosis." The most useful common denominator that ideodynamic signaling provides for healers of all persuasions is that a convincing, overt behavioral signal is generated by the patient whenever a useful bit of therapeutic progress has been experienced.

New approaches to the ideodynamic accessing of therapeutic states and the resolution of mind-body problems utilize a variety of ingenious head, hand and arm signaling procedures (Erickson, 1961/1980). These approaches are especially useful because they can be experienced so easily by most people as a mildly dissociated or state-dependent expression of their creative unconscious. The "double bind induction with the moving hands approach to ideomotor signaling," for example, was originally developed as a fail-safe approach to therapeutic hypnosis (Erickson & Rossi, 1981, pp. 126-142). Between 70 to 81% of the subjects tested are successful in experiencing the "moving hands" and the "hand lowering" items when they are presented as an ideomotor suggestion on the Stanford Hypnotic Susceptibility Scale (Hilgard, 1965). When head, hand, and arm signaling is used in a flexible manner with the implied directive and the conscious-unconscious therapeutic double bind, almost all patients can experience a fascinating and enjoyable approach to accessing their own creative resources.

This chapter has been written entirely by Rossi.

35

The *implied directive* (see Box 9) and the *conscious-unconscious double bind* (see Box 10) (Erickson & Rossi, 1979, 1981; Rossi & Ryan, in preparation) can be utilized either separately or together, with infinite variations for facilitating the experiencing of ideodynamic signals by the fingers, hands, arms, shoulders, head, mouth, eyelids, or any other part of the body that can move. Whenever spontaneous tics or apparently involuntary movements are made during therapeutic hypnosis, they can be utilized as an approach to initiating ideodynamic signaling with a question such as:
"And you can simply wonder if that movement was a signal from your unconscious. Was it a yes or no response to something I have said? . . . Or was it an expression of your own private experience?"

BOX 9: THE IMPLIED DIRECTIVE

The implied directive is a means of accessing and facilitating the expression of inner resources that are not normally under voluntary control. The implied directive can be regarded as a general, permissive and nondirective means of helping patients explore and realize their healing potentials. It has three recognizable parts:

1. A time-binding introduction:
   As soon as
2. The implied suggestion initiating an unconscious search taking place within the patient:
   your unconscious has reached the source of that problem,
3. The behavioral response that signals when the implied suggestion has been accomplished:
   your finger can lift [head can nod, arm can lower, etc.].

Useful Alternative Implied Directives:
"When you have found a feeling of relaxation and comfort, your eyes will close all by themselves."
"As that comfort deepens, your conscious mind can relax while your unconscious reviews the problem."
"And when a relevant and interesting thought reaches your conscious mind, your eyes will open as you carefully consider it and share only as much with me as I need to know to help you further."

As can be seen from these examples, the patient's own unconscious processes actually solve the problem that the conscious mind could not handle.

BOX 10: THERAPEUTIC BINDS FACILITATING CREATIVE CHOICE

The therapeutic double bind is a permissive, non-authoritarian approach to facilitating creative choice that is in tune with the humanistic, existential, and transpersonally oriented psychotherapies. These permissive approaches are ideally suited for facilitating personality development, mind-body healing, and the nondirective exploration of human potentials. As can be seen in the following general format, the therapeutic double bind consists of a series of implied directives presented in such a manner that all possibilities of response are covered; the subject is channeled in a healing, creative direction regardless of what choices are made. The "conscious-unconscious double bind" is involved because inner healing is facilitated even if the conscious mind is not aware of how, when, or what is done on an unconscious level.

1. *An implied directive . . .*
   "When your unconscious is ready to let you go into a state of inner healing (or therapeutic trance), you'll find yourself growing quiet, with your *eyes closing all by themselves.*"
   [If eyes do not close within 30 seconds or so, continue:]

2. *Becomes a therapeutic double bind . . .*
   "If the unconscious first needs to review another important issue, you'll find yourself *discussing an interesting question* that will prepare you for deeper healing (trance) work."
   [If there is no apparent effort to speak within 30 seconds or so, continue with another double-binding alternative:]

3. *Covering all possibilities of response.*
   "If you find yourself reluctant to speak, you can continue just as you are, allowing the unconscious to do what it needs to do, with your *head slowly nodding yes* all by itself as you go deeper into healing (trance)."
   [If there is no visible head nodding, continue:]
   "Unless you are already so comfortable that your unconscious can allow you to *remain perfectly still* as it resolves all the important issues by itself. . . .
   And you may or may not be aware of all the healing, constructive inner work that is being done all by itself, with each breath you take."

(A) STANDARD POSITION FOR HAND AND ARM SIGNALING: FACILITATING AN
OPTIMAL BALANCE OF WITNESSING AND EXPERIENCING

A standard format for presenting the "moving hands accessing of creative
resources" is outlined in Box 11. As always, this outline needs to be adapted
in a flexible manner to the language and frames of reference that are most
suitable for the individual patient. Most people with whom Rossi has
worked, for example, find it agreeably fascinating to experience their head,
hands, or arms moving "all by themselves" under the real or imagined
"natural magnetic forces" of their bodies. When the therapeutic process is
conceptualized as an accessing of their "creative resources for growth and
healing," the seemingly autonomous ideomotor movements of their head,
hands, and arms are taken as a signal of the positive and constructive
cooperation of their "inner mind." Patients feel supported by their own
inner resources and are quickly oriented to exploring their autonomy and
strength in coping with their problems. Their own ideomotor signals are
interpreted as "objective proof" that they can call upon the help of their
creative sources whenever they need to.

With a comfortable standard initial position, the following open-ended
suggestions, phrases, and questions tend to structure ideodynamic processes
for problem-solving.

**"Review a happy or deeply satisfying memory and notice how those hands
will move together all by themselves to signal yes."**
Pause as hands move together with the slow, hesitant, sometimes jerky
movements.

**"Now review an unhappy situation to which you wish to say no, and experi-
ence how those hands move apart."**
If there is no apparent movement, the hypnotherapist can shift this situation into a double bind by continuing with:

**"Or is the unconscious already so deeply involved that it is more important
to allow those hands to remain just as they are, as the inner work continues
all by itself in a way that you may or may not be aware of? [Pause] And will
one of those hands drift down to your lap to signal that the inner work is
progressing as well as possible at this time?"**
Occasionally the hands will slowly oscillate back and forth a centimeter or
two (or a few inches), as if the inner mind is shifting back and forth, sorting
things out. The therapist can then comment:

**"That's right, that interesting process can continue just as it is, and when
your unconscious has resolved that issue satisfactorily, I wonder which hand
will drift down all by itself, just to let me know."**

If the patient seems stuck or excessively uncomfortable, the therapist can
simply ask for a verbal report of what is being experienced. The patient is
encouraged to make whatever physical adjustments or shifts in inner attitude that may be necessary to facilitate optimal balance of conscious and

BOX 11: MOVING HANDS ACCESSING OF CREATIVE RESOURCES

1. *Readiness signal for inner work*

   a. **"Place your hands about six to eight inches apart, and with great sensitivity, tune into the real or imagined magnetic field developing between them [therapist demonstrates]. If your creative (healing) unconscious is ready to begin therapeutic work, you will experience those hands moving together all by themselves to signal yes."**
   [Pause. If hands do not move together, continue with the following.]

   b. **"But if there is another issue that you need to explore first, you will feel those hands being pushed apart to signal no. In that case, a question will come up in your mind that we can deal with."**

2. *Accessing and resolving problems*

   a. **"As your unconscious explores the sources and important memories about [whatever problem], one of those arms will begin drifting down very slowly."**
   [Pause. When one arm does begin drifting down, continue.]
   "That arm can continue drifting down very slowly so that it will finally come to rest on your lap only when you have completed a satisfactory inner review of that problem."
   [Pause after arm has come to rest on lap]

   b. **"And now your other arm will begin drifting down all by itself as your unconscious explores all the therapeutic possibilites for resolving that problem in an ideal manner that is most suitable for you at this time."**

   c. **"When your unconscious has resolved that problem in a satisfactory manner, that arm will come to rest on your lap."**

3. *Ratifying problem-solving*

   a. **"Does your unconscious want to let your head nod yes all by itself to verify the value of your therapeutic progress?"**

   b. **"When your unconscious and conscious minds know they can continue to deal with that problem in a satisfactory way, you will find yourself stretching and coming completely awake as you open your eyes."**

unconscious activity. The patient usually operates on two levels or parts: (1) There is a witnessing consciousness that watches what is being experienced, and (2) there is a receptive, experiencing part that is surprised by the autonomous ideodynamic movements that seem to have a life of their own. If the patient seems to be getting too fearful, the therapist can help restore equanimity by structuring a carefully controlled therapeutic dissociation, somewhat as follows:

"You can simply watch what is happening calmly and objectively. . . . You can experience that, and simply witness it as an inner drama. . . . You can watch what is happening as if you were seeing it in a movie. . . . One part of you can experience that very deeply while another part of you can talk to me about it, as you learn to relate to your own emotions with clarity and understanding."

This type of "partial regression in the service of inner development" is ideal for ideodynamic therapy. As patients witness the autonomy of their ideomotor movements, unusual sensations, perceptions, and inner emotional processes, they learn that they can be experienced safely in an informative and creative manner. This process may become *cathartic* and lead to *insight* in the Freudian sense, but much more is involved: *The patient is encouraged to acquire new skills by turning on, turning off, and relating to his own inner process in new ways. The patient learns to develop a fuller and richer inner life wherein there is a more optimal interaction between conscious and unconscious processes. Mind and consciousness are experienced as a creative process of self-reflective information transduction* (Rossi, 1986d).

Sometimes the hands will drift off into unusual positions and other kinds of spontaneous movements. The therapist and patient may or may not be aware of the metaphorical or symbolic significance of these movements. The therapist can facilitate whatever is involved, somewhat as follows:

"And we can wonder just what is involved with this interesting development. Sometimes the unconscious can tell a story with movement . . . sometimes it becomes clear what that is about. . . . There may or may not be images, memories, thoughts, voices, or feelings associated with those movements. . . . As that continues, you may begin to experience certain feelings more (or less) strongly . . . simply allowing that to continue all by itself until you know. . . . Allowing the creative healing forces (inner mind, higher self, etc.) to continue in just that way, until the inner work is completed for now. . . . And as those hands finally come to rest [when it is obvious that they are], **your unconscious can make available just one or two thoughts that we need to understand so that we can further facilitate the healing next time."**

As is obvious from the above, the therapist can easily facilitate the inner accessing and resolution of problems with very general, nondirective suggestions. When more specific focusing is required for dealing with an issue, the therapist may proceed with whatever style of questioning is most appropriate for the particular dynamics of the patient.

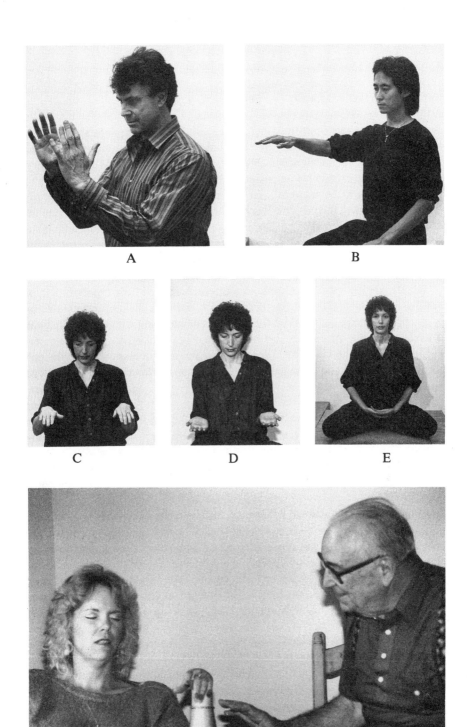

Figure 1: Hand and finger signaling positions.

41

(B) MONITORING POSITION FOR MEASURING
AND MODULATING INTENSITY OF EXPERIENCE

An optimal balance of witnessing consciousness and experiential being can be further facilitated by using one hand and arm as a gauge to measure the depth of trance or emotional involvement. With one arm held at a comfortable, neutral level, the patient is encouraged to experiment with raising or lowering the arm as a measure of inner experience. One could say the patient is learning to measure the right cerebral hemisphere's more unconscious processes with the left hemisphere's more linear, alphanumeric processes. The possibilities are endless. In general, the therapist encourages the patient to allow an arm to carefully gauge or modulate the degree to which any feared emotional process or inner experience is expressed.

In one workshop, for example, a woman described how a previous hypnotic experience with another therapist had left her in a strange state for hours afterwards — she could only cry without knowing the reason. She was afraid to go back into trance lest she go out of control again. Obviously, she needed to learn how to relate to her own inner processes with more ego control. I asked if she were willing to learn how to do this. She agreed that would be most desirable.

She was shown how to extend one arm at a neutral level to indicate her current level of consciousness. She was then asked to

"Wake yourself up now, even more than you usually are. As you feel yourself waking up, let that arm move slowly up like a lever measuring how much more aware you are becoming. Wake up more and more. . . . As your arm goes up, tell me how you can tell that you are becoming more and more alert!"

She opened her eyes widely and began to note how she could see things in greater detail — she was more acutely aware of sounds, colors, sights, etc.

"Now let yourself go back down to your normal state of awareness as your arm lowers to the neutral position."

When her arm returned to the neutral position, she was encouraged to wake up again even more, as the arm slowly raised again. She was given this exercise of waking up and returning back to normal several more times, with her arm measuring her level of consciousness. She was finally permitted to experiment with trance as follows:

"Now, if your unconscious feels it's perfectly safe to allow yourself to go into trance just a little bit, your arm will let you know by drifting down below the neutral level all by itself . . . but not too low . . . not too deep, yet! . . . Now return to normal wakefulness and tell me what it was like. . . . Now if your unconscious feels it is okay to let yourself go back into trance a little deeper this time, then that arm can go down again. . . . And with each noticeable change in your awareness, you can tell me what is happening. Keep your eyes open for now, so that you can accurately verbalize the process of going into trance."

" . . . Now return to normal wakefulness and tell me what it was like. . . . Now if your unconscious feels it is okay to let yourself go back into trance a little deeper this time, then that arm can go down again. . . . And with each noticeable change in your awareness, you can tell me what is happening. Keep your eyes open for now, so that you can accurately verbalize the process of going into trance."

She did, in fact, describe carefully the process by which her peripheral vision gradually became more and more constricted until she was experiencing a classical "tunnel vision" that is characteristic of trance experience (Erickson, 1980a, Volumes I and II). At that point she was returned again to her normal state of awareness and again asked if her unconscious was willing to let her go even deeper next time. In this manner, alternating between normal, super-awake, and trance states of various depths, the woman was supported in exploring her obviously great talent for experiencing altered states of awareness.

This ideomotor gauging approach can be used to modulate practically any subjective dimension of human experience. A natural consequent of this process is that patients learn to relate to their own inner experience in a safe, flexible, and creative fashion. Anxiety, fear, anger, depression, energy level, and psychosomatic symptoms of all varieties can be modulated, transformed, and resolved with insight and a growing sense of self-guided development.

(C) CHANNELING POSITION FOR CONSTELLATING AND RESOLVING CONFLICTS

Problems are often expressed as conflicts between the polarities of human experience: approach and avoidance, love and hate, strength and weakness, male and female, instinct and spirit, elation and depression, child and adult, good-me and bad-me, conscious ego and unconscious self, the individual and society, and so forth. The so-called "channeling position," with arms extended comfortably and palms facing downward, is an interesting way to experience and express inner conflicts in an outer, behaviorally observable form. The therapist can facilitate the situation as follows.

"Let yourself become very aware of what's happening in those arms and hands, and let's see what happens all by itself. . . . You can wonder whether one side or the other can experience and express [whatever polarity or conflict with which the patient is dealing]."

[Pause to note what minimal behavioral responses become evident. Comment and query any observable response somewhat as follows.]

"That left arm seems to be moving up. . . . Can you tell me what part of your conflict that arm expresses — for example, is it the child-you or the adult-you? Does the arm moving up mean that the child is becoming more expressive at this moment? . . . What does the child seem to be saying? . . . [etc.]"

In a workshop demonstration being given by David Cheek, a psychiatrist in his forties seemed to freeze helplessly when his arms expressed a dream he had had about the conflict between himself and the demands of society. It soon became evident that his left arm represented himself feeling helpless and hurt. And, in fact, his left arm began to ache more and more, while his right arm that represented society became increasingly "numb."

At that point he was asked if his right arm could be tested since Cheek happened to be seated on his right side. He slowly nodded his assent. When Cheek tried to move his right arm, it was rigid and immovable. Cheek asked if another workshop participant seated to his left would test his other arm. This, too, was found to be rigidly fixed in a cataleptic position. A series of suggestions for the various ways the arms might move to express and resolve the conflict were without any apparent effect. The subject began to sweat profusely; he alternately blushed and blanched; tics and twitches popped up spontaneously across his face, to his helpless amazement. The situation appeared to be getting out of his control. His observing and witnessing consciousness was not able to help him maintain a therapeutic level of equanimity or further insight.

In this stressfully worsening situation, Cheek continued as follows. **"This extreme state of tension is *as adequate an expression of the conflict as can be experienced at this time.* As soon as your unconscious and conscious mind realize this, those arms will begin to relax . . .** [pause as relaxation does begin to take place]. **And when the conscious and unconscious parts of your mind know they can continue the inner work of resolving this conflict in your future dreams and with yourself and others** [pause], **it will be interesting to see which of those arms begins to drift down to your lap first. . . . And when your unconscious is ready to allow you to wake up and return to your usual awareness, feeling refreshed and alert, that other arm will drift down. And you may or may not wish to share any more of this experience with the group."**

During the next two days of the workshop, this psychiatrist reported a sense of inner work being done but felt he was still too "stubborn" to do any more ideodynamic channeling of the conflict. Finally, on the last day of the workshop, he felt ready to deal with the "unfinished business" and experienced a process of ideodynamic conflict resolution, with his arms and hands moving easily as he gained a profound insight into how his so-called negative trait of stubbornness was actually his only defense against an authoritarian father now projected onto society.

The important point of this case is that patients are not always ready to resolve an issue when it is first constellated and channeled into ideodynamic movement. They may need more time for inner work on their own before problem resolution can take place. *The therapist's "suggestions" do not have the power to force the premature resolution of inner issues.* Often, the most significant value of these ideodynamic approaches is focusing the patient on the significant issues. This focusing may take place on a conscious or unconscious level; sometimes it is a combination of both. The initial work with this workshop participant, for example, simply accessed a state-dependent conflict that he could only express as a stubborn and rigid catalepsy. Over the next few days, he had a sense of "inner work being done." A conscious resolution was finally possible only after the unconscious had done its share of the inner work privately, on its own.

(D) THE EVALUATION POSITION FOR EXPRESSING CREATIVE OPTIONS

Having the palms face upward is an appropriately symbolic position for evaluating the various possibilities and creative options that are pressing for expression in one's life. For example, patients can be asked to simply tune into those palms with great sensitivity to determine whether "energy" is being received from the universe, or whether they are transmitting energy outward. Their response to such questions is often of diagnostic value. A very dedicated but depressed professional person, for example, admitted that energy was being "drained out and there wasn't much left."

Another patient who was concerned about sorting out all the positive and negative aspects of a marriage was facilitated as follows.
"Let us see which of those hands expresses the positive and which expresses the negative aspects of your marriage."
[Pause as patient makes slight postural adjustment and replies that the right hand holds the stronger and better aspects, while the left hand contains those weaker features that need help.]
"Fine. Now, to prepare for the work that needs to be done to help the weaker features, it will be of value to first explore all the stronger aspects of your marriage. As you review them appreciatively, you will find that right arm moving expressively."
[Pause as patient's right arm moves downward as he outlines the strong features of his marriage. This prepares a constructive context and hints about how he will later be able to use these strong features to help the weaker. As the right arm continues downward and finally comes to rest in his lap, the "weaker" arm drifts aimlessly about.]
"Now, with all those strong features *activated* within you, let's see how they can help those weaker aspects that seem to be drifting so aimlessly about. Let me know when it happens."
The patient's left arm now comes to an abrupt halt as he verbalizes how his wife's faithful attentiveness to his every need is a feature that has aroused an ambiguous response in him. He suddenly realizes that he had been holding back on his sexual assertiveness with her because he felt her faithful solicitousness implied that she was too weak to take too much sex. He now visualizes a satisfactory sexual fantasy with her, and with a broad smile he says, "This is probably enough therapy for today!"

(E) UTILIZING THE PATIENT'S CHARACTERISTIC POSITIONS AND MOVEMENTS FOR
ACCESSING STATE-DEPENDENT MEMORY, LEARNING, AND BEHAVIOR

All the above positions for initiating ideodynamic signaling are somewhat
arbitrary, although the therapist attempts to explore those that seem most
appropriate for a particular patient. With increasing skill in observing the
patient's individuality and characteristic positions and movements, however,
the therapist can learn to select those behaviors that are most suitable as
starting points for accessing and facilitating a state-dependent inner process.

An obvious example is when one patient spontaneously assumed a classical lotus posture for meditation when she volunteered for "ideodynamic
work." The therapist took that cue and utilized it as follows.

**"That's right. You've had experience in meditation, so it would be best to
begin with that for your inner work. Continue with your favorite form of
meditation; stay with it in a pure manner for as long as you can. [Pause]
And when your unconscious is ready to explore those issues that sometimes
interfere with your meditative practice, you will notice something happening
with your hands."**

Within a few minutes, her fingers began to make a series of minimal involuntary movements that were channeled into ideodynamic signals by the
therapist as follows.

**"Now, if your unconscious is willing to let that finger signal yes, it will move
up again all by itself. [Pause as the finger does so.] Now let's see what other
finger on that hand moves up all by itself to signal no. [Pause as another
finger does so.]**

A series of questions that could be answered with yes and no finger signals
were then asked about the way her meditation practice could be facilitated in
the future. It was learned, for example, that unfinished daily problems
typically intruded. In response to a few nondirective questions, she was able
to conclude that in the future she could allow her spontaneous finger signals
to determine whether she needed to spend some time writing and clearing
her mind of "practical issues" before she practiced her formal meditation.

This experience led the author, in cooperation with Charles Tart and
Shinzen Young of the Community Meditation Center of Los Angeles, to
explore the use of ideodynamic signaling with a group of meditators who
had a wide range of experience (between six months and 15 years). In this
previously unpublished study, it was found that an unusually high proportion (about 35%) of this population (N=70) scored on the high end of the
Standard Hypnotic Susceptibility Scale, Form C (scores of 10 to 12). A
variety of exploratory approaches combining classical methods of Buddhist
Vipassana meditation (Goldstein, 1983) with ideodynamic hypnotic accessing was experienced by most meditators in this group as a very fruitful
harmony in integrating the goals and methods of East and West for facilitating mind-body healing and the evolution of consciousness (von Franz, 1987).

RESEARCH

Basic Research in Ideodynamic Signaling:
Research Projects: 1–9

Although hundreds of workshops by Cheek and others have been conducted to train thousands of clinicians in the use of ideodynamic signaling for over a generation, there has never been a systematic program of research in this area. Because of this we will end each section of this volume with suggestions for a number of fundamental research projects. These will range from investigation of the basic parameters of ideodynamic signaling to a study of its most significant therapeutic applications.

Project 1 As indicated in the theory portion of this section, there is a very long tradition in hypnosis of studying the relationship between the physiological, muscular, and verbal levels of responsiveness that Cheek adopts as his basic clinical hypothesis. Many other scientific investigators, however, have noted similar relationships in a completely independent manner, using very different methods of research. A recent statement by Robertson (1986, pp. 65–66) is typical:

> Biologist/psychologist Jean Piaget (1955) has carefully studied children's behavior and development. He has argued, in opposition to Chomsky among others, that language develops out of motor actions. The synthesis that seems to be emerging among many linguists and psychologists is that both are right; there is a "deep structure" that underlies language, and that *this "deep structure" is inborn, but it is evidenced first in motor actions and only gradually develops into a spoken language.* Anthropologist Edward T. Hall has shown how large a part of language is nonverbal (Hall, 1959). [Italics added]

A comprehensive review of these many independent lines of empirical investigation would yield new sets of hypotheses that could be adequately tested with the recent technological developments for studying mind-body relationships (Pribram, 1986; Rossi, 1986d).

Project 2   Most investigations of the fundamental nature of hypnosis that involve the construction and analysis of standardized scales of hypnotic susceptibility have isolated a statistical factor called "ideomotor action" (Hilgard, 1965). Although one would expect ideodynamic signaling to be highly loaded on this factor, we are not aware of any research that tests this hypothesis. Simple correlation of scores on such standardized scales with our procedures for establishing ideomotor signals with the pendulum (Box 4) and fingers (Box 5) would be an important first step in identifying the factorial identity of ideodynamic signaling.

Does ideodynamic communication also have a significant factorial loading on a cognitive factor in standardized scales of hypnotic susceptibility? What implications would evidence for such a cognitive factor loading have for Cheek's basic clinical hypothesis about how ideodynamic communication works?

Project 3   Evaluate the validity and reliability of ideodynamic signaling by the standardized approaches used in developing psychological tests and diagnostic procedures. What criteria for validity (other than those discussed by Cheek in this section) could be developed?

Project 4   Evaluate basic parameters of ideodynamic signaling, such as frequency of occurrence in relation to age, sex, handedness, mental and personality factors, mental disorders, patient populations, etc.

Project 5   What sets of attitude, expectancy, and instructions facilitate and retard the experience of ideodynamic (ideosensory and ideomotor) responsiveness (Erickson & Rossi, 1981; Weitzenhoffer, 1957)?

Project 6   Evaluate the phenomenological characteristics of ideodynamic communication. Create and standardize a scale of subjective responses to ideosensory and ideomotor questioning. How well does this scale correlate with Spiegel and Spiegel's (1978) Hypnotic Induction Profile, with Tart's (1972) Subjective Scale of Hypnotic Depth, and with Rossi's (1986b) Indirect Trance Assessment Scale (ITAS)? What proportion of which population groups experience their ideodynamic responses as completely autonomous and involuntary? Is the experience of involuntariness necessary for the reliability and validity of ideodynamic signaling in hypnotherapy?

Project 7   Cheek (1978) has explored the hypothesis that half of the adult population may have been left-handed before submitting to repetitive training for right-handedness. He believes that, under hypnosis, states of regression, or traumatic life situations, adults may revert to their original handedness. He hypothesizes that in automobile emergency situations this could be a source of confusion contributing to accidents. He summarizes his findings as follows (Cheek, 1978, p. 17):

The thumb uppermost in a simple handclasp test appears to be a valid indicator of primary handedness before the origin of conscious memory. An exploratory study with age regression to birth was conducted with 142 adults. The results suggest the hypothesis that converting children from their natural left-handedness to right-handedness could lead to communication and learning difficulties. Procedures are outlined for assessing the validity of ideomotor signaling and suggestions are made for further research in this area. This pilot study should be replicated with more adequate controls.

Replicate Cheek's research and test his hypothesis that hand dominance may change during hypnosis.

Project 8   Test the clinical hypothesis that the retrospective ideodynamic approach facilitates desensitization of traumatic memories while the prospective chronological approach yields more emotional catharsis.

Assess the relative merits of the retrospective and prospective ideodynamic approaches to each of the major classes of clinical problems investigated in the following sections of this volume. Is one approach more reliable than the other in any of these problem areas? Are there patient variables to be considered in the choice between these two approaches?

Project 9   Is the experience of involuntariness and/or amnesia in finger signaling necessary for symptom and problem resolution to take place? This is very important from a theoretical point of view.

An experience of involuntariness and/or amnesia implies that a significant hypnotic dissociation has taken place. The classical view derived from Janet and psychoanalysis is that because a hypnoidal dissociation was present at the origin of the problem, a similar hynotherapeutic dissociation is required to access, reframe, and resolve the problem. Because of the practical problems they encountered, however, Freud went on to develop free association and Jung developed "active imagination" to replace their earlier authoritarian approach to hypnotic therapy. From our modern Ericksonian perspective, we would now regard free association and active imagination as varieties of the more permissive, naturalistic, indirect or *utilization* approach to "light" therapeutic trance. Indeed, this therapeutic trance is so light that many traditional psychoanalysts respond with indignation when it is suggested that their patients are in continually varying states of trance as they free associate on the couch.

If it is found that involuntariness and/or amnesia is not required for the therapeutic effectiveness of our ideodynamic approaches, then we will have evidence for the value of the "light," permissive, naturalistic approaches to accessing the statebound condition that encodes psychological symptoms and problems; *the essentially cybernetic process of iteration and recursion rather than dissociation and involuntariness would be regarded as the necessary therapeutic agent in facilitating the accessing, reasssociation, and reor-*

ganizing (what we now call reframing) of mind-body information for problem-solving.

Research Foundations of the Psychobiology of Ideodynamic Healing in Hypnosis: Project 10

The profound revolution that has taken place recently in our understanding of the psychobiology of mind, memory, and behavior has important implications for our ideodynamic approach to healing. To understand this research frontier, we will begin by exploring the views of some outstanding researchers in neuroscience.

Francis O. Schmitt of the Massachusetts Institute of Technology is currently regarded as one of the leaders in neuroscience research. He introduces his paper on "Molecular Regulators of Brain Function: A New View" (1984) with the following words (p. 991):

> The discovery, more than 50 years ago, that contiguous neurons interact with each other at synapses not by bioelectric modalities, but by the action of chemical mediators called neurotransmitters, was for some years received with considerable skepticism by a substantial portion of the neurophysiological community. However, this now classical chemical concept has, with virtually no substantial deviation, remained a basic tenet of neurobiology. In the working hypothesis here proposed, it is suggested that neuronal intercommunication may be mediated not alone by the dozen-odd classical neurotransmitters, but by many, perhaps hundreds, of other kinds of neuroactive substances, here called informational substances (ISs), and that in some instances, they may be delivered in a nonconventional parasynaptic mode. High specificity of action is thus achieved not from specific structures (e.g., synaptic linkage in neuronal nets) but by the equally selective binding of various ISs to receptors that are arrayed not only at synaptic regions but over the entire neuronal surface. The ISs are contained in the ambient extracellular fluid.

In a more recent paper, Schmitt summarizes this new view even more succinctly (1986, pp. 240–241):

> (1) Neurons may chemically intercommunicate by the mediation not only of the dozen-odd classical neurotransmitters but also by peptides, hormones, "factors," other specific proteins, and by many other kinds of *informational substances* (ISs), a term that seemed more generally applicable than "neuroactive substances" that was previously used (Chan-Palay & Chan-Palay, 1984; Schmitt, 1979, 1982).

(2) Alongside of, and in parallel with, synaptically linked, "hard-wired" neuronal circuitry that forms the basis for conventional neurophysiology and neuroanatomy, and that operates through conventional synaptic junctions, there is a system that I call "parasynaptic." In parasynaptic neuronal systems, ISs may be released at points, frequently relatively remote from target cells, which they reach by diffusion through the extracellular fluid. Such a system has all the specificity and selectivity characteristic of the conventional synaptic mode; in the parasynaptic case, the receptors that provide the specificity and selectivity are on the surface of the cells where they can be contacted by, and bind to, the IS ligands diffusing in the extracellular fluid. . . .

It is thus apparent that we are emerging from the "transmitter centered" era of neurophysiology and neurochemistry, and are now embarking on an historic period of discovery of previously undreamed of varieties of ISs, a substantial fraction of which may be required to subserve brain function and its regulation. *Interest would be particularly high in those that may play a role in higher functions of the human brain.* [Italics added]

The enthusiasm with which other researchers have accepted Schmitt's new framework is epitomized in this recent summary by Floyd Bloom (1986) of the Scripps Clinic and Research Foundation, who has also made fundamental contributions to neuroscience (p. 296):

From the vantage point of our present location in time and space, the points made by Schmitt (1984) in his recent thoughtful essay seem clearly to define the mainstreams of the new frameworks onto which the data are presently being conceptually placed: onto the classical, hard-wired nervous system of those who got us into this era of brain research has been superimposed a much looser nervous system in which neurons may release their signals to act at some distance from the release site, not strictly as primary communicators, but rather as signals that can modify the response of the intended target cells to the classical transmitter signals they are receiving simultaneously. In less than one decade, the nervous system ceased to be a rather dry place in which, to classical physiologists, transmitters meant relatively little, since they all worked either to excite or inhibit. In its stead we have a very juicy, flexible nervous system in which transmitters act on many different receptor transduction mechanisms to provide a very enriched repertoire of signalling capabilities across widely differing spatial domains and widely variant durations of action.

This radical shift from the "classical, hard-wired nervous system" to "a very juicy, flexible nervous system in which transmitters act on many different receptor transduction mechanisms to provide a very enriched repertoire of signalling capabilities" is an apt metaphorical description of a similar transition that is currently taking place from the older stimulus-response behaviorism to a cognitive and information theory approach to therapy (Cunningham, 1986), hypnosis (Bowers, 1977), and mind-body healing (Rossi, 1986d).

Table 1 outlines some of these distinctions between the older classical view of *neural transmission* and the newer supplementary system of *parasynaptic cellular modulation*. The basic information channel in neural transmission is via the conventional electrochemical path of ionic conductance that is diagrammed in most standard textbooks (Kandel & Schwartz, 1985). This takes place in the classical neural pathways of the central and peripheral nervous system. The signal specificity between one neuron and the next is maintained by the close juxtaposition of the neural junctions between them. The amino acids, gamma-amino butyrate (GABA) and glutamate, are the messenger molecules that transmit the information rapidly between these neural synapses of the central nervous system. This rapid and narrow band of *point-to-point neural transmission* is what we usually think of as the activity of the nervous system. The typical anatomical diagrams found in most medical textbooks illustrating the peripheral and autonomic nervous systems that mediate involuntary and reflex responses (e.g., the knee jerk) are based on this model, which is now called *anatomical addressing*.

The contrast between this fast anatomical information addressing of the nervous system and the slower parasynaptic chemical addressing system is outlined by Iversen (1986) as follows (pp. xi–xii):

There have been remarkable advances in our understanding of chemical mediators in the nervous system during the past few decades. The traditional concepts of chemical transmission in the nervous system developed largely from detailed studies of the actions of acetylcholine as the fast chemical signal used at the neuromuscular junction. Fast chemical signaling, in which the neurotransmitter released at specialized synaptic junctions stimulates the opening of receptor-controlled ion channels in the post-synaptic cell within a millisecond time frame, does occur in the mammalian CNS. Indeed the amino acids glutamate and GABA may represent the principle fast signals used by most of the "main line" fast conducting circuits. However, many chemical transmitters in the CNS do not operate in this classical manner. The actions of monoamines and neuropeptides are slow (acting over periods of seconds or minutes) and rather than directly excitatory of inhibitory, they are modulatory in character (Iversen, 1984).

Furthermore, the "slow" modulators may not always be released at morphologically specialised synapses, but can sometimes act at a dis-

Table 1: Classical view of neural transmission and newer information substance-receptor system of parasynaptic cellular modulation.

	Information Channel	Localization	Signal Specificity	Information Substances	Time	Range	Behavior
CLASSICAL NEURAL TRANSMISSION: SYNAPTIC CONNECTIONS VIA NEURO-TRANSMITTERS	Conventional electrochemical neural conductance via ion channels. Signal is carried through nerves only	*Classical neural pathways* of the central and peripheral nervous systems	*Anatomical addressing* via close juxtaposition of neural synapses	(About 10) *Amino Acids:* GABA & L-glutamate *Classical Neurotransmitters:* acetylcholine dopamine norepinephrine epinephrine, etc.	*Rapid:* Milliseconds *Evolution:* Recent	Narrow: Point-to-point neural transmission between *individual neurons* of the peripheral and central nervous systems	Peripheral and autonomic nervous systems; reflex responses
THE INFORMA-TION SUB-STANCE-RECEPTOR SYSTEM: PARASYNAPTIC CELLULAR MODULATION VIA NEUROMO-DULATORS	Diffusion of *information substances* through the blood, cerebro-spinal fluid, lymph, intercellular spaces of brain, etc.	*Nodal conver-gence* at brain and body loci associated with emotion, pain, and sensory-perceptual processing	*Chemical addressing* via special classes of recognition molecules on all cellular membranes	(over 100) *Peptides:* hypothalamic, pituitary, gut, endocrine hormones, immunotransmitters, etc.	*Slow:* Minutes, hours, days *Evolution:* Ancient	Broad: Modula-tion of *neuronal networks* made up of large numbers of target cells at many loci in brain and body tissues triggering persistent metabolic responses	Organismic states; state-dependent memory and learning; fixed action genetic patterns of behavior; psychosomatic networks; psychoanalytic phenomena

tance from their sites of release. This has given rise to the concept of *"chemically addressed"* chemical transmission, in which information is transmitted by the use of a wide range of different chemical signals acting diffusely, but achieving selectivity by the uneven distribution of suitable receptors on target cells to recognise these signals. *Slow mediators also act largely by triggering persistent metabolic responses in target cells,* rather than by controlling ion channels directly. [Italics added]

The newer model of parasynaptic cellular modulation is based upon the diffusion of information substances (messenger molecules) through the extracellular fluid between neurons (rather than at their synapses only) and other tissues of the body. The signal specificity is maintained by *chemical addressing* between information substances and their receptors. All the nerves and tissues of the body have special classes of protein receptors (also called "recognition molecules") on their cell walls that receive the signals sent to them in the form of information substances. These receptors are the addressees which receive the information substances. When information substances are made and sent by neurons, they are called *neuropeptides*. Many of these information substances, however, are made and sent by the endocrine system (where they are called *hormones*) and immune system (where they are called *immunotransmitters*). This very broad class of information substances is responsible for communication between the nervous system and the endocrine system (called *neuroendocrinology*) and the immune system (now called *psychoneuroimmunology*). Because peptides and their receptors are localized at important nodal areas within the central nervous system and the body associated with emotions, pain, and sensory-perceptual processes, it has been hypothesized that they may be the basis of a new science of psychosomatics (Pert, Ruff, Weber, & Herkenham, 1985) and mind-body healing which we will discuss later in Section V.

The chemical addressing between information substances and their receptors is relatively slow in comparison with classical neural transmission. There is now good evidence that the chemical addressing of the parasynaptic system is evolutionarily much older than the anatomical addressing of the central and peripheral nervous system (Krieger & Martin, 1981a, b). What is lost in speed, however, is compensated by the much wider bond of information transfer mediated in this manner.

Figures 2 and 3 illustrate the contrast between the rapid, point-to-point anatomical addressing of the classical nervous system and the slower but broader patterns of information modulation by the chemical addressing of the parasynaptic system. This contrast emphasizes the distinction between neurotransmitters (typically, amino acids) and neuromodulators (typically, peptides). Neuroscientists have had many debates about the distinction (see, in particular, a paper on "New Concepts of Molecular Communication Among Neurons" by Dismukes [1979] and the open peer commentary pub-

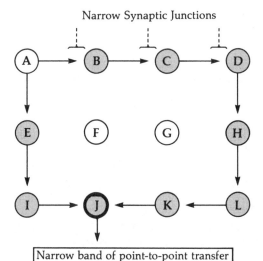

Figure 2: *Anatomical addressing.* The conventional nervous system as a network of neurons (A, B, C, D, etc.) associated via adjacent neural synapses. Amino acids and classical *neurotransmitters* mediate rapid information transfer between individual neurons via their *narrow synaptic junctions.* Only neuron J was sufficiently activated to mediate a fast narrow band of point-to-point information transfer, as is typical of the classical nervous systems. (Modified from Iversen, 1986)

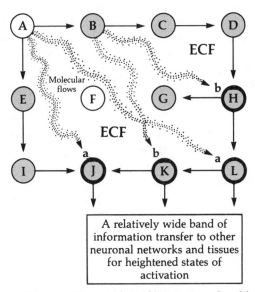

Figure 3: *Chemical addressing.* Recent view of how conventional information transmission can be supplemented by peptide *neuromodulators* that diffuse through the extracellular fluid (ECF) to activate neural networks with the appropriate recognition receptors, *a* and *b*. This relatively wide but slower band of *parasympathetic information transfer* is hypothesized to give rise to "state-dependent" effects. (Modified from Iversen, 1986)

lished with that paper). Joose has recently emphasized some of the important distinctions in the genetic origin and behavioral function of classical
neurotransmitters versus the peptide neuromodulators as follows (1986, pp.
27–28):

> At the moment there is a vivid discussion about the question of wheth-
> er classical transmitters and neuropeptide messengers have different
> functions. One of the obvious differences between the two categories is
> that the number of classical transmitters seems to be much lower (for 8
> substances this role has been proved) than that of peptide messengers
> [about 100]. Various suggestions have been presented, e.g., *neuropep-
> tides would act first of all as neuromodulators, which means that they
> have long-lasting effects on groups of neurons resulting in a change of
> behavior*. However, these effects are also known from classical transmit-
> ters. In fact, both categories of substances are able to perform all types
> of messenger roles.
> Up to now, no attention has been given to an important difference
> between the two categories. Peptides are directly coded by the genes.
> . . . In contrast, all classical transmitters, also the amino acids among
> them, are produced by more or less complex enzymatic procedures. . . .
> Therefore the essential difference between peptide and classical transmit-
> ters is that *peptides are much more appropriate for experimentation of
> animals in their adaptation to changes in the environment*. The high
> number of peptides reflects *the diversity of their functions and the wider
> range of action their flexibility in target selection*, whereas the actions of
> classical neurotransmitters are usually restricted by specific innervation
> of the targets (neuronal circuitry). [Italics added]

For the practical purposes of this book on mind-body healing methods in
hypnosis, it is important to note that the distinction between classical neurotransmission and neuromodulation has profound implications for understanding the psychobiological basis of mind-body therapy. In general, it can
be said that information substances and their receptors are the major integrators of cellular and tissue function at the molecular level (Bloom, 1980,
1986). One of the most important of the implications for mind-body healing
follows from Iversen's recognition that the neuromodulators of the parasynaptic system trigger "persistent metabolic responses in target cells."
These persistent metabolic responses are responsible for the "states" of the
organism: states of homeostasis, arousal, inhibition, pain, hunger, thirst,
sexuality, memory, learning, emotions, stress, and motivations of all sorts.
For centuries mind-body healing by hypnosis has remained controversial
because there was no scientifically acceptable means of specifiying what has
been loosely called the "psycho-neuro-physiological state" of hypnosis
(Erickson, 1980a, Vol. II; Rossi & Ryan, 1986). Evidence for the state-

dependent memory, learning, and behavior theory, however, suggests that *information substances and their receptors may be major mediators in the therapeutic state of hypnosis, just as they apparently are in all other states of the organism.*

MIND, MEMORY, LEARNING, AND THERAPEUTIC HYPNOSIS

In its bare essentials, our psychobiological approach to understanding the molecular basis of mind, memory, learning, and therapeutic hypnosis is based on four interlocking, working hypotheses about the operation of the Is-receptor communication system:

1. Localized neuronal networks of the brain are activated by information substances;
2. State-dependent memory, learning, and behavior are encoded by information substances in these neuronal networks;
3. The molecular-genetic basis of memory, learning, and behavior is modulated by information substances; and
4. Is-receptor communication systems are the psychobiological basis of state-dependent mind-body healing and therapeutic hypnosis.

We will discuss the basis for each of these hypotheses briefly.

1. *Neuronal networks may be defined in terms of the activation of specifically localized areas of neurons by information substances that reach them via diffusion through the extracellular fluid (ECF).*
The ECF makes up about 20% of the brain volume. Schmitt (1984, p. 996) has noted that information substances

can diffuse as much as 15mm from the cerebrospinal fluid . . . to any site in the cerebral cortex of the adult human brain. There would thus be ample intercellular space for the dynamic interplay of many kinds of informational substances to diffuse from release points to receptors on or in the neurons of the cerebral cortex.

In the simplest case, a 15-square mm neuronal network could be turned on or off by the presence or absence of a specific information substance. That is, *the activity of this neuronal network would be "state-dependent" on the presence or absence of that information substance.*
In actual practice, of course, the situation is much more complex. There are potentially thousands of information substances interacting with hundreds of different receptors on the brain neurons. This means that the state-dependent neuronal networks are ever-changing dynamic structures, as they would certainly have to be in order to function as the psychophysiological

basis for the phenomenology of mind, emotions, and behavior. The ever shifting somatotopic maps of the "mind-brain" that are modifiable by life experience provide particularly vivid experimental evidence for the psycho-biological dynamics of neuronal networks (Kandel & Schwartz, 1985).

2. *Information substances are contained in and transmitted through the ambient extracellular fluid (ECF) surrounding brain cells where they can encode state-dependent memory, learning, and behavior.*

There is now excellent experimental evidence in animals (goldfish) that the diffusion of information substances (glycoproteins, in this case) be-tween brain cells is responsible for encoding memory, learning, and behav-ior (Martinez, Jensen, Messing, Rigter, & McGaugh, 1981; Shashoua, 1979, 1981). The rate of release of these information substances into the extracel-lular fluid is increased during intensive learning experiences. This training results in long-term memory and learning that can be abolished when the information substances are removed from the extracellular fluid by the administration of antisera that block their ability to bind to neural recep-tors.

As has been discussed elsewhere, there is a vast body of historical and modern experimental and clinical research in support of the hypothesis that many forms of memory and learning now can be conceptualized as either overtly or covertly state-dependent (Rossi, 1986d; Rossi & Ryan, 1986). We believe that our currently developing conceptions of the modulation of the entire mind-brain-body by Is-receptor communication systems will enable us to devise new types of *experimental studies of the relationships between behavior, genes, and molecules.* Schmitt noted the relationships that now need more study when he wrote (1984, p. 994):

> The brain contains all the types of steroid hormones. . . . As ISs, they exert a duplex action: (1) a relatively fast (minutes) direct action on synaptic properties, regulating impulse traffic in particular neuronal nets, and (2) a slow (hours) indirect effect involving specific gene activa-tion leading to the synthesis of essential proteins, e.g., specific receptors. Steroid hormones regulate behavioral patterns involved in reproduction, territorial defense, mood and other affective states (McEwen, 1981; McEwen et al., 1982). For present purposes, the steroid hormones illus-trate the integrative control of both fast bioelectrical events involving the passage of impulses through neuronal nets (i.e., the neurophysiological processes that underlie specific behavior patterns), and the slow gene-activated processes that lead to the synthesis of proteinaceous material which, like specific receptors, forms the molecular substratum of behav-ioral patterns.

The implication of this passage is that the entire class of information substances may be important modulators of the fundamental mechanisms of memory, learning, and behavior on the molecular level. This is possible because most information substances trigger a common pathway in intracellular metabolism; this is the cAMP cycle—the so-called "secondary messenger system" which acts as an information transducer as well as a catalyzer of many of the most basic molecular pathways of genetically directed cellular metabolism. As we shall now review in our third working hypothesis, this same cAMP secondary messenger system has been implicated as the molecular basis of memory, learning, and behavior.

3. *The molecular-genetic basis of memory, learning, and behavior that is now called "activity dependent neuromodulation" is regulated by information substances.*

The recently proposed molecular-genetic basis of memory and learning has been variously described as "activity dependent neuromodulation" by Walters and Byrne (1983), and as "activity dependent amplification of presynaptic facilitation" by Kandel and his coworkers (Carew, Hawkins, & Kandel, 1983; Hawkins, Abrams, Carew, & Kandel, 1983; Kandel & Schwartz, 1985). The essential common feature of both of these descriptions is that the "secondary messenger" systems of information transduction within cells (such as cAMP, Ca + +, diacylglycerol) mediate the molecular-genetic mechanisms of memory and learning (Goelet & Kandel, 1986). Discovering the details of this process in terms of how the secondary messengers mediate ion transport and modulation of synaptic transmission in short- and long-term memory, as well as in genetically based "fixed action patterns" of behavior (Kupfermann, 1985), is one of the most fruitful areas of current psychobiological research.

Kandel and his coworkers have found that information substances (such as the small cardiac peptides, SCPa and SCPb) can facilitate the molecular-genetic basis of memory, learning, and behavior (Castellucci et al., 1986; Goelet, Castellucci, Schacher, & Kandel, 1986; Goelet & Kandel, 1986). Their work in this area is just beginning, but they have already developed experimental techniques that will enable them to assess the role of other Is-receptor systems on the molecular-genetic basis of all the major types of learning. In a pioneering paper, Kandel (1983) has proposed how these molecular-genetic mechanisms could account for many of the classical phenomena of acute and chronic human anxiety and neurosis. He summarizes the prospects for the future as follows (Kandel, 1983, p. 1291):

> Moreover, I have suggested that normal learning, the learning of anxiety and unlearning it through *psychotherapeutic intervention, might involve long-term functional and structural changes in the brain that result from alterations in gene expression.* Thus, we can look forward in the next decade of research into learning, to a merger between aspects of molecular genetics and cellular neurobiology. This merger, in turn, will have important consequences for psychiatry—for psychotherapy on the one hand and for psychopharmacology on the other. [Italics added]

Kandel's theoretical and experimental work is the clearest expression of the possibilities of the "mind-gene connection" that was originally formulated independently by Rossi (1983–1985, 1986d) as the molecular basis of therapeutic hypnosis. An outline of this mind-gene cybernetic network that we now hypothesize as operative in therapeutic hypnosis is presented in Figure 4. More specific illustrations of the actual locus of the tissues and information substances involved in particular mind-body systems of communication are presented later in Figures 8, 12, and 15. A more general outline of how the mental experiences of state-dependent emotions, imagery, words, and symbols are part of the same cybernetic process is illustrated in Figure 18.

This leads us to propose that the interaction between Is-receptor systems and Kandel's "activity dependent amplification of presynaptic facilitation" is the molecular-genetic basis of all the major classes of state-dependent memory, learning, and behavioral phenomena that are encoded and modulated by information substances. Table 2 lists a number of the classical experimental paradigms of memory, learning, and behavior that now can be categorized as state-dependent. This is the exact reverse of conventional wisdom among current-day theorists and researchers in psychology.

Conventional theory would conceptualize state-dependent memory and learning as a subclass of Pavlovian conditioning or associative learning. The unrecognized role of Is-receptor systems in all previous theorizing about the fundamental nature of memory and learning changes this picture dramatically, however. The types of research that are now required to uncover the usually unrecognized state-dependent effects in Pavlovian conditioning will be discussed later in Section III.

4. *Is-receptor communication systems are the psychobiological basis of the state-dependent aspects of therapeutic hypnosis.*

Table 2 juxtaposes a very wide range of experimental and clinical data from previously independent lines of research which we now hypothesize to be related via a common psychobiological factor: the Is-receptor communication systems that integrate mind, brain, body, and behavior. Over the past 40 years, psychopharmacologists have used the classical state-dependent memory and learning experimental paradigm to assess the psychological and behavioral effects of psychoactive drugs, which we now know are mediated primarily by Is-receptor systems (Ho, Richards, & Chute, 1978; Lowe, 1987; Overton, 1968, 1978). Of central significance for our working hypotheses is the fact that when animal or human subjects are given memory/learning tasks while under the influence of many psychoactive drugs that mimic or modulate Is-receptor systems, there is a varying degree of amnesia and apparent loss of learning when the drug has been metabolized out of the system. That is, when memory/learning is encoded under drugged conditions, it tends to become state-dependent or statebound to that psychobiological condition; such memory/learning behavior becomes dissociated or

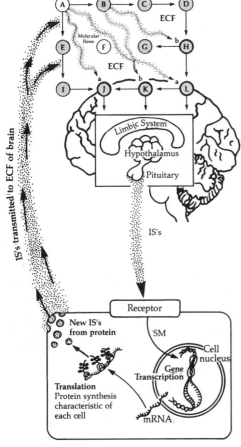

I   THE MIND-BRAIN CONNECTION

1. Neural networks of the brain's cortical-limbic systems encode state-dependent memory, learning and behavior of "mind" (words, images, sensations, perceptions, etc.) with the help of cybernetic information substances from cells of the body.

II   THE BRAIN-BODY CONNECTION

2. Neuroendocrinal information transduction in the limbic-hypothalamic-pituitary system of the brain. The information in neural networks of the brain is transduced into molecular (hormonal) information substances of the body.

3. Information substances (IS's) travel to cells of body with appropriate receptors.

III   THE CELL-GENE CONNECTION

4. Cellular receptors binding IS's

5. Intracellular secondary messengers (SM) lead to activation of "housekeeping" genes

6. Transcription of genetic information into mRNA

7. Translation: protein synthesis characteristic of each cell.

8. New IS's from proteins flow to brain to cybernetically encode state-dependent aspects of mind and behavior.

Figure 4: Three levels of the mind-gene-molecular cybernetic network of information transduction that we hypothesize to be operative in therapeutic hypnosis.

Table 2: Classical types of memory and learning that became state-dependent when modulated by information substances.

Type of Memory and Learning	Definition	Information Substances	References
HABITUATION	A reversible decrease in the strength of a natural response upon repeatedly administering a stimulus that evokes it.	β-endorphin	Izquierdo et al., 1984; Kesner & Baker, 1981
SENSITIZATION	A temporary enhancement of a natural response by a strong or noxious stimulus that evokes it.	Morphine and endogenous opiates (?)	Groves & Thompson, 1970; Kesner & Baker, 1981; Siegel, 1978
IMPRINTING	Sometimes called *programmed learning* because it is genetically predisposed to take place at a specific early life period.	ACTH and related peptides; corticosteroids; testosterone	Kuperfermann, 1985; Martin, 1978, 1981
CLASSICAL CONDITIONING	Also called *Pavlovian* or *associative conditioning* wherein an unconditioned stimulus (meat evokes salivation in dogs) is associated with a conditioned stimulus (bell sound) so that the bell soon evokes saliva.	Endogenous opiates and their analogs; epinephrine and analogs; SCPa, SCPb	Gold, Weinberger, & Sternberg, 1985; Kesner & Baker, 1981; Spiegel, 1978

INSTRUMENTAL CONDITIONING	Also called *operant* or *Skinnerian conditioning* in which positive or negative reinforcement is used to change the frequency of a behavior (passive avoidance learning cited here)	Substance P; angiotensin II	Huston & Staubli, 1981; Sagen & Routtenberg, 1981
AVOIDANCE LEARNING	A combination of classical and operant conditioning. A more cognitive type of learning wherein the animal avoids a punishing stimulus.	Vasopressin, oxytocin and related peptides, a-MSH, cholecystokinin (CCK)	Burbach et al., 1983; de Wied, 1984; de Wied & Gispen, 1977; Flood et al., 1987
CIRCADIAN MEMORY AND LEARNING	Memory and learning that take place at one time of day can be better recalled at a similar time on succeeding days.	ACTH and related peptides; endorphins; luteinizing hormone?	Ananth, Bartova & Rastogi, 1982; Folkard, 1982; Rasmussen, 1986
SOCIAL LEARNING	"Avoidance-of-attack" and social submissiveness in mice in a standard passive avoidance paradigm.	ACTH and corticosterone, VIP, β-endorphin, substance P	Leshner, Merkle & Mixon, 1981; Stewart, 1985

apparently "lost" after the drug is metabolized. Readministering the drug reestablishes the original encoding condition and typically results in some gain of memory/learning.

While it is not always recognized, essentially the same experimental dynamics are operative in studies of the neurobiology of memory and learning (de Weid, 1984; Gold, Weinberger, & Sternberg, 1985; McGaugh, 1983). The molecular basis of memory, learning, and behavior are now known to be mediated by Is-receptor systems in the broadest sense (Martinez et al., 1981). When one aspect or another of a critical Is-receptor system is blocked in these experimental studies of the neurobiology of memory and learning, the resulting dissociated or state-dependent behavior is often identical with that found in the full classical paradigm of state-dependent memory/learning (Rossi, 1986d; Rossi & Ryan, 1986).

What is most interesting about such experiments is that they enable us to study the parameters of "reversible amnesia," which have been used as criteria of therapeutic hypnosis (Braid in Tinterow, 1970; Rossi, 1986d). Just as most experiments in state-dependent memory/learning demonstrate that this "reversible amnesia" is only partial (that is, there is usually some memory/learning available even in the dissociated condition after the drug is out of the system; it is simply improved when the original encoding condition is reestablished by reintroducing the drug), so most of the hypnotic literature documents that hypnotic amnesia is usually fragile and partial in character (Erickson & Rossi, 1974/1980; Hilgard, 1965). A full amnesia that is completely reversible is relatively rare in state-dependent memory/ learning experiments as well as in therapeutic hypnosis.

This fragile and partial characteristic of reversible amnesia is also highly typical of many phenomena of post-traumatic stress syndrome (Figley & McCubbin, 1983; van der Kolk, Greenberg, Boyd, & Krystal, 1985) and psychosomatic problems (Selye, 1976, 1982) that are encoded in a state-dependent manner by the stress-released information substances (e.g., ACTH, β-endorphin, and epinephrine) of Selye's General Adaptation Syndrome (Izquierdo & Dias, 1984; Izquierdo et al., 1984; McGaugh, 1983). Selye (1976) believed that just as a shock evoked such psychosomatic problems, another shock or heightened arousal level could sometimes heal them. The more recent approaches to mind-body healing and self-hypnosis, such as the "relaxation response" (Benson, 1983a, b) and the "ultradian healing response" (Rossi, 1982, 1986a, d) are purported to operate by the reduction of these same stress-released information substances that encode psychosomatic problems.

Analogously, many experimentalists (Blum, 1979; Fischer, 1971) and clinicians (Cheek, 1962a, b, 1965a, b; Erickson, 1980a, Vol. IV) report that altered levels of arousal and affect are responsible for the encoding and recall of stress-related problems via hypnosis. The so-called "coincidental phenomena" (highly individualized and dissociated patterns of psychosomatic behavior that appear spontaneously when deep trance phenomena are evoked) described by Erickson (1943a, b, c, d) may be further examples of how both psychosomatic symptoms and hypnotic phenomena are manifestations of the same dynamics as state-dependent memory, learning, and behavior. Table 3 outlines a matching of the basic terms and processes of SDMLB, the neurobiology of memory and learning, stress-induced psychosomatic symptoms, therapeutic hypnosis, and ultradian/circadian rhythms to illustrate how they are all essentially the same class of mind-body phenomena.

In the historical literature of hypnosis (Tinterow, 1970) and the foundations of psychoanalysis (Ellenberger, 1970), this same fragile and partial character of reversible amnesia may have been responsible for many of the puzzling and paradoxical features of memory that are at the source of continuing controversy about the validity of the various theories of depth psychology (Masson, 1984). Since the earliest days of psychoanalysis (Breuer & Freud, 1895/1955), it has been noted that a sudden fright or shock could evoke "hypnoidal states" that were somehow related to dissociated or neurotic behavior. We hypothesize that such "hypnoidal states" are phenomenological expressions of altered levels of psychobiological arousal in Is-receptor systems that can encode and release memory, learning, and behavior in a state-dependent manner. This leads us to the view that the highly individualized and continually changing character of the "software" of the parasynaptic Is-receptor communication systems can account for many of the phenomenological vagaries of human memory and behavior in general as well as for therapeutic hypnosis in particular.

The profound implications of this newly emerging understanding of how information substances can integrate and modulate human functioning at levels from the mental and emotional to the genetic and molecular will be explored in succeeding sections. We will survey the "hard" research methods and data that support this view as well as their clinical applications in the construction of a new foundation for understanding psychosomatic medicine and the general class of mind-body therapies that include therapeutic hypnosis, imagery, imagination, meditation, and biofeedback.

Project 10   The ultimate validation of our psychobiological approach to ideodynamic healing will require an extensive understanding of the molecular-genetic and Is-receptor system dynamics of each mind-body illness. Survey the classical-research literature in psychosomatic medicine to determine those illnesses that could serve as appropriate models for study. For example, an appropriate disease model might meet the following criteria:

a. We have extensive documentation regarding the molecular-genetic and Is-receptor pathways by which the illness becomes manifest.
b. We have reliable biochemical assay methods for rapidly assessing the critical molecular pathway that is disturbed during the illness.

Table 3: Matching of the basic terms and processes of SDMLB, neurobiology, psychoanalysis, stress-induced psychosomatic symptoms, therapeutic hypnosis, and ultradian/circadian rhythms. (Adapted and updated from Rossi, 1986d, and Rossi & Ryan, 1986)

Encoding Condition	Information Substance-Receptor Systems	State-Dependent Behavior/ Dissociation	Recovery Condition	References
Classical state-dependent memory and learning experiments	Psychoactive drugs that trigger natural information substance-receptor systems	Amnesia and apparent loss of learning on drug withdrawal	Gain in memory/learning with drug readministration	Ho et al., 1978; Lowe, 1987; Overton, 1968, 1978
Neurobiology of memory and learning	ACTH, β-endorphin, VIP, epinephrine, etc.	Amnesia by Is-receptor disruption	Recall/on restoring Is-receptor integrity	de Weid, 1984; McGaugh, 1983

Psychoanalysis	Trauma encoded Psychophysiologically	Reversible amnesia, dissociation, repression, complexes	Hypnosis, free association, active imagination	Freud, 1909/1957; Jung, 1960b
Stress-induced psychosomatic symptoms	Hormones of Selye's General Adaptation Syndrome	Amnesia with post-traumatic and psychosomatic symptoms	Shock; relaxation and ultradian healing response	Benson, 1983a, b; Rossi, 1982, 1986d; Selye, 1974, 1976, 1982
Therapeutic hypnosis	Arousal and affect associated with information substance-receptor systems	Amnesia with coincidental phenomena; hypnoidal states	Hypnotic ideodynamic accessing of memory	Blum, 1979; Cheek, 1962a, b, 1965a, b; Erickson, 1943a, b, c, d; Fischer, 1971
Ultradian/circadian rhythms	Hormones (LH, GnRH) and peptides encoding memory	Amnesia and other everyday trance behaviors	Same period in the ultradian/circadian rhythm	Kripke, 1982; Rasmussen, 1986; Rossi, 1986a, d, e

c. The presence or absence of the illness is easily observed and measured by the patient and doctor (pain problems, skin problems, etc.).

For each disease model, compare the clinical effectiveness of our ideodynamic approach to therapeutic hypnosis with other methods such as biofeedback, imagery, meditation, the learning methods of Table 2, and so forth. Correlate the biochemical and observable indices of each psychosomatic illness with each therapeutic method to determine the ways in which each is most effective. The actual methodological details for carrying out this clinical research will become more apparent as we discuss mind-molecular relationships in the following sections.

Repression Revisited

Our hypothesized relationships between Is-receptor systems, state-dependent memory and learning, stress, and traumatically encoded mind-body problems suggest a new psychobiological interpretation of many classical psychoanalytic concepts such as *repression, dissociation,* and *emotional complexes* (Rossi, 1986d). The foundations of psychoanalysis rest upon the phenomena of reversible amnesia associated with emotional trauma (Freud, 1909/1957). Jung's concept of the "feeling-toned complexes" as the source of psychological problems had its original experimental validation with the word association test, in which gaps or time lags in the associated process suggested the presence of blocks, repressions, or dissociations in the mind (Jung, 1960b).

Is-receptor systems provide a vivid model on the molecular level of how neural networks and cellular processes that encode psychological problems can be blocked or facilitated by endogenous antagonists or agonists. An extensive documentation of this psychobiological basis of repression and dissociation has been presented elsewhere (Rossi & Ryan, 1986). In Section VI we illustrate how Jung's "feeling-toned complexes" may be related to state-dependent memory and Is-receptor systems. The current challenge is to adapt the research methods in this and the following sections to assess this psychobiological approach to psychoanalysis.

Motivation, Stress, and Mind-Body Healing: The Mind-Molecule Connection

THEORY

An adequate approach to mind-body healing must find a way of bridging the purported philosophical gap between mind and body. In this section we will explore the pharmacological method of *structure-activity analysis* as a means of integrating the molecular, physiological, behavioral, and mental levels in mind-body therapy. Most well-trained, current-day clinicians and therapists who have been out of school for more than ten years do not understand how such a far-reaching integration between mind and molecule is supported by current scientific data. Even the laboratory researchers, who for decades have carefully graphed the mathematical relationships between the molecular *structure* of drugs (as well as of the body's own information substances) and the mental and behavioral *activity* they evoke, have difficulty believing the profound implications of their daily work for a new theory of mind-body integration.

Such is the power of two philosophical ideas that seem to have double-binded most of us into disbelieving in the validity and value of our subjective experiences of mind-body integration and healing:

1. The Cartesian dualism that maintains that there is a gap between mind and body that cannot be bridged scientifically.
2. The crudely reductionist form of Occam's Razor which maintains that the subjective experience of mind is a mere epiphenomenon of physical processes and therefore can have no potency in facilitating mind-body healing.

One notable exception to this general malaise of double-binded disbelief can be found in the views of Candace Pert, Chief of Brain Biochemistry in the Clinical Neuroscience Branch of the National Institute of Mental Health in Bethesda, Maryland. Pert played a major role in the discovery of the opiate receptor (Pert & Snyder, 1973a,b), which was responsible for initiating the current "receptor revolution" in medicine. She has continually emphasized the implications of her work as a new approach to an integrated understanding of mind and behavior (Pert, 1986; Pert et al., 1985).* Since the pharmacological technique of structure activity-analysis (Pert & Herkenham, 1981) is of essence for many of her ideas about mind-body integration, we will focus on it in this section.

This short excursion into the world of biochemistry and molecular biology may seem far removed from the concerns of therapists who believe they deal only with the mental, emotional, and behavioral problems of their patients. We know, however, that the therapist's own belief system is one of the most potent factors in the effectiveness of therapy (Locke & Colligan, 1986; White, Tursky & Schwartz, 1985). Therapists and clinicians reading this section are exploring a new research base that will enable them to construct a more potent, personal therapeutic belief system that can be translated into more effective therapeutic work with their patients.

The Structural-Activity Analysis of Mind-Body Communication and Healing

A basic form of biological communication occurs via the release of *information substances* by nerves, organs, or tissues in one part of the body, which are received by "mailbox" receptors in the cell walls of nerves, organs, or tissues of another part of the body. Once a cell wall receptor has been "activated," it turns on other "secondary messenger systems" within the cell to carry out the characteristic metabolic activities of the cell: Nerve cells produce neurotransmitters for neural conductance; endocrine cells produce hormones; muscle cells initiate the biomechanical process of contraction, and so forth. Until fairly recently, the cell wall receptors were only hypothetical constructs; they were assumed to be present, but no one had ever seen them.

In the 1970s investigators began to use radioactive molecules to localize these receptors with great success. With this approach, Lefkowitz and his colleagues (1970) found how peptide hormones bound directly to endocrine receptors. Miledi and colleagues (1971) localized the acetylcholine receptors that mediate transmission at neuromuscular junctions and ganglia of the autonomic nervous system. The opiate receptor was characterized in the same manner (Pert & Snyder, 1973a,b; Simon, Hiller, & Edelman, 1973; Terenhius, 1973). There are a number of features about the characterization of the opiate receptor, however, that make it ideal for our study of the molecular basis of mind-body communication and healing. Because of this fact, we will examine it in more detail.

The opiate receptor and the information substances that bind to it (there-

*See also the semi-popular presentations of her work in Cordes, 1985; Hooper & Teresi, 1986; and Kanigel, 1986.

by activating cellular and tissue metabolism) are of special interest because they have easily measurable characteristics on the molecular, physiological, behavioral, and mental levels. On the molecular level, there are literally thousands of natural, synthetic, and semi-synthetic opiate analogs that have been isolated and manufactured for decades for possible use as analgesic drugs. Pharmacologists map the analgesic potency of such drugs with what they call *structure-activity analysis*: they correlate the analgesic potency (a mental-behavioral experience) with the molecular structure of the opiate analogs. An edited version of Pert and Herkenham's description of this process is as follows (1981, pp. 512–513):

> The construction of such structure-activity correlations became an important criterion for identifying and characterizing a biologically significant receptor.
> Opiate analogs, for example, have been tested for the ability to cause analgesia in mice on the so-called hot plate test; the mouse is placed on a hot plate and the number of seconds are counted until it makes a characteristic "hop, skip, and a jump" indicative of pain. Figure 5 shows a superb correlation between the analgesic potency of these compounds and their ability to displace tritiated naloxone-binding [naloxone is a morphine antagonist that blocks the uptake of opiates and their analogs by cell receptors; it can interfere with the normal binding of the body's own natural information substances and their cell wall receptors as well] in an opiate receptor assay; this provides a measure of the affinity or tightness with which these opiate molecules are capable of binding to the opiate receptor. The possibility of producing such excellent correlations between a biological response and an *in vitro* binding phenomenon leaves little doubt that the binding in the test tube is the same initial binding event that occurs *in vivo* to initiate the biological response.

Structure-activity analysis thus allows us to correlate the molecular structure of drugs with their biological responses. Opiate drugs and the body's own natural versions of them (endorphins and enkephalins), however, are messenger molecules (information substances) that mediate responses on the behavioral and mental-emotional levels, as well as on the biological. During the shock and stress of any traumatic experience, for example, the endorphins and their molecular analogs modulate a wide range of responses on all these levels, as illustrated in Table 4. A careful study of this table reveals that virtually all the responses on the behavioral and mental-emotional levels are manifestations of problems with motivation and stress. Most of these problems are of the type that traditionally has been ameliorated with therapeutic hypnosis.

Table 4 thus enables us to make interesting inferences about the relationship between molecular *structure* and *activity* on the behavioral and mental-

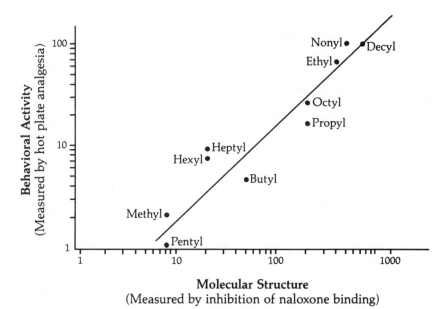

Figure 5: The structure-activity analysis of opiate analogs and their receptors. The *behavioral activity* of hot plate analgesia is highly correlated ($r = 0.95$; $p < 0.001$) with the *molecular structure* of the opiate analogs methyl, pentyl, hexyl, etc. (Adapted from Wilson, Rogers, Pert, & Snyder, 1975)

emotional levels. In effect, this suggests that we can begin thinking about the "mind-molecule connection" as the basis of ideodynamic healing in therapeutic hypnosis. We will explore this fascinating concept in more detail as a research issue at the end of this section. There we will learn that structure and activity analysis has enabled researchers to study many other classes of drugs (and the body's own natural versions of them) that integrate mind-body communication and healing on the molecular, biological, behavioral, and mental-emotional levels.

From this exhilarating foray into the molecular dynamics of mind-body communication in pain, stress, anxiety, and healing, we now return to the practical issues of how these factors can be related to our current practice of ideodynamic methods in therapeutic hypnosis. In this section, we will find that a concern with motivation and stress is the major psychobiological common denominator between the molecular biologists working with structure-activity relationships and psychotherapists working with patients on the behavioral and mental levels of emotional trauma and psychological problems.

Motivation, Stress, and Ideodynamic Healing

Patients are usually in a special psychobiological state of stress when they explore the sources of their psychological problems. This stress-induced state of arousal may provide the motivational energy for much of the suc-

Table 4: A sampling of endorphins and their molecular analogs that mediate a common psychobiological core of responses on the biological (anatomical/physiological), behavioral, and mental-emotional levels. All these responses are manifestations of problems with motivation and stress that have traditionally been ameliorated with therapeutic hypnosis.

Molecular	Anatomical/Physiological	Behavioral	Mental/Emotional	Research
β-Endorphin	Tonic depression of reflexes; EEG modification	Animal hypnosis, catalepsy	Sensory-perceptual alterations	Carli, 1977; Carli et al., 1984
β-enkephalin and β-endorphin	Anterior pituitary	Exercise stress; menstrual disturbance	Mental/emotional correlates of stress	Howlett et al., 1984
Endorphin and analogs	ACTH-endorphin neurons from hypothalamus to limbic and midbrain nuclei	Stress and sexual organism; instinctive behavior	"Agonal" orgasm; memory, learning	Murphy, 1981; Stewart, 1981, 1985
Endorphin analogs	"Nodal points" in limbic-hypothalamic system, periaqueductal grey of brain and dorsal horn of spine	Analgesia	Pain, comfort, relaxation; all sensory-perceptual experience	Chau, 1982; Henry, 1982; Pert et al., 1985

(continued)

TABLE 4 (*continued*)

Endorphin analogs	Endorphin receptor changes throughout the body	Affective disorder	Panic, anxiety and depression; mania	Gerner et al., 1982; Gold et al., 1982; Pickar et al., 1982
ACTH and endorphin analogs	Hypothalamic-pituitary adrenal axis	Ultradian and circadian rhythms	Mood shifts, memory, learning, motivation	Ananth, Bartova, & Rastogi, 1982; de Wied, 1980
Endorphins and analogs; peptides and hormones	Receptors on all neurons and organ systems of the autonomic, endocrine, and immune systems	Classical psychosomatic problems	Cognitive conflict and emotional stress; post-traumatic stress disorder	Figley, 1986; Pert, 1986; Pert et al., 1985; van der Kolk et al., 1985
Endorphins and analogs	Interactions with neurotransmitters of CNS	Schizophrenic behavior	Depersonalization, emotional sensory-perceptual alterations, hallucinations	Shah & Donald, 1982; Verhoeven & Van Praag, 1982
Endorphins and analogs	Limbic lobe and cortex	Stress and near-death experiences	Complex (mystical?) psychological experience; euphoria, memory, hallucination, dissociation	Carr, 1981; Davis, 1984

cess of hypnotherapeutic work. We would hypothesize that the relatively mild stress arousal that patients experience as they ideodynamically review their problems releases a pattern of information substances (peptides and stress hormones) similar to that which originally encoded their problem in a statebound form. The release of these information substances that modulate memory and learning accesses the statebound amnesias that have blocked the patient's previous efforts at self-understanding. We hypothesize that the seemingly spontaneous healing and recovery of traumatic memories as the patient moves through Cheek's three stages of *physiological response, ideomotor response*, and finally, *verbal recall* is the hypnotherapist's way of formulating the pharmacologist's understanding of the relationship between the molecular, physiological, behavioral, and mental levels via structural activity analysis.

With unusually traumatic events, we might hypothesize that the reverse can also take place. That is, the traumatic memories can be so disturbing to the patient that the conversational hypnotherapeutic methods used by most clinicians will be warded off. In Chapter 6, it is proposed that this is, in fact, often the source of "resistance" to hypnosis. When an especially secure hypnotherapeutic situation is created with ideodynamic finger signaling, wherein the patient need go only as "deep" as feels comfortable, however, it is possible to access even these traumatic memories in a safe, stepwise manner. Once traumatic and painful memories have been accessed in this way, the therapist may then appeal to the patient's more secure adult points of view and understanding to therapeutically reframe the significance and meaning of the original trauma.

The most significant aspect of the art of accessing the statebound sources of emotional problems can be found in the ideodynamic questions that are asked. As indicated in Section I, a simple "yes," "no," or "I don't know" frequently does not allow the patient sufficient "inner space" to do the therapeutic work that is needed. Permitting a wider range of ideomotor responses, such as "I do not want to answer," "I'm not ready to answer *yet*," or "I will be able to answer in [X amount of time]," gives the patient's unconscious an inner task it can continue to process autonomously even while the therapist offers other lines of questioning to deal with the issue. These other lines of questioning should be constructed so as to facilitate the assembling of the patient's inner resources — memories, mental skills, natural and learned psychobiological associations and processes — so that they can be integrated for problem-solving (Cheek & LeCron, 1968; Erickson & Rossi, 1979, 1981).

Questions that activate an ideodynamic response are therefore not merely a procedure for "getting the right answer." Getting the right answer is frequently only the final, conscious, verbal end-product of the ideodynamic process of healing. The activation of inner psychobiological processes of mind-body communication and healing that the patient must engage in to get the right answer is the more significant part of ideodynamic hypnothera-py.

Since most ideodynamic questioning spontaneously evokes a state of concentration or light trance, the therapist can be sure that the patient's conscious attention is frequently focused on wondering what the answer will be. *This wondering allows the patient's autonomous, unconscious healing processes to operate, to some extent, free from the usual conscious sets and learned limitations (the maladaptive patterns of previous life experience that are causing the current problem).* Ideodynamic signaling is an effective ther-apeutic tool not only because it accesses many psychobiological levels of state-dependent memory and learning, but also because it allows the patient to reassociate, reorganize, and reframe his understanding and inner re-sources in an optimal manner for problem-solving (Erickson, Rossi, & Ros-si, 1976).

This rationale for ideodynamic questioning mandates a very clear role for the therapist as a facilitator of the patient's own healing capacities. A psychobiological approach to mind-body therapy is in striking contrast to traditional hypnotic theory, which was based on the idea that suggestion, influence communication, and overt and/or covert conditioning were the fundamental mechanisms of cure. In this traditional view the patient's mind, in essence, was to be programmed by the more powerful and superior information and will coming from the therapist as the healing agent. This view has given rise to generations of highly directive "hypnotists" who were supposed to be dominant and charismatic in leading the inadequate patient into health (Milne, 1986). This misleading traditional view has tended to alienate the most knowledgeable scientists and the more sensitive therapists from the entire field of hypnotherapy. It has earned the suspicion of society in general and the derision of the media in particular.

Even today this misguided traditional view is responsible for perpetuat-ing the debilitating myth of "the usefulness of suggestion in therapy." Ever enthusiastic young therapists invariably make an initial exploration of the "fascinating field of hypnosis," only to abandon it ignominiously after a short period because they found that "suggestion" did not work the "magic" it was supposed to work. Somehow, they believe that they just were not able to get patients deep enough into "trance," which was supposed to function as a sort of "vulnerable blank slate" on which the words of the therapist were to be imprinted to effect the cure.

The truth, however, is that such a blank state does not usually exist in typical hypnotherapeutic work; the therapist's words do not effect cure by being accepted and followed in an automaton-like manner by the suscepti-ble patient. To the contrary, the true therapeutic potential of the patient can be found in that ever active and eager part of the inner mind that, like a creative child, is still flexible enough to receive, explore, and develop a few generative cues and guidelines that are offered by the therapist. When the therapist focuses his efforts not on his own power and prestige but on his skill in facilitating the patient's own inner resources ideodynamically, then, with surprising efficacy, cure and problem-solving manifest themselves as a natural healing process.

PRACTICE

4

Motivation and Healing in Therapeutic Hypnosis

Approximately one in five people can experience deep hypnosis at the first session. In group demonstrations with volunteers this ratio remains fairly constant. This is an average figure reflecting the frequency of high hypnotizability in the general population. *The percentage of people who can experience therapeutic hypnosis will approach 100 when there is strong motivation and a clear understanding of its value.* Patients who are critically ill are universally responsible to hypnotic suggestion, even when they have had no previous instruction or appreciation for its value. The relief of pain and apprehension in the trance state seems to mobilize defense mechanisms in the critically ill patient similar to the physiologic protective mechanisms seen in lower animals in hibernation or the apparently spontaneous trancelike "freezing" for camouflage in time of danger.

In a group of seriously ill patients there is the great advantage of being able to alter the abnormal physiologic patterns due to the illness. In addition, the discouraged patient, seeing the dramatic changes brought about through hypnosis, is given renewed hope of achieving the apparently impossible. The ego strength of such a patient is increased by the participation in the therapy, and this in turn can lead to subsequent use of hypnosis in gaining insight into faulty personality reactions.

The entire field of autonomic-endocrine-tissue resistance factors in such illnesses as diabetes, tuberculosis, cancer, allergy, and the collagen diseases can be profitably explored with hypnotic techniques. In none of these diseases can series of cases be studied and compared because each individual patient has a host of shifting physiological variables. With hypnosis, the individual patient can be studied and the variables evaluated under different imagined emotional circumstances.

Just before the advent of ether, chloroform, and nitrous oxide as anesthetic agents, James Esdaile (1850/1957) successfully used hypnosis to prevent pain in more than one thousand surgical operations. A state of hypnotic trance deep enough to permit surgery was easier to achieve in 1846 than it is now because incentive was greater—the patient could choose only between hypnosis and the agony of being held down by several attendants while the surgeon worked. Today under ordinary circumstances there is no such incentive. It is easier for a patient to take a sedative and an expertly administered anesthetic than it is to work with the induction of hypnotic anesthesia. During the war years, however, hypnosis came to the aid of the surgeon when anesthetic agents were unavailable (Sampiman & Woodruff, 1946).

In childbirth, hypnosis is the safest means of controlling pain (Heron & Abramson, 1950; Kroger & DeLee, 1943). It can have no harmful effect upon the unborn infant. Even when it is not completely effective for pain relief, it still allows the mother to get along with less analgesic drug than would otherwise be necessary. Obstetrics hypnosis has a limited use unless publicity makes a fad of it. It takes time to teach hypnotic techniques to an obstetric patient and time is often at a premium. The subject may be most enthusiastic during the prenatal course and may achieve complete control of sensation in the trance state only to give it all up and ask for medication on arriving at the hospital in labor. The knowledge that drugs are available decreases the incentive to persevere.

Although prestige of the operator, previous knowledge of hypnosis, and popularity of the method are important, the value of motivation is of prime importance, for it makes the difference between success and failure in critical situations of clinical medicine. At the present time, when hypnosis is still regarded as a psychologic curiosity by many physicians, the strength of the motivation to accept hypnosis must be supplied by the physician. He must be convinced of its value before he can sell it to the patient. His task is made easier by the unconscious needs of the critically ill patient.

Case 1: Diabetes and Blood Sugar Control

ANESTHESIA, AGE REGRESSION AND INSIGHTS; PROBLEM-SOLVING AND SURGERY

A 33-year-old diabetic woman was seen in the fourth month of her third pregnancy in consultation with two other physicians, who felt that her pregnancy should be terminated because of severe toxemia and two serious episodes of diabetic coma which had occurred in her second pregnancy. Because the patient had shown marked instability with any regimen of treatment and because she had to live a long distance away from a medical center, I (DBC) agreed that her pregnancy should be terminated. The patient's 36-year-old brother had died of a coronary occlusion within the year. The patient's father had died from a complication of diabetes following an appendectomy. Six years earlier, after a gallbladder operation, this patient had required insulin every 15 minutes and had remained in critical condition for several days.

Because the present pregnancy had advanced to the fourth month, vaginal therapeutic abortion seemed dangerous. On the other hand, an abdominal operation seemed dangerous because of the unfavorable psychologic conditioning of this patient. She wanted a third child but was convinced that the risk of carrying through to term would be a serious one. She was, however, afraid of undergoing an abdominal operation.

With the hope of understanding her psychological reactions better, I talked with the patient and her husband about using hypnosis to help control pain and thus help control her insulin needs. Their interest and response was favorable. During a two-hour session, the patient was trained in achieving complete anesthesia of her abdomen. She was taught to awaken from hypnosis if a nurse or physician should enter her room in order that she might not give a dangerous impression of being in diabetic coma. She was much impressed by her ability to produce anesthesia. On admission to the hospital she was taking 180 units of insulin a day, using 60 units of protamine zinc, and filling out her requirements with regular insulin.

The response to the surgery was remarkable. She maintained a normal temperature, pulse, and respiration after a total hysterectomy under spinal anesthesia. Her blood sugar never went over 117 mg./100 cc., although she was eating a regular hospital diet from the day of surgery. A 3-plus glycosuria on the day of operation dropped to zero on the second day. No insulin was used during the hospital stay. During the next 11 months, she used only an occasional dose of insulin during periods of emotional stress.

This patient showed remarkable willingness to accept hypnosis. Possibly this was due to her unfavorable experience with previous types of therapy. She was excited by her discovery that her blood sugar level had been controlled. She developed a zest for living which had been notably absent in preceding months.

During a hypnotic session on the day following surgery, a chance question was asked regarding her mother. There was an immediate outpouring of resentments toward her mother which were found, by age regression, to date back many years. During subsequent interviews, she was able to reorganize her thinking at an adult level in terms of these resentments and was able to achieve a warmer relationship with her mother. The patient took renewed interest in her garden, making clothes, and enjoying activities with her two children. She stated that she felt she would now live a long time. The untimely death of her brother and her unpredictable diabetic course had reduced her to a state of constant fear. Wondering if the diagnosis of diabetes might have been incorrect, I admitted the patient a few weeks later to the hospital for a glucose tolerance test. This test showed a definite diabetic curve but a rebound of apparent insulin output that dropped her blood sugar to a level below the initial fasting sugar after five hours. Hypnosis had allowed the patient a means of developing insight into important personality reactions which seemed to have been influencing her diabetic state.

Although the emotional instability of young diabetics has long been recognized (Heyer, 1954; Mieth, 1954; Mohr, 1954), the possibility of helping such patients to develop an understanding of their personality reactions seems to have been overlooked by clinicians in this country. Hypnotic suggestion of environmental patterns with a diabetic under carefully controlled test conditions offers fruitful possibilities for better understanding of this disease. The chance that diabetes in the early stage is a reversible functional disorder should offer more hope, particularly in view of the recent research that indicates that diabetes can be an autoimmune disease (Foulis, 1987). In any chronic disease, hope diminishes as time elapses, but hope should be nurtured.

Case 2: Motivation for Hypnotic Analgesia in Pregnancy

A 23-year-old nulliparous woman who had been a psychology major in college was told told that hypnosis could be used to relieve the pain of labor and give her baby the best chance of survival when the breech presentation was discovered. She accepted this possible means of pain relief with enthusiasm, partly because of her previous training in psychology and partly because of her understanding of the value of keeping drug sedation at a minimum. She was trained in the use of autohypnosis and was able to go comfortably through her entire first stage of labor at home before the membranes ruptured and she realized that she was close to delivery. She delivered a six-pound baby in excellent condition. The total medication was 100 mg. of Demerol, given as she entered the hospital.

In her second pregnancy the fetus presented in normal vertex position. Again she was interested in using hypnosis and was rehearsed with the technique previously used. She knew, however, that in a second pregnancy there is less to be feared both in terms of duration of labor and risk to the baby. Early in the first stage of labor she began complaining of pain and, lacking the motivation to persevere with her hypnosis, begged for analgesia. This is an example of the difference of susceptibility of the patient depending upon the incentive to use hypnosis.

Case 3: Immune Response Facilitation in Peritonitis

ANALGESIA, VOMITING CONTROL, FEVER, PULSE, AND
BLOOD FLOW IN DEEP HYPNOSIS

A 38-year-old nulliparous woman who had a ruptured tubal pregnancy after five years of sterility was referred to me. During surgery she was found to have a congenital absence of one tube. Knowing the patient's desire for a child, I removed the conceptus from the junction of the middle and distal thirds of the tube and left a new ostium at this point. Saline solution containing penicillin was injected into the uterus two days after surgery in order to keep the tube open. The patient became pregnant a few months later and went through to term. She was extremely apprehensive during the first four months and frequently had pain simulating that of the tubal pregnancy until it was obvious that the pregnancy was within the uterine cavity. During this time the patient also had persistent vomiting. I talked with her enthusiastically about the use of hypnosis and she was able to control the vomiting, but at no time did she reach a deep hypnotic level. On the third day following delivery there was a hemorrhage associated with a temperature rise to 105°F. due to an intrauterine infection which continued in spite of massive antibiotic therapy and transfusions of blood. The temperature fluctuated between 102 and 103.8°F. The pulse remained around 120 per minute until the fifth day, when it began increasing. At this time there were signs of spreading peritonitis. The patient was discouraged by her poor response to treatment.

Again I talked to her about the use of hypnosis, explaining that the pelvic inflammation was possibly causing so much spasm of the blood vessels that the antibiotic drugs were unable to get to the source of infection. I explained to her that with hypnosis we could free her of pain and, as the muscles in the abdomen and pelvis relaxed, there would be a better circulation of blood. She was immediately interested in this possibility and, contrary to her previous reaction to hypnosis, went into a very deep trance during which she was trained in inducing anesthesia of her abdomen.

This patient was hypnotized at nine o'clock in the evening. She slept that night without sedation. The temperature the next morning was 99.6°F. and the pulse had dropped to 108. Twenty-four hours later the temperature was 97.6°F., with the pulse 90. Three days after induction of deep hypnosis this patient was allowed to go home. There was no further temperature elevation and the course was from then on uneventful.

Although it is possible this dramatic response in a critical illness might have been spontaneous or might have represented a lysis as a result of the continued antibiotic therapy, it seemed from the behavior of the patient that her response was due to a change of attitude and a renewed hope upon discovering that it was possible to control pain with hypnosis.

Three cases have been presented here to illustrate the value of motivation. The first patient (Case 1) had no previous instruction in hypnosis. She had no knowledge of the obstetric merits of the operator. There was no possible prestige effect other than the dubious one of being a consultant to her physicians. In this instance she had been coerced for medicolegal reasons into seeking obstetric opinion regarding need for therapeutic abortion. She had no free choice in the matter and was initially antagonistic in this relationship. She appreciated the need for surgery under the circumstances, however, and welcomed hypnosis as a reasonable means of making the surgery safer for her. The motivation was supplied by the operator and aided by the patient's apprehension.

Cases 2 and 3 illustrate the importance of motivation at a clinically critical time in patients who were ideally prepared in terms of prestige factors and interest in hypnosis. In each case the operator succeeded once and failed once, and the difference in result depended on motivation as appreciated by the patient.

Hypnosis can be of life-saving value in obstetric emergencies. The mechanics of hypnosis can be taught to all obstetric patients and all patients with major surgical problems. The occasional frightened patient, who could develop untoward complications because of unrecognized fears, will usually accept hypnosis willingly and may help uncover and explain the fears before the critical occasion arises.

In this day of generalized lay enthusiasm for exploring the possibilities of hypnosis in age regression and recovering memories of "previous lives," it seems fitting to declare that hypnosis should be used with profound respect for its great value to the critically ill patient and to the patient whose previous therapy has been unsuccessful. We should remember that hypnotism must not be cheapened by widespread and uncritical usage. It can be of life-saving value in the very ill patient. Such a patient is the one most likely to respond in developing a deep trance.

Hypnosis offers a valuable means of exploring the reactions of patients under varying personality-environment situations. *The percentage of good hypnotic patients approximates 100 when the operator is convinced of the advantages hypnosis can offer and when he imparts this motivation to his patient. The response is best in the seriously ill patients who have lost hope for recovery or who have lost faith in the treatments used so far.* This is the group to which James Esdaile (1850/1957) was referring when he stated; "Mesmerism often comes to the aid of my patients when all the resources of medicine are exhausted and all the drugs of Arabia useless; and therefore, I consider it to be my duty to benefit them by it."

This is the surgeon whose operative mortality from infection in major surgery was 5% in the pre-Lister days, when all the surgeons of Europe were experiencing a mortality rate of 25 to 50% from infection! It would be interesting to discover why the hypnotic trance improves the resistance to infection and seems to speed wound healing. Recent research on the modulation of the immune system competency by emotions appears to be of essence when we succeed in activating a patient's motivation for healing (O'Regan, 1984, 1985).

5

Assessing and Facilitating Therapeutic Hypnosis

The hypnotic state is usually more pleasant than the normal awake state. When the hypnotized subject is warned that he will soon be expected to awaken, he will often drop into a deeper level just before awakening.

Most hypnotic subjects will respond at their best capacity if suggestions are given in a permissive way, unless the situation is critical and comparable to that of combat, where life may depend upon immediate acceptance of orders given by a superior officer.

While teaching the techniques of hypnosis induction and trance deepening, the writer (DBC) has been impressed by the indications given by hypnotized students that they have reached their deepest level just after receiving the suggestion that the session would end. Before the present experiment was set up, the observations were made with a Chevreuil pendulum as the indicator. The student was asked to hold the chain of the pendulum between pointer finger and thumb with eyes closed. The statement was made to the subject, as well as the two or three students in the group, that the unconscious knows what hypnosis feels like, even when there has been no formal exposure to it. I state that I am going to ask the unconscious of the subject to force the fingers apart when he is in hypnosis deeply enough for him to shut out all sounds except my voice. I point out that the ball will then fall to the floor without disturbing him.

Some form of induction technique is then presented in order that the students might shape their practice session along parallel lines. Some subjects drop the ball during induction. Others hold it till the end. A few hold on till the suggestion, **"In a few moments I will count from ten down to zero. As I count, I would like to have you gradually awaken until at the count of zero you are wide awake, comfortable, and relaxed."**

A large proportion of those who continue to hold the chain until this time relax their grip and drop the ball shortly after the direction stated or after the counting has started. The dropping of the ball seems to symbolize achievement of a greater depth.

There are two reasonable possibilities of explanation here. One would be that there had been a gradual deepening of the hypnotic state which happened accidentally to coincide with the command to awaken. Another would be that the signal to awaken had brought about a deepening of the level.

LeCron and Bordeaux (1949) have pointed out that there may be an accurate perception of the depth of hypnosis on an unconscious level. There seems to be a reasonable basis of clinical evidence to support this hypothesis. Thus, by utilizing the ideomotor response of finger movement, it was felt that some clarification of the "ball dropping" phenomenon might be obtained.

Toward this end the subjects could help by giving two distinct signals. A movement of the right pointer finger could give a constantly readable indication of depth similar to the alcohol weather thermometer, and a single flick of the left pointer finger could be given when the subject recognized his maximum depth for the day comparable to the maximum reading clinical thermometer. The right arm is placed in such a position that the index finger can move down as well as up. The subject is asked to lift this finger progressively as the trance is deepened and lower it progressively as the trance decreases toward the awake state. The left index finger is to lift momentarily when the impression of greatest depth is perceived.

As a further check upon the mechanism of trance deepening, the subjects were asked after awakening when they thought they were deepest and what they thought made them go deeper.

Evaluating Trance Depth Via Finger Signals

Ten successive gynecological patients without previous training in hypnosis were chosen for the experiment of evaluating depth level with finger signals. Their ages ranged from 22 to 54. Hypnosis was presented to them as a means of improving tolerance for conditioned pain and for helping uncover psychic factors in various gynecological and urological complaints. Except in the case of teaching professional men and women, (it is felt) that hypnosis should be used only when there is a real need recognized by the subject as well as the therapist (Cheek, 1957). The mechanics of hypnotic suggestion are explained to my patients as being adaptive processes serving the purpose of mobilizing defense mechanisms similar to responses found throughout the animal kingdom (Cheek, 1958a, b). If interested, my patients then listen to a 15-minute tape recording which explains hypnosis further as being a state of improved concentration enabling the subject to use effectively the tremendous ability of the brain to alter physiological processes in a beneficial way. At the conclusion of the tape, the patient is given an example of an induction with the recommendation that she listen to it objectively in order that she may see how simple, familiar words are used to call upon memories of places associated with peace, quiet, and relaxation. Toward the end of this example, the suggestion is given that she might be interested in noticing how she can alter the sensation in the left arm by pretending she has been lying on it for a long time and remembering how it might feel if it were numb in this way.

If the subject states her interest in learning more about hypnosis, she is taken through graded steps of learning outlined in Box 12.

With this sequence of tests and demonstration of personal achievement, the stage is set for the induction of therapeutic hypnosis. Any technique would suffice as further experience has shown, but for the purpose of standardizing the present group management, I asked each subject what sort of place she would like to remember. It was explained that I would like to know whether she would be most relaxed in the mountains, near a river, in a forest, or on the beach. The patient was in this way allowed to start her own induction by answering questions with autosuggestive, ideodynamic content. Then she was asked to close her eyes and visualize that place. Additional relaxing suggestions were given for three or four minutes. The right arm was then moved by the operator to a vertical position resting with the elbow flexed on the arm of the chair.

Now the suggestion was given that the right forefinger would be moved by the unconscious in an upward direction if the depth of the trance were increased, and the finger would lower if the level were decreased. Another suggestion was given that the left forefinger would raise momentarily if the unconscious sensed at any time that the level was greater than any previously experienced that day.

After continuing with suggestions that the hypnotic state would be deepened as the operator continued talking, a lapse of approximately 30 seconds was allowed to watch for the signal of increasing depth. In none of the ten cases did this occur. The suggestion was then given: **"In a few moments I will count from ten down to zero, and I would like to have you awaken feeling comfortable, relaxed and refreshed."** Another pause of 30 seconds was allowed, and then the reverse count started with intervals of 20 seconds between each of the first three counts.

Two subjects signaled with the left forefinger that the maximum depth had been reached just after the suggestion of impending reverse count had been given. The other eight gave the signal between the beginning of the count and the count of five. The right index finger was approximately elevated at the same time.

Discussion

There may be three factors accounting for this drop to a deeper level after the suggestion for awakening has been given. Erik Wright has pointed out to me that the signal to awaken may afford relief from the fear the subject may have had of being unable to awaken. This is quite possible and should be explored further. It is probably not tenable under the circumstances of

---

**BOX 12: ASSESSING COOPERATION AND RESISTANCE
TO IDEODYNAMIC SUGGESTION**

1. *Accessing ideodynamic sensitivity and cooperation*
   a. While the patient is seated with arms extended forward and parallel to each other at shoulder height, ideodynamic suggestions are given that a heavy weight (a book, box, or purse) is pulling one arm down.
   b. This ideodynamic suggestion can be enhanced by saying **heavier** and **lower** as the patient *exhales*.
2. *Assessing and reframing resistance*
   a. With the patient's arms again extended in their original starting position, it is suggested that an imaginary string on one wrist is pulling the arm toward the therapist.
   b. When the arm has moved significantly, the suggestion is given with a dubious tone to, **"Try to move the arm back to its original position."**
   c. When the patient smiles in recognition of the resistance to "trying," further suggestions are given to imagine the string being cut and a strong rubberband stretched between the arms and pulling them together.
3. *Ratifying cooperation and resistance*
   a. All successful ideodynamic movements made by the patient are ratified as good examples of sensitivity and potential for further therapeutic responsiveness to hypnosis.
   b. Any unsuccessful responses are interpreted as a conscious or unconscious need for a deeper understanding of the process of therapeutic hypnosis.
   c. After clarifying negative misconceptions, ideodynamic movements can be assessed again via the pendulum approach outlined in Box 4.

---

the present experiment because all the patients were given a clear explanation of their controlled role in hypnosis. Their training was gradual and they had already been exposed to a tape recording which contained a sample of the ending of hypnotic induction.

A second factor may be motivation. All students of hypnosis and all of the patients in this experiment were interested in experiencing hypnosis. During the early part of the hypnotic session, each may have been trying too hard to experience the trance state envisioned by the beginner. It could be that the suggestion of awakening came as a relief in terminating this seemingly unsuccessful effort. The greater depth reached may have resulted from relaxation of the effort to succeed and the freeing of a wish to go deeper.

A third possibility is that the hypnotic state is more pleasant than the awake one. Whenever a direction is given which will lead a person from a pleasant to a potentially less pleasant state, there is a mobilization of resistance against the coercive move. This has been the explanation volunteered by physician and dentist students of hypnosis when they were asked what they thought during the session. The usual statement has been, "When you told me to wake up, I just felt I wanted to stay that way." When the subjects in this experiment were asked for their reaction, they stated that they thought they had gone deepest just about the time I had told them I would awaken them. At a later session under hypnosis, all ten of the experimental subjects indicated with finger signals that it felt better to be in hypnosis and that there had been a rebellion against the command to start waking up.

6

Resolving Resistance to Therapeutic Hypnosis

Outwardly cooperative subjects may be unconsciously afraid of entering a therapeutic trance state. They often develop violent fluttering movements of the eyelids and complain of discomfort when asked to keep the eyes closed. Some will keep their eyes open after they have been asked to close them, as though the lids were in rigid catalepsy. Some will enter a light trance and then find some pretext for scratching an ear or adjusting the clothing in order to escape to an unhypnotized state. Some will give indications of hostility toward the hypnotist, when previous behavior has been friendly. Some will show a fear reaction similar to that occurring in the excitement stage of inhalation anesthesia. Some may show a frightening appearance of pseudoshock.

Occasionally these subjects may be led adequately through this troubled phase by ordinary deepening techniques. They may become used to the border zone of hypnosis, much as the timid bather may gradually enter the water after dipping in a finger and then a toe to see that it is reasonably safe. A large proportion of timid hypnotic subjects, however, will withdraw from an induced trance state and return to a more superficial level without knowing the reason for so doing. Frequently these patients are bitterly disappointed with themselves for the trouble they are causing. To stop efforts in their behalf at this point may not only be the dead-end for much-needed therapy, but may add another weight of psychological failure to burdens already present.

Two patients proved instructive in giving clues of possible reasons for this consciously cooperative but unconsciously resistant syndrome.

Sexual Trauma Reactivated in Hypnotic Induction

A 32-year-old woman traveled many miles for consultation at the request of a friend who had told her about hypnosis. Her complaints included low-back pain, vaginal discharge, fatigue, dysmenorrhea, and loss of libido.

There were no positive physical findings to account for her symptoms. Therefore, it seemed reasonable to show her a little about relaxing and how muscles could be overworking even though she believed them to be relaxed. While trying to imagine the downward pull of a heavy purse on one arm, this patient discontinued the exercise. Her manner changed as she said, "I came down here to find out what was wrong with me." With that she walked out of the office without saying goodbye.

A few weeks later I received an apologetic letter asking me to forgive her bad behavior. She wrote that while standing in my office she had suddenly been overwhelmed with a feeling of mixed fear and hostility toward me. It was not until she had nearly reached her home that the image of herself crossing an empty field on the way home from school had entered her mind. She had remembered that a man had overtaken her on the path across that field and had threatened her sexually. Although she had fainted, she knew her appearance had frightened the man away and had saved her from being molested. That experience had been separated by 21 years from the experience of using postural suggestion in my office, yet the sensations had appeared the same. She concluded her note with the question, "Do you suppose I went into hypnosis at that time?" I did not have a chance to answer this question but she stimulated me to pose some for myself and other patients.

Trauma and Spontaneous Trance

A 27-year-old woman who had been trying unsuccessfully to have a child became interested when hypnosis was recommended as a means of uncovering possible psychological factors. This patient had been interned for one year at a German concentration camp during World War II. She had seen her father led away to be killed. Because of age and graying hair, her mother's life, too, had been in constant danger.

During the third hypnotic interview this patient said, "You know, I have had this feeling before. I think we must all have been in hypnosis during the first two weeks in that concentration camp. We did not care if we lived or not. We walked around in a sort of stupor."

Here were two experiences, one demonstrating a rejection of hypnosis because it reminded the subject of what might have been a spontaneously occurring hypnotic or hypnoidal state; the second, demonstrating a recognition that a medium hypnotic trance had similarities with what may have been a spontaneous medium trance in the prison situation. From their observations I was led to search for more information about spontaneous trance states.

I have encountered 60 consecutive patients who have shown conscious cooperation but unconscious resistance to entering hypnosis. Two of these did not permit further study, but 58 were able to discover the cause and subsequently became excellent subjects. Just as with the first two, these all believed their trouble stemmed from some previous traumatic experience during which they felt they had escaped into a protective trance. They all recognized that the initial frightening experience in the artificial induction with me had reminded them of the traumatic one. The natural reaction had been a wish to escape from this conditioned fear response until they learned that the hypnosis could be associated with pleasant thoughts as well.

Types of hypnosis-producing traumatic experiences include the following:

- Childhood unpleasant general inhalation anesthetic   43
- Threatened or actual frightening sexual experience (all female)   7
- Accident involving unconsciousness or broken bones   6
- Death, or serious injury, of a loved one   2

—
58

The general technique for resolving such problems involves:

a. *With totally resistant subjects unable to enter hypnosis at all*: Use of Chevreul pendulum according to methods described in Box 4.

b. *With subjects who repeatedly withdraw after entering a light hypnotic state*: Use of ideomotor finger signals described in Box 5.

Human beings first learn to communicate by muscular efforts of gesture, facial expression, and alteration of voice tone; only later are words used. It takes effort to convert thoughts into articulated words, and this effort may lift the plane of thought from unconscious relationships to more conscious ones. For example, we learn to watch for gestures and tone-inflections when studying sterility patients at the first visit when they respond to the question, **"Did you want to become pregnant during the first few months of your marriage?"** A questioning upswing of inflection on the halting "Yes" tells more than the articulated word. Some will emphatically answer, "Oh yes, I've always wanted children," while their heads are contradicting this with a side-to-side negative gesture.

With ideomotor questioning techniques it is possible first to learn if there is some cause for resistance to hypnosis, then to bracket the time of origin for that cause. Usually memory for the event can then be brought up from the unconscious level to a conversational level where it can be described. A systematic yet flexible approach to uncovering and resolving unconscious resistances to therapeutic hypnosis is outlined in Box 13.

Physical Trauma Reactivated in Hypnotic Induction; Correcting the Therapist at an Ideomotor Level

A Mexican student in a symposium on hypnosis was one of three who were anxious to experience it before practicing inductions with each other. Using the suggestion that their unconscious minds would force apart their fingers

**BOX 13: UNCOVERING AND RESOLVING RESISTANCE
TO THERAPEUTIC HYPNOSIS**

1. *Assessing the sources of resistance*
   After setting up ideodynamic signaling, explore as follows:
   a. **"Does the inner part of your mind have some fear of hypnosis?"**
   b. **"Would it be all right for you to know what causes this fear?"**
   c. **"Would it be all right for me to know?"**
   While answering the first question, there may be a further block with a "no" or "I don't know" answer. In this event the following question will usually break through:
   d. **"Is there a deeper level of thought which knows the answer to this question?"**
2. *Reframing and resolving resistance*
   Sometimes there will be a block on the above questions caused by a spontaneous age regression to the time of the event. At the hypnotically regressed age, the event may be too traumatic to discuss, but the emotions may be made less poignant by shifting the orientation forward again to the time of interview with the question:
   a. **"Would it be all right to know about and discuss this event in terms of your knowledge and experience of [the current year]?"**
   b. **"Has there been more than one cause for your fear of hypnosis?"**
   When the source of the resistance has been recovered, the patient will usually verbalize it spontaneously as a sudden insight:
   c. **"Knowing this, can your inner mind now continue with the healing process?"**
   It is not always necessary for the resistance to be verbalized:
   d. **"Can your unconscious resolve that difficulty all by itself so that it can now proceed with the healing process?"**
3. *Ratifying the resolution of resistance*
   a. **"Having resolved those difficulties (misconceptions), will you be able to continue using therapeutic hypnosis effectively?"**
   Any further difficulty at this level can be left for resolution by suggesting that more time may be needed for the unconscious to continue its own inner exploratory work so that these issues can be resolved in the next therapeutic session.

while holding the pendulum as they entered a trance deep enough for them to produce some phenomena, I went through the motions of describing a peaceful place in the mountains. Two of the men dropped their pendulums and entered hypnosis. Dr. R grasped his pendulum more tightly. Beads of perspiration appeared on his forehead. His face and hands turned an ashy-gray color. I asked him to open his eyes and let the pendulum answer some questions. I asked him:

Q: Have you ever felt like this before?

A: (Yes.)

Q: Was this before you were 20 years old?

A: (Yes.)

Q: Before you were 15?

A: (No.)

Q: Does your unconscious mind now know what that was?

A: (Yes.)

Q: Let your eyes close now, and if your inner mind will let you know what the experience is, it will pull your fingers apart. As the pendulum falls to the table, the noise will bring that memory up to a conscious level where you can talk about it.

I remained silent for about 20 seconds. As his fingers released the chain, he appeared disturbed. A split second later, as the plastic ball of the pendulum struck the table, he lifted his left hand to the side of his head, opened his eyes, and said: "I know now. I was in gymnasium exercises and I was the top man in one of those pyramids. The man below stumbled, and I landed on the side of my head on the cement floor." There seemed to be no further comment. I asked him to pick up the pendulum and answer this question:

Q: Do you now think you can enter hypnosis comfortably, and be free of the reaction you had a little while ago?

A: (Yes.)

The doctor promptly put himself into hypnosis and repeated the self-hypnosis several times that evening without further reaction. It should be noted that positive, optimistic questions were used, implying that there might be some previous experiences to account for his evident fear during the first induction. Positive suggestions were continued in the formation of questions so that he might understand that there would be a solution and that this solution would help him to be a good subject. This method might indicate to the uninitiated that I was forcing his conscious mind to choose a reason in order to satisfy my needs and relieve the pressure upon him to find an acceptable reason, no matter what it might be. However, those who have used therapeutically slanted ideomotor questioning will agree, I think, that it is not easy to force answers of an artificial nature from the unconscious mind.

Indeed, when forced into the wrong direction by an overly authoritarian and misleading question from the therapist, the patient will typically begin to give contradictory and confusing ideomotor responses, or shut down completely.

I have frequently been contradicted and corrected verbally by patients in deep hypnotic states when I have purposely tried to force a conclusion at variance with their own observations. It must be underlined here that at a conversational level it is possible to force acceptance of ideas from the hypnotized subject. Ideomotor responses are more honest and they are often at variance with verbal answers to questions.

RESEARCH

Motivation, Stress, and Ideodynamic Signaling: Research Projects 11–19

Project 11 Is responsiveness to therapeutic hypnosis more a function of the therapist's *suggestions* or the patient's *sensitivity*?

Design an experiment to determine whether there are significant differences in response to our procedure for "Assessing Cooperation and Resistance to Ideodynamic Suggestion" (Box 12) when the word *sensitivity* is used instead of *suggestion* to describe the task.

Project 12 Although hypnotherapists have been facilitating hypnotic induction via hand levitation by associating their suggestions for "lifting" with the patient's inhalation and "lowering" with the patient's exhalation for at least two generations, since Erickson first developed this approach, we are not aware of any experimental studies in this area (Erickson & Rossi, 1979, 1981).

Does a positive association (conditioning) of the therapist's voice and suggestions with behavioral inevitabilities (suggesting "lifting" when it is inevitable that the arm will tend to lift slightly during inhalation) really lead to a more satisfactory therapeutic trance?

Project 13 How does the validity and reliability of ideodynamic signaling change when motivational variables change? What is the difference, for example, in questioning people about what they had for breakfast versus how their sex life is going? How do reliability and validity change over time (e.g., questions about yesterday, last week, last year, and so forth)?

Project 14 Evaluate the problem of resistance and negative sequelae to hypnotic induction by replicating Cheek's studies on uncovering and resolving resistance to hypnosis (Box 13). Do his findings about the source of such problems in previously traumatic and hypnoidal experiences hold? What independent checks on the validity of such experiences can you develop? One could "follow up" emergency room patients who had been in an accident, for example. Would a higher proportion of such patients experience difficulties during hypnotic induction because they tended to reexperience their traumatic accident?

Project 15 What independent lines of empirical data can you assess for determining whether accident victims are actually in a "hypnoidal state" during the initial shock phase of their trauma?

Project 16 Does resolving such previously traumatic experiences change a subject's scores on standardized scales (objective and subjective) of hypnotic susceptibility? Does it change the patient's "comfort level" with therapeutic hypnosis?

Project 17 Are patients who are more highly motivated for therapeutic hypnosis (because they are desperately ill) able to achieve higher scores on appropriately designed clinical scales of hypnotic susceptibility? How would one design a "motivated scale" of hypnotic susceptibility for the critically ill?

Project 18 Design an experimental study to determine whether stress-related hormones and information substances are actually released during hypnotic induction and/or the use of the ideodynamic finger signaling approach. Are such information substances released more when the *traumatic source* of a problem is being investigated? Would they be released more when we are "following up" emergency room patients, for example (see research project 14)?

Project 19 Numerous studies in the field of psychoneuroimmunology have now demonstrated the effects of negative and positive stress and motivation on the immune system (Ader, 1981, 1985; Rossi, 1986d; Stein, 1986). Design an experimental study to assess the degree to which the resolution of traumatic statebound memories via our ideodynamic approach can facilitate immune system competence.

Structure-Activity Analysis and Mind-Body Relationships: Project 20

The relationship between molecular structure and activity on the physiological, behavioral, and mental-emotional levels is well documented for many other classes of psychoactive drugs besides the opiates and their endogenous endorphin analogs. Pert and Herkenham discuss two examples as follows (1981, pp. 514–516):

> When characterizing structure-activity relationships for brain receptors, most often one must resort to using behavioral phenomena to correlate

with binding data. Somewhat surprisingly, correlations can be quite excellent. Figure 6 shows that the receptor for "angel dust," a frequently abused animal tranquilizer, phencyclidine (PCP), correlates reasonably well with two quite different measures of biological response (Zukin & Zukin, 1979). In the mouse rotarod test, shown on the left, mice balance on a slowly turning rod for several minutes. A dose of PCP analog required to make half of the mice fall off within the allotted time is recorded. In a discrimination test, shown on the right, rats are required to perform a prescribed response if a drug reminds them of PCP. The threshold dose required to elicit this recognition is recorded. While the correlations of 0.81 and 0.92, respectively, are less impressive than the 0.98 correlation obtained in the above example, it is still fairly amazing that such gross behavioral parameters can be traced to the interaction of one group of small molecules with their specific receptor sites in the brain.

The behaviorist, of course, would accuse us of anthropomorphizing if we assumed there were mental aspects to the animals' experiences of analgesia (Figure 5), and balance and stimulus discrimination (Figure 6). The structural-activity analysis of the relationship between the human mental-emotional experience of anxiety and the molecular structure of the benzodiazepine analogs, however, does give us a quantifiable measure of mind-molecule connections. Pert and Herkenham discuss it as follows (1981, p. 516):

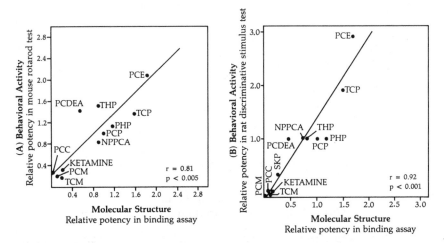

Figure 6: The structure-activity relationship between behaviors (such as balance and stimulus discrimination) and the molecular structure of psychoactive drugs. (Adapted from Zukin and Zukin, 1979)

Figure 7 illustrates the correlation between the binding data and the average therapeutic dose of benzodiazepine analogs required for alleviating anxiety in patients (Mohler & Okada, 1978). The correlation of "only" 0.79 must be considered in light of the crudeness of the response data—it does not take into account errors in prescribing appropriate dosages of Librium, Valium, etc.

Structure-activity analysis, then, is a general approach to studying the relationships between molecular *structure* and *activity* on the physiological, behavioral, and mental-emotional levels. In any particular study, however, it may not be practical to map all of these relationships. Table 5 presents interesting recent studies utilizing structure activity analysis which, when taken all together, validate the general conception of the relationships between the molecular, physiological, behavioral, and mental levels.

Project 20   Structure-activity analysis is a routine experimental procedure conducted almost daily by many pharmaceutical firms and pharmacology laboratories. Cooperate with such researchers by incorporating ideodynamic signaling as an independent variable in any of their experiments

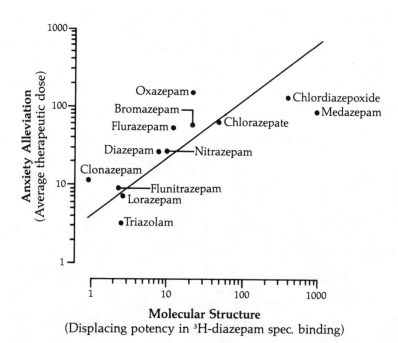

Figure 7: The structure-activity analysis of the mind-molecule connection between anxiety and the molecular structure of tranquilizing drugs such as Librium and Valium. (Adapted from Mohler & Okada, 1978)

utilizing structure-activity analysis with human subjects (see Table 5). To what degree can the ideodynamic approach facilitate and/or retard responses on the molecular, physiological, behavioral, and mental-emotional levels? What are the implications of such research for Cheek's basic clinical hypothesis, and for the state-dependent memory, learning, and behavior theory of ideodynamic healing in hypnosis (Rossi, 1986d; Rossi & Ryan, 1986)? What new testable predictions can you now formulate to assess the parameters of a more comprehensive theory of the "mind-molecule connection"? We will continue to explore the possibilities of using structure-activity analysis as a method of facilitating our understanding of mind-body healing in Section IV on psychosomatic medicine.

Table 5: Studies utilizing structural-activity analysis to trace the flow of information transduction through the anatomical/physiological, behavioral, and mental/emotional levels.

Molecular	Anatomical/ Physiological	Behavioral	Mental/Emotional	References
1. ACTH and its analogs and peptide fragments, vasopressin, oxytocin, endorphins, etc.	Limbic-hypothalamic-pituitary system and its cortical extensions	Sensory-perceptual discrimination tasks, conditioned and avoidance behavior, etc.	Attention, memory, learning, motivation, stress, anxiety, depression, schizophrenia, post-traumatic amnesia	de Wied, 1980; Greven & de Wied, 1973, 1977, 1980; Walter, Van Ree, & de Wied, 1978
2. Opiates and their analogs; all psychoactive drugs	Limbic-hypothalamic pituitary; periaqueductal grey matter; dorsal horn of spine; gastrointestinal tract; endocrines; immune system	Pain avoidance and sensory-perceptual tasks; homeostatic regulating behavior (eating, drinking, temperature, activity level, etc.)	Sensory-perceptual, emotional-motivational, and cognitive processes; stress; schizophrenia(?)	Pert & Herkenham, 1981; Pert et al., 1985; Wilson et al., 1975; Yim & Lowy, 1984; Yim et al., in press; Zukin & Zukin, 1979

3. Luteinizing and gonadotropin releasing hormones (LHRH & GnRH) and their analogs	Hypothalamic-pituitary-ovary (gonad) axis	Sexual behavior	Inferred perceptual-emotional-cognitive processes	Bex & Corbin, 1984; Geiger, 1984; Nestor et al., 1984; Peter, 1986
4. Peptides and their synthetic analogs	White blood cells (neutrophils)	Movement of neutrophils *in vitro*	Basis of psychoneuro-immunology (?)	Aswanikumar et al., 1977
5. Benzodiazepines (Librium, Valium, etc.)	Cortical receptors	Activity level reduction	"Hypnotics"; stress and anxiety reduction	Mohler & Okada, 1978
6. Anti-psychotic drugs (butyro-phenones, phenothiazines, etc.)	Dopamine receptors (?)	Reduction of psychotic symptoms	Reduction of stress and psychotic symptoms	Snyder, 1978

SECTION III

State-Dependent Memory, Meaning, and Healing

THEORY

The chapters in this section are a record of the careful refinement of procedures to access ideodynamically patients' traumatic memories while under full, general anesthesia during operations. Perceptive surgeons (Crile & Lower, 1914, 1947) have long reported cases in which their patients were apparently able to hear and remember significant events and conversational remarks while under general anesthesia. Even though deeply anesthetized patients may lose all motor reflexes, all sense of pain, and all ability to communicate with the outside world, their auditory modality may still be functioning to record any real or falsely perceived threat during this particularly vulnerable situation. The careless conversational remarks of surgeons, anesthesiologists, or other significant medical personnel can easily be misinterpreted by fearful patients. Erickson, LeCron, and Cheek found that these negative "imprints" could have significant effects on the patient's rate of recovery, as well as on the incidence of secondary life-threatening complications that accompanied surgery.

These findings were naturally greeted with great skepticism by the medical community in general when Cheek published his first papers in the late 1950s. Over the past 30 years, however, clinical evidence has continued to accumulate (Bennett, 1984, in press; Levinson, 1965a, b) and well controlled experimental work (Gold, 1984; Weinberger, Gold, & Sternberg, 1984) is currently uncovering the state-dependent psychobiological processes that may account for memory under anesthesia.

The major obstacle to a general acceptance of data in this area is the lack of consistent findings (Trustman, Dubovsky, & Titley, 1977) regarding memory and learning under general surgical anesthesia. Cheek has maintained that an important reason for this lack of consistency is that many investigators have ignored the *meaning factor*: They have failed to understand that it is the primarily *meaningful* and particularly *threatening* stimuli of conversational remarks by *significant medical personnel* that are received and recorded in memory when patients are under life-threatening stress during surgery.

The recent experimental work of Weinberger and his colleagues has dealt with many of these previously uncontrolled variables and demonstrated how epinephrine, which is released during stress, is an effective facilitator of memory and learning under general anesthesia. In essence, they found that the peripheral administration of epinephrine to deeply anesthetized rats led to a dose-dependent modulation of memory for avoidance tasks (*threatening* shock). They described the implications of their findings as follows (Weinberger et al., 1984, p. 223):

> These results may help explain the difficulty in obtaining consistent findings of learning during surgical anesthesia in humans despite anecdotal reports of such learning. It is possible that some surgical episodes result in the release of epinephrine some minutes after anesthesia has been induced, and that in such cases patients can learn and remember events taking place within the operating room. Agents other than epinephrine may also be effective in enabling learning under anesthesia. Finally, our findings demonstrate that a severely depressed brain can quickly acquire Pavlovian defensive conditioning.

These findings support the contention by clinicians that it is the fearful and obviously stressed patient approaching the operation with a fear of dying who is at greatest risk for experiencing negative side-effects during and after surgery.

To deal with the fears and stresses that can lead to the damaging release of epinephrine during an operation, Cheek originally developed his "Use of Preoperative Hypnosis to Protect Patients from Careless Conversation" (1960b). He suggested to patients that they would ignore all conversational remarks during surgery except those spoken directly to them by the surgeon or anesthetist. While he was able to report some success with this approach, he later concluded that it was not an advisable procedure to teach others since the suggestion went against patients' natural psychobiological need to protect themselves. Therefore, that paper was not incorporated into this volume. In its place, Cheek has substituted the more positively oriented "Preoperative Hypnosis to Facilitate Healing" in Box 15.

Recent experimental research on the neurobiology of learning and memory (Gold et al., 1985; Lynch, McGaugh, & Weinberger, 1984) is accumulating the clearest evidence for the highly significant role of epinephrine (an information substance utilized in parasynaptic cellular modulation) in the state-dependent and statebound phenomena that occur in human behavior. The first explicit statement regarding the "endogenous state-dependency hypothesis" based upon rigorous experimental data was made by Zornetzer in 1978 (p. 646):

> In normal memory formation, the specific pattern of arousal present in the brain at the time of training may become an integral component of stored information. The neural representation of this specific pattern of arousal might depend on the pattern of activity generated by brainstem acetylcholine, catecholamine, and serotonin systems. It is this idiosyncratic and unique patterned brain state, present at the time of memory formation, that might need to be reproduced, or at least approximated, at the time of retrieval in order for the stored information to be elaborated.

More recently, β-endorphin (Izquierdo et al., 1984) and ACTH (Izquierdo & Dias, 1984; Richardson, Riccio & Steele, 1986), which are released together during stress, have been found to encode state-dependent memory. Rigter and Crabbe (1979) summarized a series of experimental studies indicating that a variety of endocrinal hormones and their peptide analogs (ACTH-like peptides, vasopressin-like peptides, and oxytocin) are similarly involved in memory and modulation. All these peptides, of course, belong to the class of information substances (or parasynaptic neuromodulators) (Table 1) that are responsible for modulating the "state" of the organism.

Zornetzer's psychobiological hypothesis about endogenous state-dependent learning appears to be the clearest forerunner of the *state-dependent memory, learning, and behavior theory of mind-body healing in therapeutic hypnosis* (Rossi, 1986c, d; Rossi & Ryan, 1986). Although state-dependent memory, learning, and behavior (SDMLB) has been investigated in well-controlled research for the past 40 years (Izquierdo et al., 1984; Izquierdo & Dias, 1984; Martinez et al., 1981; Overton, 1978; Rossi & Ryan, 1986), most clinicians are less familiar with it than with the classical types of learning, such as Pavlovian and Skinnerian operant conditioning. At the present time, most researchers still regard SDMLB as an exotic and highly specialized form of learning that is a minor variant of the classical types. A little reflection, however, will indicate that the reverse better fits the facts. SDMLB is the broader, more generic form of learning that takes place in all complex organisms that have a cerebral cortex and limbic-hypothalamic system modulating the expression of Pavlovian and Skinnerian conditioning (Mishkin, 1982; Rossi, 1986d). Humans in particular do not always and forever react in a rigid stimulus-response manner to behavioral conditioning. The current perspective in psychobiological research reviewed in Section I suggests that it is the information substances (hormones and messenger molecules of parasynaptic cellular modulation) that are responsible for the flexible encoding of Pavlovian and Skinnerian conditioning, and which provide the flexibility characteristic of state-dependent human memory and learning.

The State-Dependent Physiology

Biological researchers have recently focused on the central significance of the state-dependent nature of normal regulatory physiology. They conceptualize the "behavioral state" as fundamental for understanding the homeostatic integration of all biological systems on a broad evolutionary level. Lydic has summarized this newly emerging view (1987, pp. 8–9):

> The concept of steady state [homeostasis] has long been appreciated in the biological sciences, but the analogous concept of a behavioral state has developed only recently. Hobson and co-workers have operationally defined behavioral state as the set of measurement values used to characterize an organism at any point in time (Hobson, Lydic, & Baghdoyan, 1986). The EEG correlates of varying levels of arousal have traditionally represented one such set of measurement values. The key concept is that endogenously generated behavioral states causally influence many aspects of regulatory physiology. Because of the often dramatic nature of this influence, the complete characterization of any physiological control system must include the effect of behavioral state. The broad applicability of the state concept is illustrated by the fact that all eukaryotic organisms [that is, all complex organisms whose cells have a nucleus containing their genetic information, versus the simpler, prokaryote organisms that do not have a nucleus, such as bacteria and virus] exhibit cyclic patterns of activity/inactivity—just as all placental, terrestrial mammals exhibit an ultradian sleep cycle. Therefore, the behavioral state concept permits the cautious integration of data concerning state-dependent physiology across a variety of species. Such integrative power is compatible with convergent evolutionary schemes, and physiological studies of animal sleep permit extrapolations for efforts aiming to clarify the basic mechanisms underlying behavioral state control in humans (Hobson, Lydic, & Baghdoyan, 1986; Hobson & Steriade, 1986).

This new conception of state-dependent physiology supports Rossi's original hypothesis (1982) that stress-related disruptions of our normal ultradian cycles lead to psychosomatic problems. An update of this view will be presented in the theory and research discussions of Section VI. Lydic goes on to note the central significance of the behavioral state concept for integrating our understanding of biological processes down to the cellular level (1987, p. 9):

The behavioral state concept has been important because it has refined our understanding of highly integrated physiological and behavioral events in terms that are amenable to analyses at the cellular level. For example, sleep, anesthesia, and coma — although superficially similar states at the behavioral level — are radically different states in terms of neuronal activity levels. Such state-specific neuronal differences suggest the potential for ultimately deriving an understanding of the concomitant changes in regulatory physiology at the cellular level.

In this seminal paper, Lydic documents how the state-dependent approach to understanding cardiovascular, respiratory, and thermoregulatory systems is not merely descriptive; rather, the conception of state-dependent physiology is "essential for the complete characterization of the cellular and molecular mechanisms underlying regulatory physiology" (p. 6).

The State-Dependent Theory of Mind-Body Therapy

The integration of mind-body communication down to the cellular-genetic level via state-dependent physiology, memory, learning, and behavior led Rossi to formulate the psychobiological basis of mind-body therapy (1986d, p. 55):

> State-dependent memory, learning, and behavior processes encoded in the limbic-hypothalamic and closely related systems are the major information transducers between mind and body. All methods of mind-body healing and therapeutic hypnosis operate by accessing and reframing the state-dependent memory and learning systems that encode symptoms and problems.

From this formulation we can now better appreciate the significance of Cheek's pioneering research. The ideodynamic approaches he has developed can be seen as specific probes of the state-dependent patterns of physiology, memory, and learning that have been encoded during circumstances of stress-released epinephrine by the autonomic nervous system and related responses by the endocrine and neuropeptide systems. The most striking clinical examples of state-dependent memory, learning, and behavior are the *post-traumatic stress disorders* (see *DSM-III-R*). Any stressful life situation (surgery, war, natural disaster, accident, rape, malnutrition, etc.) that stimulates excessive arousal by the autonomic and endocrine systems can lead to the varying clinical symptomatology of post-traumatic stress (Figley, 1985, 1986; Figley & McCubbin, 1983; McCubbin & Figley, 1983). A recent survey of the psychobiology of this syndrome (van der Kolk et al., 1985) suggests that it is the basic process underlying Freud's original concept of the "traumatic neurosis" as the organic basis of psychopathology (1920/1955). This leads to the provocative insight that *the entire history of depth psychology and psychoanalysis now can be understood as a prolonged clinical investigation of how dissociated or state-dependent memories remain active at unconscious levels, giving rise to the "complexes"* (Ellenberger, 1970; Jung, 1960a, b) *that are the source of psychological and psychosomatic problems* (Rossi, 1986d; Rossi & Ryan, 1986). We will touch upon other intriguing lines of evidence for this unexpected rapprochement between psychoanalysis and modern psychobiology in the succeeding sections of this volume.

PRACTICE

7

Unconscious Perception of Meaningful Sounds During Surgical Anesthesia

A surgical procedure under inhalation or intravenous anesthesia is often accompanied by careless conversation. The surgeon may pause as he passes from the scrub room to ask, "Is the patient asleep?" before launching into his latest story. But this may be the only concern shown for the nervous system of this apparently unconscious individual until he can again make sounds and focus his eyes as the anesthetic wears off in the recovery room. It is an error to consider the anesthetized patient as being asleep and unable to hear or understand simply because such an individual may have no subsequent conscious memory for events during this period of unconsciousness. Meaningful sounds, meaningful silence, meaningful conversation are registered and may have a profound influence upon behavior of the patient during surgery and for many years after. The anesthesized patient may lose all motor reflexes, lose all ability to communicate with the outside world, lose all sense of pain, but *he is able to hear and remember important events at a deep level of unconscious thought.* This level can be uncovered and the events recalled by hypnotic techniques.

During surgical anesthesia, unconsciousness from brain trauma, coma of diabetes, drug poisoning, and insulin shock, the last resource of the human organism in maintaining contact with the external environment seems to rest with the sense of hearing. Methods of exploring this area of unconscious human perception have evolved through Erickson's work during the past 40 years. Although he repeatedly discussed this issue in his courses on hypnosis, there has been very little recognition in the literature thus far that the unconscious mind can hear and remember careless operating room conversation. The facts should be known. *The inner world of the unconscious patient should be treated with the same respect we show when the patient is fully in possession of all senses.*

Evidence for this hypothesis has been accumulating since October 1957. It has been collected from interviews with physicians and dentists during courses on hypnosis, and from private patients as well. It is not yet possible to prove that memories attributed to operating room experience are free of coloration from later experience. In some instances, they may even be manufactured to please the implied needs of the investigator. Fabrications could be drawn from ample source material in literary works, moving pictures, and radio and television broadcasts. Evidence for the material to be presented has been tape recorded for the most part and carefully reviewed with these possibilities in mind. Cases in which recollections seemed vague or could have represented conversations overheard in a recovery room have been discarded, unless it was apparent that the patient overheard something which was clearly not intended for his ears. Exact isolation of recovered memory to that period in which the patient is in a surgical plane of anesthesia is of academic interest only, and is of no practical importance in terms of the welfare of the patient.

The modern trend of anesthesiology is toward carrying surgical patients at lighter planes of anesthesia than used to be the custom. Tranquilizing drugs are being used to diminish apparent reactions to environment, and much use is being made of combinations of drugs which sedate and paralyze motor activity at the same time. The resulting effect upon the human being may be somewhat similar to that effected by the female hunting wasps upon the grasshoppers, butterfly larvae, and spiders which they paralyze long enough to supply fresh food for their own young. Now more than ever, we should be careful of what our patients hear. Not only are their fundamental sensoria affected to a lesser degree by our anesthetics, but the patients today have been subjected to more medical education through more channels than ever before. The resulting potential for dangerous and unrecognized fears originating in and about our operating rooms is of enormous magnitude.

Consciousness During Surgical Anesthesia

Sometimes it is difficult for an experienced anesthesiologist to know whether a patient is really in a surgical plane or is just behaving as though anesthetized.

Doctor R. B. Lindsay (1957) of Montpelier, Idaho, tells of complimenting his anesthetist on the excellence of his work just as the patient's appendix had been removed and placed in a pan. As he finished saying, "That was an excellent anesthetic," the patient pulled her head away from the ether mask and joined the conversation with a cheerful, "It certainly was." She then put her head back into the mask while the abdomen was closed.

Expectancy and Anesthesia

Rudolph Selo, M.D., an anesthesiologist of Council Bluffs, Iowa, tells of giving a general anesthetic (1957) to a patient who was scheduled to have a caesarean section because of placenta praevia. Since the patient had been losing blood, she was receiving oxygen through the mask as Selo was assembling his equipment. He started a blood transfusion, checked the blood pressure, and wrote his notes while waiting for the abdomen to be cleaned and draped. To his horror, as he finally looked up to see if all was ready, he found the surgeon holding the baby while the assistant was manipulating the uterus. After checking his machine and finding that the patient was really only getting oxygen, he decided to let well enough alone. The uterus and abdomen were closed without incident and the patient suffered no pain.

These may be examples of spontaneous hypnoidal states which, though probably exceptions, tend to underline the fact that patients may tolerate surgery with less than maximum amounts of drugs. The expectancy of anesthesia may bring about dissociations of awareness for pain without affecting the ability to perceive through the other senses. The great majority of surgeries are now being performed with patients able to hear and remember.

Several hypnotized subjects have been followed through two or more remembered anesthetic experiences. Fears originating during an early operation have been found to reappear as the subject was reliving the later induction into surgical anesthesia. These fears produce changes in heart rate and respiration. From the standpoint of behavior, it would seem that the point of prime importance is not whether the patient actually heard, but rather that the patient believes he has heard. In the light of the findings, it seems of the utmost importance that we know before administering an anesthetic what attitudes a patient has carried over at an unconscious level from previous real or imagined operative experiences. Dream rehearsals of a traumatic sort may make a difference with the anesthetic reactions of a patient during the final real experience. In any case, ideomotor questioning techniques can be used to uncover unconscious fears with all preoperative patients regardless of their previous surgical experiences. The typical patient encountering major surgery will rehearse the anticipated event in his dreams as often as the quarterback will examine the possible situations for decision in a football game. Just as is the case with the uncomplaining obstetrical patient, the preoperative patient of concern to us is the one who shows no conscious evidence of fear and who asks no questions. This is the patient who may be the most frightened on an unconscious level.

Development of Technique for Recovering Surgical Memory

Why is it that some patients dislike a previous surgeon without knowing just why? During nine years, efforts have been made occasionally to evoke operative recollections from hypnotized patients. Conversational methods with age regression were used and were always satisfyingly unsuccessful. It was a relief to be convinced that thoughtless remarks in the operating room could not be remembered. Since hearing Erickson state that patients were able to hear significant material while anesthetized (1956), some misgivings were briefly activated but were easily relieved by further pleasantly unsuccessful efforts at verbal questioning in hypnosis. It was further pleasing to find that Bramwell (1956) had experienced the same difficulty in trying to uncover anesthesia experience.

Memories of operating room experience are preserved at levels of awareness so deep that they cannot be reached with ordinary conversational technique during the time usually available for investigation. As Erickson pointed out (1952/1980), it may take four or more hours to train a subject to speak without awakening from a deep trance. He believed that this fact results from the lifetime of conditioning in which verbalization is done only when awake. Another explanation might be that muscular responses of adaptation to environment are learned long before the complicated mechanisms of thought translation into articulated sounds are learned. Muscular responses are, for the most part, unconscious in origin, while those of speech are related to effort and evolve at a more conscious level in response to more complicated stimuli. Ideomotor responses at an unconscious level through gesture, facial expression, and voice inflection are perceived and utilized by the infant as a means of tuning into its environment long before it learns the word meaning of the human noises. We can reach deeper levels of unconscious thought with the help of ideomotor responses than is possible under usual circumstances with conversation in hypnosis (Erickson, 1938a, b/1980).

A patient may be requested to signal with a lifted finger the beginning of an operation, and again, with another signal, the end of the operation. When questioned at a verbal level, he may have no memory at all for the material covered in this interval. This principle has been developed and used extensively by Erickson as a means of helping patients review rapidly and extract significant material during psychotherapy. By asking a surgical patient to signal the beginning and end of surgery, as well as indicating the hearing of meaningful material, it is possible to extract important data and establish time relationships in a brief span of time. The next step is to ask permission of the unconscious to release this deeply remembered material for more conscious level evaluation and reporting.

In exploring possible traumatic memories with age regression, it is necessary to respect the decision of the unconscious mind regarding release of information. An "I don't want to answer" should be a signal to leave that recollection undisturbed, after dropping the suggestion that perhaps the experience could be reviewed later in different circumstances without emotional disturbance.

In addition, it is sometimes advisable to avoid possible dangerous physiologic reactions in certain groups of subjects by using dissociation. Subjects with hypertension, and all who are over 40 years of age, are requested to consider themselves a nurse or orderly in the hospital situation, rather than being the patient experiencing the anesthetic. Although the unconscious would probably protect the organism in the hypnotized state from critical reactions, there is so much clinical evidence that emotional stress can initiate a cerebral hemorrage or a coronary artery occlusion that it seems unwise to tempt fate in the exploration of operative experience.

In discussing deep trance phenomena, it has been our custom to select subjects who have had operations for acute appendicitis. Initially, the intent was to point out how often emotional stress has been related to the onset of symptoms. Frequently during the time available, it has been possible to achieve a physiologic regression to the point of being able to demonstrate rebound tenderness and referral of pain to the right lower quadrant on percussion over the descending colon. We have become increasingly aware of the fact that facial expressions, respiration, and pulse have reflected shifting responses to the remembered environment of the operating room. The next step is to inquire into subjective responses of the patient before and during surgery.

Accessing and Reframing Memories from Surgical Anesthesia

During a course of instruction, a physician volunteer was going through an age regression to his operation under ether anesthesia. He was asked to lift a finger if he heard anything in the operating room which might be disturbing. Verbally he answered this request by saying that there was nothing to hear. While finishing this statement, however, his finger lifted to signal the hearing of something significant. When he was asked to tell us what this might be, he again stated verbally that there was nothing audible. The question was then asked, **"Would it be all right for you to know consciously what is being said?"** He gave an affirmative ideomotor signal and then said, after a little more verbal prodding, "It's gangrenous." This was followed in approximately 20 seconds by a second finger signal and a spontaneous verbal, "Let's get out of here and go home."

In common operating room jargon, the second remark is made in reference to getting out of the open abdomen rather than out of the operating room. On further questioning, the subject indicated that he was still getting the anesthetic through his mask when the second statement was made.

Anesthesized patients seem able to differentiate between the metallic sound of respiration with the rebreather bag and that of free breathing with the mask removed. When open drop ether is used, they are aware of coolness of the evaporating ether near their skin. Patients do not seem to notice pressure of the mask, nor do they complain of an airway.

All in all, 52 surgical experiences in 37 hypnotized subjects have been investigated. Of these, there were 30 women and 7 men. All of the men and two of the women were students in courses of hypnosis. The remaining 21 women were private gynecological patients. There were six surgical recollections in which no disturbing sounds were recalled. Since, in these negative cases, the period of study exceeded 30 minutes after achievement of an age regression, it seems reasonable to conclude that the patients either did not hear anything, or that their anesthetic level was deep enough to inhibit memory or sound perception. Two of these six negative cases had been trained to have amnesia for everything relating to experience in the operating room at a time before the surgeon had learned to respect the ears of his anesthetized patients. After repeated efforts with these two cases, it has been impossible to achieve a recall of any material.

The majority of anesthetic agents used for the patients in this study has been combinations of nitrous oxide and ether. There were five with open drop ether, seven definite sodium pentothal, two definite sodium pentothal with spinal, and one with avertin and ether. Although it is not possible to be certain, there were no definite cyclopropane anesthetics in the series.

The longest period of elapsed time between surgery and hypnotic interview was 24 years, while the shortest was four years.

There would be advantages in reporting only subjects who had no knowledge of operating room mechanisms and atmosphere. Equally vivid descriptions of operating room conversation from uninitiated subjects have been elicited from patients in my (DBC) private practice. The example cases presented here are those which have been witnessed by a large number of physicians and dentists. For this reason, they are less open to question of prejudicial representation. They have all been tape recorded by at least one observer other than the doctor.

Recall of Anesthetized Patients for Meaningful Material Only

It has been evident from consideration of all the cases studied that only meaningful material seems to have been remembered. It has been impossible to get recall of such casual material as reports of golf or baseball games. Two private patients expressed amusement, one at the discomfort of the preparation nurse who was scolded by the surgeon for not adequately shaving the perineum; the other, on overhearing the surgeon laughingly saying at the end of an operation that he must have sewed up the scissors in the abdomen. These two patients must have been nearly out of anesthetic, for it is very unusual for the deeper levels of unconscious awareness to give any evidence of humor.

During this study and others, there has been a repeated demonstration of hypersensitivity to pessimistic remarks which patients have heard from lay people and to which they have given a stronger value than the reassuring statements of physicians. This is an important point if substantiated by the observation of other workers, for it should lead to more careful screening of preoperative patients for bad attitudes. It should lead to the giving of a more subtle form of reassurance than usually is employed by surgeons and anesthesiologists.

Most of the subjects in this study have demonstrated that the unconscious is acutely sensitive to nuances of voice inflection. Sometimes it is difficult to be sure this perception is based only on minimal cues. Occasionally, it seems that extrasensory perceptions may be at work. Whether by minimal cue or extrasensory, it is clear that patients under surgical anesthesia are as aware of deceit and attempts to avoid the truth as are patients with malignancy or a critical illness. There are ways of telling unpleasant truth which do not close the door to hope. *A patient has yet to be found who has not seen through a lie or failed to resent at an unconscious level the failure of his physician to trust him with the facts.*

The patient in surgical plane anesthesia is able to hear meaningful sounds made in the operating room. The deep unconscious mind is devoid of humor. It records and associates communications in a most literal way. Disturbing sounds and conversation do not always evoke physiologic responses at the moment of perception during the actual surgical experience, but the patterns of response are apparently set and may be released during reliving of the experience in age regression in hypnosis. Anticipation of another actual anesthetic experience can evoke these pre-set physiologic patterns of fear while in anesthesia.

Untoward reactions to anesthesia and surgery may be avoided in large measure through a better understanding of unconscious responses of fear. It is mandatory that we give consideration to all conversation in the operating room with the same care that we exercise when the patient is awake. There are possibilities that prognosis for surgical cancer patients could be improved if thought were given to their anxieties before surgery and optimistic conversation carried on in the operating room as though we considered the patient within earshot. This type of reassurance is acceptable. Direct reassurance from physician to patient may be acceptable to the conscious level of thought, but it is often rejected by the unconscious.

The following cases were volunteer subjects for demonstrations.

Case 1: Fear of Undiscussed Cancer During First Operation Followed by Conditioned Response to Anesthetic in Second Surgery

This subject, approximately 37 years of age, had gone through four operations at the time of the interview. Her first surgery was a breast biopsy at Mayo Clinic under sodium pentothal (approximately 1938). She had developed a lump which was to be removed. Her surgeon had not discussed her unspoken fear that the lump might prove to be malignant. Under hypnosis she signaled with her finger that the incision in the breast was being made; at this point, her respirations stopped for approximately 25 seconds. Her pulse rate was being checked by an anesthesiologist from the group of students who were observers. At the time the respirations stopped, he reported a sudden change from a regular 84 beats per minute to 140.

Suggestions were now given that the patient was a nurse in the operating room just watching what was going on. This approach to facilitating a therapeutic dissociation by suggesting the patient adopt an appropriate observer attitude (a nurse would be an appropriate observer in the operating room) is most useful when patients fall into emotional difficulty during hypnosis. The subject's respirations recommenced, and her pulse returned during the next two minutes to the former slow rate. The only verbal remark which was remembered by the subject was, "She's all right now."

The second operation under gas-oxygen-ether anesthesia was performed several days after marriage and was necessitated by volvulus of a dermoid cyst. The fact that the tumor of the ovary was probably not malignant at her age was not discussed before surgery. There was not enough time to explore the total memory for this surgery, but the patient indicated that she was having trouble after the incision was made because of her fear of cancer. The subject's husband had been in the operating room at the time of the second surgery. He reported after the hypnotic session that there had been concern over her reaction. The surgery was finally completed under very superficial nitrous oxide-oxygen anesthesia.

It would be a matter of conjecture as to whether the respiratory arrest was the sole result of an overdosage of sodium pentothal at the time of the first operation. In 1938 this anesthetic was still being given in high concentration, and rather rapidly for induction. The subjective response of the patient while reliving the experience, however, was that the fear of cancer was heightened by the realization that the nodule would soon be exposed, and that this was responsible for her stoppage of respiration. She indicated with her finger signals that the second respiratory arrest was of the same origin, even though a different anesthetic was being used.

It is noteworthy that the subject did not recognize consciously to what degree her unconscious fears were aggravated by the lack of discussion about the possible pathology. At a conscious level, she had assumed that the risks must be inconsequential if the surgeon had not discussed them. To her unconscious, however, the lack of discussion indicated that he must be worried about this possibility of cancer. In this case, there was a constant knowledge of what was going on in the operating room even though very few words were heard. She sensed the concern of the operating-room personnel.

Case 2: Traumatic Experiences Reactivated in Hypnotic Inductions

MEMORY FOR DETAILS (POSITIONS, VOICES) AND INSIGHT
FOR ATTITUDE OF THE SURGEONS

A 27-year-old dentist volunteered for investigation of his appendectomy at the age of 15. He stated that he had always wondered if a "ghost" surgeon had done the operation but he had never known just why he felt this way.

He was curious to find out if his impression was correct; his curiosity seemed free of malevolence.

During the induction, the subject related his sensation of light trance to that experienced after he had been knocked unconscious during a football scrimmage at the age of 16. Asked if there were another experience which felt similar, he indicated yes with his finger and regressed back to the induction of anesthesia for his appendectomy one year earlier. *This equating of the hypnotized state with previous experiences of delirium or with unconsciousness from diabetic coma or chemical anesthesia has been frequent in my experience.*

Q: **Where are you now?**

A: I think I'm in the O.R. — I'm not going down very well. [Respiratory rate jumps from 14–28.]

Q: **Are you scared?**

A: (No.)*

Q: **Do you hear any sounds?**

A: The fan going — they are talking back and forth — not to me.

Q: **Is there anything that worries you?**

A: (Yes.) No.

Q: **Would it be all right to hear it consciously?**

A: (Yes.) [After a pause:] "You better cut here."

Q: **Where does it come from?**

A: It seems to be coming from Sobie (the family physician). [The subject is now urged to go back over this and give the exact words as though he were replaying the record.] I think we better cut here.

Q: **Is there anything after that that disturbs you?**

A: (Yes) [after a pause of ten seconds]. It seems like they can't find it. "It's tucked under" — that comes from the doctor on the left side of the table [Sobie]. [After another pause of 25 seconds] "Come on, we got to get this out of here."

Q: **Whose voice is that?**

A: It doesn't seem to be Sobie. He seems to be on the left, and somebody else is on the right, and somebody is down at the foot.

Q: **Does this statement frighten the deep part of your brain?**

A: (No.)

Q: **Does the deep part of your brain feel anything?**

---

*Finger responses are in parentheses.

A: (No.) Just a little hyper-awareness of the lower right quadrant. [Note the adult-level choice of words.]

Q: **Do you feel any discomfort while they are looking?**

A: No.

When asked to continue his recounting, he states that nothing is being said but that he senses a feeling of relief and knows they have found the appendix.

A little later he says, "Now the light is right over my head. It didn't use to be over my head. It's brighter. I guess they must have taken the mask off, or something."

Q: **Are they finished?**

A: (No.)

The subject now seems disturbed because, although they have talked as though finished with the surgery, they decide to put another clamp on the skin.

Case 3: Differing Attitudes Towards Prognosis at Different Strata of Awareness

IMPORTANCE OF DISCUSSING PREVIOUS OPERATIVE HISTORY;
DISSOCIATION AND THE OBSERVER ATTITUDE

During the landing on the Marshall Islands in January 1943, the subject, as a medical officer, was inspecting an aid station when he was struck just above the left ilium posteriorly by a sniper's bullet. He did not realize the extent of the injury until he observed blood gushing from the abdominal wound of exit. While in a semi-stuporous state, he heard his associate instruct the stretcher bearers to move him back to the hospital ship rapidly because "he's hurt bad." On the ship he was subjected to a four-hour emergency operation under open-drop ether. Multiple perforations of bowel were discovered and closed. Because of contamination, steel wire was used for closure. He received one unit of blood and several of plasma. At the end of the abdominal closure, it was decided to introduce a nasal Levine tube while the patient was still asleep with the anesthetic. He promptly began coughing, struggling, and vomiting to such an extent that efforts were discontinued. They were unable to pass a gastric tube at any time. The resulting course was stormy.

After ten years, while jerking a golf carriage over a rough place, the subject felt a tearing sensation in his abdomen. This was followed by severe pain, nausea, and vomiting. At emergency surgery under gas-oxygen-ether anesthesia, a loop of small bowel was found torn open, apparently by one of the nonabsorbable sutures placed accidentally through the muscularis at his first operation. At the end of surgery, while the patient was still asleep, the anesthetist tried to pass a nasal tube. During the ensuing struggle, the patient tore open his incision and eviscerated on the table. His course was stormy. This history was obtained in the waking state.

After the subject had been placed in deep hypnosis, he was taken to the time of injury and asked to answer questions with finger signals as well as verbally.

Q: After you hear the medical officer say you are hurt badly, do you think you will make it all right?
A: (No.) I did, until I saw the blood coming from my abdomen, and then I knew the intestines would be torn and my chances would be poor.

Q: Is there a deeper level of your mind that has a different thought?
A: (Yes.)

The hypnotic scene is now shifted to the operating room on the ship, and the patient is asked to signal when he is asleep with the anesthetic and the doctors have commenced to work. After indicating with his finger that this has occurred, he is asked to signal again as soon as he hears something that disturbs him. After 20 seconds his finger goes up and he says, "Doctor Snider is saying 'It has perforated the colon.'"

Q: What does this mean to you?
A: Trouble.

Q: Now come up to the next thing that disturbs you. [Finger signals again after lapse of 25 seconds.]

Q: What is happening now?
A: Doctor Richardson is asking, "Do you think he needs some blood?" [After ten seconds the finger again lifts.] "We'd better put in a gastric suction tube."

Q: What does this mean to you?
A: I couldn't swallow a Levine tube in physiology class. I had sworn that nobody would ever put one in me. I knew I couldn't get the thing down—I didn't either.

The subject is now asked to progress ten years to the time of his bowel obstruction. Time does not permit covering the entire operation, but he hears the discussion about the steel wire having torn his bowel and the decision to try getting the nasal tube down. He again reacts with the thought while under anesthesia, "They will never get that thing down me!"

Case 4: Clear Memory for Discussion Under General Anesthesia

IMPORTANCE OF DISCUSSING POSSIBILITIES OF CANCER; ERROR OF USING
FIGURATIVE LANGUAGE OR MAKING NEGATIVE REMARKS DURING OPERATION

This 53-year-old dentist submitted to surgery 24 years before volunteering for interview under hypnosis. He had been suffering from peptic ulcer symptoms for about two years. With persistent findings of a defect in the stomach wall, he was advised to have surgery. The patient was consciously worried over the possibility of cancer but was afraid to ask the surgeon at the time of his preoperative interview. He was disturbed over what he assumed to be evasion of the subject when he knew the possibility of gastric cancer had to be ruled out in cases such as his own. The omission signaled to him that the surgeon must really be worrying about that possibility.

After induction into moderately deep trance, it was learned by a combination of ideomotor responses and verbal answers that he was not afraid as he was being wheeled into the operating room while anesthetized with avertin, because he felt unconsciously certain that he did not have cancer. This peace of mind was soon to be disturbed, however.

Operator: **"Signal when you hear something that disturbs you."** Subject signals and then says, "One doctor is kidding the other. The one on the left side is saying 'You're making a mighty big opening. What are you making the opening so big for?' Doctor John doesn't like to be kidded. He's saying, 'I don't want the wound to close up on me.'"

Because of his age, the patient is now dissociated to a position beside the operating table with full understanding of the patient and his reactions to what is taking place. After a ten-second pause, his finger signals another disturbing stimulus: "The intestines look like they've been burned." [Statement made by the surgeon standing on the right side of the table.]

Q: **Why does this disturb Hugh on the table?**

A: He's afraid it won't heal up.

Q: **Does this influence his heart rate or breathing?** [There is no apparent change in the subject's respiration as he is talking.]

A: I don't know, it seems to make him weak.

Q: **His abdomen is open now. Does he feel any pain at this time?**

A: Yes. It's a pain like burning.

Q: **Let your fingers answer this at a deep level. Does he really feel this?** Finger signals yes. **Could the sensation have been suggested by the remark about the bowel looking burned?**

A: Yes.

Q: **Now come up to the next thing he hears that is disturbing.**

A: [After fifteen seconds he signals and then says] They are trying to tear the adhesions loose – they are having a hard time tearing them loose.

Q: **Who is having a hard time?**

A: John

Q: **What side of the table is he on?**

A: The right side.

Q: **Let your fingers answer. Does he feel any pain now?**

A: (No.)

Q: **Does the nurse say anything?**

A: She talks to the other doctor. She says, "He can't tear the adhesions loose!"

Q: **Does he respond in any way to this conversation?**

A: (Yes.) They are going to give him ether.

Q: **Does he have a mask on?**

A: Yes.

Q: **What have they been giving?**

A: Gas and avertin.

Q: **Tell me with your finger when he is asleep with the ether.** [The finger goes up after a pause of ten seconds.] **Now signal when he hears something else.** [pause for 75 seconds].

A: The doctor says he is going to do a biopsy.

Q: **Does this disturb him?**

A: Yes. He wonders if he has cancer.

Q: **Let your fingers answer for him. Deep down, does he think he has cancer?**

A: (No.)

Q: **What is the next thing he hears?**

A: I'll *never* be able to get those adhesions loose.

Q: **Now go to the most important thing that happens during the surgery and signal.**

A: He's going to be all right.

Q: **Are you out of the anesthetic?**

A: (No.)

Q: **Do you feel that the things you heard influenced you after surgery?**

A: (Yes.)

After awakening, the subject reported that he had a stormy post-operative course with much distension and nausea.

Case 5: The Need for Honesty with Patients

A POSSIBLE RELATIONSHIP BETWEEN FEAR OF CANCER AND RESPIRATORY
ARREST DURING ANESTHESIA

A 51-year-old physician volunteered for investigation of his experience during removal of his gall bladder at a teaching institution under the care of the
professor of surgery. After returning from combat service during World
War II, the subject suffered from bouts of diarrhea and right upper quadrant abdominal pain. The gall bladder would not concentrate contrast media well enough to be visualized by x-ray studies. It was finally decided to
explore the upper abdomen with the probable aim of removing the non-
functioning gall bladder.

Before hypnosis, the subject was asked to describe his reactions to the
diagnostic procedures and his acceptance of the decision to operate. His
conscious recollections were very casual. He had confidence in the professor
of surgery and he recognized no fear of the surgery. He had been told after
the surgery of his apparent sensitivity to curare, which he was led to believe
caused a troublesome respiratory arrest.

Under moderately deep hypnosis, the subject was taken back over the
preliminary study period. With a combination of verbal and ideomotor
answers, he was surprised to find that the non-visualizing gall bladder had
symbolized the strong possibility of cancer in this area. He had expected the
professor to discuss this possibility with him but, as in the previous cases, he
was disturbed by the omission and concluded unconsciously that this was
presumptive evidence that the professor must be considering this as the
most logical diagnosis.

Because of his age, suggestions were given to the subject that he take the
role of an *observing bystander*. When asked for a finger signal to indicate
the hearing of any remarks, he raised a finger and commented on the
difficulties the anesthetist was having in getting him to breathe. He had
been receiving pentothal, but during the exploration of the gall bladder he
had been given curare. While reliving the respiratory difficulty, he is asked
whether or not he was afraid. The finger signaled no. At this point the
subject spontaneously concluded the hypnotic state. It was assumed that the
experience was too threatening for him to continue. He was, however, still
in a light trance, as indicated by his fixed expression and lack of eye movements. He was asked to let his fingers answer the following questions:

Q: **Was the difficulty with respiration due just to the curare?**

A: (No.) That's funny. I had just assumed it must have been the curare.

Q: **Was it due to a fear of cancer?**

A: (Yes.)

Q: **Was it due to anything that was said in the operating room?**

A: No.

Q: **Was it just due then to your fear that they might be finding cancer?**

A: (Yes.) [Compare this with the first case.]

In this case, it would be fair to assume that the confusion in the operating room over the respiratory arrest might have added to the problem. The subject was aware of this. The real damage, however, came from the silence of the surgeon regarding the dominant source of fear and his failure to discuss the pathology in the operating room. *Silence can be as important as careless conversation.*

Case 6: Pessimistic Attitude May Be Unrecognized at a Conscious Level Before Surgery

A dentist in his early forties volunteered for hypnotic exploration of his surgical experience with an appendectomy following rupture of appendix and generalized peritonitis. He was first questioned about the memory at a conscious level and reported how he fell on a stick of wood in his backyard while he was playing leapfrog at the age of eleven. The stick had bruised his right side. The pain spread during the night and he became increasingly ill. His uncle, a well-known surgeon in the community, came to the house on the third day of the illness. The diagnosis of ruptured appendix with generalized peritonitis was made and surgery recommended. (This occurred before the advent of the sulfonamides.) When asked, "Were you afraid when you were being taken to the operating room?", the subject answered, "No, I wasn't afraid. Everyone else seemed to be, though. As a matter of fact, I had a good time. There was a pretty nurse who used to play parcheesi with me after the operation."

Ten minutes later, while in a moderately deep hypnotic state, the subject signaled with his finger that he was reliving the experience of being pushed down the hall on the way to surgery.

Q: **Are you afraid, Ed?**

A: [Subject starts to whimper and answers yes.]

Q: **Why are you afraid?**

A: I think I'm going to die.

Q: **What makes you think that?**

A: I heard my mom talking on the telephone before I came to the hospital. She said I was very sick and that I might not live.

Q: **Didn't Doctor Ward tell you that you would be all right?**

A: Yes [inflection of voice indicating disbelief], but I thought he was just telling me that to make me feel better.

Next the subject was asked to go deeper and to go back to the beginning of surgery and indicate when something was happening. He indicated and then described the opening of the abdomen and the sounds of disgust at the color and odor of the pus. He felt as though he was seeing it and he became slightly nauseated. He was quickly dissociated from the subjective role. His nausea stopped and his respirations, which had jumped from 18 to 30 per minute, slowed down again. He was asked to go further until he heard something being said. After signaling with his finger he said: "This is a serious situation. This boy will be in danger for several days." When asked for the location of the speaker, he stated that it was Doctor Ward, and that he was standing on the right side of the operating table.

This case is an excellent example of the worthlessness of simple reassurance from a physician. To be effective with a frightened patient, reassurance must be given in a form which indirectly indicates a favorable outcome without actually saying it. An example would be telling such a patient what he should do when he awakens from surgery, and how long it will be before he can return to school.

Case 7: Respiratory and Pulse Rate Problems: A Child's Misunderstanding During Surgery

A three-and-a-half-year-old child underwent resection of a *patent ductus arteriosus* at the hands of Dr. Robert Gross, a pioneer in the development of this operation at the Children's Hospital in Boston. After three hours of anxiety, while two other operations were completed, the parents were relieved to hear that all had gone well. Dr. Gross added that auscultation with a sterile stethoscope at the conclusion of surgery had revealed a small septal defect that would cause an audible murmur but would not handicap the boy nor require surgery.

Recovery from the surgery was rapid. The child grew up healthy and strong, except for a dramatic tendency to become very short of breath accompanied by a need to lie down frequently when playing football or basketball. His pulse rate at such times would exceed 120 per minute. Usually it took about five minutes of rest in a recumbent position before he could resume play.

At the age of 10 it was possible for the boy to scan his operation at an ideomotor level of awareness in hypnosis. A finger lifted unconsciously for the beginning of anesthesia, another for placement of the intravenous needle in his ankle, another for the incision, another for any disturbing remarks he might have heard, another for the recovery from general anesthesia. He was amused at the action of his fingers until, with repetition, the events became clear enough to describe. Only one moment near the end of the operation was disturbing. The doctor on his left was doing something with the boy's heart and commented in some way. The words were long and the boy could not remember what they were, but he did remember the ending phrase, " . . . not being able to fix it." The boy recognized that the doctor did not really say he could not fix it, but that this was his "impression." When asked what this meant to him, the boy said that his heart was "so bad" it could not be "fixed." He had seen his grandfather dying of heart failure at the age of 71, the year before his own operation. His identification with his grandfather was easily recognized.

The conversation with Doctor Gross was explained and augmented by reassurance from the boy's pediatrician, who could speak with authority about the matter because of his residency training at Boston Children's Hospital. The boy is now 18 years old, and is able to exercise with normal physiologic responses.

Case 8: Awareness During Surgery and Post-traumatic Stress Disorder

An unusually vivid and well recorded case of awareness during general anesthesia that gave rise to a post-traumatic stress disorder was reported in the *Newsletter of the Society for Clinical and Experimental Hypnosis* (Dengrove, 1986) as follows:

> Mary Jo Peebles, Ph.D., adds a personal note to the recent contribution to the "New Corner" by Dabney Ewin, M.D., emphasizing the re-emerging evidence for patients' awareness under deep surgical anesthesia. In a paper and videotape in preparation, she describes the case of a woman who regained consciousness three times while under surgical anesthesia and had both auditory and pain perception. Awaking postoperatively, she remembered her experience in a fragmented, nightmarish-like way. She developed symptoms of a severe post-traumatic stress disorder and feared going crazy. It took eight sessions of hypnotherapy, combining abreaction, ego mastery, and working through techniques to lay this trauma to rest. A one-year follow-up showed her much improved, with minor resurgences of symptoms treated with self-hypnosis.

Such continuing reports of the source of post-traumatic stress disorder via the encoding of state-dependent memories during surgical anesthesia can leave no doubt about the general validity and clinical significance of this phenomenon. The resolution of such disorders through a variety of hypnotic approaches, as described by Peebles above, likewise supports our view that one of the major uses of therapeutic hypnosis is precisely in the accessing and reframing of such statebound experience.

Box 14 presents one approach to accessing and reframing disturbing memories from surgical experiences via ideodynamic methods. In the next two chapters of this section, we will provide a clinical framework for understanding how surgical patients generally behave as though hypnotized, and how we can use preoperative hypnosis to utilize this phenomenon to facilitate rather than retard healing.

**BOX 14: ACCESSING AND REFRAMING MEMORIES
FROM SURGICAL ANESTHESIA**

1. *Trance induction and deepening with finger signaling*
   a. Identification of yes, no, etc., signals.
   b. A deepening period of 30 minutes via relaxation, imagery, and so forth, with the following suggestion:
   "When your unconscious knows you are deep enough to shut out all sounds except my voice, your yes finger will lift."
   c. Age regression explored with ideodynamic signaling.
2. *Physiological and ideodynamic accessing of meaningful sounds*
   a. **"Does your unconscious mind recall having heard any disturbing sounds during the operation?"**
   b. Step-by-step ideodynamic reexperiencing of the entire operation.
   c. Therapeutic dissociation:
   "You can be a bystander just watching the whole thing. Your yes finger will lift if you hear anything disturbing to "him" (or "her").
   d. **"Will it be all right for you to hear this consciously?"**
3. *Reframing and ratifying traumatic experience*
   a. **"Please review the operation as it should have been conducted, with all the right things being said and done. As you are losing consciousness, your yes finger will lift; your no finger will lift each time something helpful is occurring; your "I don't want to answer" finger will lift as you are awakening."**
   b. **"Have you learned anything from this review that would be helpful to you, and helpful for a surgeon to learn from you?"**
   c. **"Will this more mature understanding of the situation now enable [whatever problem] to resolve itself in an entirely satisfactory way?"**

8

Surgical Patients Behave as Though Hypnotized

Hypnosis is a naturally occurring body defense mechanism, an analogue of which occurs in animals confronted by danger situations. It appears spontaneously in human beings when they are frightened, disoriented, or in situations of severe violent stress, mental or physical (Milechnin, 1962), and quite possibly even when physically or chemically unconscious. There is a growing body of evidence indicating that a state of mental activity of an unconscious or hypnotic character exists even in states of syncope or physical unconsciousness. A report indicative of this point is Erickson's hypnotic study in relation to a state of traumatic physical unconsciousness (1937/ 1980). Also in this connection, one need only to consider various undesirable startle techniques for the induction of hypnosis with what appears to be a transitional state of unconsciousness sometimes intervening between the waking and the hypnotic states. *Patients facing surgery under general anesthesia — by virtue of their spontaneous intense fixation upon their understandings of their situation and their restricted or spontaneously limited awareness of the surroundings — may well be considered to be in a prehypnotic or hypnotic-like state, or perhaps even an actual state of hypnosis.* Often, immediate postoperative developments and subsequent findings warrant this conclusion. This state of circumscribed altered awareness may develop even before the patient is readied for transportation to the operating room and may continue well after his return from surgery.

Treating Anesthetized Patients as Though They Were Conscious

Despite the extensiveness of the highly personal psychological significances of surgery to the patient, too little emphasis has been placed upon the experience it constitutes for him as a person. Extensive attention has been given only to items of surgical technique and procedure, which are important in themselves, but unfortunately equally extensive attention has not been given to the modalities for dealing with the patient as a person before, during, and after surgery. Hypnosis has been largely neglected as a significant modality for dealing comprehensively with patients, and very little instruction in hypnosis has been available to medical students and physicians in training centers. It is possible for an anesthesiologist to use hypnosis safely and effectively to meet the patient's needs without formal training, although such training would be to his and his patient's advantage. With training, he could be even more alert to behavioral changes in his patient occurring during the period of anesthesia.

It is not necessary for the anesthetist to demonstrate hypnotic phenomena, nor is it necessary for him to learn any special formulae for talking. He need only extend his usual thoughtful consideration for the fears of his patient past the period when apparent unconsciousness occurs. He should be alert for the correction of possible misunderstandings caused by careless conversation in the operating room. He should advise the anesthetized patient of any new manipulation or shifting of the patient's position. He should talk to the patient during general anesthesia just as he would talk to a conscious patient under spinal anesthesia. He should give simple directions about what he expects the patient to do upon awakening, and how to behave during the next few days of hospitalization.

With care given to these matters, and credence given to the fact that surgically anesthetized patients can hear and react physiologically to what they hear, it will be possible for the anesthesiologist to improve the operative and postoperative behavior of his patients, to diminish the need for chemical anesthesia, and particularly the need for muscle-relaxing drugs. Exploration into the possibilities of improving wound healing by diminishing the tissue reaction to trauma is just beginning. Meaningful research into the possibilities of preventing some of the accidents occurring during surgical anesthesia and during hypothermia remains to be done (Cheek, 1962a).

Traumatic Examples of Self-Induced Death

No surgeon, no anesthesiologist, really knows what the preoperative patient is thinking at an unconscious level as he is wheeled into the operating room. Nor can anyone state what influence, if any, such thinking may have upon the eventual results. The evidence is constantly growing, however, that such thinking continues and that it may significantly affect the surgical outcome. We know from psychiatry and psychosomatic medicine that unconscious attitudes, fears, and misapprehensions can manifest themselves in functional and even structural changes in the body; such alterations may very well continue through the chemically anesthetized state.

Some patients are able to verbalize their fears of death; experience has shown that these people should not be "reassured" into continuing through the surgery, except under emergency conditions. Indeed, they sometimes die

(Crile & Lower, 1914). Physiologically, the most dangerous type of fear is that which cannot be expressed verbally because it is too deeply repressed.

It has been frequently reported that oriental and primitive people are able to die without apparent cause on the day which they have set. Cardiac arrest on a voluntary basis has been reported by McClure (1959). Raginsky (1959) has reported the production of temporary cardiac arrest in another patient. An example of discrepancy between conscious and unconscious attitudes is shown by a physician who was consciously convinced that his near-fatal respiratory failure during a gall bladder surgery was due to the large amount of curare administered for relaxation (see Chapter 7, p. 00).

It is common knowledge that expectancy of death can kill. From David Rioch (1960), psychiatrist at the Walter Reed Army Hospital, we have heard about soldiers who died of superficial flesh wounds on Omaha Beach during the allied landings on "D" Day. Haggard (1929) states, "After cities are destroyed by earthquakes men and women are found dead who show no signs of injury." MacRobert (1949) has quoted two cases of human beings who died presumably as a result of foreboding thoughts initiated in dreams.

Even animals as lowly as the rat seem to react differently when they have been given hope by once being removed from an experimental whirlpool. The experiments of Richter (1956) at Johns Hopkins show that rats will die suddenly when forced to swim strenuously to stay afloat in the turbulence caused by a jet stream of water in a jar. Rats that are rescued immediately after submerging without a rallying effort rarely succumb when the experimental procedure is repeated. Richter concludes with the remark, "The results indicate that the rats die a vagal death, and that an element of hopelessness plays an important part."

That the unconscious fears of human beings are capable of causing grave physiological disturbances seems beyond any question of doubt and yet — because there has been no satisfactory way devised by psychiatrists for discovering unconscious fears during the limits of time available for investigation — we have completely discarded all concern with this matter in the extensive literature dealing with anesthetic complications. We find thoughtful observers such as Shroff (1959) wondering why 58% of operating room and recovery room deaths at the Wadsworth Veterans Administration Hospital occurred in patients with elective surgery. We find Berne, Denson, and Mikkelsen (1955) stating, "Cardiac arrest is potentially avoidable, usually reversible ventricularasystole, with or without fibrillation, precipitated by the effect of anesthesia alone, of surgery alone, or of these two in combination."

No thoughtful consideration of possible contributory patient-attitudes could be found in a survey of literature on surgical or anesthesia mortality from 1952 to 1961, yet competent surgeons and anesthesiologists have respect for this factor, and will discuss it extensively in private. But it is a topic that warrants open, not closed room, consideration.

We then must ask ourselves two questions:

1. Can we find some way of helping patients bypass potentially dangerous fears without searching out the fears?
2. Can we find some way of investigating attitudes quickly and correcting the faulty ones during the time available before surgery? Even
during surgery?

The answer to the first question is a definite "Yes." The answer to the
second question, both parts, is probably "Yes," but it must be deferred until
we have collected enough information from the subjective, unconscious
reports of patients who have survived accidents related to anesthesia and
surgery, using methods such as ideomotor questioning and other techniques
of investigation. This has been done in a relatively small series of patients.
They have all felt strongly that they reacted unfavorably to fear, which
usually was augmented by the thoughtless, sometimes very damaging conversations of nurses and surgeons. In more than 500 investigations, I have
been unable to find a single complaint against the behavior of an anesthetist. From these studies and others made with obstetrical patients (Cheek,
1961c), it has been possible to clarify somewhat our understanding of unconscious mentation and to learn something about the great potential of the
unconscious mind to enhance the personality's responses when freed from
superficial guilt, identifications, misunderstandings, and too literal understandings of carelessly uttered professional comments.

Characteristics Of Unconscious Mentation

1. Thought processes go on independently at both a conscious level and a
more child-like, literal, unconscious level while we are awake. The objective
inductive type of thinking is blocked off in serious illness, during fear, and
when the individual is unconscious, regardless of the reason for unconsciousness. A remark such as, "Don't worry about this operation, Mrs.
Jones, *it will be all over* in an hour-and-a-half," may be understood as
thoughtful and reassuring by the conscious mind. The unconscious mind,
however, may be horrified by the concept of sudden death in 90 minutes
after the beginning of surgery!
2. The unconscious mind puts together associations of thought that are
senseless to the conscious mind, and equally senseless identifications of the
self with real or imagined unfortunate people. A child who may have dis-
played a normal amount of hatred toward a parent after an unfair punishment may suffer untold agonies of guilt if a severe illness or accidental
death of the parent occurs soon after the episode. This unconscious feeling
of guilt may become dangerously activated on the eve of surgery. The

contributing factor to this danger lies in the fact that any conscious glimmer of understanding of the feeling is immediately discarded as being ridiculous. The unconscious mind decides, "I killed my father. I wished he would die that time when he was mean. He died. I deserve to die."

3. Reassurance as it is usually given by physicians and relatives is often worse than useless. It may be accepted at a conscious level but completely rejected at an unconscious level. Often, disturbing secondary questions are aroused such as, "I wonder why he said, 'This operation carries *practically* no risk'? Could it be that he is really worrying about me?"

4. Indirect reassurance by implication (Erickson, Rossi, & Rossi, 1976), on the other hand, is almost always accepted at an unconscious level, and this is the strongest weapon the anesthesiologist has against potentially dangerous fears. Most anesthesiologists seem to sense this fact, and will talk calmly about the preparation for anesthesia, and also about what the patient is to do when he awakens. This is accepted as meaning that all is well and that there will be a postoperative survival. But a common error of anesthesiologists seems to be based on the uncritical belief that the patient's hearing sense is necessarily discontinued when the patient has become seemingly unconscious with an anesthetic. Manipulations without explanation after induction of anesthesia can be frightening and dangerous for reasons to be mentioned. Dohan, Taylor, and Moss (1960) have shown a very high percentage of correlation between performance of patients and what they have been told by their surgeons about the number of days they will be in the hospital and when they will be able to work again. This same avenue for constructive suggestion is open to the anesthesiologist during preparations of the patient, during induction of anesthesia, and during the surgical phase of the anesthesia, as Wolfe and Millet (1960) have demonstrated by helping 50% of 1,500 surgical patients get through their postoperative period without medication for pain. Hutchings (1961) found 13 of 88 major abdominal cases required no medication, and 19 required less than 50 mg. of Demerol; Pearson (1961) has had similar results.

The anesthesiologist can mitigate the possible damage of careless conversation of the surgeon and assistants by explaining the intended meaning to the patient or by directing the patient's unconscious attention to constructive, acceptable instructions in a louder voice in order to channel all auditory awareness toward what is being said.

5. Hypnosis may occur spontaneously in the presence of fear, sensory or postural disorientation, and in loss of consciousness. It has been established that hibernating mammals and those assuming a reflex pseudo-death for camouflage in time of danger (for example, the opossum) are able to retain auditory capacity after they have lost all perception for pain and all muscular reflexes. On the basis of comparative zoological behavior characteristics, and from the associations of ideas in the subjective reactions of pa-

tients during the hypnotic interview, it can be concluded that anesthetized and traumatically unconscious human beings may be considered hypnotized (Cheek, 1960a).

6. The unconscious mind is able to perceive pain without necessarily passing the awareness along to the conscious part of the mind. The physiological manifestations of inflammation associated with trauma or infection may be mediated by unconscious awareness of pain. Hyperemia, edema, and muscle guarding may occur so long as the unconscious mind knows that trauma is being produced, regardless of whether or not there is conscious pain. Evidence for this has been presented elsewhere (Cheek, 1961b). It is the basis for Crile's concepts of "Anoci-Association," although Crile did not express it in these terms. It is possible to help the mind reject the unconscious awareness of pain, and to maintain a lack of attention for stimuli coming from traumatized tissue. This can be done by hypnotic suggestions recalling a previous experience of numbness to be localized in the operative area, although this type of suggestion may be completely rejected by a patient who feels he deserves to die or to suffer pain with surgery. Many hypnotic suggestions given to an unanesthetized subject seem to be censored by mentation at a nearly conscious level. Authoritative directions, however, sincerely verbalized and given sufficiently loudly and directly into the ear of an unconscious patient, seem acceptable to a large percentage of people. The extent to which we can directly improve tissue reactions to trauma by such suggestions remains to be seen. Freedom from conscious awareness of pain, and the consequent improvement in mobilization permitted by this freedom, might well be expected to improve circulation and, hence, the healing processes in an indirect manner.

In addition to suggesting the hallucination of numbness or lack of pain, it is possible to dissociate awareness. Dentists and anesthesiologists frequently use this method when working with children. It is a mechanism of hypnosis, and it is often spontaneously discovered by children who pretend that they are somewhere else, or that they are some imaginary animal when they have been injured or feel unhappy. Schizophrenic and deeply depressed human adults may also use this mechanism of release from stress. The technique of dissociation for pain control has been discussed extensively by Erickson in his papers and lectures on the topic (see, in particular, Section IV of Volume IV in Erickson, 1980a; Rossi, Ryan, & Sharp, 1984; Rossi & Ryan, 1985, 1986). It has been well described by August (1960), and also by Coulton (1961). It is possible, for example, to ask a patient to describe in detail the experiences associated with a pleasant vacation during the induction of a general anesthesia with sodium pentothal. This is an acceptable tacit type of reassurance, and it sets the pattern for separation of perceptions away from the operating room experience and, therefore, away from awareness of what is being done to the operative area. Another advantage of this approach is that it seems possible to block the association of the immediate anesthetic experience with earlier traumatic experiences.

Spontaneous Hypnoidal State in Patients

It is not dangerous for a human being to enter hypnosis spontaneously during a time of stress, provided that there is freedom from frightening suggestions during the time that he is in hypnosis. It is only reasonable to expect that the person in charge be fully aware of what is happening to his patient and be fully qualified to utilize it to the patient's advantage. It is also reasonable to assume that such spontaneous hypnosis, unrecognized and ignored by those properly responsible, could become a source of danger not in itself, but as a result of professional unawareness of significant changes in the patient.

Hypnosis — with its diminished oxygen requirements, its diminished capacity for feeling pain, its diminished tendency for bleeding, its diminished voluntary muscular activity, and its exclusion of all non-meaningful stimuli — could be used to great advantage by surgeons and anesthesiologists. For these reasons, among others, we should know when to expect a spontaneous hypnoidal response, how to recognize its manifestations, and how to utilize it for the benefit of our patients.

Unrecognized, hypnotic responses can be a detrimental force for several reasons. In the first place, a hypnotic trance is deepened by any sudden sensory perception which is out of context with the environment of the moment (Erickson & Rossi, 1976/1980). A deeper trance may be produced by anything that disturbs the individual's normal proprioceptive relationship in space.

It may occur when a paralyzed and lightly anesthetized person has his head forcibly hyper-extended for introduction of a laryngoscope prior to intubation. It may occur when an anesthetized person is unceremoniously dragged or jolted into gallbladder, kidney, lithotomy, laminectomy, or Trendelberg position. Suddenly dropping an unconscious patient from the operating table onto a carriage, or from the carriage into the bed, can produce a hypnotic state so deep that it simulates the suspended animation of the oriental religious man or the pseudo-death of the so-called "vampires" described by Hudson (1893). At such a time, the behavior of the patient may so simulate death that the attendants become frightened. This fear, in turn, may be perceived by the acutely sensitive unconscious part of the patient's mind, and this communicated alarm can then produce dangerous physiological responses or even complete collapse. *Stimuli tending to deepen a hypnotic state in an unanesthetized person may produce a very deep trance in the anesthetized patient. At such a time, the patient can seem to stop breathing, become pulseless, and lose readable electrical discharges from the myocardium.* Information is lacking with regard to how much the actions of a surgical team, confronted with this situation, might contribute to true cardiac arrest or physiological collapse. Information derived from the reports of Hudson (1893) and of Quackenbos (1908) suggest that it might be worthwhile to attempt talking authoritatively to the patient before pressing, thumping or excavating the thorax.

Secondly, upon entering hypnosis, or upon becoming unconscious, there may be a release of memory associations with earlier experiences in life which have been frightening. In inducing hypnosis in timid or frightened subjects, it is fairly common for them to experience a vivid recollection of a past traumatic or terrifying event, or even a whole series of past unhappy memories, sometimes to an overwhelming degree. The human being losing consciousness with sodium pentothal anesthesia under pleasant surroundings at the age of 46 may have a coronary occlusion during the emotional reliving of a traumatic ether anesthetic for a tonsillectomy at the age of six. He may show no outward signs of dismay because of the muscular paralysis due to the anesthetic. An adult patient may go into respiratory collapse during positioning for laminectomy, as he is reminded of a similar jolting after loss of consciousness in an automobile accident which injured his back and contributed to the need for surgery. A patient, paralyzed by a curare-like drug, may go into shock reliving the childhood panic experienced while wrapped in a rug by playful companions. All these examples may be conceptualized as the unintended accessing of state-dependent memory, learning, and behavior systems (Rossi, 1986d; Rossi & Ryan, 1986).

Thirdly, *the subjective mind, representing unconscious thought, is literal in its understanding of words. It interprets everything which could be significant as relating to itself.* For these reasons, any conversation overheard in the hallway of the surgical floor may be interpreted as applying directly to the patient. During surgical anesthesia a remark by the surgeon, "This thing won't work" may be intended to describe the jimber-jawed Kocher clamp, but it will probably be interpreted as relating to some imagined part of personal anatomy by the anesthetized patient. Fears induced in this manner may play a damaging part in the postoperative behavior of the patient.

With these considerations in mind, we may proceed to a detailed recommendation for the handling of surgical patients who may require intubation, positioning for surgery, and exploration for the ruling out of possible malignancy. This constitutes, potentially, the most vulnerable group of patients.

Beneficent Physical and Psychological Handling of Surgical Patients

Let us assume that we have a 35-year-old woman with cholelithiasis. (The words in bold face type are hypnotic suggestions to be emphasized.) On the evening before surgery, she would be told that the staff of anesthesiologists at this hospital like to have her surgeon's patients **because they always seem to do so well**. This remark is defensible because it relieves unspoken unconscious fears about the patient's correctness in choice of a surgeon. Many patients are bombarded by the well-meaning questions of relatives, who wonder why the patients have not taken the relatives' advice about the choice of a surgeon. These questions stir up anxieties which can be removed by thoughtful comments of hospital attendants.

The anesthesiologist may next explain to the patient that his job as a specialist in anesthesiology is to get her through surgery in the safest way, with a minimum of chemical anesthesia and with **complete** freedom from discomfort. The word **complete** is a suggestion and should be verbalized emphatically. She will be given a hypodermic in the morning and will not care if "school keeps or not" on the way to the operating room. It is explained that she may hear commotion in the hallways and talking in the operating room, but **she must pay attention** to conversation **only** when the anesthesiologist or her surgeon **speak directly to her by name**. Everything else will be **just a jumble of noises that do not matter**. The anesthesiologist may then explain that patients are occasionally worried because they can hear voices for quite awhile after they have **lost all ability to feel pain**. She is to remember this, and realize that her anesthesiologist is not going to let any surgery start **until he knows she cannot feel any pain**, that he will keep her posted about happenings after she is asleep, if she wants to know, but that she will find it more pleasant to take an imaginary vacation or to remember some voyage **during the time she is asleep**. It is explained that the healing processes after surgery are greatly improved if the brain has been **kept from thinking about the operation**. It is explained that **the appetite and normal digestive function** are resumed very quickly when patients let their imagination work for them in this way.

He explains further that she will go to sleep with sodium pentothal introduced by vein, and that a **little tube** will be placed in her throat so that she will be assured a constant, safe supply of oxygen at all times during the operation. He will tell her when this is to be done, **but she will be too sleepy to care about it**. The tube will be coated with a special anesthetizing lubricant which keeps the throat and trachea numb for at least two days. She will have her abdomen treated with a cool liquid. The area washed by the liquid will be surgically clean, but it will also help her to know that the area is to be kept **completely relaxed and absolutely insensitive**.

When the **surgery is finished** (never say "when it is all over," since this colloquial phrase may have implications of death) she will be told about it, and she is to listen carefully to the instructions at this time. She will awaken in the recovery room, where she may find that she is still being given some fluids in the vein. If this is the case, she will help the nurses by **letting that arm remain absolutely relaxed and immobile**. If she still has an airway in her mouth when she awakens, **she can push it out with her tongue or pull it out with her free hand**.

When she is back in her own room or ward, she is to move her toes and legs, turn from side to side if she likes, and direct her attention to the recollection of some time when she was really **hungry and looking forward to a particularly appetizing type of food**. It is explained that every bit of attention she directs to the movement of her extremities or to the imagination of hunger or thirst will be sending reparative messages to places of importance while preventing her from paying attention to the possibility of pain in the operative area. The brain has the capacity for appreciating a certain volume of sensory perceptions. The average patient tunes the brain in full volume on misery, and has nothing left over for constructive thoughts. It is explained that she is not going to be like the average patient. She will know how to direct all her awareness to helpful channels of feeling, and have little or no attention left over for the feeling of discomfort.

On the way to the operating room the anesthesiologist may comment that the worst part of the surgery is already over—her period of being uncomfortable with the gallstones and her deciding about when to have the operation. From now on, **she can relax while the crew works for her, and in a few days she will be home.** The worst type of answer to a question about duration of hospitalization is, "Well, it may be somewhere between five and nine days." This means that the surgeon really does not know what he will find, and implies that he really does not know what will happen afterward. In this day of frightening legal threats about the dangers of omissions of information in obtaining "informed consent," there are too many specialists who become more concerned over possible expensive complications and self-preservation than with their responsibilities as hope-giving, productive healers. The anesthesiologist need not commit the surgeon on the length of hospitalization, but the remark about "a few days" means that it need not be very long and, more important, that there will be a period of hospitalization **after the operation**. This is reassuring in the most acceptable way to the unconscious mind. We have no positive way of knowing which patient thinks she will die, or thinks she should die in punishment for some real or imagined sin, but the deepest core of unconscious thinking always wants to live. Discussion of what is expected of the patient in the future tacitly implies the surety of the future. The patient will reason that such discussion would not be so cooly and surely spoken if the anesthesiologist were really concerned about the dangers of surgery.

9

Preoperative Hypnosis to Facilitate Healing

The now well-established evidence for the significance of mind-body inter-actions during surgery indicates that we may use ideodynamic approaches in a positive manner to facilitate healing. A general procedure for using preop-erative hypnosis to facilitate healing and recovery from surgery is outlined in Box 15. The entire procedure—beginning before the patient enters the hospital, to the day of surgery, and finally to the postsurgical follow-up—is illustrated in the following case reported by Cheek (1964).

The patient was 34 years of age, Catholic, divorced, but planning to marry a bartender who was an only child of a dominating mother. The patient was working as an elevator operator, but could not adequately sup-port her three children without financial help from her fiancé. His attitude toward the possibility of their having more children was so violently negative that she had become increasingly anxious. After a delayed menstrual period, she had developed *trichomonas vaginitis*. In addition, she had been suffer-ing from lower back pain, bladder frequency, urgency, and some stress incontinence at times when she could not leave her elevator. Physical find-ings included a mild cystocele and urethrocele with a first degree descensus of the uterus. The unalterable emotional factors rather than the organic findings prompted choice of total vaginal hysterectomy rather than simple amputation of the cervix and a plastic procedure.

Preparation for Surgery

The patient was cooperative, slender in build, very interested in hypnosis, and motivated toward recovering from the surgery as quickly as possible. Her three pregnancies had been uncomplicated by any fear. There had never been abnormal vaginal bleeding; she had voided easily after each delivery, and she looked on the surgery as a blessing rather than as a threat. These attitudes were probably more responsible for her remarkable postoperative behavior than was the preparation with hypnosis.

Most patients requiring vaginal surgery have had some difficulties with bowel elimination, and it is therefore rare for such a patient to have spontaneous bowel evacuation without even the need of a laxative, as did the patient in this report. Many gynecologists routinely insert vaginal packing and a retention catheter after vaginal surgery. In my opinion this is not necessary.

Training Steps

FIRST SESSION (15 MINUTES)

The patient was placed in light hypnosis and asked to imagine the feeling of numbness associated with lying on the left arm long enough to make it "go to sleep." She was asked to have her yes finger lift unconsciously when this had been accomplished, and to indicate verbally when it really felt numb. Reinforcing suggestions were given with the testing until she was able to tolerate the grip of an Allis clamp. It was explained to her that anesthesia of this sort, continued in the operative area after surgery, would greatly diminish the inflammatory reaction and hasten recovery. After awakening from hypnosis, she was told that she would be shown how to effect this control of her reactions to surgery in her next session.

SECOND SESSION (15 MINUTES)

On the day of admission to the hospital, she was given an appointment for her postoperative check-up one month hence. She was then taken to the consultation room for hypnotherapy before the routine physical examination. She quickly entered light hypnosis and reproduced the analgesia of her left arm. It took 45 seconds between the request and the ideomotor signal of accomplishment, and another 65 seconds before her change of facial expression and change of posture indicated conscious acceptance of the analgesia.

The next step was to associate the left arm analgesia with the same degree of analgesia for her abdomen, vagina and rectal area. It took approximately 60 seconds before her yes finger lifted to acknowledge unconscious acceptance of the additional zone of analgesia. The suggestion was then given that analgesia would permeate the operative area any time she made her left arm numb, and this effect would last as long and be as complete as she wanted it to be.

In addition to this type of "willed" numbness, it was explained that there was another type of numbness with a different purpose. Her unconscious brain could only pay attention to a limited number of things, and she would be paying no attention to noises or remarks about her operation area if she were busy taking a vacation trip. She quickly chose a fishing trip near Antioch, California. We rehearsed this hallucination. Later she reported that this trip occurred on a cold day, but I had not known that she felt a little chilly during the rehearsal. She was awakened and sent to the examining room where pressure on the areas of the vagina and perineum further fixed in her mind the zone to be anesthetized during and after surgery. She was given an account of the procedures she would experience in being admitted to the hospital, examined by the house officer, given an enema, shaven and tapped for routine blood tests.

THIRD SESSION (10 MINUTES)

The preoperative visit is usually scheduled near bedtime. I live near enough to the hospitals in which I work to make this practical. It gives me a chance to discover unconscious fears which may be accidentally aroused by maladroit questions and remarks of hospital personnel. I assure the patient of a good night's sleep. If the intern has been delayed in taking his history and performing his examination, he usually has enough time at this hour to watch a demonstration of hypnosis and learn something about the philosophy of using hypnotism in the preparation of surgical patients. The explanations of how ideomotor questioning methods can uncover and correct "unreasonable" fears and identifications of *other* surgical patients—ostensibly being directed to an interested intern at the bedside—is also a helpful way of indirectly stimulating the patient to wonder about such possibilities without suggesting them to her by direct methods.

By way of inducing hypnosis, I can also demonstrate ideomotor action by asking the patient to think *yes* until her yes finger lifts. The next question consists of an indirect search for potentially dangerous fears and identifications. It is worded as follows:

"After the sort of surgery I plan for you tomorrow, most of my patients are all well and ready to go home in five days. Does the unconscious part of your mind know you may do even better than that?"

This is a helpful way of learning attitudes without suggesting pessimistic thoughts which might be implied by direct questions. The answer to this question was a confident lifting of her yes finger. A signal of "No" or "I don't want to answer," would be a warning.

The patient was asked to rehearse the combined arm and operative-area analgesias. Following this, she was asked to have an ideomotor signal of acceptance when she knew she could sleep deeply and well through the night with pleasant, or perhaps even no dreams at all. I asked her to let the hypodermic injection in the morning be her signal to start off on the fishing trip to Antioch and to give all of her attention to the details of that trip, the fishing, and the trip back to her home. I wanted this review to take up all her time between the moment she got her injection until the time she found herself back in her room after surgery—about three hours of real time. I said that she should only notice and react to conversation or requests when they were addressed to her directly, using her first name. It used to be my hope that such suggestions might always work; but it seems impossible to prevent surgical patients from scanning noises associated with their surgical experience. If they are worried over a possibility that cancer might be found, they will resent any effort made to keep them from listening to all conversation in the operating room. With ordinary operations such as the one here, however, it seems helpful to incorporate suggestions directed for the ignoring of conversation, because it tends to make the patient part of the team responsible for optimum results.

Day of Surgery

I stopped to ask the patient where she was. We were at the entrance to the surgical suites. She sleepily answered, "We are just getting into Antioch."

The anesthesiologist assigned to my case had helped me work with hypnosis as the sole means of controlling pain, and had been much impressed with the lack of bleeding during a breast biopsy. He had not known that hypnosis was being used in the preparation of the patient for this day. At rounds the previous night he had ordered a cross-match for a unit of blood because he thought I might have forgotten to include that with my orders. He stopped to let me know about this detail in the scrub room before going to prepare the patient for anesthesia. He was acting in accordance with good hospital rules which emphasize such precautions. I said that I did not anticipate much loss of blood but thanked him for his thoughtfulness.

The patient was anesthetized when I came into the room ten minutes later to put on gown and gloves. Her legs were up in the braces. She gave no indication of feeling the vigorous vaginal clean-up being administered by the nurse. The anesthesiologist was walking around to put a piece of tape over the needle in her left arm. He said, *"Oh, Dave, that unit of blood is all ready any time she needs it."*

"Thanks, Alex," I said. "She won't need any blood. She is fishing over near Antioch. I know it's cold over there and people who are cold don't bleed." The remark had taken me by surprise, and I was groping for some answer to inactivate what might have been a frightening statement. Suggestions of numbness and coldness have repeatedly been effective in diminishing surface bleeding and inflammation. The idea of coldness at Antioch had just popped into my mind because I had never been anything but cold on passing through Antioch. I added some embroidery to the remark by saying, "I have asked her to put a snowball in her vagina to make the tissues there even colder." I had not made any such suggestion but I thought the patient would not mind this addition.

At this, the anesthesiologist laughed but added, "Don't laugh, you nurses, he knows what he is talking about. I've seen what he can do." This was a most helpful comment and was thoughtfully given.

Bleeding was minimal. Relaxation of the tissues allowed easy exposure of the major vessels but there was very little oozing from the capillaries and smaller vessels. At the conclusion of surgery the first assistant, a gynecology resident, asked if it wouldn't be wise to put some packs in the vagina "just in case." He was holding a rubber catheter in his hand expecting me to leave it in the patient, as do most other gynecologists he has known. I said, "Vaginal packs make patients feel as though their bladder is full, no matter how empty it is kept with a retention catheter. I don't use either because I do not want patients to be thinking about their inability to void at a time when they are just waking up from their anesthetic. This patient is a good hypnotic subject. She will void all right when she is ready to go to her bathroom downstairs."

I returned to look at the patient in the recovery room after dictating a note and making some telephone calls. Two hours had elapsed since discussion over the unit of blood and the snowball. Temperature in the recovery room was 76°F. Three other patients in the same room were perspiring. My patient had "gooseflesh" on her arms, abdomen, and legs. I thanked her for her cooperation in making the surgery easy and told her to warm up and start coming back from that fishing trip. She was unable to speak but did open her eyes. I did not stay long enough to see what happened to her skin reaction, but she reported later that she did not really feel comfortably warm until her return to her room.

Approximately seven hours after completion of the surgery, the patient got out of bed without evidence of discomfort and voided in the bathroom.

Review of the Experience in Hypnosis

On the second postoperative day the patient was asked to go over the surgical experience. She remembered telling me about arrival at Antioch but also knew that she was in the entrance to the operating room suites. Disparity in these awarenesses did not trouble her—a comparable reaction to the similar and usual lack of concern over the dual awareness of the hypnogogic state. She stated that she continued with the hallucinated experience because she trusted my judgment in asking her to do so. She was beginning to feel chilly in accordance with her experience of the weather at Antioch before she heard me talking in the operating room.

I asked her to give a yes signal as she reproduced falling asleep with the pentothal induction of anesthesia, to signal with another finger if she heard any talking in the operating room, and to have her no finger lift when she knew she was waking up after the operation. Immediately on giving the initial signal about induction of the anesthetic, she became very much agitated. Her pulse rate jumped from about 80 per minute to 126 per minute. Her calm initial respiratory rate changed to 32 per minute. Tears came to her eyes and her chin was trembling. Her reaction was too strong at first to

BOX 15: PREOPERATIVE HYPNOSIS TO FACILITATE HEALING

1. *Initial training in anesthesia and well-being*
   a. Ideodynamic signaling for exercises in anesthesia and/or analgesia:
   "Your yes finger can lift when you can feel the numbness (coldness, stiffness, etc.)."
   b. Ideodynamic exploration and correction of misconceptions and fears about surgery.
2. *Accessing and utilizing inner resources*
   a. **"After surgery of this kind, most patients are well and ready to go home in X days. Does your inner mind know it can facilitate healing so you may do even better than that?"**
   b. **"Let your inner mind now select a time when you've gone on a vacation. Your yes finger will lift when you are leaving; your no finger will lift when you are back in your home again. The injection you receive before surgery will be your ticket to leave on that trip. Your yes finger can lift when your unconscious knows this. All the sounds of the operating room will translate into background noises associated with your trip."**
   c. **"Your yes finger can lift when your unconscious knows it can ignore all conversation in the operating room unless I speak to you using your first name. I will keep informed about the operation but I want you to pay all your attention to the things you see, the people you are with, and the enjoyable food you eat during that trip. As you do this, you will be using all the normal biological processes for healing your body."**
3. *Ratifying postoperative healing*
   a. **"Does the inner part of your mind know that you can ignore sensations of discomfort in the surgical area after you have regained consciousness?"** (If the answer is no, it is time to check on possible resistance; but it may be only that more time and rehearsals are necessary.)
   b. **"Elimination of postoperative pain with hypnosis allows the most rapid healing to occur because inflammation is minimized. Is your inner mind willing to work on this for the sake of yourself and the people who love you?"** (A no answer indicates an unconscious need to suffer or to punish someone else. The source must be found and removed.)
   c. **"Does your inner mind know you can go home as soon or even sooner than surgical patients who have had no preparation such as you have had?"** (This projects your confidence in the patient's ability to do well. It strongly suggests that the patient will live through the surgery and will be going home.)

permit speaking but finally she said, "The doctor is saying something about a blood transfusion. You didn't tell me I would have to have blood. He's saying, *'That blood is ready, Doctor Cheek.'*"

Since this was not exactly the conversation, I asked her to go over this part again, signaling the beginning and the ending. Then she heard the doctor speaking from her left side. She said that he seemed to be walking away from her as he spoke. When asked if he had called me Doctor Cheek she smiled and said, "I don't really know you that well to say it but he said, 'Dave.' Then he said something about me needing a blood transfusion."

I asked, "Does this remark disturb you during the operation?"

"Yes, because I didn't know I might have to get some blood and I thought something more than you had told me must be wrong." She went on to state that my tone of voice in answering the doctor made her feel better because she knew I was not worried about her. The sensations of cold became much more intense at this moment. She thought I had said something about snow but her awareness of the cold wind and the cold water at Antioch seemed to block off the remaining details of operating room experiences. She had no memory at all for the remarks about packing or the catheter. I did not, however, search here particularly because she had been adequately prepared in ignoring this type of relatively inconsequential talk.

Effort and time will be wasted if research workers insist on patients' verbatim parroting of conversations that have been recorded in the operating room as an invariable criterion of genuine recall. It might be possible, however, to learn much from information registered by electrocardiographic and electroencephalographic variations. Changes in electrical potential in eyelid, throat, and diaphragmatic muscles might be correlated with happenings in the operating room as they happen and then on review with ideomotor gestures indicating significant happenings. It is important to remember that surgical patients will report what they *think* was said or done, and their ability to report on these matters may depend in some measure upon their recognition of the sincerity of the investigator who lets them know that something is possible in the way of such memory.

RESEARCH

Classical Conditioning as a Form of State-Dependent
Learning: Research Projects 21 and 22

Current research on the unconscious perception of meaningful sounds during surgical anesthesia appears to be progressing at two levels:

There is the psychobiological level of research that usually deals with the facilitation of "unconscious learning" by studying the effects of administering hormones (such as epinephrine) while experimental animals are under general anesthesia (Weinberger et al., 1984). These studies have important implications for our view that the post-traumatic stress syndrome is essentially a form of state-dependent memory, learning, and behavior. From the broadest point of view, they suggest that the classical paradigms of Pavlovian and Skinnerian conditioning are actually varieties of state-dependent memory, learning, and behavior.

There is also the human, psychological level whereby patients under general anesthesia are first exposed to meaningful and/or unmeaningful tape-recorded sounds and verbal messages. After they have awakened from the anesthesia, they are questioned for memories of the sounds to which they were exposed.

Our suggestions for research will deal with both of these levels.

In the theory portion of this section we expressed the view that most Pavlovian and Skinnerian conditioning actually involves an important element of state-dependent memory, learning, and behavior (SDMLB) that frequently is not recognized by researchers. The pioneers in animal conditioning during the early part of this century, for example, were not aware of the role that stress hormones of parasynaptic cellular modulation played in the learned association between the sound of a bell and the shock that the experimental animal received. Pavlov's early decision to remain in the role of a "pure physiologist" (see the context of this quote in Chapter 10 in the next section) led to an oversimplification of his basic conditioning experiment as a model for learning and memory. While it may have been of value for outlining some of the significant variables in the conditioning process so that they could be studied experimentally in the early years of this century, it is clearly detrimental to our current efforts to understand mind-body communication and healing. The misleading conclusions to which such Pavlovian oversimplification can lead, even today, in conditioning studies with animals is illustrated in the following discussion.

Recently Gold et al. (1985) and Weinberger et al. (1984) have conducted a series of experiments in "Pavlovian fear conditioning" under anesthesia that illustrates the hidden role of SDMLB in current research. An abstract of the experimental design and results of their adversive fear conditioning (that would be called *traumatic* if experienced by humans) was outlined as follows (Gold et al., 1985, p. 1019):

> While under deep barbiturate anesthesia, rats received a series of 10 classical conditioning trials in which white noise was paired with intramuscular shock. The anesthetized animals received either saline or epinephrine injections prior to the training trials. Independent sets of animals were tested for retention performance 2, 7, or 15 days after training. In these test trials, a conditioned suppression measure was used in which the white noise was turned on while the animals were drinking. The results indicated that the animals that had received saline while trained under anesthesia exhibited no evidence of later retention. Animals that had received epinephrine injections prior to training under anesthesia suppressed their drinking in the presence of the white noise when tested 2 or 7, but not 15, days later. Thus, the results indicate that epinephrine can enable learning under anesthesia and, in addition, forgetting occurs within 15 days.

The results of this experiment apparently demonstrate that epinephrine facilitates (enables) learning under anesthesia but this learning is forgotten in about two weeks. If such results were to be generalized to humans under surgical anesthesia, it could be cited as evidence against the overall significance of traumatic memories so acquired. It could be argued that while traumatic imprints may be acquired under surgical anesthesia, they are of only short duration.

Careful reflection, however, indicates that the experimental design used by these researchers is actually a form of SDMLB that was not carried to completion (see Overton, 1978, for an overview of SDMLB paradigms). We would hypothesize that the peripheral epinephrine that was injected into the rats just prior to their training trials led to parasynaptic cellular modulation of the Pavlovian fear conditioning, just as stress-released epinephrine during any traumatic incident would encode SDMLB. The researchers found that after 15 days, this fear conditioning apparently was extinguished. Note, however, that when testing for the fear conditioning, they used only the white noise (now the conditioned stimulus) that had been associated with the epinephrine and intramuscular shock (the unconditioned stimulus). While this test fits the classical Pavlovian paradigm of classical adversive conditioning, *it completely ignores the crucial role of the major experimental variable, epinephrine, that enabled the conditioning in the first place.* As reported, this experiment was incomplete in that it did not test for the role of epinephrine in the recall of the fear conditioning, and therefore suggests a number of research projects, as follow.

Project 21   The altered psychobiological state induced by epinephrine (with its many associated internal cues encoded by parasynaptic cellular modulation that mediate "endogenous" learning) during the original fear conditioning is an excellent experimental model of SDMLB. We would therefore predict that the Pavlovian conditioning that apparently was extinguished after 15 days would be reinstated if the experimental animals were again administered epinephrine prior to testing, just as they were injected prior to training. The administration of epinephrine prior to testing would complete the overall experimental design so that it would fit the more general paradigm of SDMLB.

Project 22   An interesting extension of this type of experiment could serve as a model for the study of the post-traumatic stress syndrome, which we believe is the most clinically significant form of SDMLB. A classical illustration of a post-traumatic stress symptom acquired during war is when a former soldier experiences stress whenever a loud noise or helicopter suddenly roars overhead. The peripheral epinephrine acts as a parasynaptic cellular modulator that rein*states* a traumatic "flashback memory" of the original war situation. In severe cases, *any stress* may release sufficient epinephrine to reinduce an anxiety response even when the loud noise and helicopter (the conditioned stimuli) associated with battle are not present.

An extension of the Gold et al. experimental design would be to expose animals who apparently have extinguished their fear response after 15 days to any form of stress unrelated to the original fear conditioning situation (e.g., excess running, swimming, or startle situations). We would predict that the epinephrine that is naturally released during such stress would reactivate the apparently extinguished fear response.

A similar realization of the significance of the state-dependent nature in physiological studies has been noted by Lydic (1987, p. 14):

> Considered together, the evidence reviewed here suggests that physiological studies that ignore organismal states may be analogous to the experiments of physics that ignored time. Statics [*sic*: *statistics* is probably correct] are important, but the state-dependent aspects of regulatory physiology remind us that biological systems are highly dynamic and

notoriously nonlinear. In the past, the complexities of changing behavioral states were often dealt with by surgical or pharmacological elimination, but today we have come to appreciate that the behavioral state effect comprises a major independent variable influencing regulatory physiology.

The implications of our proposals for a more thorough investigation of the state-dependent aspects of Pavlov's classical conditioning experiments of learning are profound:
They would require an important expansion of our basic paradigms for investigating physiological homeostasis, memory, learning, and behavior. The simple stimulus-response experiments of classical conditioning and cognition that are currently used in the behavioristic model of human memory and learning may no longer be sufficient. A psychobiological model (Rossi, 1986d) of memory and learning that includes the state-dependent nature of physiological homeostasis as well as of memory and learning will be required for a more complete understanding of the clinical phenomena of depth psychology and psychosomatic medicine.

If we follow Sir Karl Popper's (1965) view that "the criterion of the scientific status of a theory is its falsifiability, or refutability, or testability" (p. 37), then the above will be crucial for assessing the general significance of SDMLB in learning and conditioning experiments. In particular, our predictions about the outcome of a more complete assessment of the Gold, Weinberger, and Sternberg experiments will be of central significance for evaluating our proposal that *SDMLB is the essential basis of the posttraumatic stress syndrome*, and the many more subtle dysfunctions associated with it. In a recent personal communication, Paul Gold expressed interest in our view of the need to complete these Pavlovian fear conditioning experiments as a model of the more general paradigm of parasynaptic cellular modulation that mediates SDMLB.

Recent Research in Human Memory During General Anesthesia: Research Projects 23–27

A recent review of the entire area covering the "perception and memory for events during adequate general anesthesia for surgical operations" by Bennett (1987) presents an excellent assessment of the theoretical and experimental issues involved on the human psychological level. Among the most significant conclusions drawn is that there is compelling evidence from numerous experimental studies (Adam, 1979; Bennett, in press; Goldmann, 1986; Levinson, 1965a,b, 1969; Millar & Watkinson, 1983; Stolzy, Couture, & Edmonds, 1986) that the auditory modality remains operative during minimal, light, and surgical levels of anesthesia so that patients can record verbal conversations. However, patients respond to casual questioning for surgical memories after the operation with a uniform denial of having any such memories. This is why generations of medical personnel have believed that patients cannot hear and remember when under surgical anesthesia. Surgical anesthesia apparently does block "declarative" (Squire, 1982) intentional verbal memory. When such patients are assessed for surgical memory via a nonverbal "procedural" behavioral response (pulling on their ear, touching their chin, etc.), however, there is statistical evidence that verbal memories were recorded and can be accessed by ideodynamic finger signaling methods. (See Section VII for a more complete discussion of declarative and procedural memory.)

In his search for a theoretical foundation for his findings, Bennett has reviewed 30 years of selective attention research concerned with the relationship between consciousness and the encoding of information from the environment. The two major possibilities have been formulated as "early selection theory" (Broadbent, 1958, 1977) and "late selection theory" (Norman, 1968, 1976). In early selection theory, Broadbent proposed that only the sensory-perceptual experiences which are selected into consciousness are processed for meaning and permanently encoded; *consciousness is primary and necessary for memory and learning.* If an active and intentional process of conscious selective attention is not given to information from the environment, it is not encoded. The early selection theory would predict that the unselected auditory information to which anesthetized patients are exposed in surgical operations would not be encoded as memory by the central nervous system; it would simply "fall away like sound waves hitting a wall."

Late selection theory, by contrast, postulates that multiple sources of information can be simultaneously and automatically received and encoded before they reach awareness; *consciousness is secondary and not necessary for memory and learning.* Unconscious processes of selection and encoding are primary for many of the complex phenomena of human attention and consciousness as generally postulated by psychoanalytic theory. Bennett's own experimental work, as well as that of others, overwhelmingly supports late selection theory. He summarizes his view of currently available experimental data as follows (Bennett, in press):

> Work supports the capacity for multiple channels of auditory stimulus processing, sometimes regardless of awareness of the stimuli (Eich, 1984; Squire, 1982). It was learned that two verbal perceptual activities could be carried out in parallel simultaneously yet there might be awareness of only one of them (Allport, Antonis, & Reynolds, 1972; Shaffer, 1975; Hirst et al., 1980). In my own work, subjects who were consciously occupied in an auditory shadowing task were presented with an unattended message with direct statements to engage in a behavior (Bennett, 1980). Messages were maximally separated on the basis of physical characteristics of location and gender of voice. Extensive briefing of subjects

revealed lack of awareness of the unattended message, yet covert video-taping documented a significant response to the unattended suggestion (". . . when you stop talking I want you to touch your nose") compared with controls. *Together these experiments support the late selection theory of selective attention. That is, language can be comprehended and responses initiated before conscious processes are activated. In other terms, conscious processes are not always necessary for highly skilled neurological and perceptual activities which include language understanding (Schneider & Shiffrin, 1977; Shiffrin & Schneider, 1977, 1984). Therefore it is possible to understand and respond to a linguistic message without awareness of that message.*

For events taking place during adequate anesthesia and despite lack of conscious recall, there is compelling evidence that verbal perceptual processes continue during minimal, light, and surgical levels of anesthesia (e.g.: minimal: Adam, 1979; light: Bennett, Davis, & Giannini, 1984; surgical: Millar & Watkinson, 1983; Stolzy, Couture, & Edmonds, 1986; Goldmann, 1986). These perceptual processes have been demonstrated by persistence into the postoperative period of the effects of presentations of language messages during general anesthesia in the presence of a nearly uniform postanesthetic amnesia. Therefore, though obtunded, patients appear to be able to perceive messages they are asked to remember. (Italics added)

The pioneering work of Milton H. Erickson on the hypnotic alteration of audition and memory (Erickson, 1938a, b/1980, 1963/1980, 1973/1980) and the simultaneous processing of two or more sources of information (Erickson & Erickson, 1941/1980) also strongly supports late selection theory as the basis for the unconscious perception and encoding of psychodynamically meaningful material during surgical anesthesia.

Late selection theory is also of interest for our study of ideodynamic signaling and therapy because it is entirely consistent with our view of the significance of state-dependent memory, learning, and behavior theory in this area. The unconscious processing and encoding of meaningful external as well as internal sensory-perceptual information is the common denominator of both theories. Together they integrate an impressive array of clinical and experimental data that traces the entire process by which mind-body problems (particularly those associated with post-traumatic stress syndrome) may be encoded, accessed, and resolved.

In personal communications with Bennett, we agreed that further replications of his and Goldmann's clinical-experimental designs might include a more systematic assessment of the following:

Project 23 The very subtle behavioral-physiological indices of accessing unconscious memories (autonomic arousal such as sweating, blushing, or pallor; increased heart rate, etc.) which, according to Cheek's basic clinical hypothesis, actually precede the ideomotor signaling.

Project 24   The ideo*sensory* experiences that often take place in the signaling finger before a visible ideomotor response becomes manifest.

Project 25   The qualitative variations in ideomotor finger signaling. Most clinicians believe that the slow, hesitant, and twitching finger signal is a more valid indicator of the involuntary accessing of unconscious processes than the finger signal that moves quickly with what seems to be a voluntary conscious movement.

Project 26   An ideal source of clinical material for studying the formation, accessing, and ideodynamic reframing of post-traumatic stress syndromes would seem to be the emergency rooms of hospitals and clinics. Witness and police reports of accidents, for example, could be used to assess the ideodynamic accessing of traumatic experiences. We would predict that those accident victims who experienced additional trauma from thoughtless verbal suggestions and panicky responses of bystanders, relatives, and medical personnel would have (a) more post-traumatic stress syndrome; (b) more medical complications, and longer recovery times from the acute trauma. We would also predict, in addition, that the suppression of the immune system by such post-traumatic stress syndromes would lead to a significantly higher rate of viral and bacterial infections in such patients.

Project 27   The very wide range of experimental and clinical conditions under which state-dependent memory, learning, and behavior has been studied suggests many more models for exploring the efficacy of ideodynamic methods. It has been found that when learning takes place in any special situation or physiological state, retention is usually better when tested under the same conditions. Students, for example, score higher if they are tested in the same room where they originally learned the academic material. Similarly, divers who learned material on land or under water scored higher when tested in the same environment in which they first learned the material. Hilgard (1977) has discussed this relationship between state-dependent learning and his neodissociation theory of hypnosis.

   The following is a listing of some of the clinical conditions that have been found to be associated with state-dependent memory, learning, and behavior (Rossi, 1986c, d; Rossi & Ryan, 1986):

1. Manic-depressive episodes (Weingartner, Miller & Murphy, 1977).
2. Multiple personality (Braun, 1983a, b; Lienhart, 1983; Silberman, Putnam, Weingartner, Braun, & Post, 1985).
3. Psychosomatic symptoms (Cheek & LeCron, 1968; Erickson, 1943b, c, d).

4. Psychiatric states (Reus, Weingartner, & Post, 1979).

Explore the relative merits of conventional conversational hypnosis with the ideodynamic approaches to accessing and therapeutically reframing each of these clinical conditions.

The New Psychosomatic Medicine

THEORY

In the area of ideodynamic approaches to psychosomatic medicine, investigators are making exciting progress in basic research, theory, and clinical practice. We have known for centuries that hypnosis could facilitate the healing of a bewildering variety of medical psychological problems (Crasilneck & Hall, 1985). Such healing was often associated with "new" hypnotherapeutic methods developed by unusually gifted clinicians: The names of Mesmer, Esdaille, Braid, and Bernheim will be engraved forever in the foundations of hypnosis because of their innovative methods. However, because their clinical skills were not supported by a rational and verifiable scientific theory that could guide further research, their methods soon fell into disuse.

Approaches to verifiable research have been radically improved by the recent technical and theoretical advances in the psychobiology of mind-body communication and healing. Ironically, it may now be the case that, for the first time in medical history, we have more real understanding about the molecular basis of mind-body healing than we know how to put into practice. *These theoretical advances involve a fundamental reconceptualization of mind and body as a single cybernetic system of information transduction and communication at the molecular level* (Bowers, 1977; Cunningham, 1986; Rossi, 1986d).

In order to appreciate all we already know about mind-body communication in psychosomatic medicine, it is necessary to create a new way of looking at the entire process. In Table 6, an overview of mind-body communication is condensed into three stages or loci of a single system of cybernetic information transduction: the *mind-brain*, the *brain-body*, and the *cellular-genetic*. Let us explore each in turn.

The Mind-Brain Connection

How are mind and brain related? We all know that this question has been the subject of philosophical debate for centuries and probably will continue

Table 6: An overview of mind-body communication with the three major loci and pathways of information flow.

Transduction Locus	Pathways of Information Transduction	Reference
MIND-BRAIN	-The *cortical-limbic system* pathways of the brain.	Achterberg, 1985
		Bowers, 1977
	-The sensory-perceptual languages of cortical mind (imagery, kines-	Erickson (1980a)
	thetic, etc.) are *ideodynamically transduced in the cross-modal*	Mindell, 1982, 1985a, b
	association areas of the limbic system.	Mishkin, 1982
		Mishkin & Petri, 1984
	-Consciousness is a process of self-reflective information transduction	Nauta, 1964
	between the verbal and sensory-perceptual languages of mind.	Pribram, 1971, 1986
		Rossi, 1986b
BRAIN-BODY	-The *limbic-hypothalamic-pituitary system* of the brain.	Ader, 1981
		Bower, 1981
	-The neurally encoded languages of mind of the limbic system are	Erickson, Rossi, & Rossi, 1976
	transduced into the information substances of the body in the	Fischer, 1971
	hypothalamus; this involves *neuroendocrinal transduction.*	Lydic, 1987

	-State-dependent memory, learning, and behavior are encoded as "filters" in the limbic-hypothalamic and related systems.	Overton, 1978 Rossi, 1986d Rossi & Ryan, 1986 Scharrer & Scharrer, 1940 Selye, 1976 Weiner, 1977
	-The autonomic, endocrine, immune, and neuropeptide systems are the major pathways from hypothalamus to all parts of the body.	
CELL-GENE	-The *cell wall receptor-gene system* of the entire body.	Bulloch, 1985 Kandel & Schwartz, 1982, 1985 Melnechuk, 1985 Olness & Conroy, 1985 Pert et al., 1985 Schneider, Smith, & Witcher, 1984 Smith, Harbour-McMenamin, & Blalock, 1985 Walters & Byrne, 1983
	-The information substances of the body are *transduced into "second messenger systems" that move through the cell's cytoplasm to the genes in the nucleus.*	
	-Messenger RNA carries the gene's blueprints out to the ribosome protein factories of the cell's cytoplasm where enzymes, proteins, and other information substances are made.	
	-Many information substances circulate back to the limbic-hypothalamic-pituitary system to complete the information feedback loop.	

for many more centuries on the phenomenological and philosophical level. On practical, empirical, and therapeutic levels, however, we can already outline the mind-brain relationship in a useful manner.

Let us not attempt to define *mind* itself. Rather, let us simply agree that many *modalities or languages by which mind is expressed are easily recognizable.* Who would not agree that words, imagery, sensations, perceptions, emotions, thinking, memory, and learning are all expressions of mind and its "information"? We can measure the information of all these languages of mind and study their relationships with each other and with the physical brain.

We now know, for example, that many of the sensory-perceptual languages of the mind (visual, auditory, and kinesthetic information, etc.) are encoded like a map over the cortex of the brain (Pribram, 1971, 1986). Further, we know that all these languages of human experience can be transduced or transformed into one another via the "cross-modal association areas" of the limbic system (Mishkin, 1982; Mishkin & Petri, 1984). This means, for example, that I can *visually* imagine a scene and convert (transduce) it into *words*. A talented artist might even make musical sounds or movements to express visual experience. That is, the creative artist is one who can transduce the mind's visual or verbal language into the auditory and kinesthetic languages of music and dance.

"Consciousness" is another of those phenomenological concepts like "mind" and "psyche" that cannot be defined completely, once and for all. Our ways of comprehending these terms continue to change and evolve as our life experience expands to provide for richer contexts for understanding them. For the purposes of this volume on mind-body healing, we could define *consciousness as a process of self-reflective information transduction* (Rossi, 1986d). Self-reflection involves processes of recursive information transduction between the different modalities or languages of mind (von Foerster, 1984). This suggests that we can conceptualize our methods of ideodynamic healing as recursively facilitating the evolution of insight and the creation of new meaning as we access and reframe the experiential sources of psychological problems.

Consciousness presumably evolved because there was survival value in all the modalities and languages of mind being able to converse together (Rossi, 1972/1985). This suggests that consciousness becomes more complex and effective as a healing agent as it gains more experience and skill in self-reflecting all the modalities and languages of mind. Everyone experiences these processes of self-reflective information transduction with different degrees of control. Our personalities and "points of view" are expressions of our individual proclivities and talents for utilizing many of the processes of information transduction that take place in the cortical-limbic system pathways of the brain (Achterberg, 1985; Nauta, 1964). Dreams are an especially rich modality for experiencing and exploring the potentialities of these processes of self-reflective information transduction, since dreams are subject to fewer of the constraints of cultural conditioning (LaBerge, 1985; Mindell, 1982, 1985a, b; Rossi, 1972/1985).

We can generalize this point of view to conceptualize all methods of mind-body healing as means of facilitating skills in utilizing the many languages of self-reflective information transduction. All processes of meditation (Smith, McKenzie, Marker, & Steele, 1985), hypnosis (Bowers, 1977), imagery (Achterberg, 1985), active imagination (Jung, 1960b), the systems approaches to therapeutic communication (Watzlawick, 1978, 1984), and even the placebo response (White, Tursky, & Schwartz, 1985) can be understood as means of exploring, accessing, and utilizing the many modalities and languages of mind-brain communication.

The Brain-Body Connection

Most people think of the brain as being connected to the body by nerves. We also know, however, that hormones from the pituitary, the "master gland" of the brain, can regulate body processes. The previously separate fields of neurology and endocrinology came together when the Scharrers (Scharrer & Scharrer, 1940) discovered that some neural cells were able to produce hormones. They were among the first to document how certain neurons within the hypothalamus of the brain convert the neural impulses of *mind* into the hormonal *information substances* of the *body*. This conversion of the neuronal signals of mind into the messenger molecules of the body was later termed *neuroendocrinal transduction* by Wurtman and Anton-Tay (1969). The more general concept of *information transduction* in current-day psychobiological theory apparently evolved from that point.

Information transduction at this level usually refers to the conversion or transformation of information from one neuromolecular modality into another. The most familiar examples of information transduction come from the area of sensory-perceptual psychology. Information in the form of light is transduced into chemical information when it is encoded by the molecules of rhodopsin in the retina of the eye. The photochemistry of rhodopsin transduces this chemical information into neural information via the "bipolar" and ganglion cells within the retina, which, in turn, transmit the neural information through the optic nerve to the visual association cortex of the brain. All sensory-perceptual systems operate by an analogous process of information transduction.

Information transduction at this level of mind-body communication has been used to update Hans Selye's theory of stress and the General Adaptation Syndrome as the basis of psychosomatic medicine (Rossi, 1986c, d; Rossi & Ryan, 1986). Selye's life work demonstrated that there were three routes, channels, or systems by which mental stress was transmitted into the body's "psycho-somatic" responses: the autonomic, endocrine, and immune systems. We now know that the limbic-hypothalamic-pituitary system of the brain plays the major integrative role in the mind modulation of all three of these major systems. That is, the limbic-hypothalamic-pituitary system is the major mind-body information transducer; it is the major translator between the languages of mind (in the forms of sensation, imagery, verbal language, etc.) and the languages of the body (information substances such as neuropeptides, hormones, immunotransmitters, etc.).

It has been proposed that the state-dependent memory, learning, and behavior system that encodes many mind-body problems functions as an "experiential filter" modulating the activity of the limbic-hypothalamic-pituitary system (Rossi, 1986d). This leads us to conclude that *information transduction* and *state-dependent memory and learning* are the two fundamental processes that bridge the so-called "mysterious gap" between mind and body; they are the two basic channels of mind-body communication and healing.

The Cellular-Genetic Connection

All the cells of the body are now known to have numerous receptors on their surfaces that can regulate their internal activities. The information substances of the autonomic, endocrine, immune, and neuropeptide systems signal these cell receptors to "turn on" and modulate the metabolic machinery within the protoplasm and even the expression of genes within the nucleus of the cell. Complete channels of information transduction between mind, the limbic-hypothalamic system, and the gene regulation of the metabolism of each cell of the body are thus theoretically possible. This process of mind-body communication via information substances and their receptors was described in the theory portion of Section I as the system of parasynaptic cellular modulation that is now known to supplement the classical nervous system. It is the basis of what we may now call the *mind-gene-molecule communication network*, as outlined in Table 6 and Figure 8. We will use this multilevel overview of mind-body communication as a model for exploring a variety of psychosomatic problems in the following chapters.

The classic psychosomatic responses to stress as outlined in Figure 8 illustrate how this cybernetic mind-gene-molecule communication network operates. Selye found that severe stress involved a three-part psychosomatic response. There was (1) an activation of the sympathetic branch of the autonomic nervous system, leading to dysfunctions of the gastrointestinal tract (e.g., ulcers); (2) an activation of the pituitary-adrenal axis of the endocrine system leading to a hypertrophy of the adrenals; and (3) a suppression of the thymus and immune system. Figure 8 is an oversimplified view of these three types of psychosomatic response, down to the cellular-genetic-molecular level.

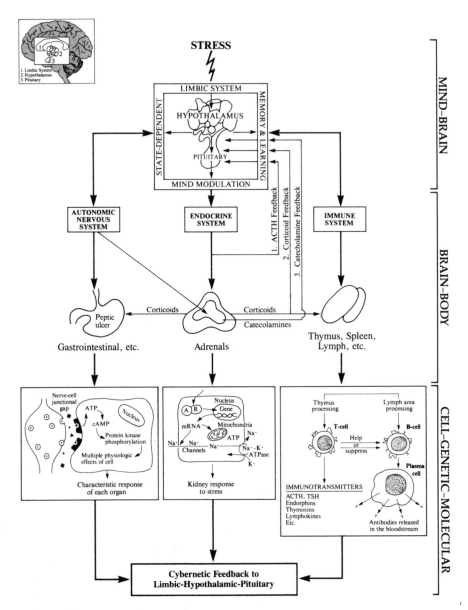

Figure 8: Three levels of mind-body cybernetic communication during stress. (Adapted from Rossi, 1986d)

Nerve endings of the *autonomic nervous system* typically are separated from the cells they signal by a narrow nerve-cell junctional gap. Neurotransmitters are released from the nerve into this gap and are received by receptors on the cell walls of the body tissue. This leads to changes in the shape of the receptor which, in turn, activate the secondary messenger system within the cell—the adensosine triphosphate (ATP) and protein kinase phosphorylation reaction—that initiates the energy dynamics and characteristic metabolism of each particular cell. Many of these cell responses involve the release of additional information substances back into the bloodstream, where they can function as a part of a recursive feedback loop to the limbic-hypothalamic-pituitary system of the brain. The autonomic system branch on the left side of Figure 8 thus illustrates a complete path of communication between the languages of mind (encoded and transduced in the state-dependent memory and learning systems modulating the limbic-hypothalamic system), and the metabolism of the cell at the molecular level.

In an analogous manner, the middle column of Figure 8 presents a simplified overview of how the *endocrine system* mediates another complete communication loop between the languages of mind and the expression of genes at the cellular level. Mental stress at the cortical-limbic-hypothalamic level leads to the formation and release of a series of hormonal information substances that ultimately modulate gene expression at the cellular level. Stress experienced as languages of mind (sensation, perception, words, images) in the cortical-limbic system is transduced into information substances in the hypothalamus. One of these hypothalamic information substances, corticotropin releasing hormone (CRH), travels via the hypothalamic-pituitary portal blood vessels to the anterior portion of the pituitary. CRH, in turn, leads to the release of adrenocorticotropic hormone (ACTH), which is the well-known modulator of the stress response in the body, where it travels via the bloodstream to the cortex of the adrenal glands to release cortisol. As illustrated in Figure 8, cortisol in turn communicates with other tissues and organs of the body modulated by the autonomic and immune systems.

Under the impact of stress, the adrenal cortex also releases hormones such as aldosterone, which modulates sodium reabsorption in the kidneys at the cellular-genetic level (as illustrated in Figure 8). All the endocrine glands of the body operate by an analogous response to regulate a wide variety of functions: basal metabolism, growth, sexuality, and so forth. The detailed analysis of how genetic expression is regulated by a variety of information substances (such as the steroid hormones) is one of the most exciting areas of molecular biology today (Roy & Clark, 1983; Sluyser, 1985). For our purposes, it is important to recognize clearly that a complete loop of information transduction between the mind-brain and the cellular-genetic-molecular level really exists. We have unequivocal evidence for the presence of what I would call the "mind-gene stress operon" (Darnell, Lodish, & Baltimore, 1986). This leads me (Rossi) to hypothesize that mind-gene healing operons also exist (see Box 16). These mind-body-gene information loops usually operate at an "unconscious" level. The ultimate goal of all mind-body healing methods is to learn how to consciously facilitate these processes for psychosomatic healing.

The *immune system* branch of mind-body communication is illustrated on the right side of Figure 8. What is most noteworthy is that recent research (Blalock, Harbour-McMenamin, & Smith, 1985) has demonstrated how all the specialized cells of the immune system (T-cells, B-cells, monocytes, neutrophils, natural killer cells, etc.) release a variety of information substances (sometimes called "immunotransmitters") that mediate communication with the autonomic, endocrine, and the central nervous system (the brain) (Ader, 1981).

Figure 8 is a simplified illustration of the major cybernetic pathways of mind-body communication involved in psychosomatic medicine. It is only now, a generation after Kroger (1963) first hypothesized about the cybernetic basis of therapeutic hypnosis, that we can trace some of the actual psychobiological mechanisms that are involved. The current challenge is to determine just how and where hypnosis enters these cybernetic loops to facilitate mind-body healing. Most of the case studies of this volume document some aspect or other of how psychosomatic problems can be resolved with our ideodynamic approaches. It would be tempting to conclude that all recursive ideodynamic approaches to therapeutic hypnosis operate by accessing the cybernetic mind-body communication networks of Figure 8. But this, precisely, is what still remains to be proven. We have a theory of mind-body communication (information substances and their receptors modulating mind-brain-body-cellular-genetic communication) and a technique of mind-body healing (ideodynamic signaling in hypnosis.) No one, however, has yet devised a convincing experiment to demonstrate that the theory and the technique are necessarily related. We will explore some ideas about how to devise such experiments in the research proposals at the end of this section. Meanwhile, let us look at the "state of the therapeutic art," as it is presented in the following chapters.

BOX 16: THE MIND-GENE HEALING OPERON

The value of a theory of science is determined by the extent to which it generates testable hypotheses. The mind-gene theory of psychobiological healing generates the testable hypothesis that *mind-gene healing operons* exist.

An *operon* is a new concept from molecular genetics that is of essence for understanding the mind-gene connection. An operon consists of a group of genes whose existence is regulated by stimuli or information substances from outside the nucleus of the cell. The existence of genes that can be turned on by environmental stress, for example, is aptly described by Baskin (1984, p. 185):

> An animal responds to stress and physical trauma on many levels, from mental to molecular. One of the most basic responses is the switching on of a gene that makes a protein called *metallothionein*, or MT. Chase a mouse around its cage for five minutes, dose the animal with high levels of toxic metals, or infect it with bacteria, and it will switch on the MT gene in tissues throughout the body.

While this concept of the operon originally was developed with bacteria, analogous processes whereby stress can modulate genetic expression of "housekeeping" proteins that continuously regulate cellular metabolism in humans are currently under intense investigation (Kandel, 1983; Watson, Hopkins, Roberts, Steitz, & Weiner, 1987). We would hypothesize that many more mind-gene stress operons exist in addition to the MT operon described above. Each time we succeed in characterizing the existence of another mind-gene stress operon, we will be adding another bit of verification for the mind-gene theory of psychobiological healing.

Since we know that positive emotions, imagery, and placebos can theoretically facilitate healing at the genetic level (Rossi, 1986d), we can also hypothesize the existence of *mind-gene healing operons*. The unequivocal experimental demonstration of the interrelated activity of stress and healing mind-gene operons in humans would validate the ultimate cybernetic basis of holistic mind-body healing.

PRACTICE

10

Psychosomatic Aspects of Surgical Emergencies

Workers in the art of medicine are aware that the mind plays an important part in maintaining physiologic adaptations to stress; yet we find little thoughtful consideration of emotional factors in the complications of anesthesia and surgery. As we read the literature, we find ourselves siding with Pavlov, who comments on his personal struggle over a course to follow in research. His early associate, Snarsky, had become overly concerned about possible subjective attitudes of dogs in their experiments (Pavlov, 1928, p. 38):

> Snarsky clung to his subjective explanation of the phenomena, but I, putting aside fantasy and seeing the scientific barrenness of such a solution, began to seek for another exit from this difficult position.
>
> After persistent deliberation, after a considerable mental conflict, I decided finally, in regard to the so-called psychical stimulation, to remain in the role of a pure physiologist, i.e., of an objective external observer and experimenter, having to do exclusively with external phenomena and their relations.

Hemorrhage, renal failure, respiratory collapse, embolism, and wound infections continue to take their toll of surgical patients. With improved operative techniques, hypothermia, and abundant blood adding to the power of our antibiotics, our tranquilizers, our paralyzers, and our blood-pressure controllers, we have opened new vistas and widened the scope of surgery for poor-risk patients. We have artificial hearts, artificial lungs, artificial kidneys, and artificial blood vessels to help us. We are lulled as we learn of the increasing mortality among anesthetized patients, for we contemplate the apparent fact that good anesthesiologists "cannot win them all." Surgeons are loath to consider the possibility that they could be contributing to the increasing number of deaths in our operating and recovery rooms because we have not yet devised an artificial brain to compensate for previous conditionings, for pessimism, for unconscious fears, for identifications with other unfortunate patients, for unconscious guilt, and for the fact that the brain is listening to everything meaningful during surgical plane anesthesia.

The honest admission by Pavlov of his conflict over emotional factors in physiologic adaptations was fostered by his inability to evaluate the psychological motivations of his animals. We are no longer in the position of discarding the "x" factor of emotion because we now have effective, quick, and safe means of exploring this area of human behavior in relation to anesthesia, surgery, and psychosomatic problems in general.

It is now time to wonder constructively about the factors that may make hearts stop beating. Perhaps we could learn from those who have survived this experience whether or not there were unconscious fears or premonitions of death prefacing the trip to the operating room. We might inquire into the subjective reactions of patients to the noise of surgical preparation, the silent, forceful extension of the head and introduction of a tracheal catheter, the jolting without explanation into kidney, gallbladder, lithotomy or prostatectomy position. We might wonder about the impact of discussions between surgeon and assistant regarding the best place to make the incision, about the operability of cancer, or the calm discussion of a recent baseball game, all the while awaiting the sounds of reassurance or terror when the pathologist returns with the verdict on a frozen section. What effect is there on the inner world of an anesthetized patient who hears there is uncontrollable bleeding and that more than one unit of blood will be needed? Could this make a heart more vulnerable to the excess potassium in bank blood (LeVeen et al., 1960), more than normally responsive to stress of all sorts?

EMOTIONAL CONDITIONING FACTORS IN SERIOUS AND
UNEXPECTED HEMORRHAGE

We have heard learned discussions about the myriad of confusing factors responsible for serious and unexpected hemorrhage in surgical patients. Paul Aggeler (Aggeler, Hoag, Wallerstein, & Whissell, 1961) has noted that 50% of patients with serious bleeding show no suspicious tendencies during the usual tests for coagulation mechanism disturbance. An American Medical Association authority gave this interesting answer to a question on bleeding tendencies (June 29, 1957):

It should be emphasized that, in order to treat "bleeding tendencies" on a rational basis, it is of the utmost importance to try to establish precisely the nature of the disturbance underlying the bleeding tendency. Thus, the hemorrhagic disease may be due to deficiency of platelets, or antihemophilic factor (hemophilia), of plasma thromboplastin component (PTC deficiency), of accelerator globulin (paraphemophilia), of fibrinogen (afibrinogenemia), of circulating anticoagulants (hemophiloid disease), of prothrombin (hypoprothrombinemia), or of proconvertin (hypoproconvertinemia or serum prothrombin conversion accelerator deficiency). These are only some of the hemorrhagic disorders associated with disturbances of the clotting mechanism.

It might be added that it is one thing to "try to establish precisely the nature of the disturbance" and another thing to correct it during surgery. We might study the mechanisms responsible for the absence of bleeding from the wounds of oriental religious zealots during their ceremonies with self-inflicted injuries. These people are in hypnotic trances. We might wonder why a frightened obstetrical patient lost 500 cc. of blood upon unconsciously discovering she was at the same stage of pregnancy on the same day of the week when she lost a previous pregnancy. Why did she stop bleeding abruptly on learning that her obstetrician would come out to see her at home rather than admitting her to the hospital? It is a curious coincidence that afibrinogenemia should occur in women whose babies have died in utero, or who have had criminal abortions and who are unconsciously sure that they have been responsible for the death of the child. Why is hemorrhage common with toxemia of pregnancy? Toxemic mothers can tell us when and why the toxemia commenced. Emotionally disturbing stresses play a major part in the production of toxemia. They play an important part in hemorrhage, in prolonged labor, in placental separation. These are obstetrical factors causing surgical intervention. Could they influence the incidence of vomiting and cardiac arrest during surgery?

The unconscious mind maintains a channel of communication to the external world through the hearing sense at all times. Fear in human beings increases bleeding tendencies; comfort and reassurance of an acceptable sort decrease bleeding tendencies. Authorities on hemorrhagic disorders inform us that the history of previous hemorrhage under stress of surgery or delivery is more important than the usual tests of blood clotting mechanisms, but no one has published reports on the emotional conditioning factors making such histories important. We have been "putting aside fantasy and seeing the scientific barrenness" of that avenue of investigation. We might reevaluate our concepts of scientific barrenness, if we dared to look.

Recording of Perinatal Experiences Associated with Fear or Injury

Those working with ideodynamic methods for accessing deeply repressed material are discovering that verifiable detailed information of prebirth, birth, and neonatal experiences have been recorded when the events have been associated with fear or injury. It appears that the sensations, the physiologic responses to maternal hormones, and difficulties with respiration are somehow "tape-recorded" and coupled with the noises of voices. When these experiences are recalled during ideodynamic age regression, the sounds made by the voices are translated into subsequently learned language.

In this way, we have found that some individuals with emphysema, asthma, and tendencies for respiratory complications with anesthetics have had their initial focusing experiences of respiratory difficulty at birth. Respiratory anxiety was caused by the doctor and attendants showing concern about their breathing. We have found that respiratory difficulties occurring during a traumatic anesthetic experience may recur during a thoughtfully conducted induction of anesthesia under good conditions merely because the human mind, entering a frightening situation or losing spatial orientation, goes into hypnosis (Cheek, 1959, 1960a; Rodger, 1961). The hypnotic state releases defensive mechanisms which may be very helpful if they occur under appropriate circumstances, but the reflex level of thinking, released during an induction with a general anesthetic, does not use reason in analyzing appropriateness of reaction. The mechanism is much like, "I am losing consciousness. This is the same feeling I had when they once held me down and smothered me with an ether cone! I am scared. Let me out of here!"

These relationships of the hypnotic state with stress situations and the associated physiologic reactions have been discussed in relation to using ideomotor questioning in overcoming unconscious resistance with patients who are consciously willing to use hypnosis (Cheek, 1960a). Patients have become ashy white, have had accelerated pulse and respiratory rates, and have concluded that hypnosis was dangerous for them because they experienced these frightening feelings even as they were lulled with peaceful descriptions of beautiful mountain meadows in the springtime. When asked to orient their thoughts to another time when they felt something like this before, these individuals have all learned that it occurred in association with a frightening experience from which they had "escaped" by entering a hypnotic trance. A subsequent trance, *no matter how induced*, can recall all the feelings associated with the earlier experience.

It is a simple matter to help these subjects understand that hypnosis can be a pleasant experience in itself, and that it can be used constructively without evoking frightening and useless memories. This facet of psychologic behavior is dangerous when unrecognized by the anesthetist or surgeon; it is of enormous value to the physician who needs to know what traumatic experiences in the past have contributed to emotional or physical disturbances later in life.

Childhood Anesthesia Trauma as Source of Adult Trance Induction Problems

There have been many jokes about the hypnotist being hypnotized by his subject. Any human being whose sensoria are concentrated on a single object will enter a hypnotic state. An example will clarify this statement.

A physician, aged 63, attending a symposium on hypnosis techniques came forward during an intermission on the second day to report a disturbing faintness and tachycardia which he had experienced each time we had given a demonstration of hypnosis. He added that he had been interested in hypnosis for 30 years, but had given it up after his first attempt at an induction with a patient. He had experienced then the same feelings that he now had during the symposium.

He was asked to sit down and establish finger movements to answer yes and no. This he readily did, but while concentrating in an expectant state on the appropriate fingers to lift, he again felt uneasy. He was asked to let the fingers answer the question, "Have you ever felt like this before your first experience hypnotizing your patient 30 years ago?" After a 24-second pause, his yes finger lifted in the characteristic trembling way; he showed the usual surprised facial expression associated with this type of investigation when the conscious mind does not expect the answer given by the ideodynamic response. A single incident was accessed by appropriate questions and localized between the ages of six and seven years in the summer and during the morning. At this moment, the subject's face indicated recognition and he said, "Now I know! My parents dressed me for a shopping trip to town but they took me to a doctor's office instead. He clapped an ether mask on my face while I struggled to get away. It was the same feeling!"

He was then asked to let his fingers answer the question, "Can you now use hypnosis comfortably without being reminded of that incident?" His finger answered yes. He went comfortably into hypnosis, and thereafter found himself comfortable working with his patients.

A hypnotic trance can be induced by stroking the body. This was the method of the old mesmerists, and it is used by mammals licking their young. In addition, hypnosis can be produced by the sudden appearance of great danger, by disorientation during a fall, or by being dropped suddenly from a surgical carriage into bed. It can be produced by a sudden blow to the face or neck, by hyperventilation, and by monotonous lulling sounds. A trance approaching the suspended animation of Hindu and Yoga religious men may be produced by suddenly dropping an unsuspecting subject a few inches, as he allows himself to be slowly lowered from a sitting to a recumbent position. These individuals may show all the appearances of shock. These signs, however, are always associated with a bradycardia in this deep trance state. The subject, although appearing quite unconscious, is in complete contact with the hypnotist and will quickly awaken on request. An identical phenomenon will occur sometimes after cyclopropane anesthesia.

The deep trance state is seen with patients after other forms of anesthesia. It usually occurs when an anesthetized patient is suddenly dropped or is shifted abruptly during positioning on the operating table. Blood pressure, pulse, and respiration will return to normal with calm, authoritative directions, but it is far better to explain to the seemingly insensate anesthetized patient what is going to be done before moving him. Fear, released by previous conditioning or surprised comments of worried surgical attendants, can convert such a defensive trance state into true surgical shock, or something worse.

Psychosomatic Kidney Failure and Indirect Suggestion

A urologist, dating his prodromal conditioning for gastric ulcer to his infantile distress over assumed rejection by his mother when she was too ill to nurse, overheard his surgeon's comments on the suspicious appearance of the lesion at the operating table.

Knowing that patients in uremia seem to die painlessly, he decided to die by shutting off his kidneys. Anuria was complete during four days until he heard the resident physician inform his surgeon in the hall outside his door that the pathology report was all right. He put out 30 cc. of urine in the next 20 minutes and thereafter functioned normally.

Box 17 presents the psychosomatic basis of such kidney failure, which could be correlated by the indirect suggestion of overhearing that "the pathology report was all right."

Bleeding Control Via Ideodynamic Questioning Methods and Indirect Suggestion

The wife of an obstetrician was being interviewed in hypnosis to discover, if possible, the cause for severe migrane headaches dating from the time of hysterectomy after the birth of her third child. It was learned that she had always wanted a large family, but her husband had urged surgery because of her continued vomiting during pregnancy and the fact that she had nearly expired from hemorrhage during delivery of the third child. It was decided to explore the emotional reactions to the pregnancy, and particularly the period of anesthesia for the delivery and the hysterectomy, in the search for misunderstandings possibly causing the headaches.

She was asked to review the delivery at an unconscious level and signal with a finger when she came to some part of that experience which might, in some way, have been related to the onset of serious bleeding. After about 20 seconds, she signaled with her finger that she had selected some phase of the anesthesia period. She was asked to bring the memory to a verbal level, if she thought it still pertinent. A moment later she said, "George is asking my obstetrician if I'm all right. He sounds worried. George is an obstetrician. There must be something wrong with me." Further questioning revealed that there had been no heavy bleeding until this moment. Her husband verified this point.

She was then asked to come up to the moment when the bleeding stopped, and to signal if any thought came to her mind unconsciously that

BOX 17: PEPTIDES IN THE PSYCHOSOMATICS OF SURGERY: ANGIOTENSIN IN BLOOD FLOW, CARDIAC, RESPIRATORY AND KIDNEY FUNCTION

The peptides angiotensin I and II may be common indicating factors in the seemingly unrelated psychosomatic aspects of hemorrhage, cardiac and kidney failure, and respiratory collapse in surgical emergencies. It is now known (Vander, Sherman, & Luciano, 1985) that specialized cells lining the small blood vessels (arterioles) of the kidneys synthesize the enzyme *renin* and secrete it into the blood. Renin splits off the small peptide *angiotensin I* from the larger blood plasma protein *angiotensinogen*. The lung capillary endothelium then converts angiotensin I into angiotensin II as blood flows through the lungs. Angiotensin II, in turn, stimulates the adrenal cortex to secrete aldosterone. Aldosterone is a factor in the regulation of sodium reabsorption and water balance by the kidneys and the blood pressure regulating reflexes that influence cardiac output and possible cardiac failure. The role of angiotensin II as one of the biochemical mediators of emotion is discussed by Pert (Pert et al., 1985, p. 823s) as follows:

Neuropeptides as the biochemicals of emotion. Charles Darwin assumed that the physiologic basis of emotions — so invariant and identifiable in humans of all cultures as well as other primates — would one day be understood. The striking patterns of neuropeptide receptor distribution in mood-regulating areas of brain, as well as their role in mediating communication throughout the whole organism, makes neuropeptides the obvious candidates for the biochemical mediation of emotion. Does each neuropeptide bias information processing uniquely when occupying receptors at nodal points within the brain and body? If so, each unique neuropeptide's "tone" might produce a typical mood state. The opiate peptides clearly mediate a state of intensely reinforcing pleasure, while substance P release has been associated with pain and indeed has a reciprocal relationship with opiatergic neurons at most levels of the neuroaxis. Neuroinjections of the neuropeptide angiotensin II through narrow cannulae implanted precisely in the angiotensin receptor-rich subfornical organ of rat brain induces drinking behavior in seconds, while angiotensin receptors in the kidney with the identical structure-activity relationship of those in brain apparently mediate retention of water from the kidney's collecting tubules. Thus, enhanced angiotensinergic tone appears associated with thirst and the conservation of water at several levels in the whole organism.

The multiple roles of information substances such as angiotensin I and II on many foci of mind-body homeostasis and emotion suggest that we will need to develop computer models to study their complex interactions in normal and stress situations.

might help us understand the reason for its cessation. She signaled within a few seconds and stated, "It is when my anesthetist says, 'She's O.K. now.' That is right after the blood transfusion has been started."

Now the subject was asked to review the entire experience to make whatever changes were necessary to let her have a simple delivery with a minimum of bleeding. She signaled the start of the anesthetic and then signaled a thought. "I believe there would have been no bleeding," she said, "if my husband had not been in that room. I knew he was concerned about me because I was his wife, but, when he sounded worried, it frightened me because I thought of him as a specialist in obstetrics."

We have only begun to understand the reasons for surgical hemorrhage and the simple means of verbal comfort and reassurance which can control threatening hemorrhage, even when we have not the time or energy to search out all the possible minutae of chemical and physical changes which accompany the threats causing such hemorrhage. The role of the peptide messenger molecule-receptor systems involving angiotensin I and II, as well as other factors mediating blood flow and clotting, which are now understood well enough for systematic investigation by ideodynamic signaling methods, are outlined in Box 17.

Although we know that patients fearful of death will often die if forced into surgery, we have not yet attempted to discover what fears of death are too deeply repressed to be expressed verbally. Dohan (Dohan et al., 1960) and others have shown us that surgeons' answers to questions of patients about length of hospital stay and duration of convalescence show an 80% correlation with patient performance. As mentioned previously, unconscious feelings of guilt and identification can kill; we should know how to discover them.

Misunderstanding Causing Disturbed Induction into Anesthesia

The patient had accepted the endotracheal catheter without distress but she became cyanotic, began bucking, and then fought her way up from a surgical plane of anesthesia. Asked in hypnosis to go over this experience at an unconsious level, signaling the induction with one finger and any disturbing stimulus with another, she gave the "disturbed" signal and stated, "I felt perfectly comfortable until I heard the doctor ask the anesthetist, 'Is she ready now?' I knew I could hear and I guess I thought I would feel pain. I wanted to tell them I was not ready but I could not get the words out."

This is only one of many reports from patients who have not been instructed before anesthesia that the awareness of pain is the first perception to be lost. This is the first lesson given to physicians and dentists using hypnosis for the relief of pain. They are instructed to inform patients that they may feel pressure or touch but there will be no sense of pain. Patients undergoing surgery under general anesthesia will respond very well to the explanation that, when they realize how little anesthetic is needed to free them from any sense of pain, they can use less chemical anesthetic and feel like healthy human beings much sooner after surgery. When they know that the anesthesiologist is trained to know just when the analgesia level is reached, and that his judgment can be trusted, then they can be instructed as to what to do with their other perceptions. For example, they could be instructed to send their imaginations out on a picnic which they had enjoyed several years ago, to experience every minute of that time, and to pay absolutely no attention to anything pertaining to the day of operation unless their help is needed. At such a time, they will be addressed by the first name (Cheek, 1960b). Reasons for doing this to diminish tissue reactions to surgery are always acceptable to patients.

Misunderstanding Causing Excitement-Stage Behavior During Surgical Plane Anesthesia

A menopausal woman under general anesthesia for hysteromyomectomy was well relaxed and breathing at the rate of 24 per minute with a pulse rate of 86. The surgeon was gently palpating the freely movable uterus. He commented, "This is an easy one, the kind we used to turn over to the assistant resident." Immediately after this statement the patient's pulse rate accelerated, she held an inspiration, tightened the abdominal muscles, and forced most of the ileum out of the incision. The first assistant said, "Bob, you better explain to her that you are really going to do the operation yourself."

The abdominal muscles relaxed, the respiration recommenced, and the ileum sucked back into the abdominal cavity. There had been no traction on the uterus; the anesthesiologist had made no change in the anesthetic and had given no muscle relaxant.

Importance of Subjective Reports on Anesthesia

These are incomplete reports. There are probably other factors which could have influenced behavior, but similar subjective evaluations by patients might be helpful in avoiding anesthetic complications in future anesthetic or surgical experiences with the same patient. If repeated observations with many patients showed constantly recurring phenomena under recurring similar circumstances, we might use constantly repeated recommendations of many patients to help us prevent accidents in our operating and recovery rooms. More clinical cases documenting the relationships between emotional stress and the psychophysiological emergencies experienced by the critically ill will be presented in the next chapter.

Psychophysiological adaptations to stress generally occur at a level of thought too deep to be reached by ordinary psychologic investigation. With newer techniques of ideodynamic questioning in hypnosis, it is possible to investigate the subjective reactions of patients who have survived surgical and anesthetic complications.

We are now in a position to understand some of the psychologic factors contributing to potentially fatal accidents. The exploration of cardiac arrest, hemorrhage, and respiratory collapse are now open for productive psychiatric research. Such research might profitably explore the role of the angiotensin peptides in mediating the psychosomatic aspects of surgical emergencies.

11

Mind-Body Healing with the Critically Ill

Until 1935 physicians relied heavily on God and the deep-seated, instinctive will of patients to survive grave threats to life. Since the advent of sulfonamides, antibiotics, corticoids, blood banks, biologic monitoring devices, intensive care units, and computers, there has been a tendency to forget the patient. This is a plea for recognition of the fact that patients are people who can be frightened to death, condemned to long hospitalization, or helped to overcome great odds according to the quality of information they receive from their attendants.

Frightened people need no formal induction of hypnosis; they are already in hypnosis by the time we see them. Their understandings are childlike and literal.* Their external appearance of apathy may mislead us into careless talking or terrifyingly silent activity. We should prepare carefully for treatment of the critically ill. Their subjective thinking makes them wonderfully responsive to helpful suggestions; it also makes them vulnerable to harmful ones. In critical illness the forces of guilt, self-punishment, and negative identifications may overpower the will to survive. Better recognition and use of spontaneously occurring trance behavior can make an important, beneficent difference in the experience of the critically ill.

Psychiatrically oriented nurses and physicians know that fever can be psychogenic in infants (Bakwin, 1944). There is a considerable literature dealing with such fevers in adults as collected by Dunbar (1954). Professional, intelligent, highly trained men and women in teaching institutions, however, often ignore the role of pyramiding child-like fears and night terrors in their treatment of critically ill adult patients.

An example of this was the case of a 23-year-old unmarried woman who ran a peculiar, intermittent fever and tachycardia for nearly three weeks after a therapeutic abortion by amniocentesis and saline replacement. She was depressed and under psychiatric care when she entered the hospital. Peculiarity of the febrile response was that the pulse rate did not seem to fit the degree of fever. Her white count remained relatively low. When a uter-

*See Section 2 of Volume III in Erickson, 1980a, for a discussion of literalism in hypnosis.

179

ine culture grew anaerobic streptoccocus, it was decided she was getting intermittent showers of bacteria. Scores of millions of units of aqueous penicillin G. were given intravenously without changing the picture. Clearly this was a resistant organism that might then respond to something else. Ampicillin and Kefalin were used, but the patient became visibly worse and the peculiar recurring fever continued. It was then thought that there must be infected decidua in the uterus to be curetted. She went into shock after this operation under general anesthesia. She awakened in the intensive care unit with a catheter in her neck to measure central venous pressure. Blood, corticoids, and more consultation were followed by signs and x-ray findings compatible with pelvic phlebo-thrombosis and pulmonary emboli. Hysterectomy, pelvic vein ligation, and use of heparin were discussed at length by the consultants.

The patient suddenly got well either because of the heparin or the threat that she might lose her uterus. One consultant decided her supportive therapy had improved her immune responses to the supposed organism; another thought she might just have decided she could make it in spite of all her medical attention.

Some of the nurses who knew this patient wondered if the original fever could have been caused by fear and guilt. They commented on brief remissions coinciding with any treatment offered with apparent confidence that it would help. They noted that the condition of the patient worsened when consultants indicated lack of confidence in a pro-tem working diagnosis.

Such problems are frequent in modern hospitals. We can only speculate on factors and effects in this one. Let us consider some definitions of critical illness and the way critically ill patients behave. What do we know about emotion creating the picture of critical illness and its role in causing death? What do such people need to help them recover? We can never be sure of what makes people get well from any kind of illness or injury, because there are too many factors at work. We can make more educated guesses when we find a patient who does consistently poorly with all standard methods of treatment but then makes an abrupt recovery. We can obtain significant information when we review the sequences of illness at an ideodynamic level of awareness in light hypnosis. We pay careful attention to the ideodynamic signal indicating the moment the patient recognizes at an unconscious level that recovery is taking place. *If this occurs after addition of a drug or some physical treatment, we must conclude that the treatment gets the credit. If the change occurs after a change of subjective attitude and before the treatment, we should credit the patient rather than the drug or physical treatment.* Methods of applying this approach will be mentioned here in the case reports and presented in greater detail in the handbook by Cheek and LeCron (1968).

A critically ill person is any person who fits the following categories:

1. Unconscious from trauma, infection, endogenous toxic substances, or general anesthesia.
2. Seemingly unconscious due to spontaneous trance state or "suspended animation" ("vampire state" of Hudson).
3. Not responding well to medical, surgical, or spiritual treatment.
4. Running a constant or intermittent "unexplained fever" or hearing the ominous sounding initials "F-U-O," meaning "fever of unexplained origin."
5. Awakening from unconsciousness breathing through a tracheostomy, receiving a blood transfusion, or finding an unexplained catheter emerging from the side of the neck to measure central venous pressure.
6. Profuse bleeding from any body orifice, any cause.
7. Conscious but unable to move or unable to coordinate movements of extremities.
8. Conscious but unable to see or unable to hear.

People in the above categories may look as though they do not care about their surroundings but such people always care. They may appear deaf to conversation. If they had intact hearing to begin with, they will be hearing what they consider meaningful and may be able to do so with more acuity than is normal for them.

They are peculiarly vulnerable to psychic insult, as may occur when attendants work without talking to them.

Their understandings are childlike and literal. They may misunderstand meaning of words, facial expressions, and voice tones which would be correctly understood by them when healthy or conscious.

Usually they have had no prior experience with this type of emergency and are therefore highly vulnerable to potentially lethal panic.

Emotion and Death

Unconscious, sick and frightened animals do poorly or may die as a result of their emotional reactions to environment. Some species of bird die within seconds of unexpected handling by humans. Richter (1957) has told of wild rats which he studied during World War II. Many of these died while being held for clipping of their whiskers. With careful habituation they could survive this process but would die a sudden, cardiac arrest–type of death in the panic of trying to escape from a whirlpool tank. At autopsy their lungs showed no evidence of water, as would be the case if they had drowned in exhaustion. Once having been removed from the tank at the end of a working day, the surviving rats apparently took on an element of hope. If replaced later in the tank, they would swim much longer. If they died, it was due to exhaustion and drowning.

Meerloo (1950) has commented on the silent panic that killed 200 of 600 people in a London bomb shelter in the spring of 1943. A bomb exploding near the shelter cut off the supply of electricity to the lights and exhaust fans. Apparently someone stumbled on a stairway in the silence that followed. A wave of silent, motionless panic swept through the shelter. There was no struggle. Autopsy showed no evident cause of death. Hyperactivity of the vagal reflex to the heart is the most logical explanation for this tragedy.

Walter Cannon (1957) has reported instances where expectancy of death brought about the expected result in primitive people. Death could be prevented when the medicine man removed the curse. We might wonder whether similar things can happen to civilized people. I know of a nurse in the Hawaiian Islands who died of ileus on the fifth anniversary of her curative surgery for breast cancer. Her sister, also a nurse, had tried to change the unreasoning conviction that five-year-survival meant exactly what it said. It seemed probable that this woman had overheard a discussion on this matter while she was under the influence of her general anesthetic. There was no evidence of cancer at autopsy.

Hopeless telling of the truth to a patient with cancer can kill. Rarely, it might evoke a fighting will to live. Evasion of the truth in communicating with cancer patients is a greater evil because it is too easy for such patients to see hopelessness in the eyes and words of relatives. They are denied the helpful strength of hope as well as the fighting response to challenge.

Dreams and Disease

Freud believed that organic disease often made itself known in dreams before it was clinically recognizable. Although this is a reasonable speculation, there is also the possibility that thoughts derived from daytime experiences may produce organic disease during the intensely vivid and seemingly real reliving of suggested trouble during dreams and thought processes occurring at deeper than REM phases of sleep (Cheek, 1963). Elsewhere I have discussed this matter and the means of gathering evidence in a chapter on sleep and in relation to some complications in pregnancy (Cheek, & LeCron, 1968).

Jake Belogorsky, M.D., of Los Gatos, California has told me of a man who died of massive hemorrhage from spontaneous rupture of his spleen. All physical findings pointed to a lesion within the thoracic cage. None of the consulting experts paid attention to the seemingly casual announcement by the man that he had dreamed on the night before admission that he was bleeding from a ruptured spleen. The man was a laborer with no knowledge of anatomy. He had received no injury to his abdomen; he had had neither mononucleosis nor leukemia, in which spontaneous splenic rupture can occur. He had felt well when he went to bed. It was a shock to the attending physician, the cardiologist, internist, and surgeon when autopsy proved that the unfortunate patient had been correct. Did he have foreknowledge of an already subclinical process during sleep, or did fear created by the dream put too great a burden on his engorged spleen?

Pseudo-Death and Suggestions for Recovery from Coma

Hudson (1893) has said that chronically ill patients become hypersuggestible and may mimic all the signs of death when their relatives and medical attendants give up hope. He interviewed several people who had been revived by someone speaking helpfully to them. One young woman had been pronounced dead by six medical attendants. She remained in a state of suspended animation for 14 days while relatives converged for the funeral. On this day the little brother, not accepting the reality of her death, cried "What do you want, sister?" Her mouth moved, asking faintly for water. She revived and lived out a normal span of life.

In the days before embalming, pseudo-death was rather common. A church yard in Bordeaux, France contained well-preserved contorted bodies exhumed after nearly 200 years in the arsenic-bearing earth. There is the grisly story of Thomas à Kempis, author of *The Imitation of Christ* in the 15th century, who missed being canonized as a saint in the Roman Catholic Church because his crypt clearly showed evidence of his struggle to get out. Decision not to canonize him hinged upon his unsaintly efforts to save his life after burial. Even today we find evidence of this phenomenon in news reports. One of these, from a Reuters dispatch to the *San Francisco Chronicle* of October 3, 1961, is an example:

Caracas: When grave-diggers shoveled the first spadefuls of earth into a grave in the village cemetery at Pecaya, Venezuela, the "dead" man, Roberto Rodriguez, victim of a heart attack, burst open the lid of the coffin, scrambled out of the grave and ran home shouting and swearing. His mother-in-law, who was standing at the graveside, dropped dead from shock.

That the ramifications of hopelessness and fear could fall short of death certainly suggests itself from these and other experiences. Quackenbos (1908), a physician-hypnotherapist of New York City, reports an interesting example:

In June, 1905, the author was called to the bedside of a young woman who, during the month preceding, had passed through a series of infections culminating in pneumonia. Her condition equivalented a death-sentence. The temperature had risen to $107\frac{1}{2}$, the pulse to 160, the respiration to 60, and the attending physicians had withdrawn from the case with the statement that she could live two hours. The patient had been unconscious for weeks. . . . When I entered the room she was unconscious, her eyes were turned up so that only the white, sclerotic coats were visible; she was from a medical point of view beyond the pale of hope.

As I looked at the girl, an inspiration came to me. I took her by the hand, learned her first name from the nurse, and said with great incisiveness: "Adele! Where are you going? You cannot die! Come back, you have work to do on earth. Come back at once!" In answer to the summons, the upturned eyes resumed their natural angle and became riveted on mine. The voice that had for days uttered only the ravings of a delirium now spoke coherently, "It is too late," it murmured.

"It is not too late; stay where you are. Assume immediate control of your physical functions, and get well. You are going to recover," . . . all this in an imperative, forceful tone. The directions were immediately accepted and implicitly followed. A change for the better supervened. Gradually the mental mist cleared away, the physical strength returned, and today the young lady is perfectly well, filling an important position in the musical world.

Those who do not understand the childlike simplicity and literalness of understanding among critically ill patients might be amused by the wording of these ideodynamic commands by Quackenbos. He was a wise man, strongly influenced by the concepts of Hudson, whom he quotes as a reference in his interesting book.

Treating the Critically Ill

As with all situations involving danger, critically ill patients have certain requirements for achieving a constructive goal:

1. *Preparation.* There should have been prior experience with a similar threat, or there should have been some briefing on what dangers to expect.
2. *Current instruction.* Patients should be kept aware that something helpful is being done; their minds should be kept occupied with external matters as much as is possible. Telling them the intended purpose of therapeutic measures helps to put them in the role of an assistant rather than in the role of victim.
3. *Briefing on expectations for the future.* Discussion of what you expect patients to do in the future tacitly implies that you believe things will turn out satisfactorily. We should not concern ourselves with fears that we may be wrong in sounding hopeful about the future. Outlining simple, sequential goals may stop the processes leading to shock, massive thrombosis, or exsanguinating hemorrhage.

It is seldom possible for a person to have had prior experience with a critical illness. It is a natural trait for human beings to avoid thoughts about dangerous illness or injury as applying to them personally. Bad things always happen to other people. For this reason, we should consider all critically ill patients as unprepared for their trouble and presently on the edge of panic. They need all we can offer.

Objective and Subjective Thinking During Emergencies

Hudson referred to *subjective thinking* with patterned responses of unconscious behavior as opposed to *objective thinking* of the conscious mind. Breuer was probably the first to observe what he called "hypnoid" experiences capable of crystalizing hysterical behavior. A simple induction of hypnosis might evoke a total or nearly total reliving of a traumatic experience. I have pointed out this phenomenon (Cheek & LeCron, 1968, p. 225) as a major factor in unconscious resistance to induction of hypnosis, and have repeatedly emphasized the dangers of "flash-back" behavior during the unconsciousness of sleep and of general anesthesia.

The discriminative use of experience in deciding a course of action is essentially the product of reason. This is a cortical activity involving the highest and most recently acquired parts of the brain. This virtue, the power of reason, is the first to be pushed aside in acute emergencies. From one standpoint of teleology, this exclusion of cortical reasoning may save time in situations where thinking about which course to take might be fatal. A cat cannot wonder whether to sit still, climb a tree, or run into the bushes when approached by an enthusiastic dog. It is likely to act out the most recent behavior that ended in safety after a similar threat. The teleology breaks down when its reflexly chosen avenue is not there.

The power of reason is gainfully used *after* we have escaped from danger and have had a chance to think about the experience. Then we weigh the factors involved, decide what should have been done better, and what mistakes to avoid in the future. We may tell others about it and profit from their knowledge of similar experiences. These preliminary steps are followed by multiple unconscious reviews in daytime ruminations and nocturnal dreams.

Eventually several agglomerations of appropriate responses are set aside and preserved in unconscious limbo for immediate recall in future moments of critical need. Some football philosopher has said, "There is no instant replay in the football game of life." He was referring to the chance of doing something over again in a better way. There are plenty of instant replays of potentially dangerous and unproductive actions during life when we are frightened or unconscious and have pushed aside our ability to think in a conscious, reasoning way.

We react well in an emergency when we have rehearsed a situation and its appropriate response, or are familiar with the general problem and have had time to think of various possible responses. We panic when we run out of things to do in an emergency. We may "freeze" in a hibernating-like state of inaction, or we may expend our energy in misdirected wild activity.

Direct Suggestions in Emergencies with the Critically Ill

1. The critically ill are already in a state of hypnosis. Learn to recognize and utilize the spontaneous expressions of hypnotic behavior.
2. Avoid conversation and actions that might suggest pessimism. Suggest hope and optimism, but do so sincerely since the threatened human is canny in recognizing reassurance that is phony.
3. Collect your thoughts and marshal a plan of action before touching or speaking directly to the patient. You may be breathless in your hurry to get to the patient; you may not know exactly what to do. Take a few moments to give directions to bystanders. Your voice will be confident with them because you know more than they do. The quality of your voice will then give confidence to the patient in accepting reassurance from you. You also have gained time to control the expressions of your haste.
4. Tell the patient what has happened and that he will be all right. Outline what you are doing now and what your reason is for so doing. This implies that you respect his knowledge and his ability to understand your actions. Allow time to outline what steps to take as you plan for the patient tomorrow and in the future. There is no better reassurance than the tacit suggestion that you expect a future for which to plan.

   Instruction and promise of a future should be given to unconscious people, even when they show no pupillary reflex to light. Congratulate the unconscious person for being so relaxed, and tell him specifically how long you expect him to remain in this relaxed state before awakening with feelings of hunger and thoughts of food.
5. Give medication for pain if possible. This is a form of communication showing that you are interested in taking constructive action. Tell him what you are giving and for what purpose. The patient will know that it takes a little time before medication works; he will be able to focus attention better on your actions during the interval. The time taken in giving an injection allows you time to collect your thoughts and control any outward signs of alarm.
6. If he is able to talk, get the patient talking about work, hobbies or his family. The human mind can be taught to ignore pain and sources of shock if it is directed to concern itself with times and places where pain and fear did not exist.

Box 18 contains a concise summary of direct healing suggestions that can be given during emergency situations.

BOX 18: DIRECT HEALING SUGGESTIONS IN EMERGENCIES

All injured, frightened, hemorrhaging, shocked, and unconscious people may be considered critically ill. They enter a hypnotic state spontaneously and need no formal induction.

1. *Accessing healing sources*
   a. Outline simply and briefly what you are going to do for them *now*.
   b. Designate a finger (by touching it lightly) to lift all by itself when the inner healing source (mind, brain, etc.) carries out the following:
   c. **"Your inner healing source can let this finger lift when the bleeding (and/or pain, etc.) has been turned down by half."**
   d. **"That finger can lift again when your comfort can continue getting better and better in every way."**

2. *Therapeutic facilitation*
   a. **"Your inner mind knows exactly what it needs to do to continue recovery by returning your blood pressure (or whatever) to normal. It can lift a finger to indicate that healing is continuing now all by itself."**
   b. Congratulate the patient for being so relaxed and doing so well in allowing the healing to take place.
   c. Outline a series of steps (signs) by which the healing process will continue in the immediate future.

3. *Ratification with posthypnotic suggestion*
   "You will feel yourself going into a deep, comfortable sleep for four hours and then awaken feeling refreshed and alert with a good appetite." (Appropriate suggestions for each patient's particular situation are added at this point.)

Examples of Constructive Communication During Critical Illness

FEVER AND APPARENT PERITONITIS FOLLOWING ILLEGAL ABORTION

A 22-year-old, unmarried German woman was seen at her boarding house approximately ten hours after undergoing a uterine curettage in a border city of Mexico adjacent to California. Her roommate, at approximately the same stage of pregnancy, had gone to the same abortionist on the same day.

She was brushing her hair in preparation for going out to dinner with her fiancé; her only concern was for the German woman, whose fiancé had deserted her on learning of the pregnancy.

The patient was in great distress. She was lying on a sofa with her legs flexed and her hands pressing against the lower abdomen. Her temperature was 100.4, pulse rate 96, and respiratory rate 24. Her abdomen was rigid and there was definite rebound tenderness over the entire lower abdomen. She was obviously depressed over her need for having the abortion. Her parents in Germany did not know about it. She was apprehensive about the possibility that I would report her to the police. She did not have money for hospitalization and did not know she could have emergency care at the local county hospital, if necessary.

The first step in communication was to assure her that I would not be reporting her to the police. Abortions performed in other countries do not fall under police jurisdiction. I knew the abortionist by reputation. His work was always competent, as she could see by results with her happier and more secure roommate. I added my conviction that time would bring about a change in our laws that would permit women to decide for themselves whether or not to carry a pregnancy; that our mental hospitals are full of unhappy adults who were unwanted babies.

I told her she would have to learn a little about relaxing now in order to let the medicine I intended giving her to get into the tissues where it might be needed. **She was told to let her hands relax and have the right index finger lift unconsciously when her unconscious mind had relaxed every muscle in her abdomen.** She did not think this would work, but was surprised a few minutes later when the finger started to tremble and lift. **Next she was asked to have the same finger lift when all the pain was gone.** This took about 80 seconds to accomplish. Tenderness and rebound tenderness were gone within 30 minutes of initial examination. Her temperature was 98, pulse rate 84, and respiration 16 by the time I gave her the shot of penicillin she expected. She was back at work the next day.

In this case the entire picture may have been emotional, but my experience with criminal abortion cases has made me respect the role of fear, depression, and guilt in lowering resistance to pathogenic organisms within the bowel and vagina. This was the third instance of abrupt termination of fever and pain in an atmosphere of uncritical acceptance rather than punitive overtreatment.

HEMMORHAGE AND SEPTIC COURSE FOLLOWING CESAREAN SECTION
2/1/62 TO 2/12/62

It was my turn as obstetrical consultant in a San Francisco hospital, and it was my first day on this service. I was called to the delivery room by a general practitioner because his 27-year-old nulliparous Mexican patient was hemorrhaging during an attempted forceps delivery under spinal anesthesia. There were six student nurses present when I arrived, and the doctor was greatly distressed. The patient, who could speak no English, was frightened. Examination showed that the cervix was incompletely dilated. The due date of the patient was four weeks past and the baby seemed very large.

I told the doctor that I would like to return the patient to her room and give her another couple hours trial of labor. There was no progress during this time. Since the doctor did not know me, I asked another consultant to perform the cesarean delivery, a man that the doctor knew and trusted. An 11 lb. 5 oz., healthy female infant was delivered without difficulty through a transverse uterine incision. A unit of blood was given the patient after surgery. Her temperature was 101.3 and pulse rate 100, four hours postoperatively. The baby developed a staphylococcus pyoderma but recovered with active chemotherapy.

At this stage we learned that the husband had become worried as time had passed beyond her expected date of delivery. His first wife had died because of obstetrical complications. He had been doing vaginal examinations for 14 days before his wife had gone into labor. We felt this might have been reason for the complications that followed.

The patient was given 1.2 million units of penicillin per day intramuscularly and 4 grams of Gantrisin per day. In spite of this, her temperature fluctuated between 98.6 and 100.4, with a peak of 103.8 on the third postoperative day. Blood cultures were negative. Uterine culture grew E. coli and anaerobic streptococcus. Penicillin was stopped on day five. Achromycin, 500 mg. every four hours was started on day six, 500 mg. of Chloromycetin every four hours with one gram of Streptomycin every four hours were given on day seven, but her fever continued with a range of 99.8 to 103 and her pulse rate averaged 99. Her abdomen was distended, her appetite was poor, and she complained of left lower quadrant pain. A mass approximately 8 cms. in diameter appeared in the left lower quadrant. An intravenous pyelogram showed good function and no evidence of obstruction of the left urinary system.

On the tenth postoperative day she was transferred from private care to the teaching service under my direction. The perceptive, morning charge nurse on the floor drew me aside and said, "Doctor Cheek, everybody has been going in and out of her room without explaining anything to her. I think you could help her get well if you would just talk to her."

I answered that I would be glad to talk with her but, unfortunately, I could not speak Spanish. A bilingual Mexican nurse solved the problem. She came to see the patient with me and translated the following remarks: "You are having much pain. When you are in pain, your muscles are held very tightly in your abdomen. The medicine we are giving you is very good, but it cannot get to the place where there is infection because your muscles are too tight. Your baby had an infection also, but she is well now. I want you to relax your muscles so that the medicine can make you well. Then you can go home with your baby."

The patient smiled as the words were translated. She seemed to accept my explanation for her failure to get well. I continued: "When you are in a beautiful place where you have nothing to do, your muscles in your neck, shoulders, and abdomen are relaxed. Please tell Celie (the aide) where you have been in such a place."

I heard the patient say, "Acapulco." The aide translated my words in about the same tempo as I continued speaking: "Now, put yourself there on the beach. You have nothing to do but enjoy the warmth of the sun. Listen to the sound of the waves breaking on the beach. Feel the warmth of the sun on your body. Numbers help you to relax even more. The more you relax, the quicker the medicine we give you will make you well."

I counted; the numbers were translated. The patient drifted into a moderately deep trance state. She was asked to have a finger lift when she had turned off all the pain in her abdomen. After about three minutes the finger lifted in the usual trembling, intermittent way. We left her sleeping. Two hours later her temperature was 98.6; her pulse rate remained at 90 until the next day when it dropped to 76. Within 24 hours the abdominal mass had disappeared. It was our assumption that the mass must have been a hematoma in the left broad ligament of the uterus.

A second translated interview took place two days later. At this time finger signals were set up for "Yes," "No," and "I-don't-want-to-answer." I asked, "When I came into the delivery room at the time you were bleeding, were you afraid in any way?" Her head shook from side to side and she answered, "No." She did not notice that her yes finger was lifting at the same time to contradict.

"Let a thought come to you to say why you might have been frightened. When you know what it is, your yes finger will pull up. As it lifts, you can tell us what the thought is."

She came out of hypnosis to say, "My sister in Mexico died in labor 15 years ago; the baby was too big."

"When I come in to see you the first time in the delivery room, are you thinking that your situation is something similar to your sister's?"

Her head again shook as she verbally answered, "No," but her yes finger was lifting as she spoke. She was surprised at the finger movement. Now she was told to relax a little more, and to send her thoughts forward to Christmas next year when she would be home with her baby and her husband. Her finger soon indicated achievement of that goal. She was then asked to go even further into the future and see the easy delivery of her next child. There was some delay, followed by a no signal. She explained that her doctor had warned her not to have another baby. She indicated a yes when I asked if her inner mind knew she could have a second baby perfectly safely.

Her course was afebrile from the time of her first interview. Eighteen months later she delivered her second child, a normal male infant, without incident.

No formal induction of hypnosis was used with this patient. She was ready for help and quickly accepted each suggestion. Discovery that she had been unconsciously identifying herself with her sister and her husband's first wife helped to fortify the suggestions given her. She had not realized the strength of her conscious denial of the possibility that she might die in the course of labor. This denial could easily explain the long delay of the birth and the enormous size of her baby. Frightened patients can hold back labor.

HEMORRHAGE AND SHOCK ASSOCIATED WITH GUILT

A 42-year-old single woman was first seen at the request of her internist at 6:30 A.M., New Year's morning. The doctor had told me that the patient had been found unconscious on the living room floor in a pool of blood. Her last pelvic examination had been done about four months earlier and had revealed no abnormalities.

The ambulance crew was wheeling the patient down the corridor toward the emergency room when I arrived. She appeared to be unconscious, her eyes were closed, her skin cold and mottled in appearance. Her respiration was shallow and rapid, her pulse rate 140.

I leaned over her as they moved her along the hall and asked, "Have you been under any emotional stress lately?" This is always a safe opening remark to an unconscious patient in apparent shock.

She opened her eyes and answered feebly, "Oh, I'm so ashamed. I've been going with my friend now for two years, and I had intercourse with him last night."

I laughed and said, "For goodness sakes, you are a big girl now. Why did you wait so long?"

A little color came into her cheeks, and she smiled momentarily before begging me not to tell her roommate what she had just revealed. Her blood pressure was 120/82 by the time she was on the examining table; her pulse rate had dropped to 100.

An estimated 250 cc. of blood saturated the bath towel between her legs and another 75 gm. of blood clot was pushed out of her vagina. The ambulance crew estimated approximately 200 cc. of blood on the floor of the patient's apartment. As I inserted a speculum to see where the bleeding was coming from, there was a massive flow of fresh blood that obscured the field. It seemed logical that there must be a deep vaginal laceration, but I could not swab away the blood fast enough to visualize the vaginal vault.

I stood up to make clear that I was addressing her when I spoke. "Look up there at that spot on the ceiling," I said, "and stop that bleeding because I can't see what I am doing." She looked up at the ceiling. Her facial expression smoothed out as she went into a hypnotic state. I added, "Now close your eyes, but keep your attention on the spot and continue to relax your scalp, neck, and shoulders."

As I sat down, the bleeding quickly diminished. It stopped within the space of 60 seconds. Two small lacerations were visible now in the right fornix. I removed the speculum and used a sterile glove to palpate the depth of the lacerations. This manipulation did not cause any more bleeding. I awakened the patient and then inserted the speculum again to decide whether sutures were necessary in the vagina. A second episode of profuse hemorrhage occurred just as the speculum was inserted. Again the patient was told to look at the ceiling and to stop the bleeding. She entered hypnosis again as she did so. It took approximately 60 seconds for the brisk bleeding to stop this time. It was not necessary to suture the lacerations. Some oxycel was placed against them and the patient was admitted to a ward room for observation overnight.

A week later I had a chance to talk with the patient in some detail, and learned that both she and her roommate were very inhibited and antagonistic toward males. An interval of 20 minutes had occurred between the sexual experience and the onset of profuse bleeding. The bleeding occurred only when the patient started thinking about the reaction her roommate might have in case the roommate discovered what had happened.

Blood Flow in Acute and Chronic Illness

The relationship between hemorrhage and emotion has been considered in relation to dreams (Cheek, 1963). John Hunter observed it in relation to fluid blood after death from trauma. Yudine (1937) rediscovered the effect of great fear in causing fibrinolysis of blood after death and allowing use of cadaver blood for blood replacement after massive hemorrhage. McKay (1965) has discussed the role of great stress in disseminated intravascular coagulation of blood. MacFarlane and Biggs (1946) have wondered about the possibility of sublethal emotion causing increase in circulating fibrinolysins resulting in surgical and postoperative hemorrhage. The matter of accelerated tendency for thrombosis under stress has been discussed by Schneider (1951).

Recently, Banks (1985) has described a useful approach to using direct and indirect hypnotic suggestion to control bleeding during routine examinations requiring angiography (x-ray studies of blood vessels). On the basis of an extensive review of the mind-body healing literature, Barber (1984) has hypothesized that hypnosis operates primarily by modulating blood supply. We will explore this hypothesis in the following research section.

RESEARCH

The Mind-Body Modulation of Blood Flow: Research Project 28

The continued finding of a central role of blood flow in a wide variety of acute and chronic illnesses that are ameliorated by hypnosis has led Barber (1978, 1984) to hypothesize that altering blood flow by directed thinking, imagining, and feeling is a common factor in most methods of mind-body healing. Table 7 is an expansion and updating of the types of clinical and experimental data he uses to support this view. We can use this accumulated data to outline the process of mind-body communication mediating blood flow as follows.

The *mind-brain level* modulating blood is illustrated by metaphors of everyday speech. Everyone knows what we mean when we say that we feel "warm" or "cool" about a person or situation. Biofeedback research indicates that these feelings of warmth and coolness are associated with an actual dilation or constriction of blood vessels to increase or decrease blood flow. This can take place because a positive response on the cognitive-emotional level can be associated with positive life experiences of warmth on a sensory level. Taken together, Tables 6 and 7 document how the sensory-perceptual languages of mind at the cortical level can be ideodynamically transduced in the cross-modal association areas of the limbic system (Mishkin, 1982; Mishkin & Petri, 1984) to facilitate mind-body healing. That is, the thought of warmth can be transformed into an actual emotional, sensory, and physical experience of warmth. As we shall see, this experience of warmth is related to the actual dilation of blood vessels and capillaries that allows warm blood from the body core to reach the skin, which frequently becomes "flushed" when we experience the warmth. Thoughts of coldness, on the other hand, can constrict blood vessels. Mental-emotional experiences of fear and stress can dilate some blood vessels and constrict others.

The *brain-body level* of blood flow modulation takes place in the limbic-

Table 7: Acute and chronic illnesses that have been ameliorated by a variety of mind-body methods that alter blood flow.

Acute Illnesses and Emergency Situations
  1. the alarm response (Cheek, 1960a, c; Rossi, 1973/1980);
  2. hypertension and cardiac problems (Benson, 1983a, b; Gruen, 1972; Schneck, 1948; Wain, Amen, & Oetgen, 1984; Yanovski, 1962);
  3. controlling bleeding in surgery (Banks, 1985; Cheek, 1969b);
  4. minimizing and healing burns (Barber, 1984; Cheek, 1962a; Moore & Kaplan, 1983);
  5. producing localized skin inflammations similar to previously experienced burns (Barber, 1984);
  6. aiding coagulation of blood in hemophiliacs (Banks, 1985; Barber, 1984);

Chronic Illnesses
  1. headaches (by warming and cooling different parts of the body) (Barabasz & McGeorge, 1978; Barber, 1978, 1984; Erickson, 1943c/1980);
  2. controlling blushing and blanching of the skin (Barber, 1978, 1984; Erickson, 1980b);
  3. stimulating the enlargement and apparent growth of breasts in women (Barber, 1984; Erickson, 1960/1980; Williams, 1974);
  4. stimulation of sexual excitation and penile erection (Barber, 1978, 1984; Crasilneck, 1982);
  5. warts (Johnson & Barber, 1978; Ullman, 1959);
  6. producing and curing diverse forms of dermatitis (Barber, 1984; Cheek, 1961a, b; Ikemi & Nakagawa, 1962);
  7. congenital ichthyosis (Barber, 1984; Mason, 1952, 1955);
  8. Raynaud's disease (Conn & Mott, 1984; Jacobson, Hackett, Surman, & Silverberg, 1973);
  9. enhancing the immune response (Black, 1969; Bowers & Kelley, 1979; Goldberg, 1985; Hall, 1982-1983; Lewis, 1927; Mason, 1963; Schneider, Smith, & Witcher, 1983, 1984)

---

hypothalamic system. The hypothalamus has some of the major control centers (e.g., the anterior and posterior hypothalamus) for regulating the autonomic nervous system. As illustrated in Figure 9, the autonomic nervous system, through its sympathetic and parasympathetic branches, can mediate the alarm response that contributes to the psychosomatic aspects of surgical emergencies and critical illnesses. The sympathetic branch, for example, can signal the adrenal medulla to secrete epinephrine and norepi-

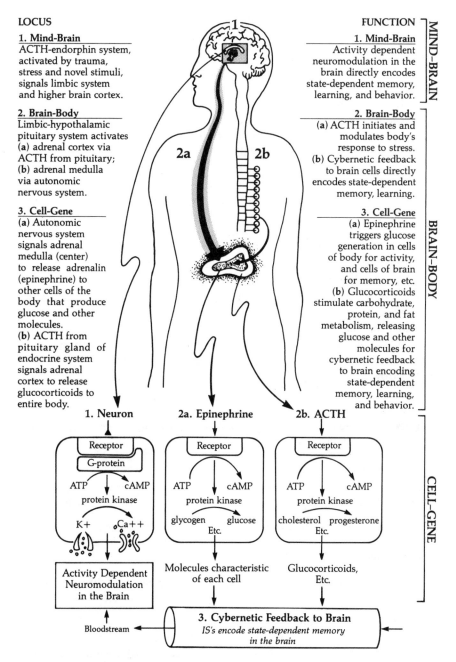

LOCUS

1. Mind-Brain
ACTH-endorphin system, activated by trauma, stress and novel stimuli, signals limbic system and higher brain cortex.

2. Brain-Body
Limbic-hypothalamic pituitary system activates (a) adrenal cortex via ACTH from pituitary; (b) adrenal medulla via autonomic nervous system.

3. Cell-Gene
(a) Autonomic nervous system signals adrenal medulla (center) to release adrenalin (epinephrine) to other cells of the body that produce glucose and other molecules.
(b) ACTH from pituitary gland of endocrine system signals adrenal cortex to release glucocorticoids to entire body.

FUNCTION

1. Mind-Brain
Activity dependent neuromodulation in the brain directly encodes state-dependent memory, learning, and behavior.

2. Brain-Body
(a) ACTH initiates and modulates body's response to stress.
(b) Cybernetic feedback to brain cells directly encodes state-dependent memory, learning.

3. Cell-Gene
(a) Epinephrine triggers glucose generation in cells of body for activity, and cells of brain for memory, etc.
(b) Glucocorticoids stimulate carbohydrate, protein, and fat metabolism, releasing glucose and other molecules for cybernetic feedback to brain encoding state-dependent memory, learning, and behavior.

MIND-BRAIN

BRAIN-BODY

CELL-GENE

1. Neuron

Receptor
G-protein
ATP → cAMP
protein kinase
$K+$ $Ca++$

Activity Dependent Neuromodulation in the Brain

2a. Epinephrine

Receptor
ATP → cAMP
protein kinase
glycogen → glucose
Etc.

Molecules characteristic of each cell

2b. ACTH

Receptor
ATP → cAMP
protein kinase
cholesterol   progesterone
Etc.

Glucocorticoids, Etc.

Bloodstream ←

3. Cybernetic Feedback to Brain
IS's encode state-dependent memory in the brain

Figure 9: The cybernetic pathways encoding state-dependent memory, learning, and behavior during surgical emergencies, critical illness, and severe stress.

nephrine into the blood, where they function as information substances that can regulate blood flow by signaling the receptors on vessels in the skeletal muscles and liver to dilate or constrict the diameter of the arterials in other parts of the body. Table 8 summarizes a variety of the factors that regulate blood pressure and flow in arteries and the smaller arterioles. It is well-established that socio-cultural factors, social interaction and speech (Lynch, 1985), and personality variables (such as "Type A") can influence blood pressure (hypertension) and cardiac activity at this level.

The *cellular-molecular level* is illustrated through the action of a number of information substances on the receptors of the capillaries that carry the blood through all the tissues of the body. In an early pioneering study on "changes in tissue vulnerability induced during hypnotic suggestion," Chapman, Goodell, and Wolff (1959b) concluded that "proteolytic enzymes and a bradykinin-like polypeptide are implicated in these enhanced reactions" (p. 104). In Section V, we will review clinical studies that illustrate the molecular mechanisms by which bradykinin and histamine open the spaces between capillary cell walls in inflammatory reactions.

It is now known that the formation and metabolism of bradykinin is interwoven with the metabolic processes that mediate the conversion of angiotensinogen to angiotensin I and II (seen Ganong, 1985, for a review), as outlined in Box 17. The interrelationships of the kinins (particularly, bradykinin and lysylbradykinin), histamine, and angiotensins in regulating blood flow at the cellular level suggests how all the information substances

Table 8: Summary of information substances modulating blood pressure and flow. (Adapted from Ganong, 1987)

Constriction	Dilation
Increased norepinephrine	Decreased norepinephrine
Circulating catecholamines (except epinephrine in skeletal muscle and liver)	Circulating epinephrine in skeletal muscle and liver
Circulating angiotensin II	Activation of cholinergic dilators in skeletal muscle
Locally released serotonin	Histamine, kinins, decreased O_2 tension, increased CO_2 tension, decreased pH, lactic acid, K^+, adenosine, etc.
Decreased local temperature	Increased local temperature

in Table 8 may be modulating blood flow in well coordinated communication patterns on all levels from mind to molecule. The conventional view has been that while all these substances may be coordinated in their activity, this coordination takes place on an entirely mechanical, involuntary, or unconscious level. Recent research demonstrates, however, that children can voluntarily and consciously modulate even the most mechanical, molecular levels of oxygen in their blood.

Project 28 One would not ordinarily think of the oxygen levels of the blood functioning as an information substance. A recent "pilot study of voluntary control of transcutaneous PO_2 by children" (Olness & Conroy, 1985), however, suggests that, in fact, oxygen and carbon dioxide are part of the mind-molecular communication cycle that modulates blood flow. Olness and Conroy found statistically significant support for their two hypotheses (p. 1):

(a) Children can voluntarily change tissue oxygen as reflected by a transcutaneous oxygen monitor, and
(b) children, experienced in use of self-hypnosis exercises, will be able to change tissue oxygen to a greater degree than children unfamiliar with such exercises.

Their preliminary results suggest that the mind-molecular basis of healing via the modulation of blood flow will continue to be a fertile field for future research. The current challenge is to devise experimental paradigms that can trace the paths of information transduction that modulate blood flow in a variety of acute and chronic illnesses, where we have some way of measuring the actual information substances that are involved at the molecular level.

The Mind-Molecular Basis of Psychoneuroimmunology: Research Project 29

Advances in medicine and psychology have usually developed around new methods of analysis. This is particularly the case in understanding and ameliorating disease. The medical researcher's first goal is to find an appropriate animal model or biological preparation of the disease process so that it can be studied in the laboratory. A number of models for studying mind-body healing has been outlined by Weiner (1977), but none has been entirely satisfactory. The Cartesian gap between mind and body looms as large as ever in all of them.

With the recent breakthroughs in our understanding of the genetic and molecular mechanisms of disease, however, it may now be possible to create new models of mind-body communication and healing. We will therefore outline what appears to be one such emerging model centered around *information substances and their receptors as a new psychosomatic system* (Plotnikoff, Morley, & Kay, 1986). Such a model has not been articulated clearly by anyone yet, but the work of Candace Pert and her colleagues continually generates hints about it (Pert, 1986; Pert & Herkenham, 1981; Pert et al., 1985). This emerging model has as much if not more to say about normal functioning as it does about malfunctioning; because of this, it can provide us with fundamental insights into mind-body communication, the nature of memory and learning, sensory-perceptual functioning, and the nature of emotion.

In what follows we will outline a number of stages or facets of this new *mind-molecular model* and illustrate it with ongoing research in psychoneuroimmunology (Ader, 1985; Solomon, 1985). This model, in essence, enables us to conceptualize and explore the mind-molecular basis of psychoneuroimmunology as a pivotal aspect of mind-body healing.

Structure-activity analysis on the cellular-molecular level is the starting point for identifying the molecular structures that are the key mediators (messenger molecules, information substances) of the disease process, or of any normal activity under investigation. Aswanikumar et al. (1977) took an initial step in this direction with their structure-activity analysis of the peptide analogs that cause white blood cells (rabbit neutrophils) to migrate. The migration of such neutrophils is believed to be an intrinsic aspect of the adequate functioning of the immune system. The neutrophils are said to move or "chemotax" toward the site of a bacterial or viral invasion of the body. They are guided in this movement by a gradient or trail of peptides that are the normal waste (degredation products) of foreign invasion. Pert and Herkenham (1981) outline how this process takes place in the pharmacological context of identifying the receptors on the cell walls that receive (bind) the peptide messenger molecules as follows (pp. 512–514):

> Viewed from this perspective, only two things are really necessary to biochemically identify the receptor that is responsible for a given pharmacological response: first, a highly radiolabeled ligand [molecule] which retains its biological activity and high affinity for the receptor in question, and second, a series of structural analogs, which have been previously ranked in some biological test. Figure 10 shows a particularly elegant example of close fit between *in vitro* binding data and a biological response, in this case the ability of rabbit neutrophils to migrate in response to a series of peptide chemoattractants (Answanikumar et al., 1977). . . . The 0.98 correlation . . . strongly suggests that neutrophils contain receptors on their surface that can be measured biochemically and are in fact responsible for their ability to migrate toward bacterial invasion.

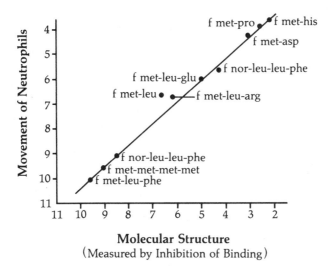

Molecular Structure
(Measured by Inhibition of Binding)

Figure 10: A structural-activity analysis of the immune response. The behavioral *activity* of white blood cells (neutrophils) is highly correlated ($r = 0.98$; $p < 0.001$) with the molecular *structure* of peptides such as f met-leu-phe. (Adapted from Aswanikumar et al., 1977)

Figure 10 clearly illustrates how the *structure* of peptide molecules (the degradation products of the invading substance) is highly correlated with the intensity of the biological-behavioral *activity* of the neutrophils as the neutrophils move toward the source of the peptides *in vitro* (in test tube). The behavior of neutrophil movement takes place through the ability of these cells to assume an alternating bipolar configuration (for movement like a single-cell amoeba) upon exposure to the chemotaxis. The neutrophils literally crawl toward the source of the chemotaxis factor (in this case, peptides) with an ameboid movement.

The structure-activity analysis of Figure 10 is on the molecular-physiological-behavioral level, but does not yet reach to the mental level of *psychoneuroimmunology*. To integrate the mental level we require another step, as follows.

Structure-activity analysis on the mental-emotional level. In a series of studies it has been found that the chemotaxis of human monocytes (a broad class of white blood cells that includes neutrophils) can be facilitated by several classes of *psycho*active molecules. The opiates and their analogs (including the naturally occurring endorphins) have been found to promote the "opiate receptor-mediated chemotaxis of human monocytes" (Ruff, Wahl, Mergenhagen, & Pert, 1985b, p. 363). The benzodiazepines, which are widely prescribed for their tranquilizing and antianxiety effects, have also been shown to be "potent stimulators of human monocyte chemotaxis"

(Ruff, Pert, Weber, Wahl, Wahl, & Paul, 1985a, p. 1281). These authors have summarized the implications of their research as follows (p. 1283):

> Neuropeptides have been studied for their behavioral and neuroendocrine effects and are increasingly being shown to exert effects on immune system function. Because these ligands [molecules] and their receptors are richly distributed in brain regions that mediate emotion and higher cognitive functions, it seems plausible that the same neurohumoral mediators of various mood states in the brain may also communicate to monocytes and other cells involved in healing and homeostatic processes. Short signal peptides (neuropeptides) and their surface receptors define a group of cells whose function may be to integrate information from the central nervous, immune, and endocrine systems through a psychoimmunoendocrine network, thereby altering the behavior of the whole organism.

How is it possible to make such broad generalizations? The key concept underlying the generalizations concerns the central role of information substances and their receptors as the basis of information transduction within all living organisms. Peptides and their receptors are now regarded as the earliest evolutionary form of communication that developed in the most primitive one-cell organisms (Moon-Edley, Hall, Herkenham, & Pert, 1982; Niall, 1976, 1982). Broad patterns of evidence suggest that this early communication system of information substances and their receptors is the phylogenetic precursor that is common to both the central nervous system and the endocrine system (Le Roith, Shiloach, & Roth, 1982; Roth et al., 1985). As the central nervous and endocrine systems evolved into the specialized forms of information transduction and communication we see today, they conserved and incorporated the older information substance-receptor system. In the central nervous system, for example, we have synaptic neurotransmission as the more rapid, newly evolved form of specific point-to-point communication, along with the older, slower parasynaptic information substance-receptor system (review Table 1 and Figures 2 and 3). The older information substance-receptor system integrates the genetic, biological, behavioral, and sensory-emotional-mental levels of functioning that generate most "states" of the organism. Evidence for this idea is assembled by studying the brain-body pathways of information substances and their receptors. Ruff and his colleagues summarize this view as follows (1985b, p. 365):

> Neuropeptides (most demonstrably, the opiate peptides) appear to cause mood and behavior alterations when acting within the brain while mediating various emotional and physical states when released within the body. Because these peptides have potent effects on macrophages, as well

as on other cells of the immune system and body, these compounds may represent a major class of biochemicals which subserve information exchange between the brain and the body. It is becoming clear that in addition to their role in nervous system function, neuropeptides have pleiotrophic effects, functioning as transmitters, growth hormones, and signal agents for several body systems. As such, neuropeptides and their receptors are envisioned as the key biochemical components of a network linking psychological and somatic functions.

There is nothing in all this, however, that directly proves that mind can really move molecules. The evidence is still correlational and inferential. Peptide messenger molecules that are released during stress and a variety of other mental, emotional, and behavioral states may be simultaneously evoking a variety of physiological responses in the autonomic, endocrine, and immune systems because they all have receptors that receive the same peptides. That is, there is a "concomitance" of physiological processes mediated by the same peptide messenger molecule-receptor system. This concomitance is a form of *psychophysical parallelism* (Boring, 1950; Weiner, 1977); mind does not directly move molecules in this model. Rather, mind and body are moved together in parallel by the same information-receptor system. If psychophysiological parallelism proves to be the predominant mode of mind-body relationship we may have, at best, only a weak basis for using mind to facilitate physiological healing.

A strong case for mind-body therapy methods requires proof for *psychophysiological interactionism*. To establish that the *mind can intentionally move molecules* for healing, we need more direct evidence for psychophysiological interactionism than we have at present. This would require that we establish that a mind method (for example, hypnosis or meditation) could purposefully direct the release of the peptide messenger molecules, which, in turn, would be received by the receptors on the cells of the body to evoke their characteristic physiological responses.

No one has yet done a crucial experiment wherein x mental level activity was demonstrated to facilitate y molecular response. So far, we have only been able to infer that this interaction must be taking place, since mind methods do seem to facilitate physical healing. Structural-activity analysis has thus far only demonstrated that there is an apparent molecular path of information transduction between the mental, behavioral, and physiological levels, but it has not yet shown how a human can purposefully use the mind to mediate such-and-such molecular process on such-and-such a cellular level.

A recent series of studies by Minning (1982) and by Schneider, Smith, and Witcher (1983, 1984), however, does seem to be moving in the direction of formulating just such a crucial experiment. These workers, without any apparent knowledge of the work of Pert and her colleagues (personal communication with Smith in 1987), demonstrated that highly motivated college students with specific training could learn to use their mental imagery to mediate significant changes in white blood cell count and the *movement (chemotaxis) of neutrophils*. These pioneering studies were complex and the results not yet as clear as we would like, but Schneider, Smith, and Witcher were able to conclude the following (1984, pp. 11–12):

> It is unlikely that it is simply a general relaxation effect or a general immune system activation that can explain these results. . . . It is possible that specific types of cells, like neutrophils, can be the focus of an imagery training procedure, and reveal shifts in function and availability as a result. Replications with other types of white blood cells and other procedures, such as hypnosis, as demonstrated by Hall (1982–1983) with lymphocytes, can further aid in understanding this effect. . . . It was apparent that those subjects who noted that they actually "felt" something going on inside of their bodies were more likely to show changes in blood function as well. . . . Clinically, some of the issues raised involve to what extent can people be trained prior to illness to be more aware of their bodies, even on a cellular level. . . . The capacity of individuals to know their own physiological potential even on the cellular level deserves further study.

Project 29 Although these studies relate a purposeful and well motivated imagery to neutrophil movement, no tests were conducted to demonstrate which molecular structure functioned as the messenger to mediate neutrophil chemotaxis. From the Ruff et al. studies (1985a, b), and from Pert's general conception of neuropeptides and their receptors as a psychosomatic network, we would hypothesize that peptide information substances were the connecting link. We will provide further evidence for this conception in Section V.

Meanwhile, it is important to recognize that the three connections between *mind-brain, brain-body*, and the *cellular-genetic* levels, as illustrated in Table 6 can serve as outlines for the types of studies now needed in the field of psychoneuroimmunology. In particular, we now need studies that will demonstrate how mind methods (imagery, hypnosis, meditation, etc.) can direct the distribution of peptide information substances to turn on the receptors of the white blood cells so that they can chemotax to the places in the body where healing needs to take place.

Notice that we are not saying more studies are needed to demonstrate that mind and emotions are related to an immunological response. Decades of research have established the general validity of the psychoneuroimmunological response well beyond any reasonable doubt (Ader, 1981; Guillemin, Cohn, & Melnechuk, 1985; Locke, Ader, Besedovsky, Hall, Solomon, & Strom, 1985; Locke & Hornig-Rohan, 1983). What we now need to know are the specific mind-molecular mechanisms that are mediating the psycho-neuroimmunological response. We need to determine how much of it is mediated by an automatic and involuntary process of psychophysiological parallelism (Boring, 1950; Weiner, 1977), and how much can be modulated by a voluntarily initiated and purposefully directed healing process of psychophysiological interaction. Only when the relative contributions of these voluntary and involuntary components of mind-molecular mechanisms are known will we have a genuine science of psychosomatic medicine and a systematic approach to mind-body therapy.

Ideodynamic Approaches with the New Psychosomatic Networks: Research Projects 30–32

Project 30 In Chapter 10, Cheek concluded that the exploration of cardiac arrest, hemorrhage, renal failure, and respiratory collapse is now open for productive psychiatric research. Search the research literature for everything that is known about the mind-body information transduction processes in these four acute sources of life distress. What are the specific information-substance-receptor systems of each? Trace the entire pathway between mind-brain, brain-body, and the body-cellular-genetic connection for each. Devise experimental-clinical research projects that could test specific hypotheses about the information substance-receptor systems that are accessible via the ideodynamic signaling in each of these conditions. How would you determine at what mind-brain, brain-body, or cellular-genetic level the ideodynamic approach operates? Formulate direct healing suggestions (Box 18) for each condition when it is manifest in emergencies and the more indirect ideodynamic approaches for exploring and ameliorating these conditions in psychotherapy.

Project 31 For all the classical psychosomatic disorders (Alexander, 1950/1987; Weiner, 1977), survey what is currently known at each of the three stages of mind-brain, brain-body, and cellular-genetic-molecular levels of information transduction. Use Table 6 as a guide for organizing this information. Such surveys could provide a clear map of what is actually known about each mind-body problem and immediately highlight the gaps that future research must cover.

Experts in each of these psychosomatic problem areas will need to coordinate this knowledge to determine whether the mind-body methods of healing are all working at the same level or at different levels. Much conventional opinion at this time suggests that mind-body healing takes place at the mind-brain level to reduce stress hormones at the brain-body level. Is this really the case? What actual experimental tests can you devise to determine that x mind method (imagery, meditation, hypnosis, etc.) results in a change in y molecules associated with stress via structure-activity analysis at the mind-brain and brain-body levels?

Project 32 The ultimate desiratum is to create new experimental designs that could assess the locus at which our ideodynamic approaches are facilitating mind-body healing in each of the classical psychosomatic problems. Design a clinical-experimental study that compares the effectiveness of ideodynamic signaling in facilitating the resolution of psychosomatic problems with that of imagery and conventional verbal hypnosis. Is there an interaction effect between these three approaches that is greater than the therapeutic value of each alone? Can it be demonstrated that the *involuntary* component of ideodynamic signaling can access mind-body healing that is not available to the more *voluntary* aspects of conventional hypnosis and meditation? How does this involuntary component of ideomotor signaling compare with the information guided physiological responses facilitated by the use of biofeedback instrumentation?

Psychosomatic Networks: Perception, Pain, and Pleasure

THEORY

In sections I and II we traced theoretical pathways between mind, brain, body, gene and molecule that make up the new psychosomatic medicine. We explored how our ideodynamic mind-body therapy methods might facilitate healing via these pathways. We surveyed the kinds of research that are needed now for further progress. In this section we will examine in greater detail just how information substances integrate psyche and soma to bridge the so-called Cartesian gap between mind and body. We will study this matter carefully because it involves some fundamentally new and ingenious solutions to age-old philosophical-psychological problems that have reached an impasse in all previous theorizing about the mind-body problem.

Our new understanding of mind-body integration finds its clearest expression in the recent conceptualizations of Candace Pert and her colleagues at the National Institute of Mental Health (Pert et al., 1985; Pert, 1986). In brief, their view is that neuropeptides and their receptors are a newly discovered psychosomatic network that modulates many aspects of sensation, perception, emotion, and behavior, as well as the autonomic, endocrine, and immune systems (Pert et al., 1985, p. 820s):

> A major conceptual shift in neuroscience has been wrought by the realization that brain function is modulated by numerous chemicals in addition to classical neurotransmitters. Many of these *informational substances* are neuropeptides, originally studied in other contexts as hormones, "gut peptides," or growth factors. Their number presently exceeds 50 and most, if not all, alter behavior and mood states. . . . *We now realize that their signal specificity resides in receptors* [distinct classes of recognition molecules] rather than the close juxtaposition occurring at classical synapses. Rather precise brain distribution patterns for many neuropeptide receptors have been determined. A number of brain loci, many within emotion-mediating brain areas, are enriched with many types of neuropeptide receptors suggesting a convergence of information

at these "nodes." Additionally, neuropeptide receptors occur on mobile cells of the immune system; monocytes can chemotax to numerous neuropeptides via processes shown by structure-activity analysis to be mediated by distinct receptors indistinguishable from those found in the brain. *Neuropeptides and their receptors thus join the brain, glands, and immune system in a network of communication between brain and body, probably representing the biochemical substrate of emotion.* [Italics added]

Pert and a number of other leading investigators in neuroscience (Schmitt, 1984, 1986) now use the term *informational substance* to describe the essential messenger function of this neuropeptide network. This is their way of integrating the data from a number of previously separated fields of psychology, neurology, anatomy, biochemistry, and molecular biology. This research over the past 15 years has led to the gradual recognition of a number of new principles about mind-body communication that are currently in the process of being formulated. In this section we will discuss a number of these principles that suggest how psychosomatic networks operate as "the biochemical substrate of emotion" and a possibly profound resolution of the mind-body problem.

Four of the new principles that are implied in the above quotation by Pert and her colleagues (Pert et al., 1985) and more recent summaries of her talks (Pert, 1986, 1987) could be stated as follows:

1. Mind-body functions modulated by information substances reside in receptors activated at the cellular level.
2. All information substances coordinate mind-brain-body functions.
3. The convergence of information substances and their receptors at specific loci throughout the brain-body makes up a "nodal network of psychosomatic communication."
4. A "relational network" rather than a hierarchy of control is more descriptive of mind-body relationships.

Let us now discuss each of these principles in turn.

1. *Mind-body functions modulated by information substances and their receptors reside within the cellular level.*

Since it was the discovery and isolation of the opiate receptor in the brain (Pert & Snyder, 1973a, b) that ushered in this new view of psychosomatic medicine, it may be best to begin with it.

Figure 11 illustrates seven loci within the mind-body that are especially rich in cells with opiate receptors. That is, these are the tissue areas whose functions are most clearly modulated by the endogenous opiate information substances such as endorphins. A glance at the wide range of mind-body processes modulated (listed in the righthand column of Figure 11) appears

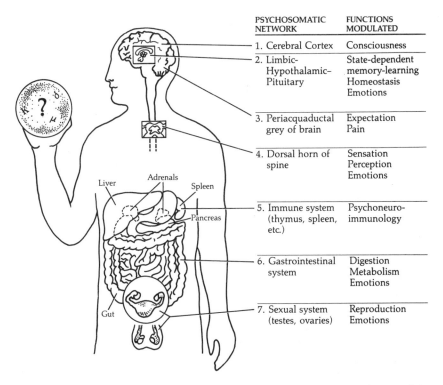

PSYCHOSOMATIC NETWORK	FUNCTIONS MODULATED
1. Cerebral Cortex	Consciousness
2. Limbic-Hypothalamic-Pituitary	State-dependent memory-learning Homeostasis Emotions
3. Periacquaductal grey of brain	Expectation Pain
4. Dorsal horn of spine	Sensation Perception Emotions
5. Immune system (thymus, spleen, etc.)	Psychoneuro-immunology
6. Gastrointestinal system	Digestion Metabolism Emotions
7. Sexual system (testes, ovaries)	Reproduction Emotions

Figure 11: Seven major nodes of the peptide psychosomatic network and some of the mind-body processes modulated by them. The endogenous "opiates" such as the endorphins and many other neuropeptides function as *information substances* integrating the entire mind-body as a holistic unit on all these levels almost simultaneously. There is still a question about the fundamental nature of the opiate receptor that may oscillate between three or more states designated as κ, δ, and μ.

to be a bit overwhelming. How is it possible, one immediately asks, for one relatively small group of substances such as the endorphins to influence so many significant life functions?

The answer to this question comes from the first new principle to emerge from the study of how information substances and their receptors operate. This is *the principle of receptor specificity* (Pert et al., 1985; Schmitt, 1984, 1986): *the functions modulated by information substances reside in receptor-activated cells rather than in the information substances themselves.*

An analogy may make this clear. A messenger arriving on horseback at a medieval castle delivers the important information that an enemy approaches. But that is all the messenger need do. It is the receiver of this information who then actually stirs the castle to action. Similarly, the opiate information substances simply signal the receptors in the cell walls to activity. These cell receptors now turn on the various functions that are characteristic of each cell type. Signal the opiate receptors on brain cells and they will modulate mental activities; signal the same opiate receptors in the gastrointestinal or sexual systems and *their* characteristic functions will be modulated.

It is now known that information substances can trigger receptors at three locations on the cellular-genetic level: the cell wall, the cytoplasm, and gene sites within the nucleus of the cell. Most of the classical peptide information substances that modulate homeostasis and metabolism, such as ACTH, vasopressin, thyroid stimulating hormone, insulin, gastrin secretion, and cholecystokinin (CCK), interact with receptors on the cell walls. Steroidal hormones, such as progesterone, estrogen, testosterone, cortisol, and corticosterone, on the other hand, interact with receptors within the cytoplasm or at genetic sites within the nucleus of the cell (Darnell, Lodish, & Baltimore, 1986).

For the sake of simplification, we have thus far omitted research that suggests there may be several forms of the opiate receptor designated as δ, κ, and μ. Pert and her colleagues (Bowen et al., 1981; Quirion et al., 1982) hypothesize that these apparently different forms of the receptor could actually be transitional forms of the same receptor that can oscillate between different states to facilitate cellular metabolism (by modulating sodium ion channels and adenylate cyclase mechanisms, etc.). She speculates upon the broader implications of this hypothesis in an intriguing manner as follows (Pert, 1986, pp. 14-15):

> There are thousands of scientists studying the opiate receptors and the opiate peptides, and they see great heterogeneity in the receptors. They have given a series of Greek names to the apparent heterogeneity. However, all the evidence from our lab suggests that in fact *there is actually only one type of molecule in the opiate receptors, one long polypeptide chain whose formula you can write.* This molecule is quite capable of changing its conformation within its membrane so that it can assume a number of shapes.
>
> I note in passing that this interconversion can occur at a very rapid pace — so rapid that it is hard to tell whether it is one state or another at a given moment in time. In other words, receptors have both a wave-like and a particulate character, and it is important to note that information can be stored in the form of time spent in different states.

It is well-known that there are at least four types of bonding forces between the atoms that make up the large polypeptides and protein structures that form receptors (Vander, Sherman, & Luciano, 1985). The first two bonds, called *covalent* and *ionic*, are so strong that they probably do not contribute to the type of alternate forms and states to which Pert is referring. The third and fourth types of bonds, called *hydrogen* and *Van der Waal forces*, however, are relatively weak. These weaker bonds lead to the formation of the "tertiary structure" of receptors that enables them to fold upon themselves in interesting and easily changeable shapes or "states." These altered states contribute to their function in opening and closing ion channels in the cell wall to regulate everything from nerve conduction and basic cellular metabolism up to emotion, memory, and learning. Since these tertiary structures are so easily modifiable, they may give rise to the rapidly changing states of the receptor Pert discusses.

The Van der Waal force is the most interesting in this regard, since it arises from the relatively *weak electromagnetic field* which surrounds the atoms within the receptor proteins. It has always been a puzzle to determine just how the so-called energy from healers, shamen, acupuncturists, and a variety of other exotic mind-body therapists could contribute to holistic healing. It is only the wildest speculation at this point, but conceivably such healing energies could operate via the easily modifiable shapes and states of the receptors that modulate all cellular-genetic metabolism.

The history of hypnosis, of course, is replete with hypotheses about the "animal magnetism" as a source of healing (see Mesmer in Tinterow, 1970). Virtually all of these earlier hypotheses have been disproved by well-controlled experimental investigations. The study of the electromagnetic basis of hypnosis and healing continues in ever more subtle electronic studies (Becker & Selden, 1985; Erickson & Rossi, 1981; Ravitz, 1950), however, so we must reserve final judgment until more conclusive research is conducted.

What is most fascinating from theoretical and practical healing points of view is how *alternating states of the receptor may be a psychobiological mechanism whereby energy and information could be converted into one another in living systems*. If validated, this hypothesis could become a most significant foundation for many mind-body methods of psychosomatic healing. Until further research clarifies this issue, we are left with a question mark about the fundamental nature of the receptor, as illustrated in Figure 11.

2. *All information substances coordinate mind-brain-body functions.* The most surprising principle that has emerged in this area is that *all information substances coordinate mind-brain-body functions*. In fact, the concept of "information substance" was defined to include terms such as *neurotransmitter, neuromodulator, neurohormone,* and *hormone* in order to focus on this "coordination of mind-brain-body functions" as their common denominator. This principle of information substance coordination is simple, yet it has profound implications for understanding many of the so-called mysteries of mind-body communication and healing.

Another look at the major loci of the opiate receptor and some of the psychobiological processes they modulate in Figure 11 will help us understand this principle of mind-brain-body coordination. We can conceptualize Figure 11 as a kind of mind-body map that illustrates how an information substance such as endorphin can modulate an incredible range of apparently different psychological and physiological functions. Endorphin that is released into the bloodstream along with ACTH by the pituitary during stress, for example, can be received within a minute by all the major endorphin loci around the body to modulate their characteristic functions.

Consciousness, memory, emotions, digestion, and immune functions, for example, could all be modulated almost simultaneously. Let us now examine these seven major loci for a broader understanding of how they can operate as a psychosomatic network.

3. *The nodal network of psychosomatic communication* The convergence of neuropeptide information substances and their receptors at a number of common loci throughout the entire brain-body could be called "the nodal network of psychosomatic communication." This idea was first formulated by Pert et al. (1985, p. 821s):

> *Fundamental feature of neuropeptide receptors—enrichment at "nodal points": nodal points in the limbic system of brain.* A fundamental feature shared by all neuropeptide receptors whose brain distribution has been well studied is profound enrichment at a number of the same brain areas. Many of these neuropeptide receptor-rich areas can be found within an intercommunicating conglomerate of brain structures classically termed "the limbic system," which is considered to mediate emotional behavior; in unanesthetized humans undergoing brain stimulation as a preclude to surgery for epilepsy, far-ranging emotional expression can be elicited by stimulation of cortex near the amygdala, the core of the limbic system. The amygdala, as well as the hypothalamus and other limbic system-associated structures, were found initially to be enriched in opiate receptors in monkey and human brain. Later maps of numerous other neuropeptide receptors in brain (including substance P, bombesin cholecystokinin, neurotensin, insulin, and transferrin have continued to implicate the amygdala and other limbic system-associated structures (e.g., the cingulate cortex) as a source of receptor-rich sites where mood presumably is biochemically modified.
>
> . . . Numerous studies have shown that it is the rule rather than the exception that sites of neuropeptide storage in brain lack physical juxtaposition with their receptors; thus the classical, closely juxtaposed synapse between the neurotransmitter acetylcholine and its receptor on skeletal muscle is not at all typical of neuropeptides. Classical synaptic neurotransmission produces information transfer very rapidly on a time scale measured in milliseconds. The separate discipline of endocrinology has featured a general theoretical framework in which peptide hormones are synthesized, stored, and released from one organ while acting elsewhere, the clarity of communication residing in the specificity of receptors rather than physical juxtaposition. Neuropeptides probably share an analogous communication principle, with receptors serving as targets for

circulating levels of neuropeptides, themselves produced at other loci in the brain and body. Thus, intercellular communication throughout networks of neuropeptide-rich nodes which extend from the brain to the endocrine and, as we shall see, the immune system, may integrate the internal milieu of the whole organism.

Let us now survey each of these seven major nodal points that Pert and her colleagues describe, wherein a variety of neuropeptide information substances come together to coordinate mind-brain-body communication.

a. *Cerebral cortex*: Areas of the cerebral cortext that receive and integrate sensory data (vision, smell, taste, hearing, touch) from the entire body are found to be rich in opiate receptors (Pert, 1978). This has led Lewis et al. (1981) to propose that "endogenous opiates exert a progressively greater influence at successively higher levels of sensory information processing in the cortex. . . . [they] may be involved in the filtering of sensory stimuli at the cortical level and thus play a role in selective attention" (p. 1168). Selective attention, of course, is of essence as an explanatory principle for the phenomena of hypnosis (Fromm & Shor, 1979), as well as psychosomatic problems (Nemiah, Freyberger, & Sifneos, 1976; Rossi, 1986d). Information substances such as the endogenous opiates could thus function as the common molecular mechanism, along with the phenomenological processes of mind, modulating sensory-perceptual processing in health and illness. The reciprocal interaction between the cortex and the motivational centers of the limbic system are surveyed next.

b. *Limbic-hypothalamic-pituitary system*: The amygdala and hippocampus of the limbic system, which are important areas for the integration of emotions, motivation, memory, and learning, are very rich in opiate receptors in all animals studied, including humans (LaMotte et al, 1978; Pert, 1985; Pert et al., 1985). Pert (1987) has noted that the amygdala and hypothalamus together have a 40-fold higher concentration of opiate receptors than any other area of the brain. These "hot spots" correspond to the specific nuclei that have been identified as mediating basic homeostatic systems such as temperature, appetite, water balance, and sexual behavior. Lewis and his colleagues have summarized the reciprocal interaction between the higher brain cortex and amygdala of the limbic system as follows (1981, p. 1168):

Because of the participation of the amygdala in emotional-motivational and reward-related functions, and because of recent evidence indicating a reciprocal projection from the amygdala back to the cortical sensory processing areas that give rise to the amygdaloid afferents, we are considering the hypothesis that selective attention may be influenced by a

"reverse" gradient of amygdalocortical opiate-containing projections onto cortical neurons containing μ-like opiate receptors. This proposal offers a neural mechanism whereby the limbic-mediated emotional states
essential for individual and species survival could influence which sensory stimuli are selected for attention.

The cortical-limbic-hypothalamic system is thus the major locus for integrating the sensory-perceptual stimuli selected for attention with the regulation of the autonomic, endocrine, and immune systems by the hypothalamic-pituitary system. That is, signals received by the opiate receptors at
the limbic-hypothalamic level modulate the major channel of mind-body
information transduction between the sensory-perceptual and memory systems with the autonomic, endocrine, and immune systems that are of essence in homeostasis and psychosomatic problems. Since the entire cortical-
limbic-hypothalamic system is in a constant state of psychobiological flux,
the state-dependent memory and learning systems they encode are in similar
flux. The stability of memory and learning that we depend upon for daily
living is actually a precarious illusion that is dependent upon the degree to
which psychobiological homeostasis is maintained in the cortical-limbic-
hypothalamic-pituitary system.

c. *Periaqueductal gray region of the brain stem*: This brain stem area is
another well-known locus where opiate analgesia is mediated (Pert & Yaksh,
1974). Pert (1980) has noted that it is in direct point-to-point synaptic communication with the "frontal cortex and is thus thought to mediate the well-
documented effect of expectation and conscious control on pain perception"
(p. 821s). *Expectation*, of course, has long been regarded as one of the most
significant psychological factors facilitating the placebo effect (White,
Tursky, & Schwartz, 1985) and the ideodynamics of therapeutic hypnosis.
The *endogenous* peptides (B-endorphin) and their receptors in the periac-
queductal gray region may thus be the psychobiological basis of expectation
that was previously conceptualized as a purely psychological variable.

Pert has recently discussed her views of the relationships between mind,
pain, and the periaqueductal area of the brain stem as follows (1987, pp. 17–
18):

We have been talking about mind, and the question arises: Where is it?
In our own work, consciousness has come up in the context of studying
pain and the role of opiate receptors and endorphins in modulating pain.
A lot of labs are measuring pain, and we would all agree that the area
called periaqueductal gray, located around the third ventricle of the brain,
is filled with opiate receptors, making it a kind of control area for pain.
We have found that the periaqueductal gray is also loaded with receptors
for virtually all the neuropeptides that have been studied.

Now, everyone knows that there are yogis who can train themselves so that they do or do not perceive pain, depending on how they structure their experience. Women in labor do the same thing. What seems to be going on is that these sorts of people are able to plug into their periaqueductal gray. Somehow they gain access to it — with their consciousness, I believe — and set pain thresholds. Note what is going on here. In these situations, a person has an experience that brings with it pain, but a part of the person consciously does something so that the pain is not felt. Where is this consciousness coming from — this conscious I — that somehow plugs into the periaqueductal gray so that he or she does not feel a thing?

I want to go back to the idea of a network. A network is different from a hierarchical structure which has one top place. You theoretically can plug into a network at any point and get to any other point. A concept like this seems to me valuable in thinking about the processes by which a consciousness can manage to reach the periaqueductal gray and use it to control pain.

The yogi and the laboring woman both use a similar technique to control pain — breathing. Athletes use it, too. Breathing is extremely powerful. I suggest that there is a physical substrate for these phenomena, the brain stem nuclei. I would say that we now must include the brain stem nuclei in the limbic system because they are nodal points, thickly encrusted with neuropeptide receptors and neuropeptides.

The idea, then, goes like this: breathing has a physical substrate which is also a nodal point, this nodal point is part of an information network in which each part leads to all the other parts, and so, from the nodal point of the brain stem nuclei, the consciousness can, among other things, plug into the periaqueductal gray.

The concept of *nodal points* and *information networks* of peptides as the basis of mind-body communication and healing will be discussed as a basic principle in more detail later in this section.

d. *Dorsal horn of the spinal cord*: The dorsal horn of the spinal cord is the locus where neurons transmitting fast point-to-point information from the skin, endocrine glands, and other organs make their first synaptic contact with the central nervous system. That is, it is the locus where fast, classical neurotransmission makes contact with the slower system of parasynaptic cellular modulation (see Table 1). Pert et al. (1985, p. 821s) hypothesize that "although it has not previously been considered part of the limbic system, neuropeptides here, as postulated for other sensory way stations (Lewis et al., 1981), may filter and prioritize incoming sensory information so that the whole organism's perception is most compatible with survival." There appears to be a fascinating correspondence between this hypothesis and the independently formulated conception of "the state-dependent memory and learning theory of therapeutic hypnosis illustrated by the limbic system 'filter' surrounding the hypothalamus" (Erickson, Rossi, & Rossi, 1976; Rossi, 1986d, p. 26).

The essential idea here is that the endorphins, as well as other information substances and their receptors, function on many levels from the spinal cord up through the cortical-limbic-hypothalamic system as filters modulating all sensory, perceptual, and physiological information. This may be a basic psychological process by which the prefrontal cortex, with its conscious expectations and planning functions, can modulate psychosomatic processes down to the spinal cord level.

These four major loci of the opiate receptor at the cortical, limbic, brain stem, and spinal levels can be seen as one single extended mind-brain system wherein neuromodulation is continually interacting with classical neurotransmission. One could generalize this "extended brain" to a number of other rich loci of opiate receptors in the body.

e. *Gastrointestinal tract*: The entire gastrointestinal tract from the mouth through the anus is populated with a network of opiate receptors. "Gut feelings" are thus more than metaphorical; the brain-gut link has been well characterized as expressive of biorhythms (Sarna, 1985) and psychosomatic problems that are not easily available to cognition on the verbal level (Wingate, 1983, 1985). Recent experimental studies have found high hypnotizability in bulimic patients and low hypnotizability in anorexia nervosa (Pettinati, Horne, & Statts, 1982, 1985). Many anorexic as well as bulimic patients are highly responsive to hypnosis, however (Pettinati, 1986; Pettinati & Wade, 1986). Since it is established that appetite (Morley et al., 1983) and weight gain (Recant et al., 1981) are modulated by opiates, this work of Pettinati and her colleagues suggests that therapeutic hypnosis can access the opiate-rich receptor brain-gut system in ways not easily available to the patient's usual walking state of consciousness.

A recent study on the modulation of memory by the release of cholecystokinin (CCK), an octapeptide, from the upper intestinal tract emphasizes the far-reaching significance of such gut information substances for mind-body communication and perhaps for the evolution of consciousness itself. CCK is released from the upper intestine whenever fatty acids and amino acids digested from a recent meal enter the intestine. Flood et al. (1987) introduced the rationale for their study as follows (p. 832):

> One of the basic needs of even the most primitive organism is to be able to find food. The advantage to the animal of maintaining a vivid memory of a successful hunt is obvious. We thus hypothesized that feeding an animal after an aversive training session would enhance memory retention.

They summarized the results of their study and some of its implications as follows:

> Our data show that both feeding and peripherally administered CCK-8S enhance memory in mice. This gastrointestinal hormone seems to produce its effect on memory by activating ascending vagal fibers. Further studies are necessary to determine if CCK-8S is responsible for the entire effect of feeding on memory, or, as appears to be the case in the regulation of feeding, if a combination of gastrointestinal hormones act synergistically to produce this effect. The concentrations of CCK-8S achieved after administration of the optimum memory enhancing dose would be well within the physiological range seen after feeding in rodents. A link may have evolved between the release of gastric peptides and memory processing in the central nervous system because of the survival advantages for an animal to remember the details of a successful food-foraging expedition. (p. 832)

It is evident that we are only beginning to see a vast new frontier on mind-molecular relationships that encode memory and learning. The leading edge of mind-body therapy is to learn to utilize these relationships to facilitate the resolution of traditional problems. How can these new mind-gut communication systems be used to help people cope with eating disorder problems, for example?

f. *Sexual system*: It is a bit amazing to learn that the human testis is as rich a source of the precursors for β-endorphin as the pituitary gland (Margioris et al., 1983). There is a large body of evidence for the existence of this brain-sexual opiate link via hypnosis, visual imagery, and a variety of other mind methods (Araoz, 1982; Henry, 1982). We will explore these relationships in more detail in Section VII.

g. *The immune system*: The recent discovery that human leukocytes (white blood cells) produce ACTH, B-endorphin, and a variety of endorphin-like molecules that can function as information substances communicating with the brain and endocrine system (Blalock & Smith, 1980; Smith & Blalock, 1981; Smith, Harbor-McMenamin, & Blalock, 1985) is a basic building block of the emerging field of psychoneuroimmunology (Solomon & Amkraut, 1981). Pert has described the relationship between the monocytes of the immune system, neuropeptides, information substances, and emotions as follows (1987, p. 16)

> A key property of the immune system is that its cells move. They are otherwise identical to the stable brain cells, with their nuclei, cell membranes and all of the receptors. Monocytes, for example, which ingest foreign organisms, start life in your bone marrow, and they then diffuse

out and travel through your veins and arteries, and decide where to go by following chemical cues. A monocyte travels along in the blood and at some point comes within "scenting" distance of a neuropeptide, and because the monocyte has receptors for the neuropeptide on its cell surface, it begins literally to chemotax, or crawl, toward that chemical. This is very well documented, and there are excellent ways of studying it in the laboratory. . . .

Now, monocytes are responsible not just for recognizing and digesting foreign bodies but also for wound healing and tissue-repair mechanisms. What we are talking about, then, are cells with vital, health-sustaining functions.

The new discovery I want to emphasize here is that *every* neuropeptide receptor that we have looked for (using an elegant and precise system developed by my colleague, Michael Ruff) is also on human monocytes. Human monocytes have receptors for opiates, for PCP, for another peptide called bombasin, and so on. *These emotion-affecting biochemicals actually appear to control the routing and migration of monocytes, which are so pivotal in the immune system.* They communicate with B-cells and T-cells, interact in the whole system to fight disease and to distinguish between self and non-self, deciding, say, which part of the body is a tumor cell to be killed by natural killer cells, and which parts need to be restored. . . .

It turns out, moreover, that the cells of the immune system not only have receptors for these various neuropeptides; as is becoming clear, they also make the neuropeptides themselves. There are subsets of immune cells that make beta endorphins, for example, and the other opiate peptides. In other words, these immune cells are making the same chemicals that we conceive of as controlling mood in the brain. They control the tissue integrity of the body, and they also make chemicals that control mood.

Pert's concept of mind and emotions being integrated with bodily processes through a network of seven major nodal areas is evident in this discussion of the immune system. Let us now examine this view in greater detail.

4. *A cybernetic network rather than a hierarchy of control in mind-body relationships.*

As has been noted earlier in her discussion of the role of consciousness in modulating pain, Pert believes that mind-body communication can be conceptualized better as a relational network rather than as a hierarchical structure of control from the top of the brain downward to the body. A relational network allows each nodal locus equal influence in the holistic functioning of the entire system. The traditional hierarchical assumption about the dominance of the higher control functions of the central nervous system over the rest of the body, by contrast, contends that what is happening in the head is more important than what is happening in the rest of the body. The implications of this mind-body network conception of neuropeptides (information substances) for a theory of consciousness, mood, and emotion have been described by Pert (1987, pp. 15–16):

I believe these findings have amazing implications for understanding and appreciating what emotions do and what they are about. Consider the chemical substance angiotensin, another classical hormone which is also a peptide and now shown to be a neuropeptide. When we map for angiotensin receptors in the brain, we again find little hot spots in the amygdala. It has long been known that angiotensin mediates thirst, so if one implants a tube in the area of a rat's brain that is rich with angiotensin receptors and drops a little angiotensin down the tube, within 10 seconds the rat will start to drink water, even if it is totally sated with water. So, chemically speaking, angiotensin translates as an altered state of consciousness, a state that makes animals (and humans) say, "I want water." In other words, neuropeptides bring us to a state of consciousness and to alterations in those states.

Equally important is the fact that neuropeptide receptors are not just in the brain, they are also in the body. We have mapped and shown biochemically that there are angiotensin receptors in the kidney identical to those in the brain, and in a way that is not yet quite understood, the kidney-located receptors conserve water. The point is that the release of the neuropeptide angiotensin leads both to the behavior of drinking and to the internal conservation of water. Here is an example of how a neuropeptide — which perhaps corresponds to a mood state — can integrate what happens in the body with what happens in the brain. (A further important point that I only mention here is that overall integration of behavior seems designed to be consistent with survival.)

My basic speculation here is that neuropeptides provide the physiological basis for the emotions. As my colleagues and I argued in a recent paper in the *Journal of Immunology* (Pert et al., 1985): The striking pattern of neuropeptide receptor distribution in mood-regulating areas of the brain, as well as their role in mediating communication through the whole organism, makes neuropeptides the obvious candidates for the biochemical mediation of emotion. It may be too that each neuropeptide biases information processing uniquely when occupying receptors at nodal points with the brain and body. If so, then each neuropeptide may evoke a unique "tone" that is equivalent to a mood state.

In the beginning of my work, I matter-of-factly presumed that emotions were in the head or the brain. Now I would say they are really in the body as well. They are expressed in the body and are part of the body. I can no longer make a strong distinction between the brain and the body.

The role of angiotensin described here in mediating mind-body emotional behavior is a striking confirmation of Cheek's assumptions about its role in the psychosomatics of stress and surgery in Section IV. This finding suggests that the growing edge of research in mind-body therapy today is to extend this process of ascertaining the specific role of information substances in modulating consciousness, mood, and emotions in everyday life as well as emergency situations. Depth psychologists such as Jung have noted that ancient systems of psychology, medicine, and human development such as kundalini yoga (Jung, 1975, 1976) have always localized consciousness, intuition, and emotion at different levels of the entire mind-body system. Many early cultures (such as the American Indians) considered that it was an aberration characteristic of the white man to believe that consciousness resided only in the head. Pert's conception of the network nature of the mind-body is an important contribution to the archetypal view of psychosomatic phenomena as a single "body-psyche continuum" (Stein, 1976), wherein all sensory, perceptual, intuitive, and emotional experience must be given equal weight for optimum functioning and healing.

PRACTICE

12

Ideomotor Questioning for Investigation of Unconscious "Pain" and Target Organ Vulnerability

The combination of ideomotor questioning methods with rapid scanning of unconscious experience makes possible some tentative explorations into areas of disturbed adaptation which so far have been closed to all but the most superficial of surveys. Work along these lines may be castigated by the organicists of medical research, who say that psychological factors are too difficult to evaluate. The skeptics could be reminded that no objective study of human behavior in health or disease can be acceptable if the personal "weltanschauung" and the subjective responses of the individual are excluded from consideration.

The organicists will point out that exclusion of this factor is necessary because there is no way of communicating with the levels of subjective reaction that relate directly with physiological adaptation. If we counter by saying that the nearest thing to this level can be reached by combining ideomotor questioning methods with hypnosis, the organicists may say that although that is possible, it is a waste of time because only a small fraction of human beings can be deeply hypnotized. This is what Freud said in his widely publicized lectures at Clark University in 1909.

The objection that few can be deeply hypnotized is untrue but it is not important anyway. The 20% figure usually quoted applies to volunteers and is not valid for those who are highly motivated by fear or severe illness (Cheek, 1957). Ideomotor questioning can be used for the induction of hypnosis, and it can be used to uncover unconscious ideation with nearly all people who have the capacity for understanding and communicating thoughts. Unconscious resistance to entering a hypnotic state or cooperating with investigation can be circumvented (Cheek & Davis, 1961).

Although most of us would agree that the brain has evolved as a central clearing house for the scanning of incoming sensations and the selection of appropriate outgoing messages directed toward adaptation, we have been handicapped in our search for knowledge about these adaptations. Environmental threats mean different things to each individual. Conscious understandings of a threat may be greatly deranged by unconscious feelings about the significance of a stress. Let us consider the areas of human adaptation which seem most in need of clarification.

Complexities of Human Immunological Responses

The immune responses are most complex and seem to have evolved with the increasing complexities of vertebrate life. In mammals, they develop after birth, although some of the mother's immune antibodies may get into the baby through the placenta or the amniotic membranes. Women may develop immune responses against the homotransplants of their husband's genetic characteristics to cause habitual abortion in some women. Erythroblastosis occurring with Rh incompatibility or AB-O incompatibility is of this type. The problem of autoimmune reaction is also hard to comprehend unless it relates in some way to self-destructive forces centering on target organs. Hashimoto disease of the thyroid reflects this type of autoimmune response directed against thyroid tissue. All of the collagen diseases seem to relate in some way to autoimmune processes. We have learned that homologous tissue grafts from adult human mammals of the same species are rejected after a time, and that repeat grafting from the same individual causes an accelerated rejection because of reinforced immune reactions to the foreign tissue. Only recently have we discovered that the grafted tissues themselves are competent to develop immune responses against the tissues of the host. We are now beginning to realize in a general way that some of the factors bearing on the abnormal growth characteristics of cancer cells and the capacity of the host to recover from cancer depend on which way the battle is turned. Removal of a majority of the cancer cells by surgery may throw the battle in favor of the host. Irradiation and the effect of radio-mimetic drugs may favor the host by interfering more with the immune responses of the cancer cells than with those of the mature host cells in the area of cancer growth. We now have knowledge of how despair and passive acceptance of cancer can shape the battle (Locke, Power, & Cabot, 1986).

Since we know there have been verified spontaneous cures without treatment in a variety of malignancies including neuroblastoma, choriocarcinoma, carcinoma of the kidney, malignant melanoma, cancer of the bladder, breast, stomach, lower bowel and uterus (Everson & Cole, 1959), we might wonder whether the victors could help us understand more about possible subjective attitudes and the course of battle.

We know that a shift from despair to hope may bring about an amazing shift from illness to health under many circumstances, but we have not explored the unconscious mechanisms responsible for this change. There is evidence that some individuals can decide to die and do so at an appointed time in the absence of disease. We have known that death may occur unreasonably soon in the aged after a stroke or disabling injury. Only since the

Korean War have we realized that American prisoners in their teens and early twenties could lose the will to live, enter a comatose state, and be dead within 48 hours if left alone by their associates. We do not know how these phenomena occur, but we do know that all of the Turkish soldiers who were exposed to the same stresses in captivity that killed 50% of our U.S. soldiers in Korea came through their trials without loss of a single soldier (Mayer, 1958).

Hypesthesia and Tissue Reaction With Scratches

Let us consider some of the possibilities for control of physiologic mechanisms of adaptation. Do we know anything about the relationship between *perception* and *tissue reaction*? The evidence is scanty but stimulating.

CASE 1

In 1952, while attempting to prove to an obstetrical patient that she was better able to anesthetize her arm hypnotically than she thought possible, I ran the point of a hypodermic needle upward from the supposedly anesthetized lower forearm to a point several inches above the antecubital space. The patient winced as the needle reached the antecubital space. The same linear scratch was made along the ventral surface of the sensitive opposite arm. The patient was convinced that there was a difference between the feeling of the arms with this stimulus. Normal sensation was suggested then and the patient discharged. When she was seen a week later at a regular prenatal visit, there was a scratch still visible along the entire length of the arm used as a control, but only the skin above the sensitive antecubital space of the previously anesthetized arm showed a scratch mark comparable to that of the unanesthetized arm. At that time, I did not know anything about the inflammatory enzyme "neurokinin," but the accidental discovery that tissues which were even partially anesthetized seemed to heal more quickly and show less immediate edema and wheal formation proved to be an asset in convincing patients that hypnosis was worthy of investigation.

At first it seemed to me that the difference in tissue behavior might be due to the increased elasticity of the skin on the "numb" side, making it yield more readily before the needle and thereby suffering less injury. There certainly was a demonstrable tensing of the muscles during injury to the sensitive skin. This could expose the skin to more trauma; the needle would encounter a more resistant bed under the skin. It was probable, too, that the dermal myofibrils contract reflexly when pain is experienced. I could devise no satisfactory way of proving to myself that tissues anesthetized by suggestion reacted less energetically than sensitive tissues. In the meantime, it was interesting and encouraging for surgical, obstetrical, and cancer therapy patients to discover that their mind could alter tissue reactions to injury in some way. I have repeated the test with better than 99% positive response in more than 1,000 personal patients since then. Box 19 summarizes the scratch demonstration of hypnotic analgesia and healing.

Pain Perception and Physiological Response

CASE 2

Use of these theoretical principles derived from accidental observation made it possible for me to speak with enough confidence to a discouraged obstetrical patient to help her change her behavior dramatically in the course of an overwhelming puerperal sepsis. The patient had been doing well after delivery of a Down's syndrome child. She hemorrhaged profusely on the third day postpartum, immediately after being told that she could go home but would have to leave her baby at the hospital for a few days. Her temperature jumped from 98 to 105 degrees after a transfusion. There was a pure growth of E. coli on urine culture and a continued septic course. Pyelitis was ruled out by absence of microscopic evidence of infection in the urine. In spite of adequate doses of penicillin and gantrisin initially, followed by chloromycetin, she went on to develop abdominal rigidity and rebound tenderness on the third day of her illness. This patient, reported elsewhere (Cheek, 1957), had been a nonresponsive subject for hypnosis. Under the circumstances of her downhill course, she either had an increased motivation for responding or else she was already in hypnosis when I began talking to her about it. I said that muscle spasm was interfering with blood supply in the uterus, that the drugs were fine drugs but that they were useless if they could not get into the area where the bacteria were causing trouble. Evidence to corroborate my fabricated theory was demonstrated to her by pressing again on her rigid abdomen. I said that the pain was tightening all the muscles in that area and blocking off the blood supply.

Within the space of time that it took to explain these matters, it became apparent that she was already in hypnosis without a formal induction. I asked her to press on her abdomen when she knew that all the pain was gone. After she carried out this suggestion, with the usual slow motion of a hypnotized subject, I asked her to go even deeper and stay in hypnosis just as she was for the next 24 hours in order to let her body best use the medication and best use the rest to rebuild her resistance to infection.

Her pulse rate, temperature, and respiration remained normal after the initial 24 hours of continued hypnotic state. It seemed noteworthy that she had lost the rigidity and rebound tenderness within five minutes of signaling that the pain was gone. Rebound tenderness and reflex abdominal rigidity are supposedly controlled through sympathetic innervation from the peritoneum through the spinal cord. I decided that I must learn more about the mediating factors in pain perception and physiological response.

BOX 19: SCRATCH DEMONSTRATION OF HYPNOTIC ANALGESIA
AND HEALING

"You need to know how much you can alter the way your body reacts to injury. It is easy to learn that once you can see how you can make one arm unable to feel an irritation while keeping the other arm normally sensitive."

1. *Accessing hypnotic analgesia*
   a. "As I touch your right arm, I would like you to experience it getting less sensitive, about the way it would feel if you had been lying on that arm for a couple of hours while you were asleep."
   b. "When your arm begins feeling heavy and kind of numb, your yes finger will lift. Notice how long it takes between the time your finger lifts and the time the message gets to your conscious mind so that you could say, 'It's numb.'"

2. *Self-testing of hypnotic analgesia*
   a. "When your arm feels kind of numb and about half as sensitive as your left arm, your no finger will lift. Say 'now' when you have done that, and then please check it yourself. Pinch the arm. Each time you notice a little difference, your confidence will grow in what you are able to do."
   b. "With your eyes closed, please notice the feeling as I touch your numb arm with the tip of a needle (or knife point). As I go up your arm, please tell me when it begins to feel sharper. [This is usually just below the elbow.] Now compare that with the sharpness as I touch your normally sensitive arm." [This reinforces the difference in feeling.]

3. *Scratch test of hypnotic healing*
   a. "I'll now make a harmless scratch on both arms so you can see the effects of hypnotic healing. Please don't move, because I want to make the scratches in the same way for you to compare, in about 20 minutes, to see the difference."
   b. In about 20 minutes, the patient will be able to see that the "hypnotized" arm has little or no redness or swelling around the scratch area, while the normal arm does.
   c. "Now your inner healing mind can let that yes finger lift again as both arms return to normal."
   d. Discuss the implications of this demonstration of hypnotic analgesia and healing in relation to the particular problem the patient is encountering.

Three years after this experience, it was possible to obtain a subjective report from this patient in a medium-trance state. Asked to orient to the time of the hospitalization and signal if she recognized some factor that might have been responsible for the bleeding, she gave a signal and said,

"You did not tell me, but I knew something was wrong with my baby by the way you said you wanted to keep her for a few days until she could gain a little weight. I did not want to leave her alone there."

The patient went on to teach me a lesson about ideomotor communication by saying, "When you did not tell me the truth about my little girl, I knew there must be something very seriously wrong."

I then asked the patient to call to mind something that might have helped her make the dramatic improvement in her condition. After giving an ideomotor signal from her designated finger, she said, "I could tell by your face that you meant what you said about my being very sick and that you wanted me to use hypnosis to let the medicine start working. I had not wanted to live because I had done so much vomiting. I thought that must have made my baby abnormal. Then I realized she would need me to take care of her. I had to get well."

Conscious and Unconscious Pain

During the course of exploring various means of helping patients control or ignore pain, it has gradually become clear that there are two forms of pain and that these share the same potential for disturbing tissue resistance and the rate of healing. Pain is commonly described as a consciously perceived unpleasant response to noxious stimuli.

CASE 3

That there could be an awareness of pain at an unconscious level, and that this could cause as much physiologic disturbance as the conscious pain, had not occurred to me until I encountered a patient several years ago who had diffuse lesions of poison oak dermatitis. She had healed all her weeping, blistered areas of skin within 48 hours of signaling with an ideomotor response that she had made all the lesions numb and that she could keep them numb for 24 hours. She had been consciously aware of the painful lesions on her face, neck, and vulva, but had not been aware of any other discomfort. This led me to wonder whether edema, vascular stasis, and limitation of motion could be caused by unconscious pain.

CASE 4

A patient with a history of rheumatoid arthritis that had occurred 20 years earlier during a time of emotional stress was now asked to perform an experiment for which she would have no conscious recollection. She was asked to awaken one day two weeks hence feeling exactly as she had felt during her illness 20 years ago. She was to have troublesome dreams the preceding night, and all of her unconscious attention was to be centered upon her left wrist. She had never had trouble with this wrist. I wanted her to focus all the physiologic responses stored in her memory upon that one wrist. She was asked to find some pretext for calling me and coming in to the office on that day to report.

On the appointed day this patient awakened after a troubled sleep. She decided her car needed a check-up. This would require her coming to the city where I was then practicing. While preparing breakfast she noticed a swelling of her left hand. Her fingers and wrist were stiff. She came to the office to inquire whether or not this might be a recurrence of her arthritis. Within an hour of being reminded that she had agreed to contribute to an experiment, she lost the edema and limitation of motion.

CASE 5

The brother of a patient under treatment with hypnosis for dysmenorrhea was permitted to sit in during the induction and preparation for therapy. He entered a deep trance while I was talking to his sister. He had undergone surgery on the previous day under local anesthesia for removal of all his third molars. Both sides of his face were symmetrically swollen. He had no conscious pain but his fingers indicated yes to the question, "Is there any pain?" I asked him to recall the feeling of the novocaine injection as it was made on the left side, to signal when it had been put in, and to signal again when the numbness was complete. He had indicated with an ideomotor response that there was awareness of pain, although there had been a verbal level denial of it. After his signal for completion of the task, a designated no finger signal was given to the question, "Is there any pain now on the left side?" A yes signal answered the same question about pain on the right side. He verbally reiterated that the right side was only painful if he opened his jaw more than an inch. Within 20 minutes of the signal for unconscious rejection of pain, there was a return of normal contour to the left side of his face. He had been reading in an adjoining room and was unaware of the changes until his sister remarked on the change in his face. He was so pleased with what he had done that he sat down in the waiting room and "put the anesthetic" into his right jaw. A telephone call from his sister the next day reported loss of all edema and return of full jaw motion within an hour of leaving the office.

CASE 6

Another example derived from these chance observations relates to pain, but also clearly shows that the brain is charged with monitoring the body situations at all times. An excellent hypnotic subject admitted to the hospital for treatment of hyperemesis of pregnancy was being rehearsed with development of anesthesia to recapture her self-confidence in being able to use hypnosis. She signaled with a finger that she had achieved an absolute anesthesia of her right arm. She gave no verbal indication of feeling pain of a needle puncture and, in fact, denied any awareness of any sort from that arm. Anesthetic effect was then augmented by a maneuver attributed to Milton Erickson, who had developed it to a high point. She was asked to hallucinate the right arm as remaining in one position after I had moved it to a new position. The brain perceives expected sensations, and the patient effecting this type of dissociation when no suggestions of anesthesia have been accepted will report pain from an imagined needle prick in the space where the arm is supposed to be but will have no awareness from the real, displaced arm. The patient adding this dissociation by hallucination to her complete anesthesia was now asked to have the index finger of her normal hand move every time she felt the needle touch her skin. She was asked also to say "Now" whenever she could feel the touch. She reported verbally every time I touched "normal" skin, and this was accompanied by a simultaneous movement of the index finger. When the displaced real arm was touched, she gave no verbal indication of awareness, but her index finger signaled even though every precaution had been taken to prevent her from knowing just where the needle was being applied.

During the past decade it has been possible to corroborate the observation of Esdaile that rejection of pain awareness at an unconscious level improves host resistance to infection and speeds the recovery from localized infection. My first glimpse of the possibility that this increased potential for combat might make the difference between life and death was offered by a patient with a spreading puerperal peritonitis which had not responded to chemotherapy (Cheek, 1957). Observations with herpes simplex, persistent urinary tract infections, skin abscesses, perirectal abscess, and acute vaginitis of several types have convinced me that this is more than a cortisol-like response which could dangerously remove the barriers to spread of infection. There has been no spread of infection in any case on which hypnosis has been used. Some research in Japan suggests that the human being in hypnosis may produce more effective immune responses to infection than is possible when energy is wasted in responses to pain and fear (Ikemi, 1959). We need to know more.

What is the Physiological Meaning of Pain?

These observations and others which have been reported elsewhere (Cheek, 1960a,b; 1961 a,b) have suggested that our concepts of pain must be altered to incorporate the evidence. Pain is usually defined as a consciously perceived sensation in response to a noxious stimulus, but this sort of definition seems worthless. George Crile (Crile & Lower, 1914) has pointed out that we cannot feel damaging stimuli in parts of the body which have not been phylogenetically conditioned for expectancy of potentially pain-producing damage. We feel pain with slow, tearing forces on the bowel or mesentery but we do not feel slow, cutting trauma with a scalpel. Attention to the stimulus, expectancy of pain, and speed of initial trauma all play a part in what we call *pain*. Authorities on pain such as Judovich and Bates (1949), Wolff and Wolf (1948), and Thomas Lewis (1942), make no mention of the spontaneous loss of pain perception in time of great danger or on entering a deep hypnotic state. Authorities writing on the subject of obstetrical analgesia have been unable to correlate the evaluations of patients. They have all been forced to lean on such artificial structures as the capacity of the patient to remember furniture in the labor or delivery room. We have seen that the capacity for consciously remembering something has no relationship to the fact.

Use of amnesia to measure the quality or intensity of pain is scientifically disrespectful to the truth. We should have some other way of recognizing the effects of trauma and inflammation. We should have some way also of understanding how these effects can be altered by expectancy, recognition, and emotion. Each of these may have conscious and unconscious components. Perhaps we should consider the unconscious as well as the conscious perceptions of pain. This will require a change in definition and some definite changes in scientific thought. Damaging stimuli of surgery may be painless by virtue of the chemical anesthesia. Preoperative anticipations of great pain, however, might lead a well-anesthetized patient to develop the same postoperative edema, vascular stasis, and muscular guarding that would have occurred in the old-fashioned way without anesthesia. A surgical team talking in an alarming way over a previously calm, sleeping patient might produce results which are even worse than those which could have been produced with anticipation and no general anesthesia (Cheek, 1959, 1960b). What, then, is pain and how can we learn more about it? For answers to these questions, we must turn to the best authorities—the patients. We must ask each individual patient about expectancy, about the feeling, and about what that feeling means. Conscious reporting is limited. We need to know more.

Thermal Burns and Tissue Reaction in Relation to Pain

CASE 7

During preliminary discussion of hypnosis prior to a demonstration of phenomena, a subject was asked whether the blister on her finger was painful. She immediately said "No," as she reached over with the other hand to rub it. After pressing on it, she corroborated the initial statement. A few minutes later she was learning how to give symbol answers with her fingers. I touched the blister and asked, "Does the unconscious part of your mind feel any discomfort as I rub this blister?" Verbally she repeated the "no" answer but her "yes" finger was slowly rising in the typical trembling response of an unconscious answer. The subject was then asked to make the blister area numb as though novocaine had been injected into it. An ideomotor signal was requested for this recognition and for the promise that the anesthetic would continue during the next 12 hours. At the end of two hours, the blister exudate had resorbed. What was responsible for this? Could it be better circulation, or something else?

CASE 8

In 1959, I was asked to see the wife of a physician for the purpose of using hypnosis to relieve the pain of second- and third-degree burns extending from her buttocks to her neck. There were large keloids encircling most of the second-degree burns. Although five weeks had elapsed since her accident, she was requiring demerol every two hours. There had been very little spontaneous epithelialization. The patient had been adamant in prohibiting attempts at skin grafting because she could not stand the thought of adding to her pain by trimming donor sites. She was afraid to take an anesthetic. With the help of a Chevreul pendulum initially, and then finger signals as she went more deeply into hypnosis, it took twenty minutes to discover that she had been punishing herself severely. When she was 17 her mother had caught her smoking a cigarette. Pointing a finger at her, the mother had exclaimed, "Some day God will punish you for this, you are not a good Mormon." The patient came out of hypnosis to tell me the burns had occurred while she was resting on a sofa in front of the television. She had finished a highball and had taken a sleeping pill to relax her after a strenuous day helping her husband in the office. She had fallen asleep, and the cigarette in the ashtray on her lap had rolled down behind her nylon dressing gown. The smoldering heat awakened her with a start. As she pulled away from the sofa, the air rushed in exploding the robe. Her back was burned as she ran along the hall to her husband.

Recovery of the memory about her mother came as a surprise. I had asked her "to orient to some reason for feeling so guilty as to suffer for five weeks like this." The thought entered her mind a few seconds after the signaling finger lifted.

After superimposing her conscious reasoning upon the unconscious one—that God was punishing her for being a bad Mormon—she was able to accept a feeling of coolness and numbness of all burned areas and to acknowledge the promise to keep the anesthesia for 24 hours. A second session reinforced and continued the anesthesia. Seventy-two hours after the initial interview, there was an interesting change in the appearance of the lesions. Where there had been keloids elevated 6 to 10 millimeters above the level of the surrounding skin, there were now depressions. This is the type of reaction which one finds after injecting cortisol derivatives beneath keloids. The response must be different in some way from the cortisol anti-inflammatory effect, however, because I have never seen spread of infection after this type of anti-inflammatory pseudo-cortisol response (Cheek, 1960a). We know that cortisol derivatives allow the spread of infections when the fibrin and vascular barriers are broken down.

This patient needed no demerol after the first interview. She permitted skin grafting a few days later. She even did better than heal: three years after the injury, there are only two small patches of scarred skin under each axilla. All the rest of her back is of uniform color and the skin is of uniform texture and mobility! This was her doing. She had sufficient pride to work at maintaining the imagery of normal skin on her back. This result is not supposed to happen after skin grafting for third-degree burns. It would be helpful to know just how guilt interfered with healing. We could reason that guilt feelings intensified the awareness of supposedly just punishment, that pain led to spasm of local muscles and stasis of blood. These are suppositions. It makes me wonder if more effort should be made to search out fears and guilt feelings with all human beings who are victims of trauma. Box 20 summarizes an ideodynamic approach to the healing of burn injuries.

Body Image and Body Awareness

Patients in hypnosis give vivid and often helpful verbal impressions of what their bodies look like and how they feel. Their unconscious idea of anatomy may be childlike and very different from the idea they render on awakening from hypnosis. Their impressions may give valuable clues to target organ vulnerability to stress.

CASE 9

While watching a demonstration of a method for teaching a child how to imagine an electric wire running from a part of his body up to the brain and then turning off a light that represented the feeling from that part, I was amused at the choice of colors used by the youngster. The color of the light was so emphatically and quickly stated that it seemed meaningful to the child. I wondered if this dissociative method of inquiry might be helpful for understanding body image and awareness in adults. It seemed reasonable to ask the subject to hallucinate a sort of telephone switchboard in the shape of a body with Christmas tree lights to symbolize the feelings from whatever organs or extremities seemed appropriate in each case.

I experimented with this approach during a symposium on medical hypnosis in the fall of 1959. It proved most interesting. The physician acting as a subject was in a medium state of hypnosis. He showed a lag of time between

BOX 20: IDEODYNAMIC HEALING OF BURN INURIES

The method will vary in relation to the surface extent and the depth of a burn. Ewin (1986) has shown that early action with hypnosis immediately after a burn and during the time the individual is in a hypnotic-like state of shock may allow even third-degree burn to heal without need for skin grafting and without scarring. If a patient is seen hours or days after experiencing a burn, proceed as follows, explaining the process as a means of eliminating inflammation and allowing healing to occur rapidly.

1. *Accessing inner healing resources*
   "Remember a time when you walked into cold water. It felt cold for a while until a time when you got used to it. That represents a degree of numbness. When you are feeling cold at an unconscious, ideodynamic level, your brain will shut down the messages that cause inflammation and interfere with healing.

   "Imagine standing in cold water up to your knees. When you are feeling that unconsciously, your yes finger will lift. When you are half as sensitive as normal, your no finger will lift.

   "Now, walk in further until the cold water is up to your hips. Your yes finger will lift when you are cold from your hips to your knees, and your no finger will lift when you are numb from your hips to your toes. Your right hand wrist will be below the water level and will also feel numb." [This will happen without explanation, even though the patient is lying in bed.]

2. *Self-testing of hypnotic analgesia*
   "Now you know how to make parts of your body alter sensations. Please place your cold, numb right hand over the burned area and experience the coldness and numbness flow into the burned area. When you know the burn is cold and numb, your yes and no fingers will lift to let you know how well you are doing."

3. *Ratifying and maintaining healing*
   a. **"That coldness and numbness will remain there for at least two hours. Then it may be necessary to repeat the exercise. You will get better each time you do it, and the result will last longer and work more effectively as you go along."**
   b. Any difficulty with this procedure may indicate a need to work through emotional problems, as in Box 13.

"seeing" the light in each area and being able to see it at whatever level is represented by the "mind's eye" where he could tell us the color and intensity of light. The head was represented by a yellow light, the arms by green lights of the same shade and intensity, but he had a great big red light above the knee in his right leg. I asked him to let his fingers answer the question, "Do you have any pain in that leg?" The answer was no. I asked him to orient back through the years of his life experience to the time when a big red light was put in for that right leg. There was a pause and then the designated finger indicated he had arrived in his thinking at that time.

A few seconds later he started to chuckle as he said, "That is the darndest thing! I played football in high school and I had a charley-horse all through school because I kept bumping that leg." Here was an apparent carry-over of an unconsciously perceived hyperawareness, conditioned by multiple injuries many years ago. Was this a key to more knowledge that might help us understand target organ vulnerability to stress?

This hallucinated switchboard body has been most useful in my practice of gynecology and obstetrics because it has revealed just that type of information. Non-orgasmic patients have reported "black lights" representing rejection of feeling from genital areas. Some have actually stated that they could see a light socket but a piece of adhesive tape was covering it. When these subjects are asked to orient back to a time when "there is a light there" or when something happens to "make the tape be placed there," there have been helpful bits of information which were readily explained by the patient in the light of later understandings at the time of interview.

Increasingly I have been impressed by the conviction of many patients that very powerful forces have influenced their attitudes toward themselves as women, according to what they think they experienced before, during and after birth. There have been many "lights" which have been changed by conversations in operating rooms while patients have been anesthetized. There have been strong hyperawarenesses for various organs because of identifications, because of material absorbed in the reading of semi-scientific reports in magazines, and because of conditioning. Box 21 summarizes a "body lights" approach to ameliorating pain and inflammation.

"Imprinting" and Posthypnotic Suggestion in Humans

In my experience, the most common examples of misdirected sexual development and physiological performance seem to relate to what Herbert Spiegel (1960) might call "imprinting." Adult females who have suffered from acne and dysmenorrhea have observed a change in their skin and have rid themselves of dysmenorrhea on realizing that they had experienced early rejection because of a parental wish for a boy, and that this did not really mean they were expected to become boys. Clinically, the matter of fact seems not as important as the *apparent* fact that the patient believed it to be fact at

1. *Accessing and transducing symptoms into "lights"*

   a. **"See yourself standing in front of a full-length mirror. See tiny
   lights in different parts of your body. The colors represent the
   feelings of those parts. When you can see the total picture, your yes
   finger will lift to let me know."**

   b. Scan the body, getting the color of each light and what that color
   represents to the patient. The process starts with unimportant parts
   of the body, ending with exploration of the organ or extremity
   suspected of having problems. For example, with rheumatoid arthritis, in which multiple joints are involved but some are more
   painful than others, one might proceed as follows, selecting the
   least painful for the first therapeutic approach. Confidence builds
   with each success from least to most painful.

   **"Look at the entire image of yourself and let your unconscious
   mind select the joint you know to be the least inflamed, the least
   painful. When you know what it is, your yes finger will lift to tell
   me which joint and what color."**

2. *Therapeutic reframing*

   a. **"Let your inner mind shift back to a time when there was a light
   that represents comfort and flexibility. When you are there, your yes
   finger will lift. [Wait for the signal.] Now come forward to the first
   moment that color (light) was put there in place of the comfortable
   light. When your yes finger lifts, please tell me how old you are and
   what is happening."**

   b. **"Now, is there any good reason why you should continue with
   pain in that joint?"**

3. *Ratifying therapeutic gain*

   a. **"Now that you know what has been happening, is your inner
   mind willing to let you turn off that unconscious pain and continue
   the process of healing?"** [If the answer is no, it will be necessary to
   orient to whatever factor is standing in the way, as in Step 2.]

   b. **"Go forward now to the time when you will not only be free of
   the pain in that joint, but will have turned off the pain in all the
   joints that have been troubling you — a time when you are no longer
   afraid of pain returning, when you are really well in every respect.
   When you are there, your yes finger will lift and you will see a
   month, day, and year, as though they were written on a blackboard."**

the ideational horizon of thinking reflected by ideomotor symbol responses.

Spiegel has likened the neurotic behavior of human beings who are disturbed by single episode experiences to the very powerful impact of some single episodes with lower animals. Lorenz (1935) found that graylag goslings exposed to a wooden decoy duck during the first day of life would select and relate to that duck in preference to their own mother thereafter. Hess (1959) explored this matter of single, significant experiences compared to the repeated conditioned types of learning in some birds and mammals. Spiegel compared the "compulsive triad" of posthypnotic behavior to this phenomenon of apparent "imprinting" in human compulsive neurotic behavior. An understanding linked with a powerful emotional stress such as birth, general anesthesia, serious illness, coma, or frightening labor may be repressed into unconscious zones of mentation and produce disturbed compulsive behavior which then has to be rationalized in some way by the patient. This is what happens with a suggestion for unusual posthypnotic behavior. There may be no amnesia for the suggestion. In this case the subject may decide intellectually to discard the suggestion. If there is posthypnotic amnesia for the suggestion then, as Spiegel points out, there is *amnesia, compulsive behavior*, dictated by the suggestion, and *conscious rationalization for the behavior*.

Continuation of the process of posthypnotic behavior varies with a number of factors, the most significant of which is probably the unconscious prehypnotic understanding that this is an experimental situation which is not expected to continue. Such a censoring mechanism may not be available for protection during great emotional stress.

Overview of Research on Tissue Trauma, Pain, and Inflammation

Let us explore some of the reasons we may hope to advance in our understanding and therapy for psychosomatic disease. First we must know why an organ or system becomes susceptible to damage, and then we must understand how damage occurs.

Esdaile observed that "mesmeric" relief of pain diminished the inflammatory reactions of trauma and infection (Esdaile, 1850/1957). The rush of enthusiasm about chemical anesthesia and what Huxley has called the "voluntary ignorance" (1956) of the medical profession held up the investigation of just what happens to make this possible. Thirty-two years went by.

In 1877 Delboeuf, Professor of Psychology at Liege (1877/1947), did some experiments with hypnosis in an effort to understand the reasons for apparent rapid healing and the failure of blisters to form when hypnotically anesthetized parts of the body were traumatized or burned. He hypnotized two volunteers and burned both arms of each subject as nearly equally as possible. Each subject had one arm normally sensitive and the other "anesthetized" by suggestion. Blisters did not form on the insensitive arms, and healing was more rapid on the insensitive arms. Reversal of the experiment using the opposite arm for control gave the same results. Seventy-three years of voluntary blindness elapsed before the next progress.

In 1950 Graham showed that reactions and permeability of minute vessels in the skin could be altered in situations perceived by the individual as threatening. The general principles of this type of reaction might be expected. We see it with the ideo-vascular reactions of blanching or blushing with emotion. Graham used conversational methods of interview.

Armstrong, Jepson, Keele and Stewart (1957) found pain-producing substances in blister exudate. In the same year, Ostfield, Chapman, Goodell, and Wolff, (1957) found pain-producing polypeptides in the scalp exudates of patients suffering from migraine headaches.

The first major contribution to our knowledge of unconsciously controllable tissue reactions came from Cornell Medical Center in New York. Chapman, Goodell, and Harold Wolff (1959a,b) reported their findings with what appears to have been an independent repetition of Delboeuf's experiment. Harold Wolff had not mentioned hypnosis in his 1948 book *Pain*, published in collaboration with Stewart Wolf of the University of Oklahoma School of Medicine.

Results were not particularly remarkable when one arm was normally sensitive and the other "anesthetized." But they added another step which is of utmost importance. They suggested to the hypnotized volunteers that something very uncomfortable would be happening to the normal arm. Anticipation of an unknown painful stimulus brought about a marked difference in tissue reaction between the insensitive arm and the perceptive arm to which the subject was giving increased attentiveness. Now when the same stimulus was applied to both arms, there was a marked inflammatory reaction in the sensitive skin and very little reaction in the insensitive skin.

Perfusates were collected from both traumatized areas of each subject by running physiological saline into the subcutaneous tissues at the upper edge of the injured skin and collecting it by gravity through another needle at the lower margin. It was possible for them to demonstrate the presence of an enzyme released by efferent nerves at the site of injury. The perfusate from the consciously painful skin area contained much of this substance, but the amount of enzyme was diminished or absent on the anesthetized side. The enzyme has specific, reproducible qualities. It produced signs of inflammation when injected into normal skin elsewhere in the body. The perfusate from the "anesthetized" skin did not cause an inflammatory reaction.

In reference to the meaning of their work, these investigators state that release of this enzyme which they have called "neurokinin" probably represents an adaptive mechanism for protection of the organism: Chapman, Goodell, & Wolff (1959b, p. 104) say:

Such adaptive reactions at times may be essential to survival, but if evoked inappropriately or excessively may contribute to disease, since non-noxious stimulation becomes noxious and mildly damaging stimuli result in greater injury.

Conclusion

We have discussed some techniques of ideomotor questioning and their values for communication with levels of awareness approximating those where perception and attitude govern physiologic adaptations. Consideration has been given to some applications of hypnosis and ideomotor techniques of analysis in areas of medicine where we need to understand better the emotional forces and their influence. *Not all evidence derived from the use of ideomotor questioning methods and hypnosis is valid. It is increasingly evident, however, that hypnosis is a natural phenomenon occurring spontaneously and often helpfully during times of emotional and physical stress.* It is a phenomenon relating to self-protection for the individual through camouflage and restriction of energy waste. In the hypnotic state, imagery and tissue memory can be mobilized for immediate use, just as they are in times of stress. For this reason, the combination of hypnosis with ideomotor communication permits more rapid and complete access to associations of imagery and physiologic response to stress than any other means so far available.

13

Emotional Factors in Persistent Pain States

Physicians are often disturbed and made angry by the seeming perverseness of patients who fail to get well under the best of treatment. Intractable pains of headaches, tic-douloureux, disc syndrome, bursitis, rheumatoid arthritis, reflex sympathetic dystrophy, phantom limb, and Raynaud's phenomenon are among the most frequent sources of therapeutic frustration. Neurosurgical attempts to relieve pain with problem patients are sometimes comparable to dynamiting the power house to turn off the kitchen light. The distress of sensory deprivation with nerve section may be worse than the original pain.

Treatment restricted to conscious outcroppings of pain may be successful with any mode of therapy. *The problems of pain states to be discussed here relate to the unconscious meanings and the usually unrecognized unconscious elements of pain. These may continue unabated long after the patient has stopped complaining.*

Livingston (1943) has given us an eloquent lament over the problems of persistent pain states:

> I have been increasingly impressed with the dynamic characteristics of pain, its urgency and its remarkable ability to find a new route when the customary channels have been blocked. Sometimes, when one thing after another that I do to relieve pain has failed, there seems to be a malicious insistency about it. I feel almost that it acquires a personality, like a spoiled and stubborn child which fiercely resents interference and punishment, and deliberately goes ahead seeking means to break over restraint.

The ability to find new routes for the pain rests with the many emotional factors which come into action as soon as pain has acquired a meaning. There is no easy way to understand or correct these factors, but an attempt will be made to suggest some working plans which the author (DBC) has found helpful during 23 years of experience with utilizing hypnosis as a psychotherapeutic modality in the treatment of pain states.

General Considerations

Any injury or infection coupled with strong feelings of fear, guilt, anxiety, depression, or dramatized identification becomes a potential source of subsequent disability. The syndrome known as *reflex sympathetic dystrophy* is a good example of general principles relating to the onset and continuation of pain states. The initial injury is often minor in extent but is coupled with great emotional stress. The emotional stress sets a limited pattern of responses to an initially simple, triggering mechanism. There is an injury and the cause of injury, plus a group of associated thoughts relating to what the victim was doing at the moment of injury. In time, the triggering mechanism is associated with more and more external, often ridiculous stimuli capable of reminding the patient, unconsciously, to be alarmed. The physiological alarm response to these is unconscious and totally beyond the ordinary conscious, willed controls, totally out of reach of reason. The widening circle of sensitizing or triggering stimuli eventually confuses the patient and medical attendants into believing there is no resolution for the problem.

To understand this series of developments we must know that *the presence of great emotional or physical stress evokes a state which is indistinguishable from that of hypnosis.* The unconscious response to injury is similar to the effect of a strongly given posthypnotic suggestion. Unlike ordinary learning by repetition, this memory is completed (learned) on initial impact.

Single-shot type of learning was observed in chicks by Spalding in 1873 and in graylag goslings by the ornithologist Lorenz in 1935. Lorenz called it "imprinting." It is apparently useful in nature by permitting young animals an immediate, fixed recognition of their parent after one visual experience. It appears that something similar to imprinting occurs at times of great stress with mammals and birds, and we may speculate on the possibility that imprinted action and reaction have the fortuitous effect of permitting immediate response to a repeated threat without waste of time in attempting to learn via repetition, which takes time. However, the response may not always be appropriate to the situation. With increasing scope and variation of the threatening stimuli, it is increasingly necessary to recognize differences between threats and to discriminate between responses. In nature and in human life, the preparation for variable threats and appropriate responses occurs during games of war. The young of all carnivorous and omnivorous mammals exercise each other with variations of attack and response. In higher development, this type of exercise occurs with fire drills, military training, and all competitive sports. Never are animals or human beings trained to vary their physiological responses to injury or disease. The primitive reactions of inflammation occur with any kind of noxious stimulus and result in changes which are more or less appropriate for contaminated wounds. Inactivity, muscle guarding, vascular stasis, fibrin deposition, fluid and electrolyte retention, and local tissue necrosis are shared by human beings with the lowest of birds and mammals. The only difference is that lower mammals have some advantage in licking their wounds. The reactions of human tissues and regional muscles are the same in contaminated wounds as in sterile surgical wounds. We have no unconscious exercises to help us discriminate between various possibilities of response to a given injury.

Herbert Spiegel (1960) has suggested that imprinting is comparable to the classic posthypnotic suggestion, and that it may be the basis of neurotic behavior. What he has said of neuroses may be transposed to considerations of psychosomatic disease. With imprinting and posthypnotic suggestions there are:

1. amnesia for the activating stimulus;
2. compulsion to reproduce the imprinted reaction;
3. rationalization for the evoked behavior.

With disease we find something making the tissues vulnerable. There may be no conscious knowledge of the first stimulus to cause this vulnerability. Then follows an unconscious compulsion to adapt as the alarmed, primitive brain dictates. The original associations are unknown to the conscious mind of the patient. For this reason, the patient may go through life rationalizing in necessary ways for the uncritical and unhealthy "package deal" of responses which were determined by the initial experience.

Unconscious Awareness of Disease

The human mind seems able to detect where tissue damage has occurred, even when there is no conscious awareness of disease or pain. There are so many variations in types of pain and ways in which it is described that we must wonder if our understandings and use of the word *pain* are justified. (See also, Erickson, 1980a, Vol IV.) By definition, pain is a consciously perceived awareness of noxious stimuli. We ignore everything that has caused tissue damage in the absence of consciously perceived pain. If we are to develop a comprehensive view of pain, we must think of it in terms of unconscious and histological components as well as the conscious elements. We should measure pain with myograms, electrical field potentials, pH of tissue fluids, changes in electrolytes, and variations in infrared radiation. We should also know as much as possible about the emotional factors capable of alleviating or aggravating the effects of disease.

Tissues in vulnerable parts of the body may be visibly and biochemically cured between episodes of conscious pain while the unconscious mind is still sending out an increased flow of protective responses. At times of stress, these efferent messages from higher centers are augmented in ways which may not be helpful in relation to the threat (Chapman, Goodell, & Wolff, 1959a).

Inflammatory Enzymes

Overactive efferent messages from higher centers release histamine, heparin, and possibly serotonin at the sensitized site. Enzymes in the area break up proteins at their peptide linkages into bradykinin-like proteolytic enzymes which are responsible for vasodilatation, diapedesis, and localization of leucocytes (Duthie & Chain, 1939). Enzymes such as bradykinin, neurokinin and fibrinolysin (plasmin) cause muscle guarding which restricts circulation of blood around the sensitized area. These enzymes are also capable of causing pain in parts of the body which are conditioned for transmitting consciously painful stimuli. Predominantly, however, they are inflammatory enzymes, regardless of their consciously painful effects. Tonic contraction of regional muscles, stasis of circulation, extravasation of fluid and cells tend to interfere with spread of infection, but they also handicap healing of injured tissues. These changes go on without regard for conscious awareness of discomfort.

Ideomotor Methods of Recognizing Subliminal Pain and Tissue Vulnerability

There is logical evidence to support the speculation that expectation of injury or disease has much to do with target organs being vulnerable. Research workers with the late Harold Wolff at Cornell have found that expectation of unknown pain increased neurokinin release at the point of trauma with hypnotized subjects (Chapman, Goodell, & Wolff, 1959a). Identification with other sufferers may lay the groundwork for the onset of disease in specific organs or parts of the body. Apprehension releases fibrinolysins in the blood which are capable of causing pain in addition to causing surgical and obstetrical hemorrhage (MacFarlane & Biggs, 1946; Margolis, 1957). Particularly impressive have been the guilt-associated genito-urinary disorders which confront urologists and gynecologists in their practice. These include fungal, protozoan, and viral infections of the penis and vagina, specific and nonspecific prostatitis, recurrent urinary tract infections, pelvic congestion syndrome, uterine myomata, and endometriosis. Thought-provoking also are the occurrences of identical malignant tumors in husbands and wives of different genetic backgrounds. The French have recognized this phenomenon and call it "carcinomea-deux." It is usually attributed to similar factors of food intake and habit. The author has known two couples with this coincident sharing of malignant disease. One couple shared a bronchogenic, squamous cell cancer, and the other couple doubled up with cancer of the larynx.

With respect for these facets of disease, our investigations of pain should include unconscious evaluations of the disease plus a long-range scanning of its meaning in the past as well as in the present. Ideomotor methods can be used quickly and with very light levels of hypnosis. Resistances are easily recognized. An unconsciously hallucinated pseudo-orientation into the future is of great help in evaluating willingness to get well and in uncovering sources of resistance.

The unconscious mind seems to possess keen awareness of time sequences and associated environmental stimuli relating to onset or recurrence of disease. Scanning of experience can be rapidly carried out at ideomotor levels of awareness. Significant incidents can be located and designated by finger signals without necessity of having the patient talk about the events, or even know consciously what is being reviewed.

The methods of uncovering information at deep levels of awareness and bringing it up to ideational zones of awareness where it can be put into verbal communication has been discussed by the author (Cheek, 1959, 1962c,d).

Persistent Pain and Natural Sleep

It is possible to break the amnesia for repressed dreams and connected thought processes in natural sleep. Variations of unconscious pain and organ function are recognized and are spatially recorded during natural sleep. Exploration of this area has clearly shown that alarm reactions during natural sleep profoundly affect physiological adaptations unless the sleeper can awaken and expose the thoughts to conscious reason. Potentially destructive thought processes in sleep are nearly always repressed. The patient awakens in a panic, does not know why, and has great difficulty getting back to sleep. Disturbing thoughts usually occur during the first half of the night when sleep is deepest. Patients usually object to the word *dream*, stipulating that these thoughts are more real than dreams and seem to occur at levels of sleep which are deeper than are usually associated with conventional dreaming as described by Aserynsky and Kleitman (1955).

Since it is now possible to search the thought sequences in natural sleep, we should attempt to understand what is going on during sleep and to respect the physiological disturbances initiated by alarming thought sequences. We should know that it is possible to break up habit patterns capable of destroying the effects of daytime therapy for mental and physical illness. Ideation in natural sleep has been ignored by most physicians, and it has been most inadequately explored in relation to remembered dreams of psychiatric patients. Remembered dreams are usually garbled and difficult to understand. They usually screen the significant thought processes which are too traumatic for release to conscious levels of awareness.

The method of scanning sleep experience is simple. It can be used to induce and deepen a trance state. As with search of chemo-anesthesia experiences, the therapist must use words carefully to avoid avenues of escape for the patient. Suggestions are given with full expectation that the job will be done. *Patients are quick to discover that the doubting investigator will be willing to accept "no" for an answer to, "Do you remember anything?" or, "Are there any disturbing dreams?"* The patient is asked to have one finger lift to indicate the beginning of sleep, another for each dream or thought sequence, and another finger to indicate the awakening in the morning. The next request is for indication of any thoughts which are important in relation to the problem at hand.

Sources of Resistance to Therapy

Before we can treat persistent pain states, it is necessary to recognize and respect some of the forces capable of disturbing or stopping the march toward relief and ultimate restoration of a comfortable adaptation to environment.

DEVALUATION OF HYPNOSIS BY MEDICAL PROFESSIONALS, RELATIVES, AND FRIENDS

Hypnosis plays a friendly part in the undergraduate education of medical students in only six of the 84 medical schools in the United States of America at the time of writing (around 1964). Since acceptance of hypnosis as a valid tool in medical practice by the 1958 American Medical Association Delegates at the convention in San Francisco, the author has been unable to find the word *hypnosis* mentioned in the lists of more than 1,200 recognized courses published each year by the *Journal of the American Medical Association* in the section on "Conti ·ing Education."

Small wonder, then, that many patients can undergo, year after year, various medical and surgical procedures aimed at relief of pain without hearing a doctor of medicine mention the possibility of hypnotherapy. It is only natural that the patient should have some doubts about its value when it is finally brought up by a friend or relative. In spite of sincere efforts to desuade the patient, however, the doctor may make a friendly call or send a disarming letter. This will mislead the hypnotherapist into believing the doctor chose this method of treatment.

Under such circumstances we will find the patient a very good hypnotic subject at the first session. Results will be limited, however. The patient can usually manifest all sorts of phenomena except any that might lead toward a successful alleviation of the pain. Shame and a need to justify the course are responsible for this lack of success. At the next visit there is total inability to get into hypnosis and it may be impossible to evoke ideomotor responses to questions. The interval between first and second visits has been filled with misgivings and discussions about a matter in which the patient is peculiarly vulnerable to doubts.

It is wise to talk about various attitudes toward hypnosis in the medical profession with care to avoid bitter words about seeming rigidities in medicine. The secondary difficulties of the patient can be explained away as an example of Bernheim's Law of Reversed Effort, due to lack of confidence. The next step is to build that confidence by starting the training as though this were the first visit. The patient should be thoroughly trained for autohypnosis aimed at simple relaxation before making any attempts at analysis of psychological factors in the illness. The author usually asks the patient not to discuss hypnosis with anyone until he is very confident of what he can do with it. Only then will he be safe from the jokes or the scoffing of friends, relatives, and doctors.

"YOU-WILL-HAVE-TO-LEARN-TO-LIVE-WITH-THIS" TYPE OF RESISTANCE

One of the most frustrating types of resistance is also iatrogenic. It is the culmination of long and fruitless efforts to overcome unrecognized resistances with time-honored methods of controlling pain. Reasons for previous failures often have been attributed to personality defects or willful obstruction within patients. Eventually an unhappy consultant gives the coup-de-grace to hope by making a remark that absolves the therapist and places all the responsibility where it seems to belong. Three of the author's patients have quoted the same disheartening words issuing from the lips of a highly-regarded neurosurgical consultant. The words were, "Well, _____, we've done all we can for you. You'll just have to live with this pain or you will end up jumping off the Golden Gate Bridge."

This statement has the unconscious meaning that the consultant is angry with the patient for failing to get well. It also carries the consciously unrecognized connotation that death will follow if there is ever freedom from the pain. Over and over, this second understanding has been discovered as a powerful force militating against acceptance of comfort. I now regularly inquire about the possibility of this having been said to the patient at the initial interview. *Very few physicians are aware of the fact that exhortation to "live with pain" carries with it the shadow of meaning, "When you are free of pain, you will be dead."** If the remark were made at the very first confrontation, there would be no difficulty. The failed attempts to relieve

---

*This "shadow of meaning" is a form of implication that is the essence of indirect suggestion (Erickson & Rossi, 1976/1980).

pain are the reason for this sinister connotation. This cause for resistance to therapy can be removed by open discussion and the hopefully slanted question, "Now, does the inner part of your mind feel willing to be free of this pain and continue to live comfortably?" The ideomotor answer to this question determines the next steps of therapy.

RESISTANCE DUE TO GUILT AND PASSIVE ACCEPTANCE OF DISEASE

Pain originating with some accident due to carelessness or some habit of which the patient is ashamed is nearly always coupled with guilt feelings. Even when there is no initial cause for guilt, the mere repetition of pain or continuation of an illness will eventually make the patient unconsciously begin to think that God is punishing him for something. Such patients may lose the willingness to get well at upper levels of unconscious thought. They may initially reject hypnosis and block ideomotor, symbol movements. Sometimes they accept definite signals initially but change them repeatedly during the interview. *Here again, a patient may be able to enter hypnosis deeply but will withdraw the moment an effort is made toward relieving pain or discovering its origin. Sudden withdrawal from hypnosis at the first approach toward the goal is a warning that the distress has assumed a special meaning.*

It is necessary to learn whether or not the pain is being used to punish someone. If so, is it the patient or someone else? If it is punishing someone else, we have a new problem discussed in the next area of resistance. If it is self-punishment, the therapist is usually able to edge the patient toward accepting relief for the benefit of loved ones. Emphasis is placed on the selfish and generally injurious qualities of self-punishment and passive acceptance of disease. It is better to do this in an indirect manner with slanted questions which require an obvious intellectual answer but which sometimes reveal interesting unconscious attitudes at levels of awareness reflected by ideomotor responses.

The author learns the first names of all friends and relatives who are loved and respected by the patient. The first name of each is incorporated in the following general types of question:

1. Does this illness help _____ or make _____ happier?
2. Would _____ be happy if you were well and happy?

A break in self-punitive resistance occurs when the patient can agree via an ideomotor signal that enough punishment has been absorbed or that it can gradually be diminished in intensity toward an hallucinated endpoint when cure has been effected.

RESISTANCE DUE TO MANIPULATIVE PAIN STATES

A disease or injury may initially serve a helpful purpose of alarming or injuring an important person. Associative processes will then cause subsequent distress for the patient when there are frustrations or causes for resentment against the original target. Pain may be rekindled after this by any emotional difficulty caused by anyone; it may occur during a period of nonspecific depression.

Therapy for manipulative pain states is difficult under any circumstances, but it may be doomed to failure when the origin is a person or an entire way of living from which there is no visible means of escape. Continued illness may have taken too great a toll of financial and spiritual resources for escape. Fear of an unknown future may be greater than current misery.

Hostility-bound pain states should be handled entirely by psychological means, but they are often challenged medically or surgically with unsatisfactory results. Temporarily successful efforts by any means may precipitate acts of violence by the patient directly in suicide or indirectly by injuring others. A therapist who is psychiatrically oriented may be alerted to the problem by the words, facial expressions, and gestures chosen by the patient. An initial warning may be given by the relative who has been the target for hostility. This person usually calls to make the appointment and then comes in with the patient. When this happens, it is wise to interview them both together. The patient who glances from time to time and generally seems friendly toward the relative may simply be overly dependent upon the relative. Red flags are waving, however, if the patient turns away from the relative, behaves as though the relative were not in the room, and appears irritated when the relative tries to help with information. A clinching sign of trouble is a glowing eulogy about the departed one when the relative has left the room.

The author has made his greatest mistakes in judgment with manipulative persistent pain states. It is a great temptation to sound hopeful and to jump to the task of trying to deserve thanks for helping such patients immediately. Patients sometimes contribute to the errors of the therapist at the first visit. They may need help so desperately that their defenses are disarmingly lowered. They may seem to want help genuinely and may seem totally relieved when they leave the office after a glorious beginning. The therapist's flame of elation is rudely extinguished a few minutes later by a telephone call, usually from the relative, stating that the pain came back as soon as the patient got home. Sometimes the original trouble is gone but the patient has a perfectly new form of distress.

In my experience, symptom substitution has only occurred with hostility-bound manipulative pain states. This does not refer to exposure of old complaints which were previously less noticeable because of lower intensity. Such "onion-peeling" of symptoms can occur with any patient harboring stratified complaints. The appearance of new symptoms or the rapid return of original pain are danger signals. Help is needed from those most qualified to handle potentially dangerous mental states.

Even hostility of the most vicious sort can be kept under control during an illness that requires sacrifice by the object of that hostility. Too rapid removal of the disability or premature confrontation with the problem are both hazardous. The therapist can probe the way by asking such questions as, "Will the unconscious part of your mind allow me now to help you with this illness?" The dangers can be diminished if it is possible to show the patient that immediate hostilities have been set up by other people with whom the object of hostility has been identified. These questions have been helpful:

1. Has there been some other person, during an early stage of your life, who may have been responsible for later hostility toward _____? (A drunken and vicious father may have made a girl hypersensitive to possibilities that her husband is headed in the same direction. A frigid and selfish mother may cause unreasonable resentment between her son and an innocent wife.)
2. What was happening, at the time the resentment first began, to make that resentment so very important?
3. Are the causes of resentment still active at the time of the interview?
4. Is it possible to discard the resentment now and begin enjoying life?

The overcoming of resistances is always a challenge for the imagination and constructive persuasiveness of the therapist. There are few rules that can be put down on paper, but two are, perhaps, worthy of mention:

1. If you feel uncomfortable with the patient or the problem, refer the patient to another therapist or limit your work to exercising the patient in learning how to relax and contemplating the positive values in living.
2. Try to obtain a commitment on a time in the near future when the patient will be willing to get well, or feel better, for the sake of loved ones.

The first is a very important rule to keep. Frightened therapists will frighten sick people. The second rule appears to be sound. Questions about the future, to be answered by ideomotor responses, seem to depersonalize the situation and allow the patient a healthful objectivity about the problems at hand.

General Principles for Alleviating Persistent Pain

Therapy for persistent pain states must be elastic and must conform to the understandings and needs of the patient and the patient's relatives. Often it must also fit into the needs and understandings of prior medical and surgical attendants in whom the patient has continued faith. It is best judgment to listen carefully to what the patient thinks can be done and what he or she expects the hypnotherapist to use as an approach to the problem. The patient is often in a hypnoidal state during the first moments of interview and may have insights of utmost value to impart. If the therapist can weather the initially critical interview and can have free rein, these are the general steps which have proved helpful:

1. Be sure the patient is unconsciously willing to be helped.
2. Discover when and what caused the illness or pain to be important in the very beginning. This may relate to the distress of another person rather than to a personal experience with pain.
3. Determine the first moment at which the patient experienced the pain. Discover whether the patient was awake or asleep at the time. (*Sleep* means either natural sleep or a period of unconsciousness as from chemo-anesthesia.)
4. Discover what reinforced the importance of that initial pain. This may have been the statement of a doctor or the consternation of relatives at the time of initial illness or injury.
5. Ask if the patient now, at the time of interview, believes cure is possible. Orient to the moment when this conclusion was drawn, regardless of the answer. Points of origin are significant whether optimistic or pessimistic.
6. Have the patient turn off all pain *at an unconscious level* and have a yes finger lift when this has been accomplished. Ask for a verbal report when it is *known consciously* that all the pain is gone (Cheek, 1961d, 1962d).
7. Ask the patient to turn the pain back on again but to make it twice as strong as it was at first. The patient may balk at this until it is made clear that the pain will again be turned off, and that it is helpful to know how to turn pain off by first learning how to turn it on. (Prior experience has been with uncontrolled fear of uncontrolled pain, a fear of the unknown.)*
8. As soon as the patient has developed confidence in being able to turn the pain on and off, it is helpful to have him select a cue word or thought which will automatically turn off the pain. This is rehearsed several times in the office, but the patient is told to avoid trying it on

---

*See Rossi, 1986d, for a discussion of the paradoxical approach of *symptom prescription*.

his own until the instructor knows it is going to be successful. (There are several implications to this bit of instruction. Most important is the implied confidence that such a day will come. Next in importance is the warning that simple experiences in the office setting do not indicate that the task is now finished.)

9. A pseudo-orientation into the future is requested and the patient is asked to have the yes finger lift when he is forward to the time when there is good health and total freedom from pain. (Refusal to select a time may indicate discouragement or resistance which have not previously been apparent. Acceptance of a date commitment reinforces the other placebo elements of optimistic hope.)

10. Train the patient carefully with autohypnosis induction and simple use of brief periods for complete relaxation. This should be restricted to three minutes, at the most, from onset of a medium trance to the moment when the eyes feel like opening. The author insists that the patient stick to the time limits rather than drifting off into natural sleep or prolonged reverie. If too much time is lost during these exercises, the patient will tend to discredit results and will give up the rehearsals as a needless waste of time. The two- or three–minute exercises should be repeated after each meal and at bed time, four times a day. This is no more time than might be taken in smoking five cigarettes during the day.

It may suffice to make office appointments for one hour once a week if the patient is first seen during an interval of relative comfort. If the patient is in severe pain, the author usually arranges for admission to the hospital for a period of two or three days. This separates the patient from unrecognized triggering stimuli at home, permits more than one visit a day if necessary, and allows use of pain-relieving drugs to augment effects of suggestion.

Value of Unconscious Review

The author usually has the patient review the discussion and experiences of the previous interview at each session by giving ideomotor signals for the beginning and ending. This is a valuable means of helping the patient enter hypnosis without a formal induction, and it often seems to speed up the release of significant information stimulated during the previous interview. This approach is another great contribution made by Milton H. Erickson (1980a, Vol. I) to our understanding of unconscious mental processes.

Similarly, it is helpful to have the patient give an ideomotor answer to the question, "Have you learned anything today that might be of help to you in getting well?" This question is asked at the end of each interview. The patient is forced to review the elements of the interview in order to answer this question. Furthermore, the voice inflection and manner of asking the question imply that something good is expected.

The author avoids asking about pain at successive interview sessions. The idea of pain is itself an unfavorable suggestion. Sufficient information can be obtained by asking the patient to scan the time between the last interview and the present moment and have a designated finger lift "each time" there is unconscious relief from pain. It usually surprises the patient to see how often the finger lifts when there is conscious conviction that there has been continued discomfort all the time. When pain-free periods are discovered in this way, it is helpful to learn what started and what terminated them.

Protecting against the "Slip-Back" Phenomenon

Dramatic improvement after any form of therapy for prolonged disability is followed by an insecure period of wondering just how long the good luck will last. Symptoms may then recur because of expectation. The patient and relatives may combine discouragement at this time and decide that the recently successful treatment is a failure like all the other ones. Patients should be protected against this mistake, should be warned that slip-back will occur, and should be told how to use the recurrence to learn more about their problem.

The author requests that the patient report in at once when there is return of discomfort after what seems to have been a peak of good results. During the telephone conversation the patient is asked to orient to the moment before unconscious pain began again, to have a finger lift, and to report what seems to be associated with the onset. Often it is a friend asking, "Are you still feeling all right?" After the initial exploration, the patient is instructed to use every tendency for recurrence as a learning process, as added insurance that eventual cure will be permanent.

Protection Against Postural Conditionings

Human beings in pain learn certain postures which are relatively comfortable. These postures soon become habits and may strongly militate against successful therapy. Accidental resumption of an old posture will ring old bells and recommence unconscious associations of expectation for pain. Particularly is this true with painful back and neck conditions. It is a well-known phenomenon among athletes. The therapist should point out the rigidity of shoulder and neck muscles for the patient who has a whiplash or cervical disc syndrome. The patient with low back pain should be shown how the lumbar curve is lost and how this amplifies the damaging effects of walking. On walking down a hill, the patient with a rigid back transmits each impulse along the axis of the spine instead of dissipating the force in pendulum movements of the hips and lumbar spine. The patient with sciatic pain puts most of his weight on the comfortable leg while standing. The patient with pelvic congestion syndrome maintains constant hypertonicity of the glutei muscles, the perineal and upper thigh muscles. In time, any muscles unable to relax will be the source of pain. Patients should be exercised in unconsciously relaxing hypertonic muscles at the beginning of an interview. They can be asked to have an ideomotor response indicate unconscious recognition that the muscles are relaxed, and they should be shown how tense muscles respond when patients think they are relaxed. A lag of five minutes commonly occurs between the time a patient thinks muscles are relaxed and the moment when there is an unconscious movement of the designated finger.

There can be no assurance that pain of an orthopedic origin will remain cured because a back has been rendered rigid with surgery, a herniated nuclus pulposus has been removed, a cartilage has been removed from a knee, or a Smith-Peterson operation has replaced the head of a femur.

It is a common orthopedic ritual to force patients with bad backs to sleep on mattresses made rigid by boards. This is helpful to the extent that it keeps the patient moving to find a restful position. It thereby prevents prolonged hypertonicity of the back muscles, but it is an unkind way to treat uncomfortable patients. I permit patients to continue use of boards only when they refuse to listen to reason or feel they need to continue penance for real or imagined sins. It is a personal feeling that the other ritual of putting patients in a modern version of the rack is unkind and unfair. Traction on the head and legs will overcome muscle spasm by sheer persistence but it is an undignified way to treat human beings. It changes no habits and it teaches people to resent doctors.

Crutches and canes should be relinquished as soon as possible because they are unconscious reminders of disease and inappropriate posture. Patients who need a cane seem to do better when they shift the cane to the opposite hand. Similarly, patients with sciatic pain will improve more rapidly when they practice standing with weight evenly distributed, or even with most of their weight on the painful leg. *Reversal of postural habit opens the way for new learnings.*

Case Illustration of Persistent Pain Following Surgery and Unconscious Hearing under Anesthesia

The following case of persistent pain after surgery correlates with the material in Chapters 6 and 7 which discusses the meaning of persistent hearing under general chemo-anesthesia. The patient's continuing and increasing pain after an operation seemed due to misunderstandings of expressed and implied ideas while the patient was in a presumed surgical plane of chemo-anesthesia. These misunderstandings were responsible for repeated, consciously unrecognized dreams. Symptomatic and physiologic relief followed the correction of these misunderstandings.

Miss C was a 27-year-old single white woman who worked as a bank secretary under great pressure. She was first seen on August 12, 1965, complaining of almost constant occipital headache with pain through her shoulders and the back of her neck. She was desperate because she had undergone a laminectomy for removal of a cervical disc in October of 1963, followed by a fixation of the neck vertebrae in April 1964, and a second attempt at fixation in August of 1964. All the surgeries had been done by an eminent orthopedic surgeon. She hoped hypnosis might help control the pain which had persisted for five years since her automobile accident in July, 1960.

The patient, a tall, attractive woman, came in with and maintained a constant frown. She kept her head in a fixed position, turning her body and shoulders in order to turn her head. To look down she would bend her body rather than tip her head forward. Clearly there were physical habit patterns of posture that needed correction. She presented an appearance of a constant alertness that was reflected in posture and facial expression.

Patients with persistent pain states often give important clues about their condition at the first interview while they are explaining their trouble. This patient stated that it had all begun as she, her *married older* sister, and the sister's daughter were on their way to a drive-in theater. (She emphasized the fact that her sister was married and had a daughter.) A car in her lane stopped abruptly to make a turn-off. The next car stopped in time to avoid collision, as did the patient's car. They were struck by the following car, causing a jolting-backward and rebound-forward thrust effect on the heads of the passengers. No one seemed injured. The patient added that the woman *causing the accident kept right on driving and was never apprehended. The owner of the other car had no insurance.* Immediate notes were made that the patient, who was driving the car, might have been jealous of her older, married sister, or may have felt guilty over hostility for her sister. It was also noted that she might have harbored resentments toward the unfairness of the situation allowing escape for the woman who caused the accident and for the man who carried no insurance. (It was later found that these were unimportant factors.)

A highway patrol officer told them at the scene of collision that they were lucky to have stopped in time to avoid collision with the car in front. He said that she and her sister in the front seat might have been thrown through the windshield and then thrown backward as they were hit from behind. (Influence of this suggestion was greater than I first suspected.)

They decided to go on with their plan to see the movie, and did so in comfort.

The next day the sister complained of pain in her neck but the patient had no distress of any sort. She drove her sister to the orthopedist, who examined both of them. He explained that the sister had a slight whiplash injury, but that nothing was wrong with the patient. (At this point, it was decided to interrupt conscious history-telling in order to combine hypnosis with a review of events at an unconscious level.)

After demonstrating postural suggestion and setting up ideomotor finger signals, the patient was asked to orient to the very first moment she was aware of pain "in her neck, shoulders or head." A signal of accomplishment occurred within 30 seconds. It surprised her to learn that the onset of pain was a few minutes after a dream about being in a very serious accident. The dream was at 3 a.m., she believed, on the second day after the accident. Now, circumstances were changed. Instead of a repetition of the real incident, this was the accident as suggested by the patrol officer. The patient had been unable to stop in time. Her sister and niece were uninjured, but she had been thrown forward with such force that her chest broke the steering wheel and her head smashed into the windshield. A few minutes later she awakened with severe head and neck pain, but she had no conscious recollection of the dream. (This phenomenon of traumatic dream repression is frequent following accidents of all sorts; it is an important factor in the complications of pregnancy [Cheek, 1963, 1965].)

SUCCESSFUL SURGERIES THAT FAILED: MISUNDERSTANDINGS LEADING TO
CONDITIONAL PAIN RESPONSES: IDEOMOTOR INVESTIGATION AND RESOLUTION

Later that second day the patient accompanied her sister to consult the orthopedist, who now showed concern over the new symptoms after 36 hours of comfort. This delayed onset of pain meant that there had been some injury to the cord or to the nerve roots. Simple neck strain would have been reflected by immediate muscle guarding and rigidity, as was shown by her sister. She did not help his diagnosis because she could not associate the dream with pain. Her sister recovered swiftly, but the patient continued with pain in spite of traction and medication. After three years it was discovered that she had a herniated disc in the cervical region. The surgeon, in explaining the situation, told her that an incision would be made anteriorly in order to approach the trouble in the most direct and safe manner. The patient did not recall being told that constant pain and muscle guarding could have caused the degeneration of the annulus of the disc. She assumed the herniation had been there for three years. When she asked the surgeon why he would not go in from the back of the neck, which seemed the logical place, he explained that the best approach was anteriorly where there *could be no possible damage to the spinal cord.* Entry from behind *could risk paralysis if blood vessels supplying the cord were accidentally injured.*

The surgery of October 1963 was "successful," but the pain persisted, as might have been expected. In April, 1964, an anterior procedure was again

MIND-BODY THERAPY

done under general anesthesia in order to place bone chips between the transverse processes to *limit motion of the neck*. The surgery was again considered a success, but there was no diminution in the pain. X-rays eventually showed that there had not been a satisfactory fusion. The orthopedist then decided on an immediate revision of the surgery. The abruptness of his decision alarmed the patient. She felt that if he decided so quickly on surgery there must be something more seriously wrong than he was willing to admit. When she asked him what would be done, he answered that he would go in *from the back of the neck* this time. When she asked him if this would be dangerous to the nerve roots or the spinal cord, as intimated in his first explanation, he answered that he would be nowhere near the nerve roots or the cord this time. He would simply be putting some more bone chips around the vertebrae, and would use wire to support them further. This was consciously acceptable but unconsciously alarming in view of her general understanding of the first discussion in 1963.

Forty-five minutes had elapsed at this point of our session. Time did not permit further analysis of the history. As the interview was concluded, she was asked to have an ideomotor response to the question, "Will it be all right for me to help you be relieved of this pain?" The yes finger lifted immediately in response, indicating that the pain was apparently not being used in self-punishment. She was then asked to turn off the pain completely at an unconscious level, to notify me with an ideomotor signal when this was accomplished, and to tell me verbally when she felt comfortable. The ideomotor response came after two minutes. A change in posture and smoothing of her brow occurred during the next 90 seconds. Her verbal report of comfort came five minutes after the ideomotor signal. (This is the usual sequence of events and about average for time lapse between unconscious gesture, change in muscle tension, and conscious awareness that pain has been blocked.)

As the patient got up from her chair, she moved her head from side to side, forward and back, and stroked the back of her neck with her right hand. She looked somewhat surprised and then added the following note as she started for the door: "You know, when I woke up after that third operation, I was horribly upset and remained upset for a week." This suggested the possibility that something could have occurred during the period of unconsciousness with the anesthetic. These last-minute bonanzas cannot be ignored safely. She was asked to sit down again for a moment to answer the question, **"While you were under the anesthetic in the third operation, was there anything said or done that could have been disturbing to you?"** There was an immediate answer with the yes finger, and an appearance of agitation in her posture and facial expression. Her neck muscles tightened as she said, "The pain is starting again." I asked again if it would be all right to turn off the pain and remain free of pain until her next appointment. The finger signal indicated a yes. Twenty seconds later she appeared comfortable and reported that the pain had disappeared. I commented on this rapid shift back to pain on the basis of a recollection, and pointed out that this is the history of conditioned pain, that she must learn about the unconscious triggers responsible for onset of pain in order to learn how to remain comfortable. An appointment was given for six days from this first visit, but she was instructed to let me know at once in case she could not handle the next recurrence of pain.

CONSCIOUS CONTROL OF PAIN TO DREAM OF TRAUMATIC OPERATION:
SEMANTICS OF THE UNCONSCIOUS; IDEOMOTOR CORRECTION OF DREAM AND
SURGICAL TRAUMA

Second visit, 8/18/65: At the second visit she reported great improvement. She recalled awakening in the early morning of the day after her first office visit with pain in her neck and head. She knew there must have been a dream, but she could not identify the dream. Realization that pain was due to an undetermined dream, however, permitted her to stop the pain as she moved about the house.

This visit was begun with a review of that night from the moment of falling asleep until the awakening with pain. There was a dream which she was able to report in detail after two unconscious reviews from beginning to end at an ideomotor level of recollection. It involved a reliving of the traumatic experiences in the third operation.

Operation #3: She has been placed on her abdomen prior to induction of anesthesia with sodium pentothal. The anesthesiologist is having much difficulty getting a tracheal catheter into position. (This is a difficult task. Usually patients are anesthetized in recumbent position, intubated, and then placed in a prone position.) Asked what makes this detail important, she answers that this is an inauspicious beginning for the operation, and indicates that the operation will probably be a failure, too. Her next signal of an important incident during the operation relates to difficulties a few minutes later. The surgeon is struggling to get a wire in place. He does not say anything, but she knows by his breathing and the way he is using his hands that things are not proceeding in the desired direction. The surgeon's assistant comments on the difficulty but gets no response, indicating that there really is some trouble. By the time the incision is made over the crest of the ilium to obtain bone fragments, the patient is greatly agitated.

Bleeding from the tissues in this secondary site of operation further delays the progress of surgery. Asked if she knows why she is bleeding so profusely, she gives a yes answer, followed by the verbal comment, "I'm bleeding because I'm afraid this operation will not work and there will be no hope for me." All during the operation she says, "I have been waiting for the surgeon to slip and cause a paralyzing injury to my spinal cord, because he is working in the back of my neck where he once said the surgery could be dangerous." Review of this operative experience points up the fact that nothing really has been said by the surgeon to cause worry. It is the difficulty of the anesthesiologist and the comment of the assistant which add to preexisting unconscious alarm. Surgeons and anesthesiologists must constantly be alert to *the semantics of the unconscious mind.*

The patient's postoperative course was troubled by her constant headache and shoulder pain. During our interview, she recognized that this pain was caused by fear that any movement would result in irreparable damage to her spinal cord. The fears were augmented by troubled dreams which were not consciously remembered. Such dreams were too threatening; they had been repressed. This phylogenetically adequate but humanly damaging defense mechanism of repression shows up frequently, and lends itself nicely to correction with ideomotor questioning techniques. It is with the help of unconscious review and ideomotor signaling devices that it is now possible to contradict the famous Freudian dictum of 1909:

> It is only if you exclude hypnosis that you can observe resistances and repression and form an adequate idea of the *truly pathogenic* (sic) course of events.

REVIEW AND HALLUCINATED REVISION OF EVENTS DURING TRAUMATIC
OPERATION

Third visit, 8/19/65: The patient had intermittent episodes of neck and shoulder pain after the second hour of therapy. At the third visit she was asked to rehearse putting herself into hypnosis, turning on and turning off the recollection of pain at an ideomotor level of awareness. She managed to keep within the two–minute time limit from beginning of hypnosis (dropping a pencil) to the moment she felt like opening her eyes. This took ten minutes of the hour.

Next she was asked to review all three of her operations to ensure that there were no alarming incidents which had not yet been discovered. There seemed to be none. The third operation again appeared as the important one. During this review, it was pointed out that both her anesthesiologist and her surgeon had shown concern and interest for her well-being. She was asked to review the operation in detail and signal with her yes finger each time she came to something troublesome. She was asked to substitute the right action or the right statement to assure that Miss C *there on the table* would have the smoothest recovery with the best results.

Patient's hallucinated revision of third surgery: The anesthesiologist explained that it was hard to stand on your head to get an airway in, but that it was working adequately now. The assistant commented on the difficulty the surgeon was having with the wire for fixation, but the surgeon just explained that he wanted to do an especially neat job this time in order to guarantee that this woman would be free of her pain. This very important phase of any review of surgical experiences took only five minutes. It is an important step because it permits us to learn the semantics of the anesthetized, unconscious brain. It is also important because it permits the patient to forgive mistakes by substituting helpful suggestions to improve the behavior of other people under similar circumstances. Further, it is an important step in obviating possible malpractice suits as long as the investigating patient can maintain personal humility in recognition of the doctor's mistakes. It can be potentially dangerous in the hands of a pusillanimous doctor anxious to "stand taller by chopping off the heads of his comrades."

The patient was next asked to review all the things that we had discussed so far during the three visits. She was asked to do this at an ideomotor level of thought, giving signals each time she came to something she regarded as important. Of significance was the fact that she had had many frightening dreams during the first weeks after her third surgery. They were always about the operation, that the neck "was all messed up," that they cannot do much with it because it has "all grown together with bone." This was interesting because it was volunteered as a substitute for my request to "go over the things we had talked about." I should have asked simply for her to consider "everything that was important since the first visit." No mention had been made of the postoperative bad dreams stimulated by the difficulties in moving her head to permit intubation, trouble with the wire, or concern about the hemorrhage at the donor site for the bone chips.

At the conclusion of the hour, she was asked to give a signal of acceptance when she knew that these dreams and fears had been completely resolved, and when she could move her head with progressively greater "freedom and comfort."

REVIEWING POSSIBLE MAJOR LIFE EVENTS AS SOURCES OF PAIN; LEARNING TO
CONTROL PAIN AT AN IDEOMOTOR LEVEL OF AWARENESS

Fourth visit, 8/27/65 (three hours used to this point): At this time, the patient was able to report that she had lost completely the feeling of occipital tension that used to come with situational pressures at work with a demanding boss. Whenever she felt the tension occurring, she would tell herself to relax, or, in special instances, she would go to the bathroom and go through the two-minute steps of autosuggestion.

I wanted to clear other possible sources of self-punishment. Her birth was unimportant; she knew that her birth had not troubled her mother, that she was perfectly acceptable although she heard her father make a remark about preferring to have a boy "this time." She indicated that her father had subsequently shown ample indications of loving her. There had been tensions in the family, mostly over her mother's alcoholism. These problems had been greater during the five years of the patient's illness, but the patient could discover no possible wish to assume any pain in the unconscious hope of sparing either her mother or father. She felt sure there had been no problem between herself and her sister. There were no concerns about her sexual adjustments and experiences. She was unconsciously sure of "cure" now.

FOLLOW-UP

The patient was asked to attend an advanced course on hypnotherapeutic methods. She willingly told the doctors about her experience, and was able to recognize the value of her contribution to our knowledge of unconscious ideation during natural sleep and the unconsciousness of general anesthesia. She demonstrated her method of brief autohypnosis for relaxation. Pain returned briefly during a time of stress in the office on September 29, but she indicated over the telephone that "her fingers knew" why she was uncomfortable, and they indicated that she could turn off this pain and remain well.

This patient is apparently cured of severe disabling head and neck pain that had lasted for five years and through three surgical attempts to relieve it with usual orthopedic methods. Initial pain seems clearly the result of a fabricated dream suggested by a well-meaning highway patrolman, and augmented by misunderstanding on the part of the orthopedist. Assumption that the injury had been more serious than first appeared reinforced the patient's unconscious alarm, and increased the painful muscle guarding which eventually led to herniation of the disc and surgical intervention. The surgeon's explanation for anterior surgical approach set reinforcing fears because he had initially told her there might be damage to the spinal cord and the nerve roots. Fear of disturbing the results of surgery maintained the painful muscle guarding and interfered with solidification of the implanted bone fragments after the second operation. Again, reinforcement of the fears came with sudden decision to operate for the third time, and from a posterior approach to the neck with all its unreal but previously implied dangers of paralysis.

Therapy consisted primarily of an optimistic general approach aimed at excluding factors of guilt and self-punishment. These were not important. The information misunderstood during general anesthesia of the third operation was of utmost significance, however. Correction of these misunderstandings and reinforcement of her self-confidence in controlling pain seemed to be the chief factors in permitting total relief of symptoms.

Conclusion

In the therapy of persistent pain states, we should consider thoughtfully all possible psychological factors that may initiate, reinforce, and continue an exaggerated awareness of discomfort. We should evaluate and correct the influence of dramatized identification, self-punishment, inverted aggressive hostilities, passive acceptance of disease, and simple habitual lack of hope. Any of these forces can set up resistance to therapy.

All people seem willing to survive and function well at their deepest core of unconscious awareness. It is up to the therapist to release this very powerful force from the handicaps of confused, frustrated, superficial ways of thinking. This can be done when we listen carefully, watch thoughtfully, and treat with dignity. Patients with persistent pain states are willing to get well. Only their emotional environment and way of viewing the world need alteration. There are times when success can be won and we can feel elated over having a part in helping a patient get well. Unfortunately, there are other times when pain acts as a sort of screen against the reality of a hopeless and meaningless future where there is no one to get well for, no one to live for. It is not easy to decide where the line of effort should be drawn. Always, there might be some other person who could ignite the flame of purposeful living again. Harvey Cushing has said that there should be no simple tribunal to decide the fate of a human being. No one person alone should take on the responsibility for lowering the curtain on hope.

RESEARCH

Mind Modulation of Pain, Inflammation, and Healing:
Research Projects 33-37

Evidence is accumulating that mind-body methods can modulate the experience of pain at all three of the major loci or levels of information transduction outlined in Table 6: the mind-brain, the brain-body, and the cellular-genetic. First, we will survey a number of research programs in experimental hypnosis that have explored the pain experience on the mind-brain level. Next, we will summarize the significant studies that investigate relationships between mind methods and information substances such as the endorphins (see Table 4) on the brain-body level. Finally, we will examine studies that specifically investigate relationships between mind methods and the cellular-genetic mechanisms. We will survey each of these levels to determine what types of clinically-oriented experimental studies are now needed.

THE MIND-BRAIN LEVEL

Early examples of well-controlled studies of how pain perception can be modulated by hypnosis at the mind-brain level were developed by Orne and his coworkers (Orne, 1976; McGlashan, Evans, & Orne, 1969). These researchers found experimental evidence to support the hypothesis that there are at least two experiential or "mind" components in hypnotic analgesia. One component is a nonspecific placebo effect that occurs when subjects know they are being treated by hypnosis. This *placebo component* is effective in subjects who are low in hypnotic susceptibility as well as those who are high, as measured on the Stanford Hypnotic Susceptibility Scale. In addition to this placebo effect, however, deeply hypnotizable subjects are able to "distort" their own perception so that they experience even deeper levels of hypnotic anesthesia. This *hypnotic component* is a form of negative hallucination that distorts or blocks information transduction at the mind-brain level.

A broad perspective on these issues has been developed in the program of laboratory research on the use of hypnosis in the relief of pain by the Hilgards (Hilgard, 1977; Hilgard & Hilgard, 1975). They found that even when their most highly hypnotizable subjects verbally reported that they were free from pain, at another ideodynamic finger signaling level they were able to report the experience of pain. This other level of responding was called the "hidden observer." Hilgard's report of how he discovered the hidden observer is an excellent illustration of Cheek's persistent clinical finding that the ideodynamic level of response is experienced before (and presumably facilitates) the verbal level. Ernest Hilgard engagingly describes how he was conducting a classroom demonstration of hypnotic deafness when he contacted the hidden observer "through an observation made almost by chance, and not perceived immediately as related to pain at all" (Hilgard & Hilgard, 1975, pp. 167-169):

One student in the class questioned whether "some part" of the subject might be aware of what was going on. After all, there was nothing wrong with his ears. The instructor agreed to test this by a method related to interrogation practices used by clinical hypnosis. He addressed the hypnotically deaf subject in a quiet voice:

"As you know, there are parts of our nervous system that carry on activities that occur out of awareness, of which control of the circulation of the blood, or the digestive processes, are the most familiar. However, there may be intellectual processes also of which we are unaware, such as those that find expression in night dreams. Although you are hypnotically deaf, perhaps there is some part of you that is hearing my voice and processing the information. If there is, I should like the index finger of your right hand to rise as a sign that this is the case."

To the surprise of the instructor, as well as the class, the finger rose! The subject immediately said, "Please restore my hearing so you can tell me what you did. I felt my finger rise in a way that was not a spontaneous twitch, so you must have done something to make it rise, and I want to know what you did." . . . This unplanned demonstration clearly indicated that a hypnotized subject who is out of contact with a source of stimulation (in this case, auditory) may nevertheless register information regarding what is occurring. Further, he may be understanding it so that, under appropriate circumstances, what was unknown to the hypnotized part of him can be uncovered and talked about. As a convenience of reference, we speak of the concealed information as being available to a "hidden observer."

It should be noted that the "hidden observer" is a metaphor for something occurring at an intellectual level but not available to the consciousness of the hypnotized person. It does not mean that there is some sort of secondary personality with a life of its own—a kind of homunculus lurking in the shadows of the conscious person. The "hidden observer" is merely a convenient label for the information source tapped through experiments with automatic writing, and here through the equivalent, automatic talking.

This quotation illustrates another profoundly important but little appreciated aspect of hypnotic phenomena that has been repeated again and again by talented investigators for over 200 years (Ellenberger, 1970; Tinterow, 1970). Virtually all the classical phenomena of hypnosis were originally *discovered* as spontaneous manifestations of altered states in everyday life (e.g., daydreaming, sleepwalking, traumatic stress syndrome, etc., Rossi, 1986a). Only after they were so discovered were efforts directed to elicit the phenomena by "suggestion." Thus, while suggestion can sometimes artificially evoke hypnotic phenomena in some subjects under some circumstances, *suggestions and so-called "hypersuggestibility" are not the essence of hypnosis* (Erickson, Rossi, & Rossi, 1976).

The erroneous equating of suggestibility with the phenomena of therapeutic hypnosis is an unfortunate artifact of our need to develop experimental measures of hypnosis by the use of *scales of hypnotic susceptibility*. We tend to forget that this artificial use of suggestion to measure hypnotic *susceptibility* is not necessarily a measure of the phenomena of therapeutic hypnosis. This distinction between the artificial but experimentally useful measure of hypnotic susceptibility and the natural clinical phenomena of hypnosis is of central significance for understanding *therapeutic* hypnosis. For if we believe that hypnotic phenomena are purely the product of artificial verbal suggestion, then we tend to discount the clinical conception of hypnosis as a natural psychobiological response to stress and trauma. This little understood distinction has had the unfortunate effect of dividing many of the academic and research-oriented investigators from the clinical hypnotherapists so that they have become divided into two communities (Coe, 1983; Rossi, 1986a). This division is also at the source of the state versus nonstate theories of hypnosis. Those researchers who focus on suggestibility, imagination, and social influence as the essence of hypnosis (Barber, 1972; Sarbin & Coe, 1972) tend to favor the nonstate theories, while clinicians who deal daily with the natural amnesias and dissociations that are characteristic of therapeutic hypnosis (Rossi, 1986c, d; Rossi & Ryan, 1986) tend to favor the state theories.

Project 33 The Hilgards' theoretical position as derived from their research on pain is unique insofar as it utilizes aspects of both state and nonstate approaches. As such, it provides support for the idea that the experimental and clinically based phenomena of state-dependent memory, learning and behavior (SDMLB) may be a common denominator for integrating the state and nonstate positions into a unified theory of hypnosis (Rossi, 1986a). What would be the next step in generating empirically testable hypotheses that could assess this idea? How could each of the classical phenomena of hypnosis be conceptualized as a special case of SDMLB? How could such formulations be tested empirically?

Project 34   Hilgard's (1977) neodissociation theory can be conceptualized as an experimentally derived special state view of hypnosis that is based upon the phenomena of SDMLB which becomes manifest under the stress of pain. This is entirely consistent with the chapters of this section wherein Cheek presented many clinical case histories illustrating his special state theory of hypnosis as a natural defensive psychobiological response to trauma and stress. He continually points out evidence that this defensive psychobiological response has been selected for its survival value far back into premammalian evolution. It is what we all share in common with animal hypnosis (Carli, 1977; Carli, Farabollini, & di Prisco, 1979). Since the information substances that account for the new psychosomatic network proposed by Pert and her colleagues also have their origins far back in premammalian evolution, it is tempting, once again, to infer that the general class of information substances that mediate hypnotic phenomena occurs at the cellular-molecular level.

Replicate the research of Carli and his colleagues to determine what information substances are responsible for the catatonic-like states that are called "animal hypnosis." Do the results of such research provide new leads for exploring therapeutic hypnosis with humans?

THE BRAIN-BODY LEVEL

In the introduction to this section, we surveyed Pert's psychosomatic network approach to mind-brain-body levels of communication in the experience of pain. Here we will review some of the problems that have arisen in clinical-experimental investigations of how information substances like the endorphins actually operate in the mind modulation of pain.

The discovery that endogenous opiates (the endorphins) and their receptors are a part of the pain process has prompted a great deal of research within the past decade in order to determine if the endorphins were involved in the process of hypnotic analgesia. The results of these studies have been difficult to interpret because of the extreme complexity of the issues involved. There may be not one but at least three different opiate receptors in the brain and body, as well as a variety of peptide information substances that can trigger them. Many of the early studies used naloxone as an antagonist of the endogenous opiates. The oversimplified hypothesis was that if hypnotic analgesia was blocked or diminished by naloxone, then some involvement of the endogenous opiates would be implied. The difficulty with such studies is that naloxone itself can have paradoxical effects. In low doses it can relieve pain, while in high doses it can make pain worse (Grevert & Goldstein, 1985). Placebo effects, emotional stress, and circadian rhythms (higher plasma levels of ACTH and β-endorphin in the morning hours usually means pain sensitivity is lower) are only a few of the factors that complicate the picture in ways that are not easily controllable in an experimental setting.

The early studies by Barber and Mayer (1977) and Goldstein and Hilgard (1975) reported that naloxone did not affect hypnotic analgesia. With one subject in a very deep somnambulistic trance, however, Stephenson (1978) found that hypnosis-induced analgesia was reversed by naloxone. Frid and Singer (1979) then found that hypnotic analgesia is partially reversed by naloxone when stress is introduced before pain. This stress may have facilitated the release of ACTH and β-endorphin at the hypothalamic-pituitary level. It is this endorphin contribution to the "hypnotic" analgesia that may have been reversed by the naloxone.

Project 35   More recent work by Kaji et al. (1981) and by Domangue, Margolis, Lieberman, and Kaji (1985) has sought to avoid the naloxone complications by directly measuring the increases in β-endorphin-like immunoreactive material following hypnotherapy. Domangue and his colleagues (1985) found that in a sample of 19 patients with arthritic pain, "there were clinically and statistically significant decreases in pain, anxiety, and depression and increases in β-endorphin-like immunoreactive material" (p. 235). It therefore appears that continuing research on hypnotic analgesia mediated by the endorphin-receptor mechanism will have more meaningful results when the endorphins are measured directly rather than via the naloxone effect (Rossi, in preparation).

THE CELLULAR-GENETIC LEVEL

An interesting series of studies has been conducted over the past few decades that contributes to our understanding of how information substances operate at the cellular level to reduce pain and promote healing. As Cheek notes in the clinical chapters of this section, hypnotherapists have made empirical observations about the associations between the hypnotically induced reduction of pain, inflammation, infection, and blood flow for centuries. Because they were not able to specify the physiological mechanisms involved, however, their work was never fully appreciated outside of the clinical sphere. This situation was slow to change, even after Chapman, Goodell and Wolff's (1959a, b) classical studies of "changes in tissue vulnerability induced during hypnotic suggestion."

The second Chapman study (1959b) can be viewed as the first well-controlled scientific effort to relate hypnotic suggestion to measurable changes on the molecular level. The investigators used an interesting experimental design wherein each subject could be used as his/her own control by receiving hypnotic suggestions for different responses on their left and right arms. Because their study can serve as an excellent model for replication in future research, we will quote their description of their procedure (Chapman, Goodell, & Wolff, 1959b, pp. 99–100):

Experiments were conducted in a quiet, semi-darkened, comfortably cool room. Thermocouples were attached to the subject's arms and a series of control temperatures recorded by means of a multi-channel recording instrument. Finger cuffs for recording of the plethysmograms, were attached to the middle finger of each hand and control recordings made.

The subjects were hypnotized in the conventional manner. As soon as a state of moderate to deep hypnosis had been established it was suggested that one arm was either "normal," or that it was "numb," "wooden" and devoid of sensation ("anaesthetic"). It was then suggested that the other arm was painful, burning, damaged and exceedingly sensitive, i.e., "vulnerable." Furthermore, it was suggested that severe injury to this "vulnerable" arm which would cause even greater pain and damage was about to occur. The "vulnerable" arm was then exposed on three spots blackened with India ink, to standard noxious stimulation (500 mcal-cm^2-sec for 3 sec). After an interval of 15–30 min during which hypnosis was continued, suggestions that the other arm was either "anaesthetic," or "normal" were repeated and reinforced. It was then similarly exposed on three spots to the standard noxious stimulation. In some experiments the order of exposing the "vulnerable" or "anaesthetic" arm to noxious stimulation was reversed. Also, the right arm was suggested to be "vulnerable" in some experiments, the left in others. In some experiments the suggestion of "vulnerability" for one arm and "anaesthesia" for the other were made simultaneously and the noxious stimulation was applied during the same interval alternately on the two arms.

The inflammatory reaction and tissue damage were assessed by observations and measurements of area, intensity and duration of erythema, oedema, blister formation, necrosis and when present, of residual scar formation. Coloured photographs were made approximately 20 minutes after the end of an experiment, and at 24-hour intervals for about 2 weeks.

They report the results of this study as follows (Chapman, Goodell & Wolff, 1959b, p. 104):

(1) Following standard amounts of noxious stimulation on the forearm during hypnosis, decreased inflammatory reaction and tissue damage was observed when the suggestion was made that the arm was insensitive and numb and would not be hurt, "anaesthetic," as compared to the reaction and tissue damage of the other arm which was suggested to be normally sensitive.

(2) Following standard amounts of noxious stimulation on the forearm during hypnosis, increased inflammatory reaction and tissue damage was observed in subjects who had received the suggestion that the forearm was tender, painful and injured ("vulnerable") as compared with arms suggested to be normally sensitive or "anaesthetic." Recordings of finger pulse amplitude and skin temperature indicated that local vasodilatation following exposure to noxious stimulation was larger in magnitude, and persisted longer in the "vulnerable" arm. The subcutaneous perfusate from the arm suggested to be painful, tender and damaged developed a greater increase of a pharmodynamic substance in response to standard noxious stimulation than did that from the arm suggested to be "anaesthetic."

(3) This pharmacodynamically active substance induced itching, local vasodilatation and oedema, lowered blood pressure, lowered pain threshold, induced delayed and slow contraction of the rat uterus and guinea pig ileum and resulted in relaxation of the rat duodenum. It deteriorated at room temperatures, was stabilized by boiling and destroyed by chymotrypsin. It was not acetylcholine, histamine or serotonin, although these and other relevant agents may also have been present. It had many of the properties of a polypeptide of the bradykinin type.

(4) Neural activity involving the segmental or axon levels, the brain stem and hypothalamic levels, as well as the subcortical and cortical levels can alter the reactions in the peripheral tissues subserved in such a way as to augment inflammation and increase local tissue damage in reaction to noxious stimulation. Proteolytic enzymes and a bradykinin-like polypeptide is implicated in these enhanced reactions.

Chapman, Goodell and Wolff also noted a paradoxical reaction in which one subject had greater signs of injury on the "anesthetic" side. Two subjects showed no difference between the sensitive and numb sides. Cheek believes that such unexpected or paradoxical results can be accounted for by the fact that subjects in hypnosis will sometimes spontaneously age regress so that their "handedness" shifts (Cheek, 1978). That is, subjects who were born left-handed but were converted to right-handedness in later childhood will reassert their original left-handedness during deep trance. Cheek currently comments on his process of discovery in this area as follows (personal communication, 1986):

In September of 1956 I had found that subjects in demonstrations were showing paradoxical responses. A few months later, I learned that converted left-handed people reverted to their original handedness orientation as they went into hypnosis. They were confused in understanding and physiologically confused. In one experiment I was embarrassed to find one subject reversing the scratch-inflammation effect, one making both arms look terrible, and one whose scratches disappeared as though both arms were numb! This, with three subjects in front of a hypnosis symposium group!

As we suggested in the Research discussion for Section I, more extensive and better controlled studies are now needed to assess these shifts in handedness during hypnosis. This suggestion is supported by recent research that suggests how cerebral-hemispheric dominance may shift during hypnosis (Rossi, 1986a).

The Chapman, Goodell and Wolff studies have even greater significance today because current pain research at the molecular level is validating their basic finding that "a bradykinin-like polypeptide is implicated in these enhanced reactions."

In 1960, D. F. Elliott and his colleagues at the National Institute of Medical Research in London found that bradykinin is a polypeptide composed of nine amino acids. It is informative to understand the sequence of molecular events that led to the formation of bradykinin and its effects on the surrounding tissues when an injury is experienced. This series of interrelated physiological responses may enable us to understand the multiple effects of hypnosis in facilitating analgesia as well as the immune and inflammatory responses.

Whenever the body experiences traumatic injury (burn, cut, infection, etc.), a number of proteolytic enzymes (called *kallikreins*) are released at the cite of tissue damage. These enzymes catalyze the release of bradykinin from a larger precursor molecule (called *kininogens*) that is constantly present in tissues and blood plasma. The bradykinin so released then initiates a broad cascade of molecular events leading to pain, an enhanced immune response, and inflammation due to active hyperemia (dilation of arterioles leading to increased blood flow). Let us examine this sequence in its simplest outline.

Like all information substances, bradykinin operates on the molecular level by triggering cell receptors. This is the key to understanding bradykinin's multiple actions. Bradykinin can activate the cell receptors on neurons, blood capillaries, and most cells of the immune system.

(a) When bradykinin triggers cell receptors on certain small unmyelinated or lightly myelinated (covered) neurons (sometimes called *nociceptors*), it initiates a series of molecular events leading to sensitization and an amplification of neural impulses that are interpreted as pain at the mind-brain level.

(b) Bradykinin also triggers cell receptors on the blood capillaries in the injured area. This leads to another chain of molecular responses that leads to the release of prostaglandins (a group of unsaturated fatty acids which function as local information substances — also called *paracrines* and *autocrines*). These prostaglandins, in turn, also trigger nerve cell receptors to amplify the pain response. The prostaglandins also promote sensitization and swelling of tissues and further hyperemia.

(c) Bradykinin simultaneously activates receptors on mast cells (a type of white blood cell of the immune system that is present in connective tissues). This initiates a series of responses leading to the release of histamine, which further amplifies the inflammation process. This inflammatory process takes place when histamine opens the junctions between capillary cells so that more blood plasma, white blood cells, and bradykinin precursors leak out into the damaged tissue area. The immune response is facilitated at this level when the white blood cells so released become available to destroy any potential bacterial or viral invaders entering the injured area. Histamine also operates as a neurotransmitter that can amplify pain impulses.

All the above can be considered as a primary response to injury. A secondary response to injury involves the central nervous system. The primary afferent nociceptor neural impulses coming from the injured tissues synapse onto several types of second-order interneurons when they enter the central nervous system at the spinal level. Substance P functions as a major neurotransmitter in the spinal cord. The secondary response to injury engages the mind-body levels of response up to the cerebral-limbic-hypothalamic systems. It is thought to operate as follows (Vander, Sherman, & Luciano, 1985, p. 646):

> It is hypothesized that the specific ascending pathways convey information about where, when, and how strongly the stimulus was applied and about the sharp, localized aspect of pain. The nonspecific pathways are believed to convey information about the aspect of pain which is duller, longer lasting, and less well localized. Neurons of the reticular formation and thalamus which are activated by the pain pathways connect with the hypothalamus and other areas of the brain which play major roles in integrating autonomic and endocrine stress responses and in generating the behavioral patterns of aggression and defense.

Project 36 The second-order central nervous system modulation of the primary response on the local area of tissue injury can enhance the release of substance P, which further activates the mast cells and immune system in the injured area. This leads to a secondary release of histamine and an amplification of the inflammatory response. It would seem that the mind-body approaches (hypnosis, visualization, biofeedback, meditation, etc.) operate by facilitating this secondary level of response that involves the central nervous system. It is now a question for future research to determine whether hypnosis operates on one or another or both of these response levels. In a series of interesting papers, Stewart (1981, 1984, 1985; Stewart & Hall, 1982) has outlined many of the possible pathways by which ACTH, Substance P, and the neuropeptide information substances in general can modulate memory, learning, and the stress response during injury.

Project 37 One of the simplest approaches to research in this area may be to use the scratch test as outlined in Box 19 with the experimental model used by Chapman, Goodell, and Wolff (1959b). The scratch demonstration of hypnotic analgesia and healing is one of the clinical techniques that has been used for more than a hundred years by clinicians without its parameters being assessed experimentally. An interesting doctoral dissertation might determine what relation may or may not exist between responsiveness to the scratch test and the various measures of hypnotic susceptibility, proneness to psychosomatic disorders in general, and dermatological problems in particular.

Women's Consciousness and Psychobiological Clocks

THEORY

That feminine consciousness is often unappreciated and lost in a masculine-oriented culture is not a new idea. That we may now have found a fundamental psychobiological basis for understanding some of the special aspects of feminine consciousness, however, is an exciting possibility. The most obvious psychobiological difference between women and men is that women experience an inner world of hormone-based changes in their psychology and physiology that is unknown to men. A woman's menstrual cycle, for example, is not something that suddenly takes place in isolation for only a few days a month; it is a subtle process of change that is taking place daily and even hourly. A glance at the chart of a woman's continually changing concentration levels in the blood of the four major hormones regulating menstruation and ovulation (progesterone, estrogen, luteinizing hormone, and follicle-stimulating hormone) in Figure 12 illustrates the psychobiological basis of the mood and mentation movements that modulate the normal rhythms of feminine consciousness. These four major hormones are, in turn, controlled by neuroendocrinal protohormones and hormones of the limbic-hypothalamic-pituitary system. Many of these hormones have been implicated as the types of information substances that modulate state-dependent memory, mood, and learning (Martinez et al., 1981; Rossi, 1986d; Stewart, Krebs, & Kaczender, 1971).

Depth psychologists such as C. G. Jung have long recognized the rhythmic or "wave like" biological basis of "psychological complexes" and emotional life in general. In his essay on "A Review of the Complex Theory," for example, Jung wrote (1960b, pp. 96–98):

What then, scientifically speaking, is a "feeling-toned complex"? It is the *image* of a certain psychic situation which is strongly accentuated emotionally and is, moreover, incompatible with the habitual attitude of consciousness. This image has a powerful inner coherence, it has its own wholeness and, in addition, a relatively high degree of autonomy, so that it is subject to the control of the conscious mind to only a limited extent, and therefore behaves like an animated foreign body in the sphere of consciousness. The complex can usually be suppressed with an effort of will, but not argued out of existence, and at the first suitable opportunity it reappears in all its original strength. *Certain experimental investigations seem to indicate that its intensity or activity curve has a wavelike character, with a "wave-length" of hours, days, or weeks. This very complicated question remains as yet unclarified. . . .*

The phenomenology of complexes cannot get round the impressive fact of their autonomy, and the deeper one penetrates into their nature — I might almost say into their *biology* — the more clearly do they reveal their character as *splinter psyches. . . .* Today we can take it as moderately certain that complexes are in fact "splinter psyches." The aetiology of *their origin is frequently a so-called trauma, an emotional shock or some such thing, that splits off a bit of the psyche.* Certainly one of the commonest causes is a moral conflict, which ultimately derives from the apparent impossibility of affirming the whole of one's nature. (Italics added)

We believe that Jung's "very complicated question" can now be clarified: Psychological complexes, in essence, are state-dependent memory, learning, and behavior systems that are encoded by many information substances during normal psychobiological events such as menstruation and childbirth, as well as "a so-called trauma, an emotional shock."

A striking illustration of how state-dependent mood, memory, and behavior modulated by hormones can encode a psychological complex is the role of *oxytocin*, which recent investigators (Fehm-Wolfsdorf, Born, Heinz-Voigt, & Fehm; Weingartner, 1986; Weingartner, Miller & Murphy, 1977) have found responsible for the amnesia that usually cloaks a woman's memory of her experience of giving birth. Oxytocin is an information substance that is released in massive amounts from the uterus during labor, and by the posterior pituitary after delivery, to regulate lactation and maternal behavior. Many women feel depressed by their memory loss for one of the most significant events of their lives. This sense of loss may have particular significance for some women, since oxytocin recently has been implicated in mother-child bonding. Consequently, they have consulted hypnotherapists for help in recovering their experiences of giving birth.

In one remarkable case recorded verbatim (Erickson & Rossi, 1979, pp. 282–313), the woman recovered not only the experience of giving birth but also many earlier traumatic and amnesic memories that had become associated with it. In only a few hypnotherapeutic sessions, she experienced a very deep process of personality maturation that came with apparent spontaneity when she recovered her lost traumatic memories.

Since women have many more obvious changes in the hormones of this

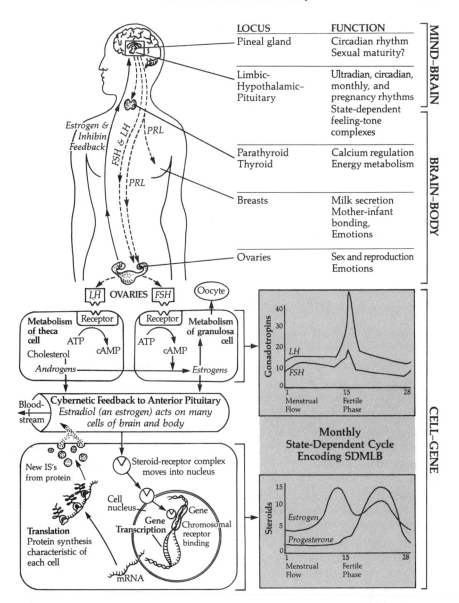

LOCUS	FUNCTION
Pineal gland	Circadian rhythm Sexual maturity?
Limbic- Hypothalamic- Pituitary	Ultradian, circadian, monthly, and pregnancy rhythms State-dependent feeling-tone complexes
Parathyroid Thyroid	Calcium regulation Energy metabolism
Breasts	Milk secretion Mother-infant bonding, Emotions
Ovaries	Sex and reproduction Emotions

Figure 12: Loci and function of some of the major sexual information substance-receptor systems in women.

mind-gene-molecular process, it is clear that the average male will be at a disadvantage in understanding them. No wonder Freud simply did not understand what they wanted. It would be all too easy to further stigmatize feminine consciousness with these psychobiological insights by citing them as evidence for the pejorative traits of changeability and indecisiveness in women. Because of unfortunate life experiences, some women could, in fact, come to mislabel themselves with such negative traits and then act them out as a self-fulfilling prophecy. With recognition of and support for their psychobiological experiences of change, however, these insights could lead women to the facilitation of the more desirable characteristics of creative flexibility and sensitivity to the emotional nuances of communication and relationship. The greater flexibility inherent in women's more delicately balanced state-dependent memory, learning, and behavior systems may also enable them to recognize more easily the new that evolves spontaneously within all of us on unconscious levels (see Rossi, 1986d, for a striking and detailed example of this point).

PMS: Premenstrual Syndrome

The significance of the way in which we interpret the state-dependent shifts in women's consciousness is especially apparent in the current controversies that are taking place about the so-called PMS—premenstrual syndrome. It is only recently that the mood and mentation shifts that occur as women approach their menses have been given the pathological label of PMS (Durden-Smith & Desimone, 1983; A. Rossi, 1980, 1984). An increasing number of professionals in health-related fields have decried this iatrogenic tendency to interpret a normal and potentially creative process of psychobiological transition in a negative and illness-engendering manner (Harrison, 1982; Laws, Hey, & Eagan, 1985; Mills, 1988; Parry, 1985; Rome, 1986; Rossi, 1986d).

These issues of correctly understanding a woman's unique psychobiological qualities are especially critical during the periods of greatest change in her life—pregnancy, childbirth, and childrearing. There is thus a special requirement made of doctors who specialize in the area of gynecology and obstetrics. As a male specialist in this area, Cheek rose to the challenge that most of his medical colleagues did not even know existed.

In the chapters of this and the following few sections that deal with the special issues raised by feminine consciousness, Cheek has pioneered many new attitudes and ideodynamic approaches to understanding. As such, his work has implications far beyond their obvious application to the professional problems of gynecology and obstetrics. It lays the groundwork for a fundamental widening of human consciousness about itself. The feminist movement, thus, has a great ally in the ideodynamic approach. Taken from this broad perspective, these therapeutic methods can be seen as prototypes for a host of new ideodynamic approaches to be developed by clinicians of the future.

The clearest model of the mind-gene communication loop involves the steroid hormones that regulate a variety of psychobiological rhythms. Three levels of this process are illustrated in Figure 12. Recent research has uncovered a number of circadian (every 24 hours) and ultradian (every 90–120 minutes) rhythms operating at each of these levels. An understanding of the relationships between these psychobiological clocks and the psychosomatic processes that are associated with them is still in its infancy. At the present time, there are many models and approaches to investigating and clinically utilizing many of these interesting relationships.

1. Thoughts at a *cortical level* modulate the multimodal sensory integration of state-dependent encoding of memories in the *limbic-hypothalamic system* (Mishkin, 1982; Mishkin, Malamut, & Bachevalier, 1984; Mishkin & Petri, 1984).
2. The *limbic-hypothalamic system* is the locus of information transduction from the neural encoding of the languages of the mind (thoughts, imagery, sensation, etc.) into the messenger-molecule languages of the body (protohormones or information substances of the hypothalamus).
3. Protohormonal information substances from the hypothalamus modulate the production and release of endocrine hormones from the pituitary (the "master gland" of the endocrine system).
4. These hormones from the pituitary in turn regulate the release of hormones from all the endocrine glands of the body.
5. Many of these endocrine glands release steroid hormones (adrenal, sexual organs, thyroid, etc.), which in turn are able to regulate the metabolism of tissues at the cellular level.
6. At the cellular-genetic level, the steroid hormones penetrate the outer cell wall into the nucleus and there signal certain parts of the gene DNA to replicate itself to form messenger ribonucleic acid (mRNA). This mRNA in turn travels out to the cytoplasm of the cell and directs the protein factories of the cell (on the endoplasmic reticulum) to produce the structural proteins and enzymes that in turn are responsible for the characteristic functions of the cell.
7. A number of these metabolic products are themselves messenger molecules that feed back information to the limbic-hypothalamic-pituitary system. Many of the larger information substances are able to move through the "blood-brain barrier" only at certain loci: certain nuclei of the hypothalamus, the pituitary and the pineal glands (Banks & Kastin, 1985; Goldstein & Betz, 1986), where they neatly complete the mind-gene information loop. Evidence is now accumulating, however, that many of the smaller peptide information substances can cross the

blood-brain barrier throughout the cortical-limbic system to modulate mood, memory, learning, and behavior (Banks & Kastin, 1985; Stewart, 1984).

This process of mind-body communication on the molecular level has been called the "mind-gene connection" (Rossi, 1986d). There are actually two distinct functions of genes that need to be carefully distinguished in this regard: (1) Genes carry the units of heredity that are distributed during sexual reproduction—there is no evidence to date that the mind-gene connection is involved in this process; (2) many genes, commonly called "housekeeping genes," are ultimately responsible for regulating cellular metabolism at every moment of life (as outlined in Stage 6 above). It has been hypothesized that the mind-gene connection is continuously operative at this cellular metabolic level (Rossi, 1986d).

The Birth Orgasm

The vast range of possible experience in women's psychobiological consciousness is illustrated by the relatively unknown phenomenon of the *birth orgasm*. Although it is seldom questioned, it is curious that so fundamental a life experience as giving birth should be associated with "labor" and pain. If the survival of the species is dependent upon giving birth, why should it not have evolved into a pleasurable experience? A number of obstetricians (LeBoyer, 1975) and hypnotherapists (Erickson, 1976/1980; Moore, 1980–1987) have spoken informally about the fact that some women actually experience a prolonged ecstatic orgasmic response when they are giving birth. Since it is still a statistical rarity, however, neither Erickson nor Moore has written about it. A number of "New Age" writers on spiritual midwifery cite examples of women who have positive-ecstatic experiences during labor (Gaskin, 1980; Kitzinger, 1962).

The following account of a birth orgasm was submitted to us by Dr. Donna Spencer. It was written by a woman who had no previous knowledge about the possibility of this type of experience. Although she describes the experience as "an ultimate ultradian moment," she had not heard of the ultradian concept at the time of the birth experience. A number of years after giving birth to three children, this woman completed her professional training and is now a practicing psychotherapist.

In the early morning hours of July 25, 1972, I watched the contractions move my abdomen in strange, push/pull undulating ways that felt different and curious—movement not quite frightening but close to overwhelming. Little did I know that this was just the "teaser." I was about to have the experience of my life.

I arrived at the hospital, received minimal anesthetic, and dilated quickly and well. As I shifted from the stretcher to the delivery table, I felt myself go deeper into a new reality—a oneness with my body that was bringing forth something so akin to its essence that it was in total astonishment. In almost a kinesthetic self-reflective posture, my body felt *evolution* folding out of itself. I was totally absorbed in this feeling of oneness within, around, through, in, and out of me. The contractions were like undulating signals of a portentous happening about to occur. The breathing rhythm and pattern only deepened my reality and my holistic experiencing of this happening with my whole mind, my whole heart, and my whole soul. As I felt this person coming forth, I experienced a total spiritual "whoof." There was no time, no sequence, no separation—all was gloriously one in a moment that knew no time. The doctor, the nurses, the others in the room became irrelevant at that moment. On a physiological level, I experienced the most fantastic sexual orgasm. Huge, warm, full undulating waves of sensual, sexual feelings, orgastic to the maximum. Simultaneously, I was also aware of the meaning of this tiny creature's being—my first born son; and even more profoundly of the physical, spiritual, cosmic link connecting this evolved human being with me and all humanity before me and all the generations that would come from him. Highly eroticized, I felt at one with him and all of humanity. It was an ultimate ultradian moment—a coming together of sexuality, reproductivity, and the deeper meaning of being part of the human species.

I wondered if I would ever feel that high again. Interestingly, each of my other birth experiences produced the same phenomena with accompanying orgasm. In many significant growth dreams since those times, I also experience the birth orgasm along with new intellectual insights.

How are we to make sense of this type of ecstatic experience that is so different from the typical labor pain experienced by most women in our Western culture? Is it just a statistical anomaly, or is it a more general life possibility for women if they understood the concept? In this and the next section, we will present further evidence for the creative, transformative possibilities of women's consciousness. Reports of heightened well-being and healing such as the above lead us to hypothesize that the *ultradian rhythms are important nodal points of mind-body interaction and integration which many people can learn how to access in a natural and spontaneous manner.* When we allow ourselves to rest during the test period of the ultradian rhythm, we can facilitate optimal health, comfort, and even bliss. If we fight our natural needs for ultradian rest, however, then we may find ourselves falling into stress, psychosomatic problems, and pain. We will explore some approaches to validating this hypothesis about the ultradian healing response in the research proposals at the end of this section.

PRACTICE

14

Ideodynamic Approaches in Gynecology and Obstetrics

With few exceptions, the use of hypnotism in medicine is merely an extension of methods long utilized by physicians who have sensed, consciously or unconsciously, the importance of psychological factors in disease. With hypnotic techniques it is possible to reach unconscious memories that cannot be reached in other ways; it is possible to control some physiological disturbances that cannot be controlled in other ways. The physician who begins to allow his patients to give him their explanations of symptoms during hypnosis will find an increasing scope to his successful work and an increasing number of patients who will be grateful for his catalytic action in helping them recover. He will discover differences in the meanings of words depending upon whether they are understood at a conscious or unconscious level of awareness. He will become increasingly sensitive to nuances of facial expression, emphasis on syllables, and inflections of voice, for these reflect more nearly the important answers to his questions. He will learn to treat seemingly unconscious patients with respect for their ability to hear. He will learn not to talk carelessly but will talk purposefully to improve their chances for recovery from trauma and to improve their responses to surgery (Cheek, 1959).

General Principles for Consideration

There are certain philosophical principles in consideration of disease and medical therapy which I will outline.

Illness represents an imbalance between an organism and its environment. Environmental stress, both physical and emotional, may lower resistance to invading organisms or damage otherwise normal physiological processes. As physicians we are concerned with two situations: On the one hand, we may find depleted reserves of energy in the individual; on the other hand, we may find a normal individual overwhelmed by abnormal levels of stress. Our task is to return the individual to as normal a balance with the environment as possible.

UNCONSCIOUS GUILT AS IMPEDIMENT TO RECOVERY

Forces of conscience, guilt, and assumed need for punishment function very strongly in all traumatic situations, and become of increasing importance whenever disease tends to continue in spite of therapy or to recur after temporary relief. It is of utmost importance that we recognize passive submission to illness occurring at an unconscious level while our patient is telling us, at a conscious level, how much she wants to get well.

The patient who was told by her aunt that lifting a heavy laundry basket an hour before a placental separation must have caused the death of her unborn child may seem consciously to have accepted a less traumatic explanation from her physician, while her unconscious mind may be feeling she is now unworthy of another pregnancy.

A 26-year-old patient with intractable pain from local recurrence of a naso-pharyngeal cancer during her third pregnancy told me, in conscious-level conversation, how much she wanted to live for her husband and child. A few minutes later, in a deep trance, she demonstrated great agitation and unwillingness to consider the possibility of recovery. With the help of ideo-motor questioning, she was able to verbalize thoughts that had never occurred to her at a conscious level. She had had intercourse with her husband before marriage, which she had been able to rationalize until she miscarried a much wanted pregnancy.

When she developed lumps in her neck in the sixth month of her second pregnancy, she "knew" that God was punishing her for her sin. She refused diagnostic biopsy and surgery until six months following delivery. The reason she had given her consultants for this delay was that she did not want to risk harm to her unborn baby by undergoing surgery. Her fingers indicated another reason. She felt that, if it were God's will to take one baby and to strike her with a malignancy during her second pregnancy, He probably wanted her to die. By asking her to pretend that she was God — a kind and forgiving one that she had been taught to revere — it was possible for her to recognize that premarital intercourse would not merit such punishment.

She began to wonder whether her exaggerated sense of guilt might have caused the abortion, or even to have had something to do with the disturbed tissue reactions leading to the cancer. She lost most of the edema of her face and her pain for a brief span of time until her dominating mother, who disapproved of hypnosis, cast doubt upon the legitimacy of her experience. She fluctuated once again between hope and abject submission to the will of that cruel, personal God. She survived the birth of her surprisingly healthy infant by a few weeks only.

Such individuals believe that the God who punishes them is stricter and more unyielding than the God of other people. Their entire picture of illness may change in the space of a few hours when they are helped to "trade places" with God during a hypnotic interview.

It should be emphasized here that religious training is not a prerequisite for assumed guilt and passive acceptance of disease as punishment. In fact, there is some evidence that religion had its beginnings in times of human dismay, in the presence of overwhelming fire, flood, war, and pestilence. I have seen two rather hard-bitten painters become enthusiastic about religion upon returning safely to the ground after swinging wildly for a time on a scaffolding at the fifteenth floor of a San Francisco building during an earthquake. Hypnotic uncovering techniques are helpful in finding and correcting misdirected religious feelings leading to submission to disease. Indeed, we have no other tool as effective as hypnosis in this respect.

DIFFERENT LEVELS OF AWARENESS

There seem to be three general levels of thought which may, at times, be contradictory, one to another. Human beings react consciously, according to experience in one way. At a very deep level of unconscious attitude, they have little sense of humor, they understand the meaning of words in a literal, almost childish way, and they seem to possess a strong drive to live or recover from illness. It is in the middle zone of unconscious behavior where confusions of thought abound. Here unresolved anxieties may fatigue the individual's resources into passive acceptance of disease or into active search for death as a lesser of evils. Within the brief scope of time available to us in clinical medicine, we are not able to indulge in protracted orthopsychiatric techniques of therapy. Communication in ordinary conversation between patient and psychotherapist can seldom gain access to deep unconscious attitudes. These levels can be accessed, however, by ideomotor questioning techniques. When we appeal to the deep, unconscious positive drives, we may aid a depressed patient in understanding her previous reasons for submission and help her decide to fight successfully for recovery.

VASCULAR STASIS

All muscles of the body must alternately relax and contract in order to maintain optimum nutrition and oxygen supply. Pathologic changes occur when either extreme of tension or flaccidity is continued too long. At one end of the scale is atrophy, which we can see causing the vaginal prolapses of widowed or non-orgasmic patients. At the other end of the scale there are sensations of pain apparently due to accumulation of metabolic waste products. Pain causes further unconscious muscle contracture. Excessive or prolonged mild muscular contraction tends to constrict the thin-walled venous channels of egress while permitting continued ingress of arterial blood under pressure through the more resilient arterial system. This disturbance of capillary pressure gradient and nutrition permits escape of fluid into the tissues causing further disturbance of circulation. The gynecologist must recognize factors that can cause increased and decreased muscular activity in order to help his patients with pelvic, back, and urologic syndromes resulting from muscle spasm pain and edema. Approach to these factors with hypnotic techniques will permit more successful surgery when indicated, and may often even make surgery unnecessary.

"THE LAW OF REVERSED EFFORT"

The achievement of any goal requiring a learning process is at the expense of many experiences of disappointing failure. Every intelligent human being has learned to walk, to avoid wetting the bed, and to eat neatly only after many failures. Thus it happens that there is a law of human behavior, called by Emile Couè, "The Law of Reversed Effort." Equally balanced forces of hope versus fear of failure will result in failure. There are myriad examples of this law. There is the difficulty in using a bedpan after surgery, or the inability of a patient to relax purposefully the contracted muscles around an injured area. It is possible that many patients develop a relative and even absolute frigidity because of the assumption that they are not performing sexually as expected. Many patients lose their sterility problem when they cease making purposeful efforts toward conception and either decide that children are not important or partially satisfy their needs through adoption. Many have demonstrated their capacity for conception by simply deciding to let a gynecological consultant take the responsibility of making necessary improvements in their performance. I have had six such patients become pregnant after two or more years of sterility during the interval between calling in for an appointment and the time they were first seen in my office. Age regression studies of these patients indicated that their conviction in ultimate medical help changed their attitude toward intercourse. They felt that conception occurred when they stopped feeling that intercourse was an unfair test of their ability to conceive.

A corollary to this law of reversed effort is the need for giving patients confidence in the eventual success of any assigned task. We cannot expect a patient to develop a continued anesthesia for a painful area unless she has learned that she could do it for a foot or an arm or some relatively unimportant area.

A second corollary relates to what I call the "slip-back phenomenon." A once diffident and defeated patient who has achieved success will soon begin thinking, *This is too good to continue and I wonder what might happen to spoil it.* Such patients should be helped to understand that relapses are normal but that even these can be instructive if a search for immediate factors is made when a relapse occurs. Patients should be told that relapses may occur but will be less severe each time and intervals between will be greater. This type of instruction proves a stimulating challenge to some patients who may nicely prove that the therapist was wrong in being so pessimistic.

ALTERING PATHOLOGICAL CONDITIONS

When one arm of the hypnotized subject is sensitive and the other arm is slightly or completely numb, we can demonstrate a difference of tissue reaction when both arms are scratched with the point of a hypodermic needle. While there may be variations in the primary reaction, the response of the scratches after two or more hours is different. Edema and redness persist along the course of the scratch on the sensitive arm but they disappear rapidly on the insensitive arm. I have repeated this test with over one thousand patients. Among two hundred consecutive patients, there were four who showed no difference between the scratches, and two who, for some reason, gave a reversed reaction. This simple demonstration is of great value with patients who have lost confidence in being able to alter a pathological condition. It can give motivation to the patient with a pelvic congestion syndrome to discover the reasons for her having become hypersensitive in the pelvic area, and to bring about the necessary improvements that can decrease the size of the uterus, improve function of the ovaries, and remove discomfort.

I have used simple training for analgesia with a patient who was running a septic course from a puerperal uterine infection and showing no response to chemotherapy. Apparently, there was enough improvement in the pelvic circulation brought about by relief from pain to permit reduction of her temperature to normal within 36 hours (Cheek, 1957). The only explanation that makes sense here is that the edema and vascular congestion had blocked the drugs from reaching the infected zone.

Suggestions of numbness lasting 24 hours permitted a patient with a perirectal abscess to lose the induration and redness after needle aspiration of the abscess. A planned operation for removal of the supposed fistula tract was not needed, and there was no recurrence during five subsequent years of observation. At one time I would have hospitalized such a patient for drainage and hot packs. (See Box 22 for an ideodynamic approach to facilitating surgical and obstetrical analgesia.)

Uses of Hypnosis With Fertility Problems

I have found hypnosis valuable in therapy for fertility problems. Infertile patients often suffer from sexual inhibitions and fears that cause non-orgasmic responses. Frustrations stemming from trying to have intercourse on

BOX 22: SURGICAL AND OBSTETRICAL ANALGESIA

1. *Accessing unconscious control of analgesia*
   a. "Walk into an imaginary, cold lake until the water reaches your knees. When you feel the cold, your yes finger will lift unconsciously. Tell me when you are feeling cold from your knees down."
   b. "When you are in cold water, you soon get used to it. It is no longer cold. You are about half as sensitive as you usually are. If you stubbed a toe or bumped your shin, you would feel a bump but there would be no pain. Your no finger will lift to let you know when you are half as sensitive as you were at first."
   c. "Now walk in until you feel the cold water up to your ribs. When you feel cold from your ribs to your knees, your yes finger will lift. When you are numb from your ribs down to your toes, your no finger will lift."
   d. "Now press your left thumb and index finger together. This associates instant coolness and numbness, and you will be able to do this with increasing speed every time you repeat this exercise."
   e. "Now loosen your pressure on the left hand, and press the index finger and thumb on your right hand to bring back, instantly, all the feelings that have been cool and numb."
   f. "Practice this at home until you know you can reproduce these sensation changes any time you wish."

2. *Therapeutic facilitation*
   a. Have patient repeat exercise until confidence is assured.
   b. Explain that making labor more like the work of sawing wood than like a long arduous experience will allow the baby to be born feeling welcome and free of guilt.
   c. "By turning off unconscious, painful stimuli, you will heal without inflammation and will be able to go home sooner."

3. *Ratifying and extending new ability*
   "Learning this skill will not only make your immediate task easier, but also will aid you in meeting unrelated tasks with confidence in the future."

pillows, in knee-chest positions, and on special days of the menstrual cycle after study of basal temperature graphs have caused secondary impotence in husbands and non-orgasmic responses in wives. Although many women with big families have demonstrated their personal capacity for conception in the absence of orgasm, from the partial knowledge of clinical observation it seems that there is a physiological advantage given to anorgasmic, infertile women when their sexual responsiveness is improved.

It is dangerous for a physician to discuss sexual problems in an unctuous tone of voice as though he were courting a girl friend. I have often spoken of this pitfall to my students; I hope the advice will be indelibly imprinted upon the unconscious minds of my readers. Another proviso of utmost importance in the therapy of these problems is that the therapist should meet the husband and be assured through firsthand observation that the husband understands the mechanisms of hypnosis and is supportive of it. It is inadvisable to proceed with hypnotherapy when a husband refuses to come in or indicates in some way that he does not believe in the value of hypnosis.

SIMPLE POSTURAL SUGGESTION DEMONSTRATING REVERSED EFFORT EFFECT

The primary steps in therapy with sterility patients are the same for anorgasmic patients, as well as those suffering from primary and secondary dysmenorrhea. It is most fortunate that we have some simple tests of postural suggestion available, because with them we can demonstrate how muscles can contract at an unconscious level. We can demonstrate that "trying" to move muscles does not achieve a result as easily as knowing that an imaginary force can bring about the movement. By showing the reversed effort effect described by Couè, we can help patients understand that past failures to conceive, to respond sexually to the degree expected, or to control the painful uterine contractions of dysmenorrhea, were not from want of trying but could, in fact, be the result of trying *too hard*. This is an emotional face-saving device of great significance because it disarms any possible counteroffensive of a patient who might feel that an emotional handicap is a disgrace. The following steps have been valuable in superficial therapy with many diseases involving hypersensitivity.

(1) The seated patient is asked to close her eyes and to hold her hands extended at shoulder height, with the thumbs about six inches apart. She is asked to pretend that a heavy purse is hanging on the arm least encumbered with jewelry. Suggestions of heaviness and the strong downward drag of the purse are given until the "weighted" arm moves down several inches. She is then asked to open her eyes and notice the difference in the position of the arms. Attention is drawn to the fact that one arm felt heavier because she was noticing more sensations from this arm than from the other one. It is explained that the muscular reaction causing a downward movement of the weighted arm was produced at an unconscious level in much the same way as

she might put her foot down on an imaginary brake if the automobile driver were approaching an intersection too rapidly. She is told that many unconscious movements are as misdirected as trying to stop a car by pressing on the floorboard. It is added that if muscles continue in a tense state, they will disturb the removal of waste products and the blood vessels will give pain because of oxygen lack.

(2) After a brief rest, the patient is asked to close her eyes and again hold her hands extended forward. The suggestion is made that there is a string tied around the wrist nearest to me, and I am going to pull steadily on the string to draw her arm toward me. After it has moved several inches in my direction, I ask the patient to keep her eyes closed and "try" to pull the outstretched arm back toward the other arm. There is usually a tremor as opposing sets of muscles go into action; the earlier suggestion having been to pull toward me, and the weaker second suggestion implying failure with the word *try* pulling toward the other arm. Usually the patient will add strength to her own suggestion by thinking, *Of course I can pull it back*. There will be a momentary movement of the arms together. At this moment I ask her to stop "trying" and let the arms move as they please while still remaining up. Generally, the arm with the imaginary string will start to drift back toward me, because that was the original suggestion.

(3) The third step takes only a few moments. The arms are kept up after the "slip-back" is demonstrated. The patient is told that she can pretend the string is cut; she can learn how to do things the easy way by pretending that she has a rubber band around her wrists, and that she is going to relax now and let the elasticity of the band pull her arms together. When her thumbs have touched, she is asked to open her eyes and observe how nicely a job gets done if she visualizes the goal as already completed and allows the unconscious mind to take care of the muscular details necessary for completion of the task. At this moment, depending on the reason for demonstrating the tests, some hints are given that there will be a living, healthy baby, or that menstruation can be normal and comfortable.

Ideomotor Techniques of Questioning and Response in Discovering and Correcting Psychological Factors

The techniques of discovery and correction of psychological factors may be carried out in the following steps:

1. Determining whether or not the patient believes that there may be some emotional factor relating to the beginning or the continuation of the trouble; ruling out the possibility of self-punishment.

2. Asking her in hypnosis to "orient back" to the first moment when she felt that something significant was occurring in relation to this problem, and letting her yes finger pull up to indicate when she is there.

3. Training the patient to speak about the thoughts triggered by the

ideomotor questioning. This can often be done with the suggestion, **"As your finger lifts, the thought can be pulled up to the more nearly conscious level where you can speak about it, if you feel it is all right."**

4. If there is refusal to discuss pertinent material, ask if it would be all right in orienting forward again to the time of interview to understand and talk about the material. Often the first memory is at the horizon of time when it was first experienced, and at that time might have been too loaded. If this is also refused, we can ask if she can go over this material at an unconscious level and work it out by herself. If she answers yes, she can be asked to signal the beginning and the ending of the experience; she can be asked to go over it rapidly many times until she thoroughly understands it in the light of all her knowledge and experience of later years. She is told that when it no longer can cause her trouble in any way, she will feel one arm lift upward as though there were balloons attached to the wrist. This technique has been helpful during a busy schedule because a patient can be asked to review the material while the therapist is working with another patient. The raised arm can indicate that the task of review has been successfully completed.

I would prefer to report that this method is universally successful. However, the optimistic signaling of the completed job of reasoning out the problem does not always assure the happy termination of the matter, but it does create an atmosphere of optimism which can be most helpful during continued therapy.

5. After the patient has reviewed unconsciously significant material, she is asked to project forward on an unconscious level to a time when the goal has been achieved (she has delivered a healthy, normal baby, or she is more responsive sexually than she has ever dreamed was possible, or she has menstruated without any discomfort, and so forth), and to signal with a finger when she is there. She is told that, as the finger goes up to signal, she will know the date and be able to say it. This mechanism of testing the optimism and confidence of the patient, as well as setting an unconsciously definite goal, is helpful in evaluating future therapeutic environment. I have frequently had consciously confident sterility patients tell me how sure they were of having a baby. A few minutes later, during hypnotic projection to the time of delivery, these same patients burst into tears, saying they don't think they can ever have a baby. It is important to achieve acceptance of the goal attainment.

Students often ask about the possible dangers of talking too confidently about the optimal results of surgery, or about the too optimistic visions of the future. It is my feeling that a gynecologist is going to use good judgment in ascertaining, as well as he can, the general possibilities of his patient before speaking out in such a manner. I would consider it poor judgment to tell a woman with endometrial carcinoma that she could stop this bleeding with some hypnosis. I would not hesitate, however, to speak of survival and eventual cure to a woman with a proven cancer, even if she had already shown evidence of recurrence after therapeutic surgery, or irradiation, or both. Extension of cancer represents only a temporary weakening of the patient's resistance to cancer growth. The battle can be swung over to the advantage of the patient by surgery, by irradiation, or by an insurgency of spirit alone. There are more than 112 valid instances of spontaneous cures of cancer in the world literature (Everson & Cole, 1959; Locke & Hornig-Rohan, 1983; Locke, Power, & Cabot, 1986; O'Regan, 1987). I talk about these to cancer patients and explain that they are being given all the best chances to win the battle. Hope is a valuable asset in all disease and should be nurtured convincingly, even at the expense of exposing ourselves to our critics as being incorrect in our judgments. I believe that if our motives are sincere, we can never harm our patients by keeping our own enthusiasm strong, and by stimulating hope.

Relation of Unconscious Attitudes and Abnormal Uterine Bleeding

For a discussion of the psychosomatic factors in abnormal bleeding, the reader should refer to Flanders Dunbar (1954) who, for 25 years, has compiled summaries of important studies relating to bodily changes with emotion. (See also, Banks, 1985; Barber, 1978, 1984; Cheek, 1962c, 1969a; Erickson, 1980b; Rossi & Ryan, 1986.) Many medical hypnotists have claimed an ability to direct menstruation to start at specific times. They probably have not reported their failures, but still the fact remains that this can be done.

A patient with pseudocyesis and amenorrhea lasting 18 months was carefully questioned during hypnosis in such a way that she discovered she really did believe she could have children, and that having children would not mean the destruction of her marriage in the same way that her mother's marriage had been destroyed. Her father had died of pneumonia a few months after her birth. She had somehow felt responsible for his death and seemed to think, with the childish superstition of her unconscious mind, that her husband likewise would be taken from her in punishment. At the time of her second interview, she decided that she could menstruate on a specific date three weeks from then. She started on the day prior to this appointed day, but menstruated a month later exactly on the chosen day. She had no further trouble.

Conversely, continued and profuse bleeding—which is often due to depression, fear of pregnancy, and fear of loss of a loved one—will respond very well to therapy after the superficial, conjoint, patient-doctor fear of cancer has been removed by the usual studies. We can tell the patient stories about other patients who learned that emotional factors caused their bleeding, and who were cured by this discovery. Usually, such patients will revert to normal menstrual cycles when their self-confidence has been improved. The original cause may not be corrected, but the patient can often make her own adjustments following ordinary conscious-level conversation. To save time, I now use ideomotor questioning with all patients who have abnormal bleeding. I will not argue with the endocrinologists who feel that there are hormonal reasons for such bleeding. I prefer to believe that hormonal changes in my patients can be brought about by feelings of sexual rejection, feelings of guilt over a protracted "stalemate" in a love-triangle, and depression over death or illness of a loved one. During ideomotor questioning, these impressions are usually yielded into "possible emotional factors in the bleeding." I have been impressed with the fear-of-pregnancy factor in continued puerperal bleeding. The reasons extracted during hypnotic questioning are important, for these patients have stopped abnormal bleeding. The subjective evaluation is always double-checked to ensure that there is no other subjectively important etiological factor. Although scientifically the study is hard to assess, the practical value of such investigation will stand against criticism.

I have had failures with hypnosis in cases of emotionally produced abnormal bleeding. One failure occurred with a lesbian whose partner had died from exsanguinating hemorrhage after what seems to have been an induced abortion. My patient's reaction probably represented a depression factor, sexual rejection shown by the girl's heterosexual complication, and a rejection of feminine symbolism. Much talk, much hormone, and several curettages were of no avail, and I was forced, in defeat, to perform a hysterectomy.

In emergency situations of exsanguinating hemorrhage, we have a tool in hypnosis which can be of life-saving value. It is easy to hypnotize such subjects, for they are often in hypnosis already. They will respond beautifully when their attention is drawn to their ability to feel comfortable and relaxed. While paying attention to the speaker's directions given in a quiet and reassuring voice, they will pay less attention to all the previous stimuli which had added to their fears. These include the sight of blood, reactions of worried relatives, and the fact that the physician was willingly available at once, or was worried enough to send an ambulance for the patient.

I have carefully explored via age regression, the experiences of patients who have survived massive gynecological and obstetrical hemorrhage. All felt that the bleeding increased as they became frightened; all felt that they "picked up" their fears from relatives and from the behavior of worried medical attendants; all felt that they would have stopped bleeding if the gravity of their condition had not evoked so much hurried and trembling-fingered attention.

Personal experience with control of hemorrhage is hard to evaluate. There were witnesses to massive obstetrical postpartum hemorrhages which I have seen terminated by a few suggestions given under the assumption that the patient was already in a trance. In my resident training, I had to apply an Allis clamp to the bleeding cuff of vagina after a total hysterectomy on one occasion, and in practice I have had to reopen the abdomen of a patient hemorrhaging from a uterine vein after a cesarean-total hysterectomy. I attempted to utilize hypnosis with the second patient, but I can well remember how worried I was over her developing signs. I was an unconvincing hypnotist, telling her to stop bleeding while I was getting the operating room staff together for emergency surgery. This patient, and one other who had contradictory feelings about sterilization through hysterectomy after her third cesarean section, have been the only problems in 1,250 successive gynecological operations, since I have been using hypnosis. I do not cite these figures in pride over the quality of my surgery, but rather in respect for the ability of properly prepared surgical patients to do well with their hemostasis when they are treated with respect for their ability to control it.

Hypnosis should be tried on patients with purpura and other forms of bleeding diatheses. Fearful responses of physicians are often perceived by such patients, and it seems reasonable to assume that these responses might be altered. These conditions can occur in conjunction with gynecological problems, but I have not seen any during 13 years of private practice. Approach to the problem could be made by stating to the patient that fear has been known to cause such bleeding, and relaxation in hypnosis seems to have a remarkable effect in improving clotting mechanisms. I would use an authoritative "shock" method, such as that of Furst and Kashiwa (1958), or a soothing conversational one, recalling for the patient pleasant times in her life when she was relaxed and having no trouble with bleeding. The method would depend upon the gravity of the situation.

The Convergence of Emotional and Organic Factors in the Spontaneous Development of a Serious Conditioning

A disturbed physiological process was altered in one patient through the use of hypnosis by first relieving pain, then discovering and resolving feelings of guilt, and finally, helping her to remember vividly the feelings of diarrhea and hunger.

The patient had been admitted to an emergency room in coma after she had injected approximately two hundred cc. of turpentine through the uterine cavity and tubes into the abdominal cavity. The admitting officer, not realizing that his patient was listening said, "Get a load of this! This patient has used turpentine to abort herself!" The younger medical attendant had answered in awe, "It will be lucky if we pull her through this." The patient, who had mistakenly interpreted her guilt-induced amenorrhea as a sign of pregnancy, reacted to this conversation rather badly. Because she had been carrying on an affair with another man while her husband was away, she felt that death was deserved.

She was seen in consultation on the eighth day of almost complete ileus. There was a doughy, indurated mass of agglomerated bowel, omentum, and peritoneal exudate palpable above the umbilicus. Her pregnancy test was negative. A probe passed easily through the cervical os into the uterine cavity, which measured only 8 cms. in length and showed absence of a pyometra. She had accidentally pulled out her naso-gastric tube the day before consultation. Standing-flat films showed distended, gas-filled small bowel with numerous fluid levels. Her urinary output was adequate and her N.P.N. [non protein nitrogen] was within upper limits of normal; but her general appearance was that of dejection, and I was concerned about her listlessness. She had been suffering constantly from abdominal pain and had required demerol regularly on schedule both day and night.

There were several fortuitous circumstances about this situation which helped motivate me, as responsible consultant, and the patient, as principal sufferer, to use hypnosis. I had seen the open abdomens of several such patients during resident training in Baltimore, where turpentine is more commonly used as an abortifacient. Edema with this type of chemical peritonitis is so marked that a dissecting finger can tear through muscularis of bowel as though it were wet tissue paper. I did not want to enter this abdomen. The patient was a member of Jehovah's Witnesses and was not at all interested in having surgery of any kind. I told her that pain might be the cause of so much tissue reaction in her abdomen, and that the bowel was not able to function well—partly because she could not feel hungry when she was in pain, and partly because demerol does not improve appetite.

I asked her if she would be interested in learning how to stop the pain with hypnosis. At first she was reluctant, but I explained that hypnosis was just a use of imagination and that it was the same thing every good actress used in making a part seem real to her audience. I was in safe territory. During our initial conversation she had told me that she had once dreamed of being an actress. It seemed wise to use this in my appeal. She reacted very well to a test of postural suggestion with an imagined weight of a purse hanging on one arm. I explained that the downward movement of her "heavy" arm was caused by unconscious movement of muscles behaving as they would if there really were a weight hanging there. I said that the difference in feeling of the two arms was the result of her paying more attention to the ordinary pull of gravity on the "heavy" arm compared to the other one, and that she could learn some tricks about paying no attention to the pain in her abdomen in a similar way. I explained that my reason for wanting her to have the sensation of a normal abdomen was in order for her to begin using the ordinary behavior of the bowel as it functioned when she was comfortable. The reasoning seemed acceptable, and the patient went into a medium trance while I explained these things to her as the test of postural suggestion was progressing.

As she drifted deeper, I asked her to let her fingers respond unconsciously to some questions, according to the technique of LeCron (1954). She gave a yes signal to the question, **"Is there some emotional reason for your pain and symptoms lasting so long?"** (The question was asked in order to convey the unconscious impression that I believed she could improve if there were such reasons. I already knew she had guilt feelings about the supposed pregnancy. I did not know about the significance of the talking in the emergency room until she brought this out a few minutes later when asked to go back at an unconscious level to the reason for her continued trouble, and signal by lifting her index finger when she was there.) The memory of the statement "It will be lucky if we pull her through this" had not been present at a conscious level, nor was it available at first with conversation during the medium trance.

We discussed the various misunderstandings between herself and her husband and the possibility that she had let herself become involved in her affair as a reprisal, which could probably be worked out and understood by both of them later on. I reiterated the fact that she had not been pregnant, and that perhaps tonight she could stop punishing herself with pain.

Her reaction to the discussion was favorable and she accepted the suggestion of a numbness for one arm as though she had been lying on the arm for a long time. After she had satisfied herself of her ability in this unimportant area, I asked her unconscious mind to imagine a numbness gradually rising upward from her feet, as though she were walking into a magic pool of fluid capable of numbing all the tissues beneath the wet skin. Her index finger finally raised to signal completion of the numbness when it had reached her rib cage. (In asking for this type of imagined analgesia, it is important, I believe, to avoid the possibility of conscious-level evaluation of the numbness. Normal pessimism will often wipe out development of the analgesia before there has been a chance to realize that it is present. The patient will accept analgesia when her unconscious has signaled its presence with a muscle movement, particularly if she has already seen that ideomotor responses reflect memory which had not been previously available.) The suggestion was given that she would be able to sleep well that night and that she could remain comfortable all night.

This patient reported happily the next morning that she had needed no demerol, and she demonstrated her continued numbness by pressing deeply into her still-distended abdomen. Her personality reaction had improved with her surprise in discovering her ability.

With this elevated platform of performance, I thought it might be helpful to have her remember how it felt to have the lower bowel active enough to expel some gas. When I saw her a few hours later she reported the passage of flatus. It occurred to me that, coming as she did from New Orleans, she might be able to remember a "good old southern summer diarrhea." With the feeling and consideration born of personal experience, I described just how actively churning her bowel could feel, and that in about ten minutes after I awakened her, she could be concerned about the possibility that she might not get to her bathroom a few feet away before eliminating a liquid stool. She had two liquid stools within an hour.

On the following morning, her tenth day of illness, she was placed in hypnosis and asked to let her imagination play with memories of a very special hunger for a particularly choice meal. She chose to contemplate a juicy steak until her mouth began to water and she complained of her growling stomach. I asked her to talk with her physician about the possibility of taking liquids by mouth. He saw her a few minutes after I left the room, and allowed her some liquid gelatin. None of this returned through her nasal tube when it was unclamped after an hour. She was allowed then to pull out her own tube. Within 24 hours she was eating a soft diet, was free of distention, and was eliminating soft stools. Although the plastic peritonitis remained palpably unchanged during the next week, there seemed to be nothing wrong with this patient's intestinal peristalsis or capacity for selective absorption once she had developed hope, freedom from pain, and freedom from guilt. She was discharged four days after beginning of hypnotherapy.

This case is presented because it exemplifies the convergence of emotional with organic factors in the development of a serious clinical problem that threatened a need for surgical intervention and possibly the patient's life. It also demonstrates some of the ways in which hypnosis can be used to alter sensation, discover emotional factors, and correct physiological misbehavior.

Gynecological Conditions in Which Etiological Psychic Factors Are Present

VULVA
Pruritus vulvae: Sexual denial and frustration.
VAGINA
Some forms of trichomonal, monilial and nonspecific vaginitis: Conditioned response of anxiety often aggravated by the fear of genital cancer or venereal disease; often aggravated by strict therapy of the gynecologist and the tacit or verbalized intimations that this may be a recurring disease.
Vaginismus: Fear.
Vaginal anesthesia: Frigidity.
CERVIX
Leukorrhea: Anxiety, fear of pregnancy, fear of venereal disease. Guilt-associated fears may be conditioned to relate any authoritative figure with the condition. Discharge may start when a mother is visiting a patient, when a husband returns from a trip, or in the presence of a strict employer.
Hypersensitive mucosa: Not a disease but a sign of unfavorable gynecological conditioning. Application of an Allis clamp to the squamous epithe-

lium is normally not painful. Painful response is caused by previous cautery or some form of genital fear.

UTERUS

Premenstrual tension, fluid, and electrolyte retention: Often related to rejection of feminine role.

Amenorrhea: Some forms are due to physical or emotional stress.

Memorrhagia: All forms which occur in absence of trauma to the uterus (see Delius, 1905, and Forel, 1949).

Polymenorrhea: All forms. These often reflect a polite rejection of husband's sexual needs.

Endometrial hyperplasia: Many women will revert to this picture during times of stress, particularly when feeling sexually rejected, and will shift back to normal progestational epithelium when the stress is over and cyclical ovulation has recommenced. They all need psychic evaluation of their cardinal attitudes toward themselves.

Adenomyosis: This condition has been associated too many times with non-orgasmic response and rejection of self as a female to be ignored. In my experience it has not always been associated with dysmenorrhea, but it has always been associated with frigidity. My statement must be qualified by saying that adenomyosis is a common pathological finding in colored people of African origin in whom true endometriosis is almost never found. I can make the above statement only in terms of private patients of other than African descent.

Myomata uteri: The possibility of uterine fibromyomata developing as a result of psychic disturbances has been considered (see Kehrer in Dunbar, 1954). Wengraf (in Dunbar, 1954) cites a case of a woman with a "plum" size myoma (case 4) which disappeared after psychotherapy. I have been impressed by the statements of patients regarding the unconscious conviction that sexual fears and inhibitions have been largely responsible for their myomata. One patient with a frigidity-sterility problem stated, "When Doctor _____ told me the fibroids were on the left side of the uterus, I just knew they had grown there because that was the side I used to lie on when I was masturbating".

ADNEXA AND PELVIC PERITONEUM

Multiple follicle cysts and giant copora lutea: It is not possible to determine accurately cause and effect of psychic factors, but I have found psychotherapy needed in the patients who have had surgery for such cystic ovaries. These patients often seem to have been laboring under the assumption that they were expected to be boys by their parents. Several of my patients have reported verbatim statements, in age regression, thought by them to come from parents at the time of delivery. Of course, the babies did not know what the words meant at the time, but were reminded of the "recorded" meaning later when being scolded normally by the offending parent.

It is my feeling from investigation with two patients having the classic indications of Stein-Leventhal syndrome (episodes of amenorrhea, male type of hirsutism, uterine hypoplasia, small breasts, normal female genitalia, bilaterally symmetrical enlargements of the ovaries, and infertility) that my next such patient will be treated only with hypnotherapy aimed at improving her attitude toward herself as a female, and helping her to realize that impressions derived from careless remarks heard in infancy do not need to be affecting her unfavorably in later life. I have wondered why the type of surgery recommended by Irving Stein (1945) resulted in such good outcomes in terms of childbearing: 64.5%, after bilateral wedge resections of the dependent part of each ovary. The area most easily accessible happens to be the area of greatest primordial follicle concentration. Some surgeons have found their results satisfactory from simple bisection of the ovaries and excision or puncture of all available cysts. The scientific reasoning involved is that removal of internal pressure allows maturation of ova because of the better blood supply.

I cannot accept this reasoning. I have watched the satisfactory reabsorption, without rupture, of a 10 cm. diameter ovarian cyst which must certainly have embarrassed the circulation of the involved ovary. I would feel more inclined to side with the psychiatrists, who might wonder what punitive needs were satisfied by this mayhem of the ovaries. Having also listened to operating room conversations of professorial as well as ordinary gynecologists justifying this pseudoscientific way of curing a general endocrine dysfunction by disfiguring one of the pituitary target organs, I have felt that the psychic needs of both the surgeon and the seemingly unconscious patient may have been satisfied. Perhaps it is reassuring for the patient to have some sort of father-figure, carrying a knife, doing something constructive with her ovaries.

Endometriosis: Many clinicians have observed the relationship of anorgasmia and sterility with endometriosis. It would be worth considering the emotional factors involved in the patients, which Sampson (1930) studied in his first theoretical contributions to our thoughts on endometriosis. He observed a continuity between endometrial peritoneal implants and the mucosa of the tubes, often in women who had experienced tubal resection for sterilization.

A patient with a 9 cm. endometrioma involving the rectus sheath, the umbilicus, and part of the underlying omentum, showed at surgery a clear continuity of endometriosis extending to the severed end of her right tube. This woman had been sterilized six months after delivery of her second child. She had a normal pelvis but her deliveries had been long and so traumatic to her emotionally that she had begged the friendly surgeon to release her from fear. The history of this woman would have made a psychiatrically thoughtful obstetrician work with her enough to permit her to have easy deliveries. I had to remove the complications resulting from a surgical approach to her problems, and this necessitated removal also of her uterus, leaving only her left ovary and adjacent normal segment of tube. Several sessions were then spent in improving her respect for herself as a female. She promptly cured her orgasmic dysfunction, which had antedated her gynecological and obstetrical problems.

We know that there is an increase in follicle-stimulating hormone from the pituitary after surgical castration, and that there may be some stimulus also to form cystic mastitis in some women. We need to know more about the imbalance that may occur when a woman with intact but unconsciously rejected ovaries is unable to resolve her sexual drives satisfactorily.

GYNECOLOGICAL CONDITIONS ASSOCIATED WITH PAIN

Dysmenorrhea: This, I feel, is psychological in origin regardless of when it occurs and regardless of presence or absence of pathological states such as myomata, adenomyosis, or endometriosis. I believe it is rarely, if ever, used consciously as a purposeful illness. It is often punitive, according to unconscious attitudes. It may be accepted in an identification pattern with someone else who has dysmenorrhea. It can frequently be handled very superficially as long as its self-punitive role has been ruled out with ideomotor-level questioning. The simple demonstration of postural suggestion, of effort effect, and then of arm anesthesia will suffice in giving confidence that the patient can control the dysmenorrhea also (Kroger & Freed, 1943; Novak & Harnik, 1929).

Pain of ovulation bleeding: This is often conditioned during a time when the pain threshold is temporarily lowered by a cold or some other disability. It may be conditioned by both sterility and the fear of pregnancy. A number of my sterility patients have discovered with dismay that they have unconsciously been avoiding intercourse during their fertile time because they felt bloated and slightly uncomfortable. Religiously constricted patients who fear pregnancy yet cannot use contraceptive methods other than the rhythm method derived from research of Knaus (1959) have often developed ovulation pain. This has proven so helpful that I have frequently taught otherwise comfortable patients to be just a little uncomfortable for protection at the time of ovulation.

Cure of this type of pain frequently follows the simple explanation of the phenomenon of intraperitoneal bleeding at the time of release of the egg from its follicle. I have seldom needed to resort to hypnosis for its cure, except to question unconscious attitudes regarding menstruation and childbearing.

Pelvic congestion syndrome of Taylor (1949). The low back pains, dragging sensations, urinary tract symptoms, and boggy enlargement of the uterus always seem related to sexually oriented emotional stresses. Hypnosis can be used with ideomotor questioning to inquire if there might be "some emotional factor" related to the trouble. Often there is thought to be a traumatic sexual experience which may only be a screen memory, but having the patient review the experience many times at an unconscious level is helpful. *There need be no ventilating of thoughts. The patient can be asked to signal with one finger each time she is starting the experience and with another finger each time she finishes. She is asked to keep reviewing the experience until she feels a designated arm start lifting upward to signal that her unconscious mind has understood the real significance of the experience and knows that it does not need to give any more trouble.*

GYNECOLOGICAL STATES ASSOCIATED WITH HYPESTHESIA

Orgasmic dysfunction: This is always psychogenic regardless of whether it is total, incomplete, primary, or secondary. The therapeutic approach varies with the individual. Husbands should be included in the therapeutic relationship and should be open to the use of hypnosis (Kroger & Freed, 1950, 1954).

Precautions: Do not accuse a patient of being non-orgasmic. Approach the problem by stating something such as the following:

"We have found that it is not easy for patients to talk about these issues but that patients with vaginal discharges, fibroid tumors, sterility, endometriosis, or polycystic ovaries often suffer from the feelings of inferiority caused by believing they are not responding adequately during intercourse. We have found that orgasmic dysfunctioning is one of the easiest of complaints to cure with hypnosis, providing a patient and her husband are otherwise on good terms with each other. We have also been happy to discover that cure of the orgasmic problem has usually cured the trouble for which the patient first requested gynecological advice."

Ideomotor questioning then can be directed in a nonthreatening way by asking, **"Does your unconscious mind feel that your responsiveness to intercourse can be improved? Do you realize at an unconscious level that the more pleasurable this experience is, the more you flatter your husband, and the stronger the bond of companionship and love between you?"**

It can be explained that stimulation of the clitoris is not an essential part of the process, and that patients who have had total excision of the vulva, including the clitoris, for cancer, have been able to experience orgasm with intercourse when properly freed from the outworn inhibitions and unconscious fears of childhood. It can be added truthfully that a patient who has never even had an orgasm in a dream can learn to reach orgasm by kissing her husband on the mouth, if the situation is appropriate. She can be rehearsed with a pleasurable experience when she "might have responded completely," if she had been free of inhibitions. The experience can be kept unconscious and indicated only by a finger signal when completed, or it can be requested to occur as a dream that night.

Patients should be warned that they may have dreams of sexual experience with some most unlikely people—such as the President of the United States, or a postman, or even their physician. They should be told that this must not disturb them; it simply represents a trick of the unconscious mind, which has to learn to accept by degrees the possibility of a successful experience with the man who has never previously been associated with success in this area. Therefore, it is only natural that the unconscious mind should select some male with whom she could not possibly, in real life, have intercourse. By explaining this as a normal phenomenon, I have found that patients are protected from thoughts that might otherwise cause some anxiety.

It is wise to finish a therapeutic session with a request for the patient to advance to a time when she is normally responsive in every way, and to signal with a finger lifting when she is there. As the finger indicates this, we can learn whether the prospect of cure of the frigidity is acceptable. We can also ask for knowledge of just when this will occur in order to commit her to the task of keeping the unconscious promise. It is possible as well to pick up missed cues by asking her to review, at this future time, everything that has been transpiring to make the cure possible. She can be asked: **"Have you learned anything that might be helpful to discuss with me, to make sure that I might be better able to help someone else later on with a similar problem?"**

This request underlines the fact that she is not alone in having been non-orgasmic, that she can help her physician to improve his therapy, and can be the means of helping other women achieve her new level of performance. These are all constructive suggestions. More importantly, it is sometimes possible to learn something which the patient was not able to reach in previous interviews. Often in the course of therapy an idea will present itself, but the patient may be trying too hard to reach significant material to realize the importance of what, at the moment, might seem trivial. Projected to the completion of therapy, the significance of the matter may become clear. Patients have often told me at a conscious level the real key to a problem just as they walk out of the office with an appointment slip in their hands; they may have sat silently or resisted therapy strongly during the hypnotic interview.

A final precaution which has been stated elsewhere is that care should be taken when discussing sexual problems in a hypnotic interview to use a normal speaking voice in order to prevent possible misunderstandings by the patient. A woman could interpret a soft "hypnotic" voice to be seductive.

15

Accessing and Reframing Unconscious Fears in Obstetric Patients

The concept that pregnant women have an extrasensory premonition regarding the gender of their unborn children has grown out of the limbo of folklore. LeCron (1959) has reported that approximately 85% of pregnant women guess correctly. Whether a larger group, now being carefully studied, will match the first one in accuracy is doubtful. But an interesting and valuable by-product of these observations has been the discovery that unconsciously frightened women are unable to commit themselves with ideomotor responses regarding the sex of the baby. By using a simple questioning method aimed at the relatively unimportant investigation of fetal sex, it is possible to expose and resolve unconscious fear. The method can be incorporated easily into the training program of an obstetrical patient, and it uncovers fear without asking about fear directly. All obstetrical patients are curious about the sex of their unborn child.

Utilizing Ideomotor Questioning Methods to Determine Sex of Unborn Child and Uncover Unconscious Fears

Ideomotor questioning depends upon the psychobiological principle that unconscious gestures and facial movements indicate deeper levels of attitude than are reflected by speech (Cheek, 1959). For example, one sterility patient, when asked if she had wanted children during the first year of her marriage, answered, "Oh, yes, doctor, I have always wanted children." As her mouth expressed this thought, her head moved from side to side in contradiction. She was surprised when this was reported to her. By using definitive muscle movements, it was then possible to show this patient that she had some unconscious conflicts which needed resolution before she could expect her body to accept and carry a pregnancy. Following seven years' extensive fertility regimens, she became pregnant after one hour of psychological exploration and rearrangement of attitude. She now has three children.

300

CASE 1: FEAR OF BABY NOT SURVIVING DELIVERY

A surprising experience with a search for unconscious predelivery knowledge of sex determination occurred in May, 1956. M. W., a 26-year-old Chinese woman, was being interviewed during a prenatal visit. I had tried vainly to present hypnosis to her a year previously because I had wanted to explore her attitudes towards herself. She had contracted pulmonary tuberculosis at 17 years of age, had undergone extensive therapy, and had been hospitalized twice for recurrence. Finally, after a radical thoracoplasty, she had maintained a remission and had married. Her first pregnancy had ended at seven months with an abruptio and intrauterine death of one twin. The second twin had expired a few hours after delivery. She was pregnant again a year later. I had withheld efforts to approach the subject of hypnosis until she had reached the stage of pregnancy comparable to that of the previous obstetrical emergency. I had reasoned that, although she seemed outwardly happy and confident, there might be a potentially dangerous unconscious fear of another accident about this time. This is a report of the interview:

Doctor: **Mary, have you thought how nice it would be to know about putting yourself to sleep and resting with hypnosis after this baby is home? You know that the mothers who are able to use hypnosis are the marvels of their neighborhood, because they always look fresh and rested when the other women with babies are haggard and tired.** (This was a planned gambit. She knew the dangers of fatigue in tuberculosis.)

The reaction to this presentation was favorable. She had not been interested the previous year when I had presented hypnosis as a means of having a baby painlessly. She responded well to the imagined downward pull of a heavy weight on her right arm and entered a light hypnotic state as she experienced this sensation. I asked her to keep her lids closed, and then went on to ask for a relaxed behavior such as she might have if she were on a vacation up in the mountains on a pleasantly warm, summer day. She entered a medium trance during the course of about five minutes. She was then asked to awaken completely as I counted from ten down to zero, but was told she could open her eyes at the count of five. I stopped counting at five and began questioning her. There is a transition from a hypnotized state to that of normal alertness. Stopping half-way interrupted the process.

Doctor: **Are you wide awake now, Mary?**
Patient: Why, yes, doctor, why do you ask?
Doctor: **Let me ask your unconscious mind to answer that question.**
Patient: (Finger signal) No.

The patient laughed as she noticed that the finger would not stay down. Her interest was excited by the discovery that her unconscious muscle response seemed to contradict her spoken answer.

I felt it might be possible to use LeCron's technique of questioning to see if she might have some hidden fears. I did not want to challenge her by asking about fear when she had already assured me, at a conscious level, that there were no fears. I believed I might find some clues to her unconscious feelings by asking about her baby. If she had a normal amount of unconscious fear under the circumstances, she should disclose this somehow in talking about what kind of baby she would have. I had been probing when I talked of being able to rest "after this baby is home." Her reaction of accepting hypnosis at this time when she had rejected it during the first pregnancy was apparently an indication that she had some motivation for this acceptance, as has been stated elsewhere (Cheek, 1957).

Doctor: **Do you have an idea, consciously, whether you will have a boy or a girl?**

Patient: Yes, it's going to be a girl.

Doctor: **Let's let your unconscious mind answer that question.**

Patient: (Looking down at her hands. The right thumb rose slowly to indicate, I don't know.)

Doctor: **Is it going to be a boy?**

Patient: (The left thumb rose slowly to indicate, I don't want to answer.)

This answer did not seem to trouble the patient. Her expression was calm, yet the unconscious lifting of that finger reflected a feeling at variance with those consciously experienced. Refusal to respond under these circumstances suggested that she had some doubts as to whether her baby would survive in order to have a sex. Subsequent careful questioning with other patients giving this type of response has shown this to be the reason.

It now seemed time to confront the patient with the evidence given by her ideomotor response. There had been no manifestation of trouble during this pregnancy. There had been no nausea, no illness of any kind. I felt that I might shift her unconscious fears into a healthier atmosphere of optimism if I now assumed she were afraid and showed, by my questioning, that I felt positive she could have a normal baby at term.

Doctor: **Let your fingers answer this question, Mary. Are you afraid?**

Patient: (Verbal) Why, no, doctor, I have confidence in you. You have told me everything is all right. I am not afraid.

As she was addressing this to me with her eyes directed at mine, I could see that her right index finger was pulling up with a grossly contradictory yes answer. At this moment she was able to feel the movement of the finger and looked down, laughing. Not only had the finger gone up but it was trembling.

Patient: I can't make it stay down!

Doctor: [Laughing] **You see, Mary, how you must pay respect to what your unconscious mind is thinking. Do you know unconsciously why you are scared?**

Patient: (F.S.) I don't know. (Verbal) My aunt said I should not have lifted that heavy laundry basket the day I started bleeding. (I ignored this indication of guilt assumption.)

Doctor: **If you could be no longer scared, will you have a nice baby?**
Patient: (F.S.) Yes. (This was a steady motion of the usual delayed type without the trembling which had accentuated the earlier answer.)
Doctor: **Then you will have a nice baby?**
This question was slanted with the tacit meaning that I felt she could get over her fear and that I expected her to have a normal child. This is an acceptable form of reassurance obliquely applied. The unconscious mind tends to reject direct reassurance. She had already demonstrated this by her earlier remarks and ideomotor responses.
Patient: (F.S.) Yes.
Doctor: **Does your unconscious mind know what kind of a baby you will have?**
Patient: (F.S.) I don't know.
Doctor: **Will it be a girl?** [Here again was a positive slant to the question.]
Patient: (F.S.) No.
Doctor: **Will it be a boy?**
Patient: (F.S.) Yes.

The unfolding of this case demonstrated an overlay of conscious attitudes in relation to those of the unconscious level. An initial, apparently deep, conviction that she would not have a live baby was shown by the "I don't want to answer" response when answering about the sex of her unborn child. Following this initial pessimistic answer, the subsequent contradiction to her consciously spoken words about fear apparently helped her recognize her fear and accept the probability of a happy outcome.

The point of asking these questions and getting the patient to express finger movements was not to determine the truth or falsity of her knowledge regarding the sex of her baby, but rather to help her to acknowledge her fears and realize that they could be overcome. Further questioning was used to help her bracket a time for delivery. The purpose of this was to reinforce her concept of labor as occurring *at term* instead of prematurely. It is always helpful to obtain this kind of commitment. Negative or doubtful answers indicate significance of unconscious fears. Discussion regarding the implication of her aunt's remark showed her normal acceptance of guilt. This was followed with later conversation, and she was found to have lost her guilt feelings.

Actually, this patient delivered four days after the date she had selected. She had a girl instead of a boy.

CASE 2: PREVIOUSLY CONFIDENT PATIENT INDICATING
UNCONSCIOUS FEAR OF DEATH WHILE IN LABOR

C. L., a 27-year-old Catholic nullipara had been married for two years when first seen for sterility workup. A 6 cm. para-ovarian cyst was removed July 2 at Hospital "A." She became pregnant three months later and attributed this to the operation. She seemed very happy and perfectly confident throughout her pregnancy. She was trained with hypnosis to develop anesthesia of her abdomen and was given the usual instructions about relaxation.

On July 16, 1957, she was admitted to Hospital "B" after spontaneous rupture of membranes. She was placed in hypnosis as a demonstration for the nurse. The following ideomotor questioning was conducted:

Doctor: **Does your unconscious know the sex of the baby?**
Patient: (No).
Doctor: **Will it be a girl?**
Patient: (I don't want to answer.)
Doctor: **Are you afraid?**
Patient: (Yes) [Note: Patient had signaled no fears during an interview in my office the previous week.]
Doctor: **Does your unconscious know what this fear is?**
Patient: (I don't want to answer.)
Doctor: **Will you be able to tell me next month at the time of your checkup?**
Patient: (I don't want to answer.) [Note: This suggested possible fear of dying before that time.]
Doctor: [I turned to the nurse in the room and explained as though the patient were not listening] **When they enter the hospital, patients often are afraid that they might have an abnormal baby or that they might die. They are often ashamed of admitting such fears lest they hurt the feelings of the obstetrician, or appear superstitious.** [Turning to the patient I continued] **Are you afraid for the baby?**
Patient: (No.)
Doctor: [I then asked the nurse to get some medication, and while alone said,] **Come now, Catherine, you'd better confess what has been worrying you. It will make your labor so much smoother for us both.**
Patient: [She smiled as she said] Last week I saw a report in the newspaper that a prominent Peninsula woman at Hospital "A" died having a baby.
Doctor: **Isn't it a sort of foolish thing to worry about, just because she had been at the same hospital? Is there anything *really* important that you are worrying about?**
Patient: (No.)
Doctor: **Is your unconscious still worried about something that you have not told be yet?**
Patient: (No.)

The husband was now asked to come in. I explained to him what had happened and told him about her identification of herself with the woman at Hospital "A." I had heard that the other patient had been suffering from ample causes for trouble. I said:

Doctor: **It is really amazing how many nice, conscientious people will seem to latch on to reasons for punishing themselves for real or imagined sins when they come into a hospital in labor.**

Now I asked the patient to demonstrate for her husband how well she could perform putting herself into hypnosis. When she was in a medium trance, I asked, **Does your unconscious mind know the sex of your baby?**
Patient: (Yes.)
Doctor: **Is it a boy?**
Patient: Yes.
Doctor: **Now go forward in time. See yourself after an easy labor with your normal little boy over there. Signal, when you are there, with your right index finger, and tell me the time you will see written up on a blackboard.**
Patient: [Signals, and says complacently] It's 7:00 P.M.
She had a boy but was wrong by three hours. Her appearance and actions were relaxed after discovery and resolution of her fear.

When it is sensed that a patient is afraid of dying during surgery or delivery, it is helpful to talk positively about actions she is expected to perform at some future time. Tacitly she will pick up the reassurance that you feel she will survive. Direct reassurance will be rejected by the unconscious mind as being given to all patients without regard to the individual needs. For this reason, I asked the patient if she could tell me about her fears "next month at the time of your checkup." Her answer indicated an unwillingness to consider the future. All the remaining conversations were aimed at letting her know other surviving patients had entertained similar fears.

CASE 3: RELATION OF FEAR IN A GROUP OF PRENATAL PATIENTS

When I was guest lecturer at the University of North Carolina in 1959, 26 pregnant women were being rehearsed with hypnosis for delivery. It occurred to me that it would be interesting to the physicians on the other side of the one-way viewer to see the responses with questioning about the sex of unborn children in this group. These were all good hypnotic subjects who had been trained previously. All were able to develop finger signals. The question was asked:
"Does your unconscious know the sex of your baby?" Twelve answered yes, eleven answered no, and three gave a signal, I don't want to answer. The 14 women with negative answers were asked to hold up their hands for identification. All of the group were then asked: "Are you afraid either for yourself or for the baby?" Fourteen patients signaling yes were the ones who had indicated either no or I don't want to answer to the first question.
I made the general suggestion to them that they talk over whatever fears they might discover in order to have a short and easy labor. I said:
"Obviously God did not intend for more than half of you to die or have dead babies, but an unconscious fear on your part could slow you down and make having a baby an unpleasant experience for you."
I then asked them to awaken. As they did so, one of the patients who had signaled, I don't want to answer, burst into tears and said:

"I know this is foolish, but my best friend died two years ago having a baby and everyone has been telling me I look like her."

This is a typical example of unconscious, unreasoning pessimistic identification. The only related fact was that her dead friend had been pregnant. Their hair, eyes, and other qualities were all different. I have found such pessimism to be a cogent cause for late pregnancy toxemia, hemorrhage, and delayed labor.

Scientific Validity Versus Pragmatic Clinical Outcomes in the Use of Ideomotor Techniques

It is not possible to prove that all answers given by muscular action with the Chevreul pendulum while awake, or by gross movements while in hypnosis, are reflections of pure unconscious attitude, free of relationship with direct or implied demands from the therapist. It would be interesting to investigate how much is spontaneous and how much is evoked by the operator. From the standpoint of effective therapy, however, this is really of little importance. It is amply clear from the arrangement of my questions that definite reactions were expected. This is not really scientific, or so it seems. The searcher after truth in psychology will have a restless and unhappy time because there are infinitely more variables in behavior of the central nervous system than there are even in the shifting variables of neuro-endocrine-organ function. Weitzenhoffer (1960a, b) has wondered if it is justifiable to think of material released during hypnosis with the aid of ideomotor questioning methods as representing true unconscious thought. This is beside the point. Let us keep a clear eye on the goal. The goal is health. If this goal seems scientifically distasteful to the sophisticated, let them carefully search their souls as they re-read Freud, Morton Prince, William James, and Janet. These great men were searching. They were capable of changing their own concepts. We do them a disservice if we freeze them into niches and measure all subsequent thought according to the horizons of their time.

We might think of the interplay of stimulus and response in hypnotherapy as comparable to the relationship between a good athlete and his seasoned coach. The athlete may have too great respect for a well-established competitor, and may unconsciously have lost the battle before the race is begun. The coach who can see no hidden qualities in his man may force his athlete to perform only in accordance with previous performance. The good coach is able to recognize promise and get his athlete to compete for victory instead of performance. The result depends upon the expectancy of victory as presented to the athlete by his coach.

Comparable relationships exist between patient and therapist when ideomotor techniques are used. The therapist stimulates helpful forces by presenting questions in optimistic terms. There is a curious, deeply-lying potential for victory and for survival which seems ever-present when we remove the more superficial confusions of pessimism, guilt, and self-punishment. When hypnotic methods of approach seem insistent, unscientific, and slanted with intent for a specific answer, we could reflect upon the results of such efforts and whether the end justifies the means.

There is yet another problem. Some patients may, like the athlete with a good coach, do better than expected, yet lose the race. What of them? Is it justifiable to treat them with expectation of a happy result even though the end apparently cannot be a happy one? Karl Menninger (1959) has written a stimulating paper on "Hope." It seems to me that the therapist with an honest faith in the unbounded potential of the human organism in the struggle for survival can never do harm in pointing constantly to hope just around the corner. We have come a long way in the last century. Brilliant breakthroughs against disease are appearing with great frequency. Our patients are capable of responding to the philosophy of hope. We should not fail them even if we seem to do an injustice to scientific thought. Scientific thought in terms of illness may tomorrow rest strongly on the capacity of the individual to fight hopefully. We can no longer argue that results with human vegetables in controlled experiments are the true measurement by which we judge results in the art of healing.

For ten years, it has been a custom of mine to ask patients to tell me of their plans about babies, the clothes, and what space will be available for the baby when it comes home. Even without hypnotic uncovering techniques, it had been clear to me that women with sterility or abortion problems seemed unwilling to purchase baby clothes or even to talk about the developing fetus, lest something would happen to justify the folklore advice against counting chickens before they were hatched. Another possible mechanism for this reaction is the, "This is too good to last" phenomenon. Women may precipitate catastrophes in subsequent pregnancies as a result of unconscious conditioned pessimism during the period when all seems to be going well.

The technique of questioning into the sex of an unborn child is readily incorporated into routine prenatal training of obstetrical patients. It seems to be a valuable way of uncovering unconscious fears and it paves the way for definitive rapid psychotherapy.

An objection has been raised by psychiatrists with whom I have communicated about this report. They have wondered whether obstetricians and general practitioners should be encouraged to delve into psychiatric matters with their patients. There could be extensive discussion of this question, but it seems reasonable to weigh the evidence from personal experience. Permissive use of the methods described here have shown no indications of being dangerous. The results in fetal salvage indicate that ignorance of, or avoidance of, the psychological factors would be difficult to defend.

16

Ideodynamic Approaches with Habitual Aborters

We have known for many years that emotional factors play a major part in the physiological sequences terminating in a spontaneous abortion. Stallworthy, in England (1959), wrote a classic paper on the fact that almost any form of treatment for repeated abortions will be successful if the physician is enthusiastic about a certain treatment regimen and conveys confidence that this will work.

Hypnosis combined with use of unconscious skeletal muscle responses (ideomotor signals) gives access to unconscious factors causing some abortions, particularly those occurring repeatedly. Recognition of the origins permits the pregnant woman to become her own psychotherapist in preventing the loss of a desired pregnancy.

There are definite organic factors that can cause abortions, and most prominent among those would be: congenital anomalies of the uterus, lethal genes in the embryo, viral infections causing severe defects in the conceptus, nutritional deficiencies, and chemical toxins affecting the embryo during the first eight weeks of gestation. If obvious organic factors have been ruled out, then careful attention must be given to the remaining psychological factors.

A woman who has had even one spontaneous or induced abortion will approach the next pregnancy with some trepidation. It is hard for her to plan for the birth of a healthy child. She may feel that she is not worthy of having a healthy normal child or that she lacks some quality of motherhood. She does not shop for baby clothes or a bassinet, for she is afraid of "counting her chickens before they hatch."

An Overview of Emotional Factors in Spontaneous Abortion

A thorough emotional history should be obtained in these patients. There are a number of factors that can have a crucial bearing on the success of a pregnancy; those that I have found to be particularly significant are:

1. A history of the patient's mother having had a serious illness or major emotional problem during or immediately after her pregnancy with the patient. There is a tendency for the daughter of such a pregnancy to assume guilt for her mother's difficulties.
2. Starting life feeling unwanted as an infant, or later, feeling unwanted as a girl. I believe that the understandings of babies at birth are imprinted and remain fixed, and that delivery room conversations, often misinterpreted, can form the bases of powerful, negative impressions.
3. A history of a serious illness during childhood, leaving the patient feeling inadequate because she was out of school or could not play like other children.
4. The death of a parent or parental divorce before the patient was 10 years old. This may cause the patient to feel responsible for what happened.
5. Parental concern if the beginning of menstruation is delayed past the age of 15 can make the child feel she is not normal and therefore cannot be sure she will have a normal child at term.
6. A history of abdominal surgery through a transverse or midline incision can make women overly concerned with their female organs.
7. Being sexually molested as a child can cause a woman to reject her femininity and feel hostility toward all males. Both forces mitigate against childbearing.
8. There may be unconscious guilt arising from an induced or spontaneous abortion, stillbirth, or delivery of an abnormal infant in the previous pregnancy.
9. Unconscious hostility toward the husband or any member of his family during the present pregnancy may cause the woman to unconsciously identify her baby with his family and may cause her to abort "his baby."
10. A history of severe menstrual cramps leading to the remark by parents or friends, "If you think that this is bad, just wait until you have a baby."

Use of Immediate Interventions to Uncover Emotional Factors in Pre-Abortion Conditions

In a retrograde study of abortion sequences some years ago, I found that more than half of the women started their bleeding and expulsive contractions during the night, usually between one and four in the morning. The majority of those who started during the day revealed, during age regression, their belief that the process really originated with troubled dreams repeated for several nights prior to the abortion.

Fortunately, thought sequences capable of causing abortion very rarely do so the first time around. They occur on repeated cycles of sleep and on successive nights of sleep. This gives the patient an opportunity to recognize that her sleep has been disturbed and to report this change in behavior to her doctor or midwife. Early intervention can prevent loss of a normal conceptus. The physician should know how to act at once during the first telephone call of alarm. In the case of a woman with a history of habitual abortion, it is far better to check out the emotional background *before* the patient begins the pregnancy.

Even if the process of bleeding and consciously perceived uterine contractions has already begun, there is usually time to expose the emotional cause and help the patient stop the progress toward abortion or delivery of a dangerously premature infant. But intervention must begin at once and should not be delayed by admission of the patient to a hospital. It can be handled over the telephone, any time, at home or even long distance when the patient is on a vacation trip.

All pregnant women, regardless of previous history, should know how to recognize that their sleep has been troubled and be shown how to check their own unconscious reactions to threatening dreams and deep sleep ideation. Their first line of correction is to ask for an ideomotor response to the question, "Is there an emotional cause for this?" If the answer is a yes with a finger signal or movement of a Chevreul pendulum, they can ask, "Now that I know this, can I stop my bleeding (or cramps) and go on with this pregnancy?"

If the answer suggests an organic beginning or inability to stop the process, there is still time to make a telephone call to the doctor or midwife who is capable of inducing hypnosis over the telephone, searching for the causal experience, and permitting the patient to make her corrections for the sake of her baby.

Consider this example: A woman who has not been to your office but has been referred to you for obstetrical care calls at 3 p.m. on Sunday to say that she has an appointment next week but started to bleed slightly this morning and is now having cramps. She would have called earlier but she did not want to bother you. She reports that her last period started ten weeks ago, that this is a planned pregnancy but she has had five previous miscarriages of planned pregnancies, and she hopes that she might be able to carry this one. She is 30 years old and has been happily married for six years.

This is an emergency and you must act quickly if you are to be of help to her. You need not be concerned about her past history. She is frightened and is therefore already in a hypnoidal state. This enables her to respond strongly to positive, hopeful suggestions given honestly and authoritatively. We should use hypnosis permissively under peaceful circumstances, but authoritative commands are necessary during an emergency.

Explain that you will show her how to stop this process but that you need to know what has started this trouble. Say to her, **"Let the unconscious part of your mind go back to the moment you are starting the bleeding. When you are there, you will feel a twitching sensation in your right index finger. Don't try to recall what is going on. Just say 'now' when you feel that finger lifting up from where it is resting."**

There is a double reason for this approach. Your words tell the patient that something can be done *right now* to prevent what has happened regularly before. The request for an unconscious gesture when reaching the moment that bleeding started centers her attention on what her finger might do and diminishes her acute attention to the contractions of her uterus and the fact that she is bleeding.

It may take less than 30 seconds before she says, "Now." You will probably notice that her voice is subdued, indicating that she has slipped into a deeper trance state. Say to her, **"Let a thought come to you about what your unconscious knows has started your bleeding. When you know it, your yes finger will lift again, and when it does please tell me what comes to your mind."**

There may be another 30-second pause before she responds. Be quiet until she reports something such as: "I'm asleep after lunch. I'm dreaming that the doctor is saying he doesn't think I will be able to carry my baby because of all the other ones I have lost. He says we can try some hormones to see if that will help."

You answer, **"That index finger can represent a yes answer to a question. Your middle finger on the same hand can represent a no answer. This is like nodding your head unconsciously when you agree with someone or shaking your head if you disagree. I want to know, is the dream occurring *after* you have started bleeding?"**

She answers, "My no finger is lifting."

"All right. This is a dream and your unconscious knows the dream is the cause of your bleeding. Sadness and fear can make a uterus bleed even when a woman is not pregnant. Is your inner mind willing now to stop the bleeding and let your baby go on developing normally?"

The patient will usually find her yes finger lifting for this question, but if she gets a no, or some other finger, that might mean she does not want to answer; then you must ask her yes finger to lift when she knows why she feels this way. It is usually some feeling of guilt or defeatist belief system at work. Simple recognition permits her to remove that factor.

You conclude the telephone call with a deepening series of suggestions and directions to relax her abdomen, stop the irritability of her uterus, and fall asleep for about 10 minutes after hanging up. You ask her to call you back in one hour with a report. Do not say any more about bleeding. Just ask her to call you in one hour. The statement often used by doctors is, "Give me a call if your bleeding continues or gets worse." Such a statement is interpreted as meaning the doctor expects her to bleed, and she will do so. She has shown five previous times how well she can bleed and abort.

You explain that this does not mean she has to miscarry again. Bleeding occurs in 30% of pregnant women at some time during their pregnancy and has nothing to do with prognosis unless they become frightened.

This presentation is easily understood by a frightened patient. The statement of a way for communicating unconscious information is also telling the patient tacitly that discovery of the cause will permit correction of the problem. This diverts her total attention from the bleeding and uterine cramps to the more constructive area of what she can do to stop the trouble and get on with the pregnancy.

The questions and the unconscious review of significant events have led the patient further away from the thought that she might lose this pregnancy.

A marvelous protective action takes place by virtue of entering a hypnotic state at a time of crisis. Coagulation mechanisms return to a normal balance and all vegetative behavior is improved. There is no need to command bleeding to stop or the uterus to remain quiet, but it helps the patient to make better use of these protective functions when you show respect for this phenomenon by saying: **"Now this is something you dreamed. Would you agree that this dream does not need to threaten the life of your baby, and that you have a right to stop your bleeding and get on with your pregnancy?"**

Treating Habitual Aborters

Now let us turn to the special situation of habitually aborting women. Women who have had six or more successive abortions with birth of a living child at term generally consider themselves hopeless cases. Their chances of having a full-term child are thought to be less than 10%. By the time there have been six miscarriages, a woman may have become so discouraged that she submits to a hysterectomy, which is often preceded by severe pelvic complaints.

I have had the privilege of working with five such women, one of whom was pregnant with her tenth trial. She was aborting when I first saw her. She had been molested by her grandfather when she was four years old, had wished she could be a boy, and had become fat and developed excess body hair. She had married a man she knew to be homosexual. After the seventh abortion she divorced her husband and shortly thereafter married a delightfully masculine and thoughtful man. The early life imprinting, however, was not corrected. She moved away from San Francisco, lost the next four pregnancies, and finally had a hysterectomy and removal of an enlarged ovary. Thereafter she adopted a child, returned to her normal weight, and lost the excess hair on her body.

The remaining five all had living, normal infants at term, although they all had frightening experiences with bleeding one or more times during the first successful pregnancy. Each was taught how to obtain ideomotor responses to questions. They called at the first sign of bleeding or cramping. They were able to discover the source of their trouble and were able to stop their bleeding within minutes of our telephone questioning. All were eventually able to hallucinate delivery of their infant as they reached their sixth month of pregnancy. This is a very good prognostic sign. Three of the four who were able to have a living child were unable to hallucinate a successful ending at the time of their first pregnancy under my care. (See Table 9)

When caring for women who have had multiple abortions, the physician must be prepared for emergency calls at any time. It is important that such women know they can call on their doctor or midwife at any time. The knowledge that they are expected to telephone if they are frightened is often enough for them to solve their own problem without calling. But it is also of utmost importance to recognize that delay in offering help may result in enough damage to the circulation to the fetus to cause abortion in spite of therapy, as happened in three of these cases.

When a distressed, frightened patient calls, your first question should be, **"What finger lifts for a yes answer?"** This takes the patient's attention briefly away from concentration on the bleeding or cramping. It also shifts her time perception to the last time you were using hypnosis and ideomotor questioning with her in the safety of your office. The next question should be, **"Does your inner mind know that your baby is OK?"** If the answer is "yes," the bleeding and cramps may stop without any further intervention. If the answer is "no," you must ask your patient to go back to whatever gave her that silly idea that the baby is not OK, and to bring the thought up to where she can tell you about it. The cause is usually constructed out of dream material or residual pessimism about the pregnancy being too good to be true.

Patients seem to know what they are able to do in a constructive way when they are pregnant. It is up to us who care for them to listen to their remarks and to know how to search for troubled dreams and unconscious sources of pessimism. The results are rewarding when we are able to project our faith in our patients' being able to find solutions to their challenges.

Table 9: Histories of habitual aborters.

Case	Age	Abortions before therapy	Abortions after therapy	Living babies
W.C.	26	7	4	0
S.W.	32	8	1	3
V.F.	37	5	1	1
G.F.	28	6	0	2
G.S.	37	8	1	1

A Stress-Reduction Program During Pregnancy

In response to the continuing problems of unconscious fears during pregnancy, habitual abortion, and the new research suggesting that sexual orientation (particularly in males) may be related to the amount of stress the mother experiences during pregnancy (Ellis & Ames, 1987; see also Section VII of this volume), I have outlined a stress reduction program for pregnant women, with suggestions for both the woman and her doctor at the different stages of pregnancy (see Table 10). A woman usually learns that she is pregnant between the fifth and seventh week. At this time, her first counseling session with her doctor should review the global issues of pregnancy and her attitudes toward the forthcoming child on a normal, waking, conversational level. The doctor then teaches the process of ideomotor signaling and reviews any problem areas that may have arisen during the initial interview.

Table 10: Stress-reduction activities for pregnant women and their physicians.

WEEKS	PREGNANT WOMAN	HER DOCTOR
5–7	Review conscious attitudes toward her pregnancy and forthcoming baby.	Counseling at normal conversational level; teaching ideomotor signaling; asking about any problem areas.
8	Establish ideodynamic communication: 1. Learn to use ultradian rest periods before lunch and dinner (this helps overcome nausea and diminishes risk of "storing food" leading to unnecessary weight gain). 2. Ask yourself if your dreams have been restful and pleasant. If not, check with your doctor.	1. **"Is your inner mind willing to give this child the best possible start in life?"** (If not, orient to cause of doubts, which can usually be easily removed.) 2. **"Does your inner mind know the sex of your baby?"** (Answer often reveals unconscious fears.) 3. Check last night's sleep for trouble.
12	1. Continue ultradian rest periods three or four times per day. 2. Search for origin of any symptom before calling doctor by orienting to first moment symptom is beginning; say to yourself, "My yes finger will lift when I am there, and as it lifts, I will know what is causing the problem." 3. If angry or disappointed, pat your abdomen and say, for example, "I am mad at your dad, but it has nothing to do with you in there" (purpose: to keep yourself aware that your feelings and hormones affect your baby).	1. Search early life impressions and attitudes of mother toward delivery and reframe if necessary. 2. Briefly rehearse mother in inducing self-hypnosis. 3. Encourage her with stress-reduction exercises.
18–20	First fetal movement: 1. Pat abdomen and talk out loud to your baby during the day, as you would to another adult (your baby is now much more receptive). 2. If possible, keep soft, classical music or folk songs playing for an hour or two each day. 3. Continue ultradian self-hypnosis exercise three or four times per day.	1. Explain about fetal activity: babies hiccup when mothers are nervous, and that near to term they will "walk" around into a head-down position if they feel everything is comfortable with mother. *(continued)*

315

Table 10 (*continued*)

24–32	Exercises:
	1. Ultradian self-hypnosis three or four times per day reviewing hallucinated labor process, making delivery nonstressful for the baby.
	2. Exercise turning "on" numbness from chest to knees with pressure at left thumb and index finger.
	3. Bringing back sensations to normal with right thumb index to pressure.
	4. Get ideodynamic-level commitment to a short, easy labor so that the baby will emerge feeling welcome and free of guilt.
	Blackboard Viewing
	-Sex of baby -Length of labor
	-Weight of baby -Time of day
	1. Check finger signals to see if baby is feeling happy.
	2. Explain how unconscious fear blocks expulsive contractions when patients are in hospital.
	3. Ask if mother has any questions.
36–40	1. Continue daily conversations with the baby and include husband's participation.
	2. Continue daily ultradian self-hypnosis.
	3. Brief daily unconscious review at finger signal level:
	a. yes finger to lift at onset of labor;
	b. no finger to lift as the baby is being held up for your welcome;
	c. I-don't-want-to-answer finger to lift as you feel baby placed on your abdomen and at your breast.
	(This is an important transition in contracting your uterus and offering the nurturing, oral gratification, and full acceptance of your baby into its new world so valuable for later sexual learning.)
	Weekly Visits:
	1. Check mother's unconscious feelings about welfare of her baby (communication is very strong between mother and infant during this period).
	2. Reinforce confidence of mother.
	3. Assure mother that she will have full control over the way her labor will be conducted; avoid any overt or implied coercion on your part or the hospital staff.
Delivery	This is now a familiar process that can simply "flow."
	Be present if possible; however, it will not be a threat if your medical associate is present instead. The mother knows that she is in charge.

316

17

The Ultradian Healing Response

The connection between ideodynamic hypnosis and ultradian (ul-trāy-dēe-ann) rhythms involves a new field of scientific investigation concerning mind-body regulation. The discovery of this connection (Rossi, 1982) was made when I (ELR) noticed that many of the "readiness for trance indicators" used by Milton H. Erickson were identical with the rest-phase behaviors of the 90- to 120-minute psychophysiological rhythms of normal everyday life.

For some time we have known that during sleep we have dreams every hour and a half, whether or not we remember them. It has recently been shown that these rhythms continue even while we are awake. In daily life we usually need to take a break every hour and a half or so, due to our natural ultradian rhythm of activity and rest. If we chronically deny ourselves these needed rest breaks, we run the risk of upsetting the delicate rhythms of mind-body regulation so that we become prone to an amazingly broad range of stress-related disorders. Overeating, sexual dysfunctions, psychosomatic pain, mood disorders, depression, and psychological problems of all varieties are in part related to a dissynchrony of ultradian rhythms. Hypnosis is useful in treating these disorders because it provides a natural way of normalizing ultradian rhythms.

Ultradian Trance Induction

Most experienced hypnotherapists intuitively recognize when hypnotic induction is appropriate. Typically, patients enter the therapy hour with a busy thrust of telling their story of "what's going on." After pouring out their problems, there comes a moment of pause when they may turn either inward in self-reflection or outward to the therapist in an appeal for an answer. This is the creative moment for an ultradian trance induction.

This chapter is written by Dr. Rossi. It is an adaptation of Rossi, 1986e.

Each patient manifests his own individual pattern of ultradian trance readiness behaviors. In general, there is a spontaneous quieting and slowing down of all body movements. The head, hands, and feet seem fixed in a natural form of catalepsy and sometimes the fingers seem to be frozen in mid-gesture. The eyelids may close momentarily or droop and blink a few times. There may be a reddening of the sclera of the eyes; sometimes a "softening" of the eyes is evident due to dilation of the pupils and/or the welling up of a slight tear film. There may be a reddening or blanching of the nose, cheeks, or neck. The facial features may become less animated as the jaw relaxes and the lips part slightly. Most importantly, there is a quiet sigh or one or two deeper breaths, as the patient spontaneously slips into an altered state of mind-body rhythms. This natural altered state results from a generalized shift toward parasympathetic and right-hemispheric dominance (Rossi, 1986a).

When such behavioral patterns are evident, the patient will readily enter therapeutic trance with permissive remarks from the hypnotherapist, such as the following:

That's right, just let yourself take a break for a few moments.

Let yourself enjoy the comfort that comes all by itself while you rest. (Pause)

And if your unconscious is willing to let that comfort deepen so that it can work on [whatever problem] **while you rest quietly in trance, you'll find those eyes closing all by themselves.** (Pause)

When patients are obviously entering the natural rest phase of their ultradian rhythms, they usually accept this type of induction with relief and gratitude. At such times it is much easier to enter trance than to stay normally awake! If patients do not close their eyes after a moment or two, the above situation can be turned into a therapeutic double bind by continuing with the following remarks:

But if your unconscious needs to bring up another issue *before* you enter trance, you'll find yourself talking about that first.

If another issue is discussed, it serves to reinforce the patient's trance readiness when therapeutic trance is next offered. This approach to hypnotherapy thus utilizes the patient's natural ultradian rhythms to turn inward, as well as the patient's own motivation and expectancy for problem-solving. In the simplest model of using the creative unconscious (Nugent, Carden, & Montgomery, 1984), the therapist need do little else. The patient is then awakened from trance with whichever of the following therapeutically double-binding implied directives seems appropriate:

When your unconscious knows it has resolved [whatever problem], **you will find yourself moving those fingers and hands, stretching a bit, and opening your eyes as you come fully awake, alert, and refreshed.**

When your unconscious knows that it has dealt with [whatever problem] to the optimum degree possible at this time, and can continue working with it successfully, you'll find yourself with an urge to move and stretch and come fully awake and refreshed.

In the more complex model of hypnotherapy (Erickson & Rossi, 1979), the therapist will "awaken" the patient one or more times during the trance period to get feedback about what is being experienced and what further hypnotherapeutic suggestions are needed to facilitate inner work. This is essentially a cybernetic recursive procedure, as discussed in Chapter 3. Whenever the patient's conscious mind seems "stuck" and needs an answer, trance can be reinduced by a significant look from the therapist and a remark such as, "Let yourself explore what your unconscious has to give you about that." Soon, whenever the therapist asks what the patient's "unconscious" feels about any issue, it becomes a signal for a permissive reinduction of therapeutic trance.

Posthypnotic suggestions are usually most effective when they are associated with the "inevitabilities" of the patient's life. What could be more inevitable than the fact that patients will experience natural shifts in their ultradian rhythms every one and a half to two hours throughout the day and night? Patients can be taught to use their ultradian rest periods as a natural form of self-hypnosis to reinforce the gains made during the therapy hour. When hypnosis and posthypnotic suggestion are associated with ultradian rhythms in this way, a very effective form of state-dependent learning and conditioning is developed. Indeed, the author has stressed that the fundamental nature of therapeutic trance can be most usefully conceptualized as a special form of state-dependent memory and learning (Erickson, Rossi, & Rossi, 1976).

The Common Everyday Trance and Self-Hypnosis

Ultradian rhythms are the biological basis of the "common everyday trance," during which we find ourselves daydreaming or just taking a break:

The housewife staring vacantly over a cup of coffee, the student with a faraway look in his eyes during the middle of a lecture, and the driver who automatically reaches his destination with no memory of the details of his route, are all examples of the common everyday trance. (Rossi, 1982, p. 22)

These normal periods of turning inward can be used as a natural form of self-hypnosis. This process can be explained to patients somewhat as follows:

"You can use a natural form of self-hypnosis by simply letting yourself really enjoy taking a break whenever you need to throughout the day. You

simply close your eyes and tune into the parts of your body that are most comfortable. When you locate the comfort, you can simply enjoy it and allow it to deepen and spread throughout your body all by itself. Comfort is more than just a word or a lazy state. Really going deeply into comfort means you have turned on your parasympathetic system — your natural ultradian healing response. This is the easiest way to maximize the healing benefits of the rest phase of your body's natural ultradian rhythms.

As you explore your inner comfort, you can *wonder* how your creative unconscious is going to deal with whatever symptom, problem or issue that you want it to deal with. Your unconscious is the inner regulator of all your biological and mental processes. If you have problems, it is probably because some unfortunate programming from the past has interfered with the natural processes of regulation within your unconscious. By accepting and letting yourself enjoy the normal periods of ultradian rest as they occur throughout the day, you are allowing your body/mind's natural self-regulation to heal and resolve your problems.

Your attitude toward your symptom and yourself is very important during this form of healing hypnosis. Your symptom or problem is actually your friend! *Your symptom is a signal that a creative change is needed in your life. During your periods of comfort in ultradian self-hypnosis, you will often receive quiet insights about your life, what you really want, and how to get it. A new thoughtfulness, joy, greater awareness, and maturity can result from the regular practice of ultradian self-hypnosis."*

Most stress-related psychosomatic and mood disorders can be ameliorated with this permissive form of self-hypnosis (see Box 23).

The Ultradian Healing Response: Mind-Body Healing of a Cervical Polyp?

The possibilities as well as the limitations of the current state-of-the-art in mind-body healing are illustrated by the following personal account written by a patient who used the *ultradian healing response* as a form of self-hypnosis (Rossi, 1988):

After beginning psychotherapy with Dr. Rossi, I was informed by my gynecologist that I had developed a small polyp on my cervix. He said that I would probably need surgery but that the polyp was small and it could wait three months in order to see if it grew or decreased in size. I sought a second opinion, this time with the "top" OB-GYN in Beverly Hills. He confirmed the original diagnosis and recommended immediate surgery.

I decided to wait the three months. During that time, I used a relaxa-

---

BOX 23: THE ULTRADIAN HEALING RESPONSE

1. *Recognizing and facilitating natural ultradian rhythms*
   "I notice your body seems to be getting quieter in these last few moments, and you're not saying much as you look out the window [or whatever ultradian rest behavior the patient is manifesting]. **I wonder if that means your unconscious is ready to enter a comfortable period of therapeutic healing?** [Pause]
   If it is, you'll find yourself getting even more comfortable, with your eyes closing."

2. *Accessing and utilizing ultradian healing*
   "You can continue allowing that comfort to deepen, just as you do when you enjoy taking a break or a much needed nap. [Pause]
   You may or may not be aware of just how your unconscious is doing exactly what it needs to do to deal with the issues that can be best resolved at this time." [Allow a five- to 20-minute period of quiet inner work.]

3. *Ratifying continuing ultradian healing and coping*
   "When your unconscious knows it has dealt with that issue to the fullest extent possible at this time, [pause]
   and when your conscious mind knows it can recognize and allow you to continue this inner healing a few times a day when it feels natural,
   [pause]
   you'll find yourself wanting to stretch and open your eyes, coming fully awake, alert, and refreshed."

Adapted from Rossi, 1986d

tion and imagery exercise that Dr. Rossi had taught me: I would relax and imagine the polyp as a small, round tumor or growth of cells. Then I would image a ray of light like a laser beam contacting the tumor and making it disappear. *When doing this visualization, I experienced a pleasurable sensation in the area of my cervix where I was visualizing the laser beam. The sensation reached a certain level of intensity and then I would stop the visualization naturally.* I did the exercise consciously about five or six times per day for about two-to-three minutes each time. But, after a week or so, I found that *the meditation was going on unconsciously most of the day. A great deal of my energy was withdrawn from involvement with social or emotional areas during this time as well. My focus was on being healed.*

Three months later, on my 38th birthday, I returned to the gynecologist. He informed me that "Mother Nature had taken care of itself" and the polyp was gone!

Documentation for this case of apparent mind-body healing was provided by this patient's unusually well-qualified doctor, who was a Fellow of the American College of Obstetrics and Gynecology and a Diplomate of the American Board of Obstetrics and Gynecology. He confirmed the disappearance of the patient's polyp with the following letter:

Dear Dr. Rossi,

On January 18, 1983, a three millimeter cervical polyp was diagnosed on _____ _____. When next seen on April 22, 1983, the polyp was no longer visible.

I hope this information will be of help to your care of this patient.

Very truly yours,

(Name withheld by request)

A follow-up telephone call to this physician established his willingness to allow his letter to be used "for research purposes," but he was unwilling for his admittedly reputable name to be cited. We can sympathize with his professional reluctance to allow his name to be used publicly regarding this case, because there are no controls or tests that could establish that the disappearance of the polyp was, in fact, related to the mind-body therapy employed. This is precisely the dilemma that clinicians have always encountered in their efforts to document their apparent therapeutic successes with mind-body healing.

How can we better document such clinical work in the future? Perhaps a review of the possible mechanisms of mind-body healing will suggest some possibilities.

The noteworthy features of this case may be conceptualized according to the mind-body model of Table 6 as follows.

(1) *The Mind-Brain Level.* We may suppose that the planning functions of the prefrontal cortical areas of the brain were well integrated with the limbic cross-modal association areas when the patient initially explored the type of therapeutic imagery that would be *meaningful and pleasurable* for her. After trying out a number of different forms of imagery, we found that the healing laser visualization was the one that was most effective for her.

(2) *The Brain-Body Level.* Since she was a highly orgasmic person, I utilized her interest and emotional investment in sexual pleasure by including it as another source of motivational energy for her therapeutic response. We may suppose that she was thereby led to utilizing those limbic-hypotha-

lamic association areas that are involved with pleasurable orgasmic responses.

She was favorably impressed with my view of the *ultradian healing response* as a naturalistic form of self-hypnosis that she could use every 90 to 120 minutes throughout the day, when there was a normal, psychobiological shift in cerebral hemispheric dominance and a concomitant activation of many healing autonomic, endocrine, and immune functions. These ultradian cycles are regulated by the suprachiasmatic nucleus of the hypothalamus (Rossi, 1986d).

This patient was particularly interested in tuning in with great sensitivity to these natural periods of rest throughout the day and utilizing them as a self-hypnosis time. When people are doing this in an optimal manner, they typically report five or six short rest periods per day. I frequently give a posthypnotic suggestion that patients will reserve "about 5-to-10% of your life energy to be continuously involved with the inner healing process, even while you go about your daily life; and no one will notice anything different in your outer behavior." I also remind patients that the inner healing can continue in dreams that come every 90-to-120 minutes throughout sleep.

(3) *The Cell-Gene Level.* All the rich neural and hormonal (information-receptor) communication networks between the limbic-hypothalamic areas of the brain and the cervix were presumably involved in her meaningful and pleasurable visualization. The genital sexual pleasure she felt during her healing laser imagery may have helped focus her mind-body information transduction systems on the area of the cervix that needed healing. We do not know what actual cellular-genetic mechanisms were involved in her healing of the polyp, but one hypnotherapeutic theory proposes that the blood supply serving the growth of the polyp could be cut off (Barber, 1984). A case could be made to support the possibility that all four of the major channels of mind-body communication (autonomic, endocrine, immune, and neuropeptide systems) were involved in the healing of this cervical polyp.

The limitations of this essentially anecdotal clinical case is that at each of the above three major loci of information transduction, we can only speculate about what mechanisms are involved. The model in Table 6 is still only a theoretical vision. It is entirely consistent with all the well-known and scientifically validated psychobiological processes that *might* be involved, but no one has yet actually applied experimental controls to determine that these are, in fact, the *actual* healing processes involved. This is the task for future research.

The skeptic also could point out that perhaps the so-called mind-body therapy was not the healing agent since there is, after all, some natural base rate of spontaneous recovery with such cervical polyps. It is difficult to get an accurate estimate of the base rate for recovery from such polyps today, however, because OB-GYN specialists prefer to remove them immediately when they are discovered. In any case, the base rate issue begs the question. One could say that the base rate of spontaneous remissions only take place because "life smiles on the patients who experience them." A change toward favorable life circumstances would reduce their stress-hormonal levels and spontaneously activate the three-stage psychobiological healing model of Table 6 (especially via the limbic-hypothalamic-pituitary-*endocrine*-cellular-gene pathway) in an unconscious manner. It has been noted that spontaneous remissions (O'Regan, 1987; O'Regan & Hirschberg, 1988), the placebo response, biofeedback cures, miracle cures, and shamanistic and holistic healing of every variety must have some sort of common mind-gene-molecular denominator, as outlined in Figure 3. The task of the future is to devise controlled clinical-experimental studies that can locate precisely where the mind-body level of information transduction takes place in each specific type of mind-body healing.

RESEARCH

Hypnosis and the Ultradian Rhythm: Research Project 38

The state-dependent features of a woman's monthly cycle comprise one instance of the more general phenomenon of psychobiological clocks. These natural rhythms provide us with a laboratory for studying the intricate relationships between mind and molecule. Information substances, mood, memory, sensitive shifts in consciousness, sensibility, and personality maturation are all a single mind-body process. Previously we have outlined the three major stages of the process of information transduction from mind to the genetic-molecular level (Table 6). Here we will explore the psychobiological clocks or rhythms that are characteristic of this process and their possible implications for ideodynamic healing in hypnosis.

The original identification of hypnotic states with natural psychobiological rhythms came about as a result of the fortuitous observation that many of the spontaneous behavioral characteristics of therapeutic trance apparently matched those of the rest-phase of the ultradian rhythms (Rossi, 1981, 1982, 1986a). While clinicians have long been familiar with the role of circadian rhythms (every 24 hours) on behavior (Kleitman, 1963), the more subtle expression of ultradian rhythms (generally, every 90–120 minutes) has been appreciated only recently (Broughton, 1975; Kripke, 1982; Rasmussen, 1986). Table 11 outlines the psychobiological, cognitive and emotional processes that have been studied experimentally in ultradian rhythm research. A broad study of the clinical literature suggests that most of these processes are modifiable by therapeutic hypnosis.

Project 38   Carefully designed empirical studies are now needed to validate this hypothesized association between the rest phase behaviors of ultradian rhythms and the characteristics of therapeutic hypnosis. Do subjects who score higher on hypnotic susceptibility scales spontaneously manifest more of the ultradian behaviors listed in Table 11? Can subjects more readily experience the classical hypnotic phenomena (amnesia, age regression, etc.) during the rest phase of their ultradian rhythms?

Psychobiological Clocks and the Ultradian Healing Response:
Research Projects 39–42

The relationships between ultradian rhythms, stress, psychosomatic problems, and healing with therapeutic hypnosis have its experimental sources in the work of a number of investigators. Ader (1964, 1967, 1971) originally found that when rats were immobilized during the peak of their ultradian cycles, they were much more likely to develop gastric ulcers than if they were immobilized during the trough period of the activity cycle. Stroebel (1969) found that the rhesus monkeys experienced a variety of "psychosomatic-like" responses (duodenal ulcers, gastritis, asthmatic attacks, and skin rashes) when their normal biological rhythms were disrupted by stress.

Their findings have been confimed by Orr, Hoffman, and Hegge (1974), who found that when subjects were stressed with extended performance tasks (complex observing responses requiring the monitoring of three panel meters), they experienced major disruptions in the amplitude and patterning of their ultradian rhythms. They found that "if there is a stable ultradian rhythm in heart rate, it is at first wiped out by the stress situation" (p. 1000). In keeping with much of the classical research on psychosomatic problems, they found highly individualized patterns in each subject's responses. This led them to conclude (Orr, Hoffman, & Hegge, p. 1000):

> . . . (a) The same stressor can produce quite different physiological and behavioral response patterns in different subjects; (b) behavioral stress can produce disruptions which are clearly manifest in terms of altered biological rhythms; and (c) there appears to be no simple relationship between a physiological response and specific behavioral responses.

The similarity between the behavioral characteristics of the rest phase of ultradian rhythms and Erikson's unwitting utilization of these characteristics as signs that his patients were ready to experience therapeutic hypnosis then led Rossi to conclude the following (Rossi, 1982, p. 26):

> The implications of this association between disruptions of the ultradian cycle by stress during psychosomatic illness are profound. If the major proposal of this section is correct—that therapeutic hypnosis involving physiological processes is actually a utilization of ultradian cycles—then we can finally understand in psychophysiological terms why hypnosis traditionally has been found to be an effective therapeutic approach to psychosomatic problems: *Individuals who override and disrupt their own ultradian cycles (by ignoring their natural periodic needs for rest in any extended performance situation, for example) are thereby setting in motion the basic physiological mechanisms of psychosomatic illness.* Most of this self-induced stress could be conceptualized as left-hemispheric processes overriding their ideal balance with right-hemis-

pheric processes and associated parasympathetic functions. *Naturalistic therapeutic hypnosis provides a comfortable state wherein these ultradian cycles can simply normalize themselves and thus undercut the processes of psychosomatic illnesses at their psychophysiological source.*

This led to clinical efforts to maximize the therapeutic effects of hypnosis by training patients to use self-hypnosis during the low activity phase of their natural ultradian rhythm. In keeping with the conventional observation that daily naps usually last about 20 minutes, it was found that most patients would find themselves going into "a healing trance" for about 15 to 20 minutes. This form of self-hypnosis was subsequently called the "ultradian healing response" (Rossi, 1986a, e).

The challenge for further research in this area has been to determine what are the sources of the ultradian and circadian psychobiological clocks that can account for this very diverse array of behavior. Are there one or a number of psychobiological clocks that regulate circadian and ultradian rhythms (Kripke, 1982)? A recent survey of the issues involved with this question indicates that these rhythms can be generated and modulated at all three of our major loci of information transduction at the mind-brain, brain-body, and cellular-genetic levels (Rasmussen, 1986).

At the mind-brain level, it is recognized that most circadian and ultradian rhythms are very "fragile"; any significant change in the environmental or emotional situation can alter them. Simply going to spend a night in a sleep laboratory changes the waking-sleep patterns of experimental subjects until they become emotionally adjusted to the new environment. Any real-life emotional or emergency situation will alter a variety of the ultradian rhythms. *It is precisely this "fragile" or easily modifiable aspect of ultradian rhythms that may enable them to operate as quantum state-dependent switching processes in mind-body communication (Bohm, 1980; Wolf, 1981, 1986). Shifts in ultradian rhythms can be understood as signaling systems as well as coordinators of mind-body processes.* As we can see from Table 11, virtually all the major psychobiological systems of the mind-body (autonomic, gastrointestinal-enteric, endocrine, immune, etc.) are modulated by ultradian and circadian rhythms that encode state-dependent physiology, memory, learning, and behavior. When we review the past 200 years of clinical research in hypnosis from this perspective (Rossi, 1986d; Rossi & Ryan, 1986), we realize that most of these psychobiological systems also have been found modifiable in one way or another by mind-body therapy. Ultradian rhythms, in particular, can thus be utilized as convenient markers of mind-body interactions. It is now necessary to design more specific experimental studies to assess the state dependent parameters of ideodynamic therapeutic hypnosis on all the ultradian processes listed in Table 11.

Perhaps the most accessible and interesting of these is the nasal rhythm. It has been found that the nasal ultradian rhythm (whereby the left and right nostrils alternate in being open and blocked) is correlated in a contralateral

Table 11: Psychobiological rhythms that have been studied experimentally in ultradian research. The clinical literature suggests that most are modifiable by hypnosis. (Updated from Rossi, 1982)

Central Nervous System
   Consciousness, Sleep and   Broughton, 1975
   Dream   Dement & Kleitman, 1957
                            Hobson, Lydic & Baghdoyan, 1986
                            Kleitman, 1963, 1969
                            Kripke, 1974, 1982
                            Lydic, 1987

   EEG   Hobson, Lydic & Baghdoyan, 1986
                              Kripke, 1972
                            Tsuji et al., 1981

   Hemispheric Laterality   Klein & Armitage, 1979
                            Kripke, 1982a

Autonomic Nervous System
   Cardiovascular   Lovett, 1980
                            Lydic, 1987
                            Orr, Hoffman & Hegge, 1974, 1976

   Eyeblink & motility   Krynicki, 1975
                            Ullner, 1974

   Nasal rhythm   Werntz, 1981
                            Werntz et al., 1981

   Peripheral blood flow   Lovett, 1980
                            Romano & Gizdulich, 1980

   Pupillary response   Lavie & Schulz, 1978
   Respiration   Feldman, 1986
                            Horne & Whitehead, 1976
                            Lydic, 1987

   Thermoregulatory   Hunsaker, Reiser & Wolynetz, 1977
                            Lydic, 1987

   Urine flow   Lavie & Kripke, 1977
                            Luboshitzky et al. 1978

Gastrointestinal-Enteric System   Friedman & Fisher, 1967
                            Hiatt & Kripke, 1975
                            Kripke, 1972
                            Lewis, Kripke & Bowden, 1977
                            Oswald, Merrington & Lewis, 1970
                            Reinberg et al., 1979

Table 11 (*continued*)

Endocrine System

Corticosterone	Shiotsuka, Jovonovich & Jovonovich, 1974
	Simon & George, 1975
Gonadotropins	Filicori et al., 1979
	Yen et al., 1974
Growth hormone	Millard et al., 1981
	Quabbee et al., 1981
	Tannenbaum & Martin, 1976
	Tannenbaum, Martin & Colle, 1976
Luetinizing & testosterone	Rasmussen, 1986
	Steiner et al., 1980
Neuroendocrine (ACTH, etc.)	Kripke, 1982a
	Lydic, 1987
	Rasmussen, 1986
	Weitzman, 1974
Plasma epinephrine	Levin, Goldstein & Natelson, 1978
Thyroid	Bykov & Katinas, 1979

Immune System

Macrophage activation	Lydic, 1987

Motor Behavior

Response latency	Globus, Phoebus & Moore, 1970
	Kripke, 1972
	Kripke et al., 1978
	Lovett & Podnieks, 1975
	Meier-Koll et al., 1978
	Orr, Hoffman & Hegge, 1974
	Podnieks & Lovett, 1975
Muscle tonicity	Katz, 1980
	Lovett, Payne & Podnieks, 1978
	Rasmussen & Malven, 1981
	Tierney, McGuire & Walton, 1978

Sensory Perceptual

	Lavie, 1976
	Lovett, 1976
	Lovett & Podnieks, 1975
Rorschach alterations	Globus, 1966, 1968
Visual illusions	Gopher & Lavie, 1980
	Klein & Armitage, 1979
	Lavie, Lord & Frank, 1974, 1975, 1977

(*continued*)

Table 11 (*continued*)

Cognitive Behavior
  Observing response   Kripke, 1972
                                      Meier-Koll, et al., 1978
                                      Okawa et al., 1981
                                      Orr, Hoffman & Hegge, 1974
  Fantasy   Kripke & Sonnenschein, 1978

Social Behavior   Delgado-Garcia et al., 1976
                                      Lavie & Kripke, 1981
                                      Maxim, Bowden & Sackett, 1976
  "Take a break" periodicity
  (90 minutes) napping time   Lavie & Scherson, 1981

---

manner with cerebral hemispheric activity (Klein, Tilton, Prossner, & Shannahoff-Khalsa, 1986; Werntz, 1981; Werntz, Bickford, Bloom, & Shannahoff-Khalsa, 1981; Werntz, Bickford, & Shannahoff-Khalsa, 1987). That is, when the left nostril is open and taking in the greatest volume of air for respiration, the right cerebral hemisphere is most active, and vice versa. Further, this cerebral hemispheric shift appears to extend to an alternating sympathetic-parasympathetic modulation of the left and right sides of the body (Kennedy, Ziegler & Shannahoff-Khalsa, 1986). It has been suggested that this may be the scientific basis whereby yogis for centuries have developed skills in modulating various trance states and bodily functions (Werntz, 1981). The possible applications of this nasal-cerebral hemispheric-autonomic system rhythm to psychosomatic problems will require an extensive program of research (see the Appendix for an outline of 64 research projects in this area).

On the brain-body level, ultradian rhythms have been traced to pacemakers in the brain stem area (pontine reticular formation, locus coeruleus, and raphe nuclei [Jouvet, 1973, 1975]). The mechanisms modulating dream sleep and the Basic Rest Activity Cycle (BRAC) are generally regarded as being generated by interations between the serotonergic, catecholaminergic, and cholinergic neurons in these stem nuclei (Hobson & McCarley, 1977; Jouvet, 1973, 1975). Rasmussen (1986) has outlined evidence that suggests that in addition to these brain stem pacemakers, the hypothalamic-pituitary system is intimately involved in the source and modulation of ultradian rhythms. He summarizes this process down to the cellular levels as follows (Rasmussen, 1986, pp. 396–397):

> In contrast to the apparent brain stem site of the BRAC, pituitary luteinizing hormone (LH) is secreted in a pulsatile fashion in response to

pulsatile neurosecretion of gonadotropin releasing hormone (GnRH) from the mediobasal hypothalamus (MBH) into the hypothalamo-hypophysial portal system. . . . This intrinsic ability of the MBH to spontaneously secrete pulses of GnRH also has been demonstrated in an experiment by Rasmussen and Malven (1983) in which fetal human MBH tissue was maintained in an in vitro flow through incubation system. . . . The isolated MBH tissue released GnRH episodically, with periods of both high and low release, demonstrating isolated MBH has the intrinsic ability to spontaneously secrete GnRH in a pulsate fashion. . . . These studies provide additional evidence that the capacity to generate pulsatile GnRH (and thus LH) secretion lies in the MBH, in contrast to the apparent brainstem origin of the BRAC. Thus, it appears that both the BRAC and GnRH secretion are capable of independently intrinsic periodicity.

It is likely that the functioning of the cellular mechanism responsible for GnRH secretion from the MBH (and probably also the mechanism responsible for the BRAC) is analogous to that of other "pacemaker" tissues with intrinsic rhythmicity. For example, the heart, most smooth muscle, and many other neuronal populations of the central nervous system are capable of spontaneous episodic activity and yet are clearly susceptible to modulation, and thus possible entrainment, by neural and humoral factors such as neurotransmitters and hormones.

Rasmussen does not discuss the relationship of his work with the nasal-cerebral ultradian rhythm to which it is apparently related. Since we have voluntary control over the nasal rhythm, it is obvious that further studies into these relationships may provide a new class of mind-methods for accessing and modulating cerebral hemispheric dominance and the lateralized secretion of gonadotropin releasing hormone (GnRH) and luteinizing hormone (LH).

Project 39 Let us now summarize some of the implications of these findings for future research. The languages of mind (imagery, words, etc.) transduced via the limbic-hypothalamic system modulate the release of GnRH, which, in turn, regulates the pulsate secretion of the two peptide hormonal information substances, luteinizing hormone and follicle stimulating hormone (FSH) from the anterior pituatary. LH and FSH are both gonadotropins. They control the function of the gonads in males via the production of testosterone, which, in turn, maintains the growth and development of the reproductive organs and the secondary sexual characteristics of males. FSH and LH in females are responsible for regulation of the menstrual cycle, ovulation, and a myriad of other functions at the mind-brain, brain-body, and cellular-genetic levels.

One frontier of research on feminine consciousness in this area would be a series of more definitive studies on the relationship between state-dependent mood and personality variables, and the concentrations of LH, FSH, estrogen, and progesterone in the different phases of the monthly cycle.

Project 40   The next step would be to determine the attitudinal differences between women who experience a comfortable menses and those who do not. Some women have reported that their menses began during an ultradian rest period. If this holds true in general, we might hypothesize that women who are easily aware of their ultradian rest periods may have an easier onset and generally more comfortable menses. Women who are not easily aware of their ultradian rest periods may be resisting this natural bodily rhythm as well as their menses. We would hypothesize these women would experience more pain and menstrual difficulties. Devise an experimental design to test this hypothesis. To what degree can an uncomfortable menses be shifted to a comfortable experience by shifts in attitudes, as claimed by some therapists (Mills, 1988)? Is the change in attitude that leads to a more comfortable menses accompanied by measurable changes in any of the information substances mediating the monthly cycle?

Project 41   Do patients more readily achieve healing of phobias and psychosomatic symptoms during the ultradian healing response? The permissive and nondirective hypnotherapeutic approach developed by Nugent (Nugent, 1987; Nugent, Carden, & Montgomery, 1984) would seem ideal for such studies.

Project 42   Compare and contrast the ultradian healing responses with Benson's relaxation response (Benson, 1983a, b). Are they the same or different on objective indices? Is Benson's relaxation response potentiated when it is carried out during the rest phase of the ultradian rhythm?

The Genetic-Molecular Basis of Psychobiological Rhythms: Project 43

Rossi (in preparation) is exploring the ultimate genetic-molecular basis of psychobiological rhythms by comparing the time it takes for the conventional synaptic nervous system versus the Is-receptor parasynaptic system to operate (see Table 1). His reasoning is as follows:

The "hardwired" neuronal circuitry is fairly fixed in its anatomical structure; it does not change its characteristics easily, but it is very rapid in its speed of information transmission (on the order of milleseconds). The Is-receptor system "software," by contrast, is always in an ongoing process of flexible change but is slower in its rate of information transmission.

The receptor protein portions of Is-receptor-communication systems are in continuous states of dynamic equilibrium and change within the normal metabolic processes of the cell. The genetic processes that govern the biosynthesis of these receptor proteins, for example, have a turnover rate on the order of "a few hours or tens of hours" (Schmitt, 1984, p. 993). The messenger RNA (mRNA), which is the template on which receptor proteins are built, has an estimated half-life of three hours in rapidly growing vertebrate cells (Watson, Hopkins, Roberts, Steitz, & Weiner, 1987). This means that a good night's sleep of six to eight hours is just about what is needed to restore the major portion of receptor proteins under typical conditions.

The information substances that trigger these receptors may require between 20 minutes to an hour for their synthesis (Johnson et al., 1980) and packaging within the cell so that they are ready for release. Once an Is-receptor system is in place, however, it will take at most about 45 seconds for an information substance released into the bloodstream to reach receptors located in any other part of the body.

These time parameters are consistent with the hypothesis that Is-receptor communication systems are responsible for the generation and modulation of a wide range of chronobiological states of the organism (Iversen, 1986). Thus it usually takes a "moment or two" to register the full impact of an emotion or the experience of a blush. When a biological system is exposed to prolonged stress that exhausts the normal storage supply of information substances and the optimal status of their receptor proteins, however, it will require a night's sleep or a bit longer for full recovery of the entire Is-receptor system via genetic resynthesis. We hypothesize that many such overlapping time parameters in the generation and maintenance of Is-receptor systems may be the ultimate biological rationale for the evolution of chronobiological rhythms in the basic metabolism of virtually all multicellular organisms.

We may state this working hypothesis a bit more formally as follows: *The time parameters required for the genetic-enzymatic-molecular processes of cellular metabolism that maintain the biological integrity of Is-receptor communication systems are the rate-limiting factors for the final common paths regarded as the "experiential states" of the organism.* In humans, for example, the monthly menstrual cycle, the daily circadian cycles (e.g., sleep and waking) and ultradian rhythms (90–120-minute activity-rest periods) are all manifestations of the final common paths or psychobiological states of Is-receptor system integrity interacting for the optimal homeostatic maintenance and development of the entire organism.

This hypothesized genetic-molecular basis of the experiential states of the organism may have profound implications for the effectiveness of mind-body healing and therapeutic hypnosis. When the Is-receptor systems required to carry out hyponotic healing are all intact and operating optimally with metabolic healing processes at the cellular-molecular level, we can expect that hypnotic suggestions will operate almost immediately (within the 45 seconds required for any information substance to travel to any part of the body). If, however, the Is-receptor systems or cellular metabolism are themselves in debilitated conditions, then we would expect that hypnotic healing would require more time. How much more time? It would seem to be a sensible speculation that it would require at least one ultradian period to optimize the genetic-molecular mechanisms that are operative at that level (e.g., regulating the gastric-motility component of appetite); at least one circadian cycle to optimize growth hormone secretion for tissue repair and healing (e.g., a good night's rest is needed since the growth hormone, soma-totropin, is released during sleep cycles); perhaps a month would be required for optimizing the LH-FSH and estrogen-progesterone cycles in a woman's menses, since that is how long it takes nature to create and secrete these hormonal information substances in an optimal balance. (On the other hand, a delayed menses could be initiated immediately by a hypnotic sugges-tion if all Is-receptor-cellular systems were already primed for this response.)

Thus, there is really nothing magical about mind-body healing and thera-peutic hypnosis; they may be the expression of normal mind-genetic-molec-ular processes of cybernetic communication. The seemingly unreliable as-pects of such healing in the past may have been due to our lack of understanding of these hidden time requirements for mind-body healing to take place. For one subject whose Is-receptor-cellular metabolism is in an optimal condition, a simple suggestion, trance, or ritual healing could initi-ate a very rapid "miraculous" response. For another subject with the same problem, but whose Is-receptor-cellular metabolism is not in an optimal and primed condition, the healing suggestion would require more time. If the subject's expectation is disappointed because the healing did not take place "instantly," however, then this disappointed expectation would act as a nega-tive suggestion that could actually halt the positive suggestion, and with it, the healing process.

Project 43   The obvious implication of these ideas is that the time required for mind-body healing may be a very crucial variable in future empirical studies. Rossi (1982) has discussed the importance of posthypnotic sugges-tion in carrying out healing mediated in ultradian rhythms. Devise a series of clinical-experimental studies with any disease process about which the Is-receptor-cellular-genetic-molecular mechanisms are known in some detail. Determine the length of the natural biological cycle for the optimization of the Is-receptor-cellular systems that are disrupted during a for any particular disease process. Finally, compare the relative efficacy of the various mind-body healing methods (e.g., visualization, Cheek's finger signaling, Rossi's implied directive and therapeutic double binds, biofeedback, meditation, Benson's relaxation response, etc.) during this optimally timed healing cycle for that particular disease.

Researchers would probably want to maximize the possibilities for suc-cess by first working with the classical psychosomatic diseases where we already know there is a large mind-body component to the overall healing process. Once we have learned to optimize the time values for psychosomat-ic healing, howvever, we will want to explore further the possibility of max-imizing the healing of any body ill. For research purposes, we want to study first those illnesses in which the Is-receptor-cellular metabolism can easily be measured and monitored with well-known and reliable bioassay methods. This will enable us to determine as specifically as possible just how and where the mind-body healing effect is taking place.

Sexual Development and Dysfunction

THEORY

In the unusually poignant case histories of this section, Cheek's ideodynamic approaches raise a host of issues that go to the very core of the entire mind-body healing enterprise. We will explore two of these issues that are of central significance for understanding the growing edge of the psychobiological approach to therapy.

(1) The sexual experience is a quintessential expression of mind-body communication that is central to most psychodynamic theories of psychotherapy since Freud. This mind-body interface has been approachable experimentally since the discovery of the relation between sleep, dreams, and sexuality that began with the investigations of Dement and Kleitman (1957; Dement, 1965, 1972). Cheek's innovative work utilizes these relationships between sleep, dreams, and sexuality to access the psychobiological sources of problems to facilitate and supplement the more conventional verbal levels of psychotherapy.

(2) Recent research on the neurohormonal basis of sexual orientation has led to a new developmental theory of homosexuality-heterosexuality (Ellis & Ames, 1987) which clarifies the role of prenatal factors in this area. We are now accumulating empirical evidence that maternal stress can lead to inverted sexual orientation of the male offspring. This finding suggests that clinical research is now required to determine whether our use of stress-reducing ideodynamic methods with pregnant women can help prevent sexual inversion. The many ideodynamic procedures that Cheek has developed over the past 40 years to explore sexual dysfunction in relation to prenatal development and the birth process are only now becoming comprehensible in the light of current psychobiological research on the developmental basis of sexual orientation.

Sex, Sleep, Dreams, and Ideodynamic Therapy

The intimate association between sex, sleep, and dreams provides us with a research base for exploring the practical therapeutic effectiveness of ideody-

337

namic healing. Cheek's work confirms the general psychoanalytic view of the almost infinite vicissitudes of human sexual expression. In keeping with the earlier hypnotherapeutic findings of Erickson (1980a, Vol. IV), Cheek's work suggests that the female sexual response is extremely adaptable, in the sense that it can be experienced over many areas of the body in a variety of ever shifting sensory-emotional-cognitive modalities. This is true even when the focal erotic tissues of the clitoris and vagina have been surgically removed.

Cheek's therapeutic work leads us to hypothesize that this is possible because an experiential encoding of the sexual and orgasmic response is localized within the brain as well as the body. It is most likely that the limbic-hypothalamic system, which has been cited as the major mind-body information transducer (Rossi, 1986d), is the locus of this encoding. This hypothesis is supported by the experimental finding that the primary effects of estrogen and testosterone on the sexual behavior of animals are produced by uptake in the ventromedial hypothalamus and the closely related preoptic regions (Carlson, 1981; Nieuwenhuys, 1985).

As can be seen in Figure 13, however, the distribution of the psychobiological, sexual Is-receptor system in the brain is much more extensive than was realized even a few years ago. All the homeostatic internal regulatory centers from the spine up through the brain stem, pons, thalamus, and hypothalamus are in communication with this vast sexual Is-receptor system. All the major behavioral states of attention, motivation, sleep, dreams, memory, and learning are likewise involved. It is no wonder that Freud was able to build a plausible case for the relatedness of sex to all these major life processes. The distribution of the male (testosterone) and female (estradiol) Is-receptor system throughout the brain as illustrated in Figure 13 can be thought of as a kind of mind-brain-body-molecular map that validates Freud's phenomenological insights. We now can use this kind of map to study in greater detail the actual psychobiological mechanisms that mediate communication between the sexual Is-receptor system and all facets of mind, emotions, and behavior throughout the body, as illustrated in Figure 13.

The flexibility and accessibility of the sexual Is-receptor system in mind-body communication are further emphasized by recent research in lucid dreaming: the experience of being aware of dreaming while dreaming and to some extent being able to direct one's own dream while dreaming. Patricia Garfield (1979) has reported that two-thirds of her lucid dreams are related to sexual themes and of these about 50% culminate in an orgasmic experience!

The question of the real physical and biological nature of these orgasmic experiences in the lucid dreams of both men and women was investigated experimentally by LaBerge (1985). Preliminary results with a limited number of subjects who were carefully monitored with 16 channels of physiolog-

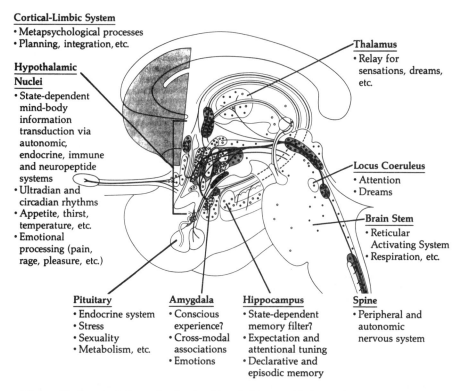

Cortical-Limbic System
• Metapsychological processes
• Planning, integration, etc.

Hypothalamic Nuclei
• State-dependent mind-body information transduction via autonomic, endocrine, immune and neuropeptide systems
• Ultradian and circadian rhythms
• Appetite, thirst, temperature, etc.
• Emotional processing (pain, rage, pleasure, etc.)

Thalamus
• Relay for sensations, dreams, etc.

Locus Coeruleus
• Attention
• Dreams

Brain Stem
• Reticular Activating System
• Respiration, etc.

Pituitary
• Endocrine system
• Stress
• Sexuality
• Metabolism, etc.

Amygdala
• Conscious experience?
• Cross-modal associations
• Emotions

Hippocampus
• State-dependent memory filter?
• Expectation and attentional tuning
• Declarative and episodic memory

Spine
• Peripheral and autonomic nervous system

Figure 13: Some of the major brain sites of the sexual information-receptor system and the state-dependent functions modulated by them: the location of female estradiol receptors (●) and male testosterone (○) (adapted from Nieuwenhuys, 1985). Similar maps of other mind-body information-receptor systems for the enkephalins, endorphins, ACTH, epinephrine, Substance P, angiotensin II, neurotensin, cholecystokinin, vasoactive intestinal polypeptide, etc., are also available in Nieuwnehuys' volume.

ical data (including the EEG, EOG, EMG, respiration rate, heart rate, vaginal EMG, vaginal pulse amplitude, penile response, etc.) clearly demonstrated that the body was indeed experiencing an orgasmic response when the subjects reported an orgasm in their lucid dreams. Most indices of sexual and autonomic system arousal corresponded closely to the lucid dream experience. The only exception was the relatively low increase in heart rate. Men do not experience an actual ejaculation, but their penile tumescence and detumescence follows their orgasmic dream experiences with remarkable fidelity (LaBerge, 1985).

This well-controlled laboratory research of the human sexual response supports the classical, historical view of hypnotherapy that ideodynamic processes are capable of evoking real body biological responsiveness. Cheek's utilization of these ideodynamic responses in the dreams of his female patients outlines a systematic procedure for the treament of both minor and major sexual dysfunctions. Let us now turn to recent theory and research on sexual orientation that will provide us with fresh perspectives on how these ideodynamic approaches may be used in the future.

The Developmental Basis of Sexual Orientation

Early efforts to explain sexual orientation by pioneers such as Von Kraft-Ebbing (1965) and H. Ellis (1915) argued that heterosexuality and homosexuality were "inborn." They reached this conclusion because sexual inversion was found to be common among many animal species and the early investigators could not detect any typical pattern of social learning that was unique to animal or human homosexuality. Freud (1905/1953), however, believed that he had found clinical evidence that homosexuality was the result of a premature fixation of one's psychosexual development during the latency stage of childhood (ages 6 to 12). With increasing knowledge about hormonal influences on sexual orientation, Hirschfeld (1920) and Forel (1924) postulated that sexual behavior was a result of a balance between male and female sexual hormones (or what we now call the sexual Is-receptor communication system). These early conjectures did not find adequate empirical support, however, because there was little consistent evidence that circulating testosterone levels were different in male heterosexuals and homosexuals. Furthermore, clinical efforts to treat male homosexuals with testosterone did not alter sexual inversion (Barahal, 1940).

The next major step in this area of research was to push the examination of hormonal factors into childhood and the perinatal period (during gestation and/or soon after birth) (Loraine, Ismail, Adamopoulos, & Dove, 1970; Saba, Salvadorini, Galeone, & Luisi, 1973). The major evidence for this view was that homosexuality could be experimentally induced in animals by altering the balance of sexual hormones during the perinatal period (Beach, Buehler, & Dunbar, 1983; Goy, 1978; Morali, Carrillo, & Beyer, 1985).

From our point of view the most interesting studies in this area are those that are pursuing the understanding of hormonal factors (informational substances and their receptors) further back into the earliest stage of neonatal life. It is now known that the genetic-molecular basis of male and female sex characteristics takes place during two phases of the development of the Is-receptor systems: (1) during the gestation period and (2) at the onset of puberty. The male and female embryos develop in a similar manner for the first two months of gestation. The embryos that contain two concordant sex chromosomes (XX) then differentiate into females, while those containing the (XY) combination become male. Genes on the Y chromosomes of the male trigger the formation of Leydig cells in the developing gonadal tissue that then begin synthesizing testosterone and its protein receptor sites within the cellular protoplasm. As illustrated in Figure 14B, this phase reaches its maximum between the second and fifth month of gestation.

What is most significant for the development of sexual orientation and behavior is that, as noted earlier, the formation of the male (testosterone) and female (estradial) Is-receptor systems takes place very extensively throughout the central nervous system and the brain (McEwen, 1981; Nieuwenhuys, 1985). As can be seen in Figure 13, the cortical-limbic-hypo-thalamic system that we have previously outlined as critical for encoding and mediating the state-dependent memory, learning, and behavioral processes of psychosomatic problems and ideodynamic healing are particularly rich in the sexual Is-receptor systems. This means that whatever mental-emotional-behavioral effects are mediated by these brain areas (as well as many others illustrated in Figure 13) are all subject to the developmental, social, and psychological factors that are encoded within the sexual Is-receptor systems.

The second phase of activating sexual orientation via the Is-receptor systems begins at puberty. During this period, the same hormones that stimulated the formation of sexual receptors initially during gestation are produced in larger quantities. When these hormones bind to their receptors, they trigger metabolic processes in the cells throughout the body that produce sex differences in bone formation, muscle mass and fat deposits, as well as mental-emotional-behavioral patterns in the developing male and female adolescents. The loci and functions of the major information substance-receptor systems in males initiated during puberty are illustrated in Figure 15.

It is now known that maternal stress during pregnancy can cause depressed testosterone production (and probably other Is-receptor systems) in a variety of species (Bernstein, Gordon, & Rose, 1983; Moore & Zoeller, 1985), as well as in humans. Maternal stress is expressed by elevated levels of ACTH, corticosterone, cortisol, and epinephrine (Stechler & Halton, 1982; Ward, 1984). Since these stress hormones can cross the placenta, they can depress testosterone production in the developing fetus. Ward and her associates (Meisel, Dohanich, & Ward, 1979; Ward & Reed, 1985) have found that subjecting pregnant rats to stress during the third trimester results in at least partial sexual inversion, particularly in the male offspring.

In a series of studies on humans, Dorner and his colleagues (Dorner et al., 1980; Dorner, Schenk, Schmiedel, & Ahrens, 1983) found statistically significant evidence that maternal stress (due to war, divorce, death of close relatives, traumatic sexual or financial experiences, feelings of severe anxiety) was associated with homosexual and bisexual behavior in male offspring. Ellis and Ames have recently summarized all the known etiological factors of sexual inversion in humans as follows (Ellis & Ames, 1987, p. 251):

We have tried to review and organize the available scientific evidence into a fairly comprehensive theory. This theory holds that sexual orientation is a fundamental component of mammalian sexual differentiation, and that inversions of sexual orientation are not unique to the human species. Without delineating all of the combinations of factors that could induce sexual inversions, we identified four categories of causes that are independent of experiential processes (from the standpoint of the individual whose sexual orientation is affected). These are (a) direct genetic-hormonally induced inversions, (b) drug-induced inversions, (c) *inversions due to maternal stress during pregnancy*, and (d) inversions caused by immunity factors. The one social experiential factor that seems to invert sexual orientation involved segregation of an individual from all members of the opposite sex throughout most of childhood. Whether or not real-life parallels to this experimental procedure exist remains to be seen.

According to our theory, complex combinations of genetic, hormonal, neurological, and environmental factors operating prior to birth largely determine what an individual's sexual orientation will be, although the orientation itself awaits the onset of puberty to be activated, and may not entirely stabilize until early adulthood. The involvement of learning, by and large, only appears to alter how, when, and where the orientation is expressed. For humans, *the crucial timing appears to be between the middle of the 2nd month of gestation and about the middle of the 5th month*, during which time the *hypothalamic-limbic* regions of the male's nervous system are permanently diverted away from their otherwise-destined female phenotype. (Italics added)

Ellis and Ames have synthesized their findings in Figures 14a and b (1987, p. 238).

Ellis and Ames conclude their theoretical statement with the following summary and admonishment regarding the premature application of their work for "preventing" homosexuality (1987, p. 251–252):

Theoretically, the behavioral dimension of sexuality primarily is a manifestation of the neurological dimension, and the neurological dimension may be conceived of in terms of two stages. The first stage establishes essentially permanent differences in the hypothalamic-limbic region, wherein sexual orientation basically is determined. The second stage, occurring during the latter half of human gestation, and apparently involving more diverse and recently evolved brain parts, pertains to behaviors that tend to complement sexual orientation, that is, sex-typical behavior patterns.

Finally, to those interested in preventing homosexuality, any use of our theory to do so at this point would be reckless. Even if the essential

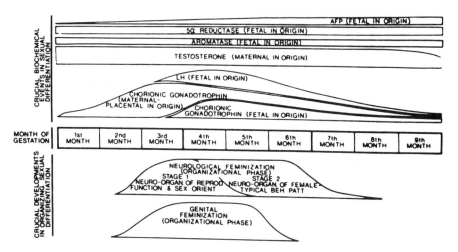

Figure 14a: Prenatal human feminine sexual differentiation. (AFP = α-fetoprotein. LH = luteinizing hormone.) (Ellis & Ames, 1987).

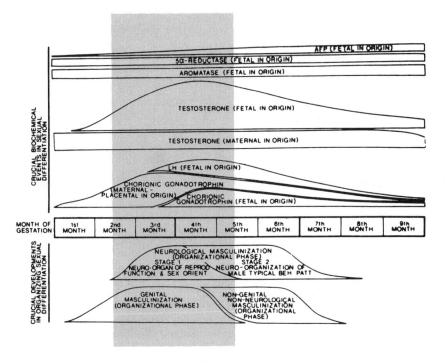

Figure 14b: Prenatal human masculine sexual differentiation. (AFP = α-fetoprotein. LH = luteinizing hormone.) (Adapted from Ellis & Ames, 1987). The shaded area between the middle of the second through the middle of the fifth month of gestation are hypothesized to be stress-sensitive for the development of male sexual orientation. (Adapted from Ellis & Ames, 1987)

accuracy of the theory were to become established, careful thought should be given to the desirability and potential hazards of intervention. Several decades of intense research may be required to adequately test the theory, and, if it is basically confirmed, to identify precisely where and when intervention might be feasible. Also, before attempting intervention, moral issues should be addressed. Although morality can never be directly derived from a scientific theory, our theory, at the very least, challenges those who are intolerant of homosexuals (see Plummer, 1975, p. 102) and those who support the retention of laws against their expressing themselves sexually (see Bell & Weinberg, 1978, p. 187). The increasing public acceptance of homosexuality apparent in recent surveys (Glenn & Weaver, 1979, p. 114; Yalom, Estler, & Brewster, 1982, p. 150) is in tune with the evidence reviewed. Ultimately, the theory implies that, were it not for delicately balanced combinations of genetic, neurological, hormonal, and environmental factors, largely occurring prior to birth, each and every one of us would be homosexual.

While we applaud the clinical caution of Ellis and Ames against the ever-present dangers of excessive therapeutic zeal, we believe it would be equally irresponsible not to explore the implications of their work. This issue is clearly one that can only be resolved with further research. The application of our ideodynamic approaches to reducing maternal stress would be a fail-safe method when used with humans. As Cheek's work has shown, reducing stress during pregnancy can facilitate a wide variety of valuable therapeutic outcomes. Researchers need only keep additional longitudinal records on reducing stress during the critical neonatal phases and its relationship to sexual orientation in the later life of the offspring. The success of these efforts may depend in large part on further advances in our understanding of how to maximize the stress-reducing potential of our ideodynamic methods. Let us now turn to an examination of some practical clinical case illustrations of how we can use the ideodynamic approaches to facilitate the resolution of sexual problems.

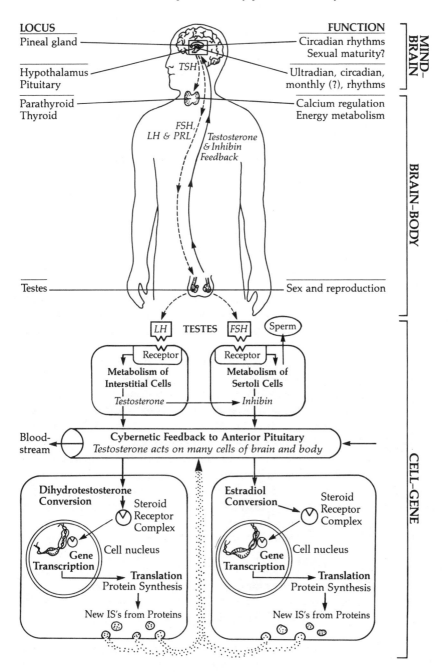

Figure 15: Loci and function of some of the major sexual information substance-receptor systems in men.

PRACTICE

18

Exploration of Early Life Attitudes in Sexual Dysfunction

Suggestion permits a hypnotized individual to remember sensations and eventually to reproduce physiological adaptive responses. These responses may be strengthened by repetition. Results with behavior modification using hypnosis appear to improve when patients are oriented first to formative experiences before attempting correction of maladaptation derived from these primal events. The alternative of working back from later toward earlier experience often leads to frustration.

Combination of light hypnosis with use of unconscious, symbol movements or ideomotor responses allows rapid access to significant information and rapid, productive rehearsal with problems of "sexual dysfunction" in the time limitations of three office visits, comprising two hours. The methods involved have been considered at length in publications by LeCron (1954, 1961) and one by Cheek and LeCron (1968).

Adequate levels of hypnosis can be achieved with 100% of women who are receptive to change and are unconsciously motivated toward continued improvement. Some women may consciously express a wish to improve their sexual feelings and may rid themselves of sexual inhibitions, yet quit therapy or continue to remain anorgasmic with a current sexual partner. They may appear to be treatment failures at the conclusion of therapy but suddenly find themselves responsive several months later. Some may discover during therapy that they have been cohabiting with the wrong man because they have never dared commit themselves to the right one.

Failures, resistances, and obscure successes occur with any problem that brings a patient to a doctor. The treatment of anorgasmia is no exception.

What Normal Women Have Taught Us During Age Regression

The plan of therapy used by the author (DBC) has been learned from women, capable of multiple orgasms, during hypnotic age-regression studies of their sexual development. All of these women reported a sense of total acceptance by their parents from their moment of birth. With this beginning they recognized that orgasm frequently occurred under circumstances that were associated with further show of loving attention. This included nursing, being gently bathed, and having diapers changed.

They all seemed to have escaped punitive action when they were exploring their genitalia with their fingers or rubbing against various objects in autoerotic maneuvers. Some thought they had experienced orgasms in dreams as early as six years of age and all knew they had before the age of ten. Through their dreams they learned that thoughts could lead to orgasm after the initial conditioning for such feelings in an environment of love and acceptance.

From the teachings of these fortunate women, the following plan of therapy evolved:

1. Hypnosis was explained to the patients as a means of understanding unconscious sexual attitudes and of improving self-confidence.
2. The sequential steps of early learning about orgasm were outlined to them.
3. They were shown about the effort effect of Coué with a demonstration of postural suggestion, and this was followed with an introduction to use of the Chevreul pendulum for discovering information that was not known to them consciously.
4. Fascination with these ideomotor responses permitted easy introduction into a light state of hypnosis without confronting patients with a formal induction.
5. At this point it could be learned if there were any fundamental difficulties between the patients and their sexual partners by orienting them to the moment of first meeting and getting their "sixth sense" unconscious reaction. The time orientation then shifted to recent feelings about the sexual partner.
6. Birth experience and later sexual feelings were next explored and sexual feelings reinforced.

Classifying Types of Sexual Dysfunction

In the beginning of this study an effort was made to divide women into classes depending on their reports during the initial office visit. Continued experience, however, has shown that there is little prognostic value in this division, with the possible exception of women who have been orgasmic in the past and are no longer responsive (A-3). Perhaps others working in this area will show whether or not this classification is worth continuing. At first it seemed probable that women who had experienced some form of orgasmic response would be fundamentally different from those who had never had an orgasm with masturbation, in dreams, or in any sexual encounter.

This division had no subgroups. The women who had experienced some form of orgasm formed Class A.

CLASS A: WOMEN WHO HAVE EXPERIENCED ORGASM

A-1 Women who have had orgasms in sleep, with petting, or with masturbation, but have never had an orgasm with a male sexual partner during intercourse.

A-2 Women who have experienced orgasm of some sort with their current sexual partner. This could be orgasm with clitoral stimulation, oral sex, or it could be the supposedly ultimate "vaginal orgasm." The standing in this group was expressed as a percentage of orgasms relative to the number of encounters.

A-3 Women who have experienced orgasm with another partner in the past or have done so in the past with their current partner but no longer are responding this way.

Some women fall into this group because of a misunderstanding associated with a gynecological operation of some sort. These may be helped over their problem easily, providing the trouble leading to surgery was not caused by conflict with the sexual partner.

Women in Class A-3 usually have very good reasons for restraining their sexual feelings. Guilt, fear of pregnancy, and resentment toward the partner are the salient factors. Sometimes it is possible to diminish resentment by helping the patient realize that she has been weighing some past injury too heavily, or has been identifying the partner unfairly with some previous male — a father, brother, or former sexual partner. Most commonly, Class A-3 women have recognized that they are with the wrong man. They may profit from extended psychotherapy that does not fall within the scope of therapy for sexual dysfunction. Most of the treatment failures belong in this group.

CLASS B: WOMEN WHO HAVE NEVER HAD ANY KIND OF ORGASM

This is not a definite group. Many women who think they have never had an orgasm will find they have had subliminal ones during sex play, petting, or in sexual dreams. Some will remember a feeling like an orgasm while being nursed, being bathed, or being leaned against by an appreciative puppy dog or a purring kitten. These feelings were stopped when masturbatory experiments drew expressions of disgust, shame or anger from a parent.

Individuals in this group may be very easy or very difficult to help toward better sexual gratification. The case to be presented was one of the easy ones. The helpful factor was her security in the rediscovered love of her first husband. All the good qualities had been there before she married him the first time. Her anorgasmia had weakened the bond as the children were born. He had assumed that she was rejecting him.

Case Example With Class B Patient: No Conscious Memory of Orgasm

Diana was a 28-year-old Caucasian woman with three children, referred by a gynecologist for her sexual problem. She had just remarried her first husband and wanted to make the marriage work this time with agreement at all levels of communication. She said she had never had an orgasm with dreams, masturbation, or intercourse. She had never tried to masturbate. Initial estimate of her prognosis with hypnotherapy was poor because of her age, multiple marriage difficulties, and 11-year history of total anorgasmia.

BACKGROUND HISTORY

Diana was the first of five children, an unplanned pregnancy when her mother was 20 years old. There were some problems that grew worse as other children arrived. Mother became involved in an affair, and the marriage broke up when Diana was eight years old—a critical time for her. She loved her father very much and felt it as a personal rejection when he moved out of the home. She resented the new stepfather, who moved in almost at once.

At 14 Diana took up Catholicism. At 17 she became pregnant after unprotected intercourse with her boyfriend, Ron, whom she married in a reproduction of her mother's plight when Diana was conceived. After birth of their third child, the marriage broke up. She married quickly again, but it was a bad union that lasted only two years.

Diana began dating Ron again and had just remarried him at the time of her first consultation. She said that she had always enjoyed sex with him but had never had an orgasm at any time in her life.

FIRST INTERVIEW AND INTRODUCTION TO HYPNOSIS

One hour had been reserved for the patient, but brief appointments for two other patients permitted two hours total time for the therapy to continue while I was out of the consultation room.

The explanation given about hypnosis so interested the patient that she was in a light state even before she was given a test of postural suggestion with her arms extended and one arm supporting an imaginary heavy weight. Her trance deepened and she appeared delighted on discovering that the heavy arm floated up toward the ceiling when the weight was replaced by "big balloons."

Finger signals were assigned on her right hand for yes, no, and I don't want to answer. Her compliance with the suggestions was checked by asking her to think the word "yes" and observing that the assigned finger rose in the typical intermittent way. Questions and directions then began as follows:

Q. Does the inner part of your mind know that you can have orgasms with intercourse just as well as or even better than other normal women?

(The phrasing was aimed at communicating my unspoken belief to the patient that she was a normal woman, capable of normal sexual responses about which I had spoken during my introduction regarding the values of hypnosis. She had already demonstrated that she could make a heavy arm feel light and that it could actually move upward against the pull of gravity without any sense of effort on her part.)

A. There was no effort made to speak but she appeared amused as she felt her yes finger lifting.)

Q. Go a little deeper now and let the deep part of your mind orient back in time to the very first breath you are taking at the moment you are born. When you are there, your yes finger will lift. Your no finger will lift each time you are hearing someone talking in that room where you are born. When you are warm and comfortable again in the nursery, your I don't want to answer finger will lift. Don't try to remember anything consciously. This is a long time before conscious memory begins.

Her respiratory rate had increased followed by the lifting of her yes finger before I had finished my directions to her, showing that she was not threatened by her memories of birth.)

Go over that entire experience quickly several times so that I can ask you some questions. Is your mother awake at the time you are born?

A. (finger signal) No.

Q. Does that little baby Diana feel welcome as a girl when she is born?

A. (finger signal) Yes.

Q. Let a thought come to you. How does that baby know she is welcome? When you know, your yes finger will lift. As it lifts, let that thought come up to where you can talk about it.

A. (The yes finger lifted quickly. Five seconds later she began to speak.) I just know she wanted a girl—even if she *didn't* nurse me. (This addition at the end of her response called for some clarification.)

Q. Does it make a difference to this baby that she is not nursed?

A. (verbalized) No. (This answer was contradicted by her unconscious gesture with her yes finger.)

Q. What is important about nursing?

A. (The level of hypnosis decreased at this moment as the patient spoke.) There is a feeling of love that goes with nursing at a mother's breast—I missed that.

This apparent biologic need for nursing, not recognized by her more conscious level of awareness, reflected by the verbal answer but indicated by the ideomotor level of thought association, demands more attention by obstetricians and pediatricians who believe breast feeding is not necessary. Denial of breast feeding has appeared too often in the age-regression evaluations of patients with peptic ulcer, gall bladder disease, and colitis (Cheek, 1975).

Q. **Now orient back to your birth again. When you are there, your yes finger will lift.** (The finger lifted in four seconds, a very rapid response.) **Come up from there to the first moment when you are having some feeling that you would later recognize as a climax or like a climax. When you are feeling that unconsciously, your no finger will lift. When it lifts, look around in your mind's eye and tell me what allows you to have that feeling.**

The wording of this direction expresses the therapist's total expectation of a positive response, an important lesson learned from the author's experience with anesthesia research (Cheek, 1959) and the search of significant dreams with obstetrical patients (Cheek, 1965b).

A. (Her yes finger lifted to indicated the reorientation, and lifted again to indicate something to report. She shifted into conversation saying) My mother is cuddling me and showing that she loves me.

Q. **Come up now to a later experience. When you are there, your no finger will lift. Tell me what is happening.**

A. My daddy is chucking me under the chin and smiling at me.

Q. **So you can see as an adult woman that pleasurable sexual feelings can be started by stimuli that are not primarily sexual: your mother cuddling you, and your daddy showing that he loves you and thinks you are cute. Come up from those early lessons telling you that you are sexually normal to the first moment when something makes you feel you cannot have those feelings. When you are there at the first important moment, your yes finger will lift and you can tell me what is happening."**

A. (After a lag of 10 seconds before lifting the finger) I'm playing with myself. Mother comes in and says, "Diana! Don't *do* that!" She looks very angry.

Q. **Come up to the next important thing that relates to your sexual feelings.**

A. I have lots of dreams that feel good. — Lots of dreams but I can't let anything happen. I always stop.

While she was still oriented to the early months of her life, it was pointed out that exploration of genital sensations by a baby is normal, that all babies are well equipped for sexual orgasm from the moment they are born. This ability continues until someone with authority makes them feel self-conscious or guilty over a process of learning that must have been started by the Creator. If mammals did not enjoy sexual intercourse, their species would die out. If they did not know that genital stimulation felt good, they would be galloping around all their lives and there would be no babies. If breast stimulation did not feel good, mother mammals would not nurse their young and their babies would die.

Q. **Now go over one of those dreams that felt good, but this time go over it as it should have been, experiencing the feelings you would have had normally if your mother had not made you feel guilty when she saw you playing with yourself. As you start the dream your yes finger will lift and** *each* **time you are reaching an unconscious climax, your no finger will lift. Do** *not* **try to feel it consciously, because you are not conscious when you are dreaming. First, you must know these feelings unconsciously before you can feel them consciously. Remember that all mammals have sexual dreams. It must be the will of God that this occur to further the knowledge learned by actual physical contact with the genital organs.**

(The patient indicated three unconscious orgasms but did not show any change in respiration or pulsations of her neck vessels.)

The next step was to ask the patient to carry the knowledge about the importance of dreams a little further. She was told that sexually normal women have told us they have experienced small orgasms as children while just holding hands with little boys they like, something "very much like what you felt when your daddy chucked you under your chin" (a thought added to reinforce her recognition that she had been "normal" before her mother scolded her about the normal autoerotic explorations). She was asked to hallucinate an experience holding hands in which she would feel a climax each time she squeezed his hand. Her no finger was to lift each time she was feeling this pleasurable sensation, which the little boy would know nothing about. Almost immediate responses were given, and now the patient was showing slight quickening of her respiration as her no finger lifted each time.

The hour was drawing to a close. She was progressing so fast that I felt it might be appropriate to deal directly with the problem of anorgasmia in relation to her husband. It was already clear that the bond between them was very good.

Q. **Would it be all right for you to really feel what a climax can be like for you and your husband if I go out of the room to examine some patients?**

A. (finger signal) Yes.

Q. **Other normal women who have never been made to feel guilty about their sexual feelings have told me that when they have felt a warmth of love between themselves and their husbands, they have had orgasms being kissed on their lips, caressed around their breasts, and kissed on their neck. They have had orgasms just as they feel his penis entering their vagina, and again as they move their hips from side to side bringing his penis in contact with the very sensitive nerves on each side of the vagina. They say they have felt a buildup to a climax as they rapidly contract and relax their vaginal muscles around the whole length of the firm penis 10 or 12 times, and that this can** be repeated. Each climax becomes stronger because a woman is able to have an orgasm repeatedly without having to wait the way a man has to wait. The strongest of all can be when you feel him swelling inside you at the moment he is reaching his climax. You can even come again just by contracting your muscles around him inside after he has ejaculated.

Please orient your memory back to some time that could have been perfect for you and your husband, had you known then what you are learning today, and as it would have been if you had never had any fears or guilt feelings given you by your mother. Let your body feel all the sensations from the top of your head down to your heels. I am going out to examine some patients and I will not need this room.

First, go over the experience, having just your fingers telling you how much you are feeling; then, as you keep going over it, you will start to feel it physically at a conscious level. When your inner mind knows that you can select what kind of climax you can have and how many you want to have, when you know that you are really satisfied, your right arm will begin to lift up as though you had those balloons attached to it. When that occurs, please let yourself come out of hypnosis and open the door so I know you are through.

It only took about five minutes after I left the room before the door opened. Ten minutes after that I found her back in her chair in a deep trance. I asked, **"Does the inner part of your mind feel that you are as normal sexually as I do?"** To this her finger answered yes. She was awakened and two more appointments were made in case she wanted to be seen later.

The interview was on Thursday. The following Monday the patient called to say she did not need to come back. She and her husband had gone to Carmel that weekend. It had been a wonderful experience for them both and she had just received some roses and a note from her husband saying, "To my new Diana."

Summation of 255 Cases of Female Orgasmic Dysfunction

Since incorporating use of ideomotor signaling methods in the treatment of female sexual dysfunction, I have worked with 255 women. There was inadequate follow-up in 124 of these, and 18 women dropped out before completion of treatment. I felt that the only good thing that could be said about this total group was that 96% of the women had learned how to induce their own hypnosis.

A much better estimate of results could be obtained on consideration of the most recent 100 cases, after I had better criteria for acceptance into the treatment regimen (see Table 12). It was soon evident that some sociological division had to be made in selection. This depended not on ability to pay but

Table 12: Estimate of results of 100 cases using ideodynamic techniques for female orgasmic dysfunction.

	Number Responding	Percent
1. Some improvement with current partner	60	60
2. No change in sexual performance	40	40
3. Dropped out before completion of therapy	0	0
4. Made worse by therapy	0	0
Change of Sexual Status	Number of total	
1. Shift from "no orgasm" (Class B) to A-2	16	22
2. Shift from Class A-1 to A-2 (all Catholic)	4	4
3. Shift from "past orgasmic but no longer" (Class A-3 to orgasmic A-2)	2	9
4. Subjectively satisfactory improvement in orgasmic Class A-2 group	38	65
	60	100

on the ability to form some meaningful relationship with a man. It is not easy to decide who should be excluded in this area, but a rough rule of thumb was to exclude those who were without attachment and those who were unmarried and had a history of multiple tenuous attachments. These women had needs for psychotherapy, but it seemed to me that their needs related to problems of self-image of another sort requiring longer-range therapy before much could be done about the sexual problem bringing them to my office.

In an attempt to justify this apparent "placebo effect percentage," it must be said that all of the women were able to use self-hypnosis. All have derived personal benefit in other areas through their being able to correct unfavorable attitudes toward their parents and themselves. Approximately 86% have corrected one or more gynecological problems having to do with hypersensitivity of the urogenital tract. These include dysmenorrhea, recurrent cystitis, vulvo-vaginitis, and Herpes genitalis ulcers. It appears that women asking for help with orgasmic dysfunction may sometimes be willing to accept a little help with something of benefit to them when they may not be ready for the goal they have consciously set for themselves.

Evaluation of Ideomotor Methods for Investigating Sexual Dysfunctions in Women

Those who are not familiar with ideomotor questioning techniques may find themselves as suspicious of information offered by hypnotized subjects as they are when such information is offered during ordinary conversational hypnosis. All who are experienced in the use of hypnosis have recognized the willingness of good subjects to comply with expressed or implied wishes of the therapist at the level of nearly conscious ideation involved in conversational communication.

It has not been the author's experience that this type of willingness extends to the level of ideation reflected by ideomotor responses. A feature of utmost importance has been repeatedly demonstrated. *Very significant experiences responsible for continued patterns of behavior are stored at a level of awareness that can be reached and reflected by ideomotor responses.* The usual steps of recall are from most recent events toward earlier ones that set the stage for the ones first recalled. If allowed to continue, the investigation may lead to strong resistances on nearing a primal event of a threatening nature.

The chance of this occurring is greatly diminished if the search starts with birth with the onus softened by a dissociated, retrospective view as from the time of interview. The knowledge of language can then be used to describe events occurring before there was such knowledge. Furthermore, it is much easier to evaluate the significance of experiences the patient discovers are related to the problem requiring investigation. The thread of pertinence remains intact with the talking part of the patient tied to the time of the interview while the much deeper zone reflected by ideomotor activity is studying evidence.

Occasionally a relatively uninhibited woman will show visible signs of reaching an orgasm while rehearsing pleasurable sexual possibilities. It should be stressed here that hypnotized subjects using ideomotor methods are always aware of their surroundings. It is their right to feel as much as they wish. It is easy to know whether or not they are embarrassed by their awakening to the concept that thoughts can evoke physiological responses. This is the goal of therapy for orgasmic dysfunction. If the patient seems embarrassed, I ask for a finger signal in answer to whether or not the patient would progress more rapidly with me out of the room. Some patients (as the one presented here) do very well when left alone. Others, however, need personal guidance and will feel rejected if the therapist leaves them. My advice here, as with all other types of doctor-patient relationships, is to decide whether or not you feel comfortable in the situation. If you are troubled, your patient will feel troubled, whether or not you are using hypnosis.

There is no danger of a patient becoming seriously dependent upon the therapist during treatment for a sexual problem unless the patient has very tenuous attachment to her sexual partner, and the therapist falls into the trap of presuming that the close relationship of therapy is a license to forget the needs and goals of the patient. Difficulties in this area do not occur when the therapist constantly involves the patient with thoughts relating to her husband or sexual partner.

Conclusion

I do not wish to convey the idea that the methods presented are more successful than others involving other modalities. I am a gynecologist with limited time for hypnotherapy. The methods described have proven of value with treatment of various gynecological difficulties; included among them are the very important problems of women who are unhappy with their sexual inhibitions.

19

Facilitating the Sexual Response After Surgery

Cancer involving the breasts and urogenital organs may have a devastating influence on the self-image and sexual attitudes of any woman, regardless of age. When the treatment is disfiguring and eliminates the possibilities of childbearing, the result may include depression, suicidal thoughts, and total orgasmic dysfunction.

It is well recognized that orgasm in women is largely dependent upon a feeling of mutual appreciation shared by both members in the sexual relationship. A woman who feels ugly or unworthy may develop a genital anesthesia even when all pelvic sympathetic and parasympathetic nerves are intact. The problem is compounded when extensive surgery cuts through or removes sensory pathways or brings about prolonged soiling because of infection, delayed healing, or urinary incontinence.

Much is gained by the surgeon who is able to prepare a woman in advance of her operation. The job is made easier for the surgeon who knows that radical surgery need not end the sexual life of a patient, even when the vulva, clitoris, and vagina have been removed. Re-education is more difficult when it has to be initiated during the postoperative period against the handicap of deeply imprinted convictions that have occurred while the patient was unconscious with a general anesthetic.

A general approach to accessing and facilitating women's inner sexual resources for coping with these problems is presented in Box 24. Two specific case examples are presented below.

Case 1: Removal of Rectum, Lower Vagina, Vulva, and Clitoris in a Woman with a Positive Attitude

A 27-year-old native of Central America had presented herself in the outpatient clinic of a northern California county hospital complaining of a small sore on her left labia. Understandably, the correct diagnosis was missed. Inguinal lymph nodes were enlarged on both sides, there were inflammatory

---

BOX 24: ACCESSING AND FACILITATING INNER SEXUAL RESOURCES

1. *Accessing inner sexual resources privately*
   a. **"As your unconscious makes available some of your most plea-surable sexual memories and daydreams privately to you, your yes finger will lift. Your yes finger will lift with each turn on."**
   b. **"Now, privately explore whatever reduces those pleasurable sexu-al feelings. Your no finger will lift with each turn off."**
   [Therapist notes whether there are more yes or no signals.]
2. *Therapeutic reframing of inner sexual resources*
   [Appropriate variations of the following format for each individual subject could be used to facilitate or modulate sexual expression.]
   a. **"Allow your yes finger to lift each time you find something new that allows you to replay that inner experience to greater and greater satisfaction."**
   b. **"Your yes finger will lift as you explore the changes you will have to make in yourself and your life to make this greater satisfaction a reality."**
   c. **"See yourself experiencing a real-life situation where everything works ideally, and let your yes finger lift with each positive step."**
   d. **"See yourself successfully dealing with whatever could interfere with your real-life satisfaction, and let your yes finger lift with each happy replay."**
3. *Ratifying therapeutic change*
   "Will your unconscious now allow you to use these private inner experiences appropriately in real life?"
   [If a long delay or a no signal ensues, return to steps 1 and 2 above.]

---

masses in both adnexal regions, and there was a positive skin test for lymph-opathia venereum.

Cancer of the vulva in women this age is very rare. During seven months of antibiotic and local treatments, the ulcer widened until it was five centi-meters in diameter, involving the left labium major, labium minor, and extending to within two centimeters of the anus. A biopsy at this time revealed a squamous cell, epidermoid carcinoma. By the time the patient was first seen by the author, the extent of induration made it necessary to include the anus and lymphatic pathways surrounding the rectum in the plan for radical vulvectomy. This would require formation of a colostomy and the rather formidable task of freeing up the rectosigmoid in the presence of extensive pelvic inflammatory disease of long standing.

One extenuating advantage of fecal diversion would be the diminished chance of infection in the wide area of gaping perineum to be left by removal of the rectum, lower vagina, vulva, clitoris and lower mons veneris. A team approach was decided upon, with a general surgeon performing the abdominal part of the operation while I worked with the vulvectomy and gland dissection from below.

The young woman was stunned by the knowledge that she had a life-threatening cancer. She did not seem to grasp the enormity of the surgery that would be involved, a fortuitous, spontaneously occurring hypnotic-like state that often protects such patients from suicidal thoughts at a time of such crisis. She jokingly remarked that she had married an 80-year-old man in order to stay in the United States and that her pelvic organs were not much use anyway. She said she had suffered so much already that she would be looking forward to an operation that would remove the trouble.

PREPARING PATIENT FOR RADICAL CHANGE BY REVIVING MEMORIES OF
PREVIOUS SEXUAL RESPONSIVENESS

During the two days of bowel preparation with neomycin, I had an opportunity to work with the patient's sexual attitudes while using hypnosis to prepare her for surgery and the recovery period. It was learned that she had been sexually responsive before the onset of her disease and had been capable of multiple orgasms during intercourse. She was told that her earlier sexual experiences had set images in her mind that were permanent and would be available in the future when she married again after the death of her husband. My experience with cancer patients during my training at Johns Hopkins Hospital had justified this concept. With reassurance, even without the help of hypnosis, these women, if normal before, would be as normal or better after removal of their cancer.

USING THE SCRATCH TEST TO TEACH HYPNOTIC ANESTHESIA
TO FACILITATE HEALING AND RECOVERY

As a means of demonstrating to her how much her mind could alter awareness and at the same time alter reaction to tissue injury, she was placed in a light hypnotic state and asked to remember how one arm would feel if she had been lying on it and it had gone to sleep. When she had satisfied herself that there really was a difference in feeling between her arms, a longitudinal scratch was carried from the wrist to antecubital space of each arm.

About 15 minutes were then taken to explain the various steps involved in the operation and what she would be expected to do in gaining mobility, feeling hungry, and eliminating easily from her bladder and bowel. At the end of this time she was surprised and pleased to discover that the scratch made on the relatively insensitive part of her "numb" arm was almost invisible, while the one on the sensitive arm was red and puffy over its entire length.

It was explained that the usual inflammatory reactions to a painful stimulus are a carryover from the responses of wild animals whose wounds are always dirty. The purpose of inflammation is to wall off an injured area to keep bacteria from getting into the circulation. An animal looks for shelter away from the light. The muscles around an injured area tighten up to prevent circulation of blood through the contaminated area. The kidneys shut down to maintain fluid until the animal is able to drink water again. The animal licks its wounds while healing from the bottom and sides in order to remove debris and necrotic tissue. It was explained to the patient that this is an outmoded way of healing a surgical wound which is initially clean. If there is pain, the wound healing is obstructed because fresh blood cannot get near enough to remove waste products and add oxygen and nutrition for the process of repair. Because of the stagnated circulation, an infection can occur and if this is the case, the antibiotics in her blood do not have a chance to work where they are most needed.

This all seemed reasonable. She went back into hypnosis and quickly indicated that she had walked into cold water and had been standing there long enough to feel numb as well as cold. She nodded acceptance of the suggestion that she could do this any time she wanted, and that she understood the deeper tissues would also feel cool and numb on command and could remain that way for at least two hours. After being told about the value of eating properly after surgery, she practiced remembering a time when she had felt very hungry. She smiled a few seconds later as she heard her stomach growling and then remembered vividly the pleasant feeling of fullness after a delicious imagined meal in Costa Rica.

The rapid progress of her confidence during these exercises in instant biofeedback allowed me to move into a convincing exercise with sexual memories. She had often had sexual dreams ending in orgasm. It was pointed out that there is no genital contact during such dreams, that she must practice not only dreaming in her sleep but remembering in hypnosis all the pleasurable feelings she had known during intercourse in order to speed up the return of nerves to her pelvic area during her recovery period. She was asked to select a very nice memory from the past now and to nod her head when she has felt an "unconscious" climax. Not only did she nod, but it was clear from her respiration and unconscious hip motions that she had a very good memory.

She was seen just prior to going into the operating room and was again placed into a hypnotic state. She was asked to make her body and legs cool and numb, and to think about that immediately on awakening after surgery. It was suggested that she pick out a very special meal that she could be thinking about while asleep in order to have a very good appetite when she awakened from the anesthetic.

The operation took four hours. In 1953 I still believed that anesthetized patients could not hear or remember conversations between surgeons and operating room personnel. There were many troubled comments during the subtotal hysterectomy and bilateral removal of the old tuboovarian abscesses during preparation of the colostomy and freeing of the rectosigmoid for removal from below. The blood pressure and other vital signs remained stable. As was expected, the following week was stormy but there were no complications. The packing was removed from the space left by the rectum and vagina on the second postoperative day. Fortunately, and possibly because of the extensive old inflammation, none of the lymph nodes contained cancer cells.

Successful Long-Term Outcome: Multiple Orgasms Nine Years Later!

At a follow-up visit to the office, it was gratifying to learn that the patient had accepted her colostomy and was glad to be alive. She was placed in hypnosis again and rehearsed with memories of a particularly pleasurable sexual experience which she was asked to relive several times while the author was out of the room examining other patients. It was stressed that a very important part of her recovery involved the frequent use of autohypnosis and the reliving of similar sexual experiences, that this directed sensory nerves back to the genital area and would be helpful in keeping the scar tissue soft and pliable.

Nine years after surgery this woman walked into the office looking young, pretty and happy. Her husband had died. She had met a man her age and was now married. She said she had multiple orgasms during preliminary sex play, that she had more feeling in her dimple of a vagina than she had ever had with all her equipment in the past.

There was no formal approach to the problem of surgical orgasmic dysfunction in this case. Rather, the discussions about sexual responsiveness were initially considered only a part of a larger scale drive to keep this young woman from dwelling on the enormity of her immediate problem by giving her confidence that she could survive the ordeal and aim for future goals of normal function as a female. Apparently some shreds of ovarian tissue must have remained after removal of her tuboovarian inflammatory masses, for she had no vasomotor disturbances to suggest that she had entered a premature menopause.

Case 2: Removal of Uterus and Vagina; Urine and Fecal Incontinence

A 22-year-old nurse went in for a routine annual checkup with her gynecologist. She had just established her independence financially, was happy in her work, was dating and looking forward to marriage. Her parents were having problems and were divorcing, but this was not a new or unexpected event.

During the examination her gynecologist found a suspicious lesion in the vagina anterior to the cervix. He asked if her mother had ever taken diethylstilbestrol. She knew that her mother had been given this drug because of a threatened miscarriage, but did not know of the recently discovered association between maternal use of diethylstilbestrol and appearance of clear-cell carcinoma of the vagina in young women. Biopsy of the vaginal lesion substantiated the fears of the gynecologist. He called her with the shocking news that she would have to have a hysterectomy and complete removal of the vagina, combined with a radical gland dissection. He added that because of the position of the lesion, it might also be necessary to remove her bladder and make an artificial bladder with a segment of small bowel. If this were the case, her bladder would open through her abdomen into a bag.

This news had a similar effect to that experienced by the first patient in this report. It seemed to her that this must be something happening to another person. She could not take action; she could make no decisions for several days. She called her mother but her mother was too concerned with her own difficulties to comprehend the needs of her daughter.

In this instance the patient had to depend entirely on her own emotional resources. Her preparation for heroic surgery consisted of a dazzlingly clear outline of the complications that might occur—this by way of obtaining "informed consent" for the operation. She would have to accept the fact that she would have no children. There could be no guarantee that she would remain cancer-free after surgery; they would not promise to save her bladder because they would have to see first if it had been invaded by the vaginal cancer. Her questions about what would happen to her sex life were fielded deftly but not answered.

At surgery the uterus, vagina, and one ovary were removed. The only memory she has had of the operation during hypnotic age regression was of a nurse in the recovery room saying, "She's dirty again." Her course was complicated by a urinary tract infection and a prolonged febrile period unresponsive to chemotherapy. The constant saturation of her bed with urine was first ascribed to leakage around the Foley catheter until it was clear that she had direct drainage from a defect in the bladder wall communicating with the space once occupied by her vagina.

In addition to the bladder drainage, she found that she had no control over her anal sphincter. Fecal incontinence added to the misery of her constant wetness. Instead of offering positive advice about what could be done to correct these problems, her surgeon impressed her with his defensive attitude. He hoped that a second operation placing skin grafts would close the bladder defect. The graft took but drainage continued. She went home to her apartment wearing rubber pants, a useless catheter in the bladder, and multiple sanitary pads to mop up excess of urine. Her depression was augmented on discovery that she could not reach a climax with masturbation. Her clitoris was anesthetic. When she asked her surgeon about this his answer was that this was *her* problem, because he had not cut any nerves to her clitoris. He continued to reassure her that the bladder openings would close in time. Months went by.

USE OF HYPNOTIC IDEOMOTOR TECHNIQUES ONE YEAR AFTER SURGERY:
"HOOKING UP THE ORGASMIC CIRCUITS AGAIN"

During the following year she consulted seven urologists. All but one advised her to accept ureteral transplant into an ileal bladder. One doctor, at the University of California in San Francisco, paying respect to her great concern about loss of her bladder, offered her a 40% chance of success in closing the fistulae and giving her back a sphincter control to her bladder. He said there was a chance but that it would take several procedures to complete the job.

It was at this stage that the patient consulted me at her father's request in the hope that hypnosis might relieve some of the discomfort of surgery and perhaps aid in the healing process. She had never accepted her father's interest in hypnosis and was obviously skeptical about its value in her case. During the initial interview she excused herself twice to visit the bathroom and change pads. Her need was great, however, and she quickly became interested in the unconscious responses of a Chevreul pendulum. It gave a yes answer to the question, "Does the inner part of your mind know that you are going to remain well and free of cancer?"

This question was posed to evaluate her past conditionings and expose iatrogenic pessimistic attitudes. Another yes signal surprised her when she was asked if her unconscious mind would allow me to help her use hypnosis successfully. She was already in a light hypnotic state before I had a chance to start a formal induction of hypnosis. She was asked to have her fingers pull apart to drop the pendulum when her unconscious mind knew she was deep enough to allow a constructive preparation for her surgery. She was told to close her eyes and wait for the results to happen, that she need not work at anything.

In the interval between closing her eyes and dropping the pendulum, an explanation about pain and inflammation was given to her. She was told that a reasonable assumption about her inability to reach a climax with clitoral stimulation was that her feelings of disgust over the urinary leakage and her unconscious fears about the chances of cancer reappearing could be giving her this genital anesthesia. Our job was to "hook up the circuits again." She was told that time would permit this to happen anyhow, but that the process would be greatly accelerated if she learned to use autohypnosis and practiced remembering pleasurable sensations as they had been in the past and would certainly be in the future after her repair work had been completed.

Fortunately there had been two other doctors who had told the patient that damaged pelvic nerves can grow back. Recognition that the process could be enhanced came a few minutes later. The pendulum slipped through her fingers. She noticed that her arm had become numb, as suggested. The feeling returned when she rubbed the arm, as had been suggested during the induction.

The next step was to have her review her original operation to see if there had been any frightening remarks made while she was unconscious. The only memory was of the nurse saying, "She's dirty again." She was then awakened and rehearsed with the technique of putting herself into hypnosis and awakening at the end of a specified time.

This was an intelligent, highly motivated young woman who had shown her need for independence in the past but was currently at a low ebb of self-respect. It seemed wise to give her the tools of autohypnosis and confidence in using them.

The next step was to have her rehearse some familiar experiences not specifically related to the immediate problems. She was asked to remember hunger followed by a feeling of fullness, thirst followed by a satisfying drink. She gave an unconscious signal for the physiological level acceptance of each sensation before she became aware, at a speaking level, that the assignment had been completed. Her success interested her. She dropped into a deeper level of hypnosis.

SUGGESTIONS FOR REGENERATING INJURED NERVES; RECALLING SEXUAL
DREAMS AND EXPERIENCING ORGASM "UNCONSCIOUSLY"

The following verbalization was used:
"The injured nerves would have grown back already if you had not been disgusted and troubled about the constant leakage of urine. Please begin opening all the sensory memories relating to your bladder, clitoris, and vaginal area. You have seen that you could diminish the feeling in your arm and then bring it back. Do the same thing with the feeling memories around the vaginal area. First, let me ask your fingers to answer this question: Is there any unconscious idea carried over from your childhood guilts or sexual fears that might be keeping you from letting your sexual feelings return? We frequently find that women who have developed problems with their pelvic organs may zero in on the assumption that some sexual experiences of the past may have been responsible for their trouble. They may unconsciously suppress their sexual feelings in order to keep from having further trouble. Has there been any such thought holding you back? Let the inner part of your mind answer that question."

There was a clear no signal given unconsciously by the appropriate finger.

This patient had known a normal sexual responsiveness before her surgery. She was first asked to orient back in time to some period of her life when she had experienced a sexual dream ending in orgasm. It is very easy for lightly hypnotized subjects to pick up this sort of memory at a level of awareness indicated by ideomotor finger signals. When her yes finger lifted to indicate beginning of such a dream, she was told to avoid trying to remember conscious feelings, that the review was to be kept at an unconscious physiological level of unawareness indicated only by the lifting of her no finger when she had unconsciously experienced an orgasm. The dream was rehearsed twice from beginning to end. She was then instructed to orient her memory back to some time before her surgery when she was most responsive with her fiancé. When her yes finger lifted in recognition of that horizon of memory, she was told to relive the experience several times while the author was out of the room working with other patients. She was told to awaken from hypnosis and open the door when she knew unconsciously that she could reproduce these feelings at will during future hypnosis exercises.

The patient opened the door about ten minutes later. She was seen again a week later, just prior to her return to Boston. At this time she was able to recognize that a major factor in her poor recovery from initial surgery was her intense feeling of isolation and rejection at not having her mother come to the hospital to visit at the time of her first surgery. Her reasoning mind realized that her mother was too troubled to make the effort, but the childlike unconscious part of her mind felt a great dependency on her mother. She believed that some of her complications may have been dictated by an unconscious feeling that if she were sick enough, her mother might come to her in the hospital. This was a surprising revelation to this highly competent, self-reliant nurse.

SUCCESSFUL LONG-TERM OUTCOME: MARRIAGE, NORMAL SEX LIFE,
AND DEDICATED CAREER

She returned to Boston where she continued to work with self-hypnosis. Her bladder incontinence continued but she was able to write a month later that she was now experiencing orgasms in dreams and also with masturbation. During the following year she underwent several operations that successfully closed the bladder fistulae and gave her control of her urethral sphincter. She married the thoughtful and understanding man who had stood by her during this troubled period and her sex life is normal. She is active now in working with disabled and discouraged people who will benefit from the spirit and determination she applies to everything she tackles.

RESEARCH

Procedural and Declarative Knowledge in Ideodynamic Signaling: Research Projects 44–51

Earlier we referred to the mind-brain connection (research portion of Section IV) as taking place via the prefrontal cortical-limbic-hypothalamic system. The neural encoding of mind in the prefrontal and many sensory cortexes of the brain is believed to be integrated in the limbic system and transduced into the information substances of the brain and body via the hypothalamus. In this section we will review in greater detail some of the more interesting ideas that have been proposed recently for exploring just how sensory-perceptual experiences, memory, and learning are processed in the limbic system. We will then provide suggestions for investigating their implications for the further development of ideodynamic signaling as a therapeutic tool with sexual problems.

Throughout this volume we repeatedly have made an effort to describe step-by-step *procedures* for the ideodynamic accessing and reframing of a variety of psychobiological problems. While they all require the therapist to introduce variations designed to utilize the patient's individuality and personal frames of reference, most of these procedures can be simply outlined in three steps, as we have done in the instructional boxes. Recent theoretical developments in the neurobiology of memory and learning on the distinction between *declarative* and *procedural* knowledge now suggest a rational basis for the special effectiveness of *ideodynamic procedures*.

The general finding of the current breakthroughs is that information is encoded and retrieved by many semi-autonomous but well integrated systems operating across virtually all the sensory-perceptual modalities of human experience. The many varieties of amnesia and mental dissociation that have been studied experimentally have given rise to a number of ways of categorizing the different systems of memory (Lynch, McGaugh, & Weinberger, 1984; Weinberger, McGaugh, & Lynch, 1985). Of these, the distinction between declarative and procedural knowledge (Squire & Cohen, 1983) may be the most significant for our understanding of ideodynamic procedures.

Declarative knowledge is described as the availability of specific information about both the time and place of an experience; it is typically represented by the verbal knowledge of the "facts and data of conventional memory experiments" (Squire & Cohen, 1983, p. 21). We would hypothesize that this is the knowledge generally accessed by conventional conversation psychotherapy. *Procedural knowledge*, by contrast, is the learning that is encoded by procedures, rules, and skills (such as perceptual-motor skills, learning rules for dealing with numbers and complex puzzles, etc.). We would hypothesize that this is the knowledge accessed by our ideodynamic procedures.

The importance of this distinction is that procedural knowledge is often spared when we experience clinical amnesias, whereas the acquisition and consolidation of new verbal declarative knowledge is severely impaired (Morris, 1984, p. 119), particularly during the stress and traumatic life circumstances that encode mind-body problems. There is a considerable complexity to the psychodynamic interplay of declarative and procedural knowledge. Kesner (1984), who has outlined many of these complexities in schematic diagrams that can be useful to the hypnotherapist, has postulated that different anatomical locations within the limbic-hypothalamic system encode these two different forms of knowledge as follows (p. 112):

> The hippocampus subserves the coding of the *external environmental context* (coding of sensory, temporal, spatial, and somatic response attributes), while the amygdala subserves the coding of the *internal environmental context* (coding of sensory, temporal, affect, and autonomic response attributes). . . . To the extent that one can dissociate the internal from the external context, one should be able to dissociate amygdala and hippocampus functions. (Italics added)

In Figures 16 and 17 we have reproduced Kesner's (1984) outline of the psychological and neural network organizations of memory mediated by the hippocampus and amygdala.

It would appear from Kesner's work that the ideodynamic signaling approach may be accessing the *internal environmental context* encoded within the amygdala of the limbic-hypothalamic system. This effort to localize the anatomical locus of a hypnotherapeutic intervention follows a long but usually unsuccessful tradition in the history of hypnosis. This is the first time, however, that hypotheses about anatomical localization have been supported by such a volume of well-controlled experimental research that can be integrated within a verifiable theory of mind-body communication and healing (Rossi, 1986d). In this broad experimental and theoretical con-

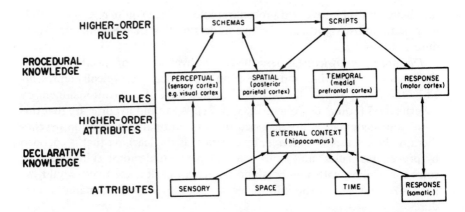

Figure 16: Psychological and neural network organization of memory empnasızıng the importance of attributes (e.g., sensory, somatic, response, spatial, and temporal), higher-order attributes (e.g., external context mediated by hippocampus), rules (e.g., spatial mediated by posterior parietal association cortex and temporal mediated by medial prefrontal context), and higher-order rules (e.g., schemas and scripts). (Kesner, 1984)

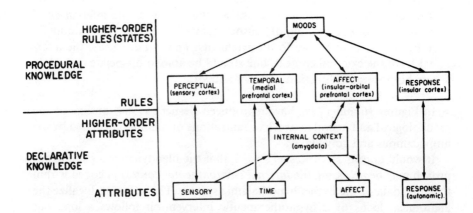

Figure 17: Psychological and neural network organization of memory emphasizing the importance of attributes (e.g., sensory, autonomic response, affect, and temporal), higher-order attributes (e.g., internal context mediated by amygdala), rules (e.g., affect mediated by insular-orbital prefrontal cortex), and higher-order rules and states (e.g., moods). (Reproduced from Kesner, 1984, p. 113)

text, Cheek's reports of the ideodynamic healing of sexual dysfunctions following radical surgery can be better appreciated as models for the development of even more informed clinical methods of the future.

Project 44 There is much to suggest that Erickson's utilization or naturalistic approach to therapeutic hypnosis (Erickson, 1958/1980, 1959/1980) was involved with the accessing of procedural knowledge. This is particularly true, for example, when he would induce hypnosis by giving a serial task (Erickson, 1964/1980); by giving a series of tasks as a posthypnotic suggestion (Erickson & Erickson, 1941/1980); by exploring mental mechanisms in his "experimental demonstrations of the psychopathology of everyday life" (Erickson, 1939/1980); and in his work on hypnotic amnesia (Erickson, 1980a, Vol. III). A very fruitful series of controlled experimental studies now could be carried out to explore the relative contributions of the procedural and demonstrative distinction to Erickson's work in each of these areas.

Project 45 As we have seen in Section I, Cheek has always insisted that a valid approach to ideodynamic signaling requires the appearance of physiological and ideomotor responses before the verbal response. It is tempting, therefore, to hypothesize that the physiological and ideomotor levels of response are indicators of accessing state-dependent *nonverbal procedural knowledge* to facilitate the final expression of *verbal declarative knowledge*. Design a well-controlled experimental study to test this hypothesis.

Project 46 Design a clinical-experimental study to test the hypothesis that the stress, traumatic, and post-traumatic stress syndromes are due to a dissociation between procedural knowledge that remains active on an unconscious level and declarative knowledge that is accessible to consciousness.

Project 47 Explore the theoretical, experimental, and therapeutic relationships between Broadbent's "early selection theory" (discussed in the research proposals of Section III) and declarative knowledge (verbal consciousness is required in both), on the one hand, and "late selection theory" and procedural knowledge (nonverbal and unconscious processes are characteristic of both), on the other. Is state-dependent memory, learning, and behavior the common psychobiological factor underlying these two independently developed experimental concepts?

Project 48 Explore the relationship between the use of the implied directive and the therapeutic double bind (as presented in Chapter 3) and procedural and declarative knowledge. Does the therapeutic double bind temporarily "freeze" the subject's conscious sets, for example, so that the less conscious processes of procedural knowledge can be accessed by the implied directive? That is, is the combined use of the implied directive and the therapeutic conscious-unconscious double bind a method for transforming unconscious procedural knowledge into more consciously expressed declarative knowledge? Can we say that all ideodynamic signaling approaches are essentially methods of transducing procedural into declarative knowledge?

Project 49 From this broadening perspective, can we say that the entire history of depth psychology has been a series of theories and approaches for converting unconscious procedural knowledge into declarative knowledge? Is the evolution of consciousness itself a reflection of this process (Jaynes, 1976; Rossi, 1972/1985, 1986d)? Is the use of analogy, metaphor, and symbol a process for converting unconscious procedural processes to declarative knowledge that is under more conscious ego control (Mills & Crowley, 1986)?

Project 50 Utilize Cheek's ideodynamic approach to stress reduction with pregnant women (Table 10) on a monthly basis throughout the gestation period to determine whether pregnancy and birth complications can be reduced.

Project 51 Utilize Cheek's ideodynamic approach to partial age regression for investigating possible sources of birth and pregnancy stress in male homosexuals. Do male homosexuals signal statistically more stress between the second and fifth months of gestation, as hypothesized by Ellis and Ames (1987), in comparison with heterosexual males? Cheek has formulated the following series of questions that might be useful for this type of investigation (see Box 25). Question 2c is crucial for determining the critical pregnancy period during which stress may affect later sexual orientation. Theoretical rationales for accessing nonverbal responses before and during the birth process are presented in Section IX on the birth experience and the construction of reality.

BOX 25: EXPLORING PREGNANCY STRESS AND
ADULT SEXUAL ORIENTATION

1. *Accessing and transducing unconscious procedural processes*
   a. "Your unconscious can review the interesting early stages of learning many skills. Your yes finger can lift all by itself while it reviews the early stage of learning to ride a bike (learning to walk, roller skate, ski; learning the letters of the alphabet, etc.)."
   b. "Let your no finger lift whenever you experience any unusual or disturbing events that interfere with your learning."
   c. "As you continue to review these disturbances, say whatever comes to you about how you're actually feeling, experiencing, and thinking. How do you deal successfully with these disturbances?"

2. *Exploring pregnancy stress and adult sexual orientation*
   a. "Although it may seem impossible, let your unconscious lift a finger when it's ready to review the entire process of your development in the womb before you were born."
   b. "Now as you grow during your mother's pregnancy, your no finger will lift whenever you or your mother are experiencing any unusual or disturbing events."
   c. Continue with appropriate inquiries to determine if the stress was experienced during the second through the fifth months of pregnancy.
   "How big are you (the embryo/fetus) during the disturbance? Is the disturbance during the beginning, middle, or end of pregnancy? What month of pregnancy is it?"

3. *Ratifying this experimental assessment*
   a. Does your unconscious recognize a relationship between these questions and your life experience as a woman (or man)?
   b. Will it be all right to discuss this further on a verbal, conscious level after you awaken?

SECTION VIII

Dreams, Illness, and Healing

THEORY

> . . . Since the beginnings of all events are small, so it is clear, are those of the diseases and other affections about to occur in our bodies . . . it is manifest that these beginnings be more evident in sleeping than in waking moments.

> . . . It is not improbable that some of the presentations which come before the mind in sleep may even be causes of the actions cognate to each of them . . . it is quite conceivable that some dreams may be tokens and causes of future events.
>
> —ARISTOTLE

Cybernetic Relationship Between Dreams, SDMLB, and Information Substances/Receptors

This ancient quotation from Aristotle's *De Divinatione per Solunum [On Prophesying by Dreams]* well expresses the experience of most clinicians who have spent some time listening to their patients' dreams. Researchers who do not study dream series over long periods of time during stressful change in people's lives, however, have had difficulty objectively investigating the role of dreams in the generation and healing of illness (Haskell, 1986). Because of this, we do not have a comprehensive and empirically verifiable theory of psychosomatic processes in dreams (Rossi, 1972/1985).

A well authenticated classical example of how dreams can express the presence of an illness was reviewed by Lockhart (1977, pp. 9–11):

In 1933, Dr. T. M. Davie submitted a patient's dream to Jung for interpretation. No other information about the patient was provided. The dream was as follows:

Someone beside me kept asking me something about oiling some machinery. Milk was suggested as the best lubricant. Apparently I thought that oozy slime was preferable. Then, a pond was drained and amid the slime there were two extinct animals. One was a minute mastodon. I forgot what the other one was.

Jung told Dr. Davie the dream indicated an organic condition and that the drainage of the pond referred to the damming up of cerebrospinal fluid. . . . Jung knew Latin and it could not have escaped his attention that the Latin word for slime is *pituita*.

From this word comes pituitary. The slimy colloidal secretions of the pituitary gland are essential to certain bodily processes. These secretions flow into the third ventricle, one of those hollow subterranean womb-like caverns through which the cerebrospinal fluid also flows. The cerebrospinal fluid has the function of lubricating these cavities and provides a mechanical barrier against shock to the brain. It is as if the brain floats in this fluid. There are many aqueducts — even named so — through which this fluid pours on its course. If cut off or blocked, the effect, as in a real aqueduct, is a drainage of the cerebrospinal pool downstream. . . . Perhaps in this dream the two extinct animals are images of the hypothalamus and the pituitary that lie beneath the cerebrospinal pond. The case was medically diagnosed as a neurological disturbance in the third ventricle.

To put this material in the form of an hypothesis, we would say that *bodily organs and processes have the capacity to stimulate the production of psychic images, meaningfully related to the type of physical disturbance and its location.* (Italics in original)

To those who are unfamiliar with the clinician's art of reaching conclusions via the language of analogy, metaphor, and symbol rather than via rational, verbal cognition, much of the above will seem to be just so much gibberish. However, there are many such well authenticated examples of how such analogical, imagistic and symbolic processes of dreams are related to sickness and health — too many to be dismissed out of hand. This example is of particular interest, moreover, because it illustrates how mind-body processes can mirror themselves in apparently accurate anatomical detail.

A new clinical approach to "amplifying" and healing the mind-body processes mirroring themselves in dreams has been detailed in a series of books by the Swiss analyst, Arnold Mindell (1982, 1985a, b). He summarizes his work as follows (1982, p. 198):

A central idea arises from this book: The body is dreaming. We discover that body processes will mirror dreams when the body is encouraged to amplify and express its involuntary signals, such as pressures, pain, cramping, restlessness, excitement, exhaustion or nervousness. Since a reduction of symptoms — and even healing — often accompany consciously unleashed body processes, we may conclude that in illness the body suffers from incomplete dreaming. The same unconscious contents that appear in dreams burden and activate the body with unexperienced forms of physical behavior and undetected insights.

The body processes, reflecting dreams and fairy tales, presented in this work indicate that human physiology is portrayed in mythology. The study of dreambody processes gives mythology a root in the flesh. We stand at the brink of new approaches to the body, approaches that are based on ancient concepts. Future research into the subtle physiology of symbols will reveal many insights about the body which I have only been able to hint at in this work. The little knowledge I have gained about physiology through the study of myths makes me painfully aware of how little we know about body processes and how much still remains to be learned about the physiological dimensions of well-defined psychological processes such as the animus and individuation.

As we have already suggested, a major difficulty the scientific mind has had in taking such clinical approaches to dream work seriously is that they are usually accompanied by analogical rather than logical explanations of how mind-body self-reflection could take place. There has been no adequate concept of how an empirically measurable process could mediate between the phenomenological experiences of mind and the organic, material, anatomical-physiological processes of the body.

Stated in this manner, the reader who has followed us thus far will be able to anticipate the solution we are about to propose. We have reviewed in great detail many of the contexts in which state-dependent memory, learning, and behavior can serve as the missing empirical link in all previous theories of mind-body healing (Rossi, 1986d; Rossi & Ryan, 1986). We now propose to combine the SDMLB concept with Pert's (1985) view of how information substances and their receptors can mediate mind-body processes. Our understanding of the role of information substances and their receptors in psychosomatic medicine suggests the next step in formulating a more comprehensive and empirically testable theory of mind-body communication in dreams as follows:

Illness and healing in dreams is mediated by the information substance-receptor activation of state-dependent memory and learning processes that modulate the cortico-limbic-hypothalamic-pituitary system of mind-body homeostasis. The phenomenological experience of dreams in the languages of imagery, metaphor, symbol and analogy is isomorphic with organic brain-body processes down to the cellular-genetic-molecular level. *Symbols, metaphor, and imagery in dreams are state-dependent information transducers that can initiate, express, and/or mediate mind-body communication in illness and healing.* These relationships are illustrated in the cybernetic loops of Figures 4 and 18.

It is important to recall here the pragmatic convention we developed

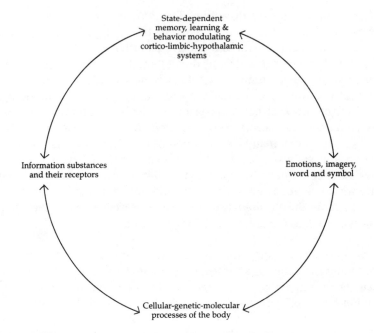

Figure 18: One way of illustrating the cybernetic loop of mutually interactive relations between the cellular-genetic-molecular level and the state-dependent encoding of "mind" in the languages of emotion, imagery, word, and symbol. The cybernetic loop between the cellular-genetic-molecular level and the state-dependent encoding of "mind" in the languages of emotion, imagery, word, and symbol. These processes are as active in dreams as in waking and fantasy states of mind. We hypothesize that the ideodynamic processes of mind-body healing utilize the languages of emotion, imagery, word, and symbol to ultimately modulate processes at the cellular-genetic-molecular level.

earlier about the use of words such as *mind, psyche, consciousness*, and now *dream experience* (see the theory portion of Section IV). Since the experiential context of such phenomenological realities is ever-changing, we cannot establish consensual and permanent definitions of them. However, we can all agree on definitions of the sensory-perceptual modalities or languages in which these phenomenological experiences are expressed. Figures 4 and 18 illustrate how languages of mind such as emotions, imagery, words, and symbols which are encoded in the neural networks of the brain can be transduced into cellular-genetic-molecular processes on the organic level. We hypothesize that the four stages of the mind-body cybernetic loop depicted in Figure 18 can make varying contributions to the many different processes of illness and health. Some processes of illness and health are more obviously determined and modulated by events on the cellular-genetic-molecular level (as, for example, the inheritance of genetic defects and genetically-based disorders in general [Baskin, 1984], and the new class of illnesses "associated with information substance-receptor problems" [Scarlett & Olefsky, 1985]). We hypothesize that even illnesses initiated and processed on such purely organic molecular levels, however, can modulate state-dependent memory, learning, and behavior (SDMLB) systems that are ultimately experienced on the phenomenological level of mind and dream via emotions, imagery, words, and symbols. This is possible because the processes that encode SDMLB and "purely organic problems" share many of the same Is-receptor-cellular-genetic mechanisms. The work of Kandel and Schwartz (1985) and others on the molecular basis of memory and learning, for example, implicates the intracellular ATP "secondary messenger system" as mediating the molecular basis of learning. This same ATP secondary messenger system is utilized by most Is-receptor-cellular metabolic systems that purportedly operate on a "purely organic level."

In this formulation we see once again how SDMLB functions as the matrix of mind-body information transduction and communication. SDMLB is the common denominator between the organic and mental levels: the information substances produced at the cellular-genetic-molecular level can modulate the state-dependent neural networks of the brain that are experienced on the mental level as emotions, imagery, and words. These mental experiences, in turn, can be transduced back into the organic level by the process of neuroendocrinal information transduction (see Figure 4). The concept of SDMLB enables us to understand how organic processes of illness and healing can be transduced into the phenomenological realm and experienced in consciousness and dreams, and how these mental experiences can be transformed back into organic processes at the molecular level. SDMLB thus bridges the so-called Cartesian gap between mind and body in a manner that can be explored experimentally in the laboratory and experienced therapeutically by the patient.

Figures 4 and 18 illustrate how SDMLB can be experienced as the vital communication link in psychosomatic illness. Trauma and stress experienced phenomenologically as emotions, imagery, words and symbols can modulate the SDMLB encoding of all the body's major homeostatic mechanisms in the cortico-limbic-hypothalamic-pituitary and related systems. Thus, experiences initiated and processed within the languages of consciousness and dreams may modulate illness and healing that is ultimately experienced at the cellular-genetic-molecular level.

Ideodynamic Approaches to Facilitating Healing in Dreams

PSYCHODYNAMIC FACTORS INFLUENCING VASCULAR AND MUSCULAR PROCESSES DURING MENSTRUATION, PREGNANCY, AND LABOR

It must be acknowledged immediately that there is a great gap between the above theoretical conceptualization about the dynamics of mind-body healing in dreams and the clinical examples of Cheek's work presented in the following chapters. As is often the case in clinical work, the successful practice comes before the rational theory. In this case, Cheek used the practical concerns of his practice in obstetrics to develop ideodynamic approaches for dealing with two specific problems of mind-body illness and healing in dreams: (1) the psychodynamics of blood pressure, clotting, and hemorrhage during the vulnerable shifts of the menstrual and pregnancy cycles, and (2) the delicate mind-body language of muscle tension and contraction during normal and premature labor and during abortion.

The seeming simplicity, rapidity, and ease with which Cheek is able to deal with these often life-threatening factors (even over the telephone!) actually veils many levels of profound psychodynamic complexity. The typical psychoanalyst who is involved with the tedious unraveling and lengthy "working through" of the complexes that are usually the result of a lifetime of psychological distortion and repression will have questions about some of these case reports. Where the classical psychoanalyst would write a whole book explicating the meaning and significance of a few dreams, together with the behavioral and transference contexts in which they occurred, Cheek writes only a few paragraphs. An example of Cheek's apparent oversimplification may help us to reconcile these differences. In the beginning of his paper on the "Significance of Dreams in Initiating Premature Labor," Cheek writes (1969b, p. 1):

> Dreams are real until they can be exposed to conscious reason. Repressed dreams, however, tend to recur. They change form with new daytime experiences and continue to affect physiological reactions.

These words do oversimplify but no one would really argue with them. Cheek then goes on to add the following:

> Repressed dreams can be discovered easily and quickly with a combination of ideomotor questioning methods and light hypnosis. We can help patients stop hemorrhaging during telephone conversations during emergencies. We can help check the progress of toxemia long enough to assure birth of a term-sized child.

Most well-trained depth psychotherapists will be taken aback by the blithe and breezy assurance of these words. And precisely therein may lay one of the important secrets of the personal effectiveness of Cheek's therapeutic work. Most of the women he has helped probably have a relatively uncomplicated positive transference to him as *the archetypal image of the doctor as healer*. His genuinely friendly, supportive, and fatherly manner automatically constellates an atmosphere of confidence, well-being, and healing within patients.

CHEEK'S UTILIZATION OF "MOOD STATE DEPENDENCY"

A second significant factor in Cheek's therapeutic work may be his utilization of what has become known in the experimental literature on hypnosis as "mood state dependency" (Bower, 1981; Gilligan & Bower, 1984). Many of the most dramatic cases in these chapters are with patients who are in a desperate emotional state or emergency situation. Cheek repeatedly notes that patients are already in hypnosis when he begins his work with them, or they very rapidly enter trance just as soon as he suggests the finger signaling procedure. That is, they are already in the midst of a process of accessing mood-state-dependent experiences that are a psychobiological expression of the problem. The so-called "stressful emotions and behavior" his patients are experiencing are actually the preverbal or noncognitive encoding of the psychobiological source of their problem. *Patients are not distressed because they have a problem; rather, their distress is the best expression of the psychobiological encoding of their problem.*

Many readers will recognize in this italicized statement an update of the James-Lange theory of emotion (James, 1890), which explained emotion as the information feedback from the peripheral effects (within the soma of the body) of the autonomic nervous system and the skeletal muscle system. This leads us to propose that the psychobiological processes that underlie the James-Lange theory of emotion can be accounted for by the state-dependent memory, learning, and behavior encoding of life experiences by the information substances and their receptors operating through the autonomic, endocrine, immune, and neuropeptide systems (see Figure 8).

THE PSYCHOBIOLOGICAL CONTEXT OF THE BIRTH PROCESS

A third major factor in the effectiveness of Cheek's therapeutic work may be the circumscribed psychobiological context in which he usually operates. As an obstetrician, he is a specialist in facilitating life's most powerful process oriented toward a definite preprogrammed biological goal: creating a baby. Evolution has selected every possible biological mechanism to ensure the success of the birth process. The cultural and psychological foibles accumulated in even the worst individual lifetime must be relatively weak in the face of millions of years of biological selection for a successful birth. Cheek is only dealing with these comparatively weak personal psychological problems that are opposing an incredibly powerful biological destiny. He delivers a few brief but effective ideodynamic taps that topple the dominos of unfortunate personal life conditioning, which are relatively fragile in the face of life's primal urge to reproduce itself.

And, yet, what a profound art there is in these few ideodynamic taps, explorations, and reframes! Throughout many of the chapters in this volume, Cheek makes short but extremely cogent comments on the care with which the therapist needs to select words and ideas for facilitating natural inner healing responses. Because of Baudouin's "law of reverse effort," it will not do to offer simple reassurance. Simple reassurance often *implies* the exact opposite to the patient who interprets it as a covert message that the doctor is really worried. There can be no lying or false postures with patients in emergency situations! Their acutely sensitized and activated unconscious processes can pick up the minimal vocal and behavioral cues about what the doctor really believes.

As one rereads many of these short case histories, one is struck by the fact that the archetypal role of the therapist as a healer is not an empty pose. We must not merely believe—we must *know*—that patients contain the healing forces within themselves. Our apparently simple ideodynamic questions implicitly communicate this knowing, which evokes a powerful expectancy that accesses and activates the patient's inner healing resources so they can become manifest even when surrounded by a lifetime of unfortunate conditioning.

In summary, ideodynamic approaches appear to be most suitable for the rapid accessing and reframing of the psychobiological encoding of traumatic and stress-related problems, particularly when they are already in the process of becoming reactivated because of current stress. Cheek's approach can be most easily generalized to any emergency (accidents, wars, etc.) or high-performance life situations (birth, sex, sports, drama, creative and artistic work, etc.). The ideodynamic approach may supplement the behaviorist, cognitive, and depth-oriented psychoanalytic therapies, but it is unlikely that it can entirely replace the lengthy restructuring and remedial work that is needed, for example, with psychotic problems and character disorders. Many of Cheek's cases, however, do suggest that long-term problems that are due to chronic stress or dissociated emotional complexes (Jung, 1960a, b; Rossi, 1986d) may also be amenable to his approach.

PRACTICE

20

Ideodynamic Approaches to Sleep Problems

There are four major sleep problems with many different causes:

1. Occasional difficulty getting to sleep;
2. Persistent, disabling difficulty in getting to sleep or awakening during the night and remaining awake;
3. Distressing tendency to get sleepy while driving a car or working at some task requiring concentration;
4. Disabling narcolepsy, often coupled with muscle weakness or cataplexy.

Occasional Insomnia

Everyone at some time is "keyed up" over tasks at hand or anticipation of things that have to be done on the morrow. Almost any dissociative process will solve this problem: taking any one of the over-the-counter sleeping pills or the seasick remedy Dramamine; getting out of bed, cooking some onion soup and then drinking it before returning to bed. It could be the boring process of counting sheep jumping over a fence, if you are good at imagery; or, some people find it is just enough to move from a bed to a couch or to a bed in another room.

The most satisfying and restful method of dealing with occasional insomnia is to get out of bed and use self-hypnosis with any induction method before asking for an ideodynamic answer to the question, **"Would it be all right for me to go to sleep when I get back to bed, and to sleep with pleasant dreams and pleasant thoughts until I awaken at ＿＿ o'clock in the morning?"** The usual answer is a yes. Now ask your yes finger to lift when you know you will keep that promise.

Habitual and Disabling Insomnia

Some people are habit-bound by insomnia. They know they cannot get to sleep and that every night will be a torture. Careful research in sleep centers has shown that such people do, in fact, achieve multiple brief periods of sleep during the night, but they focus on their difficulty and have amnesia for the sleep periods. This knowledge does not relieve their fatigue and anxiety.

With this type of insomnia there usually has been some past event that has led to an imprint-like behavior pattern of sleep avoidance. For example, a recurring traumatic dream that interrupts sleep will eventually result in a reluctance to go to sleep. People who have been assaulted, injured in an accident, or emotionally traumatized during an operation under general anesthesia will relive their experience during recurring dream cycles of sleep. Eventually, there will be such a build-up of consciously unrecognized alarm that they avoid sleep or awaken frequently with amnesia for the reason they have awakened. Because of this amnesia, they are unable to correct the problem.

MOLESTATION AS A CAUSE OF INSOMNIA

A frequent cause of habitual insomnia in women is the trauma of having been molested as a child—usually during the night with the child being frightened immediately upon awakening. Often there has been a threatening command to keep quiet and not to tell anyone about the encounter. This is another demonstration of a statebound experience that makes entry into sleep a source of troubled expectation. The causal event is rarely a part of conscious memory, but it may be quickly recognized at an ideodynamic level of awareness during an age-regression to **"the most important experience that has had something to do with your difficulty getting to sleep."**

We might expect that such a child would always have had trouble sleeping, but in fact the problem may not come into prominence until many years later, after hearing about a friend who was raped or a robbery in the neighborhood.

During a hypnotic interview it can be pointed out that it is possible for the person to sleep physiologically yet still be alert to any danger—that from now on it will be possible to trust the fact that she will awaken instantly and will know what to do if there should be a threatening intruder. Remind her that mothers will awaken when a child becomes ill during the night while the husband remains quite soundly asleep.

While there may be a difficulty in achieving recognition of a traumatic memory at a preconscious or conscious level of awareness, it usually will be elevated into consciousness when this request is authoritatively expressed: **"Go to the moment you are awakening. Recognize that that person was wrong, and was emotionally very troubled. Say out loud what would have made him stop and go away. Tell him you are going to yell until your parents come in. When you know what would have been the most powerful thing to say, your yes finger will lift. As it lifts, feel the power of scaring him away. Say it out loud, and say it again."**

Some variant of this approach, depending on the circumstances, can be created in response to individualized needs and experiences. The issue is to make clear that the client is not a victim but, rather, is in command of the situation during the hypnotic rehearsal.

Next, tell her to see how the intruder reacts after this reframing of the experience; ask her to go over the experience of awakening and giving those orders as he comes in. Notice what he does and how he reacts when she speaks up for her own needs and rights. Stress that this is the way the experience would have occurred if she had known then what she knows now. A word of caution is appropriate here. Be sure you have someone present as a witness, or let your office personnel know what you plan. It could be embarrassing if people in your waiting room heard your client yelling, "Go away! Leave me alone!"

CHILDHOOD TRAUMA: EMOTIONAL AND PHYSICAL

Death from infection often came during the night before the advent of antibiotics in the 1930s. Older people can remember being taught to say that prayer, "Now I lay me down to sleep. I pray the Lord my soul to keep. If I die before I wake, I pray the Lord my soul to take."

Children's literalness of understandings can make this prayer into a powerful reason for not sleeping, particularly as they grow old and have friends or relatives die, for death for the aging and sick comes frequently during the early morning hours.

Beatings by violent parents frequently occur at night, particularly if the parent is a father or stepfather. The victims need to recognize that the experience is "back there and no longer needs to interfere with sleep."

INSOMNIA IN PREGNANCY

When sleep problems and frightening dreams occur during the last few weeks of pregnancy, it is a clear indication that there have been fears regarding the labor, or fears that something may be wrong with the baby. It is very important for obstetricians to know how to search for the cause of these dreams, because they usually stem from ideas that would seem ridiculous if recognized consciously. If unrecognized, however, they can recur on separate sleep cycles and successive nights and may eventuate in subplacental thrombosis (abruptio), preeclampsia, premature labor, or failure to start labor at term (the unconscious reason for the latter being a desire not to face a tragedy). When this type of physiological response occurs, it is probable that the cellular receptors for oxytocin have been blocked within the uterine muscles by the mother's unconscious fears. In my (DBC) experience, this is the most common reason for continuation of a pregnancy past an expected date for labor.

INSOMNIA DUE TO SERIOUS ILLNESS OF A RELATIVE

The fear that a relative might die during the night is usually apparent as a cause of sleep deprivation without need for hypnosis. Treatment during the illness will probably be unsuccessful, but after recovery or death of the loved one, the approach would be to release the habit of alertness as no longer necessary.

IMPORTANCE OF FOLLOW-UP VISITS

With serious problems of insomnia it is necessary to set up a series of treatments to ensure that your client has been released from secondary, satellite types of triggering thoughts that might appear and threaten the client's confidence in the therapeutic program. As with most long-term problems, there is always the chance that unexpected, consciously unrecognized stimuli of lesser valence than the original trauma will appear when the major one has been discovered and eradicated. This is the factor that prompted Freud into believing that removal of one symptom would only lead to the appearance of another symptom.

To some extent, therapeutic victory depends upon the therapist's faith in the client's ability to marshall potential resources during the unconscious learning period.

Intermittent Sleepiness

This kind of sleep problem can have fatal consequences when it occurs while the sufferer is at the controls of a moving vehicle, whether on land, sea, or in the air. Most commonly it occurs during time periods when there are no alerting stimuli, and when the individual is lulled by repetitive visual or auditory input at regular intervals, such as intermittant white lane markers, the swish of windshield wipers, the steady hum of an engine.

A simple, nonhypnotic technique to counter such feelings of drowsiness is to create alerting stimuli for any of the sensory channels. For example, look from side to side, turn on the radio, sing some songs. It is unwise to fight the feeling of drowsiness because such an effort simply intensifies one's attention to the fact of feeling sleepy. Those who fly private planes should read Lindberg's account of his fight against drowsiness during his transatlantic flight in 1927. He was able to win the battle, but we have no idea how many private plane tragedies actually stem from spontaneous hypnotic states. The victim of inappropriate spontaneous hypnosis is unable to react rapidly enough for the demands in flying at high speeds. Reflexes are slower than needed; conscious responses to sources of danger peripheral to the reduced visual fields occur too late for safe reaction.

On the highway it is better and safer to stop the car on the side of the road, get out of the driver's seat, and either exercise for two minutes or give in to sleep for about five minutes. A pilot, of course, cannot do this.

When a person comes for help with a problem of intermittent and inappropriate drowsiness, it is usually adequate to place him in a moderately deep hypnotic state and ask for an ideodynamic response of acceptance to the directions:

1. **"When you know you will always stay awake and alert at the controls of a moving vehicle, your yes finger will lift."**
2. **"If your inner mind feels you cannot do this, your I don't want to know finger will answer. If that finger lifts, I want to know the reason." [It usually stems from deep-seated feelings of guilt and expectations of being punished in some way.]**
3. **"Remember that if you fall asleep driving a car, you are not only a danger to yourself, but also a threat to the people in your car and to others on the road." [This is an appeal to augment the motivation of the client toward self-preservation for the sake of others.]**

Narcolepsy

People with narcolepsy fall asleep at times that can be very troublesome and have no relationship to fatigue. This condition may be the result of organic pathology in the brain, but emotion may also trigger the mechanism. Any psychological approach to treatment should be preceded by a careful neurological study. Narcolepsy also can occur when there has been severe damage to the liver or kidneys due to disease, chemical poisoning, or circulation failure. It is a problem that should be treated by a physician.

Psychological sources of the problem may have originated in a minor drowsiness pattern that took on exaggerated importance and became amplified by medical attention and conviction that this difficulty would continue indefinitely. In this case, the therapy would be the same as that outlined above.

Therapists should learn how to search their own sleep ideation and should also practice with every client or patient. One can be very successful with daytime interventions only to discover that such efforts have been defeated by dreams occurring at night. An overview of our ideodynamic approach to facilitating a good night's sleep is presented in Box 26.

At follow-up visits it is helpful to ask for a review of the previous night's experience, as important ideas are marshalled during the night but usually lost in amnesia by the time the patient arrives for the therapy session. Since the patient enters a hypnotic state the moment he begins getting finger signals, the therapeutic session can be initiated with very little delay from superficial conversation and amenities.

BOX 26: FACILITATING A GOOD NIGHT'S SLEEP

1. *Accessing the source of the problem*
   a. "Orient your unconscious mind to the first experience in your life when something happened to make sleeping important in some way. When you are there, your yes finger will lift. As it lifts, look around in your mind's eye . . . see what is happening to affect the way you feel about sleep."
   b. When that information is obtained, ask if an earlier experience could have set the stage for the one just given.

2. *Therapeutic reframing*
   a. "Understand what you could have done to have prevented that event from troubling your sleep."
   b. "Now that you know about that, is there any other reason for the event interfering with your sleep up here at the present time?"
   c. "Now go back to some time when you slept very well and got up the next morning feeling great. As you are falling asleep that night, your yes finger will lift. Each time you are dreaming, your no finger will lift, and when you are finally awake the next morning, your I don't want to know finger will lift."
   d. "Review that wonderful night when you are ready to go to sleep. It will prepare the way for a good night of rest."

3. *Ratifying restful sleep*
   a. "Will it be all right now for you to sleep deeply and restfully at night and awaken in the morning feeling rested and relaxed?"
   b. "When you know you will keep that promise to yourself and to the people who will be pleased when you are sleeping well, your yes finger will lift."

21

Emotional Distress in Dreams

Since ancient times it has been known that unpleasant thoughts and ideas may have profoundly disturbing effects upon the body and its functions. Whatever their origin, fearful thoughts and distressing emotional states are potent forces in the physiological functioning of the body, and are not often or easily — if at all — mollified by reasoning processes. Even less likely to be mollified are the disturbing thoughts and emotions associated with terrifying dreams; hence, there is a definitely conceivable possibility of actual physical harm resulting from a dream. In this chapter we will focus on how the emotional distress initiated in dream states can be responsible for problems with hemorrhage and premature births.

Hemorrhage Initiated in a Dream

A 32-year-old divorced Canadian woman was visiting with friends while recuperating from a conization performed in Vancouver, British Columbia, eight days earlier. She felt well and had been free of vaginal bleeding after the third postoperative day. However, on the eighth postoperative day, after an uneventful visit and quiet chatting with her friends, she took a nap at 3:00 p.m. and awakened at 4:00 p.m. because of profuse vaginal bleeding. There were no cramps, and this was not the time for her expected period.

A friend transported her to the municipal central receiving station. There it was discovered she had health insurance. The attending medical officer contacted the county medical society emergency roster and she was transferred to my care and brought to the most conveniently located hospital. During the two-and-one-half-hour interval between the discovery of bleeding and the time she arrived at the hospital, there had been a loss of at least 800 cc. of blood, estimated on the basis of her description. Her hemoglobin was reported as 11.5 grams per 100 cc., and the hematocrit reading was 33 four hours after the hemorrhage had stopped. No bleeding tendency had appeared at any other time of her life and she did not bruise easily.

The patient stated that the operation had been performed to remove tissues containing intraepithelial carcinoma diagnosed on smear and biopsy. Her gynecologist had announced that it was all out and that tissue examination corroborated the conclusion that this was not malignant.

The bleeding was very profuse as the vaginal speculum was introduced. It occurred at the conization site, did not come from the fundus, and was surgical, not menstrual bleeding.

The patient was trembling, her skin was cold and moist, her pulse 118 and blood pressure 106/68. I stood up to attract her attention and said:

"You know, the last patient I examined here was bleeding just like this. I told her to look up at the ceiling at one of those spots. She went right into hypnosis and stopped her bleeding — just like turning off a faucet."

The patient relaxed a little, laughed, and fixed her attention on a point over her head. I said:

"Keep your eyes on one place until all the other objects look hazy. When you are able to concentrate that well, you can close your eyes and keep on relaxing."

The patient was probably in a hypnoidal state when I began talking to her. Her eyes closed within a few seconds. The perineal muscles relaxed. The bleeding stopped within 45 seconds. I wiped the cervix gently. All sutures were in place. I could see no suspicious areas to indicate the possibility of arteriolar bleeding nor any evidence of hematoma. A rectal examination showed no evidence of inflammation or hematoma. I said:

"There is no bleeding now, and I think you are smarter than the last patient. You have lost a lot of blood though, and I want to keep you here overnight to make sure you are all right before flying home tomorrow."

The patient was put to bed but was allowed bathroom privileges and encouraged to get up during the evening. There were only a few stains on her perineal pad two hours later when I returned to check her. She was interested in hypnosis and wanted to know more about it. I told her that I was interested in it, too, and wanted to know more about why she had started to bleed so profusely that afternoon. She said she only knew that she had awakened with blood gushing from her vagina. Ideomotor finger signaling was explained and suggested to the patient. The focusing of her attention on the problem of selecting answers unconsciously allowed her to enter into a light trance state.

Q: Could there have been any emotional reason for your starting to bleed this afternoon?

A: (Verbal) I don't think so. I was having a nice nap. I like the people with whom I was staying. (While she was saying these things her yes finger was lifting. This surprised her.)

Q: Let your unconscious mind orient back to the moment just before you

started to bleed. When you are there, your yes finger will lift. As it does, I would like to have you look around and tell me what is going on.

A: (After a lapse of 30 seconds the finger started to lift.) I'm asleep. I'm dreaming that I have cancer. I am dying of cancer. I'm feeling restless. As I turn over I can feel the blood starting to come from me.

Q: Does your unconscious mind *really* think you need to worry about having a cancer?

A: No, my doctor explained last week that I did not really have cancer. She said the operation was done to keep me from getting it someday. (While the patient was verbalizing her thoughts, her finger lifted to answer no also.)

Q: Does your unconscious mind now know that you can heal this place up with normal healthy tissue and stop having this frightened bleeding?

A: (The yes finger slowly lifted in answer to this, after a lag of 15 seconds.)

The patient slept well during the night and was ambulatory the next morning. She had no further bleeding and reported three days later by letter that there had been no bleeding after the flight home.

COMMENT

We are usually so engrossed in determining the pathological organic possibilities for causing hemorrhage that we may overlook the possibility that coagulation and fibrinolytic mechanisms as well as contractility of the capillaries, arterioles and venules may be altered by emotional factors. We may be so concerned in carrying out our offices as diagnosticians and surgeons that we give too little attention to the morbid effects such concern may have upon the physiological adaptations of our patients. In the past five years, retrograde investigations of serious surgical and obstetrical hemorrhage have indicated that subjective reactions of patients may be helpful or harmful during the experience. It is recently becoming increasingly clear that investigation with modern techniques of hypnoanalysis can be extended to reveal the subjective reactions of patients while they are unconscious from head trauma, surgical anesthesia, or chemical poisoning. The exploration of dreams can be quickly and safely done with the same methods of unconscious scanning which have permitted our growing knowledge about the other unconscious states (see Box 27).

Dreams seem to play an important part in the origin of menorrhagias, abnormal bleeding of pregnancy, fluid and salt retention of toxemia, and the onset of serious vomiting of pregnancy. The common causes of emotional problems can be quickly discovered and exposed to the saner judgment and more mature perspective of intellectual reason through simple methods of hypnotherapy, which have been outlined and discussed else-

---

BOX 27: RESOLVING SLEEP AND DREAM ISSUES

1. *Accessing the dream source of problem*
   a. "Orient yourself to the moment of falling asleep. Your yes finger will lift when you are there."
   b. "Your no (know) finger will lift each time you have a dream, as your inner mind scans your entire nighttime of sleep." [Three or four finger lifts validate the typical REM-dream sleep periods most people have each night. Repeat this nonverbal scanning process three times.]

2. *Therapeutic reframing*
   a. "If there have been any troublesome or frightening dreams or thougths, your yes finger will now lift."
   b. "Go over the entire night's sleep again, with your no finger lifting while you are reviewing the problem. Continue going over it until you are able to talk about it."
   c. A therapist-assisted review of the problem usually leads to spontaneous insights that can therapeutically reframe the problem.

3. *Ratifying the therapeutic gain*
   "Your yes finger can lift when your unconscious knows that you are entirely free of the irrational sources of that stress so that your problem can be resolved."

---

where (Cheek, 1961a, c). The factors most commonly associated with hemorrhage have been unrecognized fear, assumed guilt, and dramatized identification of self with people who have had surgical and obstetrical tragedies.

Prematurity Initiated in Dream States

The number of live births in the United States has diminished to approximately 3.5 million per year. About 7% of these infants weigh less than five and one-half pounds but more than two pounds, and are the products of what is now called "preterm" labor. More than 80% of these babies survive, but those weighing less than 1000 grams (2.2 pounds) have a high mortality, approaching 50%.

Infants weighing three pounds or less face a miserable period of hospitalization varying from several weeks to several months. The cost of intensive care for the survivors varies from $500 to $1,500 per day. The traumatic impressions made on these infants has been unknown until recently because we have not had the means of accessing their memories.

In round figures, we are considering approximately a quarter of a million vulnerable little beings who begin life with a tremendous handicap each year. They are essentially battered children from the time of birth; there is no explanation given to them that the nasogastric tube, the intravenous catheters, the bright lights, and the frequent manipulations by doctors are aimed at helping them survive.

Preterm labor is a preventable problem that with rare exceptions can be avoided by attention to the unconscious attitudes and fears of pregnant women. In essence, obstetricians must know about the early life feelings of each woman who becomes their patient. How did her mother react to the recognition that she was pregnant? What about the reaction of the father when he learned about the pregnancy? How did her mother fare during her labor with the patient who is to be a mother soon? Did the baby receive a welcome in the delivery room? Did her mother nurse her lovingly?

Only in the last 20 years have we begun to recognize the remarkable perceptions of unborn infants. We are now able to obtain verifiable evidence that there is a telepathic communication between mother and infant from the twelfth week of gestation onward. A mother who is shocked to learn that she is pregnant may change her reaction later on, but this will not alter the imprint of rejection experienced by the fetus. Imprintings are short-term learning processes that do not fade and are not normally altered by contradictory information having less hormonal impact.

With modern hypnotic techniques, we can help mothers correct their imprinted memories and assure their infants the best possible start in life in the outer world.

Twenty years of interest in this problem with babies weighing less than five-and-one-half pounds at birth suggest to the author that statistics might improve if obstetricians and generalists could separate good-risk patients who meet their stresses adequately, from the poor-risk patients who need plenty of attention early in pregnancy. Probably all women are fearful in their first pregnancy, and many are worried in successive pregnancies; but most women and their babies can compensate well for stresses. Can we recognize the ones whose backgrounds and conditionings make them vulnerable? Can we help them carry their babies to term? We should start before pregnancy begins, but we can also help during the first few critical weeks while the growing embryo is sensitive to changes in circulation and oxygen supply. Attention to the dreams of vulnerable patients must continue throughout pregnancy. The most casual and seemingly innocuous daytime experiences may evolve into potentially lethal dreams. We have not recognized the significance of dreams because patients usually consider their remembered dreams too ridiculous for reporting. Only 10% of damaging dreams are recalled on awakening; the rest are repressed. Dreams are real until they can be exposed to conscious reason. Repressed dreams, however, tend to recur. They change form with new daytime experiences and continue to affect physiological reactions. Repressed dreams can be discovered easily and quickly with a combination of ideomotor questioning methods and light hypnosis. We can help patients stop hemorrhaging during telephone conversations in emergencies. We can help check the progress of toxemia long enough to assure birth of a term-sized child.

Recognizing Poor-Risk Patient

My (DBC) initial efforts to separate good-risk from bad-risk patients were begun in a small community where I was the only physician with special training in obstetrics. Patients who seemed happily married, happy over the prospect of having a child, and those who had already delivered normal children were referred elsewhere as "good-risk" patients. Some of these good-risk patients miscarried and some delivered prematurely. Review of their histories often showed they had come from broken homes, or a mother had been seriously ill or had died when the patient was very young. Some had previously been divorced after delivery and were superstitiously afraid that another child would lead to a second divorce.

Orgasmic dysfunction and early-life sexual worries took on increasing importance as I learned to take better sexual histories. Orgasmic dysfunction, acne, childhood obesity, dysmenorrhea, and infertility were more commonly found in histories of girls whose pregnancies encountered complications. Some had no siblings. Some had names such as Jacqueline, Harriet, Henrietta or Carla, suggesting that their parents may have wanted a boy. An only child wonders why there were no siblings; the others feel they should have been boys. It did not seem to matter that such women consciously knew their parents appreciated them as female babies, that they were recognized for their beauty as adult women, and that their husbands adored them. The power of early-life imprinting was becoming apparent.

It was learned that perspiration, tachycardia, initial elevation of blood pressure, or an unexpected trace of blood in the cervical canal during initial examination seemed important warnings with the women who had later difficulties. This fear sign was used as a criterion.

About five years of private practice taught me that husbands are basically more frightened by pregnancy than are their wives. It seemed wise to ask what reaction a husband showed to the first report of pregnancy. Sometimes it was a look of silent anguish, sometimes a groan, sometimes an angry-sounding "Oh, my God!" Such reactions can shatter the beliefs and ideals of a wife. Though jokingly offered, they may be responsible for continued, unrecognized hostility on the part of an otherwise loving wife. The shocks are even greater when pregnancy occurs before marriage, or so soon after marriage that relatives and friends might raise their eyebrows. It seemed these factors were important, but they were not important to all women.

With continued probing and analysis of results, it was possible to compile criteria to help separate the good- from the bad-risk obstetrical patients.

Good-Risk Patients, Not Vulnerable

1. Happily adjusted family background; no divorce or death.
2. Happy marriage; patient looking forward to delivery.
3. Happy marriage and uncomplicated previous pregnancies.

Poor-Risk Patients to be Followed Closely

A. Serious Primary Factors. (One of these is sufficient).
   1. Death or divorce of parent before patient was age ten.
   2. Serious illness or death of mother at birth.
   3. Serious illness of patient during childhood (RHD, polio, etc.).
   4. Gynecological operation prior to pregnancy.
   5. Infertility for more than four years.
   6. Previous abortion, stillbirth, abnormal or premature baby.
   7. History of serious complication in earlier pregnancy.
B. Milder Criteria. (Must have two or more of these.)
   1. Firstborn child, or child with only female older siblings, and carrying "warmed-over boy's name" (Jacqueline, Harriet, Henrietta, Carla, etc.).
   2. Only child or only surviving child, and wondering why.
   3. Acne during adolescence (always found when child thought she should have been a boy).
   4. Tall and "skinny" or short and fat during teens (feeling unloved).
   5. History of severe dysmenorrhea (nearly always resenting being a girl).
   6. Hostile-overprotective or alcoholic mother or father.
   7. Previous divorce when this had been requested by husband (blow to self-respect not suffered when patient asks for divorce).

Comparative Results

When I moved from the small community to San Francisco, it was necessary to accept all obstetrical patients. Now it was possible to compare results in both groups. Naturally, an objection to this type of comparison is that patients quickly pick up the worries of their doctors and it is possible that my concerns over the poor-risk patients might have created the problems he wished to avoid. If this were entirely true, there should have been more premature babies and a greater fetal loss in this group. This was not the case. Blind and double-blind studies might be more acceptable for statistical evaluation, but I have directed my interest toward letting women discover their problems in order to find ways of correcting them. This seems reasonable, perhaps defensible.

The forewarning of vulnerable patients permitted them a chance to notify me at the time complications were occurring. When these occur at night, it is necessary for patients to know their call for help will not be considered an imposition. All vulnerable patients were trained early to use autohypnosis for relaxation. Trained patients will go immediately into hypnosis during a telephone conversation when request is made for ideomotor answers to questions. A state of hypnosis is often enough to permit termination of bleeding or premature labor, as has been shown by Logan (1963), Schwartz (1963), and Hartman and Rawling (1960). With repetition of abortion and with complications occurring in the second and third trimester, it is increasingly difficult to control the physiological effects of emotional stresses with ordinary, reassuring conscious communications. Stallworthy (1959) has shown that 80% of threatened abortions can be carried to successful delivery by any kind of optimistic therapy. This cannot be said when there have been four or more consecutive abortions, or when the complications have occurred late in pregnancy. Standard therapy with drugs and "reassurance" has failed consistently under such circumstances.

We need quick, accurate ways of discovering and correcting unconscious fears, guilt feelings, and identifications. We need to know all about the thoughts of pregnant women while they are asleep. We need to include husbands in our therapy.

RESULTS IN SMALL COMMUNITY: 1946–1955

There were 527 deliveries, not counting consultation or Cesarean sections done for other physicians. Of these, 34 were premature, a rate of 6.5%. One living premature baby was a Harlequin (massive scleroderma), and this died, as did two sets of twins delivered prematurely by another mother. There were three stillborn babies, one before labor and two at term during labor. Four patients had moderately severe toxemia but went on to deliver normal babies. One patient was first seen in eclampsia at term and was delivered of a normal infant by Cesarean section. Premature mortality was 15%, approximately the same as is found elsewhere. Two patients with incipient toxemia reduced their blood pressure to normal and lost their edema when they discovered relatively transparent fears. The author could not stop premature labor after the cervix had started to dilate. All patients hemorrhaging in the second and third trimester were admitted to the hospital. They seldom went home undelivered.

RESULTS IN SAN FRANCISCO: 1955–1966

Of 231 cases, there were 215 live births with six premature babies, a rate of 2.8%. Four of the six premature babies came in the good-risk group of 169 women. All of these weighed over four pounds three ounces, and their mothers were free of complications before labor. There were no deaths of premature or mature liveborn infants in the two groups. (See Tables 13 and 14.)

There was a significant difference between the two groups on the basis of numbers who hemorrhaged on one or more occasion, or threatened labor.

There were 17 times as many patients who threatened trouble in the poor-risk group, and there were nearly ten times as many who threatened serious-ly. All of the 11 serious threats in the poor-risk group had the typical picture of threatened abortion in the first trimester and threatened again later. Four of these had aborted consecutively six or more times before, and might have been expected to abort again. Two others would probably have aborted, according to criteria used by many obstetricians (ruptured membranes at 11 weeks and excessive hemorrhage). This leaves eight possible premature de-liveries for both groups, which could have changed the premature total to 7.4%.

It is fruitless to wonder what would have happened under other circum-stances. The facts are that there were six premature babies in 215 deliveries of living babies, and all of these lived. One patient who had delivered a stillborn at seven months in her first pregnancy, and whose next child was delivered by Cesarean section, had profuse bleeding after a disturbing dream. This episode occurred two weeks before delivery and was terminated by conversation and understanding of the dream. At operation, the female baby weighing six pounds was initially in good condition, but developed the typical picture of hyaline membrane disease and was in critical condition for five days. It was the belief of the pediatrician that this baby would not have had strength to survive if it had been delivered two weeks earlier when it seemed there could be placental separation. At operation there was no evidence of placental separation; the bleeding was unexplained on any or-ganic basis. Total blood lost with the first gush was estimated at 100cc.

Table 13: Personal experience fetal loss 1955–1966.

Class	Number	Abortion	Stillborn	Premature	Dead
Good-risk	169	3 (1.8%)	0	4 (2.4%)	0
Poor-risk	62	8 (13%)	5 (8%)	2 (3.2%)	5

Total liveborn incidence of prematurity = 2.8% (Total including stillbirths = 5%)

Table 14: Personal experience threatened fetal loss 1955–1966.

Class	Number	Mild Threat	Serious Threat	Carried On
Good-risk	169	6 (3.6%)	3 (1.8%)	6
Poor-risk	62	37 (59.7%)	11 (17.7%)	37

Concepts and Methods of Dream Exploration

Nathaniel Kleitman (1963) and his associates, Aserinsky (Aserinsky & Kleitman, 1953) and Dement (Dement & Kleitman, 1957), have shown that an average of eight hours of sleep is broken into four or five cycles of light and deep sleep, with approximately 90 minutes between peaks. Some years ago, I began asking patients to spend a minimum of six hours in hypnosis instead of ordinary sleep in order to control damage to skin from unconscious scratching. In 1957 I happened to ask such a patient whether or not she had followed directions. She was not sure. She was asked to put her hands on her lap and let her unconscious mind review the night of sleep and signal with one finger for ordinary sleep and one finger for hypnosis sleep. Her responses were alternating between the fingers, as though she had spent a little time in hypnosis and a little time in ordinary sleep. There were four alternations. She was asked to go through the night again. The same thing happened.

After this, an unconscious review of the preceding night was used as a rapid way of inducing hypnosis as well as setting up a means of communicating with ideomotor signals. The patient was asked to signal as she went to sleep and to signal when she knew she was dreaming. A third signal was requested to indicate final awakening in the morning. Worried patients often mobilize important thoughts on the eve of going to a doctor. It was found helpful to ask if there had been a frightening or disturbing dream that night. From this investigation came several results that seemed significant.

Signals for beginning of a dream always coincided with beginning of rapid lid movements and the kind of roving eyeball movements seen when patients are experiencing an age regression. Often the patient would lift the going-to-sleep finger at the end of the dream period; thereafter the eyes would remain immobile until the next dream period. There were four or five episodes of dreaming in an eight-hour night. Intervals were regular, and it was often possible to know how long patients had been asleep or whether their dreams had been disturbing, according to the number of dreaming signals and quality of facial expressions.

A survey of abortion sequences with hypnotic age regression to the moment of onset of bleeding showed that 54% of 125 instances began while the patients believed they were sleeping. This was more than would have been expected. At this time I was also exploring surgical anesthesia experiences. It was a short step to use of the same technique in exploring the night before onset of various complications in pregnancy. A number of patients were very much surprised to find they were aware of vaginal bleeding during the night, several hours before awakening. Several patients who had been diagnosed as having "incompetent cervix" because they had delivered immature babies in the second trimester found they had been having frightening thoughts about their baby on successive nights, and about the same time of night before the physical problem was apparent. They reviewed their sleep experiences repeatedly and noticed that they knew the quality of the normal uterine contractions changed, becoming more rapid and more forceful during their unpleasant dreams. None of these women knew they had been dreaming, and none had been aware of being in painless labor with expulsive, rather than concentric, uterine contractions.

Obstetrical patients often report headaches, onset of nausea, or facial edema on waking from sleep. Many frightened obstetrical patients find their legs going into spasms of cramps during the night after disturbing dreams. Scanning the night before these symptoms occur yields interesting information about sleep patterns, and further underlines the fact that daytime stresses may be troublesome, but they are not as troublesome as what the unconscious mind does with these experiences at night.

Hyperventilation is frequently observed during reviews of disturbed sleep sequences. Over and over again, with slowly developing complications and with the urgent problems of hemorrhage and onset of premature labor, it was emphasized by patients that the few remembered dreams were only superficial reflections of much deeper ideation usually described as "a thought" or "an experience." Reason for differentiating was usually explained on the basis that dreams are filled with symbols. Dreams may be troublesome and alarming, but the real physiological disturbances occur with the other kind of thought sequences. These must be comparable to the experiences known as "night terrors" occurring with children who do not remember what has happened and whose physiological disturbance continues long after awakening. The physiologically dangerous experiences at night seem very real, they incorporate actions of the preceding day, and they seem to be repeated on successive cycles of sleep. The great majority of emergencies originating at night are allocated by patients to the time between midnight and 4:00 a.m.

Having learned that dreams, or something like dreams, could be dangerous to unborn babies, it was necessary to protect mothers from their dreams. This can be done in two ways. We can train the mother to awaken and understand her dream, and we can train her not to have troublesome dreams. It is usually necessary to teach the mother to awaken from the dream before she can learn to substitute pleasant thoughts for unpleasant ones. Poor-risk patients are told about dreams at the first or second visit.

Frightened mothers cannot hallucinate the birth of their child. They are seen at least once a week until they are able to hallucinate a comfortable delivery at term with a living, healthy baby. They are told that 30% of women bleed during the first three months of pregnancy, and that this does not mean there is anything wrong with the baby. Great care is used with the choice of words in communicating with these patients. They are told to expect moments of fear when friends tell them about women having complications of pregnancy. They are told about the superstitious fears that follow "showers" given by friends. These are very real threats, but the aftermath of these threats can be inactivated.

Once patients have been told about their dreams and how to manage their reactions to dreams, it is not necessary to quiz them on subsequent visits unless they show sudden weight gain or begin complaining of insomnia. Since sexual inhibitions are frequently found in the poor-risk group, I make a point of telling them that intercourse is not dangerous and can continue through pregnancy, but it is important to know if it ever causes bleeding. Coital bleeding is usually caused by trauma to the delicate mucosa of the cervix. All obstetrical patients, both good- and poor-risk, are told to continue with work or sports for as long as they feel comfortable doing so. They may take trips of any sort in any type of vehicle *when they want to go on such trips*. Patients are told to use their obstetrician whenever they need support in stopping work, intercourse, or trips. They are to say, "My doctor does not want me to _____."

Comprehensive Ideomotor Training Techniques

These are described in detail in an earlier paper (Cheek, 1965b). An extended discussion of ideomotor questioning techniques may be found in Le-Cron's book, *Techniques of Hypnotherapy* (1961).

1. Demonstrate postural suggestion.
2. Demonstrate difficulty in overcoming effect of word "try."
3. Demonstrate effect of hallucinating a goal of imagining the arms pulling together with the force of a stretched rubber band around wrists.
4. Show patient how to develop a subjective hypesthesia of one arm.
5. Demonstrate difference in response of skin scratches when one arm is "numb."
6. Explain value of ideomotor responses in revealing information which is not consciously recognized.
7. Set up ideomotor symbol movements.
8. Review entire sleep period of previous night and check to see if any thoughts or dreams were disturbing.

9. Demonstrate method of inducing self-hypnosis for brief periods of rest.
10. Explain conditioning of brain, making pain equate with muscle tension, and comfort equate with muscle relaxation. This allows a rationale for purposefully relaxing muscles and using suggestions of peace and calm at a time of stress.
11. Project forward to time of "easy delivery" and obtain hallucinated commitment on the date, weight, and sex of the baby.

Pseudo-orientation to time of delivery is helpful in differentiating good-risk patients from those who must be watched. The hallucinated information may be wrong in every respect, but women who are happy at the prospect of delivering normal children will commit themselves on date, sex, and weight. Some women initially appear calm and well-adjusted, but later reveal that they should be shifted from the good-risk category to a poor-risk classification on the basis of mounting fears as they approach term. By the same token, it has been repeatedly demonstrated that the real problems are over when a patient who blocks initially on any sort of commitment, or hallucinates an abnormal baby or no baby at all, changes to an optimistic hallucinated commitment.

Emergency Therapeutic Procedures

An example will be given. It is 3:00 a.m. and a patient is in bed or in the bathroom while her worried husband is reporting that his wife awakened from sleep to find she is hemorrhaging. The husband is asked to take the telephone to his wife or bring her to the telephone.

Patient: Oh, doctor, I feel terrible. I woke up a few minutes ago and I am really bleeding.

Doctor: **Have you been mad at anybody recently?**

Patient: [Laughing] No, not really. (Purpose of the question has been accomplished: to take the attention away from bleeding momentarily and make the patient aware that emotional factors are thought to be the cause of it.)

Doctor: **Let's see what has been going on while you were asleep. Let your thoughts go back to the moment you fell asleep. When you are there, your yes finger will lift. Tell me when it goes up.**

Patient: [Lapse of 20 seconds. She is now in hypnosis.] Now.

Doctor: **Come forward now to the moment just before bleeding starts and, as your yes finger lifts, bring that thought up to where you can tell me about it.**

Patient: [After 15 seconds.] That's really crazy. My mother-in-law really wants me to have this baby now. She didn't at first, but that was six years ago when Bill was in school. I was dreaming that Mother was scolding Bill for getting me pregnant, and Bill was just standing there saying nothing. I was mad at *him*, too [laughing].

Doctor: **Let me ask your fingers now, "Will you stop this bleeding and get back to sleep with pleasant dreams?"**

Patient: [Laughing] My yes finger is going up.

Doctor: **Okay then. Give me a call about two o'clock tomorrow.** [Care is taken to avoid suggesting an expectation of further bleeding. One should not say, "Let me know if you have any more bleeding."]

Brief Clinical Reports

Helen R., 26, gravida 3, para 2, * with estimated blood loss of 1200 cc. during first trimester hemorrhages:* This patient was bleeding so profusely with an 8.7 gm. hemoglobin that 1 cc. of pitocin was placed in the first of two units of blood in order to expedite abortion. The patient had loudly stated that she did not want this baby. Her behavior contradicted her words. Under anesthesia the following morning, the cervix was tightly closed. The uterus seemed to be enlarging normally on schedule. I told the nurse at the operating table that I did not feel justified in terminating the life of this little baby. I did not know then that anesthetized patients can hear. There was no further bleeding. The patient delivered a seven-pound-nine-ounce male at term, and her term hemoglobin was 12.4 gm. Subsequent investigation revealed cumulative disturbing dreams during four nights preceding profuse hemorrhage in the daytime at work.

Sonia W., 34, gravida 10, para 0, with nine previous spontaneous abortions: Her first abortion had been induced surgically by Nazi physicians at four months of gestation, while she was interned in a Russian prison farm. She had been made to sign a statement that she would permit this abortion and would further permit surgical sterilization if she again became pregnant before the end of the war. Her next pregnancy came after termination of World War II, but she began bleeding during a dream that her baby would be taken from her by the Nazis. She had amnesia for the dream. Doctors in Italy "completed the abortion" because of profuse bleeding. This was the story of her next seven pregnancies. She lost her ninth pregnancy at 10 weeks, the day after I left town for a vacation.

The first of six major emergencies occurred at eight weeks. A profuse hemorrhage began on a Saturday, when she thought no doctor would be

*gravida=number of pregnancies; para=number of children born.

available. I answered her call and told her to stop the bleeding, and that I was coming out to give her a shot. She was told that we simply were not going to let her waste another pregnancy. The bleeding, an estimated 400 cc., had stopped before I arrived. She announced that it had stopped as soon as she hung up the receiver.

Spotting occurred at intervals until the sixth month when she had rhythmic, bearing-down contractions. She had tried to reach me to ask about some medicine. I had asked my answering service to announce that I was out of town, but had not yet gone. By the time I contacted the patient, her cervix was six cm. in diameter and a foot was visible through the delicate membranes protruding into the vagina. She was taken home and kept in hypnosis for 24 hours, after suturing the cervix together with chromic catgut, which was all I had available in the office. Four more episodes of profuse bleeding occurred and it was necessary to re-suture the cervix two more times before she ruptured her membranes. A four-pound-three-ounce female infant was delivered by Cesarean section, after she had shown indications of fetal distress during 15 hours of labor. This child survived.

The next pregnancy was totally without complications, other than one brief period of painful uterine contractions occurring after a frightening dream about losing the baby. I was away at the time. The patient reported later that she knew there had been a bad dream, and that Dr. Cheek would be angry if she did not stop the labor at this stage of seven months because the baby would be too small. The contractions stopped, and she delivered a boy weighing seven pounds seven ounces at term.

Her final pregnancy was not planned, and she had some conflict about it. There were numerous episodes of hemorrhage during this pregnancy, but her confidence was great by this time and she usually would telephone to say, "Well, I had a bad dream again. Tell me to stop." I would reply, "Ask your fingers if it would be all right for you to stop bleeding," and always obtained a yes answer. She was delivered of a normal female, weighing six pounds two ounces, by Cesarean section.

Mrs. M., 26, gravida 3, para 0: This attractive and feminine Catholic girl had been infertile for six years when first seen in my office, and this was her reason for consultation. She had felt unwanted and less attractive than her younger and older brothers. At age 11 she had engaged in mutual sexual investigation with a girl friend. After her first spontaneous abortion, she began worrying about being sexually abnormal. She had premarital intercourse with her husband and was pregnant at the time of her marriage. Her father-in-law was violently opposed to their marriage because plans had been made for her husband's further education. She aborted after bleeding had started in the night in relation to a dream about her husband dying. The Korean War had finished, but her husband was scheduled for service in Korea. Her second abortion also followed a dream that she either had to abort this baby or her husband would be killed. Unconsciously she recognized her role in aborting both babies and felt guilty, even though she had no conscious knowledge then of the dreams.

Her six years of infertility ended when she could tell me about the "homosexual experience" which had popped into her mind during each of the 16 office visits. She was relieved to know that such explorations were common and had nothing to do with homosexuality.

Her third pregnancy was complicated by many fears, many recognized disturbing dreams, and three unrecognized dreams, each of which produced hemorrhage and uterine contractions. The first serious threat occurred at 11:45 p.m. during her seventh month. She awakened from deep sleep with profuse bleeding. During the telephone call her fingers denied there had been a disturbing dream. It was not until I changed the question to "Has there been any disturbing thought?" that the answer was, "I do not want to answer that question." She indicated a desire to be admitted to the hospital and promptly stopped bleeding as she got ready to leave.

At office examination one month later her blood pressure was 160/94 and she had gained three-and-one-half pounds since the week before. Dreams were searched, and again her unconscious mind refused to reveal the content of a repeated and very disturbing set of "thoughts." A ten-year-old child with congenitally absent hands had been visiting with her since the day her blood pressure elevated and she had begun to develop edema. The dreams, however, continued to escape detection until the third day, when I insisted that her husband take a week off and stay with her in a motel near my office. I did not want her in the hospital where nurses and house officers might increase her apprehension with their frequent checking of her blood pressure. She was more than five weeks from her expected due date, and I was afraid of being forced to terminate the pregnancy with a premature baby delivered by Cesarean section.

On this third day, while her husband was out getting a lunch tray, she told me she had discovered the reason for her anxiety· and wanted to tell me before her husband returned. Her boss, a good friend of the family, had often dropped by her house for a cup of coffee. She knew he had been much attracted to her physically, but had kept him at a distance until one night during a party at the house of friends he got her into a room and very nearly had intercourse with her. She had missed her next period, and with her hypersensitive conscience had worried about whether the boss could be the father of her child. Her fears and consequent dreams had been intensified by the boss's repeated joking question, "Well, how's my baby getting along?"

We agreed to keep this information to ourselves providing she got her blood pressure down and would let this baby have the best possible blood supply. Pressure came down from the high of 156/110 with 3.8 gm. of albumen per liter of urine to 138/92. She was unable to rid her urine of albumen, but she lost her edema with the help of diuretics and continued bed rest at home until a gush of blood awakened her at 3:30 a.m., four weeks from her due date. Again it was not a dream. She had noticed some blood on a handkerchief when she blew her nose before going to bed and said to her husband, "Wouldn't it be nice if I hemorrhaged now and Dr. Cheek had to take the baby?" Bleeding stopped after uncovering the thought of hemorrhaging and my having to deliver a baby that was too small.

Fortunately the date of her last menstrual period had been incorrect. When another repressed "thought" occurred about the baby not looking like her husband, her blood pressure shot up and she had facial edema on awakening. She had a bloody show and some cramps at 8:30 a.m. Her blood pressure was 150/110. Her fibrinogen level was normal. I ruptured the membranes and she delivered a six-pound-one-ounce healthy girl three hours and 15 minutes later. She let out a whoop of glee when she saw her husband's markings—a light streak of hair over the occiput.

Her second full-term pregnancy was complicated by uterine bleeding at eight months for which she was admitted, at her request, to the hospital. Investigation revealed that the moans of her daughter during a nightmare had stimulated a fear reaction that the child, who had been exposed to chicken pox, might become ill. There was a loss of 75 cc. of blood as she turned to go to the bathroom after covering her daughter. She had gone to bed the night before with some feelings of apprehension but without knowing the cause. When asked to orient back to the time of falling asleep, she found herself concerned because I would be away at a convention for a few days. She lost her fears when she recognized them, and a month later delivered a normal male weighing six pounds three ounces. Her blood pressure rose briefly, but there was no albuminuria.

Complications of pregnancy are not always directly caused by dreams. Great emotional stress or great physical trauma from infection or injuries can certainly cause intravascular clotting, followed by rebound fibrinolytic-type bleeding and expulsive contractions of the uterus. There is one constant feature of retrograde explorations of sequences leading to complications responsible for premature labor. Thoughts and dreams during natural sleep may greatly exaggerate the impact of daytime experiences and, with vulnerable women, may be the major factor in causing fetal death through premature delivery. My premature rate has dropped from 6.5% to 2.8% since paying attention to the nocturnal fears of pregnant women.

RESEARCH

Ideodynamic Eyelid Signaling and Lucid Dreaming: Research Projects 52 & 53

The new experimental approaches to lucid dreaming utilize an important component of ideodynamic signaling that involves the use of eye movements. LeBerge describes the process by which he discovered how to do this as follows (1985, pp. 62–63):

> From the very beginning, I had been interested in the possibility, first raised by Charles Tart, of communication from the lucid dream to the outside world, *while* the dream was happening. The problem was, since most of the dreamer's body is paralyzed during REM sleep, how could the dreamer send such a message? What might the lucid dreamer be able to do within the dream that could be observed or measured by scientists? A plan suggested itself to me. There is one obvious exception to this muscular paralysis, since eye movements are in no way inhibited during REM sleep. After all, it is the occurence of rapid eye movements that gives this stage of sleep its name.
>
> Earlier dream studies had shown that there is sometimes a precise correspondence between the direction of dreamers' observable eye movements and the direction they are looking in their dreams. In one remarkable example, a subject was awakened from REM sleep after making a series of about two dozen regular horizontal eye movements. He reported that in his dream he had been watching a Ping-Pong game, and just before being awakened he had been following a long volley with his dream gaze.
>
> I knew that lucid dreamers could freely look in any direction they wished while in a lucid dream, because I had done this myself. It occurred to me that by moving my (dream) eyes in a reconizable pattern, I might be able to send a signal to the outside world when I was having a

lucid dream. I tried this out in the first lucid dream that I recorded: I moved my dream gaze up, down, up, down, up, to the count of five. As far as I knew at the time, this was the first signal deliberately transmitted from the dream world.

LaBerge's research program into the ability of lucid dreamers to influence their own psychobiological processes (anxiety, sexuality, respiration, etc.) depends on this eyelid method of ideodynamic signaling. The success of this approach in demonstrating real mind-body effects that can contribute to psychosomatic illness (Levitan, 1981) or health via dreams suggests that it may be useful in psychotherapy.

Project 52   Devise an experimental study to compare the relative merits of ideodynamic eyelid and finger signaling. The following issues might be explored: Which type of ideodynamic signaling is easier for patients to learn and use? Does either lead to deeper states of therapeutic hypnosis on objective scales?

Project 53   We have observed that eyelid movements sometimes spontaneously accompany finger signaling. What is the significance of such accompaniment for the subjective experience of the patient? Are they using imagery more than other? Do eyelid movements spontaneously occur more often when finger signaling is used to scan sleep and dreams (Box 27, p. 000)? Can the spontaneous occurrence of eyelid movements be used as a criterion for validating the significance of ideomotor finger signaling?

Psychobiological Distress in Dreams: Cardiac Emergencies: Research Projects 54–57

The experimental study of the effects of psychobiological stress in dreams can be explored with a standardized ideodynamic approach using either eyelid or finger signaling. Well-trained therapists in a medical setting would be required to carry out such investigations. An excellent and easily available research group might consist of patients who have experienced cardiac emergencies. Why should so many of these patients experience their cardiac emergency during sleep when the work load on their hearts is presumably minimal?

Research this problem with patients who have had a coronary spasm or a demonstrated infarct that began during the night and awakened them with the symptoms of pain, weakness, shortness of breath. It is possible that troubled dreams during sleep can constrict coronary arteries or lead to localized occlusive coagulation in coronary veins or terminal arteries. Blockade of circulation may lead to fatal arrhythmias or infarction, or death of muscle cells. Most coronary emergencies occur during the day. We need to know more about those that first occur at night while the patient is asleep.

In either case, patients usually survive an initial crisis, and we need to know more about what happens to their sleep patterns at night after recovery.

Nurses in coronary care units have noted telemetric signs of arrhythmias while a patient is asleep. When they awaken the patient, they have had reports that sleep was troubled *before* the electrocardiogram showed something had gone wrong.

Research is now needed to answer the following questions:

Project 54 In what percentage of patients admitted with a diagnosis of coronary occlusion did the first symptoms awaken the patient from sleep at night or during a daytime nap? Can we demonstrate with ideodynamic signaling that dreams have caused coronary attacks?

Project 55 Does alarm caused by the initial cardiac crisis set the stage for subsequent, potentially dangerous dreams after recovery? Does ideodynamic signaling indicate that this is a matter of importance with a significant number of patients?

Project 56 Using ideodynamic signaling, check the nighttime sleep of patients during recovery in coronary care units to see if they do or do not have recurring troubled dreams. Show patients on coronary care units how to use hypnosis for relaxation and symptom control. Can this improve their care?

Project 57 Teach cardiac patients how to search their previous night of sleep by using ideodynamic signaling, and how to awaken immediately if the threatening sleep pattern occurs. Can we thereby avoid a recurrence of a cardiac emergency?

Birth Experience and the Construction of Reality

THEORY

We have reserved the presentation of Cheek's papers on the birth experience to almost last in this volume, because his contributions here are, frankly, the most speculative. But then, as we have seen in each of the previous sections, Cheek's ideas always seemed speculative and "beyond the pale" of conventional medicine and psychology when they were first proposed. We have seen how controlled experimental studies and the theories based upon them have usually caught up with Cheek's clinical findings about a generation after he first proposed them. In this section, too, we will explore how recent research might be developing verifiable strategies for assessing Cheek's work in another highly controversial area of hypnotic investigation: age regression and the significance of the birth experience for memory and construction of psychological reality.

Belief in the validity of the possibility of age regression is one of the major areas of discrepancy between clinicians and experimentalists in hypnosis. Clinicians dealing with real patients highly motivated to resolve emotional issues (encoded, as we have seen, in state-dependent memory, learning, and behavior systems) have frequently cited anecdotal cases in which it seems apparent that patients can assess and experience earlier age levels. Researchers in academic environments, on the other hand, usually study normal students who know they are participating in an experiment and are not highly motivated by their real problems to age regress (hence, there usually is no accessing and experiencing of personal and state-dependent memory, learning and behavior systems). Such subjects dutifully try to follow the hypnotic suggestions but rarely provide valid evidence that they experience a genuine age regression, even when they role-play it convincingly to the casual observer (Sarbin & Coe, 1972; Silverman & Retzlaff, 1986).

In the papers of this section, Cheek pushes clinical observations of age regression to what would seem to be the ultimate: the birth experience itself, and even the prenatal life of the fetus. He uses his typical ideodynamic tri-level approach of facilitating responsiveness on the physiological, ideo-

411

motor, and verbal levels. But what sense can there be in an adult patient verbalizing vividly about experiences in the womb before there was any knowledge of language? Surely such "memories" must be confabulations.

The use of the pejorative word *confabulations*, of course, immediately prejudices the situation. If we use a more neutral word, such as *construction*, the above statement would become "surely such 'memories' must be constructions." But this is the currently developing view of the essential nature of *all* memory, learning, and behavior: They are all creative constructions (Bruner, 1986). Memory is not some sort of literal photocopy or auditory recording of an objective reality that exists "out there" independently of our constructing minds (Watzlawick, 1984). We are actually re-creating our memory each time we use it.

One of Cheek's most original papers in this section, "Sequential Head and Shoulder Movements Appearing With Age Regression in Hypnosis to Birth," is a profound demonstration of this constructivist approach to understanding the mind-body in sickness and health. After having delivered hundreds of babies, Cheek made the apparently incredible observation that the characteristic head and shoulder movement of the birth process could be unknowingly reproduced by adults when they were asked to ideodynamically review their birth process in hypnosis. His subjects were usually not aware they were reproducing their birth movements. Cheek believes that they were reproducing nonverbal patterns of procedural "memory" behavior.

Farfetched as this notion may seem, it is at least conceivable that some people are imprinted with the highly restricted patterns of physical movements at their births. A recent review of the developmental plasticity of the emotional-memory-behavioral patterns associated with the limbic system suggests how this may be possible. Livingston describes it as follows (1978, p. 19):

> The rapid postnatal development of the limbic system in many mammalian and nonmammalian forms may contribute to *the remarkable capacity of young animals to store, lastingly, idiosyncratic patterns of perception, judgement, and behavior, especially social behavior. This is what ethologists—for want of a word for superfast, superefficient learning—call imprinting.* The attachment of young to real or foster parents, to a varied and peculiar environment, and in many forms to a culture, including in humans the facile initial acquisition of a language, is considered to represent an experiential linkage between limbic development and its capacity to attach values to biologically significant experiences. The role of limbic mechanisms in learning provides an infantile endowment for all brain systems according to any reinforced experiences. This means, by definition, that any biologically meaningful experience will tend to be stored throughout all brain systems engaged in that particular experience. There it will be available for immediate or later access. This

generalized laying down of memory stores is thought to be critically served or advantaged by limbic mechanisms. (Italics added)

Evidence consistent with this possibility is the recent interesting finding that ACTH (which is released during the stress of the birth process) is one of the information substances that is responsible for mediating imprinting in newly hatched ducklings (Martin, 1978; Stewart, 1985). This, in turn, means that imprinting can be conceptualized as a form of state-dependent memory, learning, and behavior in our hypothesized experiential "filter" (see Figure 9), modulating all limbic-hypothalamic-pituitary processes of mind-body communication. Given that there is much evidence that hypnosis leads to spontaneous states of partial age regression, it is at least theoretically possible that Cheek's ideomotor methods are capable of accessing the behavioral imprints of the birth experience. It is simply an empirical question of doing the necessary well-controlled experimental research to determine the degree to which it is so.

Cheek, however, goes much further than this. He has patients repeat their nonverbal ideomotor birth experience a number of times (a recursive process) and when conditions seem optimal, he uses the *implied directive* with a most unusual expectation: "When you know all about what you need to know, and are able *to talk with me about it*, your 'yes' finger will lift. . . . Notice how the doctor holds you after you are born. Pay attention to the voices you hear." Many of Cheek's patients then proceed to describe all sorts of circumstances, emotions, behaviors, and *conversations* they heard at their births as if they were witnessing these with their adult levels of understanding. Most professional psychologists would say that the patients are, of course, "confabulating these memories." Cheek, however, takes these ideodynamically evoked verbal responses as being in some way isomorphic with "real memories." He believes that they can be psychobiologically accurate reports of events that really happened at birth. When these memories center about stress and trauma to a particular organ system, then that organ system is prone to manifesting a psychosomatic illness later in life when the patient is stressed (e.g., a birth with respiratory problems predisposes one to asthma; a feeding problem predisposes one to ulcers, and so forth).

What can we say of such ideodynamically reported memories of "conversations" during or immediately after birth? Is there any sense in which the newborn and perhaps even the fetus in the womb is already "constructing" a psychobiological memory that could later be reconstructed in adulthood as a "conversation"? In the discussion of research issues at the end of this section, we will explore a number of theoretical developments and lines of recent experimental data on in utero learning that have bearing on this question.

But let us first take a careful and tolerant look at the clinical observations and studies undertaken by Cheek in the following chapters.

PRACTICE

22

Sequential Head and Shoulder Movements Appearing with Age Regression in Hypnosis to Birth

The appearance of obstetrically appropriate head and shoulder movements during age regression to birth can lend support to the factual nature of impressions described by subjects after repetitive unconscious review according to methods developed by LeCron and myself (Cheek & LeCron, 1968).

I was troubled by scientific bias when I first heard Leslie LeCron in 1956 talking about the recovery of birth experience apparently related to such complaints as migraine and tension headache, persistent bronchitis, and asthma. LeCron said that his method of approach to the conviction that newborn babies are perceptive was dictated by the patients coming under his care. Abundant exploration during the past 30 years has substantiated his contentions when ideomotor questioning methods using repetitive unconscious review have been used. Occasional volunteer appearance of head and shoulder movements seemed worth studying and reporting.

LeCron would set up ideomotor responses with a Chevreul pendulum or with finger signals representing "yes," "no," and unwillingness to talk about something. Initially he was adding a symbol movement for "I don't know," but this was eventually discarded because hypnotized subjects have a tendency to use it as a polite way of getting out of work. He could ask if there were any past experience relating to the problem at hand. If there were, he would bracket the time of experience with questions such as, "Did it occur before you were 20 years old?" following along with further questions until the time of onset was located. Sometimes patients ended with birth as the time of origin. Understanding and reappraisal of the factors involved often permitted rapid and sometimes permanent relief after a single evaluation. The time taken in bracketing the time of origin mobilized hitherto amnesic information. This process probably allowed deepening of the hypnotic level, as did the mounting interest of the hypnotized subject.

In a 1959 hypnosis symposium, a nurse anesthetist helped me overcome residual belief that babies had too little central nervous system development to know about their births. The search for possible factors in successive third trimester stillbirths using the LeCron questioning method led to the subject's terrifying experience in a home breech delivery. After putting up considerable resistance to learning the cause of her terror, she finally recalled a seemingly endless period of silence and futile efforts to get her breath before she realized that she had been born. *In reviewing both fetal losses, she recognized that fetal movements had stopped within a few moments of ending a dream about this period of panic during her birth. She sensed, as have other patients with similar history of fetal death* in utero, *that her uterus had gone into a tight and prolonged contraction during the dream.* Other studies have convinced me that experiences at birth have influenced fertility and obstetrical behavior.

Initial Experiments

In the beginning I was mainly interested in learning what patients might believe had happened, regardless of its being real or fabricated. This partial open-mindedness seemed justified in that patients often felt guilty thinking they had caused great pain to their mother at birth. Obviously many of them had heard about this from mothers and relatives many years after birth, yet some had shown evidence of a fixed assumption of guilt that had seriously affected their lives. These negative attitudes would sometimes change dramatically when it was explained that mothers and their obstetricians are the cause of painful labor, that no baby should ever be made to feel at blame for being an unwilling passenger.

Verbalization of requests after setting up ideomotor responses were modeled after those found effective in exploring surgical anesthesia experiences (Cheek, 1959). They were aimed at discovering what might have been happening at the moment the first breath was drawn. The yes finger was to lift at this point, the no finger each time the baby heard someone talking in the delivery room, and the I don't want to answer finger was to lift when the baby was "warm and comfortable in the nursery."

SPONTANEOUS APPEARANCE OF POSTURAL CHANGES

Occasionally, very good subjects with active skeletal muscle responses would spontaneously turn their head, lift their face upward, or shrug a shoulder before indicating with a finger that they were taking their first breath. Sometimes they would show distress by respiratory changes, increased speed of neck pulsations, and appearance of perspiration on forehead or finger tips before signaling the moment of the first breath.

Since I was an obstetrician, I naturally wondered if the postural changes might reflect a conforming of the head and shoulders to the pelvic planes of greatest diameter, and whether or not the physiological changes might relate to hearing a mother in distress. *It also seemed possible that the unborn baby might be reacting to maternal epinephrine crossing the placenta to give the baby a chemical fear response.* A study was begun with obstetrically naive subjects and more care given to the orientation to the beginning of labor rather than the end. The method has proven useful, and the results with the first ten subjects studied will be presented along with a discussion of criteria and findings based on more than 17 years of investigations into these matters.

Three of the first ten subjects were headache sufferers; two were asthma patients. All five had indicated conviction that their trouble originated at birth. The remaining five included three private patients with gynecological problems, and two psychology students who had no complaints but were members of my class at the California School of Professional Psychology in San Francisco.

MECHANISM OF NORMAL VAGINAL DELIVERY

For those not familiar with the fetal postural changes during vaginal delivery, a brief summary will be given here for so-called *right occiput anterior* presentation (ROA). The mechanisms for left occiput anterior would require only the transposition of head and shoulder movements. "Head first" or occiput anterior is the most common type of vaginal delivery at or near term. Because of the configuration of the fetal head and the ability of the cranial bones to overlap, the majority of deliveries take place in the following steps for initial ROA mechanism. Figure 19 juxtaposes the illustrations of a baby experiencing ROA delivery with photographs of a young woman reliving her own ROA birth.

1. The head, with its saggital plane at right angles to the plane of the shoulders, usually has entered the pelvis by the beginning of labor. The head is flexed slightly toward the chest permitting the occiput, or crown of the head, to form a dilating wedge for the cervix of the uterus. At this point, the fetal back will be facing the mother's right abdomen.

2. As descent occurs into the pelvis during labor, the fetal head turns as though looking toward its right shoulder. This permits the greatest diameter of the head to enter the greatest anterior-posterior diameter of the lower pelvis. In relation to the mother, its face is looking directly at her sacrum. Meanwhile the fetal shoulders are entering the pelvis in one of the two diagonal greatest diameters. In ROA presentation, the shoulders come down in the diagonal, which runs from the right side of the maternal sacrum to the midpoint of the left pelvic inlet. The fetal back is still facing her right side of the abdomen.

3. On approaching delivery, the curve of the sacrum and coccyx, like a schoolyard slide, force the fetal head to extend or look upward. At the moment of delivery, the crown of the head is presenting anteriorly beneath the pubic symphasis and the face is toward the coccyx.

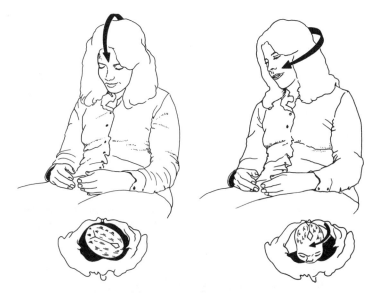

1/ The patient is in a medium trance, oriented to the feelings she is experiencing just before birth. Her head begins to bend forward in its normal right-angle relation to the plane of the shoulders.

2/ The stage of internal rotation to accommodate to the greater diameter of the outlet of the pelvis. Head passing through the outlet. The baby's back is on the mother's right side.

3/ Her head has now delivered and is returning to its right-angle relation to the plane of the shoulders, known as "restitution" or "external rotation." The obstetrician watches for this and furthers the turn to allow the shoulders to enter the anterior-posterior greater diameter.

4/ The obstetrician pulls downward to lock the anterior (left) shoulder under the symphysis pubis before lifting upward to deliver the right arm over the perineum.

Figure 19: Head and shoulder movements in the ideodynamic reliving of the birth experience.

Restitution, the return of the head to its normal right angle relation to the plane of its shoulders, now occurs after the head is completely delivered. In ROA mechanism the rotation would make the baby turn as though looking toward its left shoulder. The obstetrician looks for this rotation to tell him that the back is on the maternal right. He then accentuates the rotation by continuing the head rotation a little beyond its normal relation to the back.

5. This accentuated head rotation brings the back toward the maternal right flank to allow the shoulders to conform to the anterior-posterior greatest diameter of the outlet.

6. With small babies, the rest of the delivery is completed with simultaneous escape of both shoulders. When the fetus is over six pounds in weight, however, the obstetrician will pull down on the head, cocking it toward the fetal right shoulder. This brings the left (anterior) shoulder down and locks it under the symphasis of the pubis. Now as the obstetrician lifts up on the head, the right (posterior) shoulder will be delivered. When babies are in good condition, the right arm may be flexed with the hand near the face. In this case, the wrist is grasped and the arm is gently delivered. If both arms are at the sides, the right arm (lower arm) will fall free as the delivery is completed.

Not all the movements will appear during the time usually available for a review of labor and delivery. Sometimes the delivery is assisted by application of what is referred to as "outlet forceps." The subject may volunteer information that "something hard and cold is being placed alongside my face."

In summary, look for the most easily recalled changes in position:

For Right Occiput Anterior (ROA):
1. extension of the head (just before delivery);
2. rotation of the head, looking toward the left shoulder;
3. shrugging of the right shoulder to indicate that arm is being delivered first (small babies will shrug both shoulders).

For Left Occiput Anterior (LOA):
1. extension of the head;
2. rotation of the head, looking toward the right shoulder;
3. shrugging of the left shoulder (small babies will shrug both shoulders).

More than 80% of deliveries occur in one of these positions. More complicated deliveries can be reviewed by obstetricians who might be interested. Only rarely have I been able to evoke reports on subjective attitudes of babies that are delivered by Cesarean section. These have only come from babies whose mothers were in labor before the operations were performed. One could speculate that there is not enough stimulation to make the impressions memorable. This might be the reason babies delivered by Cesarean section before labor have a higher incidence of dangerous circulatory and respiratory system complications.

VERBALIZATION FOR OBTAINING INFORMATION ABOUT BIRTH

Finger signals are set up by either assigning fingers to represent yes, no, and I don't want to answer, or by asking subjects to keep repeating the words to themselves until "some finger lifts by itself." Subjects are asked not to lift any fingers purposefully.

Selection of the signals is interesting enough to allow subjects an easy access to a light hypnotic state without need for a formal induction. The trance is deepened when the suggestions in Box 28 are given, probably because subjects do not expect the therapist to display this form of apparent insanity.

Discussion

From my explorations of surgical anesthesia memories since 1957, it has been apparent that memory recall of deeply repressed information follows a natural sequence. The first indication that something meaningful is being recalled comes from the very deep zone of central nervous system reaction to a sensory stimulus involving physiological adaptations. Perspiration and increased respiratory and heart rate are the reflections *before* there is an ideomotor finger signal to show recognition of the stress. The more conscious horizon of thinking that can translate a feeling into speech is the last to get the message. This is a triad of greatest importance when it comes to trusting validity of final verbalization.

If the therapist asks for verbal information as soon as the finger indicates arrival at an important episode, he will greatly delay learning about it. Subjects may awaken from hypnosis and lose the memory, or they may shake their heads and say that nothing is coming to them. Repetition of the review at the ideomotor level of reaction mobilizes the information and allows eventual elevation to talking levels of thought.

Experience with surgical and birth experiences which subjects block on revealing or refuse to elevate after a show of physiological distress has shown that these are the most important memories to review and eliminate as sources of subsequent physiological disability. It is, therefore, highly important for a therapist to know ways in which the resistance can be depotentiated without further threatening the subject.

HANDLING OF RESISTANCE

The elevation to more superficial verbal levels of thought takes a variable time and depends very much on the intensity of the threat. At first it may seem immense but it may turn out to be a very slight one, perhaps a misun-

---

BOX 28: ACCESSING BIRTH IMPRINTING EXPERIENCES

1. *Accessing labor and birth experience*
   "Please orient your inner mind back to the moments before you are born. Babies are able to hear sounds transmitted through the mother's abdominal wall and the fluid in the uterus for several weeks before birth. Pay attention to the sounds as well as to your feelings during labor. Notice how your head feels, whether it wants to move in any direction. When you are at the moment you feel the pressure of labor is starting, your yes finger will lift. Each time you feel or hear something important, your no finger will lift. When you know you are outside breathing for the first time, your I don't want to answer finger will lift."

2. *Reexperiencing and reviewing labor and birth events*
   At first there may be no head movements. If they do occur, their type and sequence are noted. After the appropriate finger signals occur (usually within a minute of starting the request), the suggestion is given:
   "Please go over the entire labor again. Each time you go over it, you will be learning more useful things. You need not feel uncomfortable. You can stop any time you wish, but I would like to have you know as much as possible about your reactions and your feelings. As soon as you know your head is outside, notice which shoulder and arm is born first. You can just lift the shoulder that feels it is being born first."

3. *Verbalizing labor and birth experience*
   A request is made for further review sequences depending on whether or not the head movements occur. During the third review, the subject is usually in a very deep hypnotic state and in possession of a wealth of information that was not at first available. This accumulation of material occurs very rapidly when the therapist delays asking for verbal reporting. This suggestion can usually be made during the third review sequence:
   "When you know all about what you need to know and are able to talk with me about it, your yes finger will lift. I will ask then if it is all right to tell me about it. Please notice if you have any assistance in being born. Notice whatever comes in contact with your head or face. Notice also whether your mother is awake or asleep at the time you are born. Notice how the doctor holds you after you are born. Pay attention to the voices you hear."

derstanding of a nonthreatening remark. At the time of its beginning, however, it will always exert a suppressive effect on information in proportion to the understood gravity at the ideomotor level of thought.

It seems reasonable to infer that partial age regression and revivification occur at the ideomotor level of response even though the subject is lightly hypnotized and still may be remembering things from the time orientation of the interview when asked to talk. This dichotomy — whole and part regression — is of value. There is little value in having a subject relive experience just as it occurs, reacting with narrow understandings of an early age. Great therapeutic advantage results from experiencing the full thrust of some event that has imprinted unfavorable patterns of reaction to environment, experiencing the origin at a physiological and ideomotor level of awareness, and then subjecting it to more mature perspective at a talking level of nearly conscious understanding. *Repeatedly LeCron and I have seen spontaneous reorganizations of reaction made by the subject without need for explanation or therapeutic effort from the therapist beyond being present in a setting of optimism.* *

An initial refusal to bring information upward for discussion as shown by a no or I don't want to answer signal may be changed in a few seconds to willingness when the question is rephrased, **"Will it be all right for you to know about this up here at the time we are talking together?"**

Sometimes there will be refusal to know about it at the time of interview but acceptance when the therapist asks if it might be all right next year or several years from now. When this is found acceptable, subjects can be asked to orient forward to that time, to know about it and decide whether or not to discuss it with their therapist then. This pseudo-orientation in time, used extensively by Milton Erickson, is very helpful and can be rapidly accomplished at an ideomotor level of thinking.

The hypnotized subject always will be looking for ways to avoid reviewing unpleasant experiences. Motivations for continuing with the task must be supplied by the therapist. It may be necessary to bring friends and loved ones into the questioning. For example, a patient may be willing to live through the birth experience that set the pattern for disabling headaches if it is asked whether or not cure of the headaches might benefit a husband, son, or daughter. While the fingers are answering the questions, a reorganization of attitude is taking place at a near-cortical level of reaction.

Conclusions

In the ten consecutive explorations directed toward determining if obstetrically appropriate sequential head and shoulder movements occurred during age regression in light hypnosis, such movements presented in every case.

---

*See Rossi, 1986d, for a theoretical rationale for the principle, *every access is a reframe.*

None of the subjects had any knowledge of the mechanisms involved in vaginal, head-first delivery.

It is suggested that discovery of these ideomotor reflections of memory for the birth experience is of more than esoteric value, and that other investigators will derive immense therapeutic dividends when they give their patients a chance to reassess the origins of misplaced guilt and disabling imprinted reactions to environmental stimuli. Obstetricians will find themselves changing their handling of obstetrical patients and giving much more care to the end of delivering happy and comfortable babies in a setting of immediate acceptance.

23

Maladjustment Patterns Apparently Related to Imprinting at Birth

There is no single path to our understanding and correction of disease origins. We keep moving in our medical attitudes. Even the computer cannot diminish the humility we are forced to maintain as we consider various fancies of bygone years, the amputations of breasts to mitigate the effects of eclampsia, the marching of tuberculous patients up mountains to enlarge their hearts, the enthusiasm on finding "laudable pus" in a surgical incision.

I (DBC) offer the following with full respect for the possibility that the ideas here presented may now seem or will eventually be as wrong as these examples of our past ignorance. It has long been my belief that the basic factors in healing include willingness on the part of a sick person and optimism in the end result as communicated by the "healer." Sometimes the optimism springs from within in rebellion to depressing medical opinion, and the healer is the patient. Most of the time, the potentiating forces for healing come from faith shown by the doctor either in a mode of treatment or in the deep unconscious drive for survival that can be released by a doctor who recognizes this force.

The matter of disturbed response to environmental stimuli has been my concern since interning in obstetrics at Johns Hopkins Hospital in 1942. There I witnessed an exsanguinating hemorrhage at delivery of a red-headed Irish woman who had been prepared for this trouble by our concern over her history of a "bleeding tendency." Subsequently I learned that bleeding tendencies are created by the alarms of doctors and can be prevented or terminated in midstream by attendants who believe in the capacity of people to conserve blood with delivery or injury.

After joining the panel of instructors in hypnosis symposiums formed by Leslie M. LeCron in September 1956, I learned that unconscious symbol movements of a Chevreul pendulum could indicate information about the beginnings of an illness (LeCron 1954). This could occur while the patient was consciously wondering why the pendulum was apparently swinging to give answers that were not expected. Fascination with the ideomotor responses permitted rapid entrance of the subject into hypnosis, if there were a need. If this happened, LeCron switched to using unconscious movements of designated fingers for the answers yes, no, and I don't want to answer.

LeCron was of the opinion that most physical illnesses stemmed from some sort of initial preparation associated with a dramatic aura or with great emotional stress. His "20 questions" method of approach to a problem would go something like this:

Q. **Does the inner part of your mind feel your trouble came from some past experience?**

A. Yes [given by the pendulum].

Q. **Was this before you were 20 years old?**

A. Yes.

Q. **Was it before you were 10 years old?**

The questions and affirmative answers would continue until the answer was a no. Knowing that hypnotized people are economical in energy output and will try to stop an inquisitor from going too close to a troublesome event, LeCron would then ask, **"Is there a deeper part of your mind that knows about something earlier than this age?"**

Sometimes it would not be necessary to narrow the site of origin beyond the initial bracketing. The patient might suddenly look surprised, put the pendulum down, and say something like, "I know what it was!" Then he would explain some early life experience. When he was finished LeCron would ask, **"Is there some event before this that might have prepared the way for your trouble to begin?"** Frequently, this revealed an otherwise suppressed birth experience.

This apparent nagging of the hypnotized subject into admitting something earlier bothered me very much at first. My training from the authorities on neurological development made the idea of a birth trauma unacceptable. I already knew from prior biased explorations with hypnosis that patients under general anesthesia could not hear or be troubled by noises in the operating room. LeCron and Milton Erickson had both told me they knew that anesthetized patients can hear and be harmfully affected, but one was a psychologist and the other a psychiatrist. They seemed pretty bold to make such ridiculous assertions.

At a symposium in Houston in October 1957, a hypnotized doctor proved to me that he had heard his surgeons talking (1959). Two months later during a cruise back from a workshop in Honolulu, LeCron was investigating the origins of severe headache with one member of our group. In the course of pursuing the "past event" that might have some bearing on the headache, the physician recalled a severe eye infection caused by some dirt accidentally kicked into his eye by playmates. When asked if there might be some earlier related event, he went into a deep trance and described his very difficult delivery. He could hear his mother's cries, and in addition to feeling very nervous, he was aware also of head pain as forceps were being applied to his head. The blades were not applied to the sides of his face, as is usual with a low forceps delivery, but were misplaced as might have been the case with a high forceps delivery. One blade pressed very hard just above the eye that had later been infected; the other blade pressed against his occiput.

LeCron now asked the doctor to review some of his headaches to see what connection there might be between these two events. The eye infection was not important beyond the fact that this eye, perhaps, had a heightened vulnerability to injury or infection. What was immediately clear was that headaches always occurred when this very conscientious doctor became worried about a patient or felt upset over some personal trouble. *It seemed that this might be a conditioned type of response associating his head pain at birth with the influence of his mother's adrenal hormones passing through the placenta into his circulation.*

Any doubts I had about the validity of traumatic birth memory were dispersed on our arrival at San Pedro. The physician was met at the dock by his mother. She verified the difficulty of his birth and the fact that high forceps had been applied in an effort to preserve his life. *That the search was productive was established by the doctor's subsequent relief from headaches. When one would start at a time of pressure, he would recognize the cause and stop the headache.* Further investigations by LeCron and myself established, to our satisfaction, that migraine and ordinary tension headaches are related to pain experienced by the baby at birth in the majority of instances. Box 29 provides an ideodynamic approach to transforming a symptom into a signal.

When we observed that a handclasp with interdigitated fingers revealed primal handedness in relation to which thumb was uppermost, there was an interesting byproduct of research that seemed to warrant mention. In testing more than 2,000 individuals in groups ranging from 50 to 500 people, we found that an average of 50% would find their left thumb uppermost. Of these, roughly 7% remained left-handed. The remaining 43% were functionally right handed and usually did not know when they had converted. About 1% found their right thumb uppermost but were functionally left-handed. When they were age-regressed to about six months of age, I found a consistent correlation between the thumb-uppermost test and the hand that wants to reach out for a coveted object when the patient is remembering the child sitting up and is able to use either hand in grasping. This is a matter needing careful research with consideration of factors we could not study. The feature of interest to me was that patients with true migraine or one-sided headache often change sides. When reliving a headache, they indicate awareness of unconscious pain on the consciously painless side. Better than 90% of patients I have studied have been converted left-han-

---

BOX 29: TRANSFORMING A SYMPTOM INTO A SIGNAL

1. *Scaling to transform symptoms into signals*
   a. **"On a scale of 1 to 100, where 100 is the worst, what number expresses the degree to which you are experiencing that symptom right now?"**
   b. **"Your yes finger can lift when you recognize that symptom intensity is actually a signal of just how strong another deeper part of you needs to be recognized and understood right now."**

2. *Accessing and inquiry into symptom meaning*
   a. **"When your inner mind (creative unconscious, etc.) is ready to help you access the deeper meanings of your symptoms, you'll find yourself getting quiet and comfortable with your eyes eventually closing."** [Pause]
   b. **"Your yes finger can lift when you review the original sources of that symptom [pause], you can ask your symptom what it is saying to you [pause], you can discuss with your symptom what changes are needed in your life."**

3. *Ratifying the significance and value of new meaning*
   a. **"How will you now use your symptom as an important signal?"** [The significance of whatever new meanings come up usually can be recognized intuitively by the subject. New meaning is invariably accompanied by affects (tears, enthusiasm, thankfulness). A rescaling of symptom intensity at this time will usually ratify the value of this form of inner work with a lower number.]
   b. **"When your inner mind knows it can cooperate with your consciousness in resolving that problem, your yes finger will lift."**

---

ders. The obvious possibility here might be that converted left-handers are more vulnerable to insult and might be more sensitive to laterality than a child maintaining its original laterality.

Another possible area for research would be the significance of early conversion from left- to right-handedness in terms of learning ability. Converted males seem to have a difficulty with spelling and reading that I have not found in females, probably because they are more readily able in grade school to make the adjustment in recognizing differences between printed *b* and *d*, *p* and *q*, *m* and *w*. Freeway intersection dividers frequently attest to confusions some drivers experience on suddenly being told a direction to follow at the last moment. At a time of crisis, there is spontaneous regression to the earlier dominant handedness.

Search for earlier and earlier experiences relating to maladjustment problems often leads to birth as the causal stimulus in the following classes of problems.

Birth Sources of Various Disorders

Here there is a frequent history of a painful and difficult delivery for the mother. She may be so heavily drugged that she is unable to speak to the baby. The baby's assumed responsibility for maternal difficulty in labor may be immediate, but usually is accumulated later from hearsay or when punished by mother for misdeeds. There is a tremendous feeling of rejection that occurs when a newborn baby is not able to hear its mother talk. This is variously described as "lost," "I feel confused," "everything seems dead."

In every instance of gastrointestinal pathology that I have explored, the mother has either been unwilling or unable to nurse her baby at her breast. This seems to be the steering factor that makes the gastrointestinal tract vulnerable to subsequent emotional stress effects.

CASE EXAMPLE: GASTRIC ULCER

A physician who was consciously aware of a deepseated resentment toward all women had suffered from gastrointestinal upsets since childhood. He was operated upon for gastric ulcer shortly after learning that his wife was interested in another man. Without any request to do so, he spontaneously regressed to his premature birth on a farm. His mother was very ill during the first weeks of his life and was unable to nurse him. He felt not only very hungry during this time, but resentful of the fact that his grandmother was the one trying to get him to nurse a bottle. Although there were many demonstrations of love when his mother was able to care for him, he refused to believe her sincerity. During his adult life he recognized his need to attract pretty women, but he could not allow himself any firm attachment to a woman he believed could be loving and loyal to him. It was better not to reach out for something lest he be hurt again.

Box 30 summarizes an ideodynamic approach to gastrointestinal disorders.

BREATHING PROBLEMS

The feeling of physiological alarm involving a sense of not getting enough air, combined with a feeling of being responsible for maternal difficulty, are augmented when the mother has been put to sleep for the actual delivery. A woman who has been worried about the outcome of her pregnancy will mobilize all her fears if she is rendered unconscious before she has had a chance to see her baby. *Her catecholamines profoundly affect the baby.*

BOX 30: GASTROINTESTINAL DISORDERS

1. *Accessing source of problem*
   a. "Orient time horizon before birth when your body is totally comfortable. You are warm, well-nourished, protected. When you are there, your yes finger will lift."
   b. "Now come forward in time to the first moment food was important in some way. When you are there, your yes finger will lift."

2. *Therapeutic reframing*
   a. "Now come forward in time to the first moment your symptoms begin. When you are there, your yes finger will lift. Pay attention to what is happening and what happens in your body. This is the original model for what has troubled you. When you know the problem, you can do something about it."
   b. "Shift back in time to the most recent trouble you have had. When you are there, your yes finger will lift. Notice whether you are awake or asleep." [Encourage the patient to reexperience that moment. If asleep, get the dream or thought sequence that triggers the symptom.]
   c. Transform the symptom into a signal, as in Box 29.

3. *Ratifying therapeutic gain*
   a. Get a commitment on a future date of complete freedom from symptoms. A hallucinated date on an imaginary blackboard tells you that the patient is willing and ready for change and confidence.
   b. Follow-up with weekly review and checking to rule out unrecognized negative trigger experiences.

Long ago, Joseph DeLee pointed out that general anesthesia for delivery of a baby carries the highest morbidity and morality for both mother and baby. I am sure the reason relates to the emotional stress added to the physical pain that is always greatest when a mother has been unhappily pregnant or has had fears that her child will be abnormal.

*Rehearsal of the original stress, coupled with explanations about the right of babies to be born with a feeling of freedom from guilt, are very helpful in the corrective training program.**

---

*This is an unusually clear statement of Cheek's essential approach of accessing a stress-encoded state-dependent problem and reframing it for "corrective training."

CASE EXAMPLE: SEVERE ANGINA PECTORIS OF THREE MONTHS' DURATION

An executive for a large producer of farm seed sat next to me on a flight from Omaha to Denver. He announced to the stewardess that he could not eat the cheese sandwich because he was on special medicine for his heart. He had looked uncomfortable and pale as he got into his seat. Shortly after the sandwich exchange, the pilot announced that the weather in Denver was bad and we would have to hold a while. I learned that this gentleman was on his way to tell a subordinate that his field of sales activity would have to be shared with another man because results had not been up to expectations. He was troubled over the way this man would take the news. Chest pain with radiation down his left arm had been getting worse since he had been out of bed that morning.

Although I do not usually hypnotize people on airplane trips, this seemed an appropriate moment to do so, particularly after the gentleman had reported to me that his cardiologist had found nothing wrong with his heart but had prophesied that he would be dead within six months. I prepared the way by saying I had had the opportunity of working one time with a man who had been discharged from the navy as a cardiac cripple and was confined to his house until a friend brought him to a course we were giving in Carmel. After learning that a "silly" early life experience was a reason for his heart trouble, this man had been hiking several miles a day and was free of angina three years later when I met him at a wedding.

I showed my plane mate how to get his fingers moving to answer questions, and then asked if he might be using the chest pain in some way to punish himself or someone else. He was surprised that self-punishment was involved, that it involved concern over hurting other people, and that the origin of the angina was long before he was consciously aware of the chest pain and dyspnea. The real symptoms began a short time after his mother had died but the conditioning for this was his birth. He could feel the tight constriction of his chest before he was born. He could hear the screams and protestations of his mother. There was the typical hierarchy of response as he relived this event giving signals of beginning labor, hearing voices, and ending with the comfort of a warm blanket after birth. First he began breathing more rapidly, neck pulsations became faster, and perspiration appeared on the fingertips of the designated fingers. *The physiological expression of stress came before the finger signals and both occurred before he was able to tell me what he was recalling.*

He observed that the feeling he had with his recently acquired angina was exactly the same feeling he had experienced during the birth, and that it had become sharper when he could hear his mother crying out. After coming out of hypnosis, he recalled that his mother had always been an emotional and very verbal person. I asked his fingers to answer the question,

"Would you agree that a mother's trouble in labor is related to her

attitudes and her choice of an obstetrician, who does not help her to have an easy labor?"

His finger answered yes. I asked,

"Wouldn't your mother want you to be well and comfortable now?"

He went right back into hypnosis. I continued,

"When you know you have wiped out every sense of guilt you had, and have recognized that you had a right to be born free of responsibility for your mother's trouble, your yes finger will lift."

The finger lifted. He then turned his angina pain on and off four times on his own initiative and was delighted with his accomplishment. As we prepared to leave the plane he said, "You know, I feel much better about my man in Denver. By dividing his work, he will be much more productive and he will probably live a lot longer. I am going to present this idea to him instead of making him feel he is being demoted."

This man wrote me a thank-you letter several weeks later and reported that all had gone well and he had been surprisingly free of discomfort.

GENITOURINARY PROBLEMS

Cases relating to this class of problems have been discussed elsewhere (Cheek & LeCron, 1968). They are mentioned to alert the investigator to the fact that *problems seeming to originate later in life may have their preparation at birth, with a long intervening latent period.* It would be logical to speculate that some genitourinary system problems in men — particularly premature ejaculation and impotence — might have similar origins. My experience as an obstetrician has been restricted in dealing with men. I have found, however, that males who believed they had caused great distress to their mothers during birth were overly apprehensive when their wives approached the time of labor. It was urgently necessary to check their guilt feeling and their identifications of their wives with their mothers.

OB-GYN PROBLEMS

Obstetrical and gynecological problems including leukorrhea, recurrent vaginitis, failure to tolerate contraceptive pills, severe acne, and repeated postcoital cystitis can frequently be traced to a sense of feeling unwanted as a female at the time of birth. It does not matter how much love and acceptance is shown later. The child will imprint on such remarks as, "We wanted a boy this time" or, "We did not select a name for a girl." Such children distrust subsequent shows of appreciation and always have trouble accepting compliments graciously.

HYPERACHIEVING

Hypnotized people often feel subjectively that their drive stems from a feeling of not amounting to much at birth, or feeling that they must prove their worth to a parent who was either unconscious or seemed disinterested in them. One such was a physician in my section of an American Society of Clinical Hypnosis workshop at an annual convention. As I was working with another physician in a demonstration of age regression, this doctor asked if a tremendous need to succeed could be traced to attitudes at birth. His pendulum swings indicated this to be a fact. He went into hypnosis and I quote his words:

"During the session I was hypnotized and regressed back to the time of birth. I could see very vividly the conditions that existed at that time. I was in the bedroom of my grandmother's house, my mother was lying there on the bed, the doctor was standing on the right side of the bed, and the nurse at the foot of the bed, to the lefthand side. She was holding me in some towels and rubbing me briskly while the doctor was wiping his hands and putting some things away. As she worked with me the doctor remarked, 'Don't waste too much time, I don't think he is worth saving.' I was a seven-and-one-half-month premie, weighing three and a half pounds, delivered at home."

In a letter the doctor explained that he had run his father's ranch at age 16. At 30 he had expanded operations into five counties. He decided to become a physician at age 40 and obtained his degree at 44, after which he practiced as a family doctor, but this was not enough. He built and organized one of the most popular ski resorts in Utah. The doctor added in his letter, "You have asked if the hypnosis has made any difference in the way that I have been living. The answer is unequivocally 'yes.' I find myself with a better understanding of why I do things. However, I have to fight to keep myself from getting too involved."

Discussion

The purpose of this report is not to itemize personal experiences or to classify disease entities according to their relation to birth experience. I want only to suggest therapeutic possibilities. After earlier approaches via the "20 questions" route, it is my custom now to explore birth memory and the subjective feelings of patients immediately when I start therapy. The reasoning here is twofold. Experience has shown that many hours can be wasted by letting patients climb around the branches of memory and getting nowhere at the top of the tree of life. *I now feel that it is possible to trust the subjective reports about birth memory if physiological and ideomotor responses appear before the subject is able to know and talk about the memory at a higher level of thought association.*

A second value is discovery that attack on a primary conditioning process may allow rapid dissipation of unfavorable responses that occurred with the initial experience. Approaching from the top of the "tree" is not as satisfactory. By that later time, more rigidly fixed patterns of disturbed behavior have developed.

24

Ideomotor Questioning Revealing an Apparently Valid Traumatic Experience Prior to Birth

There is no doubt that maternal poisoning, infection, and disability can influence growth and development of the unborn embryo and fetus (Montague, 1962). Sontag and his associates (1935, 1938, 1962) have shown that the fetus reacts physiologically to sounds transmitted through the maternal abdominal wall, and that the fetus reacts when its mother is smoking cigarettes. Is it possible that traumatic events coupled with strong emotional and physiological reactions of a mother can influence her unborn baby to the extent that physical and emotional behaviour in later life are modified?

The case to be presented suggests the possibility that a critical event during the sixth month of gestation prepared a mental set of unworthiness and expectation of rejection that lasted through 41 years of pain, guilt, and multiple surgeries.

A 35-year-old, married registered nurse was first seen in my office asking for hypnotherapy in the hope it might relieve her almost constant back pain. In addition to the pain, she was suffering from clinical periods of depression and was constantly fatigued. She had a lovely two-year-old child and she loved her husband. But she felt was ruining her marriage because of her lack of libido and sexual responsiveness.

At the first visit, most of the time available was used in taking a history of major medical and surgical events. She was born on July 4, 1923, into a Catholic family. Her father was an alcoholic and usually out of work. When she was three years old, her parents divorced. Two years later her mother remarried. The patient's physical problems started at the age of seven, when she was hospitalized for three months because of pneumonia. At 13 she underwent her first of 11 surgeries with an emergency appendectomy. Later she had two illegal abortions while in training as a nurse. At 23 she married her present husband. At 26 she had emergency surgery for an ectopic pregnancy. Two years later she started a planned pregnancy that was terminated by abortion after emergency surgery for a twisted myoma of the uterus. At about this time she began her long history of back pain, which started as though it might be a herniated disc. A mylogram was negative. She was hospitalized for traction and then wore a body cast for nine months before the first of two unsuccessful spinal fusions. A few months later she was back having her eighth surgery, this time for an empyema of the gall bladder. There were no gallstones found. Two years later, in 1955, she had her second spinal fusion. Then she became pregnant and went through an uneventful pregnancy to deliver a healthy ten-pound female child. Back pain continued, and because her uterus was not prolapsed, a vaginal hysterectomy was done in the hope it might be the answer to her back problem. It was not.

At her first visit on June 18, 1958, I pointed out that there were a number of problems and asked what she would select as the number one priority in working with hypnosis. It was a surprise to hear her say she wanted immediate help with her weight. She was an excellent hypnotic subject. Finger signals were easily set up, but I noticed that they moved very quickly and without the trustworthy trembling repetitiveness of good ideomotor responses. She gave a no signal when I asked if there might be some connection between her weight, her sexual feelings, and her back pain. She kept interrupting to question me about my methods of using hypnosis. Often she came out of hypnosis to say something not germane to the subject at hand.

Another appointment was set for three weeks later. At this visit she was asked to orient her memory to some important event having something to do with her lack of libido. This time her signals were typical. She found herself thinking about her grandfather. He had enticed her into the basement when she was five and had licked her vulva with his tongue. They both heard her mother coming down the stairs. Grandfather escaped to the back yard, leaving Dorothy to be discovered in the act of buttoning up the sides of her underpants. Her mother scolded her for masturbating. Six years later, this grandfather hanged himself in the garage. Dorothy discovered him and ran for help. The newspaper report announced that she might have saved his life if she had immediately cut him down.

Another month passed before she revealed that, beginning when she was seven, her stepfather had made numerous sexual advances to her, each time threatening her with physical harm if she ever told anyone. She was afraid to confide in her mother and was terrified whenever alone in the house with him.

Finger signals repeatedly indicated a close relationship now between sexual guilt feelings, her weight, and her back troubles, but she would always evade my efforts toward getting her to accept a target day for relief. Now she began to have trouble entering hypnosis. She did not return until February of 1962, when pain in her back and neck was very severe. She was able to turn off the pain, but again I had the feeling she was asking for help on something she was unaware of consciously, and that she was unconsciously blocking every effort on my part to search it out. While talking about this with her toward the end of the interview she blurted out, "When will I stop punishing myself?" I asked her then to go back into hypnosis, back to whatever it was that seemed the most cogent reason for her self-punishment.

She described vividly a scene in the kitchen. She was two years old, hearing her father screaming, "I hate you!" Her mother had just told him they could not go to a dance adding, "We have no money and there's Dorothy." This seemed to be a powerful event, but there had been still earlier experiences paving the way. My time had run out. It was three months before she returned. Two visits were wasted searching her anesthetic experiences. She had felt insulted over her surgeon's caustic comments about her excess weight, but finger signals indicated these were not important matters. I asked her to do some searching with autohypnosis at home.

On May 27, 1962 she wrote, "I was very depressed with the use of autohypnosis. I discovered my mother did not want to have me. She tried aborting by the use of a button hook. I could see this clearly and also my trying to escape this hook. After having me, she loved and protected me. At the age of a few months my father was saying, 'I'll kill her.' The word *strangling* appears. He didn't touch me or attempt this, however. I questioned myself as to the person to whom he was referring. It was myself. My mother was standing close by. There was a basket of some sort that I was in." She went on to write, "My mind is wound up like an eight-day clock. I feel the need to talk and talk to get the whole situation out in the open."

She was seen three times, however, without anything being revealed. She was now enthusiastic about her painting. On May 29, 1963, a year after her revealing letter, she came into the office on an emergency visit because of pain so severe she could barely walk. She was hypnotized quickly and asked to orient at an ideomotor level to the origin of this episode of pain. She had given a show of her paintings, had sold two, and had been receiving a number of compliments on her work. Her art teacher, however, in spite of all this success of her pupil, seemed angry. She recognized that her teacher was jealous. With a few suggestions of relaxation and some congratulation about her painting, she indicated that all the pain was gone. I asked her fingers if there was anything else we should do before I sent her home. There was something. She wanted more help with her lack of libido and sexual responsiveness. She was asked to go a little deeper, and to give a signal with her yes finger when she was deep enough to accept suggestions about these matters. She gave the signal and I proceeded to suggest that she would be increasingly responsive to her husband, that she would have sexual dreams to orgasm, that she would lose weight from the rest of her body but would put on some flesh in her breasts, about whose lack of development she had always been self-conscious. At the mention of enlarging her breasts, she came out of hypnosis expressing irritation. I responded by asking her to go to whatever it was that made the thought of breasts repulsive to her.

At this point she burst into convulsive sobs. After several minutes of uncontrolled sobbing she said, "She tried to kill me, she tried to kill me, I know it now. I see breasts everywhere, filling the whole room. She tried to smother me under her breasts, then I'm unconscious and she is shaking me saying, 'What have I done?'" I said that to me this did not sound like a genuine effort on the part of a mother to kill her baby. It seemed much more likely to me that her mother had fallen asleep after nursing and had accidentally rolled over. Was there not something earlier than this that set the stage for her reaction?

After a few seconds she became very agitated. Her finger lifted to indicate another occurrence. She said, "It's before I'm born. My father is telling mother, 'I'm going to kill you. You can't have this baby'." Shortly after this she began screaming as she pulled her legs up to her chest. When she quieted enough to talk, she recapitulated what had been in her letter a year earlier. I asked what had happened, saying that as an obstetrician it was hard for me to believe her mother could possibly have pushed a button hook into the uterine cavity through her cervix. The patient said, "Nothing happened — only a little bleeding." I asked how she knew this. Her answer: "I know it the same way I have known other things about real people and what is going to happen to them." We terminated the interview after I had pointed out that her mother had already expressed concern about her in the breast scene, and this had been reinforced by the fact that her father's remark had demonstrated that her mother wanted to have a baby. This brought about a change in her appearance. She began to smile. I asked her to have her mother confirm or reject this account. A week later I received a letter from her mother dated June 3, 1963. I quote it exactly.

Dear Dr. Cheek:
This is to verify that the statements made by Dorothy . . . . . are true. There is one exception — when she was smothered under my breast, I was not trying to kill her. I had fallen asleep while nursing her. The statement made about her father screaming "I'll kill you" is true and happened in the early stage of my pregnancy. Dorothy had no way of knowing about these incidents:
1. Trying to abort with button hook.
2. Smothering under breast.
3. Her father saying he would kill me.
Knowing this information will be handled with discretion, I will do my upmost [*sic*] to assist Dorothy in any way possible.

The problem was not yet resolved. It would be a pleasure to be able to say that from that moment on this patient was a different person. She was, in fact, much happier in her relation to her mother, but she gained more weight to 201 pounds. I felt this reflected a continued identification of her husband with the other males who had traumatized her early life, but I was unable to get her to separate him from the others. My note of October 24, 1964 states: "Suddenly patient discovers that she does not need to be punishing herself, that her father was a sick man, that her mother was frightened by her father, and that neither had really great intent against her as an individual, that she doesn't need to go on gaining weight or punishing herself further as she has done all her life. Whether or not this is a turning point, I cannot guess. She seems greatly relieved."

The patient attended a lecture of mine at a local hospital a year later. She was still about 20 pounds overweight, but stated that her life was great now. She had no more back pain, had been painting well, and was better sexually.

Discussion: "Merry-Go-Round"-like Retrieval of Early Traumatic Events

I have given much thought to this case before deciding to report it for others to consider. In 22 years of analyzing the information supplied through the use of ideomotor questioning techniques, it has been my experience that events responsible for fixed behavioral characteristics have been easy to work with when they have occurred at birth or later. Here was a woman, highly motivated consciously to accept help, yet struggling constantly to impede the process of therapeutic assistance. She had gone through at least three life-threatening experiences, one before her birth and at least two within her first three years of postnatal life. On several occasions I had belittled her conviction that she was clairvoyant. This accounted for her refusal to return to my office for two years between 1960 and 1962. From the perspective of 1965, it seemed clear that her submission to her grandfather's enticements, the coercions of her stepfather, and the placing of herself in the position of getting pregnant twice during the time of training as a nurse were all related to her feeling of nonentity, of being the source of trouble to her mother. This was reinforced by her mother's tirade on catching her buttoning her panties after the molestation by her grandfather, and again reinforced by the newspaper criticism after her grandfather had hanged himself in the garage. If any one of these events, including the advances made by her stepfather, had been the main reason for her multiple surgeries, her lack of libido, and her overweight, I believe the work done during her many visits to the office would have made it possible for her to have become free of the self-punitive fugue that continued during her treatment period from 1958 until 1965. There had to be something else much earlier, but she steadfastly refused to face it until she had a chance to do her own searching with autohypnosis in 1963. Even then she covered it up for another year.

It has been my experience that truly significant experiences tend to make themselves known repeatedly like the posters around a merry-go-round. At first they are ignored or their message misunderstood. After many repetitions, whether in hypnosis or in repeated dream sequences, they take on meaning, and finally the most important "poster" is recognized with therapeutically positive results.

I am reporting this case with no intent to prove that prenatal memories are valid but rather that we must keep an open mind about the possibility. When therapy is lagging, when patients seem to put up unreasonable resistances to reassurance and seemingly appropriate therapy, we should consider the possibility that something very important has happened at birth or prior to birth. In some instances the problem may even have taken place either in an earlier life experience or been picked up from what the followers of Jung call the "collective unconscious." When we use ideomotor questioning methods, we can search out the subjective impressions of our patients. We must never denigrate them, as I did at first with this patient. We must observe the subjective evidence and prevent our biases from interfering with a constructive therapeutic end result.

RESEARCH

The wide scope of recent psychobiological research has many profound implications for the validation and extension of the ideodynamic signaling approach to early memories. In this overview we can only touch upon a few that we believe are of greatest significance for the newly emerging empirical paradigms of how we construct our psychological reality and how we may heal its malformations. We will explore four major areas:

a. wide-ranging experimental studies with animals and humans, which have established that the fetus in utero can learn;
b. the "neural Darwinism" approach to perception, memory, and learning;
c. a new archetypal theory of behavior and the birth experience;
d. the constructivist view of the mechanisms of memory and the ultimate nature of our human "invented reality."

In Utero Learning: Research Projects 58 & 59

Conditioning experiments have shown that the human fetus at six months can hear and learn (DeCasper & Fifer, 1980; DeCasper & Spence, 1986). Other researchers are currently investigating fetal learning in experimental animals (Kirby, 1981; Smotherman & Robinson, 1985; Smotherman, Woodruff, Robinson, Del Real, Barron, & Riley, 1985). *The human fetus in utero is responsive to sound by the third trimester of life and reaches sophisticated recognition levels with regard to human speech by birth* (Eimas, 1975). This early auditory competency is regarded as serving a variety of developmental functions, such as mother-infant bonding (Bell, 1974) and language acquisition (Eisenberg, 1976). DeCasper and Fifer (1980) state that "mother-infant bonding would best be served by (and may even require) the ability of a newborn to discriminate its mothers voice from that of other females." In more recent research, DeCasper and Prescott (1984) assessed human newborns' voice preferences as follows (pp. 488–489):

The present research allows a more precise, but unaltered, ranking of newborns' earliest voice preferences, that is, maternal voice > female voices > paternal voice = male voices. All together, these data suggest the hypothesis that the reinforcing value of perceptual salience of an early postnatal sound is significantly influenced by its similarity to frequently experienced prenatal sounds. The necessary inference is that some form of auditory perceptual learning occurs in utero.

One implication of the hypothesis is that the cues important for post-natal voice preference must be experienced prenatally. . . . The hypothesis also implies that newborns remember something about their prenatal auditory environment. We know little about the nature of the perceptual learning that must occur, about which aspects of the prenatal stimulus are stored or remembered, and about how this happens, or when these processes become effective.

Project 58   This richly developing experimental literature on human in utero memory and learning is entirely consistent with Cheek's exploratory studies of the possibility of ideodynamically accessing some sensory-perceptual aspects of the birth experience. Review this in utero memory and learning research within the cybernetic state-dependent mind-gene-molecular frameworks illustrated in Figures 4 and 18. At what stages within this network does in utero learning correlate with the work of Konrad Lorenz (1981) on imprinting, Kandel's work on the molecular basis of memory (Goelet & Kandel, 1986), and Kupfermann's (1985) genetic determinants of behavior?

Project 59   Can these in utero studies be cross-checked and/or enriched with ideodynamic signaling methods? Can the ideodynamic approach, for example, replicate the finding that the human fetus is responsive to sound in the third trimester of life? Do ideodynamic signals indicate an early life preference for the maternal voice over the paternal?

Neural Darwinianism: Research Project 60

A fundamentally new psychobiological approach to the nature of memory and learning is being developed by Gerald Edelman and his colleagues with their concept of "neural Darwinianism" (Edelman, 1978, 1985). Unlike psychology, modern biological thought is based upon the Darwinian concepts of *variation* and *selection* that can account for the facts of organic evolution from the molecular level up to the simplest (one-cell) and most complex (multicellular) levels of life. If we believe that biology and psychology are ultimately related, it is a bit disconcerting to realize that our current theories of the psychology of memory and learning are entirely divorced from these evolutionary foundations of biology. Just as physicists are currently seeking for a grand unified theory of all the forces of the universe, it is only natural that those of us who are interested in a psychobiological approach to mind-body healing and hypnosis should seek a unifying theory that can integrate all the fundamental principles of biology and psychology. Edelman's work seems to offer such a possibility.

In 1972 Gerald Edelman and Rodney Porter received a Nobel Prize for working out the complete biochemical structure of the antibody molecule. Their work led to an understanding of those portions of the molecule that are *varied* in nature to produce the millions of different antibodies that are needed to protect all higher forms of life against foreign invaders (or antigens) such as viruses, bacteria, and toxins. This confirmed a fundamental hypothesis of modern immunology: All animals are born with a complete repertoire of antibodies. When foreign invaders enter the body, they are said to "select" those antibodies that fit their molecular structure like lock and key. When foreign invaders and antibodies lock onto each other, the foreign body is neutralized and the body can get rid of it. Israel Rosenfield (1986) has recently described how this evolutionary model of immunological activity can be generalized to the psychology of memory and learning (1986, p. 22):

> Darwinian ideas have had a variable influence on psychological thinking, which has sometimes strayed away from biological explanation. Modern ethology, which studies the relation of animal and human behavior, has recaptured much of the Darwinian flavor that unfortunately left psychology when early learning theorists such as Pavlov seemed to be successful in explaining behavior without paying heed to the differences between animal species. . . .
>
> A limited number of genes, a few hundred or a few thousand at most, provide, through recombinatory mechanisms, the codes for the many millions of different antibodies. Specialized cells in the blood each produce one of the many kinds of possible antibodies that then become attached to the cell surface. An antibody molecule that happens to fit more or less closely a virus or bacterium floating in the bloodstream will bind itself to the virus or bacterium. This sets off a chain of events that causes the cell to divide and make thousands of copies (clones) of itself and more of the same kind of antibody. Other cells may carry antibody molecules that fit the virus or bacterium in different ways, and these cells, too, will bind to the virus or bacterium and produce clones. The body can only rid itself of a virus or bacterium if there is at least one good enough fit in its antibody repertoire. Usually there are several fits and some of them may overlap.
>
> So the immunological system is not taught what antibodies it has to make to rid the body of a particular virus. The invading virus *selects* the appropriate antibodies and these will be different in each individual. An unfortunate organism may not have any antibodies in its repertoire that can bind the virus, and this could be fatal. Scientists were generally

pleased with this solution to the immunological question because it was consistent with Darwinian principles of selection that have formed the basis of modern biology. Theories of immunology based on a process of learning or instruction were not.

Comparison of those findings on immunology to the theory of evolution suggested to Edelman that the brain too may function as a selective system and that what we call learning is really a form of selection. The theory he worked out is based on three fundamental claims: 1) during the development of the brain in the embryo, a highly variable and individual pattern of connections between the brain cells (neurons) is formed; 2) after birth, a pattern of neural connections is fixed in each individual, but certain combinations of connections are selected over others as a result of the stimuli the brain receives through the senses; 3) such selection would occur particularly in groups of brain cells that are connected in sheets, or "maps," and these maps "speak" to one another back and forth to create categories of things and events. . . . At higher levels in the brain, the stimuli must be organized in ways that will be meaningful and useful for the organism.

The brain performs this organizing operation by using maps made up of neuronal groups. A map is a collection of neuronal groups in the brain which are arranged in a way that preserves the pattern of relationships either between a sheet of sensory receptors (such as those in the skin of the hand) and a sheet of neural tissue in the brain to which the sensory stimuli have been transmitted, or between two sheets of neural tissue. Groups are arranged in maps that "speak" back and forth to one another so as to create categories of things and events. Different kinds of maps are found in different parts of the brain, and an analysis of how such maps interact is an essential and final part of Edelman's theory.

Edelman's view that there are maps, categories, or frames of reference but no fixed contents of memory in the brain (as there are, say, in a tape recorder) is identical with the independent conclusions of recent theoretical and experimental developments in psychology (Pribram, 1986). There are no fixed memories of the contents of our life experiences. Rather, memory is actually a sensory and perceptual selection process of categorization. Edelman presents a psychobiological theory of memory as a constructive process at the neural level. If, as Edelman maintains, *it is not the contents of experience that are encoded in memory, but, rather, neural organizations that can process experience in certain ways,* then we may at last have a way of understanding many of the paradoxes of age regression in hypnosis. From this perspective, it becomes reasonable to hypothesize that fetal learning and the birth experience can imprint neural organizations that are later "selected" by Cheek's "implied directives" to repeatedly review the birth process and bring it up to a verbal level.

So-called "conversations" projected onto birth imprints may reveal something about the structure of the original imprint even though the actual contents (the words) came from later learning. This is analogous with the situation wherein an archeologist pours a modern latex modeling material onto a fragile fossil imprint. No one looking at the latex model that results would say that it was the original; everyone would agree, however, that it was an interesting facsimile that could reveal something important about the structure of the original. Likewise, a study of many such "conversational" reconstructions of early life imprints may reveal something useful about the evolution of a patient's mental life and how we may therapeutically reconstruct or reframe it for healing.

Project 60 Design a research study to determine how well so-called "age regression" in hypnosis is actually a selection of later life experiences by neural networks formed earlier in life. Is this the mechanism by which the popular hypnotherapeutic method called the "affect bridge" (Rossi, 1986a; Watkins, 1971) works?

A New Archetypal Theory of Behavior and the Birth Experience: Research Project 61

Edelman's neural selection theory of memory, learning, and behavior has echoes in Jung's archetypal theory of the collective unconscious. There is an almost exact parallelism between the selection and cloning of antibodies for expression in Edelman's theory of immunology, and Jung's view that the archetypes (or typical patterns) of human behavior are all equally present as potentials for expression that are selected later by significant life challenges (Jung, 1959, 1960b).

A number of Jungian students have already noted this correspondence between the immune system and an archetypal theory of psychosomatic medicine (Fordham, 1957, 1974; Stein, 1967). As we have reviewed above, Edelman now finds that the entire repertory of an organism's bank of antibodies is already present in the body at birth in minimal amounts. The challenge presented to the body by viruses or microbes that have surface antigens or molecules that fit (or select) these antibodies leads to their vast multiplication (cloning) or expression. The body does not learn to make a new antibody to fit whatever invading microbe it encounters; rather, it simply proliferates the expression of those natural antibodies that already exist that can best "fit" and neutralize the invaders' challenge.

Likewise, Jung would say that the unconscious does not generate new archetypal patterns for dealing with every new environmental circumstance, problem, or challenge it encounters. Rather, the environmental problem selects (activates or constellates) whatever built-in archetypal process the collective unconscious already possesses for dealing with that type of challenge (Jung, 1959; Stevens, 1983).

According to neural Darwinianism, the process of evolution over millions of years has allowed for the selection and survival of those higher organisms (organisms with eukaryotic or nucleated cells with extensive gene information bands that are "molecular memories" of the cell's history) that could provide the widest range of antibodies to defend against any invading microbe. Similarly, Jung would maintain that all life species including humans have evolved a "collective unconscious" consisting of built-in archetypal patterns of typical mind-body behaviors that have been selected over millions of years of evolution for their survival value in coping with whatever challenges the physical and social environments were most likely to present.

From these considerations, we would infer that Cheek's ideodynamic method of accessing the birth experience may be tapping into or "selecting" evolutionarily important, built-in archetypal patterns of mind-body experience. Over four million years of evolution, the archetypal experience of birth has become attuned to imprinting all sensory-perceptual experiences that may be important for the baby's survival. We need only hypothesize that the highly focused and mildly stressful process of ideodynamic signaling under medical circumstances can access this archetypal pattern, which has already organized much of the person's dominant frames of reference, life attitudes, and so forth. Practically any adult issue or problem can be linked associatively to the primordial shaping experience of birth. Investigating virtually any mind-body problem by ideodynamic signaling, therefore, would eventually find its original sources in the birth experience. Thus, it is only natural that after 40 years of experience with the ideodynamic approach, Cheek would find it empirically expeditious to take a "short-cut" by beginning most of his therapeutic work with an ideodynamic review of the birth experience. The characteristic patterns of adaptation that were evoked and imprinted by this primordial experience act as a template or frame of reference for organizing later life experience (Rank, 1959).

Project 61 Design an anthropological-clinical-experimental study that would ideodynamically investigate the birth process in many cultures. One would first have to establish the validity and reliability of ideomotor signaling methods, and then apply them by using each culture's unique frames of reference to assess the archetypal commonalities of the birth process and its significance for later life experience in that culture.

The Construction of Mind and Memory: Research Project 62

The profound ramifications of the constructivist position for a general theory of mind and behavior have been developed by a number of workers in biology (Segal, 1986), psychology (Bruner, 1986; Watzlawick, 1984), and philosophy (Goodman, 1976, 1978, 1984). Bruner has expressed the breadth of the constructivist position as follows (1986, pp. 96–97):

> The constructivist view, that what exists is a product of what is thought, can be traced to Kant, who first fully developed it. . . . Kant's view of a world "out there" being made up of mental products is Goodman's starting point.
>
> But as already noted, Goodman refuses to assign any privileged status or any "ultimate reality" to any particular world that mind may create. Kant, on the other hand, argued that we all have certain knowledge, a priori, by virtue of having human minds. Such a priori knowledge, on Kant's view, precedes all reasoning. In place of Kant's a priori, Goodman offers a more relativistic notion. We do not begin with something absolute or prior to all reasoning, but, according to Goodman, begin instead with the kinds of construction that lead to the creation of worlds. And these constructions have in common that they take certain premises for granted, as stipulations. What is "given" or assumed at the outset of our construction is neither bedrock reality out there, nor an a priori: it is always another constructed version of a world that we have taken as given for certain purposes. Any previously constructed world version may be taken as given for subsequent constructions. So, in effect, world-making involves the transformation of worlds and world versions already made.
>
> Obviously, the idea of mind as an instrument of construction is (or should be) congenial to the developmental psychologist who observes different meanings being assigned to the same "event" at different ages. The clinical psychologist must always be impressed with the "reality" with which patients endow their rich narratives. And constructivism is nowhere more compelling than in the psychology of art and creativity. Blake, Kafka, Wittgenstein, and Picasso did not find the worlds they produced. They invented them.
>
> Goodman's notion of stipulation—of taking something as given—is also richly suggestive for cognitive psychologists. *One immediately thinks of the importance of mechanisms like "recursion," the process whereby the mind or a computer program loops back on the output of a prior computation and treats it as a given that can be the input for the next operation.* Theories as divergent as Chomsky's theory of grammar, Piaget's account of the development of mental functions, and Newell and Simon's idea of a General Problem Solver all have recourse to it. Any formal theory of mind is helpless without recursion, for without it it is impossible to account for thoughts on thoughts, thoughts on thoughts on thoughts, up to whatever level of abstraction is necessary. Indeed, Philip Johnson-Laird, in his excellent *Mental Models*, invokes recursion to account for how the mind turns around on itself to create the kind of summary of its capacities that might constitute something like a sense of

"self." One begins to get a glimmer from this work of how Goodman's stipulations might be used in sequences, each transforming a previously created world version into a new one, the whole providing a basis for understanding not only single acts of cognition but also complex ones that have the look and smell of real world-making. (Italics added)

The major point of connection between this constructivist view of mind and memory and Cheek's work is in *"the importance of mechanisms like 'recursion.'"* As we have seen throughout this volume, Cheek's ideodynamic finger signaling is a process of recursion. He repeatedly insists that the sought-for memory must be reviewed at the physiological ideomotor levels many times before it can be reconstructed into a verbal form.

Project 62   Utilize the background of readings in constructivism cited in this section to develop a series of hypotheses about the child's "construction of reality" that can be assessed with ideodynamic signaling. For example, one might explore the use of finger, hand, arm and/or head signaling with children at each of Piaget's stages of development. While some pioneering work in therapeutic hypnosis has been done with children (Gardner & Olness, 1981; Mills & Crowley, 1986), the entire area of ideodynamic signaling is still to be investigated. Care would have to be exercised in developing ethically aware procedures for such studies with children. It would be fascinating to compare a child's ideodynamic view of his or her birth process with the mother's view of it. What relationships might one uncover between such data and a child's social development and health?

SECTION X

Forensic Hypnosis

THEORY

Our unique psychobiological perspective on the nature of hypnosis could become the basis of new views on its use as a forensic tool. Because there has been almost no acknowledgment of the biological basis of hypnosis in the courts, we believe that the legal profession is at a great disadvantage in understanding many phenomena of human memory that are of central significance for evaluating testimony. This is particularly the case in our essentially adversarial legal system of evaluating the validity of information. The emotional pressures engendered by the adversarial legal encounter tend to bias the selection and construction of verbal memory. Because of this bias and tendency to confabulate on the verbal level, many have sought to discredit the use of forensic hypnosis entirely.

Cheek's response is to point out that there are physiological and skeletal (ideomotor) levels of memory that are not subject to the easy bias and fabrications possible at the verbal level. He believes strongly in this position because it is supported consistently over a lifetime of clinical investigation covered in all the previous sections of this volume. An appreciation of Cheek's view, however, requires a vast expansion in the usual understanding of what is to be included as hypnotic phenomena. Most laypeople and even "experts" in law still believe that hypnosis is an artificially induced psychological state brought about by a "formal process of hypnotic induction." They have little understanding of the many more subtle psychobiological varieties of "spontaneous hypnosis" that take place during any life circumstance that alters consciousness and/or selective attention. Let us list a few of these circumstances that are of particular relevance for the law.

1. Any situation of *stress* that has legal consequences will bias memory. These include any situation involving fright and/or injuries such as accidents, assault, bribery, etc.
2. Any effort to recall a *sequence of events* as is typically required of most witnesses — particularly when the person is "on the spot" talking to the

police, or talking to a lawyer or judge in front of a jury, or even when being recorded verbatim in preparation for legal action—tends to induce a hypnoidal state (Erickson, 1964/1980).

3. Any *novel or dramatic situation* such as a court appearance tends to induce a hypnoidal state as is evidenced by the fact that after giving testimony many people will experience partial amnesias and must query their lawyers or study the court transcripts to find out what they said.

The bane of the legal profession is the notorious unreliability of these witness situations. The most important contribution Cheek's psychobiological approach can make is to recognize and neutralize those state-dependent and essentially "constructive" aspects of verbal memory that can lead to witness bias and confabulation. Cheek believes he can do this via his three-level ideodynamic approach, wherein validity is checked by the sequence of physiological, ideomotor, and verbal levels of responsiveness. He even cites evidence (Cheek, 1982) of his effort to implant a false verbal level of memory on the physiological ideomotor levels. He found that after several months, his subjects reverted to the "truth" at the physiological and ideomotor levels. It would seem that further research of this type may begin to outline the parameters of "verbal memory" that can be relied upon in the legal profession in general and forensic hypnosis in particular.

A typical example of how state-dependent memory, learning, and behavior can be utilized in forensic hypnosis is provided in a verbal report by clinical psychologist Lee Pulos in Vancouver, Canada:

I do a lot of forensic work for the Royal Canadian Mounted Police (RCMP) using hypnosis to assist witnesses in recalling details associated with crimes.

Two weeks ago a 16-year-old nude female was found lying in a lot adjacent to a home just outside of Vancouver. The autopsy indicated that the victim had been choked from the rear.

A 36-year-old woman and her husband were returning home from a dinner party with friends a little after midnight on the evening of the crime. They reported seeing a van with hazard lights flashing right next to the lot where the body was found (though at the time of their sighting, they did not know that a crime had been committed). The woman got "a funny feeling in her gut," and told her husband to drive around the block again so that she could take another look at the van.

When I conducted my hypnotic interview with her, I first established her baseline memory by asking her to recall as much as she was able before I used hypnosis with her. She wasn't quite certain of the color of the van, and she wasn't sure if there were one or two occupants. However, after she entered a hypnotic trance state, she reported with certainty that the van was red and that it had a yellow trim in the writing of the letters *E-M-C-O*; she also picked up that there were three lines of cursive slanted writing underneath this yellow trim, but she wasn't able to discern the name of the company. She did recall that the right headlight was brighter than the left, that the van had "a brand new cherry red paint job" with no dents, and that there were two people inside it. The driver had long wavy hair, but she was unable to retrieve any specific facial features.

I learned that she and her husband had consumed 2½ ounces of hard liquor and a glass of wine at a friend's house. I gave them the "home-work assignment" of consuming the exact same amount of alcohol — $2^1/2$ ounces of hard liquor and a glass of wine — in order to stimulate a state-dependent memory experience of the conversation that they had had on their way home. They carried out this assignment and, in fact, were able to retrieve the additional information of the name of the company written on the car.

The RCMP have brought the owners of the vehicle in for questioning, and although they are denying any involvement, there is a strong suspicion that they will be charged.

A more detailed example of our ideodynamic approach to SDMLB is provided in the following chapter by Dr. Cheek.

25

The Forensic Use of Ideodynamic Signaling

This verbatim account of the ideodynamic approach to accessing a fleeting memory of the license plate of an alleged murderer is typical of practical forensic hypnosis. The current limitations and difficulties that are involved because of legal issues and the psychobiological nature of such memory are touched upon throughout.

Jane heard a gunshot and the thud of a body falling to the floor in the apartment above her. Her husband rushed to the door of the apartment in time to see a man running down the stairs and out of the building in the direction of parked cars. He called to Jane to get a look at the license plate of the car that would have to go by her as she stood outside on the walkway overlooking the road leading from the apartment parking lot onto the street.

Jane had approximately four seconds during which to see the car carrying the assailant go past her field of vision. The description she gave to the police investigating the murder was not very helpful. It was 7:30 p.m. on a clear November night. The lighting was poor. She saw a small car go by with its passenger door open; a man was getting into it with one leg dragging as he slid onto the seat. She knew she had seen the license plate, but was too excited and frightened to remember any of the details. She could not see the man's features, nor could she see the driver of the car, but she did remember that there was a dashboard light visible inside the car.

Six months later I (DBC) was called in the hope that I might help Jane remember the license plate of the getaway automobile. There had been four witnesses to the shooting. All had agreed on the description of the man who they claimed had done the shooting. An artist had made a composite sketch of the man. A suspect had been apprehended but he was "about five inches shorter" than the man the witnesses had described. Furthermore, the suspect had 13 people attesting to his presence in San Jose, 30 miles away, on the night of the killing. All other leads had been fruitless.

In April of 1986, the district attorney and the chief of police did not want anyone to hypnotize the four witnesses who had seen the gunman and watched him shoot the victim in the apartment. According to the Shirley decision, they would not be allowed to testify in court in the event that a valid suspect had been found. Jane, however, was regarded as a lesser or "throw-away witness." If she could remember the license characters on the car, that information might lead them to the murderer. If Jane revealed previously unknown information under hypnosis, she could not testify about those observations during a trial. Any new information given by her would be considered as admissible only if it could be substantiated by independent methods of search.

I pointed out to the police inspector who called me that the chances of getting an accurate recall of a license plate after an interval of nearly six months during which Jane had been extensively questioned were very poor. The average person pays little attention to remembering license plates in everyday life. Conscious memory and the nearly conscious memory revealed during conversational hypnosis tend to fade with the passage of time. The average person does not score well in retrieving the details of a license on a car while in hypnosis.

With this caveat, I agreed to meet Jane and interview her in a special room equipped with hidden videocamera equipment and minimicrophones attached to us. We were introduced before entering the room. It was not a situation where a witness could be expected to be comfortably relaxed.

I used a Chevreul pendulum at first with an explanation that it was used for revealing unconscious information without need for inducing hypnosis. "Yes," "no," and "I don't want to answer" responses were set up for her with the explanation that once consciously accepted, these symbol movements would reflect information that might not be consciously known. I explained that when there is a contradiction between what a subject says verbally and what the pendulum says, the pendulum is more accurate. Body movements that reflect unconscious answers to questions are more reliable than conversational-level memory. Once the symbol movements have been selected through conscious thoughts, they are relegated to unconscious associative levels in the same way our fingers eventually know where the letters are on a typewriter keyboard once we have learned them consciously. Jane was amused by the action of her pendulum and seemed comfortable with our interchange.

The guidelines for good forensic investigation involve an uninterrupted verbal narration starting with details prior to a target, following a critical sequence of events, and ending when the action is completed. This is to be done *before* there is a formal induction of hypnosis. The process is repeated after hypnosis has been induced. Interrupting the witness' narrative with a question is considered counterproductive. To answer, the witness usually comes to a lighter level of hypnosis, or comes out of hypnosis completely in order to verbalize a response.

Jane was much interested in the mysterious movement of the pendulum as I explained its use. She slipped into a light hypnotic state while the pendulum was answering some questions about her experience at the time of the murder. I knew this because of the "ironing out" of facial expression and her unblinking gaze at the pendulum. It was clear that she did not feel threatened by the idea of using hypnosis. She returned to a normal conscious alertness when I took the pendulum from her fingers. I made no comment on her spontaneous hypnotic state.

I asked for a narrative of what she could remember about her experience at the time of the murder. She told of hearing the thud of a body falling to the floor in the apartment overhead, of her going first to the door and then out to the landing overlooking the parking area on a road leading out to the street. Her husband saw a man running down the stairs and out toward the parking area to her left. He shouted to her, "Look at the license plate!"

She saw headlights go on and a car moving rapidly toward and past her. A man was getting in as the car was moving. His right leg was still outside the car. The headlights prevented her from seeing a license plate on the front of the car but she got a brief glimpse of the license on the back of the car. She had been too excited and frightened to hold the memory in her conscious mind. She remembered seeing a light inside the car, apparently a dashboard light. She hoped hypnosis would help her memory for the details. She had experienced hypnosis once in the past and was looking forward to the experience with me. As she said this her facial expression changed. She looked worried as she said, "I hope he didn't see me. It could be dangerous." I assured her that a man rushing away from a shooting and obviously afraid of being caught would be much more attentive to getting away than to observing the appearance of bystanders in the dark. This opinion was reinforced by the police officers later.

At this point I gave her back the pendulum and asked if her inner mind would be willing to reveal everything she had seen that night. The ideomotor response was a yes. She was told to hold the pendulum as long as her fingers could keep a grip on it, that they would pull apart whenever her unconscious mind knew she was in a hypnotic state deep enough for our purposes. I asked her to close her eyes and look at the sequential movements of the flame of an imaginary candle placed on a table about ten feet away.

This formal induction was used only because it would be expected by someone later viewing the tape. People enter a hypnotic state when they are remembering any sequence of events. This was demonstrated 50 years ago by Erickson (1964/1980). A light, subtle state of *hypnosis will occur spontaneously during any carefully sequential narrative offered by a witness to a crime.* This subtle state raises questions about where to draw the line between ordinary talking and the talking that occurs after hypnosis is formally induced.

In less than a minute, Jane smiled as she felt the chain of the pendulum slipping through her fingers. It dropped to the floor. Her arm remained in its original position in spite of my asking her to let the arm go down wherever it would be comfortable. This demonstrated to the camera and videotape that the subject was in a medium level of hypnosis. I then set up finger signals with Jane for the three responses of "yes," "no," and "I don't want to answer."

As noted earlier, the standard protocol for forensic hypnosis requires a repetition of an uninterrupted narrative. I have found this procedure to be unproductive and time-consuming in my work with the F.B.I. during the past five years. Instead, I asked Jane to review the entire experience at a subverbal level of memory. I asked her yes finger to lift as she started, her no finger to lift at each important moment, and her I-don't-want-to-answer finger to lift when the experience had terminated. I instructed her to make no effort at "*seeing*" or consciously "*knowing*" any of the details. She was told to keep going over the experience from beginning to the end, and that eventually the details would become clear like the developing imagery of a Polaroid photograph. I said, "Another finger will lift when you know everything you need to know about that car." I designated a finger on the hand opposite to the one used for the review.

In the following, taken from the taped interview, the name of the witness has been changed and the sentence structure has been edited for clarity.

Cheek: **"Watch the way the flame of the candle flickers with your conscious mind while the deeper part of your mind goes over that period of time. When you hear the loud noise above you, your yes finger will lift."**

Within ten seconds there is an increase in her respiratory rate. This occurs ten seconds before her yes finger lifts to indicate the next higher level of perception. If I had asked what is happening, she would have had no clear idea of what her fingers were indicating. The time sequence is important. Experience has shown that subjective understanding can be trusted when both physiological and ideomotor level signals precede conscious or verbal recognition of the information. The reported details are subjectively valid but may be factually incorrect. This is an important matter to keep in mind when using hypnosis for memory enhancement.

"There, and each time you come to something you feel is important, your no finger will lift.* Finally, when the car is gone, your I-don't-want-to-answer finger will lift.

"Keep on relaxing. One part of your mind will be back there at the scene, but I would like to keep your higher level association of understandings here with me at the time of our interview. In that way, you are viewing the entire event from a distance. You are in no danger."

---

*The mild paradox of using the *no* finger to signal when the patient *knows* something may be bridged by the no-know.

[This was said because of her expressed fear that the man escaping in the car might have seen her.]

"You will be paying careful attention to each detail of that experience at an unconscious level of memory, but please do not try to describe anything until your thumb on the other hand lifts. At that point I will ask your fingers if it would be okay to talk about what you have been reviewing."

It took two minutes of clock time for Jane to signal the moment the car was disappearing from view. Although there appeared to have been only one set of signals from beginning to ending, it is probable that there had been many repetitive unconscious scanning sweeps. I asked her to start from the beginning again and to have her I-don't-want-to-answer signal lift when the car had again disappeared from view. This time it took only 60 seconds. I continued:

"That's good. Now, please go over it again. Keep going over it. Each time you do, you will pick up more details. Your memory is very good anyhow, but you will find the memory much clearer with each repetition, as though you had all the time in the world to watch that scene. You will be picking up more information each time you go over that space of time. Don't try to think of anything yet but pay particular attention unconsciously to the moments you are looking at the back end of the car. When the car is gone, your I-don't-want-to-answer finger will lift again.

"There, now keep going over the moments from first seeing the rear license plate until you can no longer see it. Your little finger will lift up as you start to see the license plate, and when the picture is clear enough in your mind, your thumb will lift to let me know. Just keep reviewing it rapidly from the beginning to the end at an unconscious level, not working at it, just reviewing it.

"That's it. Keep looking at it as though you are just sweeping your eyes over the license plate. You are not staring at it, just glimpsing it. Your inner mind knows it is important. It will take care of remembering it for you. You were alarmed at the time. Your conscious mind would have been distracted, but that primitive part of your brain would have been acutely at attention to remember every detail of that plate. When you are ready, you can bring that information up to a level of awareness where you can tell me about it."

Her thumb lifted with the characteristic trembling motion of an ideomotor signal to indicate the image was clear enough to be raised to a talking level of awareness. This segment of the review process limited to the license plate took up two minutes of clock time.

"Go deeper now. This time, limit your attention to the left side of that license plate. When you can see that, Jane, your yes finger will lift. Notice the color of the plate. Notice about where it is on the car, high up or low down. Take in the whole back of the car for a moment. When you can see the lefthand side of that plate, your yes finger will lift again. Don't try to see anything consciously yet. When the image is clear, it will just mushroom up

into your conscious awareness after you have been looking at it at an unconscious level."

Cheek: **Now, let me ask your inner mind some questions. Do you know the color of that license plate?**

Jane: [finger signal] Yes [20 second pause].

Cheek: **What is it?**

Jane: [Verbal] Blue . . . and . . . yellow.

Cheek: **The left-hand character could be a number or a letter—**

Jane: [Verbal] *L*.

Cheek: *L*. **And look just to the right of the** *L*. **See what is next.**

Jane: [Verbal] *R*.

Cheek: **Now let's check with your fingers. Is the first part of it an** *L*? **See which finger wants to lift, but don't move anything purposefully. Is it an** *L*?

Jane: [Finger signal] Yes.

Cheek: **And next to it? As your yes finger lifts, say the first thing that comes to your mind.**

Jane: [Verbal] *R*.

Cheek: *R*—**and then just to the right of that? As you see that, your yes finger will lift and just say it. [Yes finger lifts] What's the first thought, as I snap my fingers—first thought. [Jane opens her eyes as I snap my fingers. The sound is out of context. I had intended only to have the sharp sound raise a deep level memory to a higher level for verbalization.] Let your eyes stay closed. See the next letter to the** *R*.

Jane: [Very soft voice] *U*.

Cheek: *U*. **Okay, let's ask your fingers about that. Is it a** *U*? **Does your inner mind agree with that? Is it a** *U*?

Jane: [Finger signal] No.

Cheek: **Your finger says no. Would it be all right to know what that is, just to the right of the** *R*?

Jane: [verbal] *Y*.

Cheek: *Y*. **Okay, Let's double check. Does your inner mind agree with what you have just said?**

Jane: [Finger signal] Yes.

Cheek: **Trust that. Now see what is to the right of the** *Y*. **First, see it at an unconscious level. Say the first thing that comes to your mind when your yes finger lifts.**

Jane: [Verbal] *3*.

Cheek: **All right. And look just to the right of the *3*. Each time you see it, your yes finger will lift. [Respirations increase in rate now]**

Jane: [Verbal, in a very low voice] It's blurred.

Cheek: **Blurred. Kind of get closer to the license plate. There may be some mud there, but you can get a better idea as you move closer to the car. This is the beautiful thing you can do with your mind. Let the plate be about three times as big as it actually was when you saw it. When you have magnified it as though your were looking through a magnifying lens, your yes finger will lift. As it lifts, just read that off.**

Jane: [Verbal] An *8* or a *6*.

Cheek: **An *8* or a *6*. We can make a note of that and check on it later. How about the next one to the right, just beyond the *8* or the *6*?**

Jane: [Verbal] *6*.

Cheek: **Sometimes there is a little patch on one side or the other at the top of the license plate telling the month it is supposed to be renewed. Can you see that?**
Jane: [Finger signal] Yes [followed by a verbal] *J − A − N*.

Cheek: **Where is that?**

Jane: [Verbal] On the left side.

Cheek: **Look on the right side and tell me what you see.**

Jane: [Verbal] *8* and a *6 − 86*.

Cheek: **Now see the whole thing and read it off.**

Jane: *L-R-Y*, and then *3*, a *6* or an *8* and *6*. [She remains unable to distinguish whether the middle number is a *6* or an *8* with further reviews].

Note on follow-up: On April 23, 1987, I called the chief deputy to ask what had become of the case. He said that there was a car in a parking lot with that license or a license like it (i.e., the second number *6* or *8* of another order). The chief suspect in the case had access to that parking lot. On the basis of information they have recently obtained, it is probable that one of the four men who were witnesses to the murder had been targeted. This man is known to the police but refuses to cooperate in giving helpful evidence. The deputy said that the information given by the witness in hypnosis had been valuable in running down other leads because it located a place where there were a number of cars that could have been used by the murder team.

RESEARCH

Ideodynamic Lie Detection? Research Projects 63 & 64

Milton H. Erickson told stories of how ideodynamic principles were used in the old American West as follows (Erickson & Rossi, 1981, p. 115):

> Alexander Dowie was an itinerant preacher in the colonial days of America who would enter the major saloon of a town and offer to detect thieves and murderers. He would have all present place their hands palm down on the bar. He would mention a recent local crime and then exhort them to the effect that the guilty one would not be able to keep his index finger flat on the bar. Or perhaps it would be the thumb or the little finger that would give away the guilty person. This procedure easily qualifies as the neatest early low-cost lie-detection device on record and, of course, is a precursor of the finger-signaling approaches we use today.

This story suggests that interesting experimental work could be done by comparing the results of ideodynamic signaling with body language and facial indices of prevarication (Ekman, 1981, 1985; Ekman & Friesen, 1969a, b, 1974, 1982). Cheek has summarized his approach to checking the validity and reliability of ideomotor responses to questions about stressful events by comparing our current conceptions of "refreshing recollection by the use of hypnosis" (AMA Council Report, 1986) with those of the early pioneers of depth psychology (Cheek, 1982, p. 26):

> These great and intuitive men like Breuer, Freud, Jung, Ferenczi, Janet, and many others of that period would not have been discouraged with hypnosis as a means of uncovering cause and effect relationships in mental disorders, had they known that there were ways of reviewing experience at subverbal levels and of protecting hypnotized subjects from the stress of reliving traumatic events as though they were just happening.

They did not know that a subject can be separated (dissociated) from the anguish of a very stressful scene, and can view it as though watching a moving picture of the event.

They did not know how to move a person from the moment of a very stressful experience into a later frame of reference, looking back at the event.

They did not know *how to use unconscious symbol movements of fingers (an ideomotor response) to represent the answers to questions about validity of verbally expressed memories.*

They did not know, for example, that a hypnotized subject can be asked to give an unconscious gesture any time his unconscious memory for an event differed from what had been verbally described. (Italics added)

Project 63 Carefully controlled research is now required to compare the validity and reliability of Cheek's ideomotor approach in forensic hypnosis with the methods of traditional conversational hypnosis (Hibler, 1984; Orne, 1984) and electronic (EEG) assessment (Evans, 1972; Sarbin & Slagle, 1972). Design an experimental study in forensic hypnosis to assess Cheek's clinical finding that ideomotor signals can be a way of checking the validity of a witness' report.

Project 64 A considerable literature has developed around the validity and reliability of using "leading questions" in forensic hypnosis (Hilgard & Loftus, 1979; Loftus, 1974, 1975; Loftus, Miller, & Burns, 1978; Loftus & Zanni, 1975). These studies have discussed the use of "implication" in such questioning but not the "implied directive" and therapeutic double bind as has been presented in this volume (Section I, Chapter 3). Scholarly reevaluations and experimental studies are now needed to reassess the use of "leading questions" and all the indirect forms of suggestion (Erickson & Rossi, 1980) in accessing the psychobiological sources of memory in stressful contexts of forensic hypnosis (Reiser, 1980). (See also, special issue of *The International Journal of Clinical & Experimental Hypnosis*, 1979, *27*(4), devoted to the topic of forensic hypnosis.)

APPENDIX

The Psychobiology of Transpersonal States: The Original 64 Research Projects in Search of a Graduate Student

The Nasal Cycle: "Window" of Autonomic Nervous System and Cerebral Hemispheric Dominance

The concept of hemispheric dominance, following the original work of Sperry and Gazzaniga (1967) on cerebral commissurotomy, presumed that specific functions such as verbal skills or pattern recognition were localized in each hemisphere and that these functions remained in a fixed, unvarying relationship to one another. In a series of unrelated studies, however, it gradually became clear that a spontaneous alternation in dominance over time took place between the left and right cerebral hemispheres. Goldstein et al. (1972) reported changes in interhemispheric amplitude relationships in the EEG during sleep, and this was confirmed by Gordon et al. (1982). This natural alternation in cerebral hemispheric dominance was dramatically confirmed in normal waking subjects by Klein and Armitage (1979), who found 1-1/2-hour oscillations in cognitive style.

Taking her clue from this work, Werntz (1981) measured the relative airflow through the nostrils of 43 subjects. She used identically matched thermistors (with a response range including the span 21–38°) and at the same time recorded their EEGs (Alpha, Beta, Delta, and Theta) on both cerebral hemispheres. Her results indicated that there was "a direct relationship of cerebral hemispheric activity (EEG) and the ultradian rhythm of the nasal cycle. Relatively greater integrated EEG values in one hemisphere are positively correlated with a predominant airflow in the contralateral nostril" (Werntz et al. 1982, p. 226).

In a series of follow-up studies (Werntz, Bickford, Bloom, & Shannahoff-Khalsa, 1981, 1983; Werntz, Bickford, & Shannahoff-Khalsa, 1987), Werntz took the next logical, experimental step and found that they could change nasal dominance by forced uninostril breathing through the non-

Reprinted with permission from Rossi, 1986a, pp. 119–125.

461

dominant (closed) nostril. Further, *this experimentally induced shift in nasal dominance resulted in an accompanying shift in cerebral hemispheric dominance to the contralateral hemisphere!* Not only was the ultradian nasal cycle a window on cerebral hemispheric activity, but voluntarily induced changes in nasal airflow could be used to change the relative locus of activity in the highest centers of the brain and thereby influence the all-pervasive autonomic system that regulates practically every major function of the body. Objective, Western science had finally validated the basic principles that underlay thousands of years of subjective, empirical experience by Eastern adepts! Werntz et al. (1981) summarize their work as follows (pp. 4–6):

> We feel that the correlation of the nasal cycle with the alternation of cerebral hemispheric activity is consistent with a model for a single ultradian oscillator system* and imposes a new conceptual understanding for the nervous system. . . . We propose an even more complete and integrated theoretical framework which incorporates an organization for all ultradian rhythms and their regulation by the autonomic nervous system most specifically the integration of autonomic and cerebral hemispheric activity. It could be suggested at this point that there might be some basis to believe that the "separate forms of intelligence" localized in each hemisphere require an increased metabolic support of the contralateral side of the body in terms of the overall bias they might serve. *In this context, the nasal cycle can be viewed as an easily measureable indicator or "window" for this framework.*
>
> . . . Thus the whole body goes through the Rest/Activity or Parasympathetic/Sympathetic oscillation while simultaneously going through the "Left Body-Right Brain/Right Body-Left Brain" shift. This then produces ultradian rhythms at all levels of organization from pupil size to higher cortical functions and behavior. . . . It is important to note that this represents an extensive integration of autonomic and cerebral cortical activity, a relationship not previously defined or studied. We propose that as the nasal cycle probably is regulated via a centrally controlled mechanism, possibly the hypothalamus, altering the sympathetic/parasympathetic balance, this occurs throughout the body including the brain and is the mechanism by which vasomotor tone regulates the control of blood flow through the cerebral vessels thereby altering cerebral hemispheric activity.

*Note the divergence from Kripke's (1982) views quoted earlier where he, apparently without the knowledge of Werntz's work reviewed here, finds a *multi*oscillator system to be more consistent with the total mass of ultradian data.

The Psychobiology of Transpersonal States

Both ancient and modern sources on the psychophysiology of transpersonal states implicate the autonomic nervous system on the physiological level and the cerebral cortex, the medulla oblongata, the hypothalamus, and the endocrine system (particularly the adrenals) on the anatomical level (White, 1979). . . . These are also the sources for the more "ordinary" alterations of consciousness in everyday life: sleeping, dreaming, meditation, ultradian rhythms, and the common everyday trance (Timmons & Kamiya, 1970; Timmons & Kanellakos, 1974).

Indeed, Gopi Krishna (1975) considers alterations such as psychosomatic symptoms, mental illness, and the spontaneous trances of everyday life to be malformations of a natural process whereby "normal everyday consciousness" breaks down in its ongoing evolution toward higher transpersonal states (Bucke, 1901/1967). According to this view, the transformative process is supposedly the next step in the evolution of human consciousness, but unfortunately most of humanity just does not know how to do it yet. Only the geniuses, great spiritual leaders, and mystics have successfully tapped into it. Gopi Krishna therefore calls for a concerted research effort to explore how this transformative process can be facilitated in all of humanity. It is in this spirit of search that the author now proposes the 64 research projects.

Sixty-Four Research Projects in Search of a Graduate Student

1. Replicate Werntz (1981) as closely as possible on all methodological, measurement, and subject-selection parameters for an all-important confirmation of her basic findings.

2-3. Replicate Werntz (1981) using the simpler mirror and nasal pitch methods of measuring nasal cycles to determine how reliable these techniques can be for studies of altered states of consciousness and behavior outside of the laboratory.

4-5. Replicate Werntz (1981) for very significant developmental studies on the relations between the nasal cycle and the autonomic system and cerebral hemispheric activity from infancy through old age. This can then be used as a basis for studying developmental shifts in altered states of consciousness, cognitive style, mood, and so on (London, 1963).

6-8. Replicate Werntz (1981; Werntz et al., 1981, 1983; Werntz et al., 1987) on any carefully selected clinical population with measurable alterations in autonomic system function or disease and/or cerebral hemispheric activity to (a) critically assess Werntz's new view of an integrated system of autonomic and cerebral hemispheric activity, and (b) gain further insights into the implications of this new view for the various phases of altered states in normal functioning and the variations introduced via clinical pathology (Flor-Henry, 1976; Passouant, 1974).

9-10. Replicate Werntz et al. (1981) on the use of forced shifts in nasal dominance to influence autonomic nervous function and shifts in consciousness and cognitive style via changes in hemispheric dominance.

11-12. Explore the use of forced shifts in nasal dominance to replicate the classical left-right hemispheric specialization studies that have been developed since Sperry's discovery of altered states of consciousness in patients with surgically separated cerebral hemispheres. To what extent can forced nasal dominance be used to study altered states of consciousness as a noninvasive substitute for the surgical separation of the cerebral hemispheres?

13-14. Explore the relation of nasal dominance to virtually all the other ultradian rhythms associated with altered states of cognition and affect reported in Table 11 of the research portion of Section VI.

15-17. Explore the relationship of nasal dominance to mental set and attitude in sports performance, sexual activity, meditation, hypnosis, and the common everyday trance; explore the variations, if any, produced by forced shifts in nasal dominance on these activities.

18. The author speculates that people with habitual head tilts to the right or left side may be influencing their nasal and cerebral hemispheric dominance, just as they do when lying down on their right or left sides. This leads to the testable hypothesis that subjects with habitual head tilts to the right are exhibiting a preferential use of their right hemisphere. This could be measured by EEG recordings, by modified levels of hypnotizability, and by better performance on holistic-synthetic versus analytic tasks. (The reverse would be hypothesized for subjects with habitual left-side tilts.)

19. Using the same line of reasoning as above, the author has isolated a dozen facial characteristics that may be associated with left- and right-cerebral hemispheric dominance (Rossi, 1983-1985). This association between facial laterality and hemispheric dominance could be tested by the same EEG, hypnotizability, and task performance tests as described above.

20. Is nasal dominance or forced changes in it associated with moods and clinically defined groups of mental disorders such as the alterations of manic depression? Will self-report mood scales correlate with shifts in nasal dominance (Tart, 1972)?

21-23. Are shifts in nasal dominance associated with the altered states of consciousness induced by psychedelics, alcohol, tranquilizers, and so forth? Can forced nasal dominance via uninostril breathing be used to potentiate, block, or otherwise modify psychedelic effects?

24-26. Is the nasal cycle related to the manifestations of the common everyday trance as listed in Table 11? Can forced shifts in nasal dominance change these manifestations?

27-28. Is nasal dominance shift during sleep associated with turning over and changing the side of the body one is sleeping on? Is this related to the REM-NREM cycle?

Ultradian Rhythms, the Sleep-Dream Cycle, and State-Dependent Memory and Learning

29–31. Ultradian rhythms, the sleep-dream cycle, and state-dependent memory and learning are the basic psychophysiological processes so far isolated for studies on altered states of consciousness in everyday life. How are they related to one another? Review Kripke (1982), Werntz (1981), and McGaugh (1983) as a background for designing studies to determine how the anatomical and physiological processes of the dream cycle, ultradian rhythms, and state-dependent memory and learning interact to produce altered states of consciousness in everyday life, in mental illness, and in transpersonal states.

32. Will surgical excision or drug blockage of the function of the *pontine reticular neurones* and the *locus coeruleus* (which regulate the REM-NREM sleep cycle) also interfere with the periodicity of other ultradian rhythms? This has implications for the multioscillator (Kripke, 1982) versus the unioscillator (Werntz et al., 1981) hypotheses of ultradian rhythms.

33–34. What vigilance and performance tasks will be maximized by structuring regular ultradian rest breaks throughout work periods? How long do these rest breaks need to be?

35–36. Is the continual override of the ultradian rest period the cause of stress and stress-induced psychosomatic problems? Determine the ultradian rhythms most likely associated with each of the major psychosomatic disorders, and determine if the disorder can be varied by the degree of desynchrony of this rhythm.

37. Will experimental desynchrony of ultradian rhythms result in the typical neurohormonal changes associated with stress? Which of the ultradian rhythm desynchronies is most potent in inducing stress and altered states?

38. Will experimental desynchrony of ultradian rhythms disrupt state-dependent memory and learning? Which ultradian rhythms are most influential?

39. Personal communication with Pir Vilayat Inayat Khan, the present head of the Sufi Order in the West and leader of hundreds of meditation groups around the world, confirms that a 90-minute verbally guided meditation is about optimum. Zazen practitioners report that 45 minutes (one-half ultradian cycle) is optimal for their more strenuous meditation (Kapleau, 1980). Do other meditation leaders from other backgrounds confirm this ultradian rhythm in meditation? Do ashrams and monasteries tend to have a full 90- to 120-minute ultradian periodicity, or a 45-minute half-cycle in their daily activities?

State-Dependent Memory/Learning and
Altered States of Consciousness

40. Run the classical state-dependent memory and learning experiments during different phases of the different ultradian rhythms. Which phase of which rhythms gives the most striking results for altered states?

41. Is the nasal cycle particularly significant in state-dependent learning and memory? Will forced shifts in nasal dominance result in the expected differences in the state-dependent learning of nonsense syllables, music, poetry, prose?

42. Will the selective activation of the cerebral hemispheres by forced uninostril breathing have measurable effects on the types of memory, affect, and cognition associated with each cerebral hemisphere?

The Common Everyday Trance and Hypnosis

43-46. Construct a scale from the list of manifestations listed in Table 11 to measure the common everyday trance and report on its various validity and reliability coefficients with different subject populations and age groups.

47-48. Will subjects with high scores on this Common Everyday Trance Scale (associated with the rest or parasympathetic phase of their ultradian rhythms) score higher on standard scales of hypnotic susceptibility?

49. Will the correlation attempted above be complicated by the fact that some hypnotic phenomena require sympathetic system activation rather than the parasympathetic activation assumed present in the common everyday trance? Are some hypnotic phenomena more easily experienced during the high activity phase (opposite of the rest phase) of the ultradian rhythm?

50. Will subjects high on the Common Everyday Trance Scale score higher on waking suggestions as defined by Weitzenhoffer (1957)?

51. Will subjects who have a talent for a particular hypnotic phenomenon more easily and completely experience it when they are in a high-score phase of the Common Everyday Trance Scale?

52-53. Will posthypnotic suggestion be more effective when it is administered during a high-score phase of the Common Everyday Trance Scale and when its future execution is limited to similar phases of the common everyday trance?

54-55. Will hypnotic amnesia be more effective in the high-score phase of the Common Everyday Trance Scale? What would be the implications of positive results for our theories of memory and our concept of altered states of consciousness in everyday life?

56. Run a number of classical memory and learning experiments (nonsense syllables, prose, poetry, etc.) during different phases of the common everyday trance. Does the phase account for a significant portion of the variance usually associated with such studies?

57. Do patients with psychosomatic disorders tend to experience more acute disturbances when they attempt to override the rest phase of their common everyday trance? Can psychosomatic symptomatology be ameliorated by training such patients to recognize reliable signs of their own common everyday trances and rest during these periods?

Ultradian Rhythms and Transpersonal States of Consciousness

58. *Pranayama* training that shifts nasal dominance via forced changes in nostril breathing patterns means that yogis "presumably . . . have developed conscious control over their autonomic nasal center" (Eccles, 1978) and related autonomic functions. What shifts in autonomic functioning are measurable with such training (Klein et al., 1986; Werntz et al., 1981, 1983, 1987)?

59–61. Study the effects of different forms of meditation on the nasal cycle. Do the results suggest how some forms of meditative practice lead to the altered states and psychophysiological benefits claimed? Do more highly experienced meditators evidence shifts in the nasal cycle sooner than beginners in meditation?

62. What other ultradian rhythms are found associated with transpersonal states (*samadhi, satori,* cosmic consciousness)? An unexpected breakthrough of kundalini is said to be associated with gross malfunctions of many autonomic system activities. Review the available literature to determine what autonomic functions are thrown into desynchrony.

63. Personal accounts of transpersonal states suggest that there may be two general classes: those dependent on a high sympathetic innervation (the kundalini experience) versus those associated with high parasympathetic activity (*samadhi*). This suggests a Bipolar Theory of Transpersonal States. The Zen practice of using "transpersonal double binds" called *koans* to bind the rational mind so that it can be transcended (giving rise to the enlightenment experience of *kensho* and *satori*) appears to use both. First there is an activation of the sympathetic system ("exert yourself to the utmost"), and suddenly that is reversed into its opposite with a flooding parasympathetic response (tears, "dissolving of the ego"). Can nasal dynamics be used as a window or facilitator of these experiences?

64. How can more effective double binds be formulated to facilitate the altered states of therapeutic and transpersonal experience (Erickson & Rossi, 1975; Jichaku, Fujita, & Shapiro, 1984)? Are these experiences more likely to occur during definite phases of certain ultradian cycles?

References

Abbey, H., & Howard, E. (1973). Statistical procedure in developmental studies on species with multiple offspring. *Developmental Psychobiology, 6*, 329–335.

Abel, E. (1980). Fetal alcohol syndrome: Behavioral teratology. *Psychology Bulletin, 87*, 29–50.

Abel, E. (1984). Prenatal effects of alcohol. *Drug Alcohol Dependency, 14*, 1–10.

Achterberg, J. (1985). *Imagery and healing*. Boston: Shambala.

Adam, N. (1979). Disruption of memory functions associated with general anesthetics. In J. Kihlstrom & F. Evens (Eds.), *Functional disorders of memory*. Hillsdale, New Jersey: Lawrence Erlbaum Associates.

Ader, R. (1964). Gastric erosions in the rat: Effects of immobilization at different points in the activity cycle. *Science, 145*, 406.

Ader, R. (1967). Behavioral and physiological rhythms and the development of gastric erosions in the rat. *Psychosomatic Medicine, 29*, 345.

Ader, R. (1971). Experimentally gastric lesions: Results and implications of studies in animals. *Advanced Psychosomatic Medicine, 6*, 1.

Ader, R. (Ed.). (1981). *Psychoneuroimmunology*. New York: Academic Press.

Ader, R. (1985). Behaviorally conditioned modulation of immunity. In R. Guillemin, M. Cohn, & T. Melnechuk (Eds.), *Neural modulation of immunity* (pp. 55–69). New York: Raven Press.

Adolf, E. (1967). Ontogeny of volume regulations in embryonic extracellular fluids. *Quarterly Review of Biology, 42*, 1–39.

Aggelar, P., Hoag, S., Wallerstein, R., & Whissell, D. (1961). The mild hemophilias. *American Journal of Medicine, 30*(1), 84–94.

Aldrich, K., & Bernstein, D. (1987). The effect of time of day on hypnotizability. *International Journal of Clinical & Experimental Hypnosis, 35*(3), 141–145.

Alexander, F. (1950/1987). *Psychosomatic medicine* (2nd edition). New York: W. W. Norton. (First edition, 1950).

Allport, D., Antonis, B., & Reynolds, P. (1972). On the division of attention: A disproof of the single-channel hypothesis. *Quarterly Journal of Experimental Psychology, 24*, 225–235.

Allport, S. (1986). *Explorers of the black box: The search for the cellular basis of memory*. New York: W. W. Norton.

Ananth, J., Bartova, A., & Rastogi, R. (1982). Endorphins and ACTH. In N. Shah, & A. Donald (Eds.), *Endorphins & opiate antagonists in psychiatric research* (pp. 427–437). New York: Plenum.

Araoz, D. (1982). *Hypnosis and sex therapy*. New York: Brunner/Mazel.

Aristotle. (1952). *De divinatione per somnum [On prophesying by dreams]*. In *Encyclopedia Britannica, Vol. III, Great Books of the Western World* (p. 707). Chicago: Illinois.

Armstrong, D., Jepson, J., Keele, C., & Stewart, J. (1957). Pain producing substance in human inflammatory exudates and plasma. *Journal of Physiology, 135*, 350.

Aserinsky, E., & Kleitman, N. (1953). Regularly occurring periods of eye motility and concomitant phenomena during sleep. *Science, 118*, 273–274.

Aserinsky, E., & Kleitman, N. (1955). Two types of ocular motility occurring in sleep. *Journal of Applied Physiology, 8*, 1–10.

Aswanikumar, S., Corcoran, B., Schiffman, E., Day, A., Freer, R., Showell, H., Becker, E., & Pert, C. (1977). Demonstration of a receptor on rabbit neutrophils for chemotactic peptides. *Biochemical & Biophysical Research Communications, 74*, 810–817.

August, R. (1960). Hallucinatory experiences utilized for obstetrical anesthesia. *American Journal of Clinical Hypnosis, 3*, 90–94.

Bakwin, H. (1944). Psychogenic fever in infants. *American Journal of Diseases of Children, 67*, 176–181.

Banks, A. (1985). Hypnotic suggestion for the control of bleeding in the angiography suite. *Ericksonian Monographs, 1*, 76–88.

Banks, A., & Kastin, A. (1985). Permeability of the blood-brain barrier to neuropeptides: The case for penetration. *Psychoneuroendocrinology, 10*(4), 385–399.

Barabasz, A., & McGeorge, C. (1978). Biofeedback, mediated biofeedback, and hypnosis in peripheral vasodilation training. *The American Journal of Clinical Hypnosis, 21*(1), 28–37.

Barahal, H. (1940). Testosterone in psychotic male homosexuals. *Psychiatric Quarterly, 14*, 319–330.

Barber, J., & Adrian, C. (Eds). (1982). *Psychological approaches to the management of pain.* New York: Brunner/Mazel.

Barber, J., & Mayer, D. (1977). Evaluation of the efficacy and neural mechanism of a hypnotic analgesia procedure in experimental and clinical dental pain. *Pain, 4*, 41–48.

Barber, T. X. (1972). Suggested ("hypnotic") behavior: The trance paradigm versus an alternate paradigm. In E. Fromm & R. Shor (Eds.), *Hypnosis: Research development and perspectives* (pp. 115–182). New York: Aldine-Atherton.

Barber, T. X. (1978). Hypnosis, suggestions, and psychosomatic phenomena: A new look from the standpoint of recent experimental studies. *American Journal of Clinical Hypnosis, 21*(1), 13–27.

Barber, T. X. (1984). Changing unchangeable bodily processes by (hypnotic) suggestions: A new look at hypnosis, cognitions, imagining, and the mind-body problem. *Advances, 1*(2), 7–40.

Baskin, Y. (1984). *The gene doctors: Medical genetics at the frontier.* New York: William Morrow.

Baudouin, C. (1920). *Suggestion and autosuggestion.* (Eden and Cedar Paul, Trans.) London: Allen and Unwin.

Beach, F., Buehler, M., & Dunbar, I. (1983). Sexual cycles in female dogs treated with androgen during development. *Behavioral and Neural Biology, 38*, 1–31.

Becker, R., & Selden, G. (1985). *The body electric: Electromagnetism and the foundation of life.* New York: William Morrow.

Beecher, H., & Todd, D. (1954). Study of deaths associated with anesthesia and surgery. *Annual of Surgery, 140*, 2–35.

Bell, A., & Weinberg, M. (1978). *Homosexualities.* New York: Simon & Schuster.

Bell, A., Weinberg, M., & Hammersmith, S. (1981). *Sexual preference: Its development in men and women.* Bloomington, Indiana: Indiana University Press.

Bell, R. (1974). In M. Lewis, & L. Rosenblum (Eds.), *The effect of the infant on its caregiver* (p. 1). New York: John Wiley.

Beller, J., Glas, P., & Roemer, H. (1961). Fibrinogenolysis as a cause of obstetric hemorrhage. *American Journals of Obstetrics and Gynecology, 3*, 620–624.

Bennett, H. (1980). *Selective attention: The expression of suggested action in an unattended message.* Unpublished doctoral dissertation, University of California, Davis.

Bennett, H. (1984). Can intra-operative conversation affect patients' nervous systems? *Human Aspects of Anesthesia, 2*, 7.

Bennett, H. (In press). Perception and memory for events during adequate general anesthesia for surgical operations. In H. Pettinati (Ed.), *Hypnosis and memory*. New York: Guilford.

Bennett, H., Davis, H., & Giannini, J. (1984). Nonverbal response to intraoperative conversation. *Anesthesia and Analgesia, 63*, 185.

Benson, H. (1983a). The relaxation response and norepinephrine: A new study illuminates mechanisms. *Integrative Psychiatry, 1*, 15–18.

Benson, H. (1983b). The relaxation response: Its subjective and objective historical precedents and physiology. *Trends in Neuroscience*, July, 281–284.

Berne, C., Denson, J., & Mikkelsen, M. (1955). Cardiac arrest. *American Journal of Surgery, 90*, 189.

Bernheim, H. (1886/1957). *Suggestive therapeutives: A treatise on the nature and uses of hypnotism*. (Herter, Trans.). Westport, Connecticut: Associated Booksellers. (Originally published by Putnam, New York)

Bernstein, I., Gordon, T., & Rose, R. (1983). The interaction of hormones, behavior, and social context in nonhuman primates. In B. Svare (Ed.), *Hormones and aggressive behavior* (pp. 535–561). New York: Plenum.

Bex, F. J., & Corbin, A. (1984). LHRH and analogs: Reproductive pharmacology and contraceptive and therapeutic utility. In L. Martini, & W. F. Ganong (Eds.), *Frontiers in neuroendocrinology, 8* (pp. 85–151). New York: Raven Press.

Black, S. (1969). *Mind and body*. London: William Kimber.

Blalock, E., Harbour-McMenamin, D., & Smith, E. (1985). Peptide hormones shaped by the neuroendocrine and immunologic systems. *The Journal of Immunology, 135*(2), 858s–861s.

Blalock, E., & Smith E. (1980). Human leukocyte interferon: Structural and biological relatedness to adrenocorticotropic hormone and endorphins. *Proceedings of the National Academy of Science, U.S.A., 77*, 5972.

Bloom, F. (Ed.). (1980). *Peptides: Integrators of cell and tissue function. Society of General Physiologists Series, Vol. 35*. New York: Raven Press.

Bloom, F. (1986). Chemical signalling in the spatial, temporal continuum. In L. Iversen, & E. Goodman (Eds.), *Fast and slow chemical signalling in the nervous system* (pp. 295–308). New York: Oxford University Press.

Blum, H. (1979). Hypnotic programming techniques in psychological experiments. In E. Fromm & R. Shor (Eds.), *Hypnosis: Research developments and perspectives* (2nd Ed.) (pp. 359–385). Chicago: Aldine Publishing.

Bohm, D. (1980). *Wholeness and the implicate order*. London and Boston: Ark Paperbacks.

Boring, E. (1950). *A history of experimental psychology*. New York: Appleton-Century-Crofts.

Bowen, W., Gentleman, S., Herkenham, M., & Pert, C. (1981). Interconverting and forms of the opiate receptor in rat striatal patches. *Proceedings of the National Academy of Sciences USA, 78*(8), 4818–4822.

Bower, G. (1981). Mood and memory. *American Psychologist, 36*(2), 129–148.

Bowers, K. (1977). Hypnosis: An informational approach. *Annals of the New York Academy of Sciences, 296*, 222–237.

Bowers, K., & Kelley, P. (1979). Stress, disease, psychotherapy, and hypnosis. *Journal of Abnormal Psychology, 88*(5), 490–505.

Braid, J. (1846). *The power of the mind over the body*. London: Churchill.

Braid, J. (1855). *The fascination of the critics criticized*. Manchester, England: Grant & Company.

Bramwell, J. (1956). *Hypnotism*. New York: Julian Press.

Braun, B. (1983a). Neurophysiologic changes in multiple personality due to integration: A preliminary report. *The American Journal of Clinical Hypnosis, 26*(2), 84–92.

Braun, B. (1983b). Psychophysiological phenomena in multiple personality. *The American Journal of Clinical Hypnosis, 26*(2), 124-137.

Breuer, J., & Freud, S. (1895/1955). *Studies on hysteria.* In J. Strachey (Ed. and Trans.), *The standard edition of the complete psychological works of Sigmund Freud, Vol. II.* New York: W. W. Norton.

Broadbent, D. (1958). *Perception and communication.* Oxford, England: Pergamon.

Broadbent, D. (1977). The hidden preattentive processes. *Amer. Psychologist, 32*(2), 109-118.

Broughton, R. (1975). Biorhythmic variations in consciousness and psychological functions. *Canadian Psychological Review: Psychologie Canadienne, 16*(4), 217-239.

Brun, J. (1968). Retrograde amnesia in a murder suspect. *American Journal of Clinical Hypnosis, 10,* 209-213.

Bruner, J. (1986). *Actual minds, possible worlds.* Cambridge: Harvard University Press.

Buchtel, H. (Ed.). (1982). *The conceptual nervous system: Selected papers of Donald Hebb.* New York: Pergamon.

Bucke, M. (1901/1967). *Cosmic consciousness.* New York: Dutton.

Bulloch, K. (1985). Neuroanatomy of lymphoid tissue: A review. In R. Guillemin, M. Cohn, & T. Melnechuk (Eds.), *Neural modulation of immunity* (pp. 111-141). New York: Raven.

Burbach, J., Kovacs, G., de Wied, D., van Nispen, J., & Greven, H. (1983). A major metabolite of arginine-vasopressin in the brain is a highly potent neuropeptide. *Science, 221,* 1310-1312.

Bykov, V., & Katinas, G. (1979). Temporal organization of the thyroid in the A/He mice (morphometric investigation). *Biological Bulletin of the Academy of Sciences (USSR), 6,* 247-249.

Cannon, W. (1957). Voodoo death. *Psychosomatic Medicine, 19,* 182-190.

Carew, T., Hawkins, R., & Kandel, E. (1983). Differential classical conditioning of a defensive withdrawal reflex in *Aplysia californica. Science, 219,* 397-400.

Carli, G. (1977). Animal hypnosis in the rabbit. *Psychological Records, 27*(1), 123-143.

Carli, G., Farabollini, F., & Lopo di Prisco, C. (1979). Plasma corticosterone and its relation to susceptibility to animal hypnosis in rabbits. *Neuroscience Letters, 11,* 271-274.

Carli, G., Petraglia, F., Facchinetti, F., Cerri, R., Genazzani, H., Farabollini, F., & Hupo, C. (1984). Opioid involvement in animal hypnosis in rabbits. In E. Muller, & A. Genazzani (Eds.), *Central and peripheral endorphins: Basic & clinical aspects* (pp. 133-137). New York: Raven Press.

Carlson, N. (1981). *Physiology of behavior* (2nd edition). Boston: Allyn & Bacon.

Carr, D. (1981). Endorphins at the approach of death. *Lancet, 1,* 390.

Castellucci, V., Schacher, S., Montarolo, P., Mackey, S., Glanzman, D., Hawkins, R., Abrams, T., Goelet, P., & Kandel, E. (1986). Convergence of small molecule and peptide transmitters on a common molecular cascade. In T. Hokfelt, K. Fuxe, & B. Pernow (Eds.), *Coexistence of neuronal messengers: A new principle in chemical transmission. Progress in brain research, Vol. 68* (pp. 83-102). Proceedings of the Marcus Wallenberg Symposium, Stockholm, June 1985. Amsterdam-New York-Oxford: Elsevier.

Chan-Palay, V., & Chan-Palay, S. (Eds.) (1984). *Co-existence of neuroactive substances in neurons.* New York: John Wiley.

Chapman, L., Goodell, H., & Wolff, H. (1959a). Augmentation of the inflammatory reaction by activity of the central nervous system. *American Medical Association Archives of Neurology, 1,* 557-572.

Chapman, L., Goodell, H., & Wolff, H. (1959b). Changes in tissue vulnerability induced during hypnotic suggestion. *Journal of Psychosomatic Research, 4,* 99-105.

Chapman, R., & Stern, J. (1977). Failure of severe maternal stress or ACTH during pregnancy to affect emotionality of male offspring: Implications of litter effects for prenatal studies. *Developmental Psychobiology, 12,* 255-267.

Chau, T. (1982). The endorphins and analgesia. In N. Shah, & A. Donald (Eds.), *Endorphins*

& *opiate antagonists in psychiatric research* (pp. 41–59). New York: Plenum.

Cheek, D. (1957). Effectiveness of incentive in clinical hypnosis. *Obstetrics & Gynecology, 9*(6), 720–724.

Cheek, D. (1958a). Hypnosis, an additional tool in human reorientation to stress. *Northwest Medicine, 57*, February, 177–182.

Cheek, D. (1958b). Orientation of hypnosis to practice of medicine. *Northwest Medicine, 57*, 177.

Cheek, D. (1959). Unconscious perception of meaningful sounds during surgical anesthesia as revealed under hypnosis. *American Journal of Clinical Hypnosis, 1*, 101–113.

Cheek, D. (1960a). Removal of subconscious resistance to hypnosis using ideomotor techniques. *American Journal of Clinical Hypnosis, 3*, 103–107.

Cheek, D. (1960b). Use of preoperative hypnosis to protect patients from careless conversation. *The American Journal of Clinical Hypnosis, 3*(2), 101–102.

Cheek, D. (1960c). What does the surgically anesthetized patient hear? *Rocky Mountain Medical Journal, 57*, January, 49–53.

Cheek, D. (1961a) Gynecological uses of hypnotism. In L. LeCron (Ed.), *Techniques of hypnotherapy* (pp. 126–160). New York: Julian Press.

Cheek, D. (1961b). Unconscious reactions and surgical risk. *Western Journal of Surgery, Obstetrics, and Gynecology, 69*, 325–328.

Cheek, D. (1961c). Value of ideomotor sex-determination technique of LeCron for uncovering subconscious fear in obstetric patients. *International Journal of Clinical & Experimental Hypnosis, 9*, 249–259.

Cheek, D. (1962a). Areas of research into psychosomatic aspects of surgical tragedies now open through use of hypnosis and ideomotor questioning. *Western Journal of Surgery, Obstetrics & Gynecology, 70*, 137–142.

Cheek, D. (1962b). Emotions and purpura. Editorial in *Journal of American Medical Association, 181*, 720–721.

Cheek, D. (1962c). Ideomotor questioning for investigation of subconscious pain and target organ vulnerability. *American Journal of Clinical Hypnosis, 5*, 30–41.

Cheek, D. (1962d). Some applications of hypnosis and ideomotor questioning for analysis and therapy in medicine. *American Journal of Clinical Hypnosis, 5*, 92–104.

Cheek, D. (1963). Physiological impact of fear in dreams: Postoperative hemorrhage. *American Journal of Clinical Hypnosis, 5*, 206–208.

Cheek, D. (1964). Further evidence of persistence of hearing under chemo-anesthesia: Detailed case report. *American Journal of Clinical Hypnosis, 7*(1), 55–59.

Cheek, D. (1965a). Emotional factors in persistent pain states. *American Journal of Clinical Hypnosis, 8*, 100–110.

Cheek, D. (1965b). Some newer understandings of dreams in relation to threatened abortion and premature labor. *Pacific Medicine and Surgery, 73*, 379–384. (Formerly *Western Journal of Surgery, Obstetrics and Gynecology*.)

Cheek, D. (1969a). Communication with the critically ill. *The American Journal of Clinical Hypnosis, 12*(2), 75–85.

Cheek, D. (1969b). Significance of dreams in initiating premature labor. *American Journal of Clinical Hypnosis, 12*, 5–15.

Cheek, D. (1974). Sequential head and shoulder movements appearing with age-regression in hypnosis to birth. *American Journal of Clinical Hypnosis, 16*, 261–266.

Cheek, D. (1975). Maladjustment patterns apparently related to imprinting at birth. *American Journal of Clinical Hypnosis, 18*, 75–82.

Cheek, D. (1976a). Hypnotherapy for secondary frigidity after radical surgery for gynecological cancer: Two case reports. *American Journal of Clinical Hypnosis, 19*, 13–19.

Cheek, D. (1976b). Short-term hypnotherapy for frigidity using exploration of early life attitudes. *American Journal of Clinical Hypnosis, 19*, 20–27.

Cheek, D. (1978). Were you originally left-handed? *Swedish Journal of Hypnosis*, September, 17–25.

Cheek, D. (1979). Consideration of LeCron's ideomotor questioning methods. *Swedish Journal of Hypnosis*, August, 44–51.

Cheek, D. (1980). Ideomotor questioning revealing an apparently valid traumatic experience prior to birth: A clinical note. *Australian Journal of Clinical and Experimental Hypnosis*, *8*(2), 65–70.

Cheek, D. (1982). Considerations relative to Dr. Bernard L. Diamond's opinions on the use of hypnosis as a forensic tool. *International Journal of Investigative and Forensic Hypnosis*, *5*(2), 22–30.

Cheek, D. (1986). Personal communication with Ernest Rossi.

Cheek, D., & Davis, J. (1961). Possible uses of hypnosis in dermatology. *Medical Times, 89*, 76–82.

Cheek, D., & LeCron, L. (1968). *Clinical hypnotherapy*. New York: Grune & Stratton.

Claren, S., & Smith, D. (1978). The fetal alcohol syndrome. *New England Journal of Medicine, 298*, 1063–1067.

Coe, W. (1983). Trance: A problematic metaphor for hypnosis. Invited Address, 91st Annual Conference of American Psychological Association. Anaheim, California.

Collins, V. (1960). Fatalities in anesthesia and surgery. *Journal of the American Medical Association, 172*, 549–556.

Conn, L., & Mott, T. (1984). Plethysmographic demonstration of rapid vasodilation by direct suggestion: A case of Raynaud's disease treated by hypnosis. *The American Journal of Clinical Hypnosis, 26*(3), 166–170.

Cordes, C. (1985). Chemical cruise steers emotions. *APA Monitor, 16*, 18.

Coulton, D. (1961). Subconscious use of hypnotic phenomena during labor. *American Journal of Clinical Hypnosis, 4*, 116–119.

Cox, B. (1982). Endogenous opioid peptides: A guide to structures and terminology. *Life Sciences, 31*, 1645–1658.

Crasilneck, H. (1982). A follow-up study in the use of hypnotherapy in the treatment of psychogenic impotency. *The American Journal of Clinical Hypnosis, 25*(1), 52–61.

Crasilneck, H., & Hall, J. (1959). Physiological changes associated with hypnosis: A review of the literature since 1948. *International Journal of Clinical & Experimental Hypnosis, 7*(1), 9–50.

Crile, G. (Ed.). (1947). *George Crile: An autobiography*. (2 Vols.) Philadelphia: Lippincott.

Crile, G., & Lower, W. (1914). *Anoci-association*. Philadelphia: W. B. Saunders.

Cuatrecasas, P. (1971). Insulin-receptor interactions in adipose tissue cells direct measurement and properties. *Proceedings of the National Academy of Sciences, U.S.A., 68*, 1264–1269.

Cunningham, A. (1986). Information and health in the many levels of man. *Advances, 3*(1), 32–45.

Darnell, J., Lodish, H., & Baltimore, D. (1986). *Molecular cell biology*. New York: Scientific American Books.

Davidson, J. (1980). The psychobiology of sexual experience. In J. Davidson, & R. Davidson (Eds.), *The psychobiology of consciousness* (pp. 271–332). New York: Plenum.

Davis, G., Buchsbaum, M., & Bunney, W. (1978). Naloxone decreases diurnal variation in pain sensitivity and somatosensory evoked potentials. *Life Sciences, 23*, 1449–1460.

Davis, J. (1984). *Endorphins*. New York: Dial.

DeCasper, A., & Fifer, W. (1980). Of human bonding: Newborns prefer their mother's voices. *Science, 208*, 1174–1176.

DeCasper, A., & Prescott, P. (1984). Human newborns' perception of male voices: Preference, discrimination, and reinforcing value. *Developmental Psychobiology, 17*(5), 482–491.

DeCasper, A., & Spence, M. (1986). Prenatal maternal speech influences newborns' perception of speech sounds. *Infant Behavior & Development, 9*, 133–150.

Delboeuf, J. (1877/1947). De l'origine des effets curatifs de l'hypnotisme. *Bull Acadamie Royal Belgique*, 1877. In H. Bernheim (Ed.), *Suggestive therapeutics* (p. 411). New York: London Book Co.

Delgado-Garcia, J., Grau, C., DeFeudis, P., del Pozo, F., Jimenez, J., & Delgado, J. (1976). Ultradian rhythms in the mobility and behavior of rhesus monkeys. *Experimental Brain Research, 25*, 79–91.

Delius, L. (1905). The influence of cerebral processes in menstruation. *Wiener Klinische Runcschau, 11 & 12*.

Dement, W. (1965). An essay on dreams: The role of physiology in understanding their nature. In *New directions in psychology II*. New York: Holt, Rinehart & Winston.

Dement, W. (1972). *Some must watch while some must sleep*. San Francisco: Freeman.

Dement, W., & Kleitman, N. (1957). Cyclic variations in EEG during sleep and their relation to eye movements, body motility, and dreaming. *Electroencephalography & Clinical Neurophysiology, 9*, 673–690.

Denenberg, V. (1976). *Statistics and experimental design for behavioral and biological researchers*. New York: John Wiley.

Dengrove, E. (1986). The new corner. *Newsletter of the Society of Clinical & Experimental Hypnosis, 27*(4), 4.

de Wied, D. (1980). Neuropeptides in normal and abnormal behavior. In E. Stark, G. Makara, Z. Acs, & E. Endroczi (Eds.), *Advances in physiological sciences. Vol 13. Endocrinology, neuroendocrinology, neuropeptides-1* (pp. 23–38). New York: Pergamon.

de Wied, D. (1984). Neurohypophyseal hormone influences on learning and memory processes. In G. Lynch, J. McGaugh, & N. Weinberger (Eds.), *Neurobiology of learning and memory* (pp. 289–312). New York: Guilford.

de Wied, D., & Gispen, W. (1977). Behavioral effects of peptides. In W. Gainer (Ed.), *Peptides in neurobiology* (pp. 397–448). New York: Plenum.

Diamond, B. (1980). Inherent problems in the use of pretrial hypnosis on a prospective witness. *California Law Review, 68*, March, 313–349.

Diamond, M. J. (1974). Modification of hypnotizability: A review. *Psychological Bulletin, 81*(3), 180–198.

Dismukes, R. (1979). New concepts of molecular communication among neurons. *The Behavioral and Brain Sciences, 2*, 409–448.

Dohan, F., Taylor, E., & Moss, N. (1960). The role of the surgeon in the prolongation of uncomplicated surgical convalescence. *Surgery, Gynecology, & Obstetrics, 111*(1), 49–57.

Domangue, B., Margolis, C., Lieberman, D., & Kaji, H. (1985). Biochemical correlates of hypnoanalgesia in arthritic pain patients. *Journal of Clinical Psychiatry, 46*(6), 235–238.

Dorner, G., Geier, T., Ahrens, L., Krell, L., Munx, G., Sieler, H., Kittner, E., & Muller, H. (1980). Prenatal stress and possible aetiogenetic factor homosexuality in human males. *Endokrinologie, 75*, 365–368.

Dorner, G., Schenk, B., Schmiedel, B., & Ahrens, L. (1983). Stressful events in prenatal life of bi- and homosexual men. *Experimental and Clinical Endocrinology, 81*, 83–87.

Dunbar, F. (1954). *Emotions and bodily changes*. New York: Columbia University Press.

Durden-Smith, J., & Desimone, D. (1983). *Sex and the brain*. New York: Warner Books.

Duthie, E., & Chain, E. (1939). A polypeptide responsible for some of the phenomena of acute inflammation. *British Journal of Experimental Pathology, 20*, 417–429.

Eccles, R. (1978). The central rhythm of the nasal cycle. *Acta Otolaryngol, 86*, 464–468.

Edelman, G. M. (1984). Expression of cell adhesion molecules during embryogenesis and regeneration. *Experimental Cell Research, 161*, 1–16.

Edelman, G. M. (1985). Neural Darwinism: Population thinking and higher brain function. In M. Shafto (Ed.), *How we know* (pp. 1–30). New York: Harper & Row.

Edley, S., Hall, L., Herkenham, M., & Pert, C. (1982). Evolution of striatal opiate receptors. *Brain Research, 249* (pp. 184–188). Amsterdam: Elsevier.

Eich, E. (1984). Memory for unattended events: Remembering with and without awareness. *Memory and Cognition, 12*(2), 105–111.

Eimas, P. (1975). In L. Cohen, & P. Salapatek (Eds.), *Infant perception: From sensation to cognition (Vol. 2)*. New York: Academic Press.

Eisenberg, R. (1976). *Auditory competence in early life: The roots of communicative behavior*. Baltimore: University Park Press.

Ekman, P. (1981). Mistakes when deceiving. *Annals of the New York Academy of Sciences, 364*, 269–278.

Ekman, P. (1985). *Telling lies: Clues to deceit in the market place, politics, and marriage*. New York: W. W. Norton.

Ekman, P., & Friesen, W. (1969a). The repertoire of nonverbal behavior: Categories, origins, usage, and coding. *Semiotica, 1*, 49–98.

Ekman, P., & Friesen, W. (1969b). Nonverbal leakage and clues to deception. *Psychiatry, 32*, 88–105.

Ekman, P., & Friesen, W. (1974). Detecting deception from body or face. *Journal of Personality and Social Psychology, 29*(3), 288–298.

Ekman, P., & Friesen, W. (1982). Felt, false, and miserable smiles. *Journal of Nonverbal Behavior, 6*(4), 238–252.

Ellenberger, H. (1970). *The discovery of the unconscious*. New York: Basic Books.

Ellis, H. (1915). *Studies in the psychology of sex: Vol. 2. Sexual inversion (3rd ed.)*. Philadelphia, PA: Davis.

Ellis, L., & Ames, A. (1987). Neurohormonal functioning and sexual orientation: A theory of homosexuality-heterosexuality. *Psychological Bulletin, 101*(2), 233–258.

Erickson, M. (1932/1980). Possible detrimental effects of experimental hypnosis. In E. Rossi (Ed.), *The collected papers of Milton H. Erickson on hypnosis. I. The nature of hypnosis and suggestion* (pp. 493–497). New York: Irvington.

Erickson, M. (1937/1980). Development of apparent unconsciousness during hypnotic reliving of a traumatic experience. In E. Rossi (Ed.), *The collected papers of Milton H. Erickson on hypnosis. III. Hypnotic investigation of psychodynamic processes* (pp. 45–52). New York: Irvington.

Erickson, M. (1938a/1980). A study of clinical and experimental findings of hypnotic deafness: I. Clinical experimentation and findings. In E. Rossi (Ed.), *The collected papers of Milton H. Erickson on hypnosis. II. Hypnotic alteration of sensory, perceptual, and psychophysical processes* (pp. 81–99). New York: Irvington.

Erickson, M. (1938b/1980). A study of clinical and experimental findings on hypnotic deafness: II. Experimental findings with a conditioned response technique. In E. Rossi (Ed.), *The collected papers of Milton H. Erickson on hypnosis. II. Hypnotic alteration of sensory, perceptual, and psychophysical processes* (pp. 100–113). New York: Irvington.

Erickson, M. (1939/1980). Experimental demonstrations of the psychopathology of everyday life. In E. Rossi (Ed.), *The collected papers of Milton H. Erickson on hypnosis. III. Hypnotic investigation of psychodynamic processes* (pp. 190–202). New York: Irvington.

Erickson, M. (1943a/1980). Experimentally elicited salivary and related responses to hypnotic visual hallucinations confirmed by personality reactions. In E. Rossi (Ed.), *The collected papers of Milton H. Erickson on hypnosis. II. Hypnotic alteration of sensory, perceptual, and psychophysical process* (pp. 175–178). New York: Irvington.

Erickson, M. (1943b/1980). Hypnotic investigation of psychosomatic phenomena: A controlled experimental use of hypnotic regression in the therapy of an acquired food intolerance. In E. Rossi (Ed.), *The collected papers of Milton H. Erickson on hypnosis. II. Hypnotic alteration of sensory, perceptual, and psychophysical processes* (pp. 169–174). New York: Irvington.

Erickson, M. (1943c/1980). Hypnotic investigation of psychosomatic phenomena: Psychosomatic interrelationships studied by experimental hypnosis. In E. Rossi (Ed.), *The collected* papers of Milton E. Erickson on hypnosis. II. Hypnotic alteration of sensory, perceptual, and psychophysical processes (pp. 145–156). New York: Irvington.

Erickson, M. (1943d/1980). Investigation of psychosomatic phenomena: The development of aphasialike reactions from hypnotically induced amnesia. In E. Rossi (Ed.), The collected papers of Milton H. Erickson on hypnosis. II. Hypnotic alteration of sensory, perceptual, and psychophysical processes (pp. 157–168). New York: Irvington.

Erickson, M. (1948/1980). Hypnotic psychotherapy. In E. Rossi (Ed.), The collected papers of Milton H. Erickson on hypnosis. I. The nature of hypnosis and suggestion (pp. 35–48). New York: Irvington.

Erickson, M. (1952/1980). Deep hypnosis and its induction. In E. Rossi (Ed.), The collected papers of Milton H. Erickson on hypnosis. I. The nature of hypnosis and suggestion. New York: Irvington. Originally published in L. LeCron (Ed.), Experimental hypnosis (pp.139–167). New York: Macmillan.

Erickson, M. (1956). Discussion, seminar on hypnosis. San Francisco, April.

Erickson, M. (1957). Personal communication, October.

Erickson, M. (1958/1980). Naturalistic techniques of hypnotherapy. In E. Rossi (Ed.), The collected papers of Milton H. Erickson on hynosis. I. The nature of hypnosis and suggestion (pp. 168–176). New York: Irvington.

Erickson, M. (1959/1980). Further clinical techniques of hypnosis: Utilization techniques. In E. Rossi (Ed.), The collected papers of Milton H. Erickson on hypnosis. I. The nature of hypnosis and suggestion (pp. 177–205). New York: Irvington.

Erickson, M. (1960/1980). Breast development possibly influenced by hypnosis: Two instances and the psychotherapeutic results. In E. Rossi (Ed.), The collected papers of Milton H. Erickson on hypnosis. II. Hypnotic investigation of sensory, perceptual, and psychophysical processes (pp. 203–206). New York: Irvington.

Erickson, M. (1961/1980). Historical note on the hand levitation and other ideomotor techniques. In E. Rossi (Ed.), The collected papers of Milton H. Erickson on hypnosis. I. The nature of hypnosis and suggestion (pp. 135–138). New York: Irvington.

Erickson, M. (1963/1980). An application of implications of Lashley's researches in a circumscribed arteriosclerotic brain condition. In E. Rossi (Ed.), The collected papers of Milton H. Erickson on hypnosis. IV. Innovative Hypnotherapy (pp. 315–316). New York: Irvington.

Erickson, M. (1964/1980). Initial experiments investigating the nature of hypnosis. In E. Rossi (Ed.), The collected papers of Milton H. Erickson on hypnosis. I. The nature of hypnosis and suggestion (pp. 3–17). New York: Irvington.

Erickson, M. (1973/1980). A field investigation by hypnosis of sound loci importance in human behavior. In E. Rossi (Ed.), The collected papers of Milton H. Erickson on hypnosis. II. Hypnotic alteration of sensory, perceptual, and psychophysical processes (pp. 121–141). New York: Irvington.

Erickson, M. (1976/1980). Personal communications with Ernest Rossi.

Erickson, M. (1980a). The collected papers of Milton H. Erickson on hypnosis (4 Vols.). E. Rossi (Ed.). New York: Irvington.
  Volume I: The nature of hypnosis and suggestion
  Volume II: Hypnotic alteration of sensory, perceptual, and psychophysical processes
  Volume III: Hypnotic investigation of psychodynamic processes
  Volume IV: Innovative hypnotherapy

Erickson, M. (1980b). The hypnotic alteration of blood flow: An experiment comparing waking and hypnotic responsiveness. In E. Rossi (Ed.), The collected papers of Milton H. Erickson on hypnosis. II. Hypnotic alteration of sensory, perceptual and psychophysical processes (pp. 192–195). New York: Irvington.

Erickson, M., & Erickson, E. (1941/1980). Concerning the nature and character of posthypnotic behavior. In E. Rossi (Ed.), The collected papers of Milton H. Erickson on hypnosis. I. The nature of hypnosis and suggestion (pp. 381–411). New York: Irvington.

Erickson, M., & Rossi, E. (1974/1980). Varieties of hypnotic amnesia. In E. Rossi (Ed.), *The collected papers of Milton H. Erickson on hypnosis. Vol. III. Hypnotic investigation of psychodynamic processes* (pp. 71–90). New York: Irvington.

Erickson, M., & Rossi, E. (1976/1980). Two-level communication and the microdynamics of trance. In E. Rossi (Ed.), *The collected papers of Milton H. Erickson on hypnosis. I. The nature of hypnosis and suggestion* (pp. 430–451). New York: Irvington.

Erickson, M., & Rossi, E. (1979). *Hypnotherapy: An exploratory casebook*. New York: Irvington.

Erickson, M., & Rossi, E. (1980). The indirect forms of suggestion. In E. Rossi (Ed.), *The collected papers of Milton H. Erickson on hypnosis. I. The nature of hypnosis and suggestion* (pp. 452–477). New York: Irvington.

Erickson, M., & Rossi, E. (1981). *Experiencing hypnosis: Therapeutic approaches to altered states*. New York: Irvington.

Erickson, M., Rossi, E., & Rossi, S. (1976). *Hypnotic realities*. New York: Irvington.

Escher, M. (1985). Placebo—the hidden asset in healing. *Investigations: A Research Bulletin*. Institute of Noetic Sciences, 2(1). pp. 1–32.

Esdaile, J. (1850). *Mesmerism in India and its practical application in surgery and medicine*. Hartford, Conn.: S. Andrus & Son. (Republished and retitled: *Hypnosis in medicine and surgery. An introduction and supplemental reports on hypnoanesthesia by W. Kroger*. New York: Julian Press, 1957)

Estabrooks, G. (1943). *Hypnotism*. New York: Dutton.

Estabrooks, G. (1948). *Hypnotism*. New York: Dutton.

Evans, F. (1972). Hypnosis and sleep: Techniques for exploring cognitive activity during sleep. In E. Fromm, & R. Shor. (Eds.), *Hypnosis: Research developments and perspectives* (pp. 43–83). Chicago: Aldine Publishing.

Everson, T., & Cole, W. (1959). Spontaneous regression of malignant disease. Guest editorial. *Journal of American Medical Association, 169*, 1758–1759.

Ewin, D. (1986). Emergency room hypnosis for the burned patient. *American Journal of Clinical Hypnosis, 29*(1), July, 7–12.

Fehm-Wolfsdorf, G., Born, J., Voigt, K., & Fehm, H. (1984). Human memory and neurohypophyseal hormones: Opposite effects of vasopressin and oxytocin. *Psychoneuroendocrinology, 9*(3), 285–292.

Feldman, J. (1986). Neurophysiology of breathing in memals. In V. Mountcastle, F. Bloom, & S. Geiger (eds.), *Handbook of physiology, Section 1, The nervous system, Vol. IV. Intrinsic regulatory systems of the brain* (pp. 463–524). Bethesda, Maryland: American Physiology Society.

Ferguson, J. (1961). Operating room fatalities. *Journal of American Medical Association, 176*, 483–485.

Ferrero, P., Guidotti, B., Conti-Tronconi, & Costa, E. (1984). A brain octadecaneuropeptide generated by tryptic digestion of DBI (diazepam binding inhibitor) functions as a proconflict ligand of benzodiazepine recognition sites. *Neuropharmacology*, in press.

Figley, C. (1985). *Trauma and its wake: Vol. 1. The study and treatment of post-traumatic stress syndrome*. New York: Brunner/Mazel.

Figley, C. (1986). *Trauma and its wake: Vol. 2. Traumatic stress: Theory, research and intervention*. New York: Brunner/Mazel.

Figley, C., & McCubbin, H. (1983). *Stress and the family. Vol. 2. Coping with catastrophies*. New York: Brunner/Mazel.

Filicori, M., Bolelli, G., Franceschetti, F., & Lafisca, S. (1979). The ultradian pulsatile release of gonadotropins in normal female subjects. *Acta Europaea Fertilitatis, 10*, 29½33.

Fischer, R. (1971). Arousal-statebound recall of experience. *Diseases of the Nervous System, 32*, 373–382.

Fisher, S. (1973). *The female orgasm*. New York: Basic Books.

Flor-Henry, P. (1976). Lateralized temporal-limbic dysfunction and psychopathology. *Annals* of the New York Academy of Sciences, Neurological Parallels and Continuities (II), 280, 777–797.

Folkard, S. (1982). Circadian rhythms and human memory. In F. Brown, & R. Graeber (Eds.), Rhythmic aspects of behavior (pp. 313–344). Hillsdale, New Jersey: Erlbaum Associates.

Fordham, M. (1957). New developments in analytical psychology. London: Routledge, Kegan & Paul Ltd.

Fordham, M. (1974). Jungian views of the body-mind relationship. Spring: An Annual Archetypal Psychology & Jungian Thought, 166–178.

Forel, A. (1924). The sexual question. New York: Physicians and Surgeons Book Company.

Forel, A. (1949). Hypnotism suggestion. New York: Allied Publication.

Fox, R., & Hilton, S. (1958). Bradykinin formation in human skin as a factor in heat vasodilation. Journal of Physiology, 142, 219.

Freud, S. (1909/1957). Five Lectures on Psychoanalysis. In J. Strachey (Ed. and Trans.), The standard edition of the complete psychological works of Sigmund Freud, Vol. XI (pp. 3–56). New York: W. W. Norton.

Freud, S. (1920/1955). Beyond the pleasure principle. In J. Strachey (Ed. and Trans.), The standard edition of the complete psychological works of Sigmund Freud, Vol. XVIII (pp. 3–64). New York: W. W. Norton.

Freud, S. (1905/1953). Three essays on the theory of sexuality. In J. Strachey (Ed. and Trans.), The standard edition of the complete psychological works of Sigmund Freud, Vol VII (pp. 125–243). London: W. W. Norton.

Frid, M., & Singer, G. (1979). Sypnotic analgesia in conditions of stress is partially reversed by naloxone. Psychopharmacology, 63, 211–215.

Friedman, S., & Fischer, C. (1967). On the presence of a rhythmic, diurnal, oral instinctual drive cycle in man: A preliminary report. Journal of the American Psychoanalytic Association, 225, 959.

Fromm, E., & Shor, R. (Eds.). (1979). Hypnosis: Research development and perspectives. (2nd Ed.) Chicago: Aldine-Atherton.

Furst, A., & Kashiwa, L. (1958). Case histories in hypnotherapy. San Bernadino, CA: AAA Publishing Co.

Ganong, W. (1987). Review of medical physiology. (13th Ed.). Los Altos, California: Appleton & Lange.

Gardner, G., & Olness, K. (1981). Hypnosis and hypnotherapy with children. New York: Grune & Stratton.

Garfield, P. (1971). Pathway to ecstasy. New York: Holt, Rinehart & Winston.

Garfield, P. (1979). Pathway to ecstasy. New York: Holt, Rinehart & Winston.

Gaskin, I. (1980). Spiritual midwifery. Summertown, Tenn.: The Book Publishing Company.

Geiger, R. (1984). Design and synthesis of LH-RH agonists and antagonists. In F. Labrie, A. Belanger, & A. Dupont (Eds.), LHRH and its analogues (pp. 36–49). Amsterdam: Elsevier Science Press.

Gerendai, I. (1980). Unilateral complete isolation at the medial basal hypothalamus interferes with the compensatory ovarian growth following unilateral ovariectomy. Neuroendocrinology Letter, 2, 39–43.

Gerner, R., Gorelick, D., Catlin, D., & Li, C. (1982). Behavioral effects of B-endorphin in depression and schizophrenia. In N. Shah, & A. Donald, (Eds.), Endorphins & opiate antagonists in psychiatric research (pp. 257–270). New York: Plenum.

Gilligan, S., & Bower, G. (1984). Cognitive consequences of emotional arousal. In C. Izard, J. Kagan, & R. Zajonc (Eds.), Emotion, cognitions, and behavior. New York: Cambridge University Press.

Glenn, N., & Weaver, C. (1979). Attitudes toward premarital, extramarital, and homosexual relations in the U.S. in the '70s. Journal of Sex Research, 15, 108–118.

Globus, G. (1966). Rapid eye movement cycle in real time. Archives of General Psychophysiology, 15, 654–669.

Globus, G. (1968). Observations on sub-circadian rhythms. *Psychophysiology, 4*, 366.

Globus, G., Phoebus, E., & Moore, C. (1970). REM "sleep" manifestations during waking. *Psychophysiology, 7*, 308.

Goelet, P., Castellucci, V., Schacher, S., & Kandel, E. (1986). The long and the short of long-term memory—a molecular framework. *Nature, 322*(6078), 419-422.

Goelet, P., & Kandel, E. (1986). Tracking the flow of learned information from membrane receptors to genome. *Trends in Neuro Sciences, 9*(10), 492-499.

Gold, M., Pottah, C., Extein, I., Goodwin, F., Redmond, D., & Kleber, H. (1982). Endorphin dysfunction in panic anxiety and primary affective illness. In N. Shah, & A. Donald (Eds.), *Endorphins & opiate antagonists in psychiatric research* (pp. 355-371). New York: Plenum.

Gold, P. (1984). Memory modulation: Neurobiological contexts. In G. Lynch, J. McGaugh, & N. Weinberger (Eds.), *Neurobiology of learning and memory* (pp. 374-382). New York: Guilford.

Gold, P. (1987). Sweet memories. *American Scientist, 75*, March-April, 151-155.

Gold, P., Weinberger, N., & Sternberg, D. (1985). Epinephrine-induced learning under anesthesia: Retention performance at several training testing intervals. *Behavioral Neuroscience, 99*(4), 1019-1022.

Goldberg, B. (1985). Hypnosis and the immune response. *International Journal of Psychosomatics, 32*(3), 34-36.

Goldman, M. L. (1986). Awareness under general anesthesia. Unpublished doctoral dissertation. Cambridge University, England.

Goldstein, A., & Hilgard, E. (1975). Failure of the opiate antagonist naloxone to modify hypnotic analgesia. *Proceedings of the National Academy of Sciences, U.S.A., 72*, 2041-2043.

Goldstein, A., Lowney, L., & Pal, B. (1972). Stereospecific and nonspecific interactions of the morphine congener levorphanol in subcellular fractions of the mouse brain. *Proceedings of the National Academy of Science USA, 68*, 1742.

Goldstein, G., & Betz, A. (1986). The blood-brain barrier. *Scientific American, 255*(3), 74-83.

Goldstein, J. (1983). *The experience of insight.* Boston: Shambhala.

Goldstein, L., Stoltzfus, N., & Gardocki, J. (1972). Changes in interhemispheric amplitude relationships in the EEG during sleep. *Physiology and Behavior, 8*, 811-815.

Goodman, N. (1976). *Languages of art: An approach to a theory of symbols.* Indianapolis & Cambridge: Hackett.

Goodman, N. (1978). *Ways of worldmaking.* Hassocks, Sussex: Harvester Press.

Goodman, N. (1984). *Of mind and other matters.* Cambridge, MA: Harvard University Press.

Gopher, D., & Lavie, P. (1980). Short-term rhythms in the performance of a simple motor task. *Journal of Motor Behavior, 12*, 207-221.

Gordon, H., Frooman, B., & Lavie, P. (1982). Shift in cognitive asymmetries between wakings from REM and NREM sleep. *Neuropsychologica, 20*, 99-103.

Gould, J., & Marier, P. (1987). Learning by instinct. *Scientific American, 256*(1), 74-85.

Goy, R. (1978). Development of play and mounting behavior in female rhesus virilized prenatally with esters of testosterone and dihydrotestosterone. In D. Chivers, & J. Herbert (Eds.), *Recent advances in primatology: Vol. 1. Behavior* (pp. 449-462). London: Academic Press.

Graham, J., Miller, M., Stephan, M., & Smith, D. (1980). Limb reduction anomalies and early in utero limb compression. *Journal of Pediatrics, 96*, 1052-1056.

Greven, H., & de Wied, D. (1973). The influence of peptides derived from cortocotropin (ACTH) on performance. Structure activity studies. *Progress in Brain Research, 39*, 429-442.

Greven, H., & de Wied, D. (1977). Influence of peptides structurally related to ACTH and MSH on active avoidance behavior in rats. A structure activity relationship study. *Frontiers in Hormone Research, 4*, 140-152.

Greven, H., & de Wied, D. (1980). Structure and behavioral activity of peptides related to corticotropin and lipotropin. In D. de Wied & P. van Keep (Eds.), *Hormones and the brain* (pp. 115-127). Baltimore: University Park Press.

Grevert, P., & Goldstein, A. (1985). Placebo analgesia, naloxone, and the role of endogenous opioids. In L. White, B. Tursky, & G. Schwartz (Eds.), *Placebo: Theory, research and mechanisms* (pp. 332-350). New York: Guilford.

Groves, P., & Thompson, R. (1970). Habituation: A dual-process theory. *Psychological Review, 77*, 419-450.

Gruen, W. (1972). A successful application of systematic self-relaxation and self-suggestions about postoperative reactions in a case of cardiac surgery. *International Journal of Clinical and Experimental Hypnosis, 20*, 141-151.

Guillemin, R., Cohn, M., & Melnechuk, T. (Eds.). (1985). *Neural modulation of immunity.* New York: Raven Press.

Gunnison, H. (1985, May). The uniquenesss of similarities: Parallels of Milton H. Erickson and Carl Rogers. *Journal of Counseling and Development, 63*, 561-564.

Haberman, M. (1986). Spontaneous trance or dissociation: A suicide attempt in a schizophrenic Vietnam veteran. *American Journal of Clinical Hypnosis, 28*(3), 177-182.

Haberman, M. (1987). Spontaneous trance as a possible cause for persistant symptoms in the medically ill. *American Journal of Clinical Hypnosis, 29*(3), 171-176.

Haggard, H. (1929). *Devils, drugs and doctors.* New York: Harpers.

Hall, E. (1959). *The Silent Language.* Greenwich, Connecticut: Fawcett Premier Book, Fawcett Publications.

Hall, H. (1982-83). Hypnosis and the immune system: A review with implications for cancer and the psychology of healing. *The American Journal of Clinical Hypnosis, 25*(2-3), 92-103.

Hall, M., & Stewart, J. (1983). Substance P and behavior: Opposite effects of N-terminal and C-terminal fragments. *Peptides, 4*, 763-768.

Hall, N., McGillis, J., Spangelo, B., & Goldstein, A. (1985). Evidence that thymosins and other biologic response modifiers can function as neuroactive immunotransmitters. *The Journal of Immunology, 135*(2), 806s-811s.

Harrison, M. (1982). *Self-help for Pre-Menstrual Syndrome.* New York: Random House.

Hartman, W., & Rawling, C. (1960). Hypnosis in management of a case of abruptio placenta. *International Journal of Clinical and Experimental Hypnosis, 8*, 103-107.

Haskell, R. (1986). Cognition and dream research. *The Journal of Mind and Behavior, 7*(2/3).

Hawkins, R., Abrams, T., Carew, T., & Kandel, E. (1983). A cellular mechanism of classical conditioning in *Aplysia: Activity-dependent amplification of presynaptic facilitation. Science, 219*, 400-405.

Henry, J. (1982). Circulating opioids: Possible physiological roles in central nervous functions. *Neuroscience & Biobehavioral Reviews, 6*, 229-245.

Herbert, N. (1987). *Quantum reality: Beyond the new physics.* New York: Doubleday.

Herkenham, M., & Pert, C. (1980). *Proceedings of the National Academy of Science, U.S.A., 77*, 5532-5536.

Hernandez-Peon, R., Scherrer, H., & Jouvet, M. (1956). Modification of electric activity in cochlear nucleus during "attention" in unanesthetized cats. *Science, 123*, 331-332.

Heron, W., & Abramson, M. (1950). An objective evaluation of hypnosis in obstetrics. *American Journal of Obstetrics & Gynecology, 59*, 1069.

Hess, E. (1959). Imprinting. *Science, 130*, 3368.

Heyer, G. (1954). In F. Dunbar (Ed.), *Emotion and bodily changes.* New York: Columbia University Press.

Hibler, N. (1984). Investigative aspects of forensic hypnosis. In W. Wester & A. Smith (Eds.), *Clinical hypnosis: A multidisciplinary approach* (pp. 525-557). New York: Lippincott.

Hilgard, E. (1965). *Hypnotic susceptibility.* New York: Harcourt.

Hiatt, J., & Kripke, D. (1975). Ultradian rhythms in waking gastric activity. *Psychosomatic Medicine, 37*, 320-325.

Hilgard, E. (1977). *Divided consciousness: Multiple controls in human thought and action.* New York: John Wiley.

Hilgard, E. (1985). Personal communication.

Hilgard, E., & Hilgard, J. (1975). *Hypnosis in the relief of pain.* Los Altos, CA: Kaufman.

Hilgard, E., & Loftus, E. (1979). Effective interrogation of the eyewitness. *The International Journal of Clinical and Experimental Hypnosis, 27*(4), 342-357.

Hirschfeld, M. (1920). *Die homosexualitat des mannes und des weibes.* [*Homosexuality in men and women*]. Berlin: Marcus.

Hirst, W., Spelke, E., Reaves, C., Caharack, G., & Neisser, U. (1980). Dividing attention without alteration or automaticity. *Journal of Experimental Psychology — General, 109*(1), 98-117.

Ho, B., Richards, D. III, & Chute, D. (Eds.). (1978). *Drug discrimination and state-dependent learning.* New York: Academic Press.

Hobson, J., Lydic, R., & Baghdoyan, H. (1986). Evolving concepts of sleep cycle generation: From brain centers to neuronal populations. *Behavioral Brain Science, 9*, 371-448.

Hobson, J., & McCarley, R. (1977). The brain as a dream state generator: An activation-synthesis hypothesis of the dream process. *American Journal of Psychiatry, 134*, 1335-1348.

Hobson, J., & Steriade, M. (1986). Neuronal basis of behavioral state control. In V. Mountcastle, F. Bloom, & S. Geiger (Eds.), *Handbook of physiology, Section 1, The nervous system, Vol. IV. Intrinsic regulatory systems of the brain.* Bethesda, Maryland: American Physiology Society, pp. 701-823.

Hofer, M. (1981). *The roots of human behavior.* San Francisco.

Hofstadter, D. (1979). *Gödel, Escher, Bach: An eternal golden braid.* New York: Vintage.

Hooper, J., & Teresi, D. (1986). *The three-pound universe.* New York: Macmillan.

Horne, J., & Whitehead, M. (1976). Ultradian and other rhythms in human respiration rate. *Experientia, 32* 1165-1167.

Howlett, T., Tomliln, S., Ngahfoong, L., Bullen, B., Skrinar, G., McArthur, J., & Rees, L. (1984). Exercise-induced release of met-enkephalin and B-endorphin. In E. Muller & A. Genazzani (Eds.), *Central and peripheral endorphins: Basic and clinical aspects* (pp. 285-288). New York: Raven Press.

Hudson, T. (1893). *The law of psychic phenomena.* Chicago: A. C. McClurg.

Hughes, J. (1975). An endogenous ligand for the morphine receptor. *Brain Research, 88*, 295.

Hull, C. (1933). *Hypnosis and suggestability.* New York: Appleton-Century.

Hunsaker, W., Reiser, B., & Wolynetz, M. (1977). Vaginal temperature rhythms in sheep. *International Journal of Chronobiology, 4*, 151-162.

Huston, J., & Staubli, U. (1981). Substance P and its effects on learning and memory. In J. Martinez, et al. (Eds.), *Endogenous peptides and learning and memory processes* (pp. 521-540). New York: Academic Press.

Hutchings, D. (1961). The value of suggestion given under anesthesia. *American Journal of Clinical Hypnosis, 4*, 26-29.

Huxley, A. (1956). A case of voluntary ignorance. *Esquire*, October, p. 47.

Ikemi, Y. (1959). Hypnotic experiments on gastro-intestinal disorders. *International Journal of Clinical and Experimental Hypnosis, 8*, 139.

Ikemi, Y., & Nakagawa, S. (1962). A psychosomatic study of contagious dermatitis. *Kyushu Journal of Medical Science, 13*, 335-350.

Iversen, L. (1984). Amino acids and peptides — fast and slow chemical signals in the nervous system? (The Ferrier Lecture). *Proceedings of the Royal Society of London, Series B — Biological Sciences, 221*, 245-260.

Iversen, L. (1986). Introduction. In L. Iversen, & E. Goodman (Eds.), *Fast and slow chemical signalling in the nervous system* (pp. xi-xiii). New York: Oxford University Press.

Izquierdo, I., & Dias, R. (1984). Involvement of a-adrenergic receptors in the amnestic and anti-amnestic action of ACTH, B-endorphin and epinephrine. *Psychoneuroendocrinology, 9*(1), 77-81.

Izquierdo, I., Souza, D., Dias, R., Perry, M., Carrasco, M., Volkmer, N., & Netto, C. (1984). Effect of various behavioral training and testing procedures on brain B-endorphin-like immunoreactivity and the possible role of B-endorphin in behavioral regulation. *Psychoneuroendocrinology, 9*(4), 381–389.

Jacobson, A., Hackett, T., Surman, O., & Silverberg, E. (1973). Raynaud's phenomenon: Treatment with hypnotic and operant technique. *Journal of the American Medical Association, 225*, 739–740.

James, W. (1890). *Principles of psychology*, (Vol. 2). New York: Holt, Rinehart & Winston.

Janet, P. (1907). *The major symptoms of hysteria*. New York: Macmillan.

Janus, W. (1890). *Principles of psychology*. New York: Henry Holt.

Jarvinen, K. (1955). Can ward rounds be a danger to patients with myocardial infarction? *British Medical Journal, 1*, 318–320.

Jasper, H. (Ed.). (1958). *Reticular formation of the brain*. Boston: Little, Brown.

Jaynes, J. (1976). *The origin of consciousness in the breakdown of the bicameral mind*. Boston: Houghton Mifflin.

Jichaku, P., Fujita, G., & Shapiro, S. (1984). The double bind and koan Zen. *The Journal of Mind and Behavior, 5*, 211–222.

Johnson, L., Eberhardt, N., Spindler, S., Martial, J., Dallman, M., Jones, M., & Baxter, J. (1980). Regulation of the genes for ACTH and growth hormones by glucocorticoid hormones. In I. Cumming, J. Funder, & F. Mendelsohn (Eds.), *Endocrinology 1980* (pp. 70–73). New York: Elsevier-North Holland Biomedical Press.

Johnson, R., & Barber, T. (1978). Hypnosis, suggestion, and warts: An experimental investigation implicating the importance of "believed-in efficacy." *The American Journal of Clinical Hypnosis, 20*, 165–174.

Joose, J. (1986). Neuropeptides: Peripheral and central messengers of the brain. In C. Ralph (Ed.), *Comparative endocrinology: Developments and directions* (pp. 13–32). New York: Alan R. Liss.

Jouvet, M. (1973). Telencephalic and rhonbencephalic sleep in the car. In W. Webb (Ed.), *Sleep: An active process*. Glenview, Ill: Scott Foresman & Co, pp. 12–32.

Jouvet, M. (1975). The function of dreaming: A neurophysiologist's point of view. In M. Gazzaniga, & C. Blakemore (Eds.), *The handbook of psychobiology*. New York: Academic Press.

Judovich, B., & Bates, W. (1949). *Pain syndromes*. Philadelphia: F. A. Davis.

Jung, C. (1957). *Psychiatric studies*. Translated by R. F. C. Hull. New York: Pantheon.

Jung, C. (1959). *The archetypes and the collective unconscious. Vol IX. The collected works of Carl G. Jung*. (R. F. C. Hull, Trans.). Bollingen Series XX. Princeton, New Jersey: Princeton University Press.

Jung, C. (1960a). *The psychogenesis of mental disease*. (R. F. C. Hull, Trans.). Bollingen Series XX. Vol. III. New York: Pantheon.

Jung, C. (1960b). *The structure and dynamics of the psyche. Vol. III. The collected works of Carl G. Jung*. (R. F. C. Hull, Trans.). Bollingen Series XX. Princeton: Princeton University Press.

Jung, C. (1964). *Man and his symbols*. Garden City, New York: Doubleday.

Jung, C. (1975). Critique of psychoanalysis. In *The Collected works of C. G. Jung, Vols. 4 and 18* (pp. 173–177). Bollingen Series XX. Princeton: Princeton University Press.

Jung, C. (1976). *The visions seminars*. Book 1, Part 7. Zurich, Switzerland: Spring Publications.

Jung, C. (1984). *Dream analysis*. W. McGuire (Ed.). Bollingen Series XCIX. Princeton, New Jersey: Princeton University Press.

Kaji, H., Domangue, B., Fink, G., et al. (1981). Effects of hypnoanalgesia on levels of B-endorphin-like components. Eighth International Congress of Pharmacology, Tokyo, Japan.

Kandel, E. (1976). *Cellular basis of behavior.* San Francisco: Freeman.

Kandel, E. (1983). From metapsychology to molecular biology: Explorations into the nature of anxiety. *American Journal of Psychiatry, 140*(10), 1277–1293.

Kandel, E., & Schwartz, J. (1982). Molecular biology of learning: Modulation of transmitter release. *Science, 218,* 433–443.

Kandel, E., & Schwartz, G. (1985). *Principles of neural science.* (2nd Ed.) New York: Elsevier.

Kanigel, R. (1986). *Apprentice to genius: The making of a scientific dynasty.* New York: Macmillan.

Kapleau, P. (1980). *The three pillars of Zen.* New York: Anchor Books.

Katz, R. (1980). The temporal structure of motivation. III. Identification and ecological significance of ultradian rhythms of intracranial reinforcement. *Behavioral & Neural Biology, 30,* 148–159.

Kehrer, E. (1954). Title is missing. In H. Dunbar, (Ed.), *Emotions and bodily changes.* New York: Columbia University Press.

Kennedy, B., Ziegler, M., & Shannahoff-Khalsa, D. (1986). Alternating lateralization of plasma catecholamines and nasal patency in humans. *Life Sciences, 38,* 1203–1214.

Kesner, R. (1984). The neurobiology of memory: Implicit and explicit assumptions. In G. Lynch, J. McGaugh, & N. Weinberger (Eds.), *Neurobiology of learning and memory* (pp. 111–118). New York: Guilford.

Kesner, R., & Baker, T. (1981). A two-process model of opiate tolerance. In J. Martinez, et al. (Eds.), *Endogenous peptides and learning and memory process* (pp. 479–518). New York: Academic Press.

Kihlstrom, J. (1980). Posthypnotic amnesia for recently learned material: Interactions with episodic and semantic memory. *Cognitive Psychology, 12,* 227–251.

Kirby, M. (1981). Effects of morphine and naloxone on spontaneous activity of fetal rats. *Experimental Neurology, 73,* 430–439.

Kitzinger, S. (1962). *The experience of childbirth.* Great Britain: Penguin.

Klein, M., & Clahr, J. (1959). Maternal mortality associated with anesthesia. *Obstetrics & Gynecology, 13,* 32–36.

Klein, R., & Armitage, R. (1979). Rhythms in human performance: 1 1/2 hour oscillations in cognitive style. *Science, 204,* 1326–1328.

Kleitman, N. (1963). Sleep and wakefulness (Second Ed.). Chicago: University of Chicago Press.

Kleitman, N. (1969). Basic rest-activity cycle in relation to sleep and wakefulness. In A. Kales (Ed.), *Sleep: Physiology & pathology* (pp. 33–38). Philadelphia: Lippincott.

Knaus, H. (1959). *The fertile and sterile days of the woman and their accurate calculation.* Munchen: Verlag Urban & Schwarzenberg.

Koch, M., Lepley, D. Jr., Schroder, C., & Smith, M. (1959). Study of staphylococcus infection occurring on a surgical service. *Journal of American Medical Association, 169*(2), 99–105.

Kohut, H. (1978). The psychoanalyst in the community of scholars. In P. Ornstein (Ed.), *The search for self: Selected writings of H. Kohut, Vol. II* (pp. 685–724). New York: International Universities Press.

Kohut, H. (1981). *Remarks on empathy* (Film). Filmed at Conference on Self-Psychology, Los Angeles, October 4. rieger, D., Brownstein, M., & Martin, J. (Eds.) (1983). *Brain peptides.* New York: John Wiley.

Krieger, D., & Martin, J. (1981a). Medical progress: Brain peptides (Part I). *The New England Journal of Medicine, 304*(15), 876–885.

Krieger, D., & Martin, J. (1981b). Medical progress: Brain peptides (Part II). *The New England Journal of Medicine, 304*(16), 944–951.

Kripke, D. (1972). An ultradian biological rhythm associated with perceptual deprivation and REM sleep. *Psychosomatic Medicine, 34,* 221–234.

Kripke, D. (1974). Ultradian rhythms in sleep and wakefulness. In E. Weitzman (Ed.), *Ad-*

vances in sleep research, Vol I (pp. 305-325). New York: Spectrum.

Kripke, D. (1982). Ultradian rhythms in behavior and physiology. In F. Brown, & R. Graeber (Eds.), *Rhythmic aspects of behavior* (pp. 313-344). Hillsdale, New Jersey: Erlbaum Associates.

Kripke, D., Mullaney, D., Wyborney, V., & Messin, S. (1978). There's no basic rest-activity cycle. In F. Stott et al. (Eds.), ISAM 1977: *Proceedings of the Second International Symposium on Ambulatory Monitoring* (pp. 105-113). London: Academic Press.

Kripke, D., & Sonnenschein. (1978). A biologic rhythm in waking fantasy. In K. Pope & J. Stringer (Eds.), *The stream of consciousness* (pp. 321-332). New York: Plenum.

Krishna, G. (1975). *The awakening of kundalini*. New York: Dutton.

Kroger, W. (1963). *Clinical and experimental hypnosis in medicine, dentistry and psychology*. Philadelphia & Toronto: Lippincott.

Kroger, W., & DeLee, S. (1943). The use of the hypnoidal state as an amnesic, analgesic, and anesthetic agent in obstetrics. *American Journal of Obstetrics & Gynecology, 46,* 655.

Kroger, W., & Freed, S. (1943). Psychosomatic treatment of functional dysmenorrhea by hypnosis. *American Journal of Obstetrics & Gynecology, 46,* 817-822.

Kroger, W., & Freed, S. (1950). Psychosomatic aspects of frigidity. *Journal of American Medical Association, 143,* 526-532.

Kroger, W., & Freed, S. (1954). *Psychosomatic gynecology*. Philadelphia: W. B. Saunders.

Krynicki, V. (1975). Time trends and periodic cycles in REM sleep eye movements. *Electroencephalography & Clinical Neurophysiology, 39,* 507-513.

Kupfermann, I. (1985). Genetic determinants of behavior. In E. Kandel & J. Schwartz (Eds.), *Principles of Neural Science*. (2nd Ed.) (pp. 795-804). New York: Elsevier.

LaBerge, S. (1985). *Lucid dreaming*. Los Angeles: Jeremy Tarcher.

LaMotte, C., Snowman, A., Pert, C., & Snyder, S. (1978). Opiate receptor binding in rhesus monkey brain: Association with limbic structures. *Brain Research, 155,* 374.

Lavie, P. (1976). Ultradian rhythms in the perception of two apparent motions. *Chronobiologia, 3,* 241-218.

Lavie, P. (1977). Nonstationarity in human perceptual ultradian rhythms. *Chronobiologia, 4* 38-48.

Lavie, P., & Kripke, D. (1981). Ultradian circa 1 1/2 hour rhythms: A multioscillatory system. *Life Sciences, 29,* 2445-2450.

Lavie, P., Lord, J., & Frank, R. (1974). Basic rest-activity cycle in the perception of the spiral after-effect: A sensitive detector of a basic biological rhythm. *Behavioral Biology, 11,* 373-379.

Lavie, P., & Scherson, A. (1981). Ultrashort sleep-waking schedule. I. Evidence of ultradian rhythmicity in "sleepability." *Electroencephalography & Clinical Neurophysiology, 52,* 163-174.

Lavie, P., & Schulz, H. (1978). Ultradian rhythms in the pupil. *Sleep Research, 7,* 307.

Laws, S., Hey, V., & Eagan, A. (1985). *Seeing red: The politics of pre-menstrual tension*. Dover, New Hampshire: Hutchinson and Company.

LeBoyer, F. (1975). *Birth without violence*. New York: Knoff.

LeCron, L. (1954). A hypnotic technique for uncovering unconscious material. *Journal of Clinical Experimental Hypnosis, 2,* 76-79.

LeCron, L. (1961). *Techniques of hypnotherapy*. New York: Julian Press.

LeCron, L. (1963). The uncovering of early memories by ideomotor responses. *International Journal of Clinical & Experimental Hypnosis, 11,* 137-142.

LeCron, L., Bordeaux, J. (1949). *Hypnotism today*. New York: Grune and Stratton.

Lefkowitz, R., Roth, J., Pricer, W., & Pastan, I. (1970). ACTH receptors in the adrenal: specific binding of ACTH-^{125}I and its relation to adenyl cyclase. *Proceedings of the National Academy of Science, U.S.A., 65,* 745-749.

Legemann, J. (1957). What the groundhog really tells us. *Coronet*, February.

Le Roith D., Shiloach, J., & Roth, J. (1982). Is there an earlier phylogenetic precursor that is common to both the nervous and endocrine systems? *Peptides, 3*, 211–215.

Leshner, A., Merkle, D., & Mixon, J. (1981). Pituitary–adrenocortical effects on learning and memory in social situations. In J. Martinez, et al. (Eds.), *Endogenous peptides and learning and memory processes* (pp. 159–196). New York: Academic Press.

LeVeen, H., Pasternack, H., Lustrin, I., Shapiro, R., Becker, E., & Helft, A. (1960). Cardiac arrest due to blood transfusion. *Journal of American Medical Association, 173*(7), 770–777.

Levin, B., Goldstein, A., & Natelson, B. (1978). Ultradian rhythm of plasma noradrenaline in Rhesus monkeys. *Nature, 272*, 164–166.

Levin, B., Rappaport, M., & Natelson, B. (1979). Ultradian variations in plasma noradrenaline in humans. *Life Science, 25*, 621–627.

Levinson, B. (1965a). States of awareness under general anesthesia: A case report. *Medical Proceedings, 11*, 243–245.

Levinson, B. (1965b). States of awareness under general anesthesia: Preliminary communication. *Britain Journal of Anesthesia, 37*, 544–546.

Levinson, B. (1969). An examination of states of awareness during general anesthesia. Monograph, Unpublished doctoral dissertation.

Levitan, H. (1981). Failure of the defensive functions of the ego in dreams of psychosomatic patients. *Psychotherapy and Psychosomatics, 36*, 1–7.

Lewis, B., Kripke, D., & Bowden, D. (1977). Ultradian rhythms in hand-mouth behavior of the rhesus monkey. *Physiology and Behavior, 18*, 283–286.

Lewis, M., Mishkin, M., Bragin, E., Brown, R., Pert, C., & Pert, A. (1981). Opiate receptor gradients in monkey cerebral cortex: correspondence with sensory processing hierarchies. *Science, 211*, 1166.

Lewis, T. (1927). *The blood vessels of the human skin and their responses*. London: Shaw & Sons.

Lewis, T. (1942). *Pain*. New York: Macmillan.

Lienhart, J. (1983). Multiple personality and state-dependent learning. Unpublished doctoral dissertation, U.S. International University, San Diego, California.

Lindsay, R. (1957). Personal communication. Montpelier, Idaho.

Lipowski, Z. (1986). Psychosomatic medicine: Past and present, part III. Current research. *Canadian Journal of Psychiatry, 31*, 14–21.

Livingston, K., & Hornykiewicz, O. (Eds.) (1978). *Limbic mechanisms*. New York: Plenum.

Livingston, R. (1978). A casual glimpse of evolution and development relating to the limbic system. In K. Livingston, & O. Hornykiewicz, (Eds.), *Limbic mechanisms* (pp. 17–21). New York: Plenum.

Livingston, W. (1943). *Pain mechanisms*. New York: Macmillan.

Locke, S., Ader, R., Besedovsky, H., Hall, N., Solomon, G., & Strom, T. (Eds.) (1985). *Foundations of psychoneuroimmunology*. Hawthorne, New York: Aldine.

Locke, S., & Colligan, D. (1986). *The healer within*. New York: Dutton.

Locke, S., & Hornig-Rohan, M. (Eds.) (1983). *Mind and immunity: Behavioral immunology. An annotated bibliography 1976–1982*. New York: Institute for the Advancement of Health.

Locke, S., Power, E., & Cabot, L. (Eds.) (1986). *Psychological and behavioral treatments for disorders associated with the immune system. An annotated bibliography, Vol. 2*. New York: Institute for the Advancement of Public Health.

Lockhart, R. (1977). Cancer myth and dream. In *Spring: An Annual of Archetypal Psychology & Jungian Thought*, 1–26.

Loftus, E. (1974). Reconstructing memory: The incredible eyewitness. *Psychology Today, 8*(7), 116–119.

Loftus, E. (1975). Leading questions and the eyewitness report. *Cognitive Psychology, 7*, 560–572.

Loftus, E., Miller, D., & Burns, H. (1978). Semantic integration of verbal information into visual memory. *Jnl. of Experimental Psychology & Human Learning, & Memory, 4*, 19–31.

Loftus, E., & Zanni, G. (1975). Eyewitness testimony: The influence of the wording of a question. *Bulletin of the Psychonomic Society, 5*, 86–88.

Logan, W. (1963). Delay of premature labor by the use of hypnosis. *American Journal of Clinical Hypnosis, 5*, 209–211.

London, P. (1963). *The Children's Hypnotic Susceptibility Scale.* Palo Alto, CA: Consulting Psychologists Press.

Loraine, J., Ismail, A., Adamopoulos, D., & Dove, G. (1970). Endocrine function in male and female homosexuals. *British Medical Journal, 4*, 406–409.

Lorenz, K. (1935). Imprinting. *Journal of Ornithology, 83*, 137.

Lorenz, K. (1981). *The foundations of ethology: The principal ideas and discoveries in animal behavior.* (Konrad Lorenz and Robert W. Kickert, Trans.). New York: Simon and Schuster.

Lovett, J. (1976). Two biological rhythms of perception distinguishing between intact and relatively damaged brain function in man. *International Jnl. of Chronobiologia, 4*, 39–49.

Lovett, J. (1980). Sinus tachycardia and abnormal cardiac rate variation in schizophrenia. *Neuropsychobiology, 6*, 305–312.

Lovett, J., Payne, W., & Podnieks, I. (1976). An ultradian rhythm of reaction time measurements in man. *Neuropsychobiology, 4*, 93–98.

Lovett, J., & Podnieks, I. (1975). Comparison between some biological clocks regulating sensory and psychomotor aspects of perception in man. *Neuropsychobiology, 1*, 261–266.

Lowe, G. (1987). Combined effects of alcohol and caffeine on human state-dependent learning. *Medical Science Research, 15*, 25–26.

Luboshitzky, R., Lavie, P., Soik, Y., Glick, S., Leroith, D., Shenn-Orr, Z., & Barzilal, D. Antidiuretic hormone secretion and urine flow in aged catheterized patients. *T.I.T. Journal of Life Sciences, 8*, 99–103.

Lydic, R. (1987). State-dependent aspects of regulatory physiology. *FASEB Journal, 1*(1), 6–15.

Lynch, G., McGaugh, J., & Weinberger, N. (Eds.) (1984). *Neurobiology of learning and memory.* New York: Guilford.

Lynch, J. (1985). *The language of the heart.* New York: Basic Books.

MacFarlane, R., & Biggs, R. (1946). Observations on fibrinolysis, spontaneous activity associated with surgical operation trauma. *Lancet, 2*, 862–864.

MacRobert, R. (1949). Psychiatry and intuition. *Journal of Insurance Medicine, 4*, 2–3.

Magoun, H. (1960). Caudal and cephalic influences of the brainstem reticular formation. *Physiological Review, 30*, 459–474.

Margioris, A., Liotta, A., Vaudry, H., Bardin, C., & Krieger, D. (1983). Characterization of immunoreactive proopio-melanocortin-related peptides in rat testes. *Endocrinology, 113*, 663.

Margolis, J. (1957). Plasma pain-producing substance and blood clotting. *Nature, 180*, 1464.

Martin, J. (1978). Imprinting behavior: Pituitary-adrenocortical modulation of the approach response. *Science, 200*, 565.

Martin, J. (1981). ACTH and brain mechanisms controlling approach-avoidance and imprinting in birds. In J. Martinez, et al. (Eds.), *Endogenous peptides and learning and memory processes* (pp. 99–116). New York: Academic Press.

Martin, R. (1984). A critical review of the concept of stress in psychosomatic medicine. *Perspectives in Biology and Medicine, 27*(3), 443–464.

Martinez, Jr., J., Jensen, R., Messing, R., Rigter, H., & McGaugh, J. (Eds.) (1981). *Endogenous peptides and learning and memory processes.* New York: Academic Press.

Mason, A. (1952). A case of congenital ichthyosiform erythrodermia of Brog treated by hypnosis. *British Medical Journal, 2*, 422–423.

Mason, A. (1955). Ichthyosis and hypnosis. *British Medical Journal, 2*, 57.

Mason, A. (1963). Hypnosis and allergy. *British Medical Journal, 13*, 1675–1676.

Masson, J. (1984). *The assault on truth: Freud's suppression of the seduction theory.* New York: Farrar, Straus & Giroux.

Maturana, H. (1970). Biology of cognition. BCL Report No. 9.0, Biological Laboratory, Department of Electrical Engineering, University of Illinois, Urbana.

Maturana, H. (1971). Neurophysiology of cognition. In P. Garvin (Ed.), *Cognition, a multiple view* (pp. 3-23). New York: Spartan Books.

Maxim, P., Bowden, D., & Sackett, G. (1976). Ultradian rhythms of solitary and social behavior in rhesus monkeys. *Physiology & Behavior, 17,* 337-344.

Mayer, Major. W. U.S.A.M.C. (1958). *Report on Korean war prisoners.* Freedom Foundation Lecture, Searcy, Arkansas.

McCubbin, H., & Figley, C. R. (1983). *Stress and the family. Vol 1. Coping with normative transitions.* New York: Brunner/Mazel.

McClure, C. (1959). Cardiac arrest through volition. *California Medicine, 90,* 440-441.

McEwen, B. (1981). Endocrine effects on the brain and their relationship to behavior. In G. Siegel, R. Albers, B. Agranoff, & R. Katzman (Eds.), *Basic neurochemistry* (pp. 775-799). Boston: Little Brown.

McEwen, B., Biegon, A., Davis, P., Kery, L., Luine, V., McGinnis, M., Paden, C., Parsons, B., & Rainbow, T. (1982). Steroid hormones: Humoral signals which alter brain cell properties and functions. In R. Greep (Ed.), *Recent progress in hormone research, 38* (pp. 41-85). New York: University Press.

McGaugh, J. (1983). Preserving the presence of the past: Hormonal influences on memory storage. *American Psychologist, 38*(2), 161-173.

McGlashan, T., Evans, F., & Orne, M. (1969). The nature of hypnotic analgesia and placebo response to experimental pain. *Psychosomatic Medicine, 31,* 227-246.

McKay, D. (1965). *Disseminated intravascular coagulation.* New York: Hoeber.

McLeod, W., Brien, J., Loomis, C., Carmichael, L., Probert, C., & Patrick, J. (1983). Effect of maternal ethanol ingestion on fetal breathing movements, gross body movements, and heart rate at 37 to 40 weeks' gestational age. *American Journal of Obstetrics and Gynecology, 145,* 251-257.

Meares, A. (1960). *A system of medical hypnosis.* Philadelphia: W. B. Saunders.

Meerloo, J. (1950). *Patterns of panic.* New York: International University Press.

Meier-Koll, A., Pohl, P., Schaff, C., & Stankiewitz, C. (1978). Ein chronobiologischer aspekt stereotypen vehaltens. *Archiv fuer Psychiatrie und Nervenkrankheiten [Archives of Psychiatry & Neurological Sciences],* 225, 179-191.

Meisel, R., Dohanich, G., & Ward, I. (1979). Effects of prenatal stress on avoidance acquisition, open-field performance, and lordotic behavior in male rats. *Psychology and Behavior,* 22, 527-530.

Melnechuk, T. (1985). Neuroimmunology: Crossroads between behavior and disease. Reports on selected conferences and workshops. *Advances, 2*(3), Summer, 54-58.

Menninger, K. (1959). Hope. *American Journal of Psychiatry, 116*(6), 481-491.

Mieth, N. (1954). In F. Dunbar (Ed.), Emotion and bodily changes. New York: Columbia University Press.

Milechnin, A. (1962). The Pavlovian syndrome: A trance state developing in starvation victims. *The American Journal of Clinical Hypnosis, 4,* 162-168.

Milechnin, A. (1967). *Hypnosis.* London: Bristol, Wright & Sons.

Miledi, R., Molinoff, P., & Potter, L. (1971). Isolation of the cholinergic receptor protein of Torpedo electric tissue. *Nature,* London, *229,* 554-557.

Milne, G. (1986). Hypnotic compliance and other hazards. *Australian Journal of Clinical & Experimental Hypnosis, 14,* 15-29.

Millar, K., & Watkinson, N. (1983). Recognition of words presented during general anesthesia. *Ergonomics, 26*(6), 585-594.

Millard, W., Reppert, S., Sagar, S., & Martin, J. (1981). Light-dark entrainment of the growth hormone ultradian rhythm in the rat is mediated by the accurate nucleus. *Endocrinology,* *108,* 2394–2396.

Mills, J. (1988). PMS: Symptom, or source of transformation? *Psychological Perspectives, 1,* in press.

Mills, J., & Crowley, R. (1986). *Therapeutic metaphors for children and the child within.* New York: Brunner/Mazel.

Mindell, A. (1982). *Dreambody: The body's role in revealing the self.* Los Angeles: Sigo Press.

Mindell, A. (1985a). *River's way: The process science of the dreambody.* Boston, London: Routledge & Kegan Paul.

Mindell, A. (1985b). *Working with the dreaming body.* Boston, London: Routledge & Kegan Paul.

Minning, C. (1982). Correlations between imagery, imagery ratings, personality factors, and blood neutrophil functions. Unpublished doctoral dissertation, Michigan State University.

Mishkin, M. (1982). A memory system in the monkey. *Philosophical Transaction of the Royal Society of London, B298,* 85–95.

Mishkin, M., Malamut, B., & Bachevalier, J. (1984). Memories and habits: Two neural systems. In G. Lynch, J. McGaugh, & N. Weingerger (Eds.), *Neurobiology of learning and memory* (pp. 65–77). New York: Guilford.

Mishkin, M., & Petri, H. (1984). Memories and habits: Some implications for the analysis of learning and retention. In S. Squire & N. Butters (Eds.), *Neuropsychology of memory* (pp. 287–296). New York: Guilford.

Mohler, H., & Okada, T. (1978). The benzodiazepine receptor in normal and pathological human brain. *British Journal of Psychiatry, 133,* 261–268.

Mohr, F. (1954). In F. Dunbar (Ed.), *Emotion and bodily changes.* New York: Columbia University Press.

Montague, A. (1962). *Prenatal influences.* Springfield, Illinois: Charles C. Thomas.

Moon-Edley, S., Hall, L., Herkenham, M., & Pert, C. (1982). Evolution of striatal opiate receptors. *Brain Research, 249,* 184–188.

Moore, F., & Zoeller, R. (1985). Stress-induced inhibition of reproduction: Evidence of suppressed secretion of LH-RH in amphibians. *General and Comparative Endocrinology, 60,* 252–258.

Moore, L., & Kaplan, J. (1983). Hypnotically accelerated burn wound healing. *The American Journal of Clinical Hypnosis, 26*(1), 16–19.

Moore, M. (1980–1987). Personal communications with Ernest Rossi.

Morali, G., Carrillo, L., & Beyer, C. (1985). Neonatal androgen influences sexual motivation but not the masculine copulatory motor pattern in the rat. *Physiology and Behavior, 34,* 267–275.

Morley, J., Levine, A., Yim, G., & Lowry, M. (1983). Opioid modulation of appetite. *Neuroscience Biobehavior Review, 7,* 281.

Morris, R. (1984). Is the distinction between procedural and declarative memory useful with respect to animal models? In G. Lynch, J. McGaugh, & N. Weinberg (Eds.), *Neurobiology of learning and memory.* New York: Guilford.

Moruzzi, G., & Magoun, H. (1949). Brain stem reticular formation and activation of the EEG. *EEG Clinical Neurophysiology, 1,* 455–473.

Murphy, M. (1981). Methadone reduces sexual performance in male syrian golden hamster. *Pharmacology, Biochemistry, & Behavior, 14,* 561–567.

Nance, D., White, J., Moger, W. (1983). Neural regulation of the ovary: Evidence for hypothalamic asymmetry in endocrine control. *Brain Research Bulletin, 10,* 353–355.

Nauta, W. (1964). Some efferent connections of the prefrontal cortex in the monkey. In J. Warren, & K. Akert (Eds.), *The frontal granular cortex and behavior* (pp. 397–409). New York: McGraw-Hill.

Nemiah, J., Freyberger, H., & Sifneos, P. (1976). Alexyithymia: A view of the psychosomatic process. In D. Hill (Ed.), *Modern trends in psychosomatic medicine. Vol. III* (pp. 430–439). London: Butterworth.

Nestor, J. Jr., Ho, T. L., Tahilramini, R., McRae, G. I., & Vickery, B. H. (1984). Long lasting LHRH agonists and antagonists. In F. Labrie, A. Belanger, & A. Dupont (Eds.), *LHRH and its analogues* (pp.24–35). Amsterdam: Elsevier.

Niall, H. (1976). Peptide hormone homologies and evolution. In J.arsons (Ed.), *Peptide hormones* (pp. 11–31). Baltimore: University Park Press.

Niall, H. (1982). The evolution of peptide hormones. *Annual Review of Physiology, 44*, 615–624.

Nieuwenhuys, R. (1985). *Chemoarchitecture of the brain.* New York: Springer Verlag.

Norman, D. (1968). Toward a theory of memory and attention. *Psychological Review, 75*(6), 522–536.

Norman, D. (1976). *Memory and attention* (2nd Ed.). New York: John Wiley.

Novak, J., & Harnik, N. (1929). Psychogenic origin of dysmenorrhea. *Medizinische Klinik (Munchen), 25*, 251–254.

Nugent, 1987MR: Get from Bunner/Mazel: Susan Cakarf 212/924-3444 Lankton's Ericksonian Monographs -2, 3 or 4?

Nuget, W., Carden, N., & Montgomery, D. (1984). Utilizing the creative unconscious in the treatment of hypodermic phobias and sleep disturbances. *American Journal of Clinical Hypnosis, 26*(3), 201–205.

Okawa, M., Matousek, M., Nueth, A., & Peterson, I. (1981). Changes of day-time vigilance in normal humans. *Electroencephalogry & Clinical Neurophysiology, 52*, S17.

Olness, K., & Conroy, M. (1985). A pilot study of voluntary control of transcutaneous PO by Children: A brief communication. *The International Journal of Clinical and Experimental Hypnosis, 33*(15), 1–5.

Orne, M. (1976). Mechanisms of hypnotic pain control. In J. Bonica, & D. Albe-Fessard (Eds.), *Advances in pain research and therapy, Vol. I.* New York: Raven Press.

Orne, M. (1984). The use and misuse of hypnosis in court. In W. Webster, & A. Smith (Eds.), *Clinical hypnosis: A multidisciplinary approach* (pp. 497–525). New York: Lippincott.

Orne, M. (1986). Council Report: Scientific status of refreshing recollection by the use of hypnosis. American Medical Association. *The International Journal of Clinical & Experimental Hypnosis, 34*(1), 1–12.

O'Regan, B. (1984). Inner mechanisms of the healing response. *Institute of Noetic Sciences Newsletter, 12*(2), pp. 1–20.

O'Regan, B. (1987). Healing, remission and miracle cures. *Institute of Noetic Sciences*, Special Report, May.

O'Regan, B., & Hirschberg, C. (1988). *Spontaneous Remission: An annotated bibliography of selected articles from the world medical literature. (2 vols.).* Sausalito, CA: Institute of Noetic Sciences.

Orr, W., Hoffman, H., & Hegge, F. (1970). The assessment of time-dependent changes in human performance. *Chronobiologia, 3*, 293–305.

Orr, W., Hoffman, H., & Hegge, F. (1974). Ultradian rhythms in extended performance. *Aerospace Medicine, 45*, 995–1000.

Orr, W., Hoffman, H., & Hegge, F. (1976). The assessment of time-dependent changes in human performance. *Chronobiologia, 3*, 293–305.

Ostfield, A., Chapman, L., Goodell, H., & Wolff, H. (1957). Studies in headache. Summary of evidence concerning a noxious agent active locally during migraine headache. *Psychosomatic Medicine, 19*, 199.

Oswald, I., Merrington, J., & Lewis, H, (1970). Cyclical "on demand" oral intake by adults. *Nature, 225*, 959–960.

Overton, D. (1968). Dissociated learning in drug states (state-dependent learning). In D. Effron, J. Cole, J. Levine, & R. Wittenborn (Eds.), *Psychopharmacology: A review of progress, 1957-1967* (pp. 918-930). Public Health Service Publications, 1836. U.S. Government Printing Office, Washington, DC.

Overton, D. (1978). Major theories of state-dependent learning. In B. Ho, D. Richards, & D. Chute (Eds.), *Drug discrimination and state-dependent learning* (pp. 283-318). New York: Academic Press.

Papez, J. (1937). A proposed mechanism of emotion. *Archives of Neurology & Physiology, 38*, 725-744.

Parry, B. (1985). *Women and health roundtable report, 9*(2), 1-2.

Passouant, P. (1974). REM's ultradian rhythm during 24 hours in narcolepsy. In L. Schevina, F. Halberg, & J. Pauly (Eds.), *Chronobiology*. Tokyo: Igakushoin.

Pavlov, I. (1928). *Lectures on conditioned reflexes*. New York: Liveright.

Payan, D., Levine, J., & Goetzl, E. (1984). Opinion: Modulation of immunity and hypersensitivity by sensory neuropeptides. *Journal of Immunology, 132*, 1601-1604.

Pearson, R. (1961). Response to suggestions given under general anesthesia. *American Journal of Clinical Hypnosis, 4*, 106-114.

Pert, A. (1978). Central sites involved in opiate actions. In J. Fishman (Ed.), *The bases of addiction* (pp. 299-332). Berlin: Dahlem Konf.

Pert, A. (1980). Psychopharmacology of analgesia and pain. In L. Ng, & J. Bonica (Eds.), *Discomfort and humanitarian care* (p. 139). New York: Elsevier.

Pert, A., & Yaksh, T. (1974). Sites of morphine-induced analgesia in the primate brain: Relation to pain pathways. *Brain Research, 80*, 135.

Pert, C. (1976). The opiate receptor. In R. Beers Jr., & E. Bassett (Eds.), *Cell membrane receptors for viruses, antigens and antibodies, polypeptide hormones, and small molecules* (pp. 435-450). New York: Raven Press.

Pert, C. (1981). Type 1 and type 2 opiate receptor distribution in brain—what does it tell us? In J. Martin, S., S. Reichlin, & K. Bick (Eds.), *Neurosecretion and brain peptides. Advances in biochemical psychopharmacology. Vol. 28* (pp. 117-131). New York: Raven Press.

Pert, C. (1985). Neuropeptides, receptors, and emotions. *Cybernetics, 1*(4), 33-34.

Pert, C. (1986). The wisdom of the receptors: Neuropeptides, the emotions, and bodymind. *Advances, 3*(3), 8-16.

Pert, C. (1987). Neuropeptides: The emotions and bodymind. *Noetic Sciences Review, 2*, 13-18.

Pert, C., & Herkenham, M. (1981). From receptors to brain circuitry. In R. Cagan, & M. Kare (Eds.), *Biochemistry of taste and olfaction* (pp. 511-527). New York: Academic Press.

Pert, C., Hill, J., Ruff, M., Berman, R., Robey, W., Arthur, L., Ruscetti, F., & Farrar, W. (1986). Octapeptides deduced from the neuropeptide receptor-like pattern of antigen T4 in brain potently inhibit human immunodeficiency virus receptor binding and T-cell infectivity. *Proceedings of the National Academy of Science USA, 83*(23), 9254-9258.

Pert, C., Ruff, M., Weber, R., & Herkenham, M. (1985). Neuropeptides and their receptors: A psychosomatic network. *The Journal of Immunology, 135*(2), 820s-826s.

Pert, C., & Snyder, S. (1973a). Opiate receptor: Demonstration in nervous tissue. *Science, 179*, 1011-1014.

Pert, C., & Snyder, S. (1973b). Properties of opiate-receptor binding in rat brain. *Proceedings of the National Academy of Sciences, U.S.A., 70*, 2243-2247.

Pert, C., & Snyder, S. (1974). Opiate-receptor binding of agonists and antagonists affected differentially by radium. *Molecular Pharmacology, 10*, 868-879.

Pert, C., Snyder, S., & Portoghese, P. (1976). Correlation of opiate receptor affinity with analgetic effects of meperidine homologues. *Journal of Medical Chemistry, 19*, 1248-1250.

Peter, R. (1986). Structure-activity studies on gonadotropin-releasing hormone in teleosts, amphibians, reptiles and mammals. In C. Ralph (Ed.), *Comparative endocrinology: Developments and directions* (pp. 75-93). New York: Alan R. Liss.

Pettinati, H. (1986). Hypnosis and patients with eating disorders: Mind over body? *Hypnos, 13*(4), 175-183.

Pettinati, H., Horne, R., & Staats, J. (1982). Hypnotizability of anorexia nervosa and bulimic patients. Paper presented at the Annual Meeting of the International Society for Clinical and Experimental Hypnosis, Indianapolis, Indiana.

Pettinati, H., Horne, R., & Staats, J. (1985). Hypnotizability in patients with anorexia nervosa and bulimia. *Archives of General Psychiatry, 42*, 1014–1016.

Pettinati, H., & Wade, J. (1986). Hypnosis for the anorectic and bulimic patient. *Seminars in Adolescent Medicine, 2*, 75–79.

Phillips, O., et al. (1960). The Baltimore anesthesia study committee report. *Journal of the American Medical Association, 174*, 2015–2022.

Piaget, J. (1955). *The language and thought of the child*. New York: Meridian Book, World Publishing.

Pickar, D., Extein, I., Gold, P., Summers, R., Naber, D., & Goodwin, F. (1982). Endorphins and affective illness. In N. Shah, & A. Donald (Eds.), *Endorphins & opiate antagonists in psychiatric research* (pp. 375–397). New York: Plenum.

Plotnikoff, N., Morley, J., & Kay, N. (1986). Neuropeptides and psychoneuroimmunology. *Psychopharmacology Bulletin, 22*(4), 1089–1092.

Plummer, K. (1975). *Sexual stigma: An interactionist account*. London: Routledge & Kegan Paul.

Plummer, K. (Ed.). (1981). *The making of the modern homosexual*. London: Hutchinson.

Podnieks, I., & Lovett, J. (1975). Spontaneous rhythms of perceptual motor performance in intact and damaged brain of man. *Biological Psychology, 3*, 201–212.

Popper, K. (1965). *Conjectures and refutations*. London: Routledge & Kegan Paul.

Posner, B. (1985). *Polypeptide hormone receptors*. New York, Basel: Marcel Dekker.

Pribram, K. (1971). *Languages of the brain: Experimental paradoxes and principles in neuro-psychology*. (3rd Ed.) New York: Brandon House.

Pribram, K. (1986). The cognitive revolution and mind/brain issues. *American Psychologist, 41*(5), 507–520.

Quackenbos, J. (1908). *Hypnotic therapies*. New York: Harper Brothers.

Quabbe, H., Gregor, M., Bumke-Vogt, C., Eckhof, A., & Witt, I. (1981). Twenty-four hour pattern of growth hormone secretion in the rhesus monkey: Studies including alterations of the sleep/wake and sleep stage cycles. *Endocrinology, 109*, 513–522.

Quirion, R., Bowen, W., & Pert, C. (1981). μ, δ and κ opiate receptors: Interconvertible forms of the same receptor. In *Advances in Endogenous and Exogenous Opioids*. Proceedings of the International Narcotic Research Conference, Kyoto, Japan, July 26–30.

Quirion, R., Bowen, W., Herkenham, M., & Pert, C. (1982). Visualization and solubilization of rat brain opiate receptors with a "k" ligand selectivity pattern. *Cellular and Molecular Neurobiology, 2*(4), 333–344.

Quirion, R., Hammer, R. Jr., Herkenham, M., & Pert, C. (1981). Phencyclidine (angel dust), the sigma "opiate" receptor: Its visualization by tritium-sensitive film. *Proceedings of the National Academy of Science USA, 78*, 5881.

Quirion, R., O'Donohue, T., Everist, H., Pert, A., & Pert, C. (1983). Phencyclidine receptors and possible existence of an endogenous ligand. In J. Kamenka, E. Domino, & P. Geneste (Eds.), *Phencyclidine and related arlcyclhexylamines: Present and future applications*. Ann Arbor, Michigan: NPP Books.

Raginsky, B. (1959). Temporary cardiac arrest induced under hypnosis. *International Journal of Clinical & Experimental Hypnosis, 7*, 53–68.

Ralph, C. (1985). *Comparative endocrinology: Developments and directions*. New York: Alan R. Liss.

Rank, O. (1959). *The myth of the birth of the hero and other writings*. New York: Vintage Books.

Rasmussen, D. (1986). Physiological interactions of the basic rest–activity cycle of the brain: Pulsatile luteinizing hormone secretion as a model. *Psychoneuroendocrinology, 11*(4), 389–405.

Rasmussen, D., & Malven, P. (1981). Relationship between rhythmic motor activity and plasma luteinizing hormone in ovariectomized sheep. *Neuroendocrinology, 32*, 364–369.

Rasmussen, D., Malven, P. (1983). Effects of confinement stress on episodic secretion of LH in ovariectomized sheep. *Neuroendocrinology, 36*, 392–396.

Ravitz, L. (1950). Electrometric correlates of the hypnotic state. *Science, 112*, 341–342.

Recant, L., Voyles, N., Luciano, M., & Pert, C. (1981). Naltrex-one reduces weight gain, alters "B-endorphin," and reduces insulin output from pancreatic islets of genetically obese mice. *Peptides, 1*, 309.

Reinberg, A., Migraine, C., Apfelbaum, M., Brigant, L., Ghata, J., Vieux, N., Laporte, A., & Nicolai. (1979). Circadian and ultradian rhythms in the feeding behavior and nutrient intakes of oil refinery operators with shift-work every 3–4 days. *Diabete & Metabolisme, 5*, 33–41.

Reiser, M. (1980). *Handbook of investigative hypnosis*. Los Angeles, CA: Lehi Publishing Co.

Reus, V., Weingartner, H., & Post, R. (1979). Clinical implications of state-dependent learning. *American Journal of Psychiatry, 136*(7), 927–931.

Richardson, R., Riccio, D., & Steele, J. (1986). State-dependent retention induced by postacquisition exposure to pentobarbital or shock stress in rats. *Animal Learning & Behavior, 14*(1), 73–79.

Richter, C. (1956). The phenomena of sudden death in animals and man. Abstract of unpublished paper presented at American Psychosomatic Society, *Psychosomatic Medicine, 8*, 515–516.

Richter, C. (1957). On the phenomenon of sudden death in animals and man. *Psychosomatic Medicine, 19*, 191–198.

Rigter, H., & Crabbe, J. (1979). Modulation of memory by pituitary hormones. *Vitamins and Hormones, 37*. New York: Academic Press.

Rioch, D. (1960). Fear can kill. *San Francisco Chronicle*, November 16.

Robertson, R. (1986). *C. G. Jung and the archetypes of the collective unconscious*. New York: Peter Lang Publishing.

Rodger, B. (1961). The art of preparing the patient for anesthesia. *Anesthesiology, 22*, 548–554.

Rogers, C. (1947). Some observations on the organization of personality. *American Psychologist, 2*, 358–368.

Rogers, C. (1987). Rogers, Kohut, and Erickson: A personal perspective on some similarities and differences. In J. Zeig (Ed.), *The evolution of psychotherapy* (pp. 179–187). New York: Brunner/Mazel.

Romano, S., & Gizdulich, P. (1980). Suggestion of ultradian rhythm in peripheral blood flow. *Chronobiologia, 7*, 259–261.

Rome, E. (1986). Premenstrual Syndrome (PMS) examined through a feminist lens. In V. Olesen & N. Fugate-Woods (Eds.), *Culture, society, and menstruation* (pp. 145–151). New York: Hemisphere Publishing Corp.

Rosenfield, I. (1986). Neural Darwinism: A new approach to memory and perception. *New York Times Review of Books, 33*(15), 21–27, October 9.

Rossi, A. (1980). Mood cycles by menstrual month and social week. In A. Dan, F. Graham, & C. Beecher (Eds.), *The menstrual cycle: A synthesis of interdisciplinary research, Vol I* (pp. 56–75). New York: Springer Publishing.

Rossi, A. (1984). Gender and parenthood. *American Sociological Review, 49*(1), 1–18.

Rossi, E. (1972/1985). *Dreams and the growth of personality*. New York: Brunner/Mazel.

Rossi, E. (1973/1980). Psychological shocks and creative moments in psychotherapy. In E. Rossi (Ed.), *The collected papers of Milton H. Erickson on hypnosis. Vol IV. Innovative hypnotherapy* (pp. 447–463). New York: Irvington.

Rossi, E. (1981). Hypnotist describes natural rhythm of trance readiness. *Brain Mind Bulletin, 6*(7), 1.

Rossi, E. (1982). Hypnosis and ultradian cycles: A new state(s) theory of hypnosis? *American Journal of Clinical Hypnosis, 25*(1), 21–32.

Rossi, E. (1983–1985). Unity and diversity in Ericksonian approaches: Now and in the future. In J. Zeig (Ed.), *Ericksonian Psychotherapy. I. Structures* (pp. 15–30). New York: Brunner/ Mazel.

Rossi, E. (1986a). Altered states of consciousness in everyday life: The ultradian rhythms. In B. Wolman (Ed.), *Handbook of altered states of consciousness* (pp. 97–132). New York: Van Nostrand.

Rossi, E. (1986b). The Indirect Trance Assessment Scale (ITAS): A Preliminary Outline and Learning Tool. In M. Yapko (Ed.), *Hypnotic and strategic interventions: Principles and practice* (pp. 1–29). New York: Irvington.

Rossi, E. (1986c). The new psychobiology of dissociation: The state-dependent memory and learning theory of hypnotherapy. *HYPNOS, 13*(4), 184–199.

Rossi, E. (1986d). *The Psychobiology of Mind-Body Healing: New Concepts in Therapeutic Hypnosis.* New York: W. W. Norton.

Rossi, E. (1986e). Hypnosis and ultradian rhythms. In B. Zilbergeld, M. Edelstein, & D. Araoz (Eds.), *Hypnosis Questions and Answers.* New York: W. W. Norton.

Rossi, E. (1987). Mind/body communication and the new language of human facilitation. In J. Zeig (Ed.), *The evolution of psychotherapy* (pp. 369–387). New York: Brunner/Mazel.

Rossi, E. (1988). The psychobiology of mind-body healing: The vision and state-of-the-art. In J. Zeig (Ed.), *Ericksonian psychotherapy: State of the art.* Proceedings of the Third International Congress on Ericksonian Approaches to Hypnosis and Psychotherapy. New York: Brunner/Mazel, in press.

Rossi, E. (In preparation). Information substance-receptor communication systems: A new view of mind-body healing and hypnosis.

Rossi, E., & Ryan, M. (Eds.) (1985). *Life reframing in hypnosis. Vol. II. The seminars, workshops, and lectures of Milton H. Erickson.* New York: Irvington.

Rossi, E., & Ryan, M. (1986). *Mind-body communication in hypnosis. Vol. 3. The seminars, workshops and lectures of Milton H. Erickson.* New York: Irvington.

Rossi, E., & Ryan, M. (Eds.) (In preparation). *Therapeutic choice in hypnosis. Vol IV. The seminars, workshops and lectures of Milton H. Erickson.* New York: Irvington.

Rossi, E., Ryan, M., & Sharp, F. (Eds.) (1984). *Healing in hypnosis. Vol I. The seminars, workshops, and lectures of Milton H. Erickson.* New York: Irvington.

Roth, J., Le Roith, D., Collier, E., Weaver, N., Watkinson, A., Cleland, C., & Glick, S. (1985). Evolutionary origins of neuropeptides, hormones, and receptors: Possible applications to immunology. *The Journal of Immunology, 135*(2), 816s–819s.

Roy, A., & Clark, J. (Eds.). (1983). *Gene regulation by steroid hormones II.* New York, Heidelberg, Berlin: Springer-Verlag.

Ruff, M., Farrar, W., & Pert, C. (1986). Interferon Y and granulocyte/macrophage colony-stimulating factor inhibit growth and induce antigens characteristic of myeloid differentiation in small-cell lung cancer cell lines. *Proceedings of the National Academy of Science USA, 83*, 6613–6617.

Ruff, M., & Pert, C. (1984). Small cell carcinoma of the lung: Macrophage-specific antigens suggest hemopoietic stem cell origin. *Science, 225*, 1034–1036.

Ruff, M., & Pert, C. (1986). Neuropeptides are chemoattractants for human monocytes and tumor cells: A basis for mind-body communication. In N. Plotnikoff, R. Faith, A. Murgo, & R. Good (Eds.), *Enkephalins and endorphins stress and the immune system* (pp. 387–398). New York: Plenum.

Ruff, M., Pert, C., Weber, R., Wahl, L., Wahl, S., & Paul, S. (1985a). Benzodiazepine receptor-mediated chemotaxis of human monocytes. *Science, 229*, 1281–1283.

Ruff, M., Wahl, S., Mergenhagen, S., & Pert, C. (1985b). Opiate receptor-mediated chemotaxis of human monocytes. *Neuropeptides, 5*, 363–366.

Ruff, M., Wahl, S., & Pert, C. (1985). Substance P receptor-mediated chemotaxis of human monocytes. *Peptides, 6* Supplement 2, 107-111.

Russel, G. (1979). Bulimia nervosa: An ominous variant of anorexia nervosa. *Psychological Medicine, 9*, 429-448.

Saba, P., Salvadorini, F., Galeone, F., & Luisi, M. (1973). Hormonal findings in male homosexuals. *IRCS Medical Science: Psychology & Psychiatry, 3*, 15.

Sagen, J., & Routtenberg, A. (1981). Specific anatomical and synaptic sites of neuropeptide action in memory formation. In J. Martinez, R. Jensen, R. Messing, H. Rigter, & J. McGaugh (Eds.), *Endogenous peptides and learning and memory processes* (pp. 541-561). New York: Academic Press.

Sampiman, R., & Woodruff, M. (1946). Some observations concerning the use of hypnosis as a substitute for anesthesia. *Medical Journal of Australia, 1*, 393.

Sampson, J. (1930). Post salpingectomy endometriosis. *American Journal of Obstetrics & Gynecology, 20*, 443.

Sarbin, T., & Coe, W. (1972). *Hypnosis: A social psychological analysis of influence communication.* New York: Holt, Rinehart, & Winston.

Sarbin, T., & Slagle, R. (1972). Hypnosis and psychophysiological outcomes. In E. Fromm & R. Shor (Eds.), *Hypnosis: Research developments and perspectives* (pp. 185-214). Chicago: Aldine.

Sarna, S. (1985). Cyclic motor activity. Migrating motor complex. *Gastroenterology, 89*, 694-913.

Scarlett, J., & Olefsky, J. (1985). Polypeptide hormone receptor-associated disease states in man. In B. Posner (Ed.), *Polypeptide human receptors* (pp. 553-587). New York, Basel: Marcel Dekker.

Scharrer, E., & Scharrer, B. (1940). Secretory cells within the hypothalamus. *Research Publications of the Association of Nervous & Mental Diseases.* New York: Hafner.

Scheller, R., Jackson, J., McAllister, L., Rothman, B., Mayeri, E., & Axel, R. (1983). A single gene encodes multiple neuropeptides mediating a stereotyped behavior. *Cell, 32,*-22.

Scheller, R., Jackson, J., McAllister, L., Schwartz, J., Kandel, E., & Axel, R. (1982). A family of genes that codes for ELH, a neuropeptide eliciting a stereotyped pattern of behavior in aplysia. *Cell, 28*, April, 707-719.

Schmitt, F. (1979). The role of structural, electrical, and chemical circuitry in brain function. In F. Schmitt, & G. Worden (Eds.), *The neurosciences: Fourth study program* (pp. 5-20). Cambridge, Massachusetts: MIT Press.

Schmitt, F. (1982). A protocol for molecular genetic neuroscience. In F. Schmitt, S. Bird, & F. Bloom (Eds.), *Molecular genetic neuroscience* (pp. 1-9). New York: Raven Press.

Schmitt, F. (1984). Molecular regulators of brain function: A new view. *Neuroscience, 13*, 991-1001.

Schmitt, F. (1986). Chemical information processing in the brain: prospect from retrospect. In L. Iversen, & E. Goodman (Eds.), *Fast and slow signalling in the nervous system* (pp. 239-243). New York: Oxford University Press.

Schmitt, F., & Samson, F. (1969). Brain cell microenvironment. *Neuroscience Research Progress Bulletin, 7*, 277-417.

Schneck, J. (1948). Psychogenic cardiovascular reaction interpreted and successfully treated with hypnosis. *Psychoanalytical Review, 35*, 14-19.

Schneider, J., Smith, W., & Witcher, S. (1983). The relationship of mental imagery to white blood cell (neutrophil) function: Experimental studies of normal subjects. Uncirculated mimeographs. Michigan State University, College of Medicine. East Lansing, Michigan.

Schneider, J., Smith, W., & Witcher, S. (1984). The relationship of mental imagery to white blood cell (neutrophil) function in normal subjects. Paper presented at the 36th Annual Scientific Meeting of the International Society for Clinical & Experimental Hypnosis, San Antonio, Texas, 25 October.

Schneider, R. (1951). Recurrent thrombophlebitis, an experimental study of life situations and emotions and clotting time and relative viscosity of the blood. *American Journal of Medical Sciences, 222*, 562–578.

Schneider, W., & Shiffrin, R. (1977). Controlled and automatic human information processing: I. Detection, search, and attention. *Psychological Review, 84*(1), 1–66.

Schrodinger, E. (1947). *What is life? The physical aspect of the living cell.* Cambridge, MA: University Press.

Schwartz, M. (1963). The cessation of labor using hypnotic techniques. *American Journal of Clinical Hypnosis, 5*, 211–213.

Seeger, T., Sforzo, G., Pert, C., & Pert, A. (1984). In vivo autoradiography: Visualization of stress-induced changes in opiate receptor occupancy in the rat brain. *Brain Research, 305*, 303–311.

Segal, L. (1986). *The dream of reality: Heinz von Foerster's contructivism.* New York: W. W. Norton.

Selo, R. (1957). Personal communication. Council Bluffs, Iowa.

Selye, H. (1974). *Stress without distress.* New York: Signet.

Selye, H. (1976). *The stress of life.* New York: McGraw-Hill.

Selye, H. (1982). History and present status of the stress concept. In L. Goldberger, & S. Breznitz (Eds.), *Handbook of stress* (pp. 7–20). New York: Macmillan.

Shaffer, L. (1975). Multiple attention in continuous verbal tasks. In P. Rabbitt, & S. Dornic (Eds.), *Attention and performance V.* New York: Academic Press.

Shah, N., & Donald, A. (1982). Current status of endorphins and opiate antagonists in psychiatry. An overview. In N. Shah, & A. Donald (Eds.), *Endorphins & opiate antagonists in psychiatric research* (pp. 1–13). New York: Plenum.

Sharpe, G., Whitaker, H., & Parsons, W. (1957). The clinical problem of circulatory failure. *Surgery, Gynecology, & Obstetrics, 104*(5), 535–538.

Shashoua, V. (1979). Brain metabolism and the acquisition of new behaviors. III. Evidence for secretion of two proteins into the brain extracellular fluid after training. *Brain Research, 166*, 349–358.

Shashoua, V. (1981). Extracellular fluid proteins of goldfish brain. *Neurochemistry Research, 6*, 1129–1147.

Shiffrin, R., & Schneider, W. (1977). Controlled and automatic human information processing. II. Perceptual learning, automatic attending, and a general theory. *Psychological Review, 84*(2), 127–190.

Shiffrin, R., & Schneider, W. (1984). Automatic and controlled processing revisited. *Psychological Review, 91*(2), 269–276.

Shiotsuka, R., Jovonovich, J., & Jovonovich, J. (1974). In vitro data on drug sensitivity: Circadian and ultradian corticosterone rhythms in adrenal organ cultures. In J. Aschoff et al. (Eds.) (pp. 225–267). *Chronobiological aspects of endocrinology.* Stuttgart, Germany: Schattauer.

Shor, R., & Orne, E. (1962). *Harvard Group Scale of Hypnotic Susceptibility, Form A.* Palo Alto, CA: Consulting Psychologists Press.

Shroff, P. (1959). Operating room deaths. *Surgery, Gynecology & Obstetrics, 90*, 9–13.

Siegel, S. (1975). Evidence from rats that morphine tolerance is a learned response. *Journal of Comparative and Physiological Psychology, 89*, 498–506.

Siegel, S. (1978). A Pavlovian conditioning analysis of morphine tolerance. In N. Krasnegor (Ed.), *Behavioral tolerance: Research and treatment implications.* NIDA Research Monograph 18. Washington, DC: U.S. Government Printing Office.

Silberman, E., Putnam, F., Weingartner, H., Braun, B., & Post, R. (1985). Dissociative states in multiple personality disorders: A quantitative study. *Psychiatry Research, 15*, 253–260.

Silverman, P., & Retzlaff, P. (1986). Cognitive stage regression through hypnosis: Are earlier cognitive stages retrievable? *The International Journal of Clinical and Experimental Hypnosis, 34*(3), 192–204.

Simon, E., Hiller, J., & Edelman, I. (1973). Stereospecific binding of the potent narcotic analgesic (3H)etorphine to rat brain homogenate. *Proceedings of the National Academy of Sciences, U.S.A., 70*, 1947–1949.

Simon, M., & George, R. (1975). Diurnal variations in plasma corticosterone and growth hormone as correlated with regional variations in norepinephrine, dopamine, and serotonin content of rat brain. *Neuroendocrinology, 17*, 125–138.

Singer, I. (1973). *Goals of human sexuality*. New York: Shocken Books.

Sluyser, M. (Ed.). (1985). *Interaction of steroid hormone receptors with DNA*. Chichester, England: Ellis Horwood.

Smith, E., & Blalock, E. (1981). Human leukocyte production of ACTH and endorphin-like substances: Association with leukocyte interferon. *Proceedings of the National Academy of Science, U.S.A., 78*, p. 7530.

Smith, E., Harbour-McMenamin, D., & Blalock, J. (1985). Lymphocyte production of endorphins and endorphin-mediated immunoregulatory activity. *The Journal of Immunology, 135*(2), 779s–782s.

Smith, G., McKenzie, J., Marmer, D., & Steele, R. (1985). Psychologic modulation of the human immune response to varicella zoster. *Archives of Internal Medicine, 145*, 2110–2112.

Smotherman, W., & Robinson, S. (1985). The rat fetus in its environment: Behavioral adjustments to novel, familiar, aversive, and conditioned stimuli presented in utero. *Behavioral Neuroscience, 99*(3), 521–530.

Smotherman, W., Woodruff, K., Robinson, S., Del Real, C., Barron, S., & Riley, E. (1985). Spontaneous fetal behavior after maternal exposure to ethanol. *Pharmacology Biochemistry & Behavior, 24*, 165–170.

Snyder, S. (1978). Neuroleptic drugs and neurotransmitter receptors. *Journal of Continuing Education in Psychiatry, 39*, September, 21–31.

Solomon, G. (1985). The emerging field of psychoneuroimmunology with a special note on AIDS. *Advances, 2*(Winter), 6–19.

Solomon, G., & Amkraut, A. (1981). Psychoneuroendocrinological effects on the immune response. *Annual Review of Microbiology, 35*, 155–184.

Sontag, L. (1962). Effect of maternal emotions on foetal development. In W. Kroger (Ed.), *Psychosomatic obstetrics, gynecology and endocrinology* (pp. 8–13). Springfield, Illinois: Charles C. Thomas.

Sontag, L., & Richards, T. (1938). Studies in foetal behavior. Foetal heart rate as a behavioural indicator. *Monographs of the Society for Research in Child Development, 3*(72).

Sontag, L., & Wallace, R. (1935). The effect of cigarette smoking during pregnancy upon the foetal heart rate. *American Journal of Obstetrics and Gynecology, 29*, 77–83.

Spalding, D. (1873). On instinct. *Macmillan's Magazine*, February, 1873, 287–289. (Quotations from William James, *Principles of Psychology*, 1890, New York: Henry Holt)

Sperry, R., & Gazzaniga, M. (1967). Language following disconnection of the hemispheres. In C. Millikan, & F. Darley (Eds.), *Brain mechanisms underlying speech and language* (pp. 177–184). New York: Grune & Stratton.

Spiegel, D., Detrick, D., & Frischholz, E. (1982). Hypnotizability and psychopathology. *American Journal of Psychiatry, 139*, 431–437.

Spiegel, H. (1960). Hypnosis and the psychotherapeutic process. *Comparative Psychiatry, 1*, 174–185.

Spiegel, H. (1972). An eye-roll test for hypnotizability. *The American Journal of Clinical Hypnosis, 15*, 25–28.

Spiegel, H. (1980). Hypnosis and evidence: Help or hindrance. *Annals of New York Academy of Sciences, 347*, 73–85.

Spiegel, H., & Spiegel, D. (1978). *Trance and treatment: Clinical use of hypnosis*. New York: Basic Books.

Squire, L. (1982). The neuropsychology of human memory. *Annual Review of Neuroscience, 5*, 241–273.

Squire, L., & Cohen, N. (1983). Human memory and amnesia. In R. Thompson, & J. McGaugh (Eds.), *Handbook of behavioral neurobiology*. New York: Plenum Press.

Staats, J., & Evans, F. (1983). Posthypnotic amnesia in four diagnostic groups of hospitalized psychiatric patients. Paper presented at the meeting of the Society for Clinical and Experimental Hypnosis, Boston.

Stallworthy, J. (1959). Habitual abortion. *International Journal of Fertility, 4*, 237–241.

Stechler, G., & Halton, A. (1982). Prenatal influences on human development. In B. Walman (Ed.), *Handbook of developmental psychology* (pp. 177–189). Englewood Cliffs, New Jersey: Prentice-Hall.

Stein, I. (1945). Bilateral polycystic ovaries. *American Journal of Obstetrics & Gynecology, 50*, 385–398.

Stein, L. (1967). Introducing not-self. *Journal of Analytical Psychology, 12*(2).

Stein, M. (1986). A reconsideration of specificity in psychosomatic medicine: From olfaction to the lymphocyte. *Psychosomatic Medicine, 48*(1/2), 3–22.

Stein, R. (1976). Body and psyche: An archetypal view of psychosomatic phenomena. *Spring: An Annual of Archetypal Psychology & Jungian Thought*, 66–80.

Steiner, R., Peterson, A., Yu, J., Conner, H., Gilbert, M., terPenning, B., & Bremner, W. (1980). Ultradian leutenizing hormone and testosterone rhythms in the adult male monkey, *macaca fascicularis*. *Endocrinology, 107*, 1489–1493.

Stephenson, J. (1978). Reversal of hypnosis-induced analgesia by naloxone. *Lancet, 2*, 991–992.

Stevens, A. (1983). *Archetypes: A natural history of the self*. New York: Quill.

Stewart, J. (1981). Brain ACTH-endorphin neurons as regulators of central nervous system activity. In K. Brunfeldt (Ed.), *Peptides 1980* (pp. 774–779). Copenhagen, Denmark: Scriptor.

Stewart, J. (1984, February). Neuropeptides, learning and memory. McArthur Foundation Series Lecture, 23-page mimeograph.

Stewart, J. (1985). ACTH neurons, stress and behavior: A synthesis. In K. McKearns, & V. Pantic (Eds.), *Neuroendocrine correlates of stress* (pp. 239–268). New York: Plenum.

Stewart, J., & Channabasavaiah, K. (1979). Evolutionary aspects of some neuropeptides. *Federal Proceedings, 38*(9), 2303–2306.

Stewart, J., & Hall, M. (1982). Substance P: The "yin-yang" of behavior? In K. Blaha, & P. Malon (Eds.), *Peptides* (pp. 511–516). New York, Berlin: Walter de Gruyter.

Stewart, J., Krebs, W., & Kaczender, E. (1971). State-dependent learning produced with steroids. *Nature, 216*, 1233–1234.

Stolzy, S., Couture, L., & Edmonds, H., Jr. (1986). Evidence of partial recall during general anesthesia. *Anesthesia and Analgesia, 65*, S154.

Stroebel, C. (1969). Biologic rhythm correlates of disturbed behavior and Rhesus monkey. In F. Rohles (Ed.), *Circadian rhythms in non-human primates*. New York: S. Karger.

Sumner, W. (1953). Spontaneous regression of cancer. *Cancer, 6*, 1040.

Tannenbaum, G., & Martin, J. (1976). Evidence for an endogenous growth hormone secretion in the rat. *Endocrinology, 98*, 562–570.

Tannenbaum, G., Martin, J., & Colle, E. (1976). Ultradian growth hormone rhythm in the rat: Effects of feeding, hyperglycemia, and insulin-induced hypoglycemia. *Endocrinology, 99*, 720–727.

Tart, C. (1972). Measuring the depth of an altered stated of consciousness, with particular reference to self-report scales of hypnotic depth. In E. Fromm, & R. Shor (Eds.), *Hypnosis: Research, developments, and perspectives* (pp. 445–477). Chicago: Aldine.

Taylor, H. Jr. (1949). Vascular congestion and hyperemia. *American Journal of Obstetrics and Gynecology, 57*, 637–666.

Terenhius, L. (1973). Characteristics of the receptor for narcotic analgesics in synaptic plasma membrane fraction from rat brain. *Acta Pharmacology & Toxicology, 33*, 377–384.

Thakur, K. (1980). Treatment of anorexia nervosa with hypnotherapy. In H. Wain (Ed.),

Clinical hypnosis in medicine. Chicago: Year Book Medical Publishers.

Tierney, I., McGuire, R., & Walton, H. (1978). Distributions of body-rocking manifested by severely mentally deficient adults in ward environments. *Journal of Mental Deficiency Research, 22*, 243–254.

Timmons, B., & Kamiya, J. (1970). The psychology and physiology of meditation and related phenomena: A bibliography, I. *Journal of Transpersonal Psychology, 2*, 41–59.

Timmons, B., & Kanellakos, D. (1974). The psychology and physiology of meditation and related phenomena: A bibliography, I. *Journal of Transpersonal Psychology, 6*, 32–38.

Tinterow, M. (1970). *Foundations of hypnosis*. Springfield, Illinois: C. C. Thomas.

Trustman, R., Dubovsky, S., & Titley, R. (1977). Auditory perception during general anesthesia—myth or fact? *The International Journal of Clinical & Experimental Hypnosis, 25*(2), 88–105.

Tsuji, Y., Fukuda, H., Okuno, H., & Kobayashi, T. (1981). Diurnal rhythm of alpha wave activity. *Electroencephalography & Clinical Neurophysiology, 52*, S43.

Ullman, M. (1947). Herpes simplex and second degree burn induced under hypnosis. *American Journal of Psychiatry, 103*, 828.

Ullman, M. (1959). On the psyche and warts: I. Suggestion and warts: A review and comment. *Psychosomatic Medicine, 21*, 473–488.

Ullner, R. (1974). On the development of ultradian rhythms: The rapid eye movement activity in premature children. In L. Scheving et al (Eds.), *Chronobiology* (pp. 478–481). Tokyo: Igaku Shoin.

Vale, W., Rivier, C., Perrin, M., Smith, M., & Rivier, J. (1981). Pharmacology of gonadotropin releasing hormone: A model regulatory peptide. In J. Martin, S. Reichlin, & K. Bick (Eds.), *Neurosecretion and brain peptides* (pp. 609–625). New York: Raven Press.

Vander, A., Sherman, J., & Luciano, D. (1985). *Human physiology: The mechanisms of body function*. (Fourth Edition) New York: McGraw-Hill.

van der Kolk, B., Greenberg, M., Boyd, H., & Krystal, J. (1985). Inescapable shock, neurotransmitters, and addiction to trauma: Toward a psychobiology of post traumatic stress. *Biological Psychiatry, 20*, 314–325.

van Epps, D., & Saland, L. (1984). B-endorphin and met-enkephalin stimulate human peripheral blood mononuclear cell chemotaxis. *Journal of Immunology, 132*, 3046–3053.

Verhoeven, W., & Van Praag, H. (1982). Endorphins in psychiatric research and treatment. In N. Shah, & A. Donald (Eds.), *Endorphins & opiate antagonists in psychiatric research* (pp. 213–229). New York: Plenum.

von Foerster, H. (1984). *Observing Systems*. Seaside, CA: Intersystems Publication.

von Franz, M-L. (1987). Consciousness, power, and sacrifice: Conversations with Marie-Louise von Franz at 71. *Psychological Perspectives, 18*(2), in press.

Von Kraft-Ebbing, R. (1965). *Psychopathia sexualis*. New York: Stein & Day. (Original work published 1886)

Wain, H., Amen, D., & Oetgen, W. (1984). Hypnotic intervention in cardiac arrhythmias. *The American Journal of Clinical Hypnosis, 27*(1), 70–75.

Walter, R., Van Ree, J., & de Wied, D. (1978). Modification of conditioned behavior of rats by neurohypophyseal hormones and analogues. *Proceedings of the National Academy of Science, USA, 75*, 2493–2496.

Walters, E., & Byrne, J. (1983). Associative conditioning of single sensory neurons suggests a cellular mechanism for learning. *Science, 219*, 405–408.

Ward, I. (1984). The prenatal stress syndrome: Current status. *Psychoneuroendocrinology, 9*, 3–11.

Ward, I., & Reed, J. (1985). Prenatal stress and prepubertal social rearing conditions interact to determine sexual behavior in male rats. *Behavioral Neuroscience, 99*, 301–309.

Watkins, J. (1971). The affect bridge: A hypnoanalytic technique. *The International Journal of Clinical and Experimental Hypnosis, 19*(1), 21–27.

Watson, J., Hopkins, N., Roberts, J., Steitz, J., Weiner, A. (1987). *Molecular biology of the gene*. (Fourth Edition.) Menlo Park, California: Benjamin Cummings.

Watzlawick, P. (1978). *The language of change*. New York: Basic Books.

Watzlawick, P. (1984). *The invented reality*. New York: W. W. Norton.

Weinberger, N., Gold, P., & Sternberg, D. (1984). Epinephrine enables Pavlovian fear conditioning under anesthesia. *Science, 223*, February 10, 605–607.

Weinberger, N., McGaugh, J., & Lynch, G. (1985). *Memory systems of the brain*. New York: Guilford.

Weiner, H. (1977). *Psychobiology and human disease*. New York: Elsevier.

Weiner, H. (1982). The prospects for psychosomatic medicine: selected topics. *Psychosomatic Medicine, 44*(6), 491–516.

Weingartner, H. (1978). Human state dependent learning. In B. Ho, D. Richards, & D. Chute (Eds.), *Drug discrimination & state dependent learning* (pp. 361–382). New York: Academic.

Weingartner, H. (1986). Memory: The roots of failure. *Psychology Today*, January, 6–7.

Weingartner, H., Miller, H., & Murphy, D. (1977). Mood state-dependent retrieval of verbal associations. *Journal of Abnormal Psychology, 86*, 276–284.

Weitzman, E. (1974). Temporal organization or neuroendocrinal function in relation to the sleep-waking cycle in man. In *Recent studies of hypothalamic function*. Basel: S. Karger, pp. 26–38.

Weitzenhoffer, A. (1953). *Hypnotism: An objective study in suggestibility*. New York: John Wiley.

Weitzenhoffer, A. (1957). *General techniques of hypnotism*. New York: Grune & Stratton.

Weitzenhoffer, A. (1960a). Reflecting upon certain recent trends in medical hypnosis. *American Journal of Hypnosis, 2*(4), 117–196.

Weitzenhoffer, A. (1960b). Reflections upon specific and current uses of the "unconscious" in clinical hypnosis. *International Jnl. of Clinical & Experimental Hypnosis, 8*, July, 165–177.

Weitzenhoffer, A., & Hilgard, E. (1962). *Standard Hypnotic Susceptibility Scale, Form C*. Palo Alto, CA: Consulting Psychologists Press.

Wells, G., Leippe, M., & Ostrom, T. (1978). Crime seriousness as a determinant of accuracy in eye witness identification. *Journal of Applied Psychology, 63*(3), 345–351.

Wengraf, F. (1954). In F. Dunbar (Ed.), *Emotion and bodily changes*. New York: University Press.

Werbel, E. (1965). *One surgeon's experience with hypnosis*. New York: Pageant Press.

Werntz, D. (1981). Cerebral hemispheric activity and autonomic nervous function. Doctoral dissertation, University of California, San Diego.

Werntz, D., Bickford, R., Bloom, F., & Shannahoff-Khalsa, D. (1981). Selective cortical activation by alternating autonomic function. Paper presented at the Western EEG Society Meeting, February 12, Reno, Nevada.

Werntz, D., Bickford, R., Bloom, F., & Shannahoff, S. (1983). Alternating cerebral hemispheric activity and lateralization of autonomic nervous function. *Human Neurobiology, 2*, 39–43.

Wetterstrand, O. (1891). *Hypnotism and its application in practical medicine*. Vienna: Urban & Schwarzenberg.

White, J. (Ed.). (1979). *Kundalini, evolution and enlightenment*. New York: Anchor Books.

White, L., Tursky, B., & Schwartz, G. (1985). *Placebo: Clinical implications and insights*. New York: Guilford.

Williams, J. (1974). Stimulation of breast growth by hypnosis. *Jnl. of Sex Research, 10*(9), 337–342.

Wilson, R., Rogers, M., Pert, C., & Snyder, S. (1975). Homologous N-alkylnorketobemidones. Correlation of receptor binding with analgesic potency. *Journal of Medical Chemistry, 18*, 240–242.

Wingate, D. (1983). Complex clocks. *Digestive Diseases and Sciences, 28*(12), 1133–1140.

Wingate, D. (1985). The brain-gut link. *Viewpoints of Digestive Diseases, 17*(5), 17–20.

Wolf, F. (1981). *Taking the quantum leap: The new physics for nonscientists*. San Francisco: Harper & Row.

Wolf, F. (1986). *The body quantum: The new physics of body, mind, and health*. New York: Macmillan Publishing.

Wolfe, L., & Millet, J. (1960). Control of post-operative pain by suggestion under general anesthesia. *American Journal of Clinical Hypnosis, 3*, 109–112.

Wolfe, L., & Millet, J. (1961). Anesthesia. In L. LeCron (Ed.), *Techniques of hypnotherapy*. New York: Julian Press.

Wolff, H., & Wolf, S. (1948). *Pain*. Springfield: Charles C. Thomas.

Wright, M. E. Personal communication.

Wurtman, R., & Anton-Tay, F. (1969). The mammalian pinel as a neuroendocrine transducer. *Recent Progress in Hormone Research, 25*, 493–513.

Yalom, M., Estler, S., & Brewster, W. (1982). Changes in female sexuality: A study of mother/daughter communication and generational differences. *Psychology of Women Quarterly, 7*, 141–150.

Yanovski, A. (1962). The feasibility of alteration of cardiovascular manifestations in hypnosis. *The American Journal of Clinical Hypnosis, 5*, 8–16.

Yen, S., Vandenberg, G., Tsai, C., & Parker, D. (1974). Ultradian fluctuations of gonadotropins. In M. Ferin et al (Eds.), *Biorhythms and Human Reproduction*. New York: Wiley, pp. 203–218.

Yim, G., Bryant, H., Kuta, C., & Story, J. (In press) Opioid involvement in stress-induced hypercholesterolemia. *Science*.

Yim, G., & Lowy, M. (1984). Opioids, feeding, and anorexias. *Federation Proceedings, 43*(14), 2893–2897.

Young, P. (1940). Hypnotic regression—fact or artifact. *Journal of Abnormal and Social Psychology, 35*, 273.

Yudine, S. (1937). Use of cadaver blood after sudden death. *Lancet, 2*, 360–366.

Zeig, J. (Ed.) (1987). *The evolution of psychotherapy*. New York: Brunner/Mazel.

Zilbergeld, B., Edelstien, M., & Araoz (eds.) (1986). *Hypnosis: Questions & answers*. New York: W. W. Norton.

Zornetzer, S. (1978). Neurotransmitter modulation and memory: A new neuropharmacological phrenology? In M. Lipton, A. di Mascio, & K. Killam (Eds.), *Psychopharmacology: A generation of progress*. New York: Raven Press.

Zukin, S., & Zukin, R. (1979). Specific [3H]phencyclidine binding in rat central nervous system. *Proceedings of the National Academy of Science, U.S.A., 10*, 5372–5376.

obstetric patients. Reprinted from the October 1961 *International Journal of Clinical and Experimental Hypnosis*. Copyrighted by the Society for Clinical and Experimental Hypnosis, October, 1961. Cheek, D. Considerations relative to Dr. Bernard L. Diamond's Opinions on the Use of Hypnosis as a Forensic Tool. *The International Journal of Investigative and Forensic Hyposis*, Vol. 5, number 2, 22–30. Cheek, D. (1986). Using hypnosis with habitual aborters. In B. Zilbergeld, M. Edelstien, & D. Araoz (Eds.), *Hypnosis questions and answers* (pp. 330–336). New York: Norton. Rossi, E. (1986). Hypnosis and ultradian rhythms. (1986). In B. Zilbergeld, M. Edelstien, & D. Araoz (Eds.), *Hypnosis questions and answers* (pp. 17–21). New York: Norton. Cheek, D. (1980). Two approaches to causal events in disease using ideomotor responses and light hypnosis. *Swedish Journal of Clinical & Experimental Hypnosis*, August, 80–86. Cheek, D. (1957). Effectiveness of incentive in clinical hypnosis. Reprinted with permission from The American College of Obstetricians and Gynecologists. *Obstetrics and Gynecology*, Vol. 9(6), 720–724.

Permission to reprint figures:
Figures 1 and 2: Iversen, L. (1986). Introduction. In L. Iversen, & E. Goodman (Eds.), *Fast and slow chemical signalling in the nervous system* (p. xii). London: Oxford University Press. Figure 6: Zukin, S., & Zukin, R. (1979). Specific [3H]phencyclidine binding in rat central nervous system. *Proceedings of the National Academy of Sciences USA*, Vol. 10, 5371–5376. Reprinted with permission of publisher and authors. Figure 7: Mohler, H., & Okada, T. (1978). The benzodiazepine receptor in normal and pathological human brain. *British Journal of Psychiatry*, Vol. 133, 261–268. Reprinted with permission. Figure 10: Aswanikumar, S., Corcoran, B., Schiffman, E., Day, A., Freer, R., Showell, H., Becker, E., & Pert, C. (1977). Demonstration of a receptor on rabbit neutrophils for chemotactic peptides. *Biochemical & Biophysical Research Communications*, Vol. 74, 810–817. Reprinted with permission. Copyright 1977 American Chemical Society. Figure 13: Nieuwenhuys, R. (1985). *Chemoarchitecture of the brain*. New York: Springer. Reprinted with permission from publisher and author. Figures 14a and 14b: Ellis, L., & Ames, A. (1987). Neurohormonal functioning and sexual orientation: A theory of homosexuality-heterosexuality. *Psychological Bulletin*, Vol. 101(2), 233–258. Copyright 1987 by the American Psychological Association. Reprinted and adapted by permission of the publisher and author. Figures 16 and 17: Kesner, R. (1984). The neurobiology of memory: Implicit and explicit assumptions. In G. Lynch, J. McGaugh, & N. Weinberger (Eds.), *Neurobiology of learning and memory* (pp. 111–118). New York: Guilford.

Index